Penguin Books

To Lose a Battle

'One last battle,' Hitler demanded in *Mein Kampf*, 'with France.'

And in 1940 he fought and won it in six weeks of lightning
warfare, using combined operations techniques that sent the
French armies reeling.

How was this extraordinary victory possible?
Alistair Horne tells the day-by-day, almost hour-by-hour, story
of the battle, sifted from the vast Nazi archives and the
fragmentary records of the beaten Allies, so that the narrative
has all the subtlety and compulsion of a novel.

As the *Spectator* said of a previous book, this masterly chronicle
'has all the formal excellences of a work of art'. With it Alistair
Horne completes a triptych (*The Fall of Paris*, *The Price of
Glory*) of the great crises of the Franco-German rivalry, stepping
far beyond the confines of military history to form a major
contribution to our understanding of the period.

About the author

Alistair Horne was born in London in 1925, and has spent much of his life abroad, including periods at schools in the United States and Switzerland. He served with the R.C.A.F. and the R.A.F. in Canada in 1943 and ended his war service with the rank of Captain in the Coldstream Guards in the Middle East. He then went up to Jesus College, Cambridge, where he read English Literature and played international ice-hockey.

Since leaving Cambridge, Alistair Horne has concentrated on writing: he spent three years in Germany as correspondent for the *Daily Telegraph* and speaks fluent French and German. His books include *Back into Power* (1955); *The Land is Bright* (1958); *Canada and the Canadians* (1961); *Small Earthquake in Chile* (1972); and his widely praised trilogy on Franco–German conflicts: *The Fall of Paris, 1870–71*; *The Price of Glory: Verdun 1916* (winner of the Hawthornden Prize); *To Lose a Battle: France 1940* (written in the 1960s). His recent book, *A Savage War of Peace: Algeria 1954–62*, won both the *Yorkshire Post* Book of the Year Prize and the Wolfson History Award in 1978. It also earned for Mr Horne C. P. Snow's acclaim of being 'one of the best writers of history in the English-speaking world ... his new book shows him at the peak of his powers'. His other recent publications include *Napoleon, Master of Europe 1805– 1807* (1979). He has founded a Research Fellowship for young historians at St Antony's College, Oxford, and is a Trustee of the Imperial War Museum. Married with three daughters, he lives and farms in Wiltshire where he has become a passionate gardener, and paints and skis when the weeds, and publishers, let him.

Alistair Horne

To Lose a Battle
France 1940

Penguin Books

Penguin Books Ltd, Harmondsworth, Middlesex, England
Penguin Books, 40 West 23rd Street, New York, New York 10010, U.S.A.
Penguin Books Australia Ltd, Ringwood, Victoria, Australia
Penguin Books Canada Ltd, 2801 John Street, Markham, Ontario, Canada L3R 1B4
Penguin Books (N.Z.) Ltd, 182–190 Wairau Road, Auckland 10, New Zealand

First published in Great Britain by Macmillan 1969
First published in the United States of America by
Little Brown & Company 1969
Published in Penguin Books 1979
Reprinted 1982, 1984

Set, printed and bound in Great Britain by
Cox & Wyman Ltd, Reading
Set in Intertype Times

The following page constitutes an extension of the copyright notice

Grateful acknowledgement is made for permission to reprint the following copyrighted material:

Excerpts from *Panzer Leader* by General Heinz Guderian, translated by Constantine FitzGibbon. Published in the United States of America in 1952 by E. P. Dutton & Co., Inc., and reprinted with their permission.

Excerpts from *The Rommel Papers*. Copyright 1953 by B. H. Liddell Hart. Reprinted by permission of Harcourt Brace Jovanovich, Inc.

The poems 'Spring Song' (or, 'Crocus Time') and 'Baku, or the Map Game' from *Siren Song* by A. P. Herbert, published by Methuen & Co. Ltd. and Doubleday & Company, Inc. Copyright 1940 by Alan Patrick Herbert. Reprinted by permission of Sir Alan Herbert, his agents, A. P. Watt & Son, and Doubleday & Company, Inc.

Excerpts from *The Second World War* by Winston Churchill, published in the United States of America by Houghton Mifflin Company.

Excerpts from *Berlin Diary* by William Shirer. Copyright 1940, 1941 by Wiliam Shirer. Reprinted by permission of Alfred A. Knopf. Inc.

La France a perdu une bataille!
Mais la France n'a pas perdu la guerre!

(France has lost a battle!
But France has not lost the war!)

GENERAL DE GAULLE'S PROCLAMATION IN LONDON
AFTER THE FALL OF FRANCE

When at last . . . the will-to-live of the German nation, instead of continuing to be wasted away in purely passive defence, can be summoned together for a final, active showdown with France, and thrown into this in one last decisive battle with the very highest objectives for Germany; then, and only then, will it be possible to bring to a close the perpetual and so fruitless struggle between ourselves and France.

ADOLF HITLER, *Mein Kampf* (1925)

Contents

List of Tables and Maps

Tables
A. Allied order of battle 10 May 1940
B. German order of battle 10 May 1940

Maps
1   Western Front showing directions of Schlieffen Plan (1914)
    and *Sichelschnitt* (1940)
2   The opposing forces (10 May 1940)
3   The Meuse crossings (12–13 May)
4A The Dinant crossing (13–14 May)
4B The Sedan crossing (13–14 May)
5   The Panzer breakthrough (15–17 May)
6   The Panzer 'corridor' (18–21 May)
7   Counter-attack at Arras (21–23 May)
8   Encirclement of the northern armies (23–31 May)
9   The last phase (5–22 June)

*FOR
ALEXANDRA*

Tables and Maps

A. ALLIED ORDER OF BATTLE

With names of commanders principally concerned

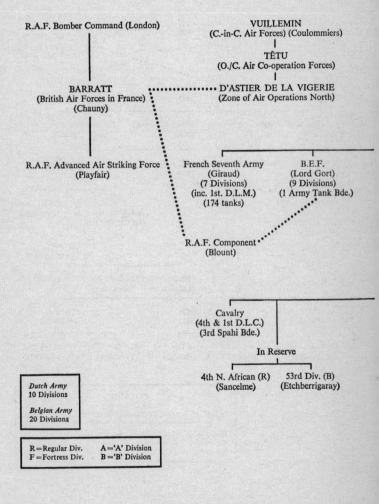

R.A.F. Bomber Command (London)

VUILLEMIN
(C.-in-C. Air Forces) (Coulommiers)

TÊTU
(O./C. Air Co-operation Forces)

BARRATT
(British Air Forces in France)
(Chauny)

D'ASTIER DE LA VIGERIE
(Zone of Air Operations North)

R.A.F. Advanced Air Striking Force
(Playfair)

French Seventh Army
(Giraud)
(7 Divisions)
(inc. 1st. D.L.M.)
(174 tanks)

B.E.F.
(Lord Gort)
(9 Divisions)
(1 Army Tank Bde.)

R.A.F. Component
(Blount)

Cavalry
(4th & 1st D.L.C.)
(3rd Spahi Bde.)

In Reserve

4th N. African (R)
(Sancelme)

53rd Div. (B)
(Etchberrigaray)

Dutch Army
10 Divisions

Belgian Army
20 Divisions

R = Regular Div.   A = 'A' Division
F = Fortress Div.   B = 'B' Division

10 May 1940

Units reading from north (left) to south (right)

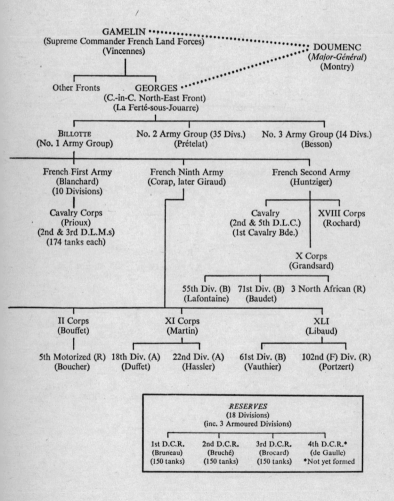

GAMELIN
(Supreme Commander French Land Forces)
(Vincennes)

DOUMENC
(*Major-Général*)
(Montry)

Other Fronts — GEORGES
(C.-in-C. North-East Front)
(La Ferté-sous-Jouarre)

BILLOTTE
(No. 1 Army Group)

No. 2 Army Group (35 Divs.)
(Prételat)

No. 3 Army Group (14 Divs.)
(Besson)

French First Army
(Blanchard)
(10 Divisions)

French Ninth Army
(Corap, later Giraud)

French Second Army
(Huntziger)

Cavalry Corps
(Prioux)
(2nd & 3rd D.L.M.s)
(174 tanks each)

Cavalry
(2nd & 5th D.L.C.)
(1st Cavalry Bde.)

XVIII Corps
(Rochard)

X Corps
(Grandsard)

55th Div. (B)
(Lafontaine)

71st Div. (B)
(Baudet)

3 North African (R)

II Corps
(Bouffet)

XI Corps
(Martin)

XLI
(Libaud)

5th Motorized (R)
(Boucher)

18th Div. (A)
(Duffet)

22nd Div. (A)
(Hassler)

61st Div. (B)
(Vauthier)

102nd (F) Div. (R)
(Portzert)

RESERVES
(18 Divisions)
(inc. 3 Armoured Divisions)

1st D.C.R.
(Bruneau)
(150 tanks)

2nd D.C.R.
(Bruché)
(150 tanks)

3rd D.C.R.
(Brocard)
(150 tanks)

4th D.C.R.*
(de Gaulle)
*Not yet formed

B. GERMAN ORDER OF BATTLE

With names of commanders principally concerned

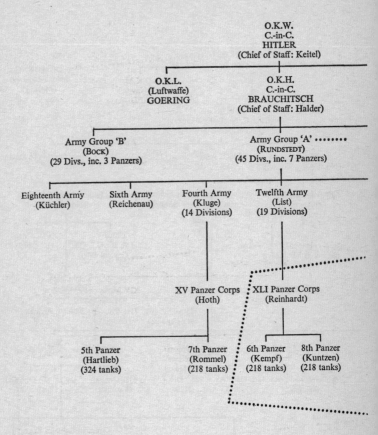

O.K.W.
C.-in-C.
HITLER
(Chief of Staff: Keitel)

O.K.L.
(Luftwaffe)
GOERING

O.K.H.
C.-in-C.
BRAUCHITSCH
(Chief of Staff: Halder)

Army Group 'B'
(BOCK)
(29 Divs., inc. 3 Panzers)

Army Group 'A' ········
(RUNDSTEDT)
(45 Divs., inc. 7 Panzers)

Eighteenth Army
(Küchler)

Sixth Army
(Reichenau)

Fourth Army
(Kluge)
(14 Divisions)

Twelfth Army
(List)
(19 Divisions)

XV Panzer Corps
(Hoth)

XLI Panzer Corps
(Reinhardt)

5th Panzer
(Hartlieb)
(324 tanks)

7th Panzer
(Rommel)
(218 tanks)

6th Panzer
(Kempf)
(218 tanks)

8th Panzer
(Kuntzen)
(218 tanks)

RESERVES
42 Infantry Divisions

10 May 1940
Units reading from north (left) to south (right)

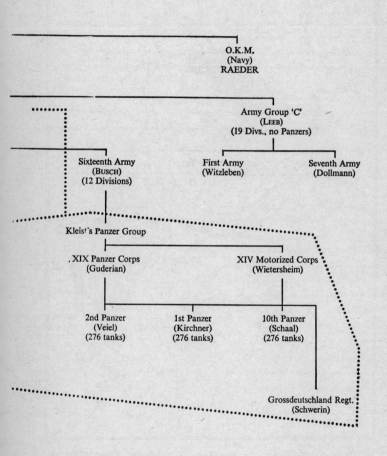

O.K.M.
(Navy)
RAEDER

Army Group 'C'
(LEEB)
(19 Divs., no Panzers)

Sixteenth Army
(BUSCH)
(12 Divisions)

First Army
(Witzleben)

Seventh Army
(Dollmann)

Kleist's Panzer Group

XIX Panzer Corps
(Guderian)

XIV Motorized Corps
(Wietersheim)

2nd Panzer
(Veiel)
(276 tanks)

1st Panzer
(Kirchner)
(276 tanks)

10th Panzer
(Schaal)
(276 tanks)

Grossdeutschland Regt.
(Schwerin)

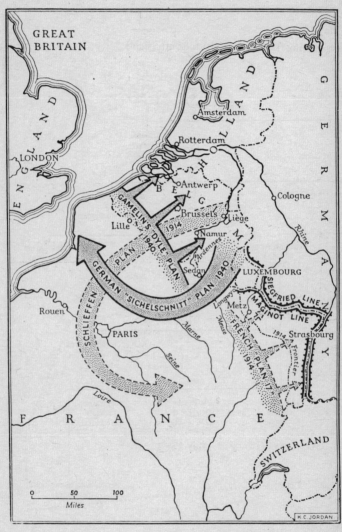

1. Western Front showing directions of Schlieffen Plan (1914) and *Sichelschnitt* (1940)

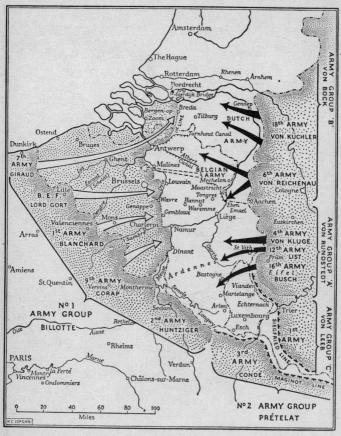

2. The opposing forces (10 May 1940)

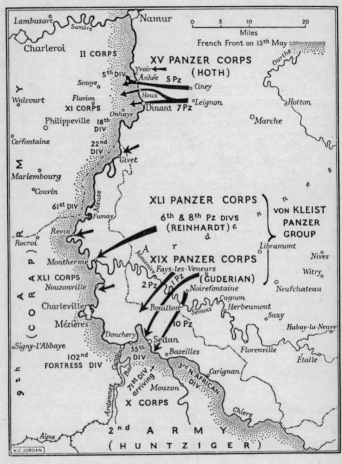

3. The Meuse crossings (12–13 May)

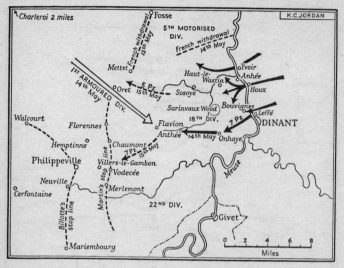

4A. The Dinant crossing (13–14 May)

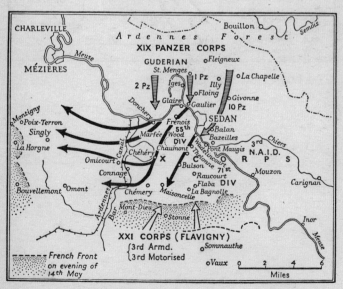

4B. The Sedan crossing (13–14 May)

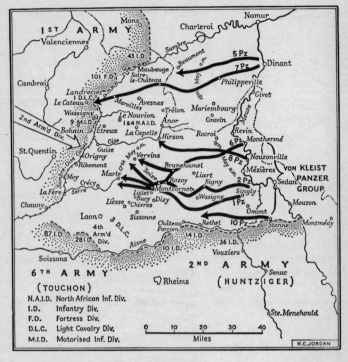

5. The Panzer breakthrough (15–17 May)

K.C.JORDAN

Terneuzen
Ostend
Bruges
Nieuport
Dunkirk
BELGIAN
Calais
Roulers
Ghent
INF.
B.E.F
Ypres
Oudenarde
DIVS
St.Omer
Courtrai
Roubaix
Boulogne
Armentières
B.E.F
Lille
Étaples
Béthune
Seclin
Montreuil
St.Amand
XVI
Berck
PANZER
B.E.F.
Lens
CORPS
attack 21st May
3 Pz
St.Pol
Douai
Valenciennes
Arras
Bouchain
4 Pz
St.Valéry
8 Pz
5 Pz
Noyelles
Achiel-
le-Grand
Solesmes
7 Pz
Abbeville
Doullens
6 Pz
Cambrai
Caudry
VON
Le Treport
Bapaume
Marcoing
Le Cateau
Cléry
Albert
Le Catelet
Busigny
Wassigny
KLEIST
Corbie
Bohain
2 Pz
Fresnoy-le-Grand
Amiens
Péronne
1 Pz
PANZER
7 N.A.I.D
Chaulnes
St.Quentin
4 C.I.D
Rosières
10 Pz
GROUP
231 D
Roye
3 I.D.
231 D
Ham
Crécy-sur-
Montdidier
Chauny
La Fère
Chéry
Serre
Sincent
Compiègne
87 I.D.
DE GAULLE attack
Laon
28 I.D
19th May
Aisne
Soissons
Fismes
6 TH   A R M Y.

Miles
0 10 20 30 40

C.I.D. Colonial Inf. Div.
N.A.I.D. North African Inf. Div.

Proposed manoeuvre
of Wegand

Allied Front
Panzer advance
19-21 May

6. The Panzer 'corridor' (18–21 May)

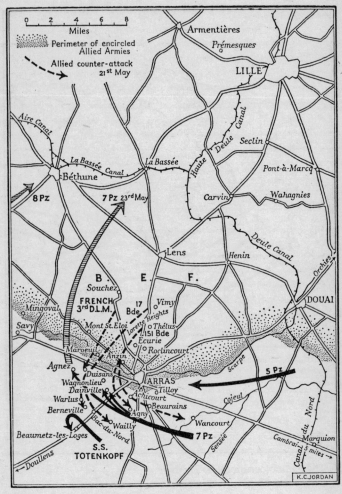

7. Counter-attack at Arras (21–23 May)

8. Encirclement of the northern armies (23–31 May)

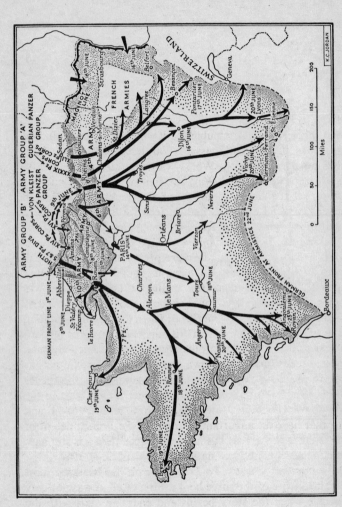

9. The last phase (5–22 June)

Preface

When this book was first published it was roughly one hundred years since the Franco-Prussian War began, fifty since Versailles concluded the First World War, and thirty since the first act of the Second World War, the Fall of France. It endeavours to tell the story of the last of these episodes. Although designed to stand firmly on its own feet, it represents the third panel of a triptych of which the other two were *The Fall of Paris: The Siege and the Commune 1870–71*, and *The Price of Glory: Verdun 1916*, and is therefore closely linked to the theme of the earlier books. During most of this past hundred years, at least until 1945, the seminal issue in Europe was Franco-German rivalry. Now it is no longer so. As I tried to explain in the Preface to *The Fall of Paris*, the original ambition of the triptych was to deal with this important chunk of modern European history, woven around three great Franco-German battles, each decisive in its own war, and in wider contexts as well. They are not, essentially, military studies. As the reader will discover from the present book, there are (at least in the author's view) various after-effects from both 1870–71 and 1916 that have an important bearing on the French defeat of 1940. And so much that has happened since then – is still happening – can find an explanation in the débâcle of 1940.

In a number of ways, *To Lose a Battle* has been the most difficult to write of the three books. First of all, it was not easy to decide when the story begins and ends. To start with the crushing superiority of the German Stukas and Panzers on 13 May 1940 leaves a lot unexplained, and the *decisive* battle was over long before Pétain asked for an armistice – even before the B.E.F. embarked at Dunkirk. After I had finished my researches I finally decided to begin with France's moment

of supreme power, as seen at the Victory Parade of 1919, proceeding to deal with only those factors in the inter-war world
which seemed relevant to France's weakness and Germany's
strength in 1940, and to end the main account with the failure
of the last Allied counter-attacks in northern France, during
21–24 May. After this date, for the Germans the campaign was
little more than a matter of marching.

The second, and by far the greatest difficulty of all, concerned source material. The Siege of Paris and the Commune
together continued, in the same setting, for nine months, Verdun for ten. Thus in both battles a multitude of chroniclers on
either side had the leisure to provide detailed day-by-day
accounts of what went on – often of superb quality. In 1870–71,
the historian is additionally aided by the presence in Paris of
many 'neutral' British and American observers whose accounts
provide a special dimension of objectivity, while for 1916 the
official war histories of either side have long been open to
scrutiny. In contrast, the decisive battle for France in 1940
lasted less than two weeks, but covered over two hundred miles
in depth alone. Many war diarists, especially on the French side,
simply had no opportunity to write up their diaries or even
scribble a letter home.

From the German side, the Allied capture of all Nazi archives
certainly provided historians with an unprecedented treasure
trove. The French, on the other hand, have not yet published
an official history of 1940,[1] and the archives at Vincennes are
not open to inspection. It is easy to understand French reticence; yet one feels it may be prompted less by what is there,
than by what is not there. However, the lack of any French
official history is in part compensated for by the plentiful personal accounts of participants granted access to the archives,
such as Generals Doumenc (*Major-Général* of the French
General Staff), Roton (General Georges's Chief of Staff) and
Ruby (Chief of Staff to the French Second Army), not to mention the lengthy memoirs by the leaders themselves, Reynaud,
Gamelin and Weygand. But because of the pressure and speed

1. The findings of such inquiries as the Serre Commission are at best only
partially satisfactory.

of events (if for no other reason), such accounts are often in disagreement, and it is therefore not easy to determine what happened, and when.

For example, recording General Weygand's crucial visit to the northern commanders on 21 May (see Chapter 18), both Baudouin and Churchill (neither of whom were there) write that Weygand's plane was attacked and forced to land at Calais. Weygand himself says he landed unchallenged at Norrent-Fontes, and then flew on to Calais. After the meeting, Baudouin says Weygand left from Ypres at 4 p.m., by torpedo-boat from Dunkirk to Cherbourg; Churchill says 7 p.m., by submarine to Dieppe; while Colonel Goutard puts the time at 'between 5 and 6 p.m.'. Churchill and others state that Lord Gort arrived, too late, at the Ypres meeting at 8 p.m.; Benoist-Méchin, 'about 9 p.m.'. These may seem like hair-splitting points, but they make the historian cautious about accuracy on the bigger issues.

Napoleon once warned: 'Above all, be distrustful of eye-witnesses . . . the only thing my Grenadiers saw of Russia was the pack of the man in front.' Obviously the advice can be taken too far, and Napoleon's Grenadiers certainly saw more of the Russian campaign than he would have liked. But one has to be cautious about the fallibility of human memory; with one or two notable exceptions (such as the late Air Chief Marshal Sir Arthur Barratt, whose reminiscences proved invaluable to me) I have in general restricted myself to what was written at the time or very soon afterwards. Even here, however, one has to exercise caution. For reasons suggested earlier, I found myself forced to lean heavily on German eye-witness accounts of battle operations, such as the crossing of the Meuse. Some, such as Rommel, seldom let one down, even though at times he stole perhaps more than his fair share of the glory. But all too often the National Socialist overtones of the moment, the vaunting of Teutonic deeds and deprecation of the enemy's – never a reverse, never the sight of a burnt-out German tank – make one recoil in distrust. On the other hand so many of the memoirs of French leaders are but one long apologia, although, set against each other, they too can be revealing.

Inevitably, there is much in this book that will be hurtful to French *amour propre*. Although many of the studies emanating from France herself could scarcely be more scorching, the French, perhaps more than most nations (and particularly at this time of resurgent nationalism), tend to regard outsiders writing about their history as the *voyeur* who peeps through other people's bathroom keyholes. And indeed, it is almost impossible for any Briton fully to comprehend the lingering wounds left by invasion and defeat in a nation as proud as France.

Again, Dutchmen and Belgians and my own countrymen too may criticize me for dealing too briefly with their part in the Battle of France; Americans may feel that I should have said more of their role in the inter-war period, and of the 1940 exchange of communications between Reynaud, Churchill and Roosevelt. I can only excuse myself by repeating that this is, like *The Fall of Paris* and *The Price of Glory*, primarily a story about France and Germany.

Acknowledgements

During my researches on this book, I was once again accorded much indispensable help, with the utmost courtesy, by Dr Rohwer and Herr Haupt of the Bibliothek für Zeitgeschichte in Stuttgart and by M. Hornung of the Bibliothèque de Documentation Internationale Contemporaine of the University of Paris. Of the libraries and archives in England, the vast collection of books and periodicals owned by the Imperial War Museum proved invaluable, and I am additionally most grateful for privileges granted me by the Ministry of Defence Library, Professor Michael Howard of King's College, London, Captain Sir Basil Liddell Hart, The Royal United Service Institution, and the London Library. In Germany, the Bundesarchiv proved a source of much vital material, and in France I am grateful to Colonel Le Goyet of the Service Historique de l'Armée at Vincennes for his answers on certain specific points. Among the people who have helped in various ways, and given advice or the benefit of their own memories, I should particularly like to record my thanks to Major-General Sir Edward Spears (who in his classical reminiscences on the French scene in two world wars deserves to rate as the Suetonius of our times), Captain Sir Basil Liddell Hart, Colonel A. Goutard, Mrs Clare Boothe Luce, the late Air Chief Marshal Sir Arthur Barratt, M. Gaston Palewski, M. Édouard Leng, Constantine FitzGibbon, and Colonel G. B. Jarrett.

I am beholden to Mr K. C. Jordan, F.R.G.S. for maps, and I and my publishers wish to thank the following for their kindness in giving permission for the use of copyright material:

Collins, Sons & Co. Ltd, for extracts from *The Rommel Papers*, edited by B. H. Liddell Hart; Michael Joseph Ltd, for extracts from *Panzer Leader*, by Heinz Guderian; and Mr William Shirer, for extracts from *Berlin Diary*.

Throughout the sifting of research material, I was enormously helped by the painstaking diligence of Mr Peter Bradley. Among those who read the manuscript and offered valuable suggestions, I am particularly grateful to Major-General the Hon. Miles Fitz-alan-Howard, who scrutinized it with a professional eye, and also to Mr Philip Whitting, as well as to my editors in London and New York, Mr Alan Maclean, Mr Richard Garnett and Mr Harry Sions, to whom I am indebted not only for their arduous work on the manuscript but also for their sustaining encouragement over the past many months. I owe a special debt of thanks to Mrs Angus Nicol for typing the manuscript, several times, in addition to providing invaluable assistance in a multitude of other ways – often at impossible hours. I am deeply appreciative of the unfailing kindness of my old friend, Mr William F. Buckley, Jr, who at a critical moment in production provided a haven of peace; and finally my wife deserves special mention for acting as map-reader during tours of the battlefields, but above all for putting up with nearly ten years of battles.

Unlike some of the principals in this story, however, the author realizes that for any disasters in the end result he has nobody but himself to blame.

London, Ashington, Château de Rougemont
1967–8

Part One *1919–40*

Chapter 1

Grandeur and Misery of Victory[1]

1919–30

Victory was to be bought so dear as to be almost indistinguishable
from defeat.

WINSTON S. CHURCHILL, *The World Crisis*

Youth could win, but had not learned to keep; and was pitiably
weak against age. We stammered that we had worked for a new
heaven and a new earth, and they thanked us kindly and made
their peace.

T. E. LAWRENCE, on Versailles

13 July 1919

Even on the Sunday afternoon preceding the next day's great
event, crowds had begun to form along the Champs-Élysées. By
3 a.m. that night an estimated 100,000 people had already taken
up positions there. The Arc de Triomphe was unapproachable.
Among the crowds, tempered by the presence of so many
women still clad in mourning for a son or a husband, a tone of
restrained, almost sober, jubilation dominated. It was all very
different from the August day of five years earlier when
frenetic Parisians had swarmed through the city singing the
Chant du Départ and shouting 'To Berlin!'

The janitors and charwomen had barely finished sweeping
away the debris of diplomacy from Versailles's Hall of Mirrors
– that great chamber where in 1871 a victorious Prussian king
had so arrogantly proclaimed himself Kaiser and which, half a
century later, France with an unsurpassable sense of theatre
had selected as the fitting stage for the final act in the tragedy
entitled Revenge. After more than four years of the most
terrible war humanity had ever known, peace was now a fact.
In London, as the guns boomed out the news that the Treaty
had at last been signed, loyal crowds had thronged outside
Buckingham Palace to hear King George V say 'I join you in

1. Title of Clemenceau's memoirs.

thanking God.' But somehow, the discussions having dragged on so tediously, details of the Treaty itself had already fallen a bit flat. The British public was as glad as the Press to get back to more immediate and appealing topics; there were the first post-war Wimbledon and Henley, even though the *Illustrated London News* mourned that the latter was 'not quite itself this year'.

In Paris especially the signature of the Treaty had swiftly become eclipsed by the imminence of this other, tangibly more magnificent occasion. 14 July 1919 was the day of the Victory Parade, France's moment of supreme triumph – to many Frenchmen, possibly the greatest triumph in all her long history. Certainly never was there to be an occasion more fitting of *Le jour de gloire* celebrated by the *Marseillaise* than this first *Quatorze Juillet* since Alsace-Lorraine had returned to the fold from the forty-eight years of bondage.

On the eve of the procession, a temporary cenotaph almost filled the mighty vault of the Arc de Triomphe.[2] Each of the four sides of the cenotaph was guarded by a Victory, the wings of which had been fashioned from the fabric of war-planes. On the surfaces of its plinth could be read the sombre dedication, '*Aux morts pour la patrie*'. Throughout the night, flames of Greek fire smouldered and flickered from urns mounted at its angles, while powerful searchlights transformed its gilt plaster into gold. Surrounding the cenotaph, soldiers of all arms of the French Army kept vigil with rifles reversed. They were watched by a silent and reverent crowd, perched upon or kneeling between the circle of captured enemy cannon drawn up around the Étoile.

14 July 1919

Shortly after midnight, the massive pylon was towed out from under the arch by tractors, so as to enable the triumphal procession to pass through it, and established a short distance

2. The idea of burying an Unknown Warrior, selected from the remains of eight fallen at Verdun, under the Arc de Triomphe was not conceived until later.

away. As the dawn prefacing a day of silver and blue broke (it recalled to some of the more romantic-minded French journalists the day of Austerlitz), a remarkable spectacle greeted the eyes of those lucky enough to have gained access to balconies high up on buildings flanking the Champs-Élysées. As far as the eye could see, down the green line of the Avenue de la Grande-Armée, and all the way along the five miles of the processional route, fluttered the flags and pennants of the Allied nations from an endless forest of white masts. On either side of the Rond-Point was heaped a huge mound of captured German guns, surmounted on one side by the Gallic cock of 1914, preening himself for the fight, and on the other by the victorious cock of 1918, crowing his ascendancy to the world. Down at the Porte-Maillot, the resplendent masses of the Allied contingents were forming up behind their leaders, greeted by members of the Municipal Council, who, like the aediles of antiquity, were opening the city to the conquering armies.

At 7.45 a.m. a car arrived at the Étoile bringing Clemenceau, the dread 'tiger' who, from the brink of defeat, had flogged France on to victory through the last desperate year of the war. Occasionally shooting fierce glances to right and left, the old tiger, followed by his inseparable lieutenant, a serious and pasty-faced young man called Georges Mandel, shambled slowly up to the official stand. Shortly after eight appeared the President of the Republic himself, Raymond Poincaré, the man of Lorraine, a symbol of all that France had fought so gallantly to regain, his open car cheered along the length of the Champs-Élysées. Accompanied by France's two glorious Marshals, Joffre and Foch, the President laid a wreath at the base of the cenotaph. The Marshals then drove off to take up their positions at the head of the parade. As the President resumed his position on the tribune, cannon began to speak out in the distance – from the Bois de Boulogne, from Mont-Valérien, from all the forts which, during the bitter winter of 1870, had endeavoured to save the city when besieged by the now humbled enemy. Rockets soared up and exploded over the Arc de Triomphe. Down at the Porte-Maillot, a captain took out his watch and gave the order heard at so many lethal dawns during the preceding four years: *Avancez!* The drums rolled, the trumpets sounded out their fanfares in those peculiarly Gallic, almost querulously high-pitched notes, and approaching the Arc de Triomphe was soon heard the music of the regimental bands playing out the stirring strains of *Vous n'aurez pas l'Alsace et la Lorraine.* An electric sense of expectancy rippled through the crowd. All the fatigue of the long wait evaporated.

The chains which had encircled the arch, ever since the day when, forty-eight years ago, the Prussians had engraved perpetual hatred in French hearts by insisting on their rights to a triumphal march through the prostrate city, had been removed. Now, for the first time since that day of shame, marching men began to appear through the sacred arch. But those who led the way across the threshold in this historic moment, they were not Joffre or Foch; not the cavalry, or the zouaves, or any Allied detachment. They were three young men, or what remained of them, unspeakably crippled by war, still in uniform, but trundled by their nurses in primitive chariots like the prams of deprived children. Immediately behind them came a large contingent of more *grands mutilés.* Officers and men of all ranks mixed together, many already in mufti, they marched – or hobbled – without precedence or any semblance of military order, twelve abreast. Hardly one had not lost an eye or a limb, and many bore on their chests France's most coveted decoration, the Médaille Militaire. The totally blind – some accorded the privilege of being ensign-bearers – came led by the one-legged, or the armless; men with their destroyed faces mercifully hidden behind bandages; men with no hands; men with their complexions still tinted green from the effects of chlorine; men with mad eyes staring out from beneath the skull caps which concealed some appalling head injury. Some were famous heroes, easily recognized by the crowd; among them, identifiable by his immense stature, limped Sergeant André Maginot, already a well-known figure in the Assembly, badly wounded at Verdun.

With a painful, halting pace the column moved by, down the Champs-Élysées to the stands specially set apart for them. As they passed a stand filled with a hundred and fifty young Alsatian girls in national costume, flowers rained down upon them. For a brief moment the terrible spectacle of the broken men was met with a kind of stunned silence. Then 'an immense cry, which seemed to spring from the very entrails of the race, arose from the vast crowd, a cry which was both a salute and a pledge'. No one who watched the *mutilés* pass that day could be unaware of what they represented: of the many thousands, more hopelessly maimed, lodged in hospitals across the country which they would never leave, of the hundreds of thousands of other war casualties, only relatively more fortunate, to whom the future could hardly offer much – and who in turn would be able to contribute but little towards the reconstruction of their exhausted nation; but above all of the lost legions of men who had not returned at all from the martyrdom of the Western Front, either whole or crippled. From metropolitan France alone these numbered 1,315,000 – or 27 per cent of all men between the ages of eighteen and twenty-seven; no combatant nation except for little Serbia had a higher mortality rate – higher than Russia, higher than Germany or her allies. It was a fact which, so brutally brought home on this luminous day of victory celebrations, would never cease to haunt the nation.

There was a long pause in the procession, 'as if to permit us to breathe – or to dry our tears'. Then came *la gloire* itself. Accompanied by a thunderous roll of drums and fanfare of trumpets a squadron of the magnificent Gardes Républicains rode through the Arc de Triomphe, and just forty yards behind them rode Joffre and Foch. Up to the eleventh hour there had been some discussion as to whether Joffre, fallen from grace during the Battle of Verdun, should take part in the parade at all. Finally Foch had settled matters by declaring with admirable magnanimity that unless Joffre rode with him, *inter pares*, he would not march either. So here they both were, riding abreast, the man who had saved France on the Marne in 1914, and the man who had brought her to final victory in 1918; France resisting, and France attacking. Each of the two leaders was wearing the uniform with which he had so long been associated: Foch all in grey, with a képi bearing three rows of oak leaves, Joffre a portly figure in black dolman and scarlet breeches. Joffre, showing his age, seemed to be much moved by the vast crowds, which he repeatedly pointed out to Foch, as if surprised they should still recognize him; Foch, rigidly upright in the saddle of his famous charger, Émir, his Marshal's baton with its seven gold stars firmly grasped in the right hand, resembled all that a victorious general should be. A few discreet paces behind – a position that had long become habitual – rode the neat and dapper figure of General Maxime Weygand, Foch's Chief of Staff. Then came the rest of the Allied Generalissimo's staff, including a Colonel Georges who, like Weygand, would also be called upon a fill a role of dreadful responsibility twenty years later.

Now it was the turn of the Allies. First, in alphabetical order, appeared the Americans with General Pershing at their head. Swinging along the route, they struck a *Times* correspondent as 'the finest American troops Paris has yet seen, and their marching is really perfect'. As the bandsmen strummed out 'Over There', something about the lilt of it reminded excited French ears of the jazz that was now all the rage in Paris. Next came the Belgians, followed after a five-minute interval by the British, led by Sir Douglas Haig. As they bore past the colours of two hundred regiments that had fought and bled in Flanders or along the Somme, the crowd showed its enthusiasm by taking up the refrain of 'Tipperary' that France had got to know so well. Then followed Italians in slate-coloured uniforms, little Japanese in khaki, Portuguese, Roumanians, Serbs and Siamese, and men wearing French tunics of *bleu horizon*, men from the 'new' nations who owed their existence to the Allied victory, and who would in turn be abandoned by these same Allies within the next two decades – Czechoslovaks and Poles. So many armies had it required to overthrow the might of the German Empire. Yet one army was missing, one without whose aid the Miracle of the Marne could never have occurred and without whose allegedly bottomless reserves of men there would not this day be any victory celebrations – Russia, now sealed off from her former allies by revolution and civil war, and apparently forgotten.

Once the initial restraint imposed by the sombre overture to the parade had passed, the crowd allowed itself to go wild. As each national detachment marched by, a fresh gust of cheering broke loose. Against all orders, cavalrymen closing intersections hoisted girls on to their saddles to provide them with a better view. Children and young women flung basketfuls of flowers on to the triumphal way and garlanded the bayonets of the soldiers with green and gilded paper crowns, so that as the morning went on it seemed as if they were marching on a carpet of blossom. On this day at least there was nothing grudging in France's gratitude to her Allies. But, understandably enough, it was the mighty French contingent bringing up the rear of the parade for which the spectators had preserved the power of their lungs. A solitary figure riding through the Arc de Triomphe on a white horse, gravely majestic, tall and magnificent in a uniform of *bleu horizon*, the austere face even paler than usual, provided the signal for the opening of the day's great climax – Marshal Pétain, the Commander-in-Chief. Behind him followed the *poilus* he had led through the ten months' hell of Verdun, had nursed through the mutinies which so nearly broke the French Army the following year. From each of France's twenty-one army corps, a company of the regiment bearing the highest battle-honours for gallantry had been selected to march in the parade. What a spectacle of triumphant glory they presented as they marched past with the regimental music thundering out *Sambre-et-Meuse* and the *Marche Lorraine*, the battle hymns that had so stirred French hearts during the years of agony! Then came the little *chasseurs* with their rapid pace and large floppy berets, men who had borne the brunt of the first German onslaught at Verdun; resplendent-looking hussars and *cuirassiers* in their glittering breastplates, who had not really had much of a chance in this war, after the first mad carnage during the Battle of the Frontiers; marvellous-looking men from France's overseas empire, Foreign Legionnaires, ferocious Moroccan *goums* in turbans and flowing white robes, Algerian and Indo-Chinese *tirailleurs*, coal-black Senegalese with an alarming reputation for not taking prisoners; artillerymen drawing a battery of the famous 75s that had halted the Germans on the Marne, and a

battery of the less elegant, stubby 155s that had played so vital
a role in the defence of Verdun; airmen, led by one of the few
survivors of the legendary aces, René Fonck, bearing an ensign;
marines in navy blue, who, cheek by jowl with the Belgians and
British, had anchored the line in the muddy swamp of Flanders.

At various intervals came the victorious commanders, whom
the crowd instantly recognized and applauded. Gouraud, the
one-armed hero; Pau, also bearing an empty sleeve, but from
1870; Fayolle and Debeney; Maistre and Mangin, once nicknamed by his troops 'the butcher'; and Castelnau, whose black
brassard, recalling that he himself had lost three sons in the
war, seemed to draw particularly warm acclaim from the
stands. All famous warrior names, and in the recognition each
received, those angry memories of the futile costly offensives,
the frightful reverses, the reproaches that the generals were
wantonly throwing away the lives of their men – all these were
submerged in this moment of sublime thanksgiving. But it was
the men, not the chiefs, that the crowd were chiefly saluting,
and particularly the infantry that made up the vast bulk of the
procession. Wave upon wave they came, the renowned cutting-
edge and very substance of the French Army, which had
fought and endured, suffered and died, in the most unspeakable conditions ever imposed upon humanity, all through the
war from the first murderous clash on the frontiers, through
Verdun and the Somme and the Chemin des Dames, to the
Second Marne and the final glorious advance of October 1918.
As the crowd watched the tattered colours of the infantry regiments file by, a kind of delirium overtook it. There were many
who began, quite instinctively, to sing *La Madelon*, with tears
streaming down their faces. What thoughts, what memories
were passing through the minds of the troops as they marched
by the statue of Strasbourg in the Concorde, now disburdened
of its mourning crêpe for the first summer since 1870! For in
all French hearts this *Quatorze Juillet* was a day of destiny that
had been dreamed about, not merely over the past agonizing
five years, but for another forty-three beyond them. Enough
Frenchmen, both watching and marching, were sufficiently old
to recall the shame of that defeat. Pétain (who, alas, would live

on to act as caretaker for France under a new and still more humiliating defeat) had been a schoolboy, but Foch as a youth had witnessed Louis-Napoleon retreat sick and defeated through Metz, and Joffre had manned a cannon on the ramparts of Paris during the four months' siege; Clemenceau had been one of the Deputies to protest against the surrender of Alsace-Lorraine in 1871, and had narrowly escaped being lynched in the civil war that followed with the Commune. But now, as President Poincaré had declared to him in a special message, 'In the light of this glorious morning, the last traces of the painful past have just been removed for ever.'

For over an hour the march-past of the French contingent continued. It was hard to realize that, in the course of the past year, France had already demobilized nearly three million men. It was also pardonable for a Frenchman to believe, watching this magnificent cavalcade of his Army, that France had won the war largely by her own efforts – and losses. Finally, to close the procession, nine of General Estienne's assault tanks rumbled through the Arc de Triomphe. The sulphurous smell of burning oil and the deafening roar and clatter that reverberated with their passage under the great archway seemed more a token of the potency of the French Army of today than a harbinger of the battles of tomorrow. Who could have any doubts that France, emerging triumphant from the inferno, now possessed the world's most powerful instrument of war on land? What a day! What a spectacle! As the dust from tanks settled and the golden cenotaph was dragged slowly back under the arch, the thought impressed itself on one onlooker that 'a sight like this will never be seen again. Because there will never again be a war.'

Light and Shadows

All through the night of 14 July 1919 revellers danced through the streets of a dazzlingly illuminated Paris, turning it (as *The Times* remarked) into 'one vast ballroom', hoping, believing, that the euphoric *vie douce* of pre-1914 would return – had returned. But sombre spectres were already casting their deep shadows. For anyone who read the small print in the news-papers, they were apparent even before the feast began. On the previous Friday there had been a disagreeable little incident at the Café de la Paix. It had been thronged with gay, chattering customers, including many Allied officers and their ladies, when a group of waiters on strike suddenly appeared on the scene, upsetting tables, breaking crockery and spilling drinks. Blows were exchanged between patrons and strikers, but the arrival of some hundred reserve police quickly restored order. The disgruntled waiters, it appeared, were striking for an eight-hour day and better food and working conditions, similar demands to those which, on the very day of the signature of the Peace Treaty, had brought about a Métro and bus strike, paralysing the city. That spring, inflation and the growing restiveness of the workers – *la vie chère* instead of *la vie douce* – had been the main topic of conversation in many a French household. Fortunately, or so it seemed to Parisian property-owners, the Government was being tough with these left-wing demon-strators. But its toughness was only embittering the atmosphere. It was clear that France, in giving her all for victory, had gravely neglected some aspects of her internal health. The *Union Sacrée*, that miraculous war-time truce between all parties and all classes, had barely survived the Armistice!

Then, on the very day of the Victory Parade, there had been disquieting reports from Berlin in the papers, telling of a street fight between wounded German ex-soldiers and some French officers. The affray had ended in the killing, by some unknown hand, of a French Serviceman. It was a nasty reminder that the Beast was still not quite dead. And meanwhile from Washington where the Senate was beginning its deliberations on the Peace Treaty, rumours were coming that President Wilson might yet have difficulty in persuading the American Congress to ratify the instrument that was to guarantee France, once and for all, against the menace of the Beast. Four months later the dreadful rumours became reality.

Left-wing Dissent

In France one important group had boycotted the victory celebrations – the political constellation of the far Left, Communists, internationalists and extreme Socialists. The recent war, in their eyes, had been but a criminal affair between the capitalist classes. The workers in their millions had died in it, but it had been no concern of theirs, and the war had not ended in a holy revolution, bringing the overthrow of the existing order, as had happened in Russia. Therefore there was no cause whatever for rejoicing. Instead, the extremists had decided to stage their own show. Together with some disabled ex-Servicemen, about a hundred strong,[3] they gathered near the Place de la Trinité. As a macabre demonstration against militarism, they had intended to roll several of the *mutilés* in their invalid carriages in front of Foch's horse as he rode past the Opéra. But they were forestalled by the police and dispersed. Reforming on the exterior boulevards, they then marched through the East End of Paris to pay tribute to the Communard martyrs enshrined at Père Lachaise Cemetery. There was a scuffle at the cemetery, and some twenty arrests were made. The next day Marcel Cachin, editor of *L'Humanité*, blazed forth in vituperation against the Victory Parade:

Bitterness! Disgust! I have recognized the crowd. It is not the crowd that took the Bastille and sang for the first time of liberty in the streets. It is not the crowd that religiously followed the bier of Zola or Jaurès. . . It is the brutish elemental crowd which does not change, which slavishly acclaims Caesar and Boulanger, which yells at the vanquished, which chooses its heroes indifferently among boxers, gladiators and captains.

Cachin's ire may well have been fanned by the poor turnout of his supporters on the 14th, but their small numbers that day were deceptively irrelevant to the intrinsic, let alone the potential, strength of the new Left in France. For in none other of the victorious nations had Russia's October Revolution

3. Despite exhortations, the vast majority of the Left appear to have been lured away by the greater attraction of the Victory Parade.

evoked stronger sympathies than among the workers of France, the home of revolution itself. It struck powerful chords with the ancient and deep-rooted revolutionary mystique of 1793, 1848, but above all with the Commune of 1871, the brutal repression of which remained stamped in the minds of the French Left wing and whose failure Lenin had now used as a textbook to perfect his own revolution. The foundation in March 1919 of the Third International in Moscow had revived hopes of successful revolution in the hearts of the spiritual heirs of the martyred Communards, while it was no accident that among the interventionist forces in Russia it was the French at Odessa who had raised the flag of mutiny. And at home there was already abundant fuel on the economic and social scene for the flames of revolution to feed upon. From the very earliest post-war days the presence of a potent new force on the French political scene was increasingly apparent, and the bourgeois, property-owning classes closed their ranks accordingly.

French Illusions

With the Armistice of 1918, a series of insidious illusions had pervaded France. Falling back on the eternal, rather arrogant dogma of it being civilization's implicit duty to come to the rescue, when necessary, of its fountain-head, she automatically presupposed that her Anglo-Saxon allies would henceforth never abandon her; that they (particularly America) would maintain their interest in reshaping Europe. But when President Wilson had come over to France to address the victorious doughboys about 'peace upon the . . . foundation of right', they had shown themselves frankly bored. They wanted to get home, and the American electorate showed that it wanted to keep them there – for ever. As the idealism of 1918 evaporated, so the Anglo-Saxon nations would retreat further and further into their shells. Even more than France, they would become pre-occupied with their own pressing internal problems. Feelings would grow (particularly in Britain) that Germany had been treated with excessive harshness at Versailles, feelings generated partly by honest altruism, partly by the dictates of commerce, but partly by instinctive concern at a victorious France's apparently annexationist tendencies, as revealed by her reaching out for the Saar and her sending troops into Germany's bankrupt and defaulting Ruhr.

Another illusion, one to which the glory of the Victory Parade doubtless added impetus, was that France felt she had won the war largely by her own superlative exertions. But the British and Americans *knew* that it could not have been won without them, and they would soon feel that the price paid, both in men and gold, had been too high. They would do almost anything rather than risk having to save France a second time, let alone regain Alsace-Lorraine for her. Hand in hand with this illusion went France's belief that, primarily through the supremacy of her Army, she could enforce the peace by herself. But she could not, because morally, numerically and economically the war had left her feebler than she realized.

As the true state of France's economy became more widely apparent, so it became popular to cherish the happy, simple illusion that 'the Boche will pay'. But Germany could not, would not pay. The Allies would not make her, and the effort to do so was to cost France herself too much. Finally, there was the mortal illusion (although, certainly, Foch for one did not share it) that vanquished, ruined, truncated, revolution-torn Germany could never again be a military menace. But had Frenchmen forgotten already how the harsh settlement imposed by Prussia in 1871, with its territorial amputations, had kept alight France's own fire of revenge for the best part of half a century? Would France indeed have been so ready to rush to the aid of her ally, Russia, in 1914, had Alsace-Lorraine not weighed heavily upon the balances? Now France's supreme grievance had been erased, but Versailles had simply transferred the burden to Germany, mourning her lost territories in the East.

Financial Stresses

Of all the sources of her illusions, probably the most consequential lay in France overestimating her own powers to
mould the post-war world – an error that was to claim Britain
too in the years following 1945. It was in fact 'a haggard
France' that faced the dawn of victory. The bare economic
facts were daunting: France had expended some 25 per cent
of her national fortune; almost 7 per cent of her territory had
been devastated by war, including some of the richest industrial areas; 3¼ million hectares (12,500 square miles, or roughly
the area of Holland) of fertile soil had been ravaged; 3,500 miles
of railway and over 30,000 miles of roads were destroyed; coal
production was down by 37 per cent compared with 1914, steel
by 60 per cent; the trade deficit had risen from 1½ million to
17½ million francs. France's Ministry of Finance estimated the
material damage caused by the Germans, and which would be
the basis for reparations, at 134,000 million gold francs, a
staggering figure compared with 5,000 million which Germany
had demanded, and got, from France in 1871. Yet, showing the
same extraordinary recuperative capacity that had amazed the
world in 1871, France after 1918 repaired her shattered industries, and her courageous peasants got her raddled fields back
under the plough far quicker than anyone could have imagined.
It was to her financial structure, however, that the really lasting
damage had been done. To pay for the war, France had ineluct-
ably allowed inflation to have its head by issuing a flood of
paper money. By the Armistice the franc had lost nearly two-
thirds of its value. This was only a beginning; whereas it then
exchanged at 26 to the pound sterling (5·50 to the dollar),
already by the time of the Victory Parade it had depreciated to
51 to the pound. By May 1926 its value had sunk to 178 to the
pound, and finally, two months later, with a hostile mob beating on the gates of the Palais Bourbon, to 220.

The causes were not hard to find. Fanned by the new viru-
lence of the revolutionary Left, the French workers' very justi-
fiable demands for better conditions and higher wages to offset
this war-time inflation gave the spiral an extra spin. Then there

were the additional millions which had to be spent in paying the pensions of the legions of ex-Servicemen, notably the *mutilés*. But the most pernicious influences here harked back to those two illusions, namely, that France's allies would always be ready to help her, and that 'the Boche will pay'. By the end of the war the public debt had reached 156,000 millions, of which 32,000 millions were owed to the United States and Britain. The Budget of 1919 had been postponed more than seven months, during which time further vast loans had been launched, so that when the Budget was finally agreed it showed an enormous deficit of 27,000 millions. Nobody viewed this too tragically. First, it was automatically assumed that the Allies would be accommodating, and generous, in the recovery of France's war debts; it was widely thought, in the words of a cynical expression popular at the time, that the Allies could not possibly expect France to repay 'the cost of overcoats in which her soldiers had got themselves killed'. But Britain for one, with nearly a million of her own men lying dead in Flanders fields and with equally grave internal problems at home, did not quite see things that way.

Hopes for Reparations

When the Budget had been postponed in December 1918, the Minister of Finance, Louis-Lucien Klotz (according to Clemenceau 'the only Jew who knows nothing about money'), made it clear that he expected France's budgetary deficits to be redeemed then and thenceforth by German reparations. At the Peace Conference, France had estimated her total war damages at 209,000 million gold francs, while the overall claims of the Allies amounted to some 400,000 million. But British Treasury experts reckoned that the most that could be squeezed out of Germany would be 75,000 million. With the British showing marked distaste for the whole subject from the outset, most bitter discord had surrounded the talks on reparations at Versailles, a discord that certainly did not go unobserved beyond the Rhine. Finally – and fatally – the sum to be paid by Germany was left open for future negotiation. It was as an open sore that the issue of reparations remained open, gaining little for France but ill-will. In 1923 Germany defaulted on her payments, and France occupied the Ruhr to force her to pay. Britain, seeing political ambition behind the financial pretexts (and indeed there were nationalist Frenchmen who openly expressed hopes that the occupation might prove permanent) dissociated herself. From the ensuing industrial breakdown resulted the final collapse of the German mark. Down in Bavaria an angry unknown Austrian acquired his first national publicity. Throughout Germany a legacy of lasting resentment was created, as well as a few martyrs of whom Hitler would later make excellent capital. Relations with Britain became chronically estranged, and would hardly regain their former cordiality before the eve of the second world crisis, while in France herself the franc threatened to run after the Reichsmark. On being forced to retreat from the Ruhr, the illusion of France's power in the post-war world received its first serious shock.

Reparations, with the international hostility they caused, did more than anything else to clear the way for the Second World War. They certainly did not result in balancing France's Budget, as Klotz and his successors had hoped. In fact, out of all the international transactions intertwining reparations with the repayment of war debts in the 1920s, Germany probably gained more than France. During the first half of the 1920s, seven different Ministers of Finance, following on each others' heels, failed to put France's house in order. Although the return of Raymond Poincaré in 1926 brought France an almost miraculous three-year period of quasi-stability (as well as prosperity), in the seventeen months after his retirement in 1929 another five governments came and went. France's financial dilemma extended itself into the 1930s, bringing down government after government, rendering impossible any consistent foreign policy – let alone any policy of reconciliation with Germany – bedevilling the Third Republic throughout the remainder of its existence, and finally hamstringing it when the necessity to rearm confronted France with desperate urgency.

Lack of Men and Ideas

'The means by which Providence raises a nation to greatness are the virtues infused into her great men.' So said Burke in his memorial to Pitt. By the end of the 1920s it was painfully apparent that the political being of the Third Republic was suffering from a grave deficit of great men, as much as it was of great ideas. Clemenceau had been rapidly dispatched, in much the same manner as the British nation was to deal with its warlord in 1945 – '*passé le péril, maudit le saint*'. Briand was tottering, Painlevé ageing, while in the same year that both Clemenceau and Foch died, 1929, ill-health forced Poincaré from the political scene. After the ceremony solemnizing the liberation of Strasbourg in 1918, he had been heard to sigh 'Now I can die.' Despite his own remarkable resurrection in 1926, the overtones of Poincaré's remark were loaded with a double significance. With the return of Alsace-Lorraine, the supreme motivating and uniting ideal had been removed from French politics. Where was there now a Holy Grail worth questing and fighting for? Balancing the Budget was hardly a substitute. At the same time, Poincaré's sigh echoed the psychological lassitude that was increasingly to beset French politics, later to be compounded with the physical consequences of France's terrible war losses; for among these, the one category bled whiter than all the rest comprised the liberal professions (of the total mobilized, 23 per cent had been killed), the source which should have supplied the new Clemenceaus and Poincarés. In her autobiography, *The Prime of Life*, Simone de Beauvoir tells of a Dr Lemaire, who, on returning from the front where he had operated on hundreds of wounded under the most sickening conditions, 'took to his bed and never got up again'. How many of France's young intellectuals lucky enough to survive the trenches and who should now be taking over the reins of government, had, like Dr Lemaire, simply slumped within themselves, mentally and morally drained?

The left-wing challenge immediately following the end of the war was succeeded in France by a brief phase of deceptive parliamentary stability. Thoroughly alarmed by fears of the

Bolshevik menace, the bourgeois parties had rallied together to form a right-of-centre *Bloc National Républicain*. At the elections of November 1919, the *Bloc* swept into power, winning nearly three-quarters of the seats in the Assembly, and furnishing France with the most right-wing parliament she had known since 1876. Meanwhile, the Left wing seemed to be tearing itself apart by internal divisions. During their congress at Tours in December 1920, the Socialist Party had split into the new *Parti Communiste Française* – uncompromising devotees of the Soviet Revolution – and the more moderate Socialists calling themselves the *Section Française de la IIe Internationale Ouvrière* (S.F.I.O.). This was followed, in 1921, by a similar split within the trade unions from which emerged the dissident Communist *Confédération Générale du Travail Unitaire* (C.G.T.U.), obedient to every instruction from Moscow and pledged to total war against management, in contrast to the more moderate line pursued by the old *Confédération Générale du Travail* (C.G.T.). Until the great reunion under the Popular Front of 1936, Communist would chastise Socialist, the C.G.T.U. would revile the C.G.T. Short-sightedly, employers and bourgeois rejoiced at this rift in the left-wing camp, and were encouraged by its apparent weakness to backtrack on essential social reforms, thereby building up for the future an explosive reserve of grievances and ill-will.

Expressing his fundamental mistrust for the League of Nations, Clemenceau once remarked: 'If you want to have a new spirit between nations, start by introducing a new spirit at home.' In fact, post-war French politicians swiftly showed an instinct to return to the old spirit of the Third Republic – only worse. Before the war, issues had at least been relatively clear-cut and simple; hardy perennials such as anticlericalism and the Dreyfus Case helped define boundaries between parties, and there was always the supreme polarizing force of Alsace-Lorraine. Now revenge – *la revanche* – was fulfilled, and anti-clericalism virtually a dead duck; issues were blurred and complex, and there was this mounting shortage of strong wills and clear minds capable of guiding their parties in the search for a coherent programme. Like amoebae, parties divided and redivided within themselves. Politicians became subject to the pull of the rapidly growing numbers of pressure groups all acting upon Parliament, and for many self-interest came, in the absence of any other grander motive, to be their guiding star. With the collapse of each successive government, it proved just that much harder (especially after Poincaré had gone) to create a majority with any promise of stability. A mad game of musical chairs ensued, to be played at a giddier and giddier rate until Hitler's Panzers finally stopped the music.

Though France's governmental instability in the 1920s was principally provoked by discord over internal matters, such as the Budget, it was upon her external policy – particularly towards Germany – that this had the most baneful effects. The overriding practical purpose of the Versailles Treaty had been to guarantee the security of France, to prevent her from ever again being swamped by the Teutonic hordes. To this end the Germans were required by the Treaty to disband their General Staff, to reduce their Army in perpetuity to a militia of only 100,000 men, and forbidden tanks, heavy artillery or aircraft. Under the separate treaties of St Germain and Trianon, the Hapsburg Empire had been broken up into a row of small nations so as to deprive Germany of any powerful potential ally in Central Europe; and it was hoped that these Poles, Czechs, Yugoslavs, Hungarians and Roumanians would all show their gratitude by remaining constant allies of France. By augmenting French industry at the cost of Germany's it was reckoned that reparations would help erase the traditional disparity between the economic power of the two countries. Finally, to secure her vulnerable eastern frontier, France had been granted a footing in Germany's Rhineland. But here she had got less than she wanted. Foch had declared: 'If we do not hold the Rhine permanently, no neutralization, or disarmament, or any kind of written clause can prevent Germany ... from sallying out of it at will.' In the future, he added prophetically, there would not be time for the arrival of Anglo-American aid to save France from military defeat. But Lloyd George and President Wilson had thrown up their hands in horror, exclaiming that they could not countenance annexations by France that would only create another Alsace-Lorraine. In the end, France had had to be satisfied with the permanent demilitarization and a temporary occupation of the left bank of the Rhine.[4] Foch boycotted the signature of the Treaty, grumbling in disgust and with some accuracy: 'This is not peace. It is an armistice for twenty years.'

As the realities of the post-war world proceeded systematically to destroy France's illusion that she was capable of maintaining the peace of Europe, so her leaders were beset by mounting anxiety that the provisions of Versailles could at best offer her only partial and temporary security. In the background there stood constantly the one unalterable fact of life from which they could never avert their gaze: even with the addition of Alsace-Lorraine's 1,800,000 inhabitants and the effects upon Germany's population of her territorial losses, there were in 1919 still only 39 million Frenchmen compared with 59 million Germans. Moreover, Germany sustained a vigorously expanding birth-rate, whereas that of France was static, so that even by 1931 she had still barely made good her war casualties. This was the one fundamental, constant factor at the back of France's European policy throughout the 1920s and into the 1930s.

But because of her chronic state of governmental instability she found herself incapable of facing this problem with any consistent strategy of her own. One moment she would show herself bent on grinding down the Germans by marching into the Ruhr; the next, she was offering the olive branch of reconciliation. She would vaunt the supremacy afforded by the offensive might of the French Army, then hide herself behind a twentieth-century Great Wall of China. She would appear to place her faith in the League of Nations, while with the other hand she endeavoured to hem Germany about by alliances with the new East European buffer states, although it was all too doubtful whether any combination of these could ever replace the weight of the Russian behemoth, France's defaulting ally now engrossed in the dream of Marxism and the nightmare of civil war. Even during the most hopeful post-

4. In fact, the last French soldier left the Rhineland in June 1930.

war period of the Briand–Stresemann entente, which stretched intermittently from 1925 to 1929, attacks from the Right and lack of support on the Left forced Briand again and again to renege on his declared aims of Franco-German rapprochement. Finally, in 1929, when Premier for the eleventh time, Briand proposed from the tribune of the League of Nations a European Federation embracing Germany. It was a grandiose ideal a generation, alas, ahead of its time, and Briand was promptly overthrown by the French nationalists. Almost simultaneously came the death of Stresemann, the Weimar Republic's most inspiring and inspired leader, and possibly the one man capable of stemming the rising tide of Nazism. Shortly before he died, exhausted and disillusioned, Stresemann summed up his dealings with France: 'I gave and gave and gave until my followers turned against me . . . If they could have granted me just one concession, I would have won my people. But they gave nothing . . . That is my tragedy and their crime.'

In actual fact, by the end of the first post-war decade France had made substantial concessions; she had, for instance, agreed to withdraw her troops from the Rhineland five years ahead of the specified time. But her concessions were so hedged about with the reservations imposed by the waverings of her diverse governments that, in German eyes, they bore no signs of genuine magnanimity or forward-looking statesmanship; rather they seemed acts of weakness and irresolution, forced upon France by her dissident allies or by the *force majeure* of external events. As the 1930s opened, Briand lamented with bitterness that despite all recent concessions made on reparations, nothing had diminished Germany's ill-will. By 1931 Germany was like the genie in the bottle, who, instead of showing gratitude to his innocent liberator, slew him by way of requital for his prolonged sufferings.

Now in the midst of France's perennial game of legislative musical chairs, there burst the malignant, irreconcilable figure of Hitler.

Chapter 2

'Thank God for the French Army'

Against an army sailing through the clouds neither walls nor mountains nor seas could afford any security.
SAMUEL JOHNSON, *Rasselas*

'Thank God for the French Army,' cried Winston Churchill before the Commons on 23 March 1933. It was two months after the coming to power of Hitler. Few statements by Churchill outraged even Tory opinion more than this one. All round the House, he observed looks 'of pain and aversion'. For it was also the year in which, having reduced her own arms expenditure to its all-time low for the inter-war period, Britain was urging France to follow suit. Preoccupied with the row over Larwood's body-line bowling in the Test Match against the Australians, the yo-yo craze, trunk murders and the amorous successes of the Rector of Stiffkey,[1] Britain had assumed a progressively detached attitude towards Europe's problems. The emotional view of the Great War as a glorious crusade had been widely replaced by the doubts voiced by Lloyd George when he declared: 'We all blundered into war', and France's role in leading Britain into this supreme blunder seemed to be illuminated with ever-increasing clarity. British public opinion, shocked at accounts by the Spenders and Isherwoods of starving, ricket-ridden children growing up in a Germany apparently broken by France's avarice for reparations, had, unlike the French, ceased to regard Germans as the eternal enemy.[2] By and large it had lapsed back into that normal, healthy Anglo-Saxon *status quo ante* of mistrusting

1. Throughout most of 1932, the middle-aged Rector of Stiffkey (pronounced 'Stewky' locally) had provided the British Press with an unending source of anticlerical entertainment through his escapades with battalions of teenage waitresses in London teashops. Defrocked, he ended his career in a lion's cage in 1937, where he was billed to give a lecture. The lion objected.
2. The inverted attitudes of post-1945 make an interesting comparison.

all French designs, a spirit of the age which, as late as July 1934, *The Times* epitomized with its forecast: 'In the years that are coming, there is more reason to fear for Germany than to fear Germany.' It was the vision of the huge French Army, still presumptively the most powerful in the world, constantly poised over European affairs, which alarmed Britons, among whom, in praising it, Winston Churchill stood for only a dissident minority.

But, as Hitler began to make it abundantly plain that he would not rest until the *Diktat* of Versailles was overthrown and Germany returned to her former ascendancy, what in fact was the state of the French Army? Was it still the superlative weapon of 1919?

The Influences of Verdun

The training and morale of an army, and even its weapons, are transient factors that can alter the balance between opposing forces within the course of one campaigning season. It is the more immutable matters of doctrine and fundamental strategy that require to be considered here. That a victorious army should, in its subsequent peace-time development, be strongly influenced by the experiences of the past war is a historical platitude and only too natural; but, to quote Frederick the Great, 'experience is useless unless the right conclusions are drawn from it'. France having borne so much of the brunt of the fighting on the Western Front, the experience there came to weigh with particular gravity upon French military minds. Predominant was that of Verdun 1916, whence arose three separate influences, in many ways self-conflicting, but each vitally affecting the post-war French Army.

The first related to the psychological consequences of Verdun emerging as the symbol and legend of ultimate glory. In most of the great Allied undertakings of the war, the glory had been shared, but Verdun, the longest and most terrible struggle of them all, had belonged solely to France. For ten agonizing months, and at a cost of over 400,000 men, she had measured herself in single combat against the full power of the German

Army and won. As well as epitomizing the very nature of the
war itself, Verdun proved to be a kind of watershed in it, 'the
walls upon which broke the supreme hopes of Imperial
Germany', as President Poincaré declared. With every justification, Verdun at once became a legend of national heroism and
virility. In the passage of years it grew to be enshrined with the
holy qualities of a miracle. It was France's Battle of Britain,
symbolizing just as much, though perhaps imbued with even
greater emotive force, and bearing the same kind of latent
peril. Just as post-1945 Britons, perplexed by imperial disintegration and adversities of trade, found (and still find) un-
reasoned comfort in the belief that whatever divinity had presided over Dunkirk and in the London skies would always, in
the end, sally forth to save them, so Frenchmen, to their peril,
came to regard Verdun as a touchstone of faith in the jungle
of the inter-war world. In the Army, as recurrent financial
crises rendered the replacement of obsolescent equipment a
constant nightmare, it was always agreeable to recall the fundamental superiority which the French warrior race had displayed over the (now disarmed) enemy in 1916. Just as the
British Navy ossified after Trafalgar, a kind of conservative
complacency was bred in France: 'What was good enough in
1916 is good enough now.' To challenge it hardly guaranteed
popularity in Army circles.

Yet parallel to the first influence, a second contained the
awareness of just how much warfare like Verdun had cost
France. More regular officers and men of the French Army had
gone through the inferno of Verdun than any other battle, and
the frequent post-war commemorations ensured that their
minds retained the full horror of those ten months: the ceaseless shelling from an enemy whom, very likely, one never saw,
the wounded men agonizing untended, the hideous mutilations,
the reliefs and ration parties never arriving, the senseless
counter-attacks to recapture at impossible cost a few yards of
shell-holes; the thirst, the hunger, the stench, the misery, the
fear; above all, always the shells. A young lieutenant killed at
Verdun scrawled in his journal: 'They will not be able to make
us do it again another day; that would be to misconstrue the

price of our effort. They will have to resort to those who have not lived these days.' Privately, the men of France's post-war Army wondered to themselves if they could do Verdun again, if any other Frenchman, if any other human being could? In the lassitude left by the war, they felt the answer, morally, was *no*. There was indeed no doubt that, numerically, Verdun was the kind of battle that France, with her depleted population, could never, never fight again. But what kind of battle could she fight?

Certainly, whatever those British critics of Churchill might have feared, it seemed increasingly improbable that France could ever herself engage in offensive warfare. Defensively, her interests were protected by the Versailles Treaty – for the time being. But the function of military staffs is to plan for contingency. France *might*, nevertheless, be attacked once again by the traditional enemy; in this event, how could she fight a defensive battle without suffering a Verdun? What new strategy, what new technique could be evolved to avoid it? In their pursuit of an alternative, the footsteps of France's military thinkers led them back towards Verdun itself. The actual lessons gained there, and the conclusions drawn from them, constitute the third, and most portentous, influence emanating from that hideous battlefield.

Most of the siege warfare of 1914–18 had surged back and forth over an amorphous line of trenches. What was peculiar about Verdun was the presence of concentric clusters of powerful underground forts. Although, for various reasons, France had grossly neglected these at the beginning of the battle, its subsequent course seemed to indicate that Verdun owed its survival to them. The mightiest of these forts, Douaumont, had actually been captured early on in an extraordinary, bloodless *coup* by a small group of Germans; its loss was later estimated to have cost the French the equivalent of 100,000 men. Its neighbour, Fort Vaux, with a garrison of only 250 men, heroically stood up to a whole Germany army corps and delayed the advance on Verdun one vital week. Others, like Souville, proved invaluable by furnishing shellproof shelters from which infantry could sally forth to repulse the attacking

Germans, while supporting them with fire from artillery mounted beneath almost indestructible carapaces of thick steel. Only the very heaviest enemy shells could penetrate them. When a French Army Commission led by Marshal Joffre visited Verdun in 1922, it was astonished at the way in which the forts had absorbed the pounding of the German 'Big Berthas', an impression reinforced by the nigh-impenetrable strength which their scrutiny of Germany's deep-dug 'Hindenburg Line' revealed. If only the French High Command could have utilized those forts properly in 1916, think how many valuable *poilu* lives might have been saved, all the while assuring the integrity of Verdun! Let these lessons not be ignored, the Commission warned itself.

The Maginot Line

There was an additional factor. From the days of the barbarians onwards, France had constantly lain open to invasion through her vulnerable eastern frontier. With the new rapidity of movement afforded by railways, it had twice been proved, in 1870 as in 1914, that a battle lost in the east could bring the Germans to the very doors of Paris itself within a matter of weeks. In Lorraine and the Nord, France's most vital industrial centres lay particularly exposed to German aggression, and deprivation of these had so nearly brought defeat in the Great War. Among a nation where the peasant voice still predominated, the soil of France – every square yard of it – assumed sacred qualities; it was the unyielding defence of this which had persuaded the French High Command to adopt such rigid and costly tactics at Verdun. After the stabilization of the fronts in 1914, the French infantry had paid out a steady and prodigious rent in blood just to hold on to that continuous line of ill-protected trenches, stretching from Switzerland to the North Sea. But at least they had held, and by doing so had ensured the inviolability of France's sacred soil. Supposing now, the Army Commission of 1922 asked itself, France should prepare to defend herself behind not shallow, hastily dug trenches, but a continuous and permanent line of forts even deeper and more sophisticated than those of Verdun? In the event of another German war, would not such a line surely save both lives and the ravaging of French territory? Might not its mere existence pose a formidable deterrent to any aggressive-minded German ruler in the future?

For seven years the Battle of Verdun was re-fought in the higher councils of French military thought, as argument swayed back and forth over the blueprints for France's new fortress line. On one premise the majority were agreed from the start: the line must represent a 'continuous front'. Above all this was the view of Pétain, appointed Inspector-General of the Army after the war, and, as age removed Joffre and Foch from the scene, for many successive years her most influential soldier. He was also the man who had been more closely concerned in the immortal defence of Verdun than any other. But although Pétain, in the years following his trial and disgrace, has come to be regarded in France as a scapegoat for all that was faulty about inter-war military thinking, it is entirely unjust to suggest that he single-handedly laced his Army into a kind of intellectual straitjacket. The French Army donned it all too willingly. For during the past war its officer corps had had no contact with the great fluid movements of the campaign in the East in which so many Germans had taken part nor had they even any direct knowledge of the highly mobile campaigns fought by Allenby and the British in Palestine. 'We had been haunted,' wrote a distinguished subsequent Army leader, General Beaufre,[3] 'by the tenacity of the German machine-guns, and the impossibility in which we found ourselves of breaking the enemy front.' From the lessons of their four years of static warfare, which even the introduction of tanks did disappointingly little to alter, had emerged the doctrine of the 'continuous front', to be espoused by the great mass of French military thought, with its experience of no other form of strategy. This, thought the École Militaire all through the

3. André Beaufre, a junior staff officer at the Ministry of War after the First World War, later became a full general and one of France's leading military intellects after the Second World War. He led the French contingent at Suez in 1956.

1920s, must prove to be the shape of future warfare; moreover, as shown above, it was a shape peculiarly expedient for the defence of the soil of France. But expediency usually turns out to be a poor strategic guide.

On 4 January 1930, a vast majority in both chambers of the National Assembly voted for a law accepting the Army's long-debated plans for a Great Wall on the eastern frontier. André Maginot, who had become one of the Third Republic's most honourable politicians, happened to be Minister of War at the time; thus it was his name that the fortress line would bear henceforth. For the first phase of its construction, the Assembly voted the immense sum of 3,000 million francs,[4] to be spread over four years. Work on the Maginot Line began at once; as Maginot himself stressed, it *had* to be completed by 1935, the date appointed by the Versailles Treaty for France finally to withdraw her troops from the Rhineland. It was to run from Basle, on the borders of Switzerland, to Longwy, close to where the Belgian, Luxembourg and French frontiers meet; why it was not intended to continue to Dunkirk, thus covering Belgium, will be seen later. The strength and depth of line varied, but for 87 miles it consisted of 'fortified regions', guarding two major invasion avenues. One covered a potential assault aimed at Metz and Nancy, while the other faced north to guard the plains of Lower Alsace. Facing directly east, a series of lesser fortifications backed up the wide river barrier of the Rhine. Just behind the frontier, the defences of the two fortified regions began with a series of anti-tank obstacles and barbed wire, backed up by reinforced barracks, known as *maisons fortes* ('strong houses') and pill-boxes, the object of these advance posts being to provide warning of an attack and delay it. At their rear came a deep anti-tank ditch and then the subterranean casemates, and forts which comprised the back-bone of the Line. Protected by up to ten feet of concrete, each casemate contained rapid-firing anti-tank guns and machine-guns firing out of underground slits with a 50-degree arc, as well as grenade-throwers to dislodge any enemy infantry approaching by means of dead ground. Their twenty-five-man garrison

4. £24 million at the then rate of exchange.

lived and slept on a floor still deeper under the earth. Superbly blended into their environment, about all that an enemy could see of these concrete casemates were two small nipples formed by the observation cupolas surmounting them.

The real pride of the Maginot Line, however, lay in its forts, which backed up the casemates at an interval of every three to five miles. Ever since Vauban, French engineers have been without rivals in the art of fortification, and the Verdun forts had been masterpieces of their time, but these new concrete and steel monsters were veritable wonders of the modern world. When troops passed through their cavernous gates placed discreetly at the base of some hill, they entered into a Wellsian civilization in which they could live, sleep, eat, work and exercise for many weeks without ever seeing the surface of the earth – not unlike nuclear submariners of today embarking on a voyage under the Pole. Electric trains whisked them from their underground barracks and canteens to their gun turrets; vast power stations, equally underground, provided them with heat and light; powerful compressor plants supplied them with air, and ensured that the forts were proof against poison gas; immense subterranean food stores, reservoirs and fuel tanks would enable them to remain cut off from the rest of the French Army for up to three months. There were three different types of forts, the biggest of which – Category 1 – housed a garrison of up to 1,200 officers and men, and contained between fifteen and eighteen concrete 'blocks', each bristling with guns mounted in disappearing turrets and of calibres that ranged from 37 mm. to 135 mm. Each fort was divided in two, connected by deep subterranean galleries lying beyond the penetration of any bomb r shell, and varying between 400 yards and 1½ miles in length. Thus even if one half of the fort should be knocked out, the other half could continue to fight, and each half was so located that it could bring down supporting fire on its twin, its neighbouring forts or casemates.

At Verdun the greatest danger experienced by the French forts had been from infantry infiltrating on to their superstructures and working their way underground. Both Douau-

mont and Vaux had been lost in this way. To prevent a
repetition, the Maginot Line plan incorporated 'interval troops',
infantry complete with field artillery, which could be moved
up to counter any threat to a particular fort or group of forts.
These were intended to compensate for what, by definition, the
Line lacked – mobility.[5]

Much has been said about why the Maginot Line failed to
save France in 1940, though not always have the right reasons
been given. It was enormously costly. Partly owing to errors of
construction due to bureaucratic jealousies, the 87 miles of
'fortified regions' completed by 1935 had already cost 7,000
million francs, far in excess of the parliamentary estimates. In
addition to its construction, the maintenance of the Maginot
Line represented a considerable financial burden. For a country
plagued by chronic budgetary difficulties and with a powerful
Left wing opposed to rearmament in any form, this overall
costliness meant that inevitably the French Army would be
forced to accept economies elsewhere. The Maginot Line also
lacked depth, with its four successive positions never occupying, even in their most advanced state, a belt larger than twelve
miles deep. This too was a consequence of expense.

But the most mortal defect of the Line lay not in its depth
but its length. Romantically, it came to be dubbed 'the shield of
France'. The essence of a shield, however, is that it can be
manipulated to protect any portion of its owner's body. The
Maginot Line obviously was incapable of motion, yet it did not
extend to cover what Clausewitz called 'the pit of the French
stomach', the classical invasion route across the Belgian plains,
over which the Schlieffen Plan had so nearly brought total
calamity in 1914. By as late as 1935, the motives for not fortifying the remaining 250 miles along the Belgian frontier were
only partially related to problems of cost. This extension would
have to run right through the heavily industrialized Lille–
Valenciennes area which straddles the frontier and would be

5. Though ironically enough, when the supreme test came, the drain imposed by maintaining the 'interval troops' was to be one of the leading
factors in depriving the French Army of the mobility it so sadly lacked.

immeasurably disruptive as well as costly. A factor carrying even greater weight, however, was that Belgium, mindful of how her neutrality had been outraged by Germany in 1914, remained France's close ally, so that a fortified line on the French side of her frontier would leave her out in the cold, abandoned on the wrong side of the ramparts. She would then have no option but to return to her former neutrality, and rely upon German morals. Pétain, despite his reputation for defensive-mindedness, made it quite clear when Minister of War in 1934 that, in the event of any German aggression, it was part and parcel of French strategy to 'go into Belgium' and to fight an offensive war of movement against the enemy there.[6] As the French Army stood in 1934, still with its crushing superiority over the Germans – who had not yet invented the Panzer corps – this strategy made excellent sense, as long as Belgium remained within the alliance. It was also clearly in France's interest (though she could hardly explain this to the Belgians) to protect her soil by fighting the battle, with all its destructiveness, as far forward of her frontiers as possible.

With the construction of the Maginot Line, the wheel of French military thought, which had started spinning in 1870, performed a fatal full cycle. In 1870, to state it in the simplest terms, France had lost a war through adopting too defensive a posture and relying too much on permanent fortifications. Fortress cities such as Strasbourg, Metz and Paris herself had been simply enveloped by Moltke's Prussians and besieged one by one. In reaction against this calamitous defeat, France had nearly lost the next war by being too aggressive-minded. Now she was once again seeking safety under concrete and steel. Rapidly the Maginot Line came to be not just a component of strategy, but a way of life. Feeling secure behind it, like the lotus-eating mandarins of Cathay behind their Great Wall, the French Army allowed itself to atrophy, to lapse into desuetude. A massive combination of factors – complacency, lassitude,

6. Both in 1927 and 1932, Pétain, the President of the Army Council, had stressed the importance of having 'a mobile force near the frontier and to make sure of its swift advance into Belgium'.

deficiencies of manpower and finance – conspired to rust the superb weapon which the world had so admired on that *Quatorze Juillet* of 1919.

The French Army: Men and Arms

By the end of 1935, the eve of France's first major confrontation with Hitler, her Army was below par both in numbers and quality of manpower. The call-up was just beginning to suffer the full effect of the 'hollow classes' caused by the drop in births during the Great War. In Germany, for instance, the 1915 class available for conscription (if it were not for the restrictions imposed by Versailles) amounted to 464,000 men; in France, it was only 184,000, a ratio that would continue right the way through to the Second World War. Yet politics had forced a reduction in the length of military service from three years to one, and hopes that the population deficit of metropolitan France could be made good by a vast colonial army were never quite fulfilled. Thus instead of a total strength of over 300,000 men, about two-thirds of this was the most the French could muster. As far as the hard core of professionals was concerned, there was certainly little enough inducement for good men to stay on. With a captain paid approximately £11 a month, and a major in command of a whole battalion paid only £16,[7] officers without private incomes lived in desperate straits. They had no vote, and now that the supreme goal – revenge – had been achieved, wherein resided the glory of an Army career?

Composed of all too many officers whom the previous war had left drained of *élan vital*, the French General Staff allowed itself to become bogged down in bureaucratic methods; *paper-asserie*, as the French call it, the blight to which all armies are susceptible, flourished. It was difficult to see exactly where the power of decision lay. The once omnipotent and cohesive *Conseil Supérieur de la Guerre* (Supreme War Council), from whose members would be designated France's senior commanders in time of war, no longer filled anything but a con-

7. Even in the underpaid British Army at this time, a captain (unmarried) received a basic pay of £38 a month, a major £53.

sultative role. Divided by mutual antipathy and jealousies, its generals had little contact with each other; their staffs followed suit, each existing in its own watertight compartment. There was not much discussion on a higher strategic and tactical plane, and what there was tended to follow abstract intellectual paths from which little practical use ever emerged. General Beaufre, writing of his own experiences at that time, states that

At the Ministry of War, the General commanded in theory, but had not the money, the administration, the personnel or the equipment; the Permanent Secretary had the money and the administration, without the responsibility of command; the various departments had personnel and equipment, but neither money nor command. The Minister stood at the head of all this, but could achieve nothing without obtaining unison from the whole orchestra, the complexity of which helped to paralyse all initiatives. The ensemble possessed only one force – that of inertia.

In this state of inertia, the Army tended to rest content with the techniques and equipment of 1918. To a large extent the financial strain imposed on successive military budgets by the Maginot Line provided it with little alternative.[8] Although, with the taxis of the Marne and later by her victualling of Verdun along the *voie sacrée* – the 'sacred road' – the French Army had pioneered warfare by road, as its post-war mechanical transport aged and was not replaced it regressed to relying for mobility once more on railways – and horses. While other armies (notably the German) were experimenting with radio communications, the French clung to the telephone, even despite the lessons gained from 1914–18, when operations had so often failed after the severing of lines by artillery barrages, and regardless of the new threat to land communications which modern air power and tanks posed. In 1924 the Army decided to replace its automatic rifle and to modify the standard infantry cartridge; the new weapon came into service by 1932, but – typical of the prevailing inertia – the rifle, intended to utilize the same cartridge, was not selected until 1936. As late as 1939,

8. Arms credits for 1936 totalled 1,492 million francs, roughly a fifth of what had already been spent on the Maginot Line.

only a few hundred thousand had been issued. General Weygand, before he retired as Inspector-General of the Army in
1933, had prescribed that five infantry divisions be motorized
and a cavalry division be converted into a *Division Légère
Mécanique*;[9] but otherwise the rest of the Army showed little
advance on that which had processed so resplendently through
Paris in 1919.

Tanks and Doctrine

There is no weightier problem common to the General Staffs
of all peaceably-minded countries in modern times than the
decision for what year to plan the re-equipment of its forces
with a new armoury.[10] Weapons designed too long before the
moment of crisis, becoming speedily obsolete, are almost as
useless as those that arrive too late. In its tank production
policy, the French Army had remained for many years a
prisoner of the mass of machines left over from 1918. With the
rise of Hitler, it adopted the expedient of building prototypes
while year by year postponing their mass-production until such
time as the threat of war seemed imminent, a notional date
which self-deception and appeasement would constantly defer.
So long as Germany obeyed Versailles, binding her not to build
tanks, France's obsolete armour was quite sufficient for her
purposes. In any case, she could hardly afford to replace it. But
the most insidious long-term consequences – and it would be
hard to find any single military factor contributing more
directly to the defeat of 1940 – of this residuum lay in the
shadow it cast over the development of France's doctrines of
armoured warfare. The bulk of the tanks inherited from the
war consisted of the Renault F.T. model, lightly armoured,

9. 'Light mechanized division' – which was something of a misnomer, in
that the D.L.M.s were largely equipped with the excellent Somua medium
tank, more heavily armoured than most of its German counterparts. They
also had a strength of 220 tanks each, compared with only 150 for each of
the subsequently created French 'Armoured Divisions'.

10. In Britain, for instance, up to 1932 the Services worked on the simple
assumption each year of not having to anticipate a major war for at least
another ten.

slow and strictly limited in operational radius. It was useless against concrete fortifications, or in battle against other tanks; it was predominantly an instrument of infantry support. In the culminating battles of 1918, the F.T.s moved up with the infantry after the usual heavy bombardment. When the infantry had advanced beyond the range of their artillery (and the tanks had run out of petrol), the attackers would consolidate and wait for the guns – drawn by horses – to move up and prepare for the next laborious step forward. At each pause, the hard-pressed Germans were given a respite in which to repair their defences. Never was the rhythm of attack maintained; never were the French tanks, numbering over 4,000 but spread out all along the front, concentrated for a breakthrough; and never did any deep penetration occur. Again and again, in the French communiqués there appeared sentences like the following: 'The tanks put to flight the defenders, but the infantry did not reach the objective.' Against an enemy that was already beaten, losses in both tanks and infantry were disheartening, the conclusions drawn discouraging.

In his post-war 'Instruction' of 1921, Marshal Pétain, then Supreme Commander, dismissed the future role of armour in two lines: 'Tanks assist the advance of the infantry, by breaking static obstacles and active resistance put up by the enemy.' For the next fourteen years this was to remain the accepted creed of the French Army. As at Verdun, the plodding infantryman dominated. But meanwhile, in England, a prophet had arisen with a new and revolutionary concept of warfare. A twenty-four-year-old ex-regular officer invalided out of the Army as a result of gassing on the Somme, Captain Basil Liddell Hart, was invited to help draft the British Army's post-war infantry training manual. The manual gave him a first opportunity to propound his 'expanding torrent' theory of deep, swift penetration as an antidote to the static warfare of 1914–18. As his thoughts evolved, Liddell Hart saw offensive operations being spearheaded by powerful concentrations of fast-moving, wide-ranging tanks, no longer mere adjuncts of foot soldiery, and backed by equally mobile self-propelled guns and infantrymen transported in armoured carriers. Instead of battering away along a wide sector with the old, methodical siege techniques, the attacker, having probed out a weak spot in the enemy's defences, would pour through it at top speed with his 'expanding torrent' of mobile firepower, creating vulnerable new fronts deep in the defenders' rear. If Liddell Hart's theories – and those of his contemporary Major-General J. F. C. ('Boney') Fuller – should be proved viable, it obviously meant the death of the 'continuous front' school of thought, on which the whole of France's inter-war strategy was based.

Harried by this awkward and gangling guru and his small band of supporters within the walls, the British Army decided in 1926 to lead the way by establishing an experimental mechanized force. Within two years, however, the conservative factions of the Army 'Establishment' reasserted themselves and this force was disbanded. In France, there was an even smaller body of bright young officers who, in Beaufre's words, found Liddell Hart's doctrine 'as dazzling a discovery as the rediscovery of antiquity must have seemed to the men of the Renaissance after the conformist sterilities of medieval scholasticism'. But otherwise, comforted by the unreceptiveness of orthodoxy in England, the shapers of French military policy were able to ignore his teachings. Only elsewhere, in Germany, was their full import immediately grasped. In an attack upon proposals for the creation of an armoured corps, Pétain's successor as Minister of War, General Maurin, summed up French attitudes prevailing in 1935 when he asked the Chamber of Deputies, amid loud applause, 'How can we still believe in the offensive when we have spent thousands of millions to establish a fortified barrier? Would we be mad enough to advance beyond this barrier upon goodness knows what adventure!' Yet if the offensive was damned and its mechanical requisites neglected, how then was the French Army to carry out that essential component of Maginot Line strategy – the march into Belgium – against a presumptively rearmed and re-equipped Germany?

Alliances Undermined

The significance of the defensive posture the French Army had adopted by the end of 1935 far exceeded simple military considerations of protecting France's own soil. Most important, it gravely impinged upon the system of alliances painfully constructed since 1919 as breakwaters against possible German aggression. From the very beginning, the Quai d'Orsay had realized that they could no longer count on the traditional ally of 1914, Russia, to contain Germany by means of the deterrent which the threat of a war on two fronts imposed. The Allies' policy of intervention, their subsequent instinctive mistrust of Bolshevism, and Russia's own multitudinous internal problems all made this quite clear. By way of a substitute, France had had to rely on diplomatic accords with the small nations of Eastern Europe, which had been carved out of the rump of Austria–Hungary, Germany and Russia herself. On paper, the combined sum of their military forces seemed impressive enough, and the Poles (advised by General Weygand) had, for instance, proved themselves doughty warriors against the Red Army; but, as the aftermath of Munich was to prove, they would never be combined, in so far as they would just as soon cut each other's throats as form a coherent front against Hitler's Germany. In 1914, as the Germans surged through Belgium to the Marne, it was Russia who came to France's aid by taking the offensive. Now, it should have been obvious to any amateur strategist, France was faced with a reversal of the situation, and in the event of war she would in all probability have to rush to the aid of her weaker eastern allies. Yet with that all too typical Gallic arrogance, all she asked was 'How can they help us?' and never 'How can we help them?' And France's defensive posture of the 1930s made it increasingly doubtful whether she could effectively help her allies at all. Ironically, the creation of Poland was to benefit Germany more than the Allies; instead of providing a *cordon sanitaire* to protect Russia from the Germans, it meant that, when the crucial moment came in 1939, Russia would be unable (even if she had wanted) to help France, because a mistrustful Poland lay in the way. For France, the only hope of helping her eastern allies, threatened by Hitler's Germany, was for her to replay 1923 (and how unpopular that had been!) by marching into the Rhineland, the one part of Germany directly vulnerable to her. Yet, as General Maurin had revealed with painful clarity, the Maginot Line strategy virtually discounted this possibility. So, as with Poland in the east, in the west the Maginot Line indirectly came to be a *cordon sanitaire* protecting Germany, as well as France!

Herein lay a fatal contradiction between France's diplomatic and military policies. And exploiting this contradiction, Hitler was soon to slam the door to the Rhineland in France's face by one swift, brutal act.

Reoccupation of the Rhineland

On 5 March 1936, William Shirer, the C.B.S. correspondent in Berlin, noted down in his diary: 'Very ugly atmosphere in the Wilhelmstrasse today, but difficult to get to the bottom of it.' Two days later the mystery solved itself, and Shirer could add, melodramatically: 'Tonight for the first time since 1870 grey-clad German soldiers and blue-clad French troops face each other across the Upper Rhine.' Acting with the lightning speed which was to characterize all his subsequent actions, Hitler had moved into the demilitarized Rhineland. Although rearmament had already been overtly under way for the past year, the new Wehrmacht was still a feeble infant which could only afford three battalions with which to make the initial crossing of the Rhine, and these had orders to withdraw immediately in the event of any French reaction. As yet unarmed planes of the Luftwaffe flew from airfield to airfield to create an impression, and (so some German sources allege) as soon as they landed new identity marks were painted on them. Three battalions and a handful of planes cocking a snook at what was still rated as the world's most powerful land force! It was one of the most remarkable gambles in history. Would it come off? Extreme nervousness gripped the German Army. During the crisis, Shirer met General von Blomberg, the Minister of War, 'walking along with two dogs on the leash. His face was white, his cheeks twitching. "Has something gone wrong?" I wondered.' Later even Hitler admitted that 'the forty-eight hours after the march into the Rhineland were the most nerve-racking in my life'. All the world looked at France to see how she would meet this gross breach of the Versailles Treaty.

In her turn, France looked towards Britain. But Britain was preoccupied with Italy and Abyssinia; besides, had not France declared impatiently, just two years previously, thereby killing the Disarmament Conference, that 'France will henceforth guarantee her security by her own means'? [11] In any case, a large portion of Englishmen thoroughly agreed with Lord Lothian's historic comment about the Germans 'only going into their own back-garden'. So Britain told France that this was her problem. The French Government called in General Gamelin, Weygand's successor as Army Commander-in-Chief. Gamelin, already revealing himself a master of political if not military manoeuvre, temporized and equivocated in the style that was to prove so fatal to France four years later. Of course his Army was ready for instant action; but did the Government realize that the Germans had nearly a million men under arms, 300,000 of them already in the Rhineland? It was an absurd exaggeration (see below, p. 75), deliberately intended to avoid action and pass the responsibility on to the politicians. Without conceding that the Army might in any way be unfit for a swift offensive operation, Gamelin pointed out that it was numerically under strength owing to the reduction in military service (of course the fault of the politicians, he implied). Then he dropped the bombshell that, if it were to act over the Rhineland, the Government would have to face up to the prospect of general mobilization.[12] The French Ministers looked at each

11. For sheer arrogant folly, the Barthou declaration of 17 April 1934 is hard to beat; A. J. P. Taylor remarks: 'The French had fired the starting pistol for the arms race. Characteristically they then failed to run it.' Yet it has its parallel in more recent times, when in 1966 de Gaulle informed the North Atlantic Alliance that henceforth he felt strong enough to dispense with its benefits. There are moments when one feels that – like the Bourbons, only worse – France has learned nothing and forgotten everything.

12. In retrospect, Gamelin's torpor becomes all the more criminal when

other in horror. Mobilization! And six weeks before an election? It was madness. The electorate would never stand for it. Parliamentary defeat would be certain – why their very jobs were at stake! It was impossible. Now both the military and the politicians had their excuses. It remained to blame Britain for their joint paralysis of will. This was, however, said Churchill, 'an explanation, but no excuse'; and indeed, at least in the opinion of Paul Reynaud, had France acted alone, in defence of her vital interests, Britain would have been bound to back her up.

Belgium Opts Out

So France did nothing, and Hitler got away with his first and most desperate gamble. The consequences were not long delayed. The most immediate followed with the reaction of France's ally, Belgium. That gallant sovereign who signed the Franco-Belgian Alliance of 1920, King Albert, had died tragically in 1934, and his son, Leopold III, did not inherit the full measure of his wisdom and moral courage. Instead of the protective belt of the demilitarized Rhineland, the new King now saw armed German soldiers once again on Belgium's frontier, while behind him he saw an apparently impotent France. Wherein lay the security of Belgium? On 14 October 1936, Leopold III revoked the Franco-Belgian Treaty, thereby opting for a return to the neutral status of pre-1914. Said the King, with the optimism of the imprudent little pigs: 'This policy should aim resolutely at keeping us apart from the quarrels of our neighbours . . .' For France it meant that, in the event of war, she could not enter Belgium until Hitler had already invaded. In one stroke the whole of her Maginot Line strategy lay in fragments. Belgium's neutrality now confronted France with two fearful alternatives. No longer could there be any

it appears that, as long as two months in advance of the reoccupation of the Rhineland, he had predicted to a French general (Armengaud) the likelihood of Hitler's move. Flandin, too, is purported to have raised the possibility in a Cabinet meeting of January 1935. Why then did the French Army allow itself to be taken by surprise?

'rush into Belgium' carefully co-ordinated with the army of an ally; instead, either she would have to meet the invading Germans somewhere on the defenceless Flemish plains, in a hastily improvised battle of encounter, such as her defensive-minded Army was least suited for, or prepare to meet them once again on French soil, the prospect dreaded above all others. The only way to certain safety now lay in prolonging the Maginot Line to the sea. But the 87 existing miles of 'fortified regions' had already cost 7,000 million francs, and it was obvious that to extend the Line all the way to the sea, through the industrialized north, would prove infinitely more expensive. So the politicians of the Third Republic resorted to that time-honoured expedient of deceiving their constituents – and their allies – by *pretending* to do something which they recognized to be beyond their powers.

Meanwhile, in the reoccupied Rhineland itself, Hitler hastened the construction of his own powerful line of concrete forts, opposing the Maginot Line – the West Wall, or 'Siegfried Line'. As Churchill predicted in a remarkable prophecy on 6 April 1936, those fortifications would

enable the German troops to be economised on that line, and will enable the main forces to swing round through Belgium and Holland. Then look East. There the consequences of the Rhineland fortification may be more immediate ... Poland and Czechoslovakia, with which must be associated Yugoslavia, Roumania, Austria and some other countries, are all affected very decisively the moment that this great work of construction has been completed.

Indeed, its completion would make it virtually impossible for France to render any effective aid to her eastern allies. Hitler could henceforth mop up in the East at will, then, with his rear secured, deal with an isolated France when the moment came.

The reoccupation of the Rhineland marked the watershed between 1919 and 1939. No other single event in this period was more loaded with dire significance. From March 1936, the road to France's doom ran downhill all the way. In Germany, Hitler was rearming with terrifying speed.

Chapter 3

Fortune Changes Sides

Before the year was out it seemed as if Fortune, recognising her masters, was changing sides.
  WINSTON S. CHURCHILL, *A History of the English-Speaking Peoples*, Vol. iii (on the coming of Pitt)

There are only two powers in the world . . . the sword and the spirit. In the long run, the sword is always defeated by the spirit.
  NAPOLEON

Sunday, 17 March 1935 was Heroes' Remembrance Day in Germany. At a ceremony in Berlin's State Opera House, Hitler presided, flanked on the right by the veteran August von Mackensen, Germany's last surviving Field-Marshal, and on the left by Crown Prince Wilhelm, the heir to the deposed Kaiser and one-time commander of the army attacking Verdun. The whole of the stalls was a sea of military uniforms; to William Shirer, it was 'a scene which Germany had not seen since 1914'. Far from being one of sober commemoration of the Great War dead, the atmosphere was charged with jubilation and thanksgiving. Amid powerful acclaim, Blomberg declared: 'The world has been made to realize that Germany did not die of its defeat . . .' It was a fact; for the previous day Hitler, in full defiance of Versailles, had announced to the world his intention to rearm, and to do so by introducing conscription.

Hitler Rearms

The sequence of events which led to the nightmarish rise of the Third Reich lies still too close to us for anything new to be added here – even if it belonged to this story. But, having sketched in the decline of the French Army up to the Rhineland crisis of 1936, one needs to examine briefly the awe-inspiring process by which Hitler, within the following four years, was to create a force not only crushingly superior to the combined might of France and Britain, but indeed the most dazzling instrument of war the world had yet seen. By the end of his first year in power Hitler had already secretly ordered the Army to treble its statutory strength of 100,000 men, imposed by Versailles, before October 1934. During that year the defence budget was drastically raised from 172 million Reichsmarks to 654 million. Then, on 10 March 1935, Hitler deliberately leaked to the British Press, as a *ballon d'essai*, the news that he already possessed an air force in the shape of the infant Luftwaffe.

His pretext was that France had just 'expanded' her own Army by retaining a class of conscripts (which had been done, in fact, simply to mitigate the consequences of the 'hollow classes'). No more than a blast of protest was registered by either France or Britain, so, on 16 March, Hitler went ahead and published his brief decree announcing the creation of a new German Army, based on compulsory military service. In peace-time alone, the number of its divisions would comprise the imposing total of thirty-six. This was many more than was wanted by even the grateful generals congregated in the State Opera the next day; they realized the mountainous difficulties that digesting this huge expansion would present to the small regular cadres. In fact, as has already been seen, by the time of the reoccupation of the Rhineland the new Wehrmacht was still a relatively feeble, small and lightly armed force; as yet no more than 5 per cent of Germany's national product was being spent on rearmament. But then, as later, what Hitler lacked in actual hardware he made up for by the loudness and terrorizing effect of his boasting. After 1936, there followed the 'quiet' two years of semi-respectability, the years of no territorial adventures, during which the expanding Wehrmacht assumed its definitive shape. By the beginning of 1937, its Army divisions numbered thirty-nine; by 1939, fifty-one.[1] By 1939 it had also added to its potential the manpower of both Austria and the Sudeten Germans.

1. Upon mobilization in August 1939, this number was doubled.

Seeckt's Bequest

When Hitler began the task of rearming Germany, daunting though it was, he was presented with a number of advantages denied to the French. First, as the vanquished party, the German Army was not saddled with the victor's impedimenta of obsolescent ideas and equipment. Secondly, Hitler inherited some remarkably solid groundwork in the shape of Colonel-General Hans von Seeckt's Reichswehr. As Mackensen's Chief of Staff on the Russian front, Seeckt had been responsible for the spectacular breakthrough at Gorlice in 1915. His monocle and hard features, making him seem like a traditional, rigid Prussian Junker, in fact concealed a remarkable elasticity and breadth of vision. From the moment of taking over command of the Reichswehr on the morrow of defeat, his guiding principle had been to 'neutralize the poison' in the clauses of the Versailles Treaty by which the German Army had been disarmed, and to create a nucleus from which a new and greater army could one day be formed. When the Allied terms had forced the Reichswehr to purge some 20,000 of its officers, Seeckt made sure that it was the élite who remained. Every subaltern was trained to command a battalion, and every field officer a division. At one moment, out of the 100,000 men permitted by Versailles, 40,000 were N.C.O.s, and each of these was regarded as potential 'officer material'. Mistrustful of the unwieldy mass armies of conscripts of 1914–18, so lacking in mobility, Seeckt selected the rank and file of the Reichswehr all from carefully vetted volunteers. Determined to safeguard traditional values, at the same time he introduced a new, closer and more comradely relationship between officers and men, based on mutual confidence. Gone was the stiff social segregation, which to a large extent still afflicted the French Army, and gone too was much of the harsh bullying, or *Kommiss*, of the old days. The result was a remarkably professional, technically efficient force in miniature.

Considerable ingenuity was employed to surmount the Allied restrictions imposed on heavy equipment. In Reichswehr manoeuvres right up to 1932, soldiers could be seen trundling along 'dummy tanks' mounted on bicycle wheels. After protracted arguments with the Allies, the Germans were permitted to construct a small armoured vehicle with a revolving turret; although barred from carrying any weapon, it was of great use in teaching officers the art of armoured warfare. Barred from producing any tracked vehicles,[2] the Germans ingeniously developed eight- and ten-wheeled armoured cars, forerunners of the famous eight-wheeled reconnaissance vehicle which did such good service during the Second World War. Short of transport, Seeckt began experimenting with motor-cycle companies, later an essential component of the Wehrmacht's *Blitzkrieg* technique. But Seeckt's greatest contribution lay in guiding German military thought on to the correct lines. He insisted, wrote Churchill,

that false doctrines, springing from personal experiences of the Great War, should be avoided. All the lessons of that war were thoroughly and systematically studied. New principles of training and instructional courses of all kinds were introduced. All the existing manuals were rewritten . . .

Unlike the French with their vision fixed upon the static warfare of the Western Front, too gratified by the fact of final victory to study the military mistakes which had come so close to compromising it, Seeckt, together with many other German staff officers who had fought on the Russian front, enjoyed the advantage of having seen that there were other ways of waging war. He himself had helped devise the tactics of the great sweeping operations in the east, and had directed the breakthrough at Gorlice, leading to a depth of penetration such as was never to occur in the west. From these war-time experiences, he concluded as early as 1921 :

The whole future of warfare appears to me to be in the employment of mobile armies, relatively small but of high quality, and rendered distinctly more effective by the addition of aircraft . . .

---

2. Within a year of the departure of the Allied Control Commission in 1927, Krupp was producing the first tanks, and under the strange, secret alliance with the Soviet Union these were shipped in pieces to Kazan on the Volga, to be put through their paces there.

Guderian and the Panzer Corps

Seeckt retired for political reasons in 1926, and died ten years later. But he left solid foundations for his successors to build upon. In 1922, a thirty-four-year-old staff captain called Heinz Guderian was appointed to the staff of the Army's Motor Transport; a signals specialist, it was the first time he had had anything to do with mechanization. During the Great War, Guderian, as an Intelligence officer at the Crown Prince's H.Q., had been at Verdun throughout the German offensive of 1916. What he had seen there had been enough to convince him that the senseless carnage of this kind of static warfare should never again be indulged in. Encouraged by the ideas of Seeckt, he began ardently to study the effect of motorization on mobility, and at an early stage fell under the profound influence of the writings of the British military thinkers, Liddell Hart, Fuller and Martel. After eighteen months in the Inspectorate of Transport, Guderian was selected to assist Lieutenant-Colonel von Brauchitsch[3] at exercises in co-operation between motorized troops and aircraft. He did so well that he was next given a job lecturing on tactics and military history, which provided him with an admirable opportunity to develop his ideas further. By 1929, Guderian himself claims that he had become 'convinced' of the fundamental importance of integrated armoured divisions, in which tanks would assume the primary role instead of being subordinate to the infantry. In 1931 he received his first motorized command – of a battalion equipped with dummy tanks and dummy anti-tank guns. Meanwhile, in Britain, during 1934 some advanced experiments on deep penetration had been carried out by General Hobart's 1st Tank Brigade. Guderian kept abreast of these manoeuvres by employing at his own expense a local tutor to translate Liddell Hart's articles about them the moment they were printed in England. By the following year his own thinking had reached the point where he could both give utterance to it in an astoundingly prophetic book, and put it into practice. As has often been the humiliating story with

3. Later Field-Marshal, and Hitler's Army C.-in-C. in 1940.

British inventions and discoveries, the development of armour was now left to another, unfriendly country.

Guderian began his book, *Achtung – Panzer!*, by examining the causes underlying the success and failure of Allied tank operations (the Germans missed the boat and hardly employed any tanks at all) during the First War. He listed the following fundamental errors: the Allies did not attack in sufficient depth, and were never backed up by sufficiently powerful mobile reserves, so that they 'broke into' the enemy front, but never *through* – where they would have been able 'to knock out his batteries, his reserves, his staffs, all at the same time'; the full potential of the tanks was sacrificed by their being yoked to two such slow-moving components as foot-infantry and horse-drawn artillery; they were thrown in by 'penny packets', instead of powerful concentrations; and they were the wrong kind of tanks.

Guderian saw the remedy to all this lying in the fully mechanized Panzer divisions, all the components of which would collaborate closely together, and which had to be capable of moving at equal speeds. The Panzer division was to be built around the tank itself – not the slow, short-range 'infantry escort' tank to which the French Army was still wedded,[4] but a medium 'breakthrough' tank possessing 'armour sufficient to protect it against the mass of enemy anti-tank weapons, a higher speed and greater cruising range than the infantry escort tank, and an armament of machine-guns and cannon up to 75 mm.' From the beginning, these tanks' commanders would be trained to 'fight in large units', thus providing maximum concentration of firepower. Close behind the 'breakthrough' tanks would follow motorized infantry with the role of mopping up and exploiting the successes of the armour, and interspersed with them would be mobile anti-tank guns. These were to be rushed offensively forward, to hold the vulnerable flanks of the Panzer salient against any counter-attack by enemy tanks. The

4. It was significant that the infant Panzer Corps chose to base its procedure on the British Army manual on the use of armour rather than on the French, because of the rigidity of the French links between tanks and infantry.

unwieldy horse-drawn artillery of 1914–18 would be replaced by self-propelled guns mounted on tracks. But here Guderian, writing in 1936, was able to provide a solution which he admitted to be only partially satisfactory. The essence of the Panzer thrust, he stressed, must be surprise. Yet a prolonged softening-up bombardment, even from highly mobile artillery, was always liable to give the game away, as happened repeatedly during the set-piece offensives of the Great War. The full answer was only to come with the development, later, of the Stuka dive-bomber.

Guderian stressed the advantage of tanks attacking in mass, and, if possible, at early dawn, on account of the difficult targets they would present to the defender's anti-tank guns. He also stressed the need to strike with such speed that the tanks would get into the enemy's main defence zone before these guns could be properly sited. But he regarded 'the most dangerous opponent' of the Panzer division to be the enemy tank. If the attacker

cannot succeed in beating them, then the breakthrough can be considered as having failed, because neither the infantry nor the artillery will be able to get through any longer. Everything depends on delaying intervention of enemy anti-tank reserves and tanks and encountering them as early as possible with powerful units, i.e. Panzer units capable of taking part in a tank battle in the full depths of the battlefield, in the area of the enemy reserves and command centres.

The intervention of the defender's reserves was to be delayed by the tactical air force, which Guderian already saw as working in close co-operation with the Panzers; this delaying task would be one of air power's principal functions in the battle. He also mentions the employment of airborne troops in capturing important points in the enemy rear to open routes for the oncoming Panzer thrust.

Once the attacker had succeeded in breaking through into the enemy's defence area,

the crushing of the enemy batteries and the mopping-up of the infantry battle zone can be achieved with relatively weak Panzer units. The infantry can then exploit the successes of the tanks . . .

The endeavour to strike the enemy defence simultaneously in its whole depth [continues Guderian] must therefore be regarded as highly justified. This lofty goal is only to be achieved with numerous tanks in the necessary deep deployment, with Panzer units and Panzer leaders who have been taught to fight in large units and to break any unforeseen resistance rapidly and decisively. Apart from its depth, the breakthrough attack must also be on so great a width that the outflanking of a centre of the attack is made difficult . . . We thus sum up our demands for a decision-seeking Panzer attack in these terms; suitable terrain, surprise and mass deployment in the necessary width and depth.

Here lay an astonishingly accurate blueprint of how, four years later, Guderian himself would effect the breakthrough at Sedan. In *Mein Kampf* Hitler had already broadcast to the world his intentions to obtain *Lebensraum* by conquest in Europe; now, in detail, Guderian revealed the technique by which these conquests were to be made. Despite the admonition contained in its very title, *Achtung – Panzer!* was ignored by French and British leaders even more completely than *Mein Kampf* had been. It was never translated into either French or English, and appears never to have been properly studied by anyone in a key position in the General Staffs of either country. Yet already by February 1935, the *Deuxième Bureau* (so its chief, General Gauché, tells us) had warned the French High Command of the potential of Germany's embryo Panzer divisions; moreover, by the time of the publication of *Achtung – Panzer!*, Guderian was already a well-known military figure who had published his theories in professional magazines for all to read, and was now commanding Hitler's 2nd Panzer Division.

As early as 1933, when Hitler had attended a demonstration of Germany's earliest tank prototype, he exclaimed repeatedly to Guderian: 'That's what I need! That's what I want to have!' Hitler's own technical grasp was a constant source of astonishment to his advisers; mechanical details fascinated him, and among other things it was reputedly he who first suggested (in 1938) that the 88-mm. anti-aircraft gun be used in an anti-tank role, thereby giving birth to a weapon which was perhaps the most successful to be used on either side in the Second World War. But above all, Guderian and his theories were just what Hitler needed to execute his policy of lightning conquests effected with minimum force. With that visionary intuition of his, he had remarked to Hermann Rauschning shortly after coming to power: 'The next war will be quite different from the last world war. Infantry attacks and mass formations are obsolete. Interlocked frontal struggles lasting for years on petrified fronts will not return. I guarantee that. They were a degenerate form of war ...'; and later, even more prophetically: 'I shall manoeuvre France right out of her Maginot Line without losing a single soldier.' Although Guderian had to face opposition from conservative elements in the German Army almost as tough as anything encountered by the French and British reformers, under Hitler's patronage he received the utmost support. In October 1935, the first three Panzer divisions were formed; Guderian, still only a colonel, receiving command of one of them. By the beginning of 1938, Guderian was promoted lieutenant-general and placed in command of the mobile corps which played a leading role in the march into Austria. At the end of that year, now a full general, he received the key post of Chief of Mobile Troops on the General Staff. Guderian and the philosophy of *Blitzkrieg* had arrived.

The 'Revolutionary' Wehrmacht

In *Achtung – Panzer!* Guderian describes the highest human quality called for by the Panzer Corps as being 'a fanatical will to move forward'. It was this very quality which the strange and terrible creed of National Socialism was instilling into the new Wehrmacht as a whole. How difficult it is at this range to recapture, let alone explain, the instant magic that, in the 1930s, Hitler wielded over German youth – sublimely unaware as it was of the dark tunnel of unprecedented horror into which he would eventually lead them and all Europe! On to the fertile stock of German childhoods cast over by the miseries of hunger, crazy inflation followed by depression and mass unemployment, the humiliations of defeat and occupation, the apparent injustices of Versailles and the seeming pointlessness of life under Weimar, Hitler was able to graft the bud of intoxication. As Nietzsche said of the Germans, 'Intoxication means more to them than nourishment. That is the hook they will always bite on. A popular leader must hold up before them the prospect of conquests and splendour; then he will be believed.' Hitler was believed, and his early bloodless conquests confirmed and re-confirmed that belief. Satisfying some elemental need for mysticism in the German soul, the gigantic Nuremberg Rallies with their pageantry and colour, their hysterical, chanting masses of assenting humanity, filled young Germans with a kind of revolutionary fervour which they carried with them into the Wehrmacht. Among the older generation, for all those whose nightmare memories of the shellholes on the Western Front, implanted as deeply as in French minds, caused them to wonder fearfully where Hitler's rearmament would lead, there were many who could think only of one word – revenge! Visiting Germany in 1934, Jean-Paul Sartre was deeply shocked by the fanaticism of an ex-sergeant of the Great War: ' "If there's another war," he said, "we shall not be defeated this time. We shall retrieve our honour." ' Sartre replied that there was no need for a war; everyone ought to want peace. But ' "Honour comes first," the sergeant said. "First we must retrieve our honour." ' As Hitler's successes brought his promises to reverse the *Diktat* of Versailles ever closer to fulfilment, so did the numbers of those sharing the views of Sartre's ex-sergeant multiply. Patriotism rekindled, the Army became imbued with a new glory. A military career satisfied the young German's inherent yearning for *Kameradschaft*, as well as his passion for mechanical matters, canalizing all that tremendous fund of technical skill and imagination latent in Germany in the 1920s and early 1930s. At the same time, the Wehrmacht's programme of expansion promised swift promotion. Here, at last, was something that imparted to life a new meaning! Seeckt and Guderian had provided the Wehrmacht with a revolutionary doctrine, Hitler and Nazism a revolutionary spirit to go with it.

The training of German youth, both within the new Wehrmacht and, earlier, in various para-military organizations, was in itself revolutionary. Their regimented education began at a tender age. At ten they entered the *Jungvolk*, pledging 'to devote all my energies and my strength to the saviour of our country, Adolf Hitler. I am willing and ready to give up my life for him so help me God.' At twelve, the most outstanding members of the *Jungvolk* were picked out to be dispatched to special schools for the instruction of élite cadres. The emphasis here, as everywhere else under the Nazis' educational system, was strongly on physical culture and disciplined teamwork; among other preliminary military training, the boys also received courses in parachute jumping. At fourteen young Germans became eligible to join the vast body of the Hitler Youth itself. In 1936, a law was passed closely co-ordinating the Hitler Youth with the Wehrmacht; from local units, its members received instruction in marksmanship and leadership, visited Army barracks and were taken to watch manoeuvres. One of the liaison officers organizing these programmes was a certain Lieutenant-Colonel Erwin Rommel. At eighteen, youths became of age for conscription into the Wehrmacht or the *Arbeitsdienst* (Labour Service). Inside the *Arbeitsdienst*, while young Germans served their country by building roads and barracks, the work of inseminating corporate consciousness and para-military discipline and of preaching the essential classlessness of the New Order continued. Then, for vacation times, there was the Nazi 'Strength through Joy' welfare organization to provide still further regimented *Kameradschaft*. There was no mistaking the enthusiasm of the recipients of this massive indoctrination; even a dispassionate British journalist [5] studying 'these young Germans of 1933' was deeply impressed (as indeed were so many other observers at the time) by the

tremendous sense of comradeship amongst themselves. They were happy to learn together, play together, march together and to learn to fight together. They loved the open air and they flung away clothes from them with an abandon which would have horrified the Victorian generation . . . Their animal energy was gigantic.

By the time they reached the Wehrmacht, these spartan, dedi-

5. Terence Prittie, *Germans Against Hitler*.

cated youths were already superlative material for a 'revolutionary' force, instinctively versed in the one craft which was to pay off in Germany's early military operations more than any other – teamwork.

Anti-militarism in France

By comparison, what contrast one may glimpse in the spirit of France of the mid-1930s! The last of those rosy post-war illusions had been roughly swept aside by the revelation of her impotence during the Rhineland crisis; the urge for national *grandeur*, the desire for supremacy in Europe, were replaced by a deep longing simply to be left in peace. It was a longing widely diffused through all strata of French society, though of course the symptoms were paralleled in, and stimulated by, the mood prevailing in the England of Cliveden and Lansbury, the Peace Ballot and the Peace Pledge Union. But in France particularly the instinct for peace, or for what was later to become stigmatized as 'appeasement', remained strongly rooted in memories of the dreadfulness of the Great War, memories which, perhaps perversely, had become more rather than less potent with the passage of the years. This was to a large extent a consequence of the spate of anti-war literature which had swept Europe in the late 1920s, all telling basically the same tale of the horror and wastefulness of war, combined with the cynical callousness and sheer incompetence of the war leaders. In Germany, Hitler had been swift to stifle such books as Remarque's *All Quiet on the Western Front*, but in France the terrifying novel of Henri Barbusse, *Le Feu*, had an immeasurable impact. For the Verdun generation, here indeed was an indelible reminder of what it had really been like; for their juniors, a nightmare fantasy the re-enactment of which must be avoided at all costs. Wielding enormous intellectual influence were various anti-war associations formed by such giants of France's literary Left wing as André Gide, Paul Éluard, Louis Aragon and Romain Rolland. But Barbusse was the torch-bearer; when he died in 1935 more than 300,000 followed his coffin to Père Lachaise Cemetery.

With his instinctive genius, Hitler knew well how to play on French fears and hopes, accompanying each new adventure with barrages of peace propaganda and repeated pledges of renunciation of any claim to Alsace-Lorraine, aimed at making Frenchmen sleep all the more comfortably at night behind the safety of their Maginot Line. With the vileness of the concentration camps yet to come, the full menace of the New Order only apparent when it would already be too late to check, Hitler did not seem especially malignant to the average Frenchman. Besides, as will be seen shortly, there were other dangers much closer to home. What hatred and fear of the Nazis there existed were roughly balanced out by equal hatred and fear of war itself.

So often in history when the unpleasantness of external reality induces a state of emotional confusion, societies become irresistibly tempted to bury themselves in all manner of imaginary pleasure and internal distractions. The louder the barbarians outside hammered at the walls of Rome, the wilder grew the public diversions in the Colosseum and the private orgies within the walls. At many levels of French life during the late 1920s and 1930s, escapism reveals itself as the ruling factor. Dadaism and surrealism in art are matched by the *fantaisiste*, fairy-tale world of Cocteau and Giraudoux. The frenzy of the fox-trot *dansomanie* of the 1920s marches with the stage extravaganzas of Diaghilev; the *Ballet Russe*, the *Ballet Suédois*; Josephine Baker, the *Revue Nègre*. Anything for 'spectacle'. The circus is rediscovered. Then France suddenly finds she can play tennis and rugger; to be able to beat England provides a welcome sop to the Quai d'Orsay's growing dependence upon the Foreign Office. The sporting pages of *Paris-Soir* make it overnight the journalistic success story of the decade. Bicycling is all the rage; for the masses, the Tour de France supplies the nearest emotional equivalent to Germany's Nuremberg Rallies. In the cabarets, even the sacred fetishes of pre-1914 can be made mock of, with bearded ladies from Alsace chanting melodramatically:

> No, no, a thousand times no! My breast is French,
> I shall never give suck to a German child . . .

In literature, the passion for romantic travel, so powerful in the 1920s, gives way to an equal fascination in the personal 'heroic quest' of the agonizing man of action, as represented by such adventures as Saint-Exupéry and Malraux.

Despite its philosophy of 'engagement', no form of literature demonstrated a greater revolt away from reality than the existentialism of young Jean-Paul Sartre and his fellow inmates of the Café Flore in the latter 1930s. In her autobiography, Sartre's mistress, Simone de Beàuvoir, furnishes a revealingly honest chronicle of the attitude of French left-wing intellectuals. The autumn of 1929 had made her feel she was living in a new 'Golden Age': 'Peace seemed finally assured; the expansion of the German Nazi Party was a mere fringe phenomenon, without any serious significance ... It would not be long before colonialism folded up.' Of Hitler's coming to power in 1933, she writes: '... like everyone else on the French Left, we watched these developments quite calmly', and in the same breath that she records, in passing, Einstein's flight from Germany, she deplores the closing-down of the German 'Institute of Sexology'. Still, 'there was no threat to peace; the only danger was the panic that the Right was attempting to spread in France, with the aim of dragging us into war'. To the 'elders' of the Left, as to so many of that generation, 'the memory of the 1914–18 was stuck in their throats ... In 1914 the whole of the intellectual élite, Socialists, writers and all – no wonder Jaurès was assassinated – toed a wholly chauvinistic line ... Our elders, then, forbade us to envisage the very possibility of a war ...' In their filmgoing, this dread of war led Sartre and Beauvoir to miss Renoir's classic, *La Grande Illusion*, by preference seeking escapism in such American farces as *My Man Godfrey* and *Mr Deeds Goes to Town*.

Political Scandals

At the important elections of 1936, after Hitler's occupation of the Rhineland, Sartre had refused to vote: 'The political aspirations of left-wing intellectuals made him shrug his shoulders.' Yet while regarding the French political scene with 'disengaged'

aversion, and finding nothing 'to stir my interest' in the assassination of King Alexander of Yugoslavia and the French Foreign
Minister, Barthou, Simone de Beauvoir concedes at the same
time that 'both Sartre and I read every word' of the latest turn
in the Stavisky scandal. This duality of attitudes extended far
beyond the narrow circle of the Café Flore. Upon the futility
of the Third Republic's political jungle had now become superimposed (though perhaps 'grafted' is the better word) a miasma
of corruption cases. The first big shock came in 1928 with the
arrest of Klotz, the former Minister of Finance about whom
Clemenceau had been so scathing, on charges of issuing dud
cheques. Two years later there followed the Oustric scandal.
Oustric had built up a bogus banking empire largely propped
up on vast loans somehow obtained from the Bank of France;
when his empire crashed, the involvement of the second
Tardieu Government was sufficient to bring about its fall too.

But the greatest furore was caused by Serge Stavisky, the
son of a Ukrainian-Jewish dentist, a seductive young man with
an apparently limitless number of useful contacts in politics,
the Press and the judiciary. Already by 1933 his financial
operations had come under official scrutiny, but he appeared to
be immune from police interference and a criminal case against
him had actually been postponed nineteen times. It so happened that the public prosecutor who was failing to bring
Stavisky to justice was the brother-in-law of the current Prime
Minister, Camille Chautemps. Then suddenly, on 30 December, a major fraud, concerning the issue of millions of francs
based on the assets of a municipal pawnshop in the small town
of Bayonne, was pinned on Stavisky. The Mayor of Bayonne,
Garat, who was also a Radical Deputy, was arrested, but the
indications were that much bigger game was involved. How
else had Stavisky managed to pull off such swindles, and how
had he evaded justice for so long? Before any answers could be
provided, the police found Stavisky dead in a house in Chamonix where he had been hiding with his mistress. Suicide was
alleged, but it was widely believed that he had been shot by a
policeman – conveniently, it seemed, for Chautemps. Overnight
Stavisky became the best-known name in France since Dreyfus.

Crowds appeared outside the National Assembly, shouting 'Down with the thieves!' and spitting on Deputies. On 27 January 1934, the Chautemps Government fell – after an innings of just two months and four days.

In common with Sartre and Beauvoir, the great mass of Frenchmen indulged themselves heartily in the spectacle of political scandals as part of the nation's pursuit of escapism. Hand in hand with this indulgence went a deep disgust and disillusion with politicians and government, which was about to create a grave split in France just at the moment when the Nazi jackboots were striding out in mounting unison. By 1934 the reputation of politicians in France had sunk to a record low; but it was to sink still lower, and with it all efficacy of government. Constantly there was some new scandal and, however distantly, some Minister in what the cynics dubbed 'the Republic of Pals' always seemed to be implicated. As Pertinax pungently observed, French politicians had assumed the habit of 'dealing with their country as if it were a commercial company going into liquidation'. Recounting a typical scene of the Third Republic, Élie Bois describes how at a lunch party Georges Bonnet and Camille Chautemps 'vied with one another to succeed a Premier whose ministry had just fallen: "It's my turn!" "No, Georges, it's mine ..." ' Dizzier and dizzier became the game of musical chairs played by the little men unaware of the proportions of the tragedy moving in on them. In the eighteen months preceding 1934, there had been five different governments but with virtually the same faces in each; from mid 1932 to the outbreak of war in 1939, France's score of governments was to total nineteen, including eleven different Premiers, eight Ministers of Finance, seven Ministers of Foreign Affairs, and eight Ministers of War. A favourite insult with Parisian taxi-drivers became 'Espèce de député!' The populace loathed the politicians; the politicians loathed each other.

Beginnings of Civil War

On 6 February 1934, passions overflowed. This was the date

marking the beginning of what approximated to civil war in France, which was to have so insidious and powerful an influence on the events of 1940 that its background needs to be carefully understood. Since Armistice Day 1918, two major ideological streams, distinct and opposing, had flowed through the political life of France. One was revolutionary, the other patriotic; or, simplified in terms of the two historic events which supplied each with its most potent, fundamental inspiration, they might well be called, respectively, the streams of the Commune and of Verdun. The revolutionary, Commune stream may trace its original source back to the Great Revolution of 1789, whose spiritual heirs fought against the Establishment on the barricades in 1830 and 1848; while, as has already been suggested, its main motivating force in the post-1918 world was derived from the Russian Revolution. But it was the Paris Commune of 1871 in which resided the numen of France's Left wing, and especially of that important section comprised by the Parisian proletariat. It was the Commune which, though unsuccessful, had first pointed the way to the possibility of a Government of the proletariat, based on revolution and the destruction of the bourgeois monopoly; moreover, it was upon the achievements and errors of the Commune (as interpreted by Karl Marx) that Lenin had based his own triumphant revolution of 1917. Above all, in France it was the savage memories of the 20,000 Communards so brutally massacred by Thiers's forces of order which kept alight the flame of revolution, making the gulf between bourgeois and proletarian wider and more unbridgeable than in any other nation of the Western world. The link with the Commune has never been severed; in the 1930s (and still today), every Whitsun the leaders of France's Left wing made a solemn pilgrimage to the Mur des Fédérés at Père Lachaise Cemetery, to commemorate the summary execution there on 28 May 1871 of 147 Communards. The *Internationale* was their marching song, but the wall was the shrine to which they marched.

The Verdun stream, on the other hand, drew its main impetus from the middle-class, conservative forces which had repressed the Commune. It believed in the fundamental, indestructible *grandeur* of France (a generation later, it might be rated as essentially Gaullist); it hankered after *la gloire* as embodied by the military triumphs of Louis XIV and Napoleon. While the heirs of the Commune marched to the Mur des Fédérés, it was to the tragic glories of Verdun that this second stream turned for its (even more immediate) inspiration. It felt that France should not renounce the benefit from all the blood gloriously shed in her numerous wars, especially in this last and most terrible; though it was torn when, like the Left wing, it reflected upon the realities on the reverse of the Verdun coin. Still clinging to many of the illusions left over from that *Quatorze Juillet* of 1919, it was sickened by France's subsequent retreat from *grandeur*, sickened by the corrupt ineptness of her politicians. At the same time, it too had its memories of the Commune, which the new strength infused into the French Left by the Russian Revolution had revivified. The spectre of Bolshevism, teeth clamped upon a bloody knife, was constantly breathing down its neck.

By the 1930s, the most vocal and extreme of those Frenchmen borne along in the Verdun stream had banded themselves together in various Right-wing 'leagues'. There were the *Camelots du Roi*, shock-troops of the monarchist, Catholic and anti-semitic *Action Française* of Charles Maurras,[6] which had led the assault on Stavisky and his highly placed 'pals' in the Radical Party. Then there were the *Jeunesses Patriotes*, nationalist and violently anti-Communist, who had assumed the mantle of the fire-eating Paul Déroulède's *Ligue des Patriotes* founded to avenge the defeat of 1870. But now, with the grievance of Alsace-Lorraine eradicated, the patriotism of the *Jeunesses* was as defensive as that of any other section of the country for whom the Maginot Line had become a way of life, and their energies were directed largely towards the protection of private property against real or imagined threats of 'Bolshevism'. In 1932, the *Solidarité Française* was created by funds from the perfumery fortune of François Coty, its members wearing a para-military uniform of black beret and blue shirt. Their motto was '*La France aux Français!*' – 'France for

6. In 1945 Maurras was sentenced to life imprisonment as a collaborator.

the French' – and a newspaper also founded by M. Coty, *L'Ami du Peuple*, bore at its masthead the slogan 'With Hitler against Bolshevism'. In 1933 the *Francistes* were formed, adopting a uniform not dissimilar to that of the Nazi stormtroopers.

Less extreme politically, though still well right of centre, were various veterans' associations, whose members came largely from the *petite bourgeoisie*. But the most activist and significant of the 'Leagues' was the *Croix de Feu*, originally founded in 1928 as an association of ex-soldiers decorated for bravery. Its leader, Colonel Casimir de la Rocque, who had served on the staffs of both Foch and Lyautey, was now dedicated to the purgation of all that was corrupt in the institutions of the Third Republic. Under his impulse the *Croix de Feu* assumed a distinct political orientation. 'Honesty' and 'Order' were its twin battle-cries, and though it could not strictly be described as Fascist – unlike some of the more right-wing leagues – it shared their admiration for the vigour and efficiency that Mussolini had succeeded in instilling into Italian youth; in addition, as the scandals multiplied, the *Croix de Feu* had adopted a more blatantly anti-Republican attitude. The patrician colonel himself was certainly no rabble-rouser like Hitler. A British journalist says of him: 'His head was too narrow and unimpressive, his voice was too high, his diction too elaborate for mass appeal. His gestures were those of a romantic actor, not a tribune. He was too genteel.' Nevertheless, to the Left wing in France Colonel de la Rocque had come to epitomize everything that it understood, loathed and feared in the meaning of the word Fascism.

During the week that followed the fall of the Chautemps Government on 27 January 1934, tension had been rising in Paris. Enraged by the revelations of the Stavisky case, de la Rocque met with leaders of the other right-wing leagues to coordinate a march upon the Assembly. On 5 February there were demonstrations and various collisions with the police. The next morning, *L'Action Française* carried the most provocative headlines: 'The thieves are barricading themselves in their cave. Against this abject régime, everyone in front of the Chambre des Députés this evening.' At about 6 p.m. the first shock-troops, consisting largely of the *Camelots du Roi* and with a number of *grands mutilés* veterans placed conspicuously to the fore, attempted to force their way through police barriers drawn up on the Pont de la Concorde. They hurled bottles, stones and sections of lead piping at the police, and when the mounted police charged, the hocks of their horses were slashed with razors tied to sticks. Meanwhile, inside the Chamber the new Government, headed by Édouard Daladier, was still struggling to get a vote of confidence. By 7.30, the police were becoming increasingly hard-pressed, and, after three warnings, they received the order to fire. Seven demonstrators were killed outright, and a large number wounded. Though driven back as far as the Opéra, a counter-attack brought them once more to the Concorde. The police opened fire a second time, but it was not until midnight that the Deputies could reckon they were safe from a repetition of 3 September 1870, when the Palais Bourbon had been stormed and the Government overthrown by a Paris mob outraged by the news of Louis-Napoleon's defeat at Sedan. Out of 40,000 demonstrators, 16 had been killed and at least 655 known to be wounded; well over 1,000 policemen received injuries.

Nevertheless, the next day Colonel de la Rocque proclaimed from his secret battle H.Q.: 'The *Croix de Feu* has surrounded the Chamber and forced the Deputies to flee.' The proclamation infuriated the leaders of the other leagues, who considered that de la Rocque's men had played only the most prudent of parts in the battle. But the impact that the Colonel's braggadocio had upon the Left wing was even more dramatic. Suddenly, in the heated atmosphere of the moment, it seemed as if a new General Boulanger had arisen. Fears were greatly exacerbated on the afternoon of the 7th when, with extreme precipitance, Daladier resigned. Ex-President Gaston Doumergue, now aged seventy, took his place at the head of a 'National Government' with – as a special sop to the *anciens combattants* of the Right-wing leagues – seventy-seven-year-old Marshal Pétain, the 'Hero of Verdun', as its Minister of Defence. It was the first time since 1870 that the mob had brought about the fall of a French government, but, alas, not the last time that a disastrous display of weakness by Daladier would bely his nickname, 'the bull of Vaucluse'. Of his resignation, Daladier explained feebly: 'otherwise we should have had to shoot'.

On 6 February the Communists, sharing de la Rocque's detestation of corrupt Republican politicians, had also taken up cudgels against the Government. One eye-witness actually saw a *Camelot du Roi* and a Communist, each recognizable by his badge, jointly pulling down a lamp-post – just about the last occasion in time of peace, before de Gaulle, that the two extremes of French political life would be able to find common cause. But now, with the powerful shock administered by the fall of the Daladier Government, the entire Left wing thought in terror that it saw an imminent right-wing *coup d'état*, along the lines taken in Germany and Italy, with Colonel de la Rocque playing the role of Louis-Napoleon – or Mussolini. Abruptly it reversed its position. On the morning of 9 February, the Communist *L'Humanité* called a mass meeting for that evening in the Place de la République, to demand the dissolution both of the Chamber and of their ephemeral allies, the right-wing leagues. That night an event of major importance occurred. Near the République, two rival columns approached each other, one of Communists, the other of *Jeunesses Socialistes*, representing the two principal left-wing parties which had hardly been on speaking terms ever since the great schism of 1920–21. At first it looked as if there would be conflict. However, amid cries of 'We're not clashing, we're fraternizing ... we're all here to defend the Republic', the heads of the two columns mingled and clasped hands, then marched together chanting 'Unity of action!' On 12 February the C.G.T. called a general strike in protest against the 'Fascist peril', and for the first time since its breakaway thirteen years ago the Communist C.G.T.U. collaborated fully. In the course of that day the new pact was sealed in blood when, amid the old Communard strongholds of eastern Paris, three-cornered mêlées between strikers, right-wing layabouts and the police resulted in four deaths. 'United as at the front!' had been on the lips of Colonel de la Rocque's *anciens combattants* on 6 February; 'Unity of action!' was the slogan of the heirs to the Commune three days later. But in fact both would only lead disastrously to the greater disunity of the French nation.

After 6 February, whatever chance the Right wing had of pulling off a *coup d'état* vanished forever, but the protest march against the 'corrupt politicians' drew a mass of new, young recruits to de la Rocque's standard. In response the left closed ranks more tightly to form a 'common anti-Fascist front'. That July, Blum the Socialist leader and Thorez the Communist signed a pact of unity; by October 1934, *L'Humanité* was beginning to talk about a 'Popular Front against Fascism'. Meanwhile, other factors were lending further cohesive force to this new display of left-wing solidarity. France found herself still plunged deep into economic darkness by the world slump, while Britain and America were already emerging from the tunnel; between 1928 and 1934 French industrial production dropped by 17 per cent, between 1929 and 1936 average incomes fell by 30 per cent, and by the end of 1935 over 800,000 were unemployed. Fearful of the 'Bolshevist' threat to private property and never quite forgetting the Commune, the steely-faced managers of French industry – the *patrons* – had taken full advantage of the past splits between the Socialist and Communist trade unions to put the brake on essential social reforms. Now (although from mid 1935 onwards the economy did begin to show an upturn), the plight of the workers in many French industries was genuinely appalling.

On 14 July 1935, the *Croix de Feu* marched with smart military precision down the Champs-Élysées; de la Rocque was seen paying homage at the Arc de Triomphe. But the day belonged to the Left, demonstrating at the other end of Paris. Down from Belleville and the Faubourg Saint-Antoine they flooded to the Place de la Bastille in their thousands; some papers estimated that well over half a million turned out that day. At a mass meeting on the Bastille, beneath great red banners proclaiming 'Peace, Bread, Liberty!', the Popular Front was officially launched. That afternoon, a vast column processed from the Bastille to Vincennes. Daladier, the Radical-Socialist ex-Prime Minister whose downfall the Communists had helped bring about the previous year, marched alongside Marty, the revolutionary who had organized the post-war mutinies in France's Black Sea Fleet; arm in arm, like blood brothers, went Blum and Thorez, Herriot and Barbusse and Duclos. Such scenes of left-wing solidarity and elation had not been seen since the heyday of the Commune sixty-four years earlier. But, as Herriot grudgingly remarked later on, it did seem rather as if the Communists had dominated the proceedings.

At their congress that October, the French Radicals decided to throw in their lot with the Popular Front. Then, in March 1936, came Hitler's reoccupation of the Rhineland. On 3 May France went to the polls and the Popular Front was swept into power. Formerly with only 10 seats, the Communists now emerged with no less than 72; the Socialists, gaining another 49 seats, became the strongest party, and accordingly it fell to Léon Blum to form a government. In a frenzy of thanksgiving, some 400,000 Parisians marched on 24 May to do homage at the Mur des Fédérés, amid cries of *'Vive le Front Populaire! Vive la Commune!'*, while a contingent of soldiers from Versailles bore a banner proclaiming 'The Versailles soldiery of 1871 assassinated the Commune. The soldiers of Versailles in 1936 will avenge it.' The Left had scored its greatest triumph since 1871; but how, with the clouds growing more and more sombre beyond the Rhine, was it going to exploit this victory?

Chapter 4

Palinurus Nods

> Lost was the nation's sense, nor could be found,
> While the long solemn unison went round;
> Wide and more wide, it spread o'er all the realm;
> Even Palinurus nodded at the helm.
> ALEXANDER POPE, *The Dunciad*

> In tragic life, God wot,
> No villain need be! Passions spin the plot:
> We are betrayed by what is false within.
> GEORGE MEREDITH, *Modern Love*

France on Strike

Almost from the moment of his accession, things went badly
for Léon Blum. The difficulties of agreeing a programme meant
that subtle negotiations between the disparate members of the
Popular Front coalition dragged on all through May 1936. The
French proletariat, buoyed up with the exhilaration of victory,
now watched with extreme impatience for palpable efforts to
implement the Front's electoral promises and alleviate their
hardships. Within a week of the election, strikes broke out at
the Bréguet aircraft factory at Le Havre. At a meeting of the
Communist Party on 25 May, militants began calling for the
Party to break with the dilatory Blum. Thorez urged restraint,
but at the same time demanded immediate economic action
from the Government. The next day the Lavalette factory in
the north-west suburbs of Paris and the Nieuport aircraft works
at Issy in the south-west were paralysed by strikes. These
assumed a new form, later to become known as *grèves sur le
tas* – sit-in strikes. The workers presented their demands to the
management, which rejected them. They then sent the women
home and simply occupied the factory. Friends outside provided
them with food, cigarettes and bedding, and they settled down
for the night, arguing, playing cards or *boules*, singing and

dancing. Alcohol was banned, but the general tone was one of
en fête, again evoking memories of the first jubilant days after
the Commune seized Paris in 1871, but also related to the mood
of mass escapism then gripping France. Day by day the bizarre
situation renewed itself, the factory-owners being told, forcefully, that if they attempted to break the strike their plants
would simply be burnt down.

At first the stoppages appear to have been anarchic and
spontaneous; Simone Weil explains that as soon as the 'pressure' of management had been felt to weaken with the coming
of the Popular Front, 'immediately all the suffering, the
humiliations, the rancour, the bitterness silently built up over
the years created a force sufficient to break all restraint'.
Gradually, however, the unions assumed control. Over the 27th
and 28th, similar strikes smoothly took over the Farman aircraft works and the factories of Citroën, Renault, Gnome et
Rhône, and Simca in the Paris area (virtually all these plants,
it should be noted in passing, happened to be vital to the French
armaments industry). By the beginning of June the number of
strikers reached 500,000 (eventually they were estimated to total
2 million), affecting more than 12,000 enterprises. Parisians
began to take their Sunday promenades out to the factories to
gaze at the workers laughing and entertaining themselves
among the dead machinery.

Blum became thoroughly alarmed by events, which he later
described as 'this social explosion which slapped the Government in the face', and began hastily to prepare reformist legis-
lation. Prices on the Bourse plunged, and some *patrons* transferred their money abroad. Although at shop-floor level there
were Communist agitators at work, the Party leaders seemed
to have been taken by surprise by events – just as they were
during the Paris riots of May 1968. Then at 1 a.m. on 8 June,
Blum signed the famous 'Matignon Agreement', named after
his new official residence. Under what was undoubtedly their
greatest single advance in the history of French industrial relations, the workers were guaranteed compulsory collective bar-
gaining and annual paid holidays, a forty-hour week, and an
immediate general rise in wages of 7 to 15 per cent. Yet still

the strikes continued, until on the 11th Thorez was forced to intervene by appealing to Parisian Communists: 'You must know when to end a strike!' On 13 June the workers evacuated Renault. That *Quatorze Juillet* – at what was both the high point and the swansong of the Popular Front – the entire Left celebrated its great triumph, linking arms once again around the Bastille.

Simone de Beauvoir describes how the Matignon Agreement 'filled us with joy'. Thanks to the forty-hour week, 'couples on tandem bicycles could now be seen pedalling out of Paris every Saturday morning; they came back on Sunday evening with bunches of flowers and foliage tied to their handlebars', and Léon Blum movingly remarks: 'I had the feeling, in spite of everything, of having brought a lull, a vista, into their dark difficult lives . . . we had given them hope.' Yet in fact he had rendered the future for France as a whole more hopeless. A week after the Assembly ratified the Matignon Agreement, the Spanish Civil War broke out; in Germany, Hitler's rearmament was picking up tempo at an alarming speed. Necessary and long overdue as were Blum's reforms, they could not have come at a worse time for France. Far from producing a magical panacea for all her economic ills, if anything they aggravated them. One reasonable estimate puts the immediate additional cost of the Agreement to French employers at between 64 and 107 per cent, which in turn pushed up the cost of living by 50 per cent by the end of 1937. Finding their new gains thus whittled away, the workers at once saw the hand of the employers attempting to neutralize the new laws, and throughout 1937 another series of wild-cat strikes was sparked off. The sharply increased costs meant that French exports became less competitive abroad, with the result that, in September 1936, Blum was forced to devalue the franc (once again) by 25 per cent – to the fury of the Communists.

French industry continued to stagnate. Because they assumed it created unemployment, the Front opposed the introduction of the assembly line, which meant that much of France's badly needed new military equipment would continue to be turned out laboriously by manual processes. Most insidious of all was the impact that the forty-hour week had on French rearmament, at a time when the Germans were toiling away in Hitler's munitions industries for an average of fifty-two hours a week. By the autumn of 1938, while German production was 30 per cent higher than it had been in 1930, Pertinax reckoned that French industrial production was probably as much as 25 per cent lower; Paul Reynaud considered that the forty-hour week 'was equivalent to destroying one-sixth of French plant'. Another injurious legacy from the stay-in strikes of 1936 which contributed to the enduring stagnation of French industry was the loss of power and prestige of works foremen; less visible beneath this lay a newly acquired instinct for disobedience, a disdain for authority of all forms, whether of Government, management or union, which was certainly to bear moral fruit in 1940.

France Rearms – Reynaud, de Gaulle and Pétain: 1936–9

Amid all this political and economic turmoil, France, in alarm at the rise of Hitler and his reoccupation of the Rhineland, had begun to make tentative efforts to refurbish her armed forces. In March 1935 the period of military service had been extended to two years (though at the time the official Socialist organ, *Le Populaire*, complained that 'as in 1913, the Chamber had capitulated to the generals'). In September 1936 a mechanization programme was laid down providing for the creation of 3 D.L.M.s (light mechanized divisions) and two armoured divisions, but it was desperately slow in getting off the ground. Work began on the prototypes of some impressive new weapons, all of which were to prove actually superior on various points to their German counterparts in 1940. In 1935 came the first heavy 'B' tank; in 1936 the fast, hard-hitting medium 'Somua'; and in 1937 the 47-mm. anti-tank gun. But hesitancy on the part of the High Command, lack of co-ordination between the Army and the arms manufacturers, added to the inbuilt hostility of the Popular Front towards rearmament of any kind, plus the consequences of the strikes and the forty-hour week, resulted in the first orders for even the necessary machine-tools not being given until the year after the launching of the new armament programme. Whereas even during 1936, 120 tanks had been leaving the factories each month, by January 1937 the number fell to 19. The arms budget, which in 1936 amounted to 1,492 million francs, rose to 2,938 million in 1937 and 5,152 million in 1938, but much of it was pointlessly frittered away. In 1937, the Government decided to construct a line of unconnected light pill-boxes along the now unguarded northern frontier; the Press immediately assumed this meant the prolongation of the Maginot Line proper, and the Government wholeheartedly encouraged it in this act of self-deception.

As early as February 1935, the French *Deuxième Bureau* had notified the High Command of the appearance of the first Panzer division in Germany, and given a reasonably accurate account of its intended role. But from the leaders of government right down to the patrician French cavalry officers, with their conservative shibboleth 'Oil is dirty, dung is not', the nation in general was disinclined to believe that any combination of tanks and aircraft could alter the existing balance of warfare. Chief among the 'rebels' who dared fight against the current was that political maverick Paul Reynaud, who as early as 1924 had been calling for a mobile and offensive Army as constituting the sole means of deterring German aggression. Later he found a useful ally in an Army major, Charles de Gaulle, who had first come to notice by pleading the case of the armoured division in a review article published in 1933. Two years later de Gaulle expanded his ideas into a slender book, *Vers l'Armée de Métier*.[1] For this audacity, de Gaulle was struck from the 1936 promotion list, just as his earlier idol and patron, Marshal Pétain, had suffered before 1914 for his unorthodox views on firepower.

In assessing de Gaulle's contribution one has to exercise extreme caution. The events of the war and the Vichy era, coupled to the subsequent growth of a potent Gaullist myth-making machine, have tended to cast de Gaulle, in peace-time, as an unhonoured prophet of original genius, and in war-time as the heroic executor of his own theories, on a plane above all

1. 'Towards a Professional Army'.

other French commanders during the brief conflict of 1940. Pétain, on the other hand, emerges as the malevolent scapegoat responsible for all the military shortcomings of France in the inter-war period. Both estimates err by exaggeration. This is not the place to attempt to restore the image of Pétain, but on a few specific points it may be relevant to put the record straight. As has been noted earlier, Pétain, with his doctrine of the 'continuous front', may well be blamed for inculcating wrong-headedness in the French Army – up to 1936. But this false doctrine was shared by the vast majority of French leaders, and, one might well ask, why did even Reynaud appear to challenge Pétain's errors only in the wake of 1940? The same question could be levelled with equal force at other eminent Frenchmen. Then Pétain is accused of having gravely neglected the Army while Minister of Defence under the Doumergue Government of 1934, but in fact his term of office was a steady struggle with the politicians to obtain the necessary military credits, a struggle which he, already approaching eighty and with a life of antipathy to politicians behind him, was least fitted to wage. One of Pétain's utterances most held against him *ex post facto* was that of March 1934, when he claimed that the Ardennes Forest was 'impenetrable'. But this, too, was the general view of the French Army, and indeed, as Guderian's Panzers had not yet been invented, at the time it made reasonably good sense. Also, it should be noted, Pétain had added the essential qualification – '*provided we make some special dispositions*'. As will be seen, no such 'special dispositions' were ever made. Further, the generalization that de Gaulle foresaw the potentialities of the armoured *Blitzkrieg*, while Pétain, in his dotage, failed to do so, is also not strictly correct. Speaking at the École de Guerre in 1935 about the impact of air power and armour on the warfare of the future, Pétain made a prophecy that de Gaulle would not have improved upon; 'victory will belong to him who is the first to exploit to the maximum the properties of modern engines and to combine their action, on whatever level, to destroy the adversary's means of carrying on the struggle . . .' At St Quentin the following year he declared that

The conception of the defensive army which has had priority in France since the Treaty of Versailles has had its day ... we must direct our activity so that we have on the ground and in the air powerful forces for immediate unleashing ... for modern offensive techniques are alone capable of effectively collaborating with an ally in peril ...

But what is really important, as far as Pétain is concerned, is that during the years when the really irreparable damage was done to the French military machine – 1936 to 1940 – the old Marshal's influence had largely been removed from the councils of war.

Although the publication of *Vers l'Armée de Métier* in 1934 provoked the final breach between Pétain and his former protégé, by his heretical unorthodoxy in the book de Gaulle showed himself to be (in the view of one of his biographers) 'the spiritual heir of the Pétain of 1914'. After beginning, characteristically, with a great sweep of history, de Gaulle wrote: 'Nowadays, Germany is ceaselessly marshalling the means at her disposal with a view to rapid invasion.' To meet this menace, 'A certain portion of our own troops must always be on the alert and capable of deploying its whole force at the first shock of attack.' An inert, passively defensive Army, de Gaulle scornfully predicted, would be 'surprised, immobilized and outflanked; and thus you have ... Bazaine blocked in Metz'. He heaped derision on France's conscript Army with its 'provisional groupings', which, 'once dispersed, are re-united with difficulty, like a pack of cards continuously shuffled and mixed up'. The only hope for France, de Gaulle considered, lay in mobility – 'it is therefore in manoeuvring that France is protected' – and such mobile striking power could only be obtained by an efficient professional Army mounted on tracks. Six Guderian-style armoured divisions backed by air power would form the nucleus of de Gaulle's force; but the main point was that it had to be a *professional* corps, of some 100,000 élite troops. This point is hammered home repeatedly in *Vers l'Armée de Métier*.

Yet there is a certain romantic imprecision about all de Gaulle's ideas expounded here, and none of the meticulously technical blueprinting to be found in Guderian – or for that matter any of the original thought-content produced at an earlier date by Liddell Hart or by Seeckt. In fact, de Gaulle was a fairly late convert to the mechanized philosophy of the earlier apostles. He seems only incompletely to have understood the importance of air-armour co-operation, and in the post-war edition of his book there is a bad piece of *ex post facto* 'fudging' where he adds an important passage on the impact of air power written *after* the fall of France. Nevertheless, the real significance of de Gaulle and his pre-war writings was that, for France at that time, his views were as outstanding as his courage in stating them.

The Reynaud–de Gaulle heresy was assailed from every side. Pétain, his natural pessimism exacerbated by his unhappy experiences as Minister of Defence, considered, pragmatically, that it would be quite impossible to obtain the additional 700 million francs per year that de Gaulle's armoured contingent would require. Weygand, the retiring Army Chief of Staff, had been so obsessed by the shortage of numbers caused by the 'hollow classes' that he was prevented from giving full attention to de Gaulle's ideas. Of much more consequence were the attitudes of Daladier and Gamelin, the team which would actually lead France into war in 1939. As late as January 1937, Daladier, as Minister of National Defence, is to be found declaring to a Senate Commission that the German Panzers might be all right in the vast unprotected spaces of Eastern Europe, but never against so sophisticated a defence system as that of France. The Spanish Civil War, claimed Daladier, 'has seen the crumbling of immense hopes based on certain machines'. Outside Madrid the tanks lay 'pierced like sieves'. 'Be reassured,' Daladier added, 'our fortified works are sufficiently equipped to halt a sudden attack even on Sunday...' On Whit Sunday three years later, those words – 'even on Sunday' – would acquire an historic irony.

Following Daladier's exposition, the new Chief of Staff, General Gamelin, rallied to his support with a letter in which he stressed that the development of the anti-tank gun now meant that tanks, unless supported by ponderous artillery, would inevitably be halted, 'just as infantry is by the machine-gun'. Thus the only conclusion was to scatter armoured divisions among the various old-style infantry corps, 'that is to say, let them be melted into the *dispositif général*'. Speaking to the British C.I.G.S., General Sir Cyril Deverell, in 1936, Gamelin echoed Daladier by dismissing the German tanks in Spain as 'inadequately protected, fit only for the scrap-heap', adding smugly: 'All our information shows that it is our doctrine which is correct.' As further evidence of Gamelin's fundamental technical miscomprehension, at another time he is quoted as having said (in response to de Gaulle): 'You cannot hope to achieve real breakthroughs with tanks. The tank is not independent enough. It has to go ahead, but then must return for fuel and supplies.' Had Gamelin read Guderian, it seems doubtful that he could possibly have maintained this view. Lukewarm about armour, Gamelin never seems to have regarded it as his job to see even the 1936 mechanization programme, such as it was, executed purposefully. Perhaps nothing is more revealing than his own admission in his memoirs, where feebly he regrets not having 'demanded in 1935 the creation of an independent armoured force ... Had I known that the war would not break out before 1939, I would certainly have tackled the problem.'

In the opposition to Reynaud and de Gaulle, there were also other factors which underline to what extent the political 'civil war' in France blinded French leaders to all but internal developments. The immediate reaction of Léon Blum and his allies of the Popular Front to de Gaulle's 'professional Army' was to see in it an *armée de coup d'état*, by means of which the likes of Colonel de la Rocque might be able to emulate Louis-Napoleon in seizing power. Daladier the Radical had also backed Blum, declaring: '... we do not want any professional shock Army, more dangerous than one could believe for the security of the country', and, apart from a brief policy switch by the Communist Party during the Czechoslovak crisis of 1938, Thorez consistently opposed French military expenditure, for the same motives as Blum. 'Not a *sou* for military service,' he pronounced in 1935, adding in words that were to assume particular significance on the outbreak of war: 'We ask our followers to penetrate into the Army and fulfil the task of the working class by disrupting the Army.' Meanwhile, at the opposite end of the political spectrum, the ultra-conservative General Weygand's view of de Gaulle's 'professional Army' was: 'What a hotbed of Communism, this troop of mechanics!'

So the Reynaud–de Gaulle doctrine received but little support. At the beginning of 1937 a new Army Instruction on the 'Tactical Employment of Major Units' came into force, framed by General Georges and bearing the signature of Daladier. Baldly it stated its dogma that 'technical progress has not appreciably modified, in the tactical sphere, the essential rules laid down by its predecessors'. As before, it was the infantry which was to be 'entrusted with the principal duty in battle. Protected and accompanied by its own guns and by the guns of the artillery, and occasionally preceded by combat tanks and aviation, etc., it conquers the ground, occupies it, organizes, and holds it.' With a nostalgic glance back to 1916, it continued that the task of the infantry was 'particularly dangerous and of outstanding glory'. The Instruction gave its considered opinion that the development of anti-tank guns 'will result in the employment of tanks only in an attack after the protection and support of a very powerful artillery' – a belief that was to mislead the French High Command fatally in their assessment of the speed of the German attack in 1940.

Thus in the new Instruction, France's official doctrine of war remained the mixture as before, and this was essentially the blueprint with which she would face Germany in September 1939. The bulk of her tanks still stayed scattered among her infantry divisions; some were (reluctantly) received by the cavalry, but, as Guderian pointed out, the combination of horse and motor presented 'more disadvantages than advantages'. At the same time, Guderian rightly dismissed France's new light mechanized divisions as possessing no more striking power than reconnaissance units (though, to some extent, this deficiency would be repaired at the eleventh hour). In the remaining three years before the deluge, slow and halting attempts were made to find a formula for creating French Panzer-type divisions;

but when these did arrive they would be too little and much too late. Meanwhile, above it all, the cumbersome system of the High Command, with its duplication of channels and dispersal of powers, continued without reform under the undynamic aegis of General Gamelin. In September 1938, when war threatened over Germany's confrontation with France's Czech allies, the *Deuxième Bureau* informed Gamelin that Hitler's new Army had definitely gained military superiority over France.[2] Thus, in less than twenty years, had the European balance sheet been reversed.

The New Weapon: Goering's Luftwaffe

In 1938 the horizon was further darkened by France's sudden realization of a terrible new weapon in Hitler's armoury – the Luftwaffe. As General Spaatz of the U.S.A.F. remarks, 'It was the German Air Force which dominated world diplomacy and won for Hitler the bloodless political victories of the late 1930s,' and undeniably it was what provided the ingredient essential to Hitler's lightning victories in the early part of the war.

Before Hitler came to power, the Versailles restrictions hit the building up of a German military air force harder than they did the Army; in engine design Germany never caught up with the West the years that were lost between 1918 and 1933. Nevertheless, once again, what the Germans lacked in material they made up for in ingenuity and enthusiasm. Full use was made of the 'Black Reichswehr' Pact, in force long before Hitler, to train pilots in Russia. Aircraft designers like Ernst Heinkel and Willy Messerschmitt managed to dodge the Versailles bans either by building planes in plants abroad, or through undercover construction in Germany.[3] By 1933 the

2. At the time, the equally conservative German Army High Command certainly did not agree with this appreciation; but the important thing, from Hitler's point of view, was that Gamelin did.

3. An apocryphal story current in Germany told of a worker who thought that he was employed in a pram factory and was asked by his wife to steal pieces from the plant to make her a pram. When the stolen pieces were put together under cover of darkness, he discovered he had constructed not a pram but a Messerschmitt fighter.

French were already disquieted by Professor Heinkel's production of a 'postal' plane faster than their fastest fighter. Erhard Milch's Lufthansa empire provided an invaluable cadre of highly trained pilots, while all over Germany gliding schools were crowded out by eager young trainees. When Hitler made clear his intentions of creating an air force, the members of these schools hitched themselves to the Nazi bandwagon with passion.

The man to whom Hitler handed responsibility for creating the new Luftwaffe, Hermann Goering, had been the last commander of the famous Richthofen Squadron at the end of the Great War, and he immediately surrounded himself with other war-time fliers, men like Udet, Loerzer and Milch. Combined with Hitler's daemonic impatience for results, the get-up-and-go attitude to life of these aces paved the way for the essential early successes of the Luftwaffe; at the same time their fundamental lack of administrative and technical experience would be the cause of its ultimate failure. One thing they all agreed upon was that the Luftwaffe was to be primarily an instrument for rapid conquest in a series of short wars. Here a governing consideration was the limiting factor of Germany's industrial capacity, and as early as 1936 the Nazis adopted a policy of concentrating upon the mass-production of light and medium bombers, at the expense of heavy four-engined machines and sophisticated fighters which required large quantities of labour and material. The function of the Luftwaffe was seen to be purely offensive, flying in support of the Army in the field, rather than carrying out any long-range strategy of its own. In terms of the war to be fought in France in 1940, this philosophy was to prove ideal, though it would lose the Battle of Britain, and from then on would leave Germany increasingly deficient of air cover when she would most need it. Everything was subordinated to speed in creating the new weapon. Already by 1935, when Hitler first announced its birth, the Luftwaffe mounted 1,000 front-line aircraft and 20,000 officers and men. In March that year the first fighter group, called 'Richthofen No. 2', was formed. The same year, the civil Heinkel 111 appeared, followed by its military version a year later, and by

1939, 800 of these bombers had been produced. The forerunner of Messerschmitt's Me-109, later to become Germany's standard fighter during much of the war, was shown in 1936, and the following year it shook Britain by winning the London to Isle of Man race. During the summer of 1936 the Luftwaffe took part in the first full-scale joint manoeuvre with the Army, and a young man called Wernher von Braun persuaded Professor Heinkel to carry out experiments in rocket propulsion.

The secret of the Luftwaffe's rapid expansion lay to a large extent in its ruthless policy of concentrating on a few types – in marked contrast to France and Great Britain. Always the emphasis was on quantity, if necessary at the expense of quality. New aircraft factories were opened to build machines under licence from bigger firms rather than to develop designs of their own, while Junkers was ordered, to the delight of Heinkel, to abandon his Ju-86 and take on construction of the He-111, which Goering wanted in vast quantities. The hard core of the Luftwaffe was formed of four basic types: the twin-engined He-111, which by 1938 had a top speed of approximately 260 m.p.h. and a range of 1,200 miles, but a bomb load of only about 4,000 lb., and was supplemented in 1939 as the standard German level bomber by the Ju-88, with a top speed of 300 m.p.h.; the Me-109 fighter, which in its 1939 version could top 350 m.p.h. with a battle endurance of about one hour; the Ju-52 transport plane; and the Ju-87 'Stuka' [4] dive-bomber. As far as France 1940 is concerned, it was these last two which were perhaps most fundamental to the Luftwaffe's success. [5]

The Stuka was the brainchild of Ernst Udet. Udet was a cosmopolitan, bohemian *bon viveur* with considerable charm, who claimed to have shot down sixty-two Allied aircraft when flying with the Richthofen 'circus' (his record was second only to Richthofen's), and who after the First War had become a

4. Abbreviated from the German *Sturzkampfflugzeug*, 'dive-attack plane'.
5. Two other front-line planes engaged in France which should be mentioned in passing were the Dornier 17 medium bomber, nicknamed the 'Flying Pencil' – faster than the He-111 but carrying only half its bomb load – and the twin-engined Messerschmitt 110 'destroyer' fighter, which proved highly unsuccessful.

stunt flyer for a film company, often performing hair-raising
acrobatics in a top hat and tails. In 1936 Goering appointed
him Director of the Technical Department of the Air Ministry,
then probably the biggest arms concern in the world. Udet made
a point of personally testing all new prototypes, and in 1938
won the world speed record of over 400 m.p.h. in a Heinkel 112.
In 1933, while working in America, he had flown a Curtiss
Hawk at Buffalo, New York, and immediately saw its potential
as a dive-bomber. Overnight he became a single-minded convert to the technique of dive-bombing, and persuaded Goering
to buy two Curtiss Hawks for Germany, one of which Udet
promptly crashed. At first Udet met with the same kind of
doubting conservatism which had confronted Guderian and
his Panzers, but from the moment of his appointment as the
Luftwaffe's Technical Director, he threw all his weight behind
his conviction. Gradually the idea caught on in Germany. At
its plant in Sweden, Junkers set to work on a dive-bomber which
emerged in 1935 as the Ju-87. The following autumn, a trial was
held between the Ju-87 and Heinkel's rival He-118. The He-118
could not stand up to a power dive; Udet, flying it himself,
crashed once again, but emerged safely as usual. Henceforth
the Luftwaffe adopted the Ju-87 as its dive-bomber, or Stuka.[6]

A single-engined plane whose fixed undercarriage gave it the
appropriately sinister aspect of a bird of prey swooping with
talons outstretched, the Stuka carried a crew of two. Its top
speed was only 200 m.p.h. (later increased to 240 m.p.h.) and its
normal radius of action was limited to little more than a hundred miles. It carried three machine-guns and a normal bomb
load of only 550 lb., in its earlier versions. But it could place its
bombs on a small target with immensely greater precision than
could a level bomber. Poorly armoured and slow, its vulnerability was great, both from fighters and ground anti-aircraft
fire, provided the gunners were not panicked. Its capacity to
demoralize was quickly realized by Udet, who himself added a
siren, which he dubbed the 'trumpet of Jericho', the howling
screech of which when diving was to become all too familiar to

6. Udet, unable to face the chaos into which the Luftwaffe had fallen,
committed suicide in November 1941.

Allied troops in the early stages of the Second World War. But the principal significance of the Stuka was that it could provide the essential factor which, up to 1936, had been lacking from Guderian's Panzer doctrine – mobile artillery. Here, as Guderian himself at once realized, was flying firepower which could be brought to bear swiftly and devastatingly on any target miles behind the battlefront, and without any of the laborious preliminary concentration of gun barrels so deleterious to the element of surprise. Considering the fact that the German Condor Legion was to demonstrate in Spain just how effective dive-bombing could be, it is once again surprising that no serious notice of the new weapon was taken by the leaders of France's Army and Air Force.

Second in effectiveness only to the Stuka was that old work-horse transport, the triple-engined Ju-52, Germany's equivalent to the Dakota. Still in service with some 1970s airlines the Ju-52 first appeared in 1932, and was produced in such large numbers that already by 1936 it had given Junkers the lead over De Havillands as the firm with the largest number of civil planes in operation throughout the world. As many as fifty were used during the Spanish Civil War, both as bombing and as transport planes, ferrying Franco's troops from Morocco. Experiments were also carried out in Spain at dropping air-borne troops from the Ju-52, but the experience with the greatest relevance to France in 1940 lay in the employment of massed Ju-52s as cargo planes bringing up bombs, fuel and spare parts from airfield to airfield. Probably nothing learned from the Spanish Civil War proved of greater value to Hitler's war machine. Out of it the Luftwaffe gained the true mobility which it would require to maintain its short-range combat planes always in step with the advancing ground troops, a mobility that no other air force in the world possessed at that time.

In August 1938, on the eve of the first Czech crisis, General Vuillemin, the Chief of the French Air Staff, accompanied by Brigadier-General François d'Astier de la Vigerie, who in 1939 would be given command of the crucial Northern Zone of Air Operations, paid an official visit to Germany. At Heinkel's

Oranienburg works, Heinkel, Udet and Milch did everything to impress the Frenchmen, deploying the habitual Nazi technique of bluff combined with reality. After taking him up in an experimental He-100 fighter, Udet told Vuillemin that the model was already in full production, although in fact only three test prototypes existed. Vuillemin was then taken around workshops crammed with He-111 bombers under mass-production, and was heard to murmur as he left: 'I am shattered!' On his way back to Berlin with François-Poncet, the French Ambassador, he confessed despondently that 'should war break out as you expect late in September, there won't be a single French plane left in a fortnight'. On his return to Paris, Vuillemin's account of the stupefying power of the Luftwaffe made a profound impression, particularly upon Georges Bonnet, France's current Foreign Minister.[7]

7. No doubt aided by the exaggeration of Udet, both French and British experts feared the Luftwaffe for the wrong reasons in 1938. While they remained blind to the potential tactical significance of its dive-bombers and fighters, they were hypnotized by the carnage that Goering's He-111s seemed poised to wreak upon the civil population. In Britain in 1938, the Imperial Defence Committee estimated that the Luftwaffe could drop 3,500 tons of bombs on London within the first twenty-four hours of an attack, while the Ministry of Health was anticipating 600,000 killed and 1,200,000 wounded in the first six months. (In fact, during the whole of the London Blitz only 18,000 tons of bombs were dropped, causing a total of 90,000 deaths over a period of seven months.) The R.A.F., reckoning its fighter force to be below the minimum required for the defence of Britain in 1938, misled the Government (as indeed the exponents of strategic air power have been misleading governments ever since) on the capacity of carpet bombing to win wars, which in turn greatly influenced Chamberlain's determination not to face war over Czechoslovakia. No doubt, in the event of war in 1938, London (and probably Paris) would have been bombed, for which they were ill prepared, but the damage inflicted could not have been greater than, or indeed as great as, that which Britain suffered during the Blitz, while in 1938 Hitler still had neither Panzers nor Stukas in sufficient quantity (nor were the crews of these yet adequately trained) to risk a decisive campaign against the French Army. On military grounds alone, the passage of time makes Munich increasingly indefensible. As Churchill remarks: 'The year's breathing space said to be "gained" by Munich left Britain and France in a much worse position compared to Hitler's Germany than they had been at the Munich crisis.'

The French Air Force

Towards the end of 1935, André Maurois recalls meeting Churchill, who urged him 'to write one article a day ... saying the same thing, to warn France of the decline of her Air Force'. By that time France's Air Force had decayed for much the same reasons as her Army; only the gap between it and the Luftwaffe over the next five years grew even greater and more irremediable. As with the tanks she inherited from the Great War, France entered the 1930s with a mass of obsolete planes accumulated in the 1920s. Meanwhile aircraft design was moving ahead at an infinitely faster rate even than that of tanks. In 1934, France was fortunate to have a far-sighted and energetic Air Minister, in the shape of General Denain. Realizing the importance of fighters, Denain had ordered a large quantity of Dewoitine fighters, the best of their period, but by 1939 these were already outclassed. After Denain, French aircraft production was stricken with that malaise of the Third Republic, multiplicity of governments, which impeded the formulation of any consistent policy. The aircraft constructors wielded considerable power in the political lobbies. Successive Air Ministers found it hard to refuse their diverse propositions; thus a contract for a prototype would be followed by an order for an uneconomically small number of planes. Then, as often as not, the next Minister would cancel the order. Typically, the selection of each prototype was surrounded with an immense amount of abstract argument, so that it could well be said that the best was the constant enemy of the good so far as French air production was concerned.

As has already been noted, the French aircraft industry in particular suffered from the industrial disturbances which followed the advent of the Popular Front in 1936. The new Minister, Pierre Cot, showed himself at once more concerned with vague dreams of international disarmament and with solving the industry's problems at home by nationalization than with laying down any solid programme of rearmament. No doubt there were strong arguments for nationalizing the French aircraft industry, but the fundamental disarray into which Cot threw it was hardly to be made good before the coming of war, while the Air Force itself suffered from his injection of politics into such matters as promotion. Under Cot, the 1936 programme (which only reached the drawing-board stage the following year) resulted in two bombers, a Bréguet and a Potez. 125 of the Potez 633s were ordered in May 1938, but the order was cancelled a short time later. Meanwhile the French Press continued to delude itself and the electorate by boasting, as did *L'Intransigeant*: 'Our Air Force is the strongest in Europe!' In March 1938 the French Government attempted to implement a crash programme called 'Plan V', by which priority was given to fighter and reconnaissance aircraft, but out of 864 aircraft ordered, only one-sixth consisted of attack- and dive-bombing aircraft, and long indecision delayed the production of a three-seater attack-bomber well into 1939. In January 1938, a vigorous new Air Minister, Guy La Chambre, took over, but by then the accumulated chaos of the past was too great for anyone to set right within the eighteen months available. On his appointment, La Chambre reputedly found nothing but a disheartened industry of small workshops of which only one factory alone was equipped for mass-production. As war approached and the production gap with the Luftwaffe appeared hopelessly wide,[8] he tried to fill it by means of large-scale purchases from the United States; but even this measure of desperation met with intense opposition from the French aircraft manufacturers' lobby.

Deprived of any ruthless overriding agency such as Goering's Air Ministry, the French Air Force suffered acutely from being treated as a poor relation by the Army. As Chief of the Defence Staff, General Gamelin was nominally responsible for the well-being of the Air Force, but as a thoroughly conservative Army man, new ideas of air power did not commend themselves to him. His view was that the Air Force should look after itself, and General Vuillemin, Chief of the Air Staff, an elderly bomber pilot not over-endowed with dynamism, obliged

8. By 1939, German production of first line aircraft was already nudging the 3,000-a-year mark, while France was producing at a rate of perhaps 600 a year.

by not pestering him. The role of the Air Force was also clearly laid down in the Army's Instruction on the 'Tactical Employment of Major Units': preparation for the attack was to remain the work of the artillery, and only troop concentrations and columns on the march or in retreat at the rear of the battlefield were considered suitable targets for the Air Force. 'It is convenient,' said the Instruction, 'to leave to the Air Force commanders the initiative for launching their attack.' Here was no question of any intimate liaison between the Army and the Air Force such as Guderian and the Luftwaffe pioneers were developing in Germany.

One of the most serious faults of French pre-war air policy was its complete inability to appreciate the importance of dive-bombers. As early as the Riff War in the 1920s in Morocco, French airmen had recognized the potentialities of this weapon, and others had fully comprehended the importance of the German dive-bombers in Spain later; but they were in a minority. In his memoirs General Gamelin claims that the Army was in favour of dive-bombers, but that the Air Force opposed them on technical grounds; yet there is no evidence to show that Gamelin ever actively pushed the Army's views in this instance. Worried by reports from Spain, after much contemplation Vuillemin decided in 1938 to develop the Loire-Nieuport as a dive-bomber. But it was finally considered to be too slow, and only the Navy was equipped with it. Instead, the Air Force went ahead, belatedly, with experiments in *vol rasant* (ground-level) attack-planes. As a result of this indecision, when 1940 came France possessed a total of only fifty dive-bombers. The belief was that sufficient and fast enough fighters could be made available to destroy the slow dive-bombers and deal with the enemy's fighter cover as well. But in 1940 France's most numerous fighter, the Morane 406, was at least 50 m.p.h. slower than the Me-109, and barely able to catch up with the swifter German level bombers; yet because of the backwardness of the French production lines, each Morane required 18,000 man-hours of labour, compared to only 5,000 for the Messerschmitt. Consequently, it was also gravely lacking in numbers. Armed with one cannon and two machine-guns, the Morane carried only enough ammunition for the briefest of encounters. In equipment, the French planes were also inferior in a number of ways. During 1938 some French units were unable to use their guns during any exercise that year owing to constructional defects in their aircraft. By 1939, most French bombers were still not equipped with radio communication, so that once they left the ground they were out of touch. Ground equipment for loading them with bombs was slow and cumbersome, so that much time was wasted in getting them off the ground. In one of its most serious deficiencies by comparison with the Luftwaffe, the French Air Force possessed no proper air-transport facilities, so that in action it was highly immobile.

One further important function in which the French air defences lagged behind those of Germany was the ground anti-aircraft arm. In Germany this was fully integrated into the Luftwaffe, and its mobility and firepower, particularly of the light flak units which accompanied the Panzers in the forefront of battle, were to have a most important influence in the Meuse crossing of 1940. In France, anti-aircraft defences came under the individual armies, with a separate detachment hived off under the *Défense Aérienne du Territoire* (D.A.T.). In 1939, when the Luftwaffe possessed seventy-two anti-aircraft regiments, France had only five, and was notably short in the small-calibre 25-mm. and 40-mm. guns essential for protecting ground troops from attacking aircraft – especially Stukas.

Enter the 'Fifth Column'

As the Popular Front continued its reign, so the political chasm in France widened, Blum like so many other thoroughly honourable European leaders of that time remaining blind to the real threat of Hitler until too late. For all its declared *raison d'être* of presenting an 'anti-Fascist' front, it was constantly against the French 'Fascists' at home rather than those abroad that the Front concentrated its zeal. When it should have been feverishly stepping up its arms industry, it was preoccupied with social reform, its attitude encouraging and prolonging an indolent and illusory sense of ease among the French workers. On the other hand, the acts of the Popular Front generated in its opponents passions hard for an Anglo-Saxon to comprehend at that time. On the extreme Right, a terrorist group called the *Cagoulards* made its appearance with a series of bomb outrages. As General Spears remarked of his bourgeois friends in Paris, 'these people hated the *Front Populaire* and all it stood for', and, though he himself could never be accused of left-wing sympathies, he was shocked by their inability 'to take into account that the very violence of the socialist reaction was due to the selfish, the merciless attitude' of the *patrons*. On this subject Spears found that there simply 'could be no argument'. 'The revolution is about to break out!' had been the rallying cry of the French conservatives ever since 1934, and the experience of the stay-in strikes had done much to aggravate their terror. 'It would be difficult to exaggerate', stressed the French historian, Marc Bloch, 'the sense of shock felt by the comfortable classes, even by men who had a reputation for liberal-mindedness, at the coming of the Popular Front in 1936', while Pertinax describes a divided nation going through 'an emotional crisis comparable with the Dreyfus Affair, but more fundamental'. Dangerously, the French conservatives, in their alarm, persisted in regarding the enemy within as infinitely more menacing than the monster without. 'Rather Hitler than Blum' – became their motto, and in it Hitler himself saw possibilities that he wasted not a minute in exploiting. To the attentive Rauschning he predicted that France 'in spite of her magnificent Army could, by the provocation of internal unrest and disunity in public opinion, easily be brought to the point where she would only be able to use her Army too late, or not at all'.

One comes to that most elusive of factors in the fall of France – the bogy figure of Germany's pre-war 'Fifth Column'. (The origin of the expression came from the Spanish Civil War, when General Mola boasted that he had four columns outside Madrid, and a fifth inside.) Hitler, says Rauschning, had made a thorough study of Machiavelli's *Il Principe*; from which he concluded that 'a thorough knowledge of the weaknesses and vices of each one of my opponents is the first condition of success in any policy'. To act upon the weaknesses and vices of the Third Republic, Hitler sent to Paris a personal envoy endowed in abundance with the talents praised by Machiavelli – Otto Abetz, who, after France's defeat, was to become Nazi Ambassador in Paris.[9] Abetz, a friend of Ribbentrop who had been won over to the Nazis in 1933, had a French wife and professed deep love and admiration for all things French. 'I had a liking for the man,' admitted Jules Romains, the novelist.

First, he was cheerful . . . He might have come from French Flanders or Alsace . . . He represented himself as a real Western German who, by all his natural affinities and cultural tradition, felt a bond with the Western nations. The Belgians, the northern French, the Swiss, they were his brothers. On the other hand, he felt nothing but aversion and mistrust towards the Prussians . . .

One recognizes the type.

Tall and square-shouldered, with reddish-blond hair, a pale face and blue eyes, Abetz swiftly gained acceptance by smart Parisian café society at various echelons. He was a frequent visitor to the chic political salon of Comtesse de Portes, Paul Reynaud's influential mistress. Skilfully he played upon the snobbishness and anti-semitism of the ruling classes, upon the hatred of Socialism of the *nouveau riche* bourgeoisie, upon the deep-seated pacifism of the French as a whole. Principal among the Frenchmen in the circle which Abetz collected around him were Fernand de Brinon,[10] a journalist closely associated with Laval and Georges Bonnet, and who was the prime mover of the *Comité France–Allemagne*, which under cover of intellectual rapprochement between the two countries became an instrument of Nazi propaganda; Jean Luchaire, another journalist, who had once been Frau Abetz's boss; and Paul Ferdonnet, director of the Agence Prima, who was to establish himself during the war as France's Lord Haw-Haw, broadcasting propaganda from Stuttgart. Through this circle, Abetz

9. In 1949, a French military court sentenced him to twenty years' hard labour.

10. He later became the Vichy Ambassador to Paris.

organized flattering trips to Germany for sympathetic French intellectuals, who were also promised enticing contracts and immense German editions for their books. The *Comité France–Allemagne* sponsored superbly stage-managed reciprocal visits of ex-Servicemen, culminating in moving pledges that there should never again be war between France and Germany. Abetz encouraged, on occasions financed, and generally exploited for his own use such newspapers as Maurras's *L'Action Française* and weeklies like *Gringoire, Candide* and *Je Suis Partout* which combined a running attack on Republican statesmen and institutions with a violent Anglophobia generally guaranteed to appeal to a wide readership in France. Typical of what Abetz inspired, and France's Right wing eagerly consumed, was the line that, in case of war, a French victory over Germany would only lead to the ruin of France and the civilized world, since Germany represented the chief rampart against the bolshevization of Europe.

The direct achievements of Abetz and his circle were not great; neither he nor any other German agency succeeded in creating in pre-war France any large-scale network for espionage, sabotage or subversion and compared with what the world has since come to associate with the Kremlin, all their efforts were as child's play. But what was important about Abetz's 'Fifth Column' was not what it was, but what other Frenchmen thought, and feared it, to be. Writing in 1941, Élie Bois claimed typically: 'The traitors did not show themselves, they worked in the deepest shadow, so that the eye of justice should not surprise them. From afar they pulled the strings of puppets, some of whom did not even suspect it, while others, being aware, feigned ignorance.' These 'traitors', claimed Bois, were held together 'by a truly mystical bond'. Hitler's cunning propaganda of bluff and double-bluff, just as it made his Army and Luftwaffe seem even more imposing than they really were, helped inflate the sinister spectre of the 'Fifth Column'. In the last years of peace, Abetz's work further widened the gulf between Frenchmen; in war, it was to foster belief in the presence of a vast, malignant invisible machine of agents and 'traitors' efficiently paralysing the French war effort at every remove. In fact France had no need of villains; she was effectively enough 'betrayed by what is false within'.

Fall of the Popular Front

On 21 June 1937, after the Radicals had deserted him in the Senate, Léon Blum and his Government resigned. The Popular Front lay in fragments. Blum's refusal to intervene in the Spanish Civil War (despite pressure from his Communist allies), his attempt to come to terms with the *patrons* by temporarily pegging wages, the 'Clichy massacre' whereby six workers had fallen to police bullets, and finally the drab failure of the Great Exhibition of 1937, had provided the nails in the Front's coffin. Within the next fourteen months, another three Cabinets came and went in France, in what Jacques Chastenet, the French historian, describes as 'a sombre period marking perhaps the low point of French political life under the Third Republic'.

But although the Popular Front had disintegrated, the most pernicious of the effects of the 'civil war' associated with it remained deeply rooted in France. First, out of the wreckage the Communist Party had emerged immeasurably strengthened, principally at the cost of the Socialists of the moderate and patriotic Blum. In 1922, while the German Communist Party numbered 218,555 members, the French totalled only 60,000. After sinking to an all-time low of 29,415 in 1931 (but polling 6·8 per cent of the electoral votes), already by January 1936 the French Party's membership had risen to 32,000, and its slice of the nation's votes to 12·6 per cent; but by the end of 1937 its strength had attained the fantastic figure of 340,000, making it the strongest in the Western world, an ascendancy it would long retain. Not only had the Party gained in numbers; it had also gained vastly in wisdom, tactical skill and striking power. These were factors that were to help the Party survive the rude shock of the Nazi–Soviet non-aggression pact of August 1939, and to lend weight to its assault on the national war effort during the 'Phoney War'. Secondly, after the psychological and physical upheaval caused to French industry by the

Popular Front, its equilibrium could not be restored in time to meet the crash rearmament programme forced upon France in the wake of Munich. And thirdly, though the French Communists stood alone in opposing the Munich settlement and maintained their opposition to Hitler until the new *volte-face* of August 1939, hatred of the Party and mistrust of Russia, augmented by doubts as to her value as a potential ally, following the 1936 purges within the Red Army, inclined the French bourgeoisie more and more towards appeasement.

The Rush towards War: 1938–9

In March 1938, after two years of deceptive passivity since the reoccupation of the Rhineland, during which time his rearmament programme had gone into top gear, Hitler resumed his march of conquest by annexing Austria. At one blow, France with her static population of 42 million was confronted by a Reich of 76 million virile Germans. The powerful frontier defences of France's principal Continental ally, Czechoslovakia, were now turned. Again Britain and France stood motionless. Hardly had Hitler begun the work of digesting Austria than he was directing his attentions against the Czechs. With ever-increasing momentum, events now swept Europe once again towards the abyss of war. President Beneš appealed to France to stand by her treaty obligations to her ally. The French Government, with Édouard Daladier once more at the helm and that slippery arch-apostle of appeasement, Georges Bonnet, at the Quai d'Orsay, represented a divided and thoroughly pacifist nation. Terrified by General Vuillemin's recent revelations of German air strength, and doubtful that its defensively organized Army could strike effectively, and without suffering enormous losses, at the Germans protected by their 'West Wall', it cast about desperately for some means of evading its obligations. Salvation was granted in the shape of Neville Chamberlain, who obligingly prepared to fly to Germany to offer Hitler any sacrifice of the Czechs that might avert the unspeakable prospect of a renewed war with Germany. Nervously France watched the negotiations at Munich, the

Paris bourgeoisie already having fled the capital in their thousands, in cars with mattresses heaped high upon the roofs – a
concomitant of panic that would be all too familiar eighteen
months later. Then Daladier returned from Munich. Expecting
to be lynched, he was astonished to find himself besieged by an
enthusiastic crowd at Le Bourget. Simone de Beauvoir recalls
that 'that evening a great wave of rejoicing swept over Paris;
people sang and laughed together, lovers clung together . . .';
while she admitted that she herself 'was delighted, and felt not
the faintest pang of conscience at my reaction. I felt I had
escaped death, now and forever.' The honest Léon Blum represented a wide range of French feeling when he said that he
greeted Munich with a mixture of 'shame and relief'. In the
Chamber, only the Communists of Thorez, acting on the latest
instruction from Moscow, voted solidly against the Munich
sell-out.

After Munich, France's whole inter-war strategy of alliances
at Germany's eastern rear lay in ruins. The great Skoda arms
complex fell under Hitler's control, and the bloodless surrender
of the Czech 'Maginot Line' meant that the full weight of the
Wehrmacht could now be deployed against France, if need be.
But Poland was next on Hitler's timetable. In March 1939 he
occupied the rump of Czechoslovakia, in flagrant breach of the
Munich agreements. Though France remained mutely pacifist,
an extraordinary change of heart now swept England; enraged,
she at last girded herself for war against Hitler. Chamberlain
now extended his 'guarantee' to menaced Poland, thereby jet-
tisoning Britain's traditional policy of non-involvement in East
European affairs, and at the same time assuming direction of
the Franco-British alliance. 'Here', said Winston Churchill,
'was decision at last, taken at the worst possible moment and
on the least satisfactory grounds.' France followed Britain's lead
reluctantly.

By the summer of 1939, British war production was rapidly
catching up with that of Germany, and at last, desperately
late, a new sense of urgency began to filter through to France's
stagnant industries. She had a long way to go. Her share of
world production had fallen from 6·6 per cent in 1929 to only

4·5 per cent in 1937; because of the plunge in her birth-rate, the number of her workers had decreased, between 1932 and 1938, by nearly a million and a half; while the number of hours worked per year had fallen from 8,000 million in 1933 to 6,000 million in 1937. In that latter year, when Germany was producing 19 million tons of steel, France's total was only 6·6 million. Although the world slump of the early 1930s had hit her far less hard than Britain, it had also hit France later, so that she was only just shaking off its effects as war approached. In November 1938, a new, energetic and fearless Minister of Finance, Paul Reynaud, assumed office. At once he challenged the French worker's sacred inheritance from the Popular Front, the forty-hour week. 'Do you believe,' he asked in a broadcast, 'that in today's Europe France can maintain her standard of life, spend 25,000 million on armaments, and at the same time take two days off every week?' He followed up with forty-two decrees largely repudiating the Popular Front's reforms, and reinstating a forty-eight-hour week. On 30 November a twenty-four-hour strike, Communist-inspired, gripped France in protest against Reynaud's fiats. But the protest was a failure, and a remarkable new vitality began to make itself felt throughout the French economy. Unemployment fell rapidly, and in 1939 French productivity rose 17 per cent compared with the previous year. Would France, however, be granted enough time to set her own house in order?

In June 1939 Britain and France opened negotiations at the Kremlin in a desperate bid to put teeth into the Polish guarantee by gaining a Russian commitment. With misgiving ('I must confess to the most profound distrust of Russia,' Chamberlain had declared that March) and almost incredible dilatoriness on the part of the Western powers, the talks dragged on through the summer. Marshal Voroshilov, the principal Soviet negotiator, stated that his Government had a 'complete plan, with figures' for co-operating over Poland; but what about the others? The British and French delegates had to admit they had neither a plan, nor plenipotentiary powers even to discuss one. All propositions had to be passed back to their respective governments. How many British divisions might be available for dispatch to France? asked Voroshilov. Five infantry and one motorized, came the reply. Blandly, Voroshilov declared that the U.S.S.R. would be ready to put into the field against an aggressor 120 infantry and 16 cavalry divisions, 5,000 heavy and medium cannon, and about 10,000 armoured vehicles. Then what about Poland, the subject of the Allied guarantee? Obstinately, Colonel Beck's Government declined to permit entry into Poland of the Red Army under any pretext. 'With the Germans we risk losing our liberty,' Marshal Smigly-Rydz told the French Ambassador in Warsaw, 'but with the Russians we would lose our souls.' As post-war events have shown, his fears were not entirely ill-founded.

In Paris, that last summer season of 1939 passed with a particularly frenzied brilliance. The official receptions all seemed to have a note of unreality about them, but nothing quite rivalled the July ball held at the Polish Embassy. It appeared as if the women had all been invited for their beauty as much as for their distinction, and the Ambassador, Lukasiewicz, excited the admiration of Paris by leading his staff, barefooted, in a polonaise until three in the morning across the lawn of the Embassy. The dancers were macabrely illuminated by red Bengal lights, and one spectator could visualize Poland herself being consumed in front of his eyes, *'courageuse et légère, en danses, en fumée . . .'* Ten days later came the last *Quatorze Juillet*, an echo full of the splendid panoply of a past age: Foreign Legionnaires, Senegalese, *cuirassiers* in shining breastplates – and a detachment of British Grenadier Guards in scarlet tunics and bearskins to reassure Frenchmen as to the reality of the Entente. But there was little that offered encouragement for the immediate future. How the facts of life had changed since that *jour de gloire* of just twenty years ago!

Meanwhile, in Moscow the Russians had become exasperated by Polish intransigence and Franco-British temporizing, and were finally convinced that the Allies' object was to involve the U.S.S.R. in a war in which she could expect little or no support from them. On 17 August the talks ground to a halt; but already three days earlier Ribbentrop and Molotov were in negotiation together. On 23 August the shattering news that

Nazi Germany and Communist Russia, those apparently irreconcilable foes, had signed a pact of non-aggression. It was a crushing defeat for Anglo-French diplomacy, though at this distance it is difficult to see that this had left Russia any alternative. If Britain stuck to her guarantee to Poland, war seemed inevitable. The Pact sealed the fate of Poland, and for that matter of France too, because now the only military ally she could count on in the East was the valiant but antiquated Polish Army. As Paul Reynaud wrote later, 'The Allies had lost the game' – but he might well have added 'set and match' as well. France, on holiday, was utterly stupefied by the news of the Russian *volte-face*, which caught even the Communists momentarily off balance, though *L'Humanité* hastened to interpret it as a move of 'peace'. The full moral effects of the shock upon France would only later become felt. In Berlin, William Shirer noted that the Germans were quite bowled over by Hitler's latest and most astonishing *coup*. At one blow the German nightmare of a war on two fronts seemed to have been removed. Surely, whatever now happened to Poland, France and Britain would not dare intervene?

On 28 August, Shirer reported Berliners watching 'troops pouring through the city towards the east. They were being transported in moving vans, grocery trucks and every sort of vehicle that could be scraped up.' Three days later, the world heard that the German Army had attacked Poland without warning. On 3 September, a stricken Chamberlain announced that Britain was fulfilling her guarantee to the unhappy Poles. In a France desperately disinclined to 'die for Danzig', and even more mindful than Britain of the unreplaced dead of 1914–18, Bonnet still tried to skate upon the slippery ice of appeasement, replying to the outraged protests of Ambassador Lukasiewicz: 'You don't expect us to have a massacre of women and children in Paris . . .' But the game was up, and France too found herself in the war she had dreaded for so long, with no allies but Britain and Poland, Belgium neutral and the Maginot Line incomplete between Longwy and the sea, her Army strong on paper but weak in fact, her Air Force hopelessly outclassed, and the nation divided.

Chapter 5

'Queer Kind of War'

We talked to many of the soldiers. They were sick of the war before it had started . . . they wanted to go home and did not care a bean for Danzig and the Corridor . . . They rather liked La France, but they did not actually love her; they rather disliked Hitler for all the unrest he created, but they did not actually hate him. The only thing they really hated was the idea of war.

ARTHUR KOESTLER, *Scum of the Earth*

In London, Berlin and Paris the coming of war was accompanied with none of the hysteria, throwing of flowers or cries of 'To Berlin!' that had characterized August 1914. The memories of the Great War were still too recent. The correspondent of the *Christian Science Monitor* in Berlin, Joseph Harsch, even went so far as to claim that

the German people were nearer to real panic on 1 September 1939 than the people of any other European country. No people wanted that war, but the German people exhibited more real fear of it than the others. They faced it in something approaching abject terror.

In France there was no repetition of the mad crushes outside the recruiting offices. On the troop trains, Simone de Beauvoir declares, it was only the Negro colonials who sang, a sharp contrast with 1914. The slogan of the moment – though somewhat forced and accompanied with a resigned shrug of the shoulders – became 'Let's get it over with'. But, as Arthur Koestler remarks, 'it carried no real conviction. It was the grumbling of an entirely exasperated person rather than a programme for which to die . . .' Meanwhile, for the third time in seventy years, the Venus de Milo left the Louvre for a safer place. There were air-raid false alarms in Berlin, Paris and London on the first day of war. When the warning first sounded in Paris, Parisians rushed panic-stricken to shelters where women sat stifled and half fainting in their gas-masks. Then soon, as each alarm turned out to be a false one, they began walking around with their masks abandoned at home. Initially, all cinemas and theatres closed; within ten days they were already reopening.

France Mobilizes

Up in the forward zone beyond the Maginot Line, peasants, women and children were hastily evacuated to the interior of France, leaving the wretched farm animals to fend for themselves. In the Line itself – henceforth to be known unflatteringly as *le trou* – the reservists were arriving leisurely, with bottles of mirabelle and kirsch in their packs. Defiant slogans from another age – *'Ils ne passeront pas!'* and Pétain's *'On les aura!'* began to appear on the damp walls; meanwhile the tenants of *le trou* settled down peaceably to their duties like a vast army of *concierges*. On the whole, mobilization proceeded smoothly; on the outbreak of hostilities, 67 French divisions – plus the first contingent of five B.E.F. divisions that were arriving in the north – stood on a war footing, as opposed to an initial overall total of 107 German divisions.

In fact, if anything French mobilization was *too* efficient. Several vital war industries were brought almost to a standstill by the drafting of skilled technicians. The Bourges arsenal, for example, was so deprived that it was reduced temporarily to delivering only 10 per cent of its monthly quota of shells. At the Renault works, the numbers of workers fell abruptly from 30,000 to 8,000, and several plants producing the planes that France was to need more desperately than anything else were actually forced to close down. There were also some strange distortions: one large automobile factory which might have been building tanks continued to turn out civilian cars by the thousand throughout the winter of 1939, while, according to André Maurois, when Paul Reynaud after dinner one evening in October decided 'to make a tour of certain armament factories in the region of Paris, he was astounded to find them closed. They did not work at night . . .' On 13 September the French Government appointed Raoul Dautry, a brilliant engineer who had reorganized French Railways in the inter-war period, to co-ordinate French arms production. But the appointment was late; Dautry confided to Maurois that he would be unable to provide the armies with all they required 'before 1942'. One of Dautry's first actions was to bring back the conscripted technicians. Soldiers at the front wrote disdainfully of a 'massive recall of metalworkers to the factories'. Some divisions lost half of their reservist officers and N.C.O.s.

Here was one more by-product of France's bleeding-white of 1914–18, reflected in the scarcity of manpower of 1939. Although we now know that Hitler's arms industry in 1939–40 was far from being totally geared to the needs of all-out, prolonged warfare, as was generally believed at the time, its shortcomings would only make themselves felt midway through the war; yet by comparison, as Dautry pointed out, it would not be until 1942 that French arms production got into its stride. It was hardly an encouraging picture.

The 'Saar Offensive'

Meanwhile, fortunately it was of course in the east – not against France – that Hitler was concentrating the overwhelming power of the Wehrmacht, which, with terrifying swiftness, was slicing into Poland in two great pincer thrusts. But what were Britain and France doing to help their solitary ally in the east?

In May 1939 Gamelin had given an undertaking to the Polish High Command [1] that immediately on the outbreak of war the French Army would assume the offensive against Germany and that, at the latest by the fifteenth day after mobilisation, it would throw in the full weight of 'the majority of its forces'. In session with British military leaders after the outbreak of hostilities, Gamelin, however, declared with caution 'Certainly, we shall do all we can to help the Poles', but he would not countenance 'discouraging' the Army by any hastily prepared offensive.[2] Elsewhere he was recorded as promising 'I shall not

1. Though subsequently he took refuge behind the fact that this accord had never been officially ratified by the two governments.

2. In fact, the project of a Saar offensive had already existed for a full year, ever since the Czech crisis of 1938.

begin the war by a Battle of Verdun', again a revelation of how deeply the defensive mentality was ingrained upon the sub-conscious of France's Army leaders. To his deputy, General Georges, Gamelin telephoned a message couched in terms that were hardly those of a Foch: 'We have a duty to fulfil towards Poland. The method does not exclude action . . .' On 4 September Georges signalled Gamelin: 'All reconnaissance groups have reached the frontier from the Moselle to the Rhine.' By 7 September French forces had advanced into German territory in the Saar. As the news filtered through the apparatus of censorship and propaganda, the Allied Press promptly inter-preted this to signify the launching of a major effort. The *Daily Mail* spoke of the 'French Army pouring over the German border', while the next day the *Daily Express* headlined: 'Germany Rushes More Troops to the West.' On the 9th, the *Express* announced: 'France last night began the first big attack on the Siegfried Line', and on the 12th: 'France's secret 70-ton tanks crash through German lines.' In fact, no more than nine divisions ever took part in the vaunted Saar opera-tion, and their orders were to move up to the outposts of the Siegfried Line and no further. By the 12th, the French had advanced a maximum of five miles on a sixteen-mile front and occupied some twenty abandoned villages; including Spicheren, scene of one of the first of Louis-Napoleon's defeats in 1870.

As Fabre-Luce remarked, the Saar 'offensive' bore a certain resemblance to an eighteenth-century campaign, where 'great nations delegated a few companies to measure their arms; the rest of the nation watched and applauded'. Casualties were light, principally caused by mines and booby-traps, and with memories of France's 1·3 million dead from 1914–18 casting their ponderous shadow, it was strict Army policy to avoid losses at all costs. One regimental diary recorded: 'X Platoon tried to continue its advance; it was halted by the fire of an automatic weapon.' Commenting on this entry a cavalry officer, Marcel Lerecouvreux, remarked acidly: 'Imagine if in 1918, the attack of 18 July had been halted by a single machine-gun . . .!' Mean-while, for a few minutes each day the guns in the famous Hoch-wald bastion of the Maginot Line fired desultory rounds, but only the 75-mm. cannon had range enough to reach enemy territory, and after the first shots one of them jammed.

In the air, the Allied effort to relieve Poland was even more pathetic. Fears of Luftwaffe reprisals against Paris caused the French Government to veto any R.A.F. bombing of Germany, as later Daladier was to bar Churchill's project 'Royal Marine' to float mines down the Rhine – in case Hitler should retaliate by blowing up a Seine bridge. In Britain, when Leo Amery suggested to the House of Commons that the brutality of the German air onslaught against Poland should be countered by incendiary attacks on the Black Forest, the Secretary of State for Air, Sir Kingsley Wood, was aghast: 'Are you aware it is private property?' he exclaimed. 'Why, you will be asking me to bomb Essen next!' So the R.A.F. was employed in showering tons of non-lethal leaflets on Germany: 'truth raids', Sir Kingsley called them; ignominious 'confetti warfare' was the view of another M.P., General Spears.

Poland Abandoned

The half-hearted Allied efforts resulted in not one single German division being diverted from Poland. There, for all its bravery, the Polish Army – cavalry pitted against tanks and Stukas – was succumbing even more rapidly than the most pessimistic Allied staff officer dared imagine. For the first time the world was beginning to understand the meaning of the word *Blitzkrieg*; Guderian, now in command of XIX Motorized Corps, which provided the steel tip to one of the encircling pincers, was proving his theories in practice. Watching the Wehrmacht in action from an observation post, William Shirer wrote in his diary:

Very businesslike they were, reminding me of the coaches of a championship football team who sit on the sidelines and calmly and confidently watch the machine they've created perform as they knew all the time it would.

At the same time, he shrewdly observed how the 500-lb. bombs dropped by Stukas had proved far more lethal to Polish coastal fortifications than heavier battleship shells. On 14 September the German pincers closed behind Warsaw, and that same day Guderian's Panzers, dashing far ahead of the infantry, reached Brest-Litovsk. Visiting his protégé, Hitler expressed astonishment at the spectacle of a smashed Polish artillery regiment on the Vistula: 'Our dive-bombers did that?' 'No,' replied Guderian, 'our Panzers!' On 17 September, in fulfilment of the secret clauses of the Ribbentrop–Molotov Pact, the Red Army entered eastern Poland. On 28 September, Poland capitulated. She had resisted for twenty-eight days; Gamelin had calculated she would be able to hold out until the spring.

On 12 September Gamelin, alarmed at the ways things were going in Poland, sent a secret order to General Prételat, the commander of the Saar 'offensive', ordering him to halt and assume a defensive posture. When Poland capitulated, the French War Cabinet decided to pull back its forces to the Maginot Line; by 4 October the withdrawal had been completed without a hitch, Gamelin heaving a sigh of relief that the Germans had obliged by letting his forces go peacefully. At least France had made a gesture on behalf of the Poles; thus honour, he felt, was satisfied. Militarily, he excused the withdrawal with the comparison 'Wasn't this after all what the Germans did at the start of 1917 in withdrawing on the Hindenburg Line ...?' Speaking to Anthony Gibbs, the British war correspondent, a French general dotted the i's:

'It was simply a token invasion ... We do not wish to fight on their territory. We did not ask for this war! . . . Now that the Polish question is liquidated' – he shrugged – 'we have gone back to our lines. What else did you expect?'

Thus ended France's first and last offensive operation of the war. During it, the morale of the French troops had been promisingly high – 'We're starting to invade *them*!' wrote an infantry N.C.O. in Lorraine, René Balbaud – but frustration at the subsequent withdrawal was correspondingly great. Out of the experiences gained, the Army settled down to the dubious consolation that German anti-tank shells had been observed to bounce off French tanks. Henceforth it would be Allied war policy to wait either until their war potential matched

Germany's before launching any offensive from French territory, or for a miracle, though it was hard to gauge which, in
September 1939, seemed the less remote.

In Germany, the Wehrmacht leaders observed France's
supineness in the West with mixed amazement and relief. Aware
of their own Army's unreadiness for full-scale war, they had
viewed Hitler's lunge into Poland as one more lunatic gamble;
when Britain and France declared war, they were terrified that
this time Hitler's bluff had been called and that immediately
they would face a powerful breakthrough offensive in the West.
According to General Westphal, during the whole Polish campaign the frontier from Aachen to Basle was held by no more
than twenty-five reserve, militia and depot divisions, with not
one single tank under their command and enough ammunition
for only three days' battle. At the Nuremberg trials, Milch
declared that the Luftwaffe's stock of bombs had been so small
that the Polish campaign had consumed half of it, while Jodl
(the Wehrmacht Chief of Operations) claimed that, because of
ammunition shortages, in Poland 'we only managed solely
because there was no battle in the West'. The Siegfried Line,
despite Hitler's boasting, was nothing like as formidable as the
Maginot, and was far from complete; according to his Chief of
Staff, when Rundstedt inspected it for the first time, 'he
laughed'. If the French had seriously attacked it in September
1939, their troops would at least have gained the training which
was to prove so badly lacking eight months later, while many
responsible German generals believed (and indeed still do) that
the French could have reached the Rhine within a fortnight,
and possibly have won the war. From Berlin, Joseph Harsch
reckoned that German morale 'was probably no better able to
withstand the shock of invasion in September 1939' than French
morale the following summer. Probably he exaggerated, possibly he was right; but both Harsch and the German generals
ignored the fact that Gamelin's Army no longer possessed the
offensive capacity of Foch's of twenty years previously, let alone
the *will* of Joffre's of the Marne. Hitler, the amateur, alone
knew, and in being right he had won his first crucial war-time
round against Germany's professional soldiers.

'Queer Kind of War ...'

Whereas on the first day of war, people in France were saying
'Let's get it over with!', Fabre-Luce recalls that on the tenth
day they were remarking: 'These affairs, one knows when they
begin but not when they end.' But on the twentieth day they
confined themselves to the comment *'Drôle de guerre ...'* And
so, for the next eight months, interpolated by periodic false
alarms that Hitler was about to invade Belgium and Holland,
the *drôle de guerre* – or what United States Senator Borah
dubbed the 'Phoney War' – dragged dismally on. At sea, Britain
hung her head in shame when, on 14 October, H.M.S. *Royal
Oak* was torpedoed inside Scapa Flow; two months later the
score was evened with the cornering of the *Graf Spee* off the
River Plate. But on the Western Front action was limited to
desultory patrol actions, carried out by volunteers, so-called
détachements francs, a system hardly designed to improve the
fighting qualities of the non-élite mass of the French Army.
The Duke of Windsor visited Fort Hochwald, which honoured
him by firing four shells into no-man's-land; later there was
champagne in the officers' mess. Dorothy Thompson also came
and was allowed to fire a '75', while Clare Boothe 'adopted' a
fort to which she sent cigarettes in exchange for a 'brave flag'
embroidered in gold with those evocative words *'Ils ne passeront
pas!'* Visitors to the front were constantly astounded by the
state of truce existing there. After a trip made to the German
lines in October, Shirer wrote:

Where the train ran along the Rhine, we could see the French
bunkers and at many places great mats behind which the French
were building fortifications. Identical picture on the German side.
The troops seemed to be observing an armistice ... one blast from
a French '75' could have liquidated our train. The Germans were
hauling up guns and supplies on the railroad line, but the French
did not disturb them.

Queer kind of war ...

Some five months later President Roosevelt's peace emissary,
Sumner Welles, noted the same picture. 'There was not a sound

as we passed. Not even an aeroplane was seen in the sky.' From the French side, the inactivity infuriated British war correspondents like Gordon Waterfield:

Across the river a young German was standing in the sun, naked to the waist, washing himself. It annoyed me that it should be possible for him to go on washing calmly there with two machine-guns on the opposite bank. I asked the French sentry why he did not fire. He seemed surprised at my bloodthirstiness. *'Ils ne sont pas méchants'*, he said; 'and if we fire they will fire back.'

That the enemy were *'pas méchants'* became the keynote of the Phoney War, and it was a notion assiduously fostered by the Germans. When Strasbourg was being evacuated on the outbreak of war, they obligingly aided by turning on search-lights from their side of the river; for several months, power plants in the German Saar continued to supply French frontier villages with electricity. On the River Lauter, where the opposing troops used to do their washing in plain view of each other, there was a typical incident when a French soldier strayed over to the German side and was captured. This was immediately followed up by a note under flag of truce from his company commander, asking for his return; first, explained the French captain, the man's capture was 'against the custom', and secondly his sector was so wide that he simply could not do without him! It was hardly surprising that, by 7 November, a French lieutenant, Claude Jamet, should be writing in his diary: *'Et la guerre?* Frankly, one isn't interested in it. One does not think of it. Does it really exist?' When the bell of his fort sounded the warning of German aircraft, 'instead of taking shelter, on the contrary one rushes out, nose in the air, dazzled by the sunshine and excited, making gestures like football supporters or race-track touts . . .'

After the initial fear had passed of the Luftwaffe air-raids which never materialized, life behind the lines in France resumed something very close to its normal course. In Paris the black-out remained sombrely effective, but once outside 'the glare and dazzle of headlights was like returning from the Aldershot Tattoo', remarked Anthony Gibbs. 'Every shop in

St Germain and in the outskirts of Paris blazed to high heaven . . .' In Brittany and the remoter provinces, Simone de Beauvoir reported how 'Chic refugees cruise around in cars and complain about the lack of entertainment; what a mad twittering world they inhabit!' Driven by their age-old dread of exile, the smart Parisians soon began to return to the capital. People were earning good money there, and spending it freely. Symbolically, the hit of the season was Maurice Chevalier's *'Paris reste Paris'*. But the psychological atmosphere was far from happy. In October, Simone de Beauvoir questioned in her diary: 'What does the word "war" really mean? A month ago, when all the papers printed it boldly across their headlines, it meant a shapeless horror, something undefined but very real. Now it lacks all substance and identity . . .'

Some outside observers felt that the canker of Munich had gnawed deeply and ineradicably into the French soul. Janet Teissier du Cros, a Scotswoman married to a Frenchman serving in the Army, reflected:

I often wonder what the outcome would have been if we had fought instead of giving in over the Czechoslovakian crisis. I think the temper of France would have been very different. After the first moment of relief, Munich left people in France with a cynical taste in their mouths . . . There was no honour left in public life; all one could now do was to cling to what was left of private life. The door was open for the 'realists' who were to do so much harm . . .

Arthur Koestler agreed: 'The cynicism of the Munich era,' he declared, 'destroyed any creed worth fighting for . . .' And German Intelligence was well aware of this spirit.

To stave off boredom and lack of interest in the war, and to show *bonne volonté*, the Parisiennes busied themselves in good works of varying value to the war effort. In the Ritz, chic ladies in 'simple black dresses' shook tins for refugee relief and soldiers' canteens, then (if it happened to be a 'spiritless day', of which there were three a week) took themselves off to a champagne lunch. The Red Cross and volunteer nursing organizations were womanned to excess; according to the cynical

Fabre-Luce, much as in 1870, 'twenty thousand nurses and more were demanding the wounded. Some of them gave the impression of believing that the military authority was failing in its duties by not providing them . . .' *Le Jour* tried once again to institute *les marraines de guerre*,[3] the good women who in 1914–18 had each adopted a *poilu* whose every need they endeavoured to fulfil. As it was, most already had their soldier 'somewhere in France' – that delightful euphemism of the censor much guyed in the music-halls – to whom they sent all manner of games, detective novels, drink and handkerchiefs.

Life at the Front

Despite all this attention, conditions at the front were by no means brilliant for the simple soldiers. Initially, there was an acute shortage of boots and blankets among some units; in the Second Army on the Sedan front, owing to the lack of proper billets, men slept in the stables with their horses. Where they were lodged out in villages, it was often found that the contagious influences of civilian life from which so many reservists had been lately uprooted had a debilitating effect on discipline. In sharp contrast to the more democratic Wehrmacht, French officers seemed to look after themselves much better than their men, with whom they had deplorably little contact. Although the wearing of helmet, gas-mask and belt was obligatory at the front, officers were often to be seen strolling around in service caps, jackets unbuttoned, hands in pockets and cigarettes dangling from their lips. An American canteen worker who had been a nurse with the French Army in 1917 was shocked by the sleekly well-groomed officers, with their 'well-polished nails and brilliantined hair, compared with the soldiers in their grubby barracks and the dreary canteens in which they could spend their fifty centimes a day'.[4] Somehow the *poilu*'s pay had improved little over the scandalous wages for which he fought and died in 1914–18, and family emoluments were equally poor: a

3. Literally, 'war-time godmothers'.
4. At comparative rates of pay, a British private received 17 francs a day – a source of friction made much use of by Goebbels.

wife with two children, for instance, though living rent-free, received only 16 francs a day in the provinces and 21 francs in Paris. Soldiers would often use their ten days' leave to drive a taxi-cab in Paris, or run errands so as to make a little more money for their dependants. The officers, however, seemed somehow to manage to carry on with their civilian business, wangle official 'missions' to their home towns, run their own cars in the prohibited 'Zone of Armies', and even keep wives and mistresses in lodgings there. At least, so the stories went; and they were as implicitly believed as that hoary chestnut common to bored soldiers in all armies of the world – namely that men on leave from the front had it spoilt because their potency had been diminished by the bromides with which their officers laced the issue of wine. And, as the Phoney War dragged on, leave was the one thing the French soldier really cared about.

To add to the harsh conspiracy of Fate against France, the winter of 1939 turned out to be the coldest in nearly half a century. The English Channel froze at Dungeness and Folke-stone. Germany suffered too; clothes rationing came into force, causing, noted Shirer, 'many long German faces'. The bitter cold and an incipient coal shortage made Christmas in Berlin particularly bleak that year: 'few presents, Spartan food, the menfolk away, the streets blacked out, the shutters and curtains drawn tight . . . the Germans feel the difference to-night. They are glum, depressed, sad . . .' But for France the Arctic con-ditions were particularly undesirable; apart from their effect on military morale, they severely curtailed training and work on those neglected defences stretching from Longwy to the sea.

A French soldier described the lonely monotony of guard duty at an advance post of the Maginot Line during the bitter winter: 'Before you, an unknown countryside, a black night. The nearest post is several hundred yards away. Your feet are frozen in their stiff boots. Your helmet weighs heavily. Your eyes are tired from looking without seeing.' Night after night, the same meaningless vigil. Days turned into weeks, weeks into months. *Le Rire* printed a cartoon showing two *poilus*, one white-bearded and bedecked with many First War medals, telling the younger: 'It all began in the time of my grandfather, but no one any longer knows why.' As the winter dragged on, the whole Army became chronically tainted with that most pernicious of Gallic diseases – boredom. Commented Fabre-Luce with his customary acridity: 'We're no longer fighting the Germans, we're fighting *ennui*.' By comparison with the French sectors of the front, visitors to the B.E.F. tended to remark on the constant bustle of activity even during the period of worst weather. Possibly much of this activity may have been sense-less, of the order of digging holes then refilling them, but at least it preserved the B.E.F. from the boredom gnawing at the French. General Spears, so closely acquainted with the French Army at the time of the 1917 mutinies, in which neglect of the troops' welfare had played no inconsiderable part, noted – in contrast to the B.E.F. – the same neglect once again. He found the scenes at the French front 'horribly depressing'. And the 'unfathomable, limitless boredom' he saw there was hardly conducive to maintaining good morale.

French Army Morale

Disquieting symptoms of the state of morale in the French Army began to reveal themselves in various ways. In many units discipline left much to be desired; men did not salute their officers, and the officers often failed to exact such 'external marks of respect'. This seemed to be particularly the fault of the reservist officers: 'The events of 1936 had perhaps caused them to lose in civil life the habit of being obeyed,' suggested Marcel Lerecouvreux of the 2nd Cavalry Division, and – whether right or wrong – his was a view widely shared among the French officer corps. With horror Lerecouvreux recalled how he observed the sentry of a neighbouring unit, charged with guarding the demolition charges placed under a Meuse bridge, quietly abandon his post and his rifle to assist his mate fishing some fifty yards away. Another aspect of indiscipline manifested itself in the widespread pillaging of the evacuated areas; according to Lieutenant Jamet, serving with the Third Army, 'the Gendarmerie reports are overwhelming. Here, there are acts of vandalism; wherever the zouaves have passed, for example, not a piece of furniture remains upright; everything that could not be drunk or stolen has been smashed . . .' Already by the end of September six soldiers were reported to have been shot for pillaging villages near the Maginot Line.

Just as it had done during the Siege of Paris in 1870, alcoholism became a concomitant of boredom. 'The first reaction of the authorities' surprise by the onslaught of boredom,' noted Fabre-Luce, 'was to prolong the licensing hours.' The resultant drunkenness in the Army soon grew to be a serious headache; as General Ruby of Huntziger's Second Army wrote, 'the sight of our men in railway stations was not always comforting . . . in larger stations special rooms had to be prepared, euphemistically known as "disethylation rooms" . . .' Another disturbing phenomenon was the increasing number of young and healthy officers prepared to go to any length to get a staff job, away from the dreariness of life in the front-line cantonments, whereas in 1914–18 anyone appointed to the staff, unless badly wounded, was in danger of being condemned as an *embusqué* – a shirker. With no General Staff escape-hatch open to them, the simple soldiers registered their discontent in the steady growth of 'French leave'.[5] 'Without permission, secretly at first, and soon almost openly, they went away Saturday at midday, sometimes in the morning, to reappear Sunday evening, Monday morning, or even Monday at midday,' writes General Menu. Threats of discipline seemed to have little effect. Even President Lebrun, who had fought at Verdun, shook his head sadly after his visits to the front: 'I seemed to encounter slackened resolve, relaxed discipline. There one no longer breathed the pure and enlivening air of the trenches of 1914–18.'

Meanwhile, Lieutenant-General Alan Brooke, then commanding the B.E.F.'s II Corps and later to become Churchill's Chief of the Imperial General Staff from 1941 onwards, in whom the listlessness of the troops he had seen on the Belgian frontier had early aroused 'most unpleasant apprehensions as to the fighting qualities of the French in this new war', put his

5. Or what in France is known of course as *'filer à l'anglaise'*!

finger on a different, though perhaps equally undesirable, psychological factor within the Maginot Line – complacency. To the critical Brooke, the Line 'reminded me of a battleship built on land, a masterpiece in its way ... And yet! It gives me but little feeling of security.' Living in far greater comfort than the troops billeted outside in the mud and ice, the guardians of *le trou* maintained a higher morale; but, as Brooke noted prophetically in his diary of 6 February 1940,

the most dangerous aspect is the psychological one; a sense of false security is engendered, a feeling of sitting behind an impregnable iron fence; and should the fence perchance be broken, the French fighting spirit might well be brought crumbling with it.

Apart from boredom and the impact of winter, there were certain other readily identifiable viruses sapping military morale. There was the singularly discouraging effect of the repeated 'false alarms'. On 12 January, for example, Major Barlone, serving in Blanchard's First Army, recorded in his diary: 'All leave suspended ... the entry of the Germans into Belgium is considered imminent ... All the men, roused from their sleep on an intensely cold night, are full of enthusiasm for the idea of going to fight the Germans at long last ...'; but six days later: 'The "stand-by" is now at an end ... our men are very disappointed ...' There was the sense of resentment that for the 'civvies' behind the lines life should continue apparently unaffected by the war, while at the front the troops were suffering all the discomforts, the dislocation of their professional and private lives that war brings – and yet enjoying none of its excitements or glory. There was also bitterness at the way Britain seemed to have pushed France into the war and then – while France had fully mobilized her forces – continued to submit herself to only partial conscription. With no more than a handful of B.E.F. divisions sent to hold the line, this French grievance was certainly not without justification.

Finally, what was the *point* of the war? Since the fall of Poland, no kind of declaration of war aims had been put out by either the British or French Government. Why not? Lerecouvreux notes that the question 'Why are we fighting?' was constantly raised by the troops, but it was 'never answered by the officers, nor did they ever attempt it. By comparison, in 1914, it was quite simple: "We are fighting because we have been attacked and in order to retake Alsace and Lorraine." ' Yet although the French High Command must have been well aware how much lower morale was than in 1914, and of its causes, it did absolutely nothing about it – even to the extent of trying to improve the deplorable mail service; its inefficiency at the beginning of the war meant some troops remaining six weeks without news of their families. Perhaps the reason for inertia lay in Gamelin's subsequent mild apologia: 'I realize that as I spent my time exclusively with staff officers, I was not in sufficiently close touch with the spirit of the country and the troops.'

The Propaganda War

In its state of boredom and malaise, the French Army was eminently susceptible to the propaganda directed at it by Dr Goebbels and his experts. Throughout the Phoney War, each side made up for the lack of shells it fired at the other by a constant barrage of words. Across the Rhine, huge rival hoardings and loudspeakers confronted one another. French troops did not fire on the enemy's artifices by order; the Germans reciprocated, possibly because they found French propaganda so utterly risible. Its general tenor was to be found in the posters plastered all over France which contained a map of the world displaying the vast areas covered by the French and British Empires, overprinted with the slogan 'We shall win because we are the stronger.' This was backed up by attributing, each month, some new project of conquest to the Germans; when nothing happened, an Allied victory was then claimed. Another popular line widely disseminated, both for internal and external consumption, was Daladier's boast at the beginning of 1940: 'In 1914, we suffered 100,000 killed during the first four months. This time we have only lost 2,000'; while steady favourites were the themes that Germany was either on the brink of revolution, or of starvation induced by the Royal Navy's blockade.

Hardly less fantastical was the story recorded by Clare Boothe, much publicized by the French Press, of a miraculous spring in Lorraine which evidently 'started flowing exactly three months before the end of the Franco-Prussian War of 1870. It flowed again in August 1918. On February 19th, 1940, the miraculous spring began to flow once more. "Will Germany collapse by the end of May?" asked the papers.' If most of the French propaganda seemed insulting to so intelligent a people, to Allied sympathizers among the neutrals in Germany its sheer grotesqueness was one of the most depressing features of life.

> We heard over *Paris Mondiale* [wrote Joseph Harsch from Berlin] that Berlin was on the verge of starvation, and then went out and ate meals at any one of a dozen Berlin restaurants which were all a man could eat . . . We read in copies of English newspapers which came through the American Embassy that the German Army was undertrained . . . that it still employed the technique of the mass charge of herds of men with officers driving them forward from behind . . .

On the other hand, German propaganda was adroit, direct and immensely effective. It was based on three hypotheses: the Frenchman's lack of interest in the war, his hereditary dislike and distrust of 'perfidious Albion', and the damage done to an already divided France by the Nazi–Soviet non-aggression pact. Again and again it pounded out the simple, torpor-inducing theme which increasingly reflected the wishes of a large portion of the French Army: 'You remain in your Maginot Line, we will stay in the West Wall.' Undoubtedly the most accomplished performer in the propaganda war was Otto Abetz's old ally, Paul Ferdonnet, who had run off to Germany and whose 'Lord Haw-Haw'-style broadcasts earned him the sobriquet 'the traitor of Stuttgart'. He shocked French troops by his extraordinary knowledge of their movements. René Balbaud noted how in December Ferdonnet announced that his division was going back to rest, giving the identity of the division due to replace it; both quite correctly. On another occasion, he warned a certain corps commander that the wives and mistresses of officers under his command were joining them for the weekend in nearby towns. The general's inquiries proved Ferdonnet to be quite right. Ferdonnet's slogans, such as *'Les Anglais donnent leurs machines, les Français donnent leurs poitrines'*, stuck easily in the mind. Over the radio and their frontier loud-speakers, the Germans played cunningly on the French love of music; Gaston Palewski, then an Air Force officer and later a leading Gaullist, admitted to the author that the programmes piped from Germany used to be far and away the best the French forces could receive. Then would come the slogans: 'Don't transform France into a vast field of battle ... don't listen to perfidious England ... Your feet are cold in this mud ... *La France aux Français!'* Then some more of Tino Rossi singing *Marinella.* Meanwhile, crudely pungent cartoons would flutter down from aircraft; in November, Lieutenant Jamet picked up one, entitled 'The Bloodbath'. The first picture showed a little Frenchman and a large, pipe-smoking 'Tommy' standing on the edge of a blood-filled pond; in the second, the two were preparing to jump in, but the third revealed that the Frenchman alone had dived, leaving the Tommy standing on the bank; in the fourth, the Frenchman was up to his neck in blood while his ally walked away laughing. Another cartoon, which struck a lively chord, depicted British officers in Paris fondling half-naked women while a *poilu* kept watch in the Maginot Line. Occasionally this kind of meretricious appeal backfired; General Spears relates how the Germans once put up an enormous hoarding, informing 'soldiers of the Northern Pro-vinces' that the licentious British soldiery was 'sleeping with your wives, raping your daughters'. But the French regiment opposite promptly riposted: 'We don't give a bugger, we're from the South!'

There was, however, no mistaking the impact made by this artful propaganda onslaught. Already by mid November, Jamet noted down in his diary that the common catchword had become 'Have you seen the English?', adding that 'Anglophobia seems to be almost universal in the French Army.' Meanwhile, behind the lines, while the Government had been prompt to ban Communist newspapers on the outbreak of war, such crypto-Fascist organs as *Je Suis Partout* and *Le Petit Parisien* continued to flourish with their blatantly anti-British, anti-semitic lines. Neville Chamberlain was depicted as being in the hands of the war-lusting British Jewry, while cartoons of British soldiers, philandering with French wives and sweethearts as their men drilled for ten *sous* a day appeared under captions identical to those showered down in German leaflets.

In all the German armoury of psychological warfare against France there was, however, no weapon of greater potency than that with which – at the end of August 1939 – Hitler had been presented by the non-aggression pact with Stalin. To many intelligent non-Marxist Frenchmen, mindful of how vital Russia's assistance had been in 1914, hopes of victory had vanished with her defection to the Nazi camp; the leadership of the Communist Party, however, had been just as paralysed by the brutal shock of the Kremlin's *volte-face*. For a month, during which Stalin was cynically grabbing his share of the Polish booty, the Communist Party awaited new orders. Meanwhile, it was forced to perform, in the eyes of Arthur Koestler, like 'one of those conjurers on the stage who can produce an egg from every pocket'. The first consequences were the physical dissolution of the last bonds of the Popular Front – though its effects were still felt. On 25 September, the C.G.T. broke once again with the Communists. Léon Blum, who, however misguided in the past, was a patriot through and through, stood squarely behind the war effort and renounced his former allies. 'They are defeatists,' he declared, adding sadly: 'We can't deal with these people at all. I know them well – there is nobody who has been more thoroughly fooled by them than I have . . .' From the ranks of the Communist Party itself, during the first three months of the war, twenty-one Deputies and one Senator quit in disgust, as well as a large number of mayors, councillors and trade unionists. Into Party H.Q. flowed telegrams such as the following: 'Since Polish invasion, consequence of Hitler–Stalin Pact, await your condemnation in vain . . .' The Party suffered a severe setback. But the great accretion of power and tactical experience gained during the period of the Popular Front enabled it to survive, much aided by the maladroitness of Daladier's Government.

On 27 September the French Government decreed the dissolution of the Communist Party. Between 5 and 10 October, thirty-five of its Deputies were locked up, Thorez (having deserted from the Army to avoid arrest) was deprived of his citizenship, *L'Humanité* was closed down, and youths were sentenced to two years' imprisonment for circulating Communist pamphlets. Ilya Ehrenburg, the *Pravda* correspondent, complained that 'in reality the bourgeois was taking its revenge on the workers for the fear they had inspired in 1936', and indeed the fact that throughout the Phoney War no comparable attempt was ever made to round up the Right wing's pro-Nazi sympathizers, or to close down such malevolent rags as *Le Petit Parisien*, did lend force to his assertion. Measures against the Communists bore a strong resemblance to the fear-inspired 'spy-mania' which had swept Paris in 1870, and again in 1914. Together with the known Communists, the police in their zeal arrested thousands of non-Communist 'suspicious' foreigners, many of whom, dedicated anti-Nazis, were themselves refugees from Hitler's concentration camps. Arthur Koestler, among those rounded up, describes the French concentration camps into which these unfortunate 'scum of the earth' were flung as being 'even below the level' of those from which they had escaped in Germany; about the only difference was that 'in Vernet people were killed for lack of medical attention; in Dachau they were killed on purpose'. It took the inmates of Vernet a long time to understand 'this general and puzzling outburst of hatred against those who had been the first to fight the common enemy', says Koestler, 'and when we understood it, it laid bare one of the main psychological factors which finally led to the suicide of France.'

Of the French Communists he met during his internment, Koestler remarks how they represented several million of 'the toughest, most active and most violently anti-Nazi part of the French working class ... the best fitted to give an example of comradeship and reckless sacrifice in the struggle'. In their state of utter bewilderment and disillusion at Stalin's *volte-face*, they could have been wooed to join in the common crusade against Nazism. 'It was murderous stupidity on the part of the French

Government,' argues Koestler, 'to start a police pogrom against the Communist rank and file, instead of seizing this unique opportunity to win them over.' Oppression of the Communists and martyrdom of its leaders did in fact only help close the ranks of the party; nothing could have rendered it greater service than the banning of *L'Humanité* and *Ce Soir*, as Léon Blum for one realized. Already by the end of October 1939, *L'Humanité* was beginning to appear illicitly, while with great effectiveness Thorez continued to direct the Party, clandestinely, from a refuge in Belgium.

On 1 October 1939, Édouard Herriot, the Radical Socialist President of the Assembly, received a letter from the banned Communist Deputies, urging that Hitler's 'peace proposals' be seriously examined by the Government. This marked the formulation of Moscow's new policy for the French Communist Party: all-out resistance to the continuation of the war. Later a tract by Georgi Dimitrov, the powerful Secretary of the Comintern, calling for an end to this 'war of plunder', was passed by hand from factory to factory, as well as being widely distributed among the French Army. On Armistice Day 1939, Communist peace pamphlets appeared demanding 'Who in France would want to fight to reconstitute a Poland of reactionary and Fascist colonels?' Others found in factories at this time proclaimed in one breath *'Vive Stalin! Vive Hitler!'* Constant play was made of the theme that, for the French proletariat, there remained but one enemy, the bourgeoisie. 'Away with this Government of misery and servility to the bankers of the City of London!' cried another pamphlet. For Communist propaganda, as for Goebbels, Britain provided target number one. Always trying to create hostility between French and British troops, it harped upon the differences in pay between the two armies. As late as May Day 1940, when the German *Blitzkrieg* was poised for its lunge into the Low Countries, the Communists launched a last offensive against the 'imperialist war', in which, among other things, they charged France with having descended to the rank of a 'British Dominion'.

Although there was not much to choose in the content of Communist and Nazi propaganda, the former was considerably more effective. As well as striking a more responsive chord within the nation as a whole, its means of dissemination were vastly superior. Pamphlets seemed to be in circulation everywhere, chain-letters made the rounds at the front, soldiers coming home on leave were got at outside the Gare de l'Est, and there was even a special underground edition of *L'Humanité*, called *Les Soldats contre la Guerre*, expressly designed for the Army's consumption. Quick to realize the immense value of this ready-made propaganda machine, the Germans did all they could both to aid it and to cash in on its efforts; Luftwaffe planes were employed to drop pamphlets reporting Molotov's speech of 31 October 1939 in which he had identified himself with Hitler's peace proposals. In the progressive boredom of the Phoney War, the Communist propaganda slowly began to poison and win back even adherents of the former parties of the Popular Front which had broken with the Communists. More and more the Army was divided, as the other ranks inclined towards the Communist line; while for the officer corps the principal enemy remained 'the enemy within' – Communism. It was all very well for Somerset Maugham to write a tract from the azure and gold of Cap Ferrat claiming (for British consumption) German 'ignorance of the French temper' when they thought that 'they were fighting a house divided against itself', but there was no mistaking just how effectively joint Nazi–Communist propaganda was widening the rifts left by the Popular Front era.

Equally depressing upon French war morale were the more tangible results of that close concomitant of Communist subversion – sabotage. During the Phoney War, numerous slowdowns of mysterious origin struck at France's war production. Most of the worst cases of actual sabotage appear to have taken place at the Renault (tanks) and Farman (aircraft) works, those old hot-beds of trouble in Paris. A report on the damage wreaked upon Renault's production of the B.1, France's gravely needed new heavy tank, itemized: 'nuts, bolts, various bits of old iron put in the gear-boxes and transmissions ... filings and emery-dust in the crank-cases; saw-strokes producing incipient rupture of the oil and petrol ducts, intended to make them fall to bits after several hours' running . . .' In April 1940, a number of fatal flying accidents led investigators to the Farman factory. Here it was found that on engines ready for delivery a brass wire acting as a lock on the nut which held the petrol feed nozzle in position was severed. After a number of hours' flying, the nut, stripped of its lock, unscrewed itself with the engine vibration and allowed the petrol to drip on to the white-hot exhaust pipe, which eventually led to a lethal explosion. It was claimed that, under the very eyes of *Sûreté* investigators, a young Communist, Roger Rambaud, was caught in the act, having snipped the locking wires on seventeen out of twenty engines on the test bed. Elsewhere, at a factory producing the 25-mm. anti-aircraft gun – which the Army was to need at least as badly as the B.1 tank – one act of sabotage wrote off some two hundred barrels, the normal equipment for four divisions. In the chaos that followed the fall of France, purported acts of sabotage went either unverified or unpunished. Undoubtedly many allegations were exaggerated; but, just as with the shadowy German 'Fifth Coloumn', the constant fear of Communist-sponsored espionage and sabotage was to prove almost as effective as the weapon itself.

How many Russian lives, one might well ask in retrospect, were to be forfeited from June 1941 onwards as a direct consequence of the success of the Kremlin's whole dingy policy towards France in 1939–40?

Chapter 6

Gamelin

What kind of a nation will they make of us tomorrow, these exhausted creatures emptied of blood, emptied of thought, crushed
by superhuman fatigue . . .?
    MARC BOASSON,[1] *At the Evening of a World*

One of Napoleon's marshals once brought him a plan of campaign
in which the French Army was neatly and evenly lined up from
one end of the frontier to the other. 'Are you trying to stop
smuggling?' Napoleon asked heartlessly.
    THEODORE DRAPER, *The Six Weeks War*

As the spring of 1940 approached, French eyes, military and
civilian, turned instinctively towards the Château de Vincennes,
wondering what new Allied strategy was being evolved behind
its grim walls. Here Henry V of England had died, and as one
of France's favourite execution grounds it was against these
walls that the Duc d'Enghien, Mata Hari and the last of the
Communards had died. One of the most forbidding castles in
all France, to Spears it 'seemed to drip with blood'. Despite its
sombre historical associations, Vincennes, on the eastern outskirts of Paris, was now the home for the *Grand Quartier
Général* (G.Q.G.) of General Maurice Gamelin, Chief of the
General Staff of National Defence and, since the outbreak of
war, Supreme Commander of all French land forces. Descended on his mother's side from an old military family of
Alsace-Lorraine, Gamelin had passed first out of St Cyr in
1891, and entered the Algerian *Tirailleurs*. In 1914 he had been
on Joffre's operations staff and had drawn up the orders on
which rested the victory of the Marne; in 1916 (then aged
forty-four) he became both one of the youngest and most
competent French divisional commanders; by 1918 he had
generally come to be regarded as the outstanding officer of his

1. Killed in Flanders in 1918. The passage relates to the fighting at Verdun
in the summer of 1916.

'promotion'. Already having reached the age-limit of sixty-eight at the beginning of 1940, Gamelin was a small sandy-haired man usually clad in tight tunic and high-laced boots. To André Maurois, 'his short, stiff moustache, his small eyes and thin-lipped mouth gave him an indecipherable aspect, which no spontaneous gesture served to clarify. He had neither the sparkling vivacity of Foch nor the massive geniality of Joffre.' Nor was Gamelin, he might have added, adorned with the coldly imposing presence of Pétain. Britain's 6 ft. 4 in. C.I.G.S., General Ironside, rather patronizingly regarded his opposite number as a nice little man in well-cut breeches. (In less polite terms, Air Chief Marshal Sir Arthur Barratt, the former commander of the Advanced Air Striking Force, described Gamelin[2] as 'a button-eyed, button-booted, pot-bellied little grocer'.) Modest and unassuming, Gamelin's ideal inconspicuousness as Joffre's Chief of Operations had led Jules Romains, in his famous novel *Verdun*, to base upon him his characterization of 'Lieutenant-Colonel G—', a model staff officer. General Spears recalls him from 1914, following Joffre 'like a shadow', and it was upon his former master that Gamelin seemed to model himself. His blue eyes certainly gave an impression of calm serenity; but he possessed none of the solid basis for Joffre's legendary imperturbability – and in any case this attribute, carried to excess, had ultimately cost Joffre his job, and nearly France the war, in 1916. Like Joffre, Gamelin was taciturn; but whereas the explanation often given for Joffre's silence was that he simply had nothing in his mind, this was certainly not the case with the cerebral Gamelin. When Gamelin did speak, he had a habit of clasping his hands and moving them as if giving a benediction; indeed, there was something faintly monkish about him, which could never have been said of Joffre.

A senior French diplomat dining with Gamelin at the French Embassy on one of his visits to London was amazed to hear the Generalissimo discourse on nothing but philosophy and Italian painting. Joffre, he reckoned, would have been much discountenanced by the tenor of the conversation, while, listening to Gamelin, the diplomat 'felt a cold draught at my back'. Un-

2. To the author.

ashamedly, Gamelin was an intellectual who felt ill at ease in front of the troops (with whom his contacts were certainly kept to a minimum), much preferring the company of his fifteen adulatory staff officers where, says Pertinax, 'culture was the thing, books on the history of art'. According to de Gaulle, after a visit to the gloomy vaults at Vincennes tenanted by Gamelin, he

dwelt in an atmosphere very akin to that of a convent, surrounded by only a few officers, working and meditating, completely insulated from current events ... In his *Thébaïde* [3] at Vincennes, General Gamelin gave me the impression of a savant, testing the chemical reactions of his strategy in a laboratory.

Adding to this isolation from the outside world there was the extraordinary fact that Vincennes possessed no radio-communications centre.[4]

Gamelin considered experience to be everything, ignoring Frederick the Great's sally that if this quality 'were all a great general needs, the greatest would be Prince Eugene's mules'. To Jules Romains he dwelt upon the grave disadvantage of the Wehrmacht, because 'I can think of very few of their present generals who fought in responsible posts in 1914–18. Here we are almost all former 1918 divisional commanders ...' The tragedy of Gamelin was not that he misconstrued modern trends through stupidity; certainly, his luminous mind had *thought* deeply about tanks and their possible effect on warfare, but in a kind of abstract intellectual vacuum, and his private lucubrations had hardly helped provide the French Army with more and better tanks. When Gamelin gave orders, they sounded less like the words of a fighting man calling for vigorous action than topics for academic discussion. Worried about defects in training at the end of 1939, he had simply

3. Literally an 'ivory tower'.
4. In a letter to the Press after the war (*L'Aurore*, 8 November 1949) defending this deficiency, Gamelin challenged: 'What would we, at this level, have done with a transmitter?' He added that, in any case, there had been one at the General Staff Headquarters some twenty-two miles away: 'But we avoided using it so as not to give our position away.'

indicated to his subordinate, General Georges, 'a few ideas' phrased in a style which the Quai d'Orsay would have admired, instead of issuing clear-cut instructions. It was hardly surprising that the Army took no notice of these 'ideas'. According to Paul Baudouin, even Daladier, Gamelin's political protector, once remarked to General Weygand: 'When you speak, one has something; as for Gamelin, it is like sand running through one's fingers', while the final damning remark about Gamelin, made by Reynaud to Baudouin, was that 'He might be all right as a prefect or a bishop, but he is not a leader of men.'

Indeed, as Georges Mandel described him, Gamelin was a kind of 'military prefect' who tailored his decisions closely to the whim of the politicians. One of his officers at G.Q.G. recalled how

when he had to take a decision in the domain which interested me, I often saw him hesitate, postpone his decision to another moment, so as to weigh up all the consequences, and finally to take that which would not expose him to a subsequent conflict with the civilian powers.

It was with the express purpose of keeping a close feel on the political pulse that, whereas Joffre had stubbornly maintained his G.Q.G. out at Chantilly so as to be beyond Parliamentary interference, Gamelin selected Vincennes. Thus it was that, too close to his political masters, too remote from the zone of operations, Gamelin gravely compromised his authority over the fighting forces.

French Chain of Command

The whole French chain of command was anomalous and hardly satisfactory. The Minister of National Defence (which role Daladier filled, as well as being Premier) wielded only nominal power over the Navy and Air Force, and Gamelin as the Chief of Staff possessed no more authority than his political boss. So the French Air Force, under the depressed General Vuillemin, tended to go its own way. Vuillemin had his H.Q. at Coulommiers, outside Paris. Under him came General Têtu, with the title of 'Officer Commanding the Air Co-operation Forces', who was supposed to co-ordinate air activities with the Army's North-East Front H.Q. This front was divided into 'Zones of Air Operations', corresponding to the various Army Groups. In theory the arrangement was adequate, but in practice it meant that the individual army commanders found it impossible to obtain a sufficient concentration of air power at the right moment. The fundamental trouble, of course, was the sheer numerical shortage of French aircraft. Of the R.A.F. in France, Air Marshal Barratt's Advanced Air Striking Force came directly under Bomber Command in England, the Royal Air Force Component of the B.E.F. under the Army Commander, Lord Gort.[5]

As Supreme Commander of all French land forces, Gamelin gave direct orders to the armies in the Alps, in Syria and in North Africa. But to the great bulk of the forces grouped together under the Armies of the North-East, Gamelin issued his orders through the intermediary of his deputy, General Georges, who initially bore only the somewhat indefinite title (which had originated under Napoleon, and in the First War had been held, under Joffre, by General de Castelnau) of *Major-Général des Armées*. On the next level came the commanders of the various Army Groups. No. 1 Army Group, which, stretching from the Channel to the beginning of the Maginot Line, would play the predominant role in the battle for France, was commanded by General Billotte. Among the five armies on Billotte's front was the B.E.F.; Lord Gort, however, received his orders not from Billotte but from Gamelin, via Georges.[6]

It soon became apparent to Gamelin that he could not effectively control overall war strategy *and* exercise specific command over the Zone of the Armies of the North-East all from

5. In January 1940, command of the R.A.F. component was transferred to Barratt, although it remained under Gort's operational control.

6. In fact it was never quite clear whether the ultimate responsibility for the B.E.F. rested with Gamelin or Georges, and in any case Gort's instructions permitted him to appeal to the British Government before executing any order if it 'appears to you to imperil the British Field Force' – which was to prove an important escape clause.

one inflated headquarters. On 6 January he effected a re-organization which relieved himself of the direct command of the North-East and handed it to Georges, now entitled C.-in-C. North-East Front. It was a measure that would provide Gamelin with numerous let-outs when it came to writing his memoirs, but somehow it did not improve the efficacy of the French command. While he reserved the right to intervene in an emergency (a right he never exercised in battle until it was much too late), the reorganization meant in fact that Gamelin – in sharpest contrast to his old master, Joffre – removed himself from control of what was almost certain to become the key battle area of the war. Yet Georges, on the other hand, was never vested with full powers or responsibility. The reorganiz-ation also resulted in the immediate creation of yet a third headquarters, G.H.Q. Land Forces under General Doumenc, situated in a Rothschild mansion beside the Marne at Montry, midway between Vincennes and Georges's North-East Front H.Q. at La Ferté-sous-Jouarre, which lay forty miles to the east of Pa.is. The new H.Q., whose function was to prepare and elaborate orders, was created by fission chiefly from elements of General Georges's staff, and this breaking-up of offices that had been working well together for several months had par-ticularly lamentable effects. The *Deuxième Bureau* (Intelli-gence) was split in two, with its chief, Colonel (later General) Gauché, under Gamelin's wing at Vincennes and officers com-pelled to make the trip there from La Ferté every day to obtain his signature for documents. The *Troisième Bureau* (operations) was also divided, but even more inopportune was its separation from the *Quatrième* (transport and supply) which was removed completely to Montry, an artificial divorce that had to be rapidly rescinded when the Germans attacked on 10 May. General Doumenc too had to 'cut himself in two', directing affairs at Montry in the morning and at La Ferté in the after-noon. Visiting officers from the line, such as General Prioux, commanding the élite Cavalry Corps, were not impressed by what they saw of the new organization; obeying Parkinson's Law, the various staff adjuncts proliferated like amoebae, creating among themselves bureaux that specialized in agricultural affairs, P.T. and sports. Meanwhile, the inconveniences caused to communications by this splitting up of G.Q.G. encouraged the habit of short-circuiting Gamelin in his *Thébaïde* altogether.

General Georges

Not least among Gamelin's motives in establishing this third, buffer-state, H.Q. at Montry was the animosity that existed between himself and Georges, and it seemed to be his deliberate policy to weaken his subordinate's position by removing the more valuable members of his staff. As Gamelin's star waned in Government circles and Georges emerged as his logical successor, relations between the two worsened to the point where they could hardly exchange civilities. 'They are so busy making war on each other,' a British general quipped in the hearing of Maurois one day, 'that they have no time to make war on the Germans.' General Georges himself came of very modest origins – he was said to be the son of a gendarme – and he owed a fine career entirely to professional merit, in no way to intrigue or political pull. In the Great War he had served on the staff in Salonika and had then been picked up by Foch, and it was in his retinue that he had ridden behind the Marshal, as a colonel, in the Victory Parade in 1919. After the war he had commanded a regiment in the Rhineland, later becoming Pétain's Chief of Staff in Morocco. On 9 October 1934, fate struck a cruel blow at Georges: while accompanying King Alexander of Yugoslavia at Marseilles he was very badly wounded in the chest by the assassin who killed the King and Barthou, the French Foreign Minister. By 1940 he was still visibly suffering from the effect of his wounds; Spears noted that 'he now invariably wore a woollen glove on one hand, and had been told he must not fly'. Instead, he drove about at high speed in a 'beautiful and enormous Cadillac car, of which he was justly proud'. Because of Georges's supposed doubtful associations with the more extremist right-wing factions, Daladier viewed him with mistrust and (so Gamelin claimed) for this reason would never tolerate him as C.-in-C. of the Army.[7] In 1939 Georges's pessimism about the war was widely known in the French Army; but of the British officers acquainted with him, many considered Georges to be France's finest soldier. According to Spears, who should have known, he 'had more influence on Churchill than any other Frenchman'. There were also many senior officers in the French Army who felt that Georges – not Gamelin – should have succeeded Weygand as C.-in-C. in 1935.

Before the war, La Ferté, with its bourgeois houses topped by pretentious turrets that lent them an air of bogus castles, had been a popular summer retreat for rich Parisians. Here General Georges had established H.Q. North-East Front at Les Bondons, described by a staff officer as 'a spacious cottage in an Anglo-Norman style, sited in the middle of a park on a wooded hill which dominated the Marne', but 'as little as possible suited to be a command post in time of crisis'. In a leisurely manner, Georges's staff officers dined at the Hôtel de l'Épée, boasting a renowned chef, M. Truchet, who in 1917 had presided over Pétain's cuisine. Perhaps on account of the mentally sapping consequence of Georges's wounds, the atmosphere at Les Bondons struck visitors as being much the same as at Vincennes; here too an order was 'an excellent basis for discussion'.

Reading General Spears's incomparable accounts of the French High Command in 1940, one emerges with a feeling of a world grown old and tired. In the military corridors one runs into the same old faces one has encountered a generation earlier. Brigadiers are now army commanders, or Commanders-in-Chief; battalion commanders have divisions or corps; the captains of 1918 are now in command of brigades or divisions. But they have aged. Symbolically, here is Marshal Franchet d'Esperey, the virile hero of 1918, in his wheelchair, now aged eighty-three, and declaring to Spears and Harold Nicolson: 'Well, gentlemen, you see a ghost revisiting the scenes of his past'; Gamelin, the heir to Joffre, is sixty-eight; Weygand, the shadow of Foch, seventy-three. A French historian, Marc

7. To some extent, the bad relations between Georges and Gamelin were an extension of the rivalry between their respective political champions, Reynaud and Daladier.

Bloch, writing at the time describes a perhaps typical senior officer who had gone through the First War as 'weighed down ... by years spent in the office work and conditioned by a purely academic training'. Where then, and who, are the young men, with the young ideas?

Gamelin's Strategy

In the Entente of 1939, while conduct of the war by sea rested upon Britain's shoulders, on account of France's vast military preponderance the planning of land operations devolved in effect upon the French Generalissimo, which seemed a reasonably fair division of labour. Gamelin's long-range strategy was to wait until, in terms of men and equipment, Britain and France had caught up with the Wehrmacht before launching any serious offensive. This could not be before 1941, at the earliest; by then, who knows, perhaps neutral America might be persuaded once again to come to the rescue. The two overriding considerations behind French strategy remained the same as they had been ever since 1919: to husband French manpower so as not to permit a repetition of the slaughter of 1914–18, and to keep the war away from the sacred soil of France. But what if, while France was building up her potential, Hitler should attack first? This seemed more than likely, in which case the two avenues open to him would be to attack across the common frontier, taking the shortest route to Paris, or to repeat 1914 and sweep through neutral Belgium. In the path of the first route lay the imposing barrier of the Maginot Line; of the second, Belgian neutrality. Given the ruthlessness of Hitler, there could be little doubt as to which barrier was the least daunting; the various *Deuxième Bureau* reports from October 1939 onwards suggested that it was towards the Flemish plains that Hitler was already turning his gaze.

With the Maginot Line 'extension' between Longwy and the sea still far from reality, Pétain's prescription of 'going into Belgium' to meet a German invasion clearly continued to hold good.[8] But now, of course, King Leopold's rigid neutrality eradi-

8. As always, it was of course also very much Britain's policy not to allow the Belgian coast to fall into enemy hands.

cated any prospect of the French moving, at Belgian invitation, comfortably into their fortifications upon the German frontier as soon as war broke out. There had been no exchange consultations between the two General Staffs. The Belgians based their plans on the hope that they could hold their modern defence system along the Albert Canal, of which the powerful fortress of Eben Emael was the linchpin, at least long enough for the Allies to come to their assistance. But they adamantly declined to provide the Allies with any detailed information about these plans, and requests for French officers to visit defences in civilian clothes were invariably turned down. The same strict neutrality applied also to Holland. Ideally, Gamelin and the French military would have liked to go into Belgium without having to wait for the Germans to move first. But, quite rightly, the politicians were horrified at the impact any French violation of Belgian neutrality might have upon world (and, predominantly, American) opinion. Besides, the possibility of jeopardizing eventual collaboration with the Belgian Army simply could not be entertained, for one of Gamelin's principal motives for 'going into Belgium' at all was the indispensability to France of the Belgian Army's 700,000 men and twenty-two divisions (plus another ten from Holland in case of her involvement).

On 24 October, Gamelin issued orders to the armies of the North-East Front, telling them to be ready to advance to a defensive position along the Escaut (or Scheldt) River, running from Antwerp to Ghent. In terms of distance of approach march, the 'Escaut Plan' represented the most prudent of the Low Countries operations open to the Allies. But it was an awkwardly long line to hold, and at the same time it covered so small a portion of Belgian territory that Brussels would be abandoned and the bulk of the Belgian Army simply left, unsupported, to its fate. General Georges, however, immediately registered the strongest misgivings about any 'deeper progression into Belgium'. The Army was still not yet sufficiently ready to risk being caught by a German offensive in unprepared positions, far from its bases. Despite Georges's doubts, on 15 November Gamelin gave out his amended Instruction No. 8, in which the Allied forces were to move up to the Dyle Line, stretching from Antwerp due south to above Dinant on the Meuse. The Dyle itself was little more than a wide stream, and it involved the French Army going out still further on the Belgian limb. Once again, General Georges expressed his reservations. On the credit side of the original 'Dyle Plan', it constituted a shorter line, it protected Brussels and gave a better chance of linking up with the Belgian defenders in their Albert Canal positions, and it committed no more than ten French divisions. Gamelin himself, however, was not satisfied; it made no provision for lending a hand to the Dutch in case of attack.

Towards the end of November, Gamelin requested General Billotte, commander of No. 1 Army Group, to study an extension of the Dyle Plan northwards from Antwerp in the direction of Breda, which lay twice as far from the French frontier as from Germany. On hearing of this new inflationary development of Gamelin's Belgian strategy, Georges objected vigorously. In the margin of Billotte's report, he wrote: 'This is of the order of an adventure ... Don't let's engage our effectives in this affair', and on 5 December he sent it on to Gamelin with an accompanying memorandum which contained this highly pertinent and prescient warning:

The problem is dominated by the question of available forces ... There is no doubt that our offensive manoeuvre in Belgium and Holland should be conducted with the caution of not allowing ourselves to commit the major part of our reserves in this part of the theatre, in face of a German action which could be nothing more than a diversion. *For example, in the event of an attack in force breaking out in the centre, on our front between the Meuse and Moselle, we could be deprived of the necessary means for a counter-attack* ...[9]

Momentarily, Gamelin seems to have been swayed by Georges's arguments. But as well as the essential military considerations, there was an element of personal honour and pride pushing Gamelin along: humiliatingly, as France's top soldier, he had

9. Author's italics.

been forced to stand by while Germany crushed first Czecho-slovakia and then Poland. His enemies had never ceased taunt-ing him since the French Army's lethargy during Hitler's conquest of Poland, and he was determined not to give them cause to say he had cast Belgium and Holland to their fates too. Then, on 10 January, there occurred one of those freak acci-dents of war which change the destinies of mankind.

The Mechelen Incident

On 9 January a German major of the paratroops employed on an airborne planning staff, by name Hellmuth Reinberger, re-ceived a summons to attend a highly secret conference at Second Air Fleet H.Q. in Cologne the following morning. Rein-berger was in Münster at the time, some eighty miles distant as the crow flies. That night he was invited to the local air base. After a number of drinks, and some conviviality, the station commander, a reservist major called Hoenmanns, genially pro-posed to Reinberger that he save him a dreary train journey by flying him down to Cologne. A First War flyer, Hoenmanns had a civil pilot's licence and wanted to get in a few more flying hours; also he would welcome an excuse to visit his wife and take home some laundry. Reinberger accepted, on condition that weather conditions were perfect.

The next day dawned cloudless, with visibility over the Ruhr up to two and a half miles. The two majors set forth in a tiny Me-108, Reinberger hugging on his knees an imposing yellow pigskin briefcase, which bulged with top-secret documents relating to the air plan of a German operation to invade Holland and Belgium. Suddenly the weather closed in. Hoen-manns realized that he had probably strayed too far west from his course, and accordingly changed direction towards the east. At that moment, the engine inexplicably cut out. Narrowly missing a high-tension line and with both wing-tips ripped off by a row of poplars, Hoenmanns made a skilful forced landing in a snow-covered thicket. A quick investigation of the map revealed that they had landed just inside Belgian territory, near Mechelen, a few miles north of Maastricht. In horror, Reinberger leapt behind a bush hedge and tried to destroy the vital documents. But his lighter failed. Then an obliging Belgian peasant provided a match, and Reinberger built a small fire into which he fed the papers (always notoriously hard to burn) leaf by leaf. Soon some Belgian troops, under a captain, arrived and arrested Hoenmanns, who pretended that he had flown alone. The column of smoke from behind the thicket betrayed Reinberger, however, and the two majors were marched to a Belgian gendarmerie post. There, through what seems like extraordinary negligence, Reinberger was enabled to have another shot at destroying the documents by thrusting them into a stove. But he was interrupted by the Belgian captain, who rescued what remained. By nightfall, the papers were in the hands of the Belgian G.H.Q.; though badly charred, they contained enough to indicate that the Germans intended thrusting into northern France, via Belgium (and Holland), in what appeared to be a replay of the Schlieffen Plan of 1914.

The 'Dyle–Breda Plan'

Belgium promptly passed this information on to the Dutch and the French. The French Army was placed in a state of alert. In terrible weather conditions, Billotte's forces closed up to the Belgian frontier. Momentarily, the Belgian High Command raised the frontier barriers, and it seemed as if the Allies would be 'invited' to enter. But swiftly King Leopold reversed the order, sacking his Chief of Staff. Exasperated and despondent, the French Army drew back again. After 15 January, this apparently most menacing of the various false alarms receded into the ranks of the others. But the glimpse it gave of German operational plans proved enough to fix Gamelin in his resolve.[10] On 20 March he issued a new directive, supplementing the former 'Dyle Plan' with the 'Breda Variant'. Approved by both French and British Governments, this would in fact be the master-plan with which the Allies met the German onslaught

10. Since, as it later turned out, the French Army reacted in precisely the way Hitler wanted it to, for some years even after 1945 suspicions lingered that the Mechelen Incident was a cunning Nazi 'plant'. It definitely was not.

when it came on 10 May. Instead of the ten French divisions (plus the B.E.F.) previously earmarked for Belgian operations, now thirty would be involved, among them the very cream of the French and British Armies: two out of France's three new armoured divisions, five out of seven motorized divisions and all three of the Light Mechanized Divisions (D.L.M.s). On the extreme left flank the manoeuvre, edging the sea, was placed General Giraud's Seventh Army of seven first-rate divisions (including one D.L.M.), with the task of being ready to move at top speed through Belgium to link up with the Dutch Army. Hitherto the Seventh Army had constituted a significant part of General Georges's mobile strategic reserves; Gamelin's decision to allocate it to the 'Breda Variant' was to have the most far-reaching consequences of any part of the Allied Plan. Next in line came Lord Gort's B.E.F.,[11] which would advance up to the River Dyle roughly between Louvain and Wavre; south of it came General Blanchard's crack First Army, with the role of holding the Gembloux 'Gap' down to the fortress of Namur on the Meuse; while General Corap's Ninth Army was to wheel forwards to occupy the line of the Meuse where it runs through the Belgian Ardennes, south of Namur. The pivot of the whole manoeuvre would be just north of Sedan, where the Meuse leaves France, and where lay the boundary between the Ninth and Second Armies; to the right of Corap, General Huntziger's Second Army, stretching from Sedan to the Maginot Line anchor at Longwy, would remain static – as indeed would the rest of the French Army encamped behind '*le trou*'. In essence, the finalized plan meant that the main striking power of the Franco-British Army was to be committed to whatever might transpire in Belgium and Holland, north of the line Liège–Namur.

Up to the moment of the German onslaught, misgivings lingered in high French circles about the Dyle–Breda Plan.

11. Explaining his reasons for placing the French Seventh Army on the left of the B.E.F., Gamelin writes in his memoirs that they were 'not only strategic, but psychological and moral'. Similar doubts at the back of French minds about having the British too close to the Channel and home had also existed in 1914–18, when the French had always managed to keep Haig's army 'sandwiched' between French forces.

Following the 10 January alarm, the Belgian General Staff had been persuaded to prepare positions along the Dyle, in case the Allies should be called upon to occupy them; but General Prioux, commanding the Cavalry Corps, which with some of France's best armoured and mechanized units formed the steel tip of Blanchard's First Army, had strong doubts on the efficacy of the unreconnoitred defences the Belgians were supposedly erecting in the Gembloux Gap. General Giraud, whose Seventh Army would now have the most ambitious role to perform, complained of the difficulties in a letter to Billotte on 28 March. Billotte, whose No. 1 Army Group held direct responsibility for the whole manoeuvre, had been its most enthusiastic supporter among Gamelin's subordinates, but he too now backed up Giraud's reservations. General Vuillemin, always gloomy about German air superiority, had shared General Georges's pessimism throughout, and Georges himself remained unconvinced. But perhaps because of the lack of communication between him and Gamelin, perhaps because his will-power had been diminished by his ailing health, Georges was impotent to influence the Generalissimo.[12] In Britain, too, there were dissenting voices; but with only a handful of divisions in the field (by May 1940, Lord Gort still had no more than nine under his command), it was felt that she should keep quiet and leave the planning to the leaders of France's invincible Army.[13]

Gamelin, buried away in his *Thébaïde*, alone remained sublimely confident. On 15 April he dispatched a last letter to dispel Georges's doubts, once again reiterating that 'it seemed impossible systematically to abandon Holland to Germany'. In

12. Georges, too, seems to have suffered from his share of the unreality afflicting the French High Command, as witness a revealing marginal comment he wrote, in August 1940, to a report on the defeat: 'In the spring of 1940, did we really have the impression of being poorly prepared?'

13. Criticizing this silence retrospectively, Churchill remarks that the British War Cabinet 'ought not to have been deterred from thrashing the matter out with the French in the autumn and winter of 1939. It would have been an unpleasant and difficult argument, for the French at every stage could say: "Why do you not send more troops of your own? . . . Pray show a proper confidence in the French Army and in our historic mastery of the art of war on land." Nevertheless we ought to have done it.'

defiance of the lessons of Poland, he somehow maintained a simple faith in the Dutch and Belgian ability to defend their countries. Far from fearing a German onslaught through the Low Countries, there were occasions when he gave the impression of actually longing for it, for, as he once informed the Government, 'the enemy would be offering himself to us in open territory'.

It is difficult to conceive, however, with what forces Gamelin saw himself counter-attacking the German thrust which would thus be 'offering' itself. In expanding the Dyle Plan to embrace the 'Breda Variant' and by committing General Giraud's Seventh Army to it, Gamelin was being totally loyal to the principles of the 'continuous front'. But behind this front he retained only the scantiest of reserves. It was all right provided the front *remained* continuous, as it had done from 1914 to 1918. In Gamelin's final alignment which was to bear the brunt of the German attack of May 1940, roughly thirty divisions were committed to the Dyle–Breda manoeuvre, ten garrison divisions were permanently installed in the Maginot Line, while yet another thirty backed them up as 'interval troops', leaving only twenty-two divisions in reserve. Of these twenty-two, seven (including two out of France's three new armoured divisions) were earmarked for Belgium, and another five allocated to meet a possible German thrust through Switzerland, so that the overall strategic reserve left to General Georges amounted to between ten and thirteen divisions, or practically nothing. That an additional thirty good divisions should have to be employed 'guarding' the Maginot Line in itself seemed to point up a grave fallacy in France's whole strategic plan; as things were to turn out, the crucial phase of the battle would already be lost beyond repair before any of these thirty wasted divisions could be thrown into it.[14] Thus the overall picture of General Georges's North-East Front showed a powerful right flank on

14. In his memoirs, Gamelin tries to justify this concentration of forces on the Maginot Line by claiming that 'Its existence alone guaranteed us, in the spring of 1940, that, at the moment when the Germans attacked via Luxembourg, Belgium and Holland, they could not at the same time make a decisive effort between Longuyon and Switzerland.' But this was not an intention that ever for a moment entered Hitler's mind.

the Maginot Line (absorbing nearly half of all his effectives), and a powerful left flank facing northern Belgium. But the centre, along a front of little less than one hundred miles behind the so-called 'impenetrable' Belgian Ardennes, was held by only some four light cavalry divisions (still partly equipped with horses) and ten mediocre infantry divisions of the Ninth and Second Armies – about which more will be said later. And behind them, emptiness.

What a standing temptation the spectacle of this French line, then, so weak in the centre, might present to an opposing captain of audacity and genius!

Polish Lesson Unlearnt

Of all the attitudes struck by the French High Command during the Phoney War, none today seems more incomprehensible than its apparent refusal to take cognizance of the lessons of the Polish campaign. Nothing that had happened to the unhappy Poles made France in any way alter her basic doctrine of war, review the training techniques of combat echelons, or consider possible German offensive plans against her in the light of the strategy that had succeeded so admirably against Poland. It was not as if the French High Command was uninformed. On returning to France in the autumn of 1939, General Armengaud, an Air Force general sent to lead a mission to Poland, and who had closely observed events there, delivered a detailed oral report to Gamelin, which he then followed up with a written memorandum. In this memorandum, he warned how the Wehrmacht in Poland had proved its ability 'to break through a defensive front inadequately manned'.

It would be mad [continued Armengaud] not to draw an exact lesson from this pattern and not pay heed to this warning. The German system consists essentially of making a breach in the front with armour and aircraft, then to throw mechanized and motorized columns into the breach, to beat them down to right and left in order to keep on enlarging it, at the same time as armoured detachments, guided, protected and reinforced by aircraft, advance in front of the supporting divisions . . . in such a way that the defence's manoeuvrability . . . is reduced to impotence.

Armengaud considered that of the German armour and aircraft, it was the latter that had been the 'most decisive', by impeding the defenders' manoeuvrability, and by breaching the chain of command 'in such a way that the command is made blind and cannot get its orders through'. To Gamelin, Armengaud expressed the view that the Germans would attempt a breakthrough in the West, probably near the *centre* of the French front, and that they would then try to fan out to the rear, using a mass of material and aircraft. He thought they would be able to make such a breach very quickly, possibly within forty-eight hours.

For his pains, Armengaud was relegated to an administrative post, as commander of the Paris Air Region, where, he says, he found himself powerless to stem the feckless optimism in high places, which increased as the Polish defeat receded from memory. But Armengaud was evidently also backed up by reports submitted to Gamelin by his *Deuxième Bureau* chief, Colonel Gauché, one of which described how the effects of the German aerial bombardment had 'resulted in almost complete paralysis of the Polish High Command, which was rendered incapable either of completing mobilization or concentration, or of carrying out reinforcements or supplies, or of executing any kind of co-ordinated manoeuvre'. The *Deuxième Bureau* also pointed out the highly relevant strategic fact that the Germans had aimed *not* at capturing Warsaw, but had sought first and foremost to achieve the total destruction of the Polish Army. Here was certainly one lesson that would prove worth considering in May 1940. On more specific, but equally important, matters, the *Deuxième Bureau* warned the High Command of the effect of German tank guns on the Polish bunkers; these had 'withstood the fire of 150-mm. guns perfectly, but their machine-guns were often destroyed by shots in the embrasure fired by the tanks. It thus appears that every fortified work must be provided with anti-tank weapons . . .' It will be seen how much notice was taken of this warning.

The French High Command attitude to all this was roughly:

'We are not Poles, it could not happen here.' General Keller, Inspector-General of Tanks, wrote in answer to a memorandum written by Colonel de Gaulle:

. . . Even supposing that the present fortified line were breached or outflanked, it does not appear that our opponents will find a combination of circumstances as favourable for a *Blitzkreig* as in Poland. One can see, then, that in future operations the primary role of the tank will be the same as in the past: to assist the infantry in reaching successive objectives.

Thus inflexible remained the military doctrinaires of France. General Huntziger, commanding the ill-fated Second Army, did go to some length to circulate among his command details of the Wehrmacht technique in Poland, but few practical consequences by way of combat training ever seem to have followed.

Finland and other Distractions

No less extraordinary than the French High Command's studied and arrogant disregard of the lessons of Poland was the astonishing unreality of all the Allied schemes and projects during the Phoney War, of which Gamelin's delusive optimism is but one facet or syndrome. In both French and British Councils of War, new mad ideas of launching diversionary operations were constantly being thought up. Certainly, in France, the genesis of these schemes lay understandably in the external anxiety of keeping war away from French soil, but all were predicated upon strength which, in early 1940, the Allies simply did not possess, and, worse still, several of them would have brought Russia actively into the war on Hitler's side, a possibility the folly of which hardly bears thinking about.

On 30 November, her demands for concessions to help secure the approaches to Leningrad having been refused, Russia attacked Finland. Hitting back, the gallant Finns captured Western imagination by inflicting defeat after defeat upon the ponderous Red Army. In England, Transport House condemned with angriest indignation 'the criminal conspiracy of Stalin and Hitler', while (according to the *Daily Sketch*) at Buckingham Palace a large-scale map of Finland soon displaced one of the Western Front in the King's office. But in France emotions reached fever pitch: prayers were offered in the Madeleine for Marshal Mannerheim; ladies knitted vests for Finnish soldiers; gala charity performances in aid of the Finns were held at the Opéra and in the Carlton at Cannes. Here was a *real* war, a man's war that one could get excited about! 'The fortified front of Karelia,' wrote Fabre-Luce, 'evoked simultaneously the Maginot Line and a season of winter sports. It was like a highly seductive glossy magazine for skiing amateurs, obliged this year to remain at their hearth-sides.' From the squalor of the concentration camp at Vernet, French attitudes struck Arthur Koestler rather less favourably; the treatment of each Finnish success as 'victories of France' reminded him of 'a *voyeur* who gets his thrills and satisfaction out of watching other people's virile exploits, which he is unable to imitate'.

Ideologically, French emotions were compounded of several ingredients. At their highest, Russia's attack was regarded as just one more repellent act of aggression by the totalitarian powers; and had not France, that same September, entered the lists as champion of the spirit of the League of Nations? But, more powerfully, among the bourgeoisie and the Right wing there were those animosities left lingering by the Popular Front, and exacerbated by the Ribbentrop–Molotov deal. Here the 'Winter War' presented prospects of a holy crusade against Bolshevism infinitely more appealing than the *drôle de guerre* against the dormant and untroublesome Hitler. The Assembly, from which the Communist Deputies had just been purged, became strongly interventionist. Senator Bardoux, an independent Radical charged with 'sounding out the British', represented a fair section of French bourgeois opinion when he wrote in his diary for 23 December:

The Russian disaster in Finland is a capital event. Henceforth, far from trying to split Germany and Russia, we must, on the contrary, weld them together more tightly, for a weak ally is a

ball-and-chain and opens a breach in the common front. We must
enter into it resolutely. By intervening to aid Finland we shall
create, together with the neutrals and Italy [he added hopefully],
the definitive bloc. It is possible to offer the Crimea to Hitler, to
utilize the Ukrainians, the Transcaucasians and the Persians. We
can roll up everything, all the way to the Caucasus . . .

As the Finns continued to defeat the apparently decrepit Soviet
war machine, serious thoughts of intervention spread to the
military planners. An expeditionary force landed at the Norwegian port of Narvik could lend a hand to the Finns by
marching across northern Sweden, while at the same time a
mortal blow would be struck at Hitler by depriving him of the
Swedish iron-ore supplies essential to his war economy. Here
would be a fine sideshow to distract Hitler's gaze from France!
   On 15 January, Gamelin wrote to Daladier proposing the
opening of a front in Scandinavia. Throughout the winter discussions volleyed back and forth between London and Paris,
while the slopes at Chamonix became carpeted with British
officers and men learning to ski. Briefly, Chamberlain with his
declared anti-Communist bias favoured this happy means to
'kill two birds with one stone', but as the full gravity of the
undertaking sank in, the British Government began to try to
exercise prudence upon its more impetuous ally.[15] Meanwhile
– fortunately for all concerned – the Norwegian and Swedish
Governments stalwartly rejected every overture for the expedition to pass through their territory. By March, however, Parliamentary pressure upon Daladier was such that, without
consulting Britain, he informed the Finns that France would be
prepared to brush aside Norwegian and Swedish objections. On
the 11th, he told Halifax he would resign unless Britain toed
the line. The French, wrote Ironside (the British C.I.G.S.) in
disgust, 'are absolutely unscrupulous in everything', while the

15. Gamelin, who claims that he had reservations about the Scandinavian
venture but 'did not feel I had the right to stand up, in this domain, against a
Government decision', with extraordinary light-heartedness dismisses the
possibility of war with Russia by writing in his memoirs: 'of course, we
could not send forces to fight side by side with the Finns without colliding
with the Russians. If we wished to do anything in this direction, one had to
accept this consequence . . .'

following day he recorded that the Chamberlain Cabinet – 'a bewildered flock of sheep' – had reluctantly acceded to the Narvik expedition. Then, on 13 March, Finland signed peace with Russia. By a matter of days, if not hours, Britain and France had been saved from a war with Russia as well as Germany. As Colonel Josiah Wedgwood remarked in the Commons, 'It would have been the maddest military adventure upon which this country had ever embarked.' But in France there was bitter disappointment; in his diary, Major Barlone recorded: 'it is a heavy moral defeat for the Allies. I realize this when I talk to the men, who are bewildered by the inactivity of the Allies ... We are disheartened.' And this 'moral defeat' was enough to cause the fall of the Daladier Government.

At the other extremity of the European war theatre, the sprightly General Maxime Weygand, commanding the French Army of the Levant, had been toying with schemes hardly less realistic than the Scandinavian adventure. Somehow Turkey and Greece would be brought into the war, the dismal Salonika front of the First World War would be reactivated, and a hundred Balkan divisions would loyally march with the Allies against Hitler's 'soft underbelly'. Here again was a bright prospect (encouraged by Gamelin) of saving French manpower and diverting the course of war from French soil. Much talk ensued. But neither Greece nor Turkey, nor any of the other Balkan powers, were much moved by Allied wooing; General Weygand received only two divisions of reinforcements throughout the Phoney War, while of his army he would be the only member to take part in the war of 1940.[16]

Following the invasion of Finland, Weygand, a Catholic and politically very much to the Right, is to be found urging Gamelin by letter: 'I regard it as essential to break the back of the Soviet Union in Finland ... and elsewhere.' From here sprang notions of striking (by bombers flying out of Weygand's Syrian base) at the Caucasian oilfields which were fuelling both the Wehrmacht and the Red Army in Finland. Gamelin claims that he did his best 'to deflect our thoughts from such an action', though Weygand in his memoirs declares that he received, on

16. His army in Syria was later rounded up by the British.

13 March, a memorandum from Gamelin which 'advocated an attack on the oil-wells of the Caucasus'.

As late as 17 April, Weygand was still corresponding with Gamelin about the operation, the planes for which, fortunately, were never available. (Meanwhile Walter Lippmann, passing through Paris, was helpfully offering the French Government his advice on how to breach Black Sea Traffic between Russia and Germany.) How, with the absurdly small bomber potential then available to both Britain and France, it was imagined that any raid on the Baku oil-wells could have caused more than a pin-prick is hard to imagine. The whole lunatic venture was well summed up by a poem by A. P. Herbert published at the time:

Baku, or, The Map Game

It's jolly to look at the map
And finish the foe in a day.
It's not easy to get at the chap;
These neutrals are so in the way.
But if you say 'What would *you* do
To fill the aggressor with gloom?'
Well, we might drop a bomb on Baku,
Or what about bombs on Batum?

Refrain: I'm all for some bombs on Baku,
And, of course, a few bombs on Batum.

Meanwhile, as fervid brains in various Allied councils played 'The Map Game', in apparently blissful indifference to realities on the other side of the Rhine, fighting soldiers up at the front did sometimes also wonder precisely what form Hitler's plans for the spring might be taking.

Chapter 7

The Sickle and the Reaper

'Quiet, friend Sancho!' replied Don Quixote, 'Even more than other subjects, affairs of war are subject to continual change.'
CERVANTES, *Don Quixote*

His Majesty, Chance . . .
FREDERICK THE GREAT

Long before the war Hitler, the corporal who had endured the miseries of four years of static warfare on the Western Front, nurtured dreams of smashing France in what *Mein Kampf* predicted would be 'one last decisive battle'. To Rauschning he declared that 'with an unprecedented application of all means at his command, with the most ruthless dispatch to the front of all reserves, he would nail victory to his mast in one gigantic knock-out blow'. Veiled in mystical imprecision, Hitler's inchoate ideas as to how this was to be achieved repeatedly sent his military advisers scurrying for shelter. The overcoming of their objections and the evolution of one of the most brilliant war plans of all time is in itself an extraordinary story, in which Chance plays a part of high importance.

When war had come in 1914, Germany possessed her long-prepared Schlieffen Plan ready to roll into instant action against France while Russia was still mobilizing her unwieldy forces. But in 1939, never expecting that, on their past performance, Daladier and Chamberlain would honour their guarantee to Poland, Hitler had not instructed his General Staff to give thought to any comparable strategy. In the first place, he had no Russian foe to worry about. His generals had, however, by no means recovered from the dreadful shock of finding themselves once again at war with France and Britain when, on 12 September, Hitler told Colonel Schmundt, his chief military adjutant, that he intended attacking in the West immediately the Polish campaign was ended. On 27 September, Poland capitulated after Gamelin had conclusively shown that no threat would confront Germany from the west. At five o'clock that afternoon, Hitler held a meeting of the commanders-in-chief of the three Wehrmacht services in the map room of the new Chancellery.[1] Without any preamble, and without seeking any opinion from this constellation of military experts, Hitler gave his views for an offensive against France – this year, and as soon as possible. Casting to the winds his recent promises to respect their neutrality, Hitler pronounced that the offensive would pass through Belgium and the Dutch appendix of Maastricht. By way of justification, he pleaded the vulnerability of Germany's Ruhr and alleged evidence of French collusion with the Belgian General Staff. After the minimum of discussion, tossing into the fire the scrap of paper on which he had scribbled down his notes for the meeting, Hitler dismissed those present and instructed the Army leaders to draft an operational plan.

Directive Yellow

News of Hitler's decision was promptly greeted with wide protest in the Army. General Ritter von Leeb, commanding Army Group 'C' along the Rhine and rated as the leading defensive theoretician of the old school, was outraged at the 'lunacy' of breaching Dutch and Belgian neutrality, and (to Brauchitsch) condemned Hitler's simultaneous 'peace offer' to the Allies as 'simply deceiving the German people with lies'. Moved more by pragmatic than moral considerations, his fellow Army Group commanders, Rundstedt and Bock, declared that any early offensive would have little likelihood of success. Halder was convinced that the motorized and armoured divisions which had fought in Poland could not possibly be reorganized before mid November,[2] while the troops which had stood

1. The Army High Command (O.K.H.) was represented that day by its C.-in-C., Colonel-General von Brauchitsch, and his Chief of Staff, Halder; the Luftwaffe (O.K.L.) by Goering and Jeschonnek; the Navy (O.K.M.) by Admirals Raeder and Schniewind; the Wehrmacht (O.K.W.) by its Chief of Staff, Keitel, and Colonel Warlimont, deputizing for Jodl, the O.K.W. Chief of Operations.

2. Half their fighting vehicles were temporarily in repair shops.

defensively on the Rhine were not up to scratch, and there were serious shortages of ammunition and equipment. Even the impetuous Goering had his doubts, based on the probability of bad flying weather.

The studied view of the Army (O.K.H.) at this time was that there could be no prospect of a successful offensive against France until the spring of 1942.

But nothing would deflect Hitler. On 9 October, Warlimont relayed to the O.K.H. that Hitler had fixed 25 November as the date of the offensive. The next day Hitler delivered to Halder a 58-page memorandum, to urge on the reluctant O.K.H. in its detailed planning. Riding roughshod over all technical objections, Hitler declared that 'General Time' was on the side of the Allies, not Germany. Giving specific details for the first time he proposed that the main weight of the Panzer forces should advance on both sides of Liège, the objective of the offensive being to occupy territory on the Channel for the further prosecution of the war against England. In view of the modest limits of this goal, it seemed as if Hitler was still voicing more a wild personal desire than any calculated plan when he spoke once again of the 'final military annihilation' of the enemy. Working, for all their lack of enthusiasm, with the speed characteristic of the German General Staff, Halder and the O.K.H. produced their first plan, with the code name of 'Deployment Directive Yellow' (*Aufmarschanweisung Gelb*) by 19 October. Fundamentally, it consisted simply of an enveloping movement on Ghent, designed to separate the B.E.F. from the French, if possible, while securing air and sea bases for employment against the British Isles. The question of how the campaign would be continued in order to obtain a decision against the Allies, once the Channel had been reached, was left entirely open.

Erroneously, historians have described the first O.K.H. *Gelb* draft as a variation on the Schlieffen theme, but in fact it was nothing of the sort. Schlieffen had prescribed a great Cannae battle of annihilation in which, after crashing through Belgium and striking to the west of Paris, the German Army would swing southwards to roll up the French forces from the rear and crush them against Switzerland and the Jura; on the other hand Halder's axis of advance lay *west-north-west*, and eschewed any such bold and far-reaching strategic conception as Schlieffen's.

It was manifestly a bad plan, so conservative and uninspiring that it might well have been thought up by a British or French General Staff of the inter-war years, and through its many imperfections glimmered the half-heartedness of the O.K.H. and the Army commanders. Arguments leaped back and forth as to where the Panzer divisions were to be deployed. Hitler was far from satisfied. To an unreceptive Halder he began proposing visionary schemes of 'special operations' in which airborne troops would capture the Meuse crossings north of Liège, and cut off the Belgium Army retreating from Ghent. On 22 October he shocked Halder by announcing his intention of advancing the date of the Western offensive to 12 November. Then, at another conference three days later, Hitler suddenly asked Brauchitsch whether a main attack *on the southern Meuse only* might be able to 'cut off and annihilate' the enemy. Almost casually he injected the name of Amiens into the discussion, and then with a red pencil sketched on the map a line running from the Meuse south of Namur to the French Channel coast. According to Bock, Brauchitsh and Halder appeared 'utterly astonished'. They were then packed off to reconsider the O.K.H. plan. Meanwhile, that same day a most portentous event occurred within the Army itself: Colonel-General Gerd von Rundstedt, a sixty-four-year-old officer called back from retirement to command Army Group South during the Polish campaign, arrived in Koblenz on the Rhine to take over the newly created Army Group 'A', facing Luxembourg and the Ardennes country of southern Belgium. With him came his Chief of Staff, a brilliant and impulsive lieutenant-general who, born Erich von Lewinski, had later adopted the name of von Manstein. From this day on, two channels of thought began to flow, coincidentally and quite independently of each other, which would eventually funnel together – at Sedan.

On 29 October the O.K.H. produced its revised plan. As

before, the centre of gravity (*Schwerpunkt*) of the attack remained with Bock's Army Group 'B' in the north, but to meet the point Hitler had raised on the 25th, it had shifted somewhat to the south, so that the Fourth Army with four Panzer divisions would now cross the Meuse both north and south of Namur. The plan still, however, envisaged a frontal attack with the same limited objectives. Hitler still remained only partially satisfied, and the next day he revealed to Jodl, the O.K.W. Chief of Operations, a 'new idea' which would make use of the east-west Arlon gap in the Ardennes to reach Sedan, on the Meuse and just over fifty miles *south* of Namur, striking at it with one Panzer and one motorized division. It was the first time that the fateful name of Sedan was mentioned in German councils of war. But Jodl did not bother to pass on this latest brainwave of the Führer's to the O.K.H.

Hitler and Brauchitsch

Meanwhile, as October ended, Hitler was becoming thoroughly aware of the O.K.H.'s opposition towards his designs. On 5 November, the deadline for ordering the attack to begin on the 12th, Brauchitsch was summoned to the Chancellery for a sulphurous meeting. The Army C.-in-C. was a fifty-eight-year-old artilleryman, much decorated during the Great War (when he too had served his time at Verdun) and with a distinguished subsequent record. Of outstanding intelligence, he was also a quiet and withdrawn man, painfully correct in his external relations. Although emotional and rather too highly strung, his Junker upbringing led him to abhor violent scenes. He had a conscience and a will, but could hardly be described as combative. Both as a soldier and a man, in every way he excelled the third-rate Keitel, the O.K.W.'s Württemberger Chief of Staff, but none of his attributes were of any assistance in standing up to Hitler. Furthermore, though not a Party man, he was under some obligation to the Nazi hierarchy for having eased his divorce in 1938, the same year that he succeeded Werner von Fritsch [3] as C.-in-C. His new wife was a rabid Nazi, who

3. Disgraced on trumped-up charges of homosexuality.

exerted a dominant influence upon him. Brauchitsch's stormy sessions with the Führer in the past left him exhausted, and he tended more and more to retreat behind a passive line of 'military obedience'. But on 5 November he confronted Hitler fortified by a tour of the front two days previously, during which all his senior commanders had unanimously and vigorously declared that the Army was not ready to launch a major offensive. To Hitler he now read out a memorandum presenting the Army's views. When Brauchitsch warned him against underestimating the French, Hitler held up his hand:

Herr Generaloberst, I should like to interrupt immediately here, because I hold quite different views. Firstly, I place a low value on the French Army's will to fight. Every army is a mirror of its people. The French people think only of peace and good living, and they are torn apart in Parliamentary strife. Accordingly, the Army, however brave and well trained its officer corps may be, does not show the combat determination expected of it. After the first setbacks, it will swiftly crack up . . .

Though shaken, Brauchitsch rashly continued. In Poland, he said, the German assault troops had not matched up to the infantry of 1914; there were incidents where discipline had failed, which led one to question whether the troops would be up to the stresses of a campaign in the West. At this, Hitler lost all self-control. Brauchitsch was heaping 'monstrous reproaches' upon *his* Army. Where had there been acts of indiscipline? Hitler demanded 'concrete examples'. He then vented his rage upon Brauchitsch and the Army commanders; they had never been loyal to him, and the 'spirit of Zossen' [4] had become synonymous with defeatism. Rudely, Hitler dismissed Brauchitsch, and dictated a note sacking him – which he later destroyed. Brauchitsch tottered to his car, arriving back at Zossen in a state of total incoherence. In fact, he never substantiated his charges of 'indiscipline', and Hitler never forgave him for the slurs he had cast upon his new young Army;

4. A town twenty miles south of Berlin, where, in reinforced concrete buildings, complete with bomb-proof and gas-proof cellars, the O.K.H. was housed.

the waning influence of the O.K.H. in Nazi war councils had receded another notch. Quite unaffected by the memorandum Brauchitsch had delivered, Hitler ordered Keitel to proceed with troop movements for an attack on the 12th, as planned. But two days later, bad weather forced Hitler to delay the attack. It was the first of twenty-nine such postponements. On 9 November an enraged Hitler once again had to call off operations, this time until 19 November.

Brauchitsch's interview of 5 November represents a high point in the O.K.H.'s opposition to Hitler. Well before the war began, Hitler had already shorn his General Staff of much of its power. Although adorned with the title of Supreme Warlord, the Kaiser before him had never possessed so much influence over military affairs as did Hitler; in fact, soon after 1914 he had become the virtual prisoner of the Great German General Staff. Hitler, on the other hand, had swiftly reduced his O.K.W. to little more than a drafting office entirely subservient to himself as Supreme Commander of the Wehrmacht. In military circles, O.K.W. was liberally translated as *Oben Kein Widerstand* ('no resistance at the top'). Of the Saxon, Keitel, scornfully nicknamed *Lakeitel* (a diminutive of 'lackey') it was said that he received the appointment after the O.K.W. C.-in-C., Blomberg,[5] had remarked disparagingly to Hitler: 'He's nothing but the man who runs my office.' Hitler immediately replied: 'That's exactly the man I'm looking for.' And so, for the remainder of the war, Keitel ran Hitler's 'office' as a kind of pliable chief clerk, while below the O.K.W., the C.-in-C.s and their staffs of the three Services possessed a mere shadow of the independence they had enjoyed in Imperial days.

Once, during the Second World War, Churchill is reputed to have grumbled in aggravation against the Chiefs of Staff system:

It leads to weak and faltering decisions – or rather indecisions. Why, you may take the most gallant sailor, the most intrepid airman, or the most audacious soldier, put them at a table together – what do you get? *The sum of their fears.*

---

5. Subsequently disgraced on charges of marrying a tart.

This was indisputably Hitler's view about *his* military advisers, and, as the success of each new gamble proved their 'fears' to be groundless, so he listened to them less and less. In the long run, the diminished influence of her General Staff was to prove one of the great weaknesses ·of Germany's superb military machine in the Second World War. Certainly, the influence of the O.K.H. was never to stand as high again after the Brauchitsch–Hitler interview of 5 November 1939.

Halder and the 'Resistance'

Behind the O.K.H. opposition to Hitler's plans for a Western offensive in the autumn of 1939, there lay a complexity of motives which, because of its bearing on the evolution of *Gelb*, needs to be examined. It borders on the whole question of the German 'resistance'. At the time of the Czech crisis of 1938, the 'resistance' movement, such as it was, resided principally among the conservative elements of the Army who had always regarded Hitler as an upstart and a guttersnipe, and who were now thoroughly alarmed as to where his policies would lead the nation. At their head stood the Army Chief of Staff,[6] the honourable Colonel-General Beck, who was forced to commit suicide after the bomb plot of 20 July 1944. Had France and Britain stood firm over Czechoslovakia, the 'resistance', so we are told, would have taken action against Hitler. But Hitler triumphed, and the 'resistance' lost much of its impetus as well as many of its adherents in high places, while another devastating blow was struck at its prestige by Hitler's *coup* in pulling off the non-aggression pact with Russia.

Beck had resigned before Munich, depriving the 'resistance' of its mainspring. He was succeeded in office, reluctantly, by General Franz Halder, an artilleryman three years younger than the new Army C.-in-Ċ., Brauchitsch. Coming from an

6. Traditionally in Germany, the Chiefs of Staff at various levels occupy positions of relatively greater responsibility vis-à-vis their commanders (especially where planning is concerned) than their British or American counterparts. At the same time, the German Army was then obviously the one body physically capable of deposing Hitler.

old military family which had provided Bavaria with soldiers
for many generations, Halder set a precedent as the first Bava-
rian Catholic to break the traditional Prussian, Protestant hege-
mony and to become Chief of Staff. A shrewd, quick-witted and
precise-minded intellectual with a passion for mathematics and
botany (Shirer says Halder with his mild features and pince-
nez reminded him more of a university professor), he had had
a brilliant career as a staff officer, in which capacity he had
passed more of the First War on the static Western front than
in the East. In the autumn of 1939, he could definitely be
counted a man of the 'resistance', but he possessed neither the
determination nor the Army following to assume Beck's
mantle. He was not one to take risks, either military or political,
nor was he entirely devoid of professional ambition. Whenever
he contemplated practical means for ridding Germany of the
evil of Hitler, Halder was confronted with the choice of having
to resort either to a political *putsch*, against which his tradi-
tionalist sense of honour and obedience as a German officer
revolted, or to assassination, which his Christian conscience
overruled. Here, in the dilemma of Halder, lay the essential
tragedy of what was both best and most ineffective in the
German 'resistance' as a whole. So instead of sharper weapons,
Halder – as far as *Gelb* was concerned – settled for those of
procrastination and obstructionism.[7]

After war began, Halder and his like-thinking generals had
been associated with various peace feelers extended to Britain,
predicated upon the removal of Hitler and the restoration of the
'other Germany'. But the 'other Germany' they contemplated
was hardly the easy-going liberal republic of Weimar; it was
much more like Kaiser Wilhelm II's pre-1914 Reich. In their
'peace terms', the conspirators were not even prepared to discuss Germany's disrobing herself of Austria and the Czech
Sudetenland, while from Poland they required a return to the
1914 frontiers, which was asking even more than Hitler's pre-
war demands. So, while prepared to renounce Hitler, they were
not prepared to renounce his works. As far as British accep-

7. One is entitled to wonder whether British or American generals placed
in similar conditions would have done better.

tance was concerned, these terms were utterly unrealistic, though perhaps domestically more unrealistic still, when it came to carrying along in a *coup d'état* a German populace elated by Hitler's cheap triumphs. As it was, in the Army alone, support for the 'resistance' was very mixed. Of the Army Group commanders, Leeb (already, unbeknown to himself, under Gestapo observation) would have gone far, but Bock and Rundstedt, though sympathetic, took the conventional line of non-political involvement. At the end of October 1939, Halder had sent out his deputy, Stülpnagel,[8] to sound out feelings at the front, but on his return Stülpnagel warned him that the troops and junior officers would not follow any call to overthrow Hitler.

Towards the end of November, Halder, referring to the future offensive in the West, declared (according to Ulrich von Hassell): 'We ought to give Hitler this last chance to deliver the German people from the slavery of English capitalism . . .' This was a revealing remark, as symptomatic of the deep conflict in Halder's mind as it was of that existing in the German military 'resistance' as a whole. For the more Hitler looked like winning, both before and during the war, the less ready the 'resistance' was to resist, and conversely. Halder certainly never had any particular desire to save the Allies from humiliation; what motivated him and his fellows, both as patriotic Germans and military men, was that Germany should not suffer the horrors of another long war, ending in defeat. For all the radical brilliance that had gone into the shaping of the new Wehrmacht, with its Panzers and its Stukas, the conventional German military Establishment, of which Halder and Brauchitsch were thoroughly representative, remained fundamentally conservative, its thoughts deeply conditioned by 1914–18. In spite of the Army's staggering success in Poland, its leaders could not shake off their pessimism at the prospects of war with Britain and France; as Brauchitsch had revealed in his 5 November interview with Hitler, they could never quite suppress their awe of the once-victorious French Army. Left to

8. Later Military Governor of France, and executed for his role in the 1944 conspiracy.

themselves, Brauchitsch and Halder would have played their
game with the same caution as Gamelin and Georges; they
were, after all, educated in the same school. This excessive
professional prudence was another factor that conditioned their
planning for *Gelb* in the autumn of 1939.

If Hitler had been allowed to attack, as he wished and upon
the plan then offered by Halder and the O.K.H., in the autumn
of 1939, the chances were exceedingly slim that he would have
inflicted a decisive defeat on the French. A stalemate would
probably have resulted, and the war might well have limped on
– until, as the generals feared, it brought eventual defeat to
Germany. Thus although motivated by a desire to topple Hitler,
in stalling off an abortive offensive in 1939 the O.K.H. 'resistance' was in fact to pave the way for Hitler's greatest triumph
and prolong his survival until Germany lay in ashes, while at
the same time assuring their own emasculation. History knows
few starker ironies.

The 'Manstein Plan'

Among the professional soldiers in opposition to the *Gelb*
projects of 1939, however, another skein now emerges with a
quite different point of departure. The details of the first
O.K.H. plan had reached Rundstedt's newly-created Army
Group 'A' when his Chief of Staff, Manstein, passed through
Zossen on 21 October. Immediately the two generals took
exception to it – on purely professional and technical grounds.

Together, Rundstedt and Manstein represented the most imposing combination in the German Army; under their leadership Army Group South had formed the right, and stronger,
arm of the pincer which had smashed the Polish forces in
little more than a week. In his background at least, Rundstedt was a typical Prussian officer of the old school. There
were few wars involving Prussia in which a von Rundstedt
had not taken part; as early as 1745, there is a record of one
serving with the Hessians in Scotland. In 1914, Gerd von Rundstedt had been a captain on the staff of the 22nd Reserve
Division, which during the enactment of the Schlieffen Plan

came the closest to Paris that September. The memory of the bitter disappointment which followed after his division had actually glimpsed the Eiffel Tower in the distance, only to be thrown back by the French counter-offensive on the Marne, was to wield considerable influence upon Rundstedt all through the campaign of 1940. From 1915 onwards, Rundstedt spent the rest of the war fighting in the mobile campaigns of the Russian front. Between 1919 and 1933, he held almost every staff post in Seeckt's Reichswehr. On the advent of Hitler, he was commanding the key First Army Group in Berlin, which high post he held for six years. At the end of 1938 (having already applied to retire several times) he left the Army as a colonel-general to live in a rented apartment in Cassel. In 1939, like Hindenburg and Pétain before him, he was recalled to service. He was then rising sixty-four.

As a special tribute, Rundstedt on his retirement had been made honorary colonel of the 18th Infantry Regiment, which he had once commanded, and during the war he always preferred to wear the simple jacket of a regimental commander rather than a Field-Marshal's regalia. Frequently young officers mistook him for a colonel. With his hair parted down the centre and a heavy jowl even as a young man, Rundstedt's face reveals no outstanding intelligence. But in the Army he had a deserved reputation for being the most gifted of all the senior commanders. Despite his age, he was resourceful and flexible-minded. He knew how to profit from the advice of talented subordinates, and he confined his genius to tactical problems, while his Chief of Staff, Manstein, possessed a much wider vision on the overall conduct of war. Rundstedt also enjoyed deep respect throughout the officer corps, and would have made an ideal leader of the 'resistance'; his moral principles on the waging of war were of the highest, and he was one of the few senior Wehrmacht commanders against whom there was never to be any taint of war crimes. But, like a true Prussian officer, however much he may have despised Hitler he eschewed political involvement just as much as he regarded higher strategy to be no concern of his.

Erich von Manstein, promoted Lieutenant-General shortly

before the war, was just twelve years younger than Rundstedt. His father was an Army officer of Polish–German origin, named Lewinski, but Erich had been adopted as a child by a family friend and brother officer, whose name of Manstein he subsequently assumed. Commissioned into a Prussian regiment of Foot Guards in 1906, Manstein had served as a staff captain on General von Gallwitz's group attacking on the left bank of the Meuse throughout much of the worst fighting at Verdun. The conclusions Manstein had formed from this appallingly futile struggle lay directly opposed to those of his French contemporaries defending Verdun: attrition resulting from the old style, direct, frontal attack was no way to win a war. In 1935, then a colonel, Manstein became Army Chief of Operations, under General Beck. But extremely outspoken and with one of those minds which any army finds uncomfortably brilliant, during the military 'purge' of 1938 Manstein, although he was not one of those hostile to Hitler,[9] was dispatched to command a division. It was only with considerable difficulty that Rundstedt could bring him back on to the General Staff. In appearance, the beaky nose which dominated his features, the heavily arched eyebrows and penetrating eyes, gave Manstein something of the look of an eagle or a hawk. A harsh disciplinarian,[10] icy and unbending, he was a leader who commanded respect rather than love. Like Guderian, Manstein's interests were purely professional, and this formed the basis of his loyalty to Hitler. Guderian, seldom lavish with praise for others, regarded Manstein as 'our finest operational brain', and as the war was to bring him one higher post after another, Manstein indeed proved himself Germany's ablest commander of large bodies of troops, as well as being her outstanding strategic

9. Typical of Manstein's attitude to Hitler was his response in 1942, as a Field-Marshal commanding an army in southern Russia, to an overture from the 'resistance'; he would join in a coup against Hitler, he said – provided he were first allowed to capture Sebastopol.

10. After the war, Manstein was tried on various war-crimes charges. He was acquitted on the most serious, but sentenced to eighteen years' imprisonment (reduced to twelve), partly because he rigidly refused to enter any plea of 'mitigating circumstances'.

thinker. In fact, history is almost certain to rate him one of the great generals of the twentieth century.

On examining the O.K.H.'s 'Deployment Directive Yellow' of 19 October, Manstein's instant reaction was that, at best, it could only lead to a partial success. Unlike General von Leeb, he was not deeply concerned by the fate of Belgium, but he did believe that if Germany were to breach her neutrality for a second time in a generation, this was worth doing only if it aimed at a totally *decisive* victory. Accordingly, he sat down to draft the first of six memoranda to the O.K.H. In it he expressed the view that success of the whole operation would lie in 'defeating and *annihilating* the *whole* of the enemy forces fighting in Belgium, or north of the Somme, and not only throwing them back frontally'. With this aim, the *Schwerpunkt* of the offensive must be shifted farther to the south, with its axis running from Namur through a line Arras–Boulogne, so that the Allied wing in Belgium would not simply be rolled back to the Somme, 'but cut off on the Somme'. At the same time, the left flank of the German thrust must be strong enough to ward off any powerful French counter-thrust coming up at it from the south-west.[11] Manstein concluded that he did not expect the Allies to 'make the mistake of throwing too strong forces into Belgium on their northern flank' (which in fact, as has already been seen, was precisely the direction in which Gamelin's plans were heading); but if they did, the prospects for Germany of a 'great success' would be just that much better.

In its initial shape, the 'Manstein Plan' still allocated the *Schwerpunkt* to Bock's rival Army Group 'B' in the north. It gave no specific details as to the employment of the Panzers; it offered no comment on the timing of the offensive; nor did it mention the magic names of Sedan or the Ardennes, as did Hitler's 'new idea' of 30 October. On the other hand, Manstein was putting forward a much more precise formula. And, in his proposition to 'cut off' the northern wing of the Allied

11. This was a fear which in May 1940 was to haunt the German planners incessantly until success was finally achieved.

armies on the Somme, here was a scheme far more ambitious than anything that had yet emerged from the mind of Hitler himself.

Rundstedt entirely supported the thinking of his Chief of Staff, and on 31 October (by sheer coincidence, only a day after Hitler had voiced his 'new idea' to Jodl) the memorandum was dispatched to the O.K.H. bearing his signature. Four days later, a visit to Rundstedt's H.Q. by Brauchitsch gave Manstein the opportunity to discuss his plan in person. Brauchitsch refused to countenance any alteration to the existing directive; finally, however, he did let himself be coaxed into promising to Army Group 'A' in the south the 2nd Panzer Division and two motorized regiments. Here began the progressive escalation of Army Group 'A' at the expense of 'B' (Bock).[12] But Brauchitsch was not to be impressed by Manstein's fears of a French threat to his left flank. 'Every Army Group', commented Halder trenchantly, 'expects the maximum of enemy counter-measures on its own front', and doubtless Manstein's proposals struck the O.K.H. at first as simply a subordinate formation advancing its own parochial interest. In any case, they were sat upon at Zossen and not passed on to the O.K.W. or Hitler, nor were the new orientations in Hitler's thoughts relayed to Army Group 'A'.

Meanwhile, the Führer was still pursuing his 'new idea' of 30 October. On 11 November, after the second postponement of the offensive, the O.K.H. notified Army Groups 'A' and 'B' that Hitler had ordered a third group of fast-moving troops to be formed on 'A's' southern flank, heading for Sedan. This would be composed of Guderian's XIX Corps, consisting of two Panzer and one motorized divisions. Bock at once expressed dissatisfaction at this further erosion of Army Group 'B', but still the function of the Sedan thrust was regarded as purely secondary, designed to 'ease' the task of Army Group

12. Under the O.K.H. directive of 29 October, Army Group 'A' was allocated only 22 infantry divisions, and 'B' 43 divisions, including 9 Panzer and 4 motorized infantry divisions. By 10 May the respective proportions had shifted to: 'A', 45½ divisions (including 7 Panzer); 'B', 29½ (including 3 Panzer).

'A' (which in itself remained subordinate to that of 'B'). Guderian, the Panzer expert, who now enters the act for the first time, was asked for his opinion and declared that the forces for an advance on Sedan via Arlon were quite inadequate. On the 13th, and again on the 16th, bad weather, combined with the continued reluctance of the O.K.H. (which was undoubtedly having its effect even on Hitler), once more postponed the offensive, on the latter occasion to 26 November. On 21 November another visit to Koblenz by Brauchitsch (accompanied by Halder) permitted Manstein to deliver a second memorandum. Again, however, the O.K.H. leaders granted it no serious discussion. At this time they had still cherished hopes that Hitler would abandon all ideas of an offensive in the West, and the injection of Manstein's views into the existing plan could only lend grist to Hitler's mill. But at the same time, there was also undoubtedly an element of professional jealousy involved in Brauchitsch's and Halder's refusal to allow their subordinate generals direct access to the Führer. Relations between Brauchitsch and Rundstedt were never noticeably good, while the cautious Halder clearly evinced resentment towards the daring genius of Manstein.

Hitler Berates His Generals

Two days later, an extraordinary gathering took place in the Chancellery. By now thoroughly exasperated at the O.K.H.'s opposition to his designs, Hitler summoned together all his top Wehrmacht leaders down to corps commanders and their equivalent ranks in the Luftwaffe and Navy – totalling over 180 – and, treating them like so many small boys, delivered a scarifying lecture. He began with the reminder that without the Nazi Party, the rebuilding of the Wehrmacht (through which, he did not need to point out, those present enjoyed their present distinction) could never have taken place. Although he had always been surrounded by more 'doubters' than 'believers', his policy of annexations had paid off; now, for the first time in sixty-seven years, while the successors of Bismarck may have missed their cues, he, Hitler, had ensured that Germany would not have to fight on more than one front. He was determined to launch a crushing offensive on this one front, and 'anyone who thinks otherwise is irresponsible'. Now, the moment was favourable; in six months' time it might not be. Waving aside the question of Belgian and Dutch neutrality, he declared that 'nobody would question this if Germany were victorious'. As for Britain, she would be brought to her knees by U-boat and mine warfare (details unspecified).

Turning the heat on the Army leaders, Hitler all but accused them of cowardice; *he* had not created the Wehrmacht in order not to fight. He condemned obsolete notions of chivalry, and warned that anyone who opposed his will would be 'annihilated'. With a reference to Brauchitsch's luckless intervention of 5 November, he declared that he was 'infuriated' by any suggestion that 'his' troops had been 'inadequate' in Poland. 'Everything depends on the military leaders. With the German soldier I can do anything, provided he is well led.' Hitler ended his homily with a call for total determination: 'If we emerge from this struggle as victors – and we shall be victors! – then our epoch will enter into the history of our people. As for me', he added prophetically, 'I shall stand or fall in this struggle. I shall not survive the defeat of my people. No surrender abroad! No revolution at home!'

The generals filed away, shattered by this tirade. Brauchitsch tendered his resignation. Hitler rejected it, saying that Brauchitsch had his duty to fulfil, like every simple soldier. Later Guderian, detailed by Reichenau, one of the most steadfast of the pro-Hitler generals, went to see Hitler and voiced the 'indignation' the Army commanders felt at their leader's distrust. Hitler replied that he was principally getting at the C.-in-C. of the Army. In that case, said Guderian with some audacity, Brauchitsch should be replaced, and he went on to name some possible successors. But Hitler approved of none of these, and the interview ended inconclusively. The net effect of Hitler's taunting insults upon the generals, however, was largely to galvanize them into much more enthusiastic support of the Führer. 'The reproach of cowardice turned the brave into cowards,' scathingly remarked Colonel Hans Oster, a dedicated member of the military 'resistance'. From now on the O.K.H.'s opposition to *Gelb* waned steadily, while at the same time its past hesitancy had made its mark on Hitler, who now seemed rather less determined upon a winter offensive than he had been in October – despite his exhortations of 23 November. The only one of the three main participants in the *Gelb* plan who remained obdurate was Manstein.

In the latter half of November, Manstein invited Guderian to visit him at Koblenz, where he questioned the Panzer expert as to whether it would be technically feasible to push heavy armoured forces across the Ardennes, towards Sedan. Guderian, who knew the area from the First War, reassured Manstein, but with one proviso. The Panzer divisions deployed there must be made as strong as possible. This was an important conversation, in so far as Manstein was first and foremost an infantryman and had hitherto given little precise thought as to the use of Panzers;[13] nevertheless, as late as 18 December, he shows himself still thinking in terms of allocating seven Panzer divisions to Army Group 'B' and only three[14] to 'A', crossing the Meuse south of Dinant. On 30 November, a third memorandum from Manstein now forced Halder to pass, for the first time, some written judgement. It was noncommittal and evasive, saying that the O.K.H. did not want to decide upon where the critical *Schwerpunkt* should lie until the first encounter with the enemy. Manstein promptly followed up with two more memoranda during December. His fourth, dated 6 December, for the first time came down categorically in favour of the *Schwerpunkt* being located on the southern flank of the attack, i.e. with Army Group 'A', heading for the mouth of the Somme. By this time Halder had had enough and decided to transfer Manstein (already previously earmarked to command a corps) to Stettin in the east, about as far away from Army Group 'A' and the Western Front as possible!

13. Guderian in fact later went so far as to claim that he had provided the original inspiration for the Manstein Plan.
14. Of which one was still only rated as a 'light' division.

Gelb Postponed

During December, the vile conditions of snow, ice and fog which were demoralizing the French Army caused four more postponements of *Gelb*. No new strategic alterations to the plan were proposed by either the O.K.H. or Hitler, who was still kept unaware of Manstein's ideas. On the 28th, Hitler told Jodl that if the weather continued bad by mid-January, he would call off the offensive, perhaps until the spring. Nevertheless, on 10 January, after a period of bright, clear skies had been predicted, D-Day was finally fixed for Wednesday the 17th, at dawn. The troops began to roll, over sixty divisions strong, towards the Dutch and Belgian frontiers, the weight of both armour and infantry still preponderantly with Bock's Army Group 'B' in the north. Then, that same day, the two Luftwaffe majors made their forced landing at Mechelen. At 11.45 a.m. on the 11th, Jodl braced himself to inform Hitler. Hitler flew into a terrible rage. Threats of death sentences for the flyers were uttered; the Gestapo was dispatched to interrogate their wives; General Felmy, commanding the Second Air Fleet to which Reinberger and Hoenmanns both belonged, was sacked, and replaced by Kesselring.[15] The German Military Attaché in The Hague, Lieutenant-General Wenniger, rushed down to interview the interned majors and find out just how much information the Belgians might have gleaned. Jodl wrote nervously in his diary: 'If the enemy is in possession of all the files the situation is catastrophic.' On the afternoon of the 12th, Wenniger wired Berlin: 'Reinberger declares post burned. Remains of little importance ...'[16] In fact, the half-burned papers from Reinberger's briefcase did betray scarcely more than the bare outlines of the operation, but the Germans could never be quite sure. For one more day Hitler refused to abandon the attack. Then, yet again, the weather broke, causing

15. His Chief of Staff, Colonel Kammhuber, was similarly disgraced. After the war he rejoined the new Federal German Luftwaffe and subsequently became its Inspector-General.

16. Reinberger was repatriated from Canada as a P.O.W. in 1944; Germany capitulated before a case against him could be heard.

another three postponements. By the 16th, alarming reports were coming in about the extent of Dutch and Belgian mobilization. At last Hitler took a major decision. That afternoon he ordered an indefinite postponement of *Gelb*. The whole operation must be replanned 'on a new basis, to be founded particularly on secrecy and surprise'. This new act of Chance finally saved Hitler from what might have been the grave blunder of a premature offensive and led him conclusively towards his finest hour.[17]

For the Germans, the Mechelen Incident proved to be pure gain. First of all, the High Command could now re-examine its strategy at leisure, and try out variations on the ground by means of 'war games'. Secondly, Hitler's new priorities of 'secrecy and surprise' lent added importance to the speed with which the all-out blow should be struck. At a meeting in the Chancellery on 20 January, it was agreed to abandon the previous build-up of several days; instead, all units would have to be ready to attack with twenty-four hours' warning or less. Thirdly, the enemy reaction to the mid-January alarm now gave the O.K.H. Intelligence 'Foreign Armies West',[18] an excellent idea of the Allies' order of battle and their intentions, which it did not possess before. As the French and British units rushed up to take their positions on the Belgian frontier in the middle of January, they made it clear to the Germans that, under Gamelin's Dyle Plan, the cream of both armies was designated to be pushed into northern Belgium; while, lower down, the weakness of General Corap's Ninth Army on the Meuse became increasingly apparent. Thus, as knowledge of the Franco-British dispositions made the prospects of a frontal collision less and less attractive, so Manstein's alternative, that would in effect close a trap behind the élite of the enemy forces,

17. There is a certain historic irony about the role bad weather played in Hitler's plans for 1940. In February 1916 the delay of a week which it imposed on the Crown Prince's initial attack on Verdun probably saved the French from disaster; in 1940 it was Hitler who was saved.

18. According to its chief, General Liss, this branch of O.K.H. Intelligence had been divided on the following arbitrary basis: 'Countries who wear their shirts inside their trousers belong to the West, and those who wear their shirts outside, to the East.'

obviously gained in appeal. Finally, it was of course the Mechelen Incident's revelation of apparent German intentions
towards Holland that committed Gamelin, disastrously, to his
project of strengthening his northern wing still further by the
'Breda Variant', thus adding his best reserves to the 'bag' that
Manstein was proposing to cut off on the Somme.

But still Halder held out against the persistent Manstein.
On 12 January, the day after the news of Mechelen reached
Hitler, Rundstedt signed Manstein's sixth and last memorandum, summing up all that had gone before, and forwarded it
to Zossen with the express request that it be submitted to
Hitler. Once again, Army Group 'A' was told – rather tartly –
to mind its own business, and Rundstedt's request was turned
down. On the 25th, Brauchitsch visited Koblenz, and in what
must have been by now a chilly atmosphere, Manstein accused
the Army C.-in-C. point blank of not aiming for a 'full decision'
in the West, and referring to the 'well-known negative attitude
of the O.K.H.' to the offensive in general. He sharply criticized
the O.K.H.'s opportunist intention of leaving the *Schwerpunkt*
question open until it had been seen which way the Allied cat
would jump, citing Moltke's maxim that 'mistakes in the initial
deployment cannot be repaired'. Two days later, Manstein was
shattered to receive his posting to Stettin. It seemed as if he
had lost the battle.

Hitler Backs Manstein

Then, on 7 February, just two days before Manstein was due
to depart for his new command, Army Group 'A' held its first
'war game'. Halder was clearly impressed by what he saw, and
for the first time showed himself veering towards Manstein's
thinking. On leaving Koblenz, he at last agreed to one of the
points demanded by Manstein, namely, that the Meuse crossing
at Sedan by Guderian's XIX Panzer Corps be simultaneously
supported by the XIV Motorized Corps. Here was yet a further
step in the escalation of Army Group 'A'. Manstein left for
Stettin with at least some satisfaction. Bock uttered another
growl of displeasure. On the 14th, 'war games' were con-

tinued, this time in Manstein's absence, at Mayen near Koblenz. Now an important and lively disagreement took place between Guderian and Halder. Guderian wanted to push his Panzers across the Meuse on the fifth day of the attack. True to the doctrines of *Achtung – Panzer!*, he conceived the armoured blow as being 'concentrated and applied with surprise on the decisive point, to form the arrow-head so deep that we need have no worry about the flank'. With some asperity, Halder condemned this as 'senseless'; it would be impossible to mount a 'stage by stage' attack across the Meuse until the infantry divisions arrived, and this could not be before the ninth day.[19] Rundstedt, no longer supported by Manstein, now took Halder's side. The games ended with this point unsettled. But, if nothing else, they had proved one other point – the extreme sensitivity of the area around Sedan for the 'Red', or defending side.

There now occurred the last of the elements of chance which were to shape the course of *Gelb*. Shortly before Manstein's departure, Hitler's chief adjutant, Colonel Schmundt, happened to be on a tour of the front and called in at Rundstedt's H.Q. Here he had a prolonged conversation with Manstein, who revealed his plan at length. This was the first Schmundt had heard of it, and he was amazed how closely it paralleled Hitler's own thoughts, though in a 'significantly more precise form'. Back in Berlin on 2 February, he immediately told Hitler of the conversation. Though not hiding his own personal aversion to Manstein,[20] Hitler expressed the keenest interest; Manstein must be brought before him, but how could this be done without arousing the suspicions of the O.K.H.? Talking to Schmundt later, a Lieutenant-Colonel Heusinger[21] of the O.K.H. operations branch, who was a warm supporter of the

19. Just how akin Halder's First War thinking was to that of his French opposite numbers is revealed by the fact that Gamelin, in his appreciation of German capabilities, was also to reckon that the Germans could not cross the Meuse before the ninth day.

20. Based on some suspicion that Manstein (ex-Lewinski) had Jewish blood?

21. In 1956 he became the first Inspector-General of Federal Germany's post-war Bundeswehr.

Manstein Plan, suggested that he should be summoned along with the four other newly-appointed corps commanders to 'kiss hands' with the Supreme Commander. So, on 17 February, a fateful working breakfast took place at the Chancellery. Manstein remained until 2 p.m. pouring forth every detail of the plan he had so long been ruminating. Hitler listened raptly. The next day Brauchitsch and Halder were ordered to the Chancellery. Hitler put the Manstein Plan to them, producing it as his own homework, with no attribution to its author. The O.K.H. leaders showed that they had in the meantime swung round towards it still further (perhaps, seeing which way the wind was now blowing, they were also anxious to avoid a repetition of the painful tirades of November). With a new spring in their step, they returned to Zossen to draft an entirely revised directive. A buoyant mood of fresh confidence replaced · earlier doubts. Hitler having been navigated safely past the shoals of a winter campaign, and the Army reorganized from the war in Poland, the new design now caused a prospect of great military success to glimmer within the keenly professional mind of Halder. Thoughts of deposing Hitler receded to remoter regions. Henceforth, until the plan actually went into action, the O.K.H., Hitler, Rundstedt and the other front commanders are to be found all pulling together with that superbly smooth efficiency of the German military machine at its best.

Sichelschnitt

By 24 February the new directive was ready. As it emerged from the cautious pen of Halder, it represented an even more drastic revision of *Gelb* than anything proposed by Manstein. The disputed question of the *Schwerpunkt* had been resolved; it would lie, from the very start, on the front of Army Group 'A'. The role of Bock's Army Group 'B' was now relegated, in the admirable simile of Liddell Hart, to that of 'a matador's cloak', which would draw Gamelin into Holland and northern Belgium, while Rundstedt was striking the lethal sword-blow elsewhere. The operation of the original Schlieffen Plan in 1914 has been compared (again by Liddell Hart) to that of a revolving door; the harder the French armies pressed in Lorraine, the more forcefully the door was intended to rotate against their back with the German push swinging round through Belgium in the north. *Sichelschnitt* ('the cut of the sickle'), as the O.K.H.'s new plan was admirably christened, also functioned like a revolving door, but this time the rotation was clockwise, with the French 'pushing' in the north, the Germans in the south. Bock's forces had been whittled down from his original 43 divisions to 29⅓; from controlling all the Panzers, he was left with only three, and two of these would be earmarked for eventual transfer to Rundstedt. None the less, Bock's role remained of the utmost importance. Though substantially weaker than the numerical sum of the forces likely to be met in Holland and northern Belgium, Bock had to engage the Allied 'bull' so vigorously that he would be unable to break away in order to gore the flank of Rundstedt's thrust.

Reading from north to south, the German line-up would be as follows: Army Group 'B', consisting of Küchler's Eighteenth Army (opposite Holland), and Reichenau's Sixth Army; Army Group 'A', with its northern boundary running south of Liège, consisting of Kluge's Fourth Army (which, transferred from Bock to Rundstedt, now brought Army Group 'A's strength up to 45⅓ divisions), List's Twelfth Army and Busch's Sixteenth Army; Army Group 'C' (Leeb), running from Luxembourg to the Swiss frontier and consisting of the First and Seventh Armies. The seven Panzer divisions handed to Rundstedt were all to be concentrated from the start (as in *Achtung – Panzer!*) to break through the rugged Ardennes country of Luxembourg and southern Belgium – which the French High Command had so long considered 'impenetrable'. In a solid steel phalanx, forty five miles wide, they would breach the Meuse between Dinant and Sedan.

The main effort – no longer just a subsidiary thrust – would be made at Sedan, by Guderian's XIX Panzer Corps consisting of the 1st, 2nd [22] and the 10th Panzer Divisions, aided by Hitler's élite Grossdeutschland Regiment of motorized infantry and backed up by von Wietersheim's XIV Motorized Corps.

22. Commanded by Guderian himself in the early pre-war days.

Further north, the 6th and 8th Panzers of Reinhardt's corps were to head for Monthermé, while the 5th and 7th Panzers of Hoth's corps were to provide flank cover by crossing the Meuse at Dinant. The five Panzer divisions of Guderian and Reinhardt, comprising the main effort, were welded together under command of an integrated Armoured Group. There was some argument as to who should command this; both Guderian and Manstein were passed over (fortunately for Britain, because if either had received the key command there would most probably have been no evacuation from Dunkirk), the final choice falling upon General Ewald von Kleist. A rather conservative-minded cavalry general, Kleist had been retired at the time of the Fritsch–Blomberg 'purge', but brought back to command a corps in the Polish campaign. Though his corps had included one Panzer and one 'light' division, according to Guderian (who certainly did not welcome the thought of Kleist sitting on top of him), Kleist had never 'shown himself particularly well disposed to the armoured force'. His appointment, however, was an important success for Halder, who, always suffering some nervousness about the audacity of the new plan, reckoned that in the conservative Kleist he had a man whom he could keep on a tight rein.

At Hitler's particular instance, a major reshuffle (which would make an essential contribution to the success of *Sichelschnitt*) was ordained within the Panzers themselves. Most of the heavier, cannon-bearing Mark III and IV tanks were to be withdrawn from Küchler's Eighteenth Army facing Holland, where they would hardly be needed, and given to Kleist and Rundstedt, who would find their guns indispensable for silencing bunkers that defended the Meuse crossing areas. Also incorporated in the new plan were various 'special operations' that had been hobby-horses of Hitler from the earliest days of *Gelb*;[23] these included parachute and glider operations to cap-

---

23. In the course of its evolution Hitler had frequently cried out at the lack of imagination his generals showed whenever the issue of 'special ops' arose. 'These generals are too correct . . . No tricks ever occur to them!' This was at least one common factor which Hitler as a military mind shared with Winston Churchill.

ture key bridges and forts on the Dutch and Belgian canal defence systems, as well as communications centres lying on the route of Kleist's approach-march through the Ardennes. Hitler occupied himself down to the last detail with the planning of these 'special operations'; as will be seen, the use of 'Brandenburger' commandos wearing Dutch uniforms especially appealed to him.

Meanwhile, *Sichelschnitt* was to be accompanied by elaborate 'deception' schemes designed to keep the French constantly in fear that the *real* – or, at least, a serious secondary – attack would come from Leeb's Army Group 'C' facing the Maginot Line. In fact, Army Group 'C', containing only nineteen infantry divisions of moderate value, was to play virtually no aggressive role in the coming battle. The mighty Maginot Line upon which France had spent so much of her substance would simply not be accorded any opportunity to cover itself with battle-honours. On the other hand, if it fell for Hitler's deception plan, the French High Command, it was hoped, would be hesitant to risk withdrawing from the Maginot Line the 'interval troops', which constituted such a large portion of disposable reserves, for use against the Sedan breakthrough. Thus were both Leeb and Bock to act as foils for Rundstedt.

There remained some doubts and misgivings about the new plan. As late as April, Bock, possibly still smarting from the dilution of his command, was grumbling to Halder that

you will be creeping by ten miles from the Maginot Line with the flank of your breakthrough and hope that the French will watch inertly! You are cramming the mass of the tank units together into the sparse roads of the Ardennes mountain country, as if there were no such thing as air power! And [added Bock] you then hope to be able to lead an operation as far as the coast with an open southern flank 200 miles long, where stands the mass of the French Army!

It was, he declared, 'transcending the frontiers of reason'. Rundstedt too, deprived of the reassuring presence of Manstein, continued to worry about that 'open southern flank', deducing that it must be along the axis Paris–Châlons-sur-Marne–Verdun that Gamelin would logically mass his strongest reserves. His new Chief of Staff, Sodenstern, had his doubts about the hideous traffic tangle that might ensue from the vehicles of seven Panzer divisions all converging on the Ardennes. Even Guderian was seen to be having some second thoughts about whether his corps alone could force the Meuse at Sedan. Halder, right to the end, harboured doubts as to whether the troops would be capable of executing this plan, which called for the utmost skill and endurance. The deficiencies shown in the Polish campaign still worried him, and even by the spring of 1940 only a portion of the Army seemed to him to be up to standard, either in spirit, training or equipment, and all these élite units would be committed into the first wave of the attack.

But gradually new sand-table exercises and war games ironed out the remaining defects in the plan. Day after day the Panzer men brought themselves and their weapons to a higher pitch of efficiency; up in the Eifel Mountains, schools, dance-halls, and timber sheds were turned into workshops, keeping the vehicles in top running order, ready for action at twenty-four hours' notice as decreed by Hitler. Meanwhile, Intelligence reports brought encouraging news. By mid-March, 'Foreign Armies West' had a complete enough picture of the French order of battle to assure the O.K.H. that the most reserves Gamelin could bring to bear upon that vulnerable southern flank of the breakthrough would be 41 to 48 divisions, of which 12 to 17 could be rated as 'third wave' units only. And to muster this force, the French High Command would have to act with great speed and decision; this, 'Foreign Armies West' assessed, was not of the highest probability. A second cause for satisfaction stemmed from the results of aerial reconnaissance over the Meuse crossing zones. Throughout the winter, Luftwaffe planes flying at extremely high altitude had been busily photographing the area. From a microscopic examination of the prints, Major von Stiotta, an Austrian engineer of great ability, reported to Rundstedt shortly before the attack was due to be unleashed that the French fortifications belonging to the Maginot Line 'extension' were very far from completed.

In Rome in mid-March, President Roosevelt's peace envoy,

Sumner Welles, was told by Ciano that recently 'Ribbentrop seemed to be convinced that the German Army could achieve a military victory within five months', and Welles recalled the cockiness Goering had displayed when interviewed in Berlin, declaring that Germany now held 'all the trumps in her hands'. At the beginning of April, Halder's diary reveals a new note of confident enthusiasm, while later in the month General Fromm, commanding the Reserve Army, was heard to prophesy 'We shall push through Holland and Belgium at one stroke, and finish off France in fourteen days.' It was not least a growing awareness of the real beauty of *Sichelschnitt* as a strategy of war that lay at the root of this self-assurance. As subsequent events were to prove, *Sichelschnitt* was one of the most inspired blueprints for victory that the military mind has ever conceived.[24] In its final state, it could no longer be rated as the brainchild of any one person: without the extraordinary drive and instinctive ideas of Hitler, and without Manstein's brilliant strategic conception, the O.K.H. would never have contemplated a knock-out blow against France. Yet without Halder and the O.K.H., Hitler would probably have launched a half-cock offensive in 1939, and it was finally Halder's organizational excellence, his ability to digest and apply technical advice, and his meticulous care that brought *Sichelschnitt* to its ultimate perfection.

But in fact, *Sichelschnitt* was not *quite* perfect. Otherwise it would have won not just the Battle of France, but the whole war. Tactically perfect, strategically almost perfect, yet as an instrument of higher policy it possessed one fatal flaw. In mid-March Hitler was questioning Guderian on his plans for establishing a bridgehead across the Meuse at Sedan on the fifth day of the attack: ' "And then what are you going to do?" He was

24. Even its framers seem to have been partially unconscious of the inherent beauty of *Sichelschnitt* as it developed; for instance, to the French High Command, when Rundstedt broke through at Sedan his ultimate objective might well have been one of three almost equally attractive ones: to swing left and roll up the Maginot Line from behind, to continue straight on and seize Paris, or to swing right and head for the Channel, as in fact the plan intended. Faced with this choice, any High Command would be like a greyhound having to make a decision on three equidistant rabbits.

the first person who had thought to ask me this vital question,'
Guderian recalls.

I replied: 'Unless I receive orders to the contrary, I intend on
the next day to continue my advance westwards. The supreme
leadership must decide whether my objective is to be Amiens or
Paris. In my opinion the correct course is to drive past Amiens
to the English Channel.' Hitler nodded and said nothing more.
Only General Busch, who commanded the Sixteenth Army on my
left, cried out: 'Well, I don't think you'll cross the river in the
first place!'

Guderian adds revealingly: 'I never received any further orders
as to what to do once the bridgehead over the Meuse was captured ...' This reluctance of the German High Command to
name the Channel as its ultimate objective was typical of the
nagging fears at the audacity of *Sichelschnitt*, which, with
memories of the brilliance of the French Army of the Marne
still persisting, could never quite be suppressed. Most of the
energy that the O.K.H. had lavished upon *Sichelschnitt* had
been absorbed in planning the actual breakthrough, but little
on its immediate aftermath. Furthermore, the contingency of
Sichelschnitt leading to a *total* victory over France seemed so
remote that, beyond the operation itself, no thought whatsoever
had been given to how a knockout blow might then be administered to Britain. The vanquishing of France in one swift offensive remained altogether too startling a prospect for the First
War minds of Halder and company, and even Hitler's inspi-
rational vision for once failed him. Just three days before the
great attack began, Hitler had an interview with Admiral
Raeder, his naval chief; but neither *Sichelschnitt*, nor any possible follow-up invasion of Britain, was ever mentioned. All
Hitler could think of was the mighty engagement by land that
lay ahead.

Herein lay the Achilles' heel of *Sichelschnitt*, and the seeds
of Hitler's defeat.

By mid-March 1940, *Sichelschnitt* and its dependent forces had
already reached the necessary state of readiness. Everyone

expected Hitler to press the button in a matter of days. But his attention was temporarily distracted elsewhere. Despite the capitulation of Finland and the collapse of their crazy schemes of intervention, the Allies still appeared to be showing a disquieting interest in Narvik and the Swedish iron-ore fields. To forestall them, Hitler decided that, while the Allies dithered, he would strike in Norway first.

Chapter 8

Towards the Brink

Easy training, hard combat; hard training, easy combat.
SUVAROV

All conditions are more calculable, all obstacles more surmountable, than those of human resistance.
B. H. LIDDELL HART, *The Strategy of Indirect Approach*

Disaster in Norway

On 14 December concern about the course of the Russo-Finnish War had caused Hitler to instruct the O.K.W. to prepare preliminary studies for an invasion of Norway. His preoccupation with *Gelb* kept thoughts of any such project well in the background, until, on 16 February, the Royal Navy boarded within Norwegian territorial waters a German ship called the *Altmark*, liberating a large number of British seamen taken off ships which the *Graf Spee* had sunk. Three days later, Hitler, enraged by this *coup de main* and alarmed by Allied interest in Norway, ordered the speeding-up of plans for *Weserübung* ('Exercise Weser'), the code name for the occupation of Denmark and Norway. On 1 March he signed the directive for *Weserübung*, but for two days could not make up his mind whether it should come before or after *Sichelschnitt*. Then, upon the advice of Jodl [1] that the two operations should be kept entirely independent of each other, Hitler decided that the Norwegian operation should be implemented first, and he began to cast around for a suitable pretext for violating the neutrality of two more countries. All this resulted in further delay to *Sichelschnitt*.

Meanwhile, after months of argument, Churchill, at a meeting of the Allied Supreme War Council on 28 March, finally

1. Brauchitsch and Halder were not even consulted on *Weserübung* until the very last minute, Hitler possibly anticipating the objections which the O.K.H. would raise to this new adventure, which was even more risky than *Sichelschnitt*.

persuaded Chamberlain to permit the Royal Navy to mine the Leads, the Norwegian coastal waters, along which flowed the Swedish iron ore destined for Hitler's war plants. Warning of this breach of neutrality was to be transmitted to Norway and Sweden on 5 April. By now the advent of spring had brought a new (and quite misplaced) cockiness to the men and mouthpieces of British public life. On 4 April, Chamberlain made his famous speech informing the Conservative Party that Hitler had 'missed the bus', while on the same day it reported his speech, the *Daily Express* published an interview with the C.I.G.S., under the headline 'Come on Hitler! Dares Ironside!', in which Ironside was quoted as having said: 'We would welcome a go at him. Frankly we would welcome an attack. We are sure of ourselves . . .' But while Chamberlain and Ironside were speaking, the first of some 10,000 German troops were already 'embussed' for Norway, concealed aboard merchant ships and colliers, in what was to be one of the most daring strokes of the war.

On 9 April, Denmark was seized almost without a shot being fired. In five separate groups, the Germans landed in Norway at Oslo, Kristiansand, Bergen, Trondheim, and Narvik. Airborne forces seized the key airfields at Oslo and Stavanger. The Norwegians fought back courageously, though ill prepared and surprised. But the Allies, in spite of having had months in which to think about the problem, were equally taken by surprise. In Paris, the Secretary of the newly created War Committee, Paul Baudouin, recalled that 'for five minutes the Prime Minister and I vainly sought on the coasts of Norway for another Narvik, for we were sure that the Narvik where the German troops had been reported could not be the iron-ore port in the north' – a thousand miles from any German base. British submarines watched the German troopships creeping across the Skagerrak, but it was not until the afternoon of the 9th that they received orders to torpedo them, by which time it was too late. The fact was that the Allies, in arrogant confidence of the supremacy of the Royal Navy, had never believed that Hitler with his tiny naval forces could conceivably launch an amphibious operation of this scope. Leisurely, and confusedly, they reacted. Between 10 and 13 April the British scored a heartening naval victory by sinking all ten German destroyers covering the Narvik landings; but they carried with them no ground troops with which to follow up. It was the story of Gallipoli and Suvla Bay all over again. Further south, off Bergen, a three-hour air attack by Luftwaffe bombers on the 10th sank a destroyer and hit the battleship *Rodney* with a dud bomb. Modest as these results were, they had the critical effect of persuading the C.-in-C. Home Fleet, Admiral Sir Charles Forbes, to turn back out to sea. It was the first time in war that ground-based aircraft had proved their ascendancy over capital surface ships.

At Rosyth, four British battalions already earmarked for a Norwegian adventure were embarked, disembarked and then re-embarked, losing in the process much of their stores and departing almost without artillery or tanks. The first British contingent arrived at Narvik on 15 April; then between the 16th and 18th other feeble forces landed at Namsos and Andalsnes, on either side of Trondheim in central Norway, in hopes of cutting off the German bridgehead there. On the 19th, ten days after the Germans had landed, the first French troops arrived; but, according to Paul Reynaud,

they were completely incapable of moving off or offering any action whatsoever. Their artillery, tanks, anti-aircraft guns, their mules and even their skis and snowshoes had remained in the auxiliary cruiser *Ville d'Alger*, which had not been able to enter the harbour because of her length – a detail which had been forgotten.

By now, using 350 Ju-52 transport planes, the Luftwaffe had thoroughly established itself in central and southern Norway, and here the Stukas rendered the Allied expeditionary forces quite helpless. This extreme mobility of German air power was a depressing foretaste of what was to come, in France, a month later.

By 3 May the British had been forced to evacuate all their troops from central Norway. Narvik remained the Allies' only toehold, and indeed here things went badly against the Germans; only the exigencies of the war in France were to save General Dietl and his 2,000 mountain troops from being wiped out.

In his Norwegian gamble, Hitler lost ten out of his twenty destroyers, three out of eight cruisers. Thus on a sideshow with no decisive bearing upon the war, he had squandered his Navy, without which (even had he prepared any such strategy) an invasion of the British Isles in 1940 would be utterly out of the question. This, for the Allies, was the one net gain from an operation that was otherwise an unrelieved saga of British professional incompetence and half-heartedness – 'frivolous dilettantism' was Hitler's scornful verdict. Here, as at Gallipoli in 1915 (not to mention Suez in 1956), Britain failed at just the kind of operation for which both her history and geography should have best prepared her.[2] Worst of all, Norway was a flagrant defeat of British sea power. Its repercussions upon the forthcoming campaign in France also deserve serious consideration: first, there was the impact that defeat in Norway had upon the already impaired morale of France; and secondly, there were its stimulating effects upon the German leadership.

From Berlin on 9 April, William Shirer recorded the news of Hitler's Scandinavian move as 'stupefying'. Reactions in France were just that much more powerful. They were admirably summed up by a lieutenant accompanying André Maurois on a visit to General Corap's ill-fated Ninth Army:

It's a bad business that our first enterprise in this war met with failure. A young horse must never be defeated in his trial runs. If he is, he gets the habit, loses his self-respect and comes to consider it perfectly natural that he should stay behind.

Frivolously, Paris society affected satisfaction at Britain's

2. An intriguing field of speculation opens up if one considers what *might* have happened if, in both world wars, Britain had remained true to her amphibious traditions and maintained the bulk of her Army as a truly mobile expeditionary force, instead of committing it inextricably to the line in France. Certainly, in the Second World War, the presence or absence of the few B.E.F. divisions in France was to have little influence in events there, whereas, properly organized, they could have undoubtedly inflicted a signal defeat on Hitler in Norway.

discomfiture; Vincent Sheean noted that 'even the most sensible Frenchman seemed to take pleasure in saying that France could have managed things better'. Everything the caustic Ferdonnet broadcast from Stuttgart about '*les sales anglais*' seemed to be true. But in the Army, there was the deepest apprehension; if Hitler could worst Britain in her own element, where the Royal Navy was supposedly supreme, how could the French Army stop him on land, where the odds were by no means so favourable? Was there, in fact, no stopping this apparently invincible demon? Morale descended yet another few pegs.

Unknown to the Allies, however, for all the feebleness of their counter-efforts, Norway was in fact a much closer-run thing than it had seemed. Hitler had been significantly shaken by the few reverses suffered there. There were two periods of what Jodl in his diary describes as 'leadership chaos': from 14 to 18 April, concerning Narvik, and until the 23rd over Trondheim. Narvik threw Hitler into a complete panic, and he actually ordered Dietl to surrender; the signal was, however, suppressed by a courageous staff officer on the O.K.W. Trouble with the airborne landing in Norway had made Goering and his staff extremely nervous about the operations projected for Holland, while so large a portion of Luftwaffe strength (especially in the indispensable Ju-52 transports) had been committed to Norway that even a moderate increase in the British air effort there might well have made a considerable inroad in the air support of *Sichelschnitt*. But the most important factor was psychological. Whatever the results in Norway, they would have been unlikely to halt *Sichelschnitt*; on the other hand, the panic Hitler showed over Narvik entitles one to conclude that one or two harder knocks would most probably have persuaded both him and his generals to greater caution when it came to France. And nothing would have been more likely to spell ruin to *Sichelschnitt* than excessive caution, or bad nerves.

As it was, by 24 April the situation had improved so much that Hitler could now once again turn his eyes back to the West. On 1 May, more good news prompted him to order that steps be taken so that *Sichelschnitt* could be launched at twenty-four hours' notice at any time from 4 May.

Crises in France and Britain

If Norway led, among the German generals, to renewed confidence in their Führer, in both France and Britain it resulted in a major crisis of leadership. For Gamelin, the days of 12 and 13 April were 'among the most painful of my existence'; on being summoned to a Cabinet meeting, he found 'an atmosphere of ice. It was as though they had just pronounced "Bring in the accused!"' Following on the Finnish débâcle, public dissatisfaction had already brought about the fall of Gamelin's protector, Daladier, replaced (on 21 March) by a new Cabinet under Paul Reynaud, who was no friend of the French Generalissimo.

When France went to war in 1914, her political parties had declared a truce, forming under the *Union Sacrée* a coalition almost unique in the history of France. Poincaré had possessed no love for Clemenceau, but out of patriotism was prepared to collaborate loyally with him; in 1939, although Léon Blum had declared that he would ally himself with anyone dedicated solely to winning the war, it was typical that at a dinner party where Clare Boothe was present, half the guests refused to shake hands with poor Blum. In war, the musical chairs of the Third Republic went on as dizzily as before. Shortly after its outbreak, Daladier had managed to purge the appeaser, Bonnet,[3] from the Quai d'Orsay, though he could not get rid of him altogether, and Bonnet had lingered on as Minister of Justice. Daladier then made an attempt at re-creating the *Union Sacrée* by bringing his old foe, Édouard Herriot, into the Government in Bonnet's place. 'Come, it is your duty,' he is reputed to have said to Herriot. 'At the Quai d'Orsay we need a faith, a doctrine, a capable head, endurance; in short, a man.' Herriot retorted, ungraciously, 'What for?' but accepted with the proviso that he should be 'covered' by Pétain also entering the Cabinet. The old Marshal's response to Daladier, however,

3. Typical of the mistrust festering within Daladier's War Cabinet was Gamelin's refusal to discuss France's military deficiencies in front of Bonnet, to which Daladier commented, 'You did right. If you had exposed them, the Germans would have known about them the next day.'

was: 'I am at your orders. But veto Herriot.' Thereafter
Daladier was left with no alternative but to turn himself into
a one-man band: Foreign Secretary, as well as Premier, Minister of National Defence and Minister of War.

The Cabinet swiftly divided itself into the 'hards', as represented by Paul Reynaud and Clemenceau's former hatchet-
man, Georges Mandel, and the 'softs': Bonnet, de Monzie,
Pomaret and Chautemps.[4] These 'softs' within the Cabinet represented but a small fraction of the various dissident groups,
opposed to the war to some extent or other, with whom
Daladier had to deal: Communists, anti-militarists of the non-
Communist Left, conservatives fearful of revolution, the rich
trembling for their riches, defeatists and pro-Fascists such as
Pierre Laval, who, though still in outer darkness, wielded a
potent influence upon the 'softs' within Daladier's Cabinet.
Meanwhile, above it all, the Head of State, who could perhaps
have lent more teeth to France's war-time Government, was
manifestly senile; on visiting President Lebrun in the spring of
1940, Sumner Welles found his memory 'failing rapidly. It was
difficult for him to remember with any accuracy names, or
dates, or even facts ...' He attempted 'with a good deal of
assistance' to tell Welles about the various paintings in the
Élysée, but 'was quite unable to remember the names of any of
them'.

Daladier

Daladier himself was neither strong nor prepossessing. A fifty-
five-year-old widower and son of a baker from Vaucluse in the
south, he had taught history before going into politics. He
succeeded Herriot as leader of the Radical-Socialist Party in
1935, had been Minister of War almost uninterruptedly since
1932, and Premier both at the time of the Stavisky riots of 1934
and Munich, on each of which occasions he had capitulated to
external pressures. Daladier was a stockily-built, energetic man
with a dull-brown complexion and a greasy lock of hair that

4. In a more modern context, they would have been rated 'hawks' or
'doves'.

imparted a slight (and deceptive) look of Bonaparte. Under the strain of the Popular Front, he had come to depend increasingly on the more fiery French liquors; writing in all the bitterness of 1940, Vincent Sheean describes him as 'a dirty man with a cigarette stuck to his lower lip, stinking of absinthe, talking with a rough Marseillaise accent . . . He had a certain southern eloquence, particularly over the air when he could not be seen.' While Daladier was still in power, Harold Nicolson wrote in his diary that he looked 'like a drunken peasant. His face must once have had sharp outlines but now it is blurred by the puffiness of drink. He looks extremely exhausted and has the eyes of a man who has had a bad night. He has a weak, sly smile.' In the south, his supporters nicknamed Daladier 'the bull of Vaucluse', but as Spears remarked acidly, 'his horns bore more resemblance to the soft feelers of the snail than to the harder bovine variety'. Others said that his was a case of a 'velvet hand in a glove of iron', and certainly his rough appearance and violent fits of rage had given him a reputation for strength to which, as both Munich and the Stavisky riots had shown, he was hardly entitled. His strength, such as it was, lay in politics rather than in statecraft, and he excelled in the steamy jungles comprising the political lobbies of the Third Republic. To Pertinax, Daladier – honest but infirm and immensely jealous of his position –epitomized the average Frenchman of his time; he was 'the image of the last decade of the Republic'. For a nation as reluctantly at war as France, he was certainly not a leader to impart inspiration; in his New Year's Eve broadcast at the end of 1939, he expressed a desire to spread 'a ray of joy' in each home, but all he managed to do was propagate his own gloom. Yet as a political juggler capable of keeping the parties of the Third Republic in some sort of equilibrium, he was indispensable.

At the beginning of January 1940, Daladier took a weekend off to escape from the political pressures bearing down on him. He was out riding, when his horse slipped on frost-hardened ground and he fell, with his foot caught in the stirrup. For the next months he suffered constant pain and insomnia, which appear to have had their effect upon his control of the Govern-

ment; Senator Bardoux notes that when he saw Daladier on
6 March he was still limping and seemed 'even wearier, sadder
and less dynamic than a fortnight previously', while grumbling
'Nothing is going right.' Flandin, whose Government had once
fallen as a result of a car accident in which he broke his arm,
commented caustically that 'a politician has no right to have
accidents', and on 20 March Daladier fell again – this time
politically. Pierre Laval launched the attack, while the killing
blow was struck by a Deputy who cried tellingly: 'The men
who were able neither to prevent nor to prepare for war are not
now qualified either to stop it or win it . . .' After some talk
about Daladier being succeded by such 'softs' as Chautemps,
Laval, or Pétain, President Lebrun called for Paul Reynaud to
form the one-hundred-and-ninth Government of the Third
Republic.

Reynaud

Paul Reynaud was sixty-two when he came to power, for the
first time. His family were farmers in the Basses-Alpes, but he
had established himself as a successful barrister. He had acquired a connoisseur's taste for Chinese art, and indeed there
was something of the mandarin in his own appearance: dapper,
sharp-featured, with eyebrows that seemed to be permanently
raised in a quizzical expression. He was very fond of sport –
walking, cycling and swimming – and he rather advertised the
fact. But the important physical feature of Reynaud was his
modest stature. He had most of the attributes of the small man:
agility, combativeness, vulnerability to flatterers, the self-con-
fidence that masks a sense of inferiority – and courage. His
enemies (and they were many) called him 'Mickey Mouse'. But
to Maurois he was

a little fighting cock . . . I liked to see him, when a subject fired
his imagination, get to his feet, put his hands in his pockets, throw
back his head to raise his short figure to its full height, and hold
forth in picturesque and biting phrases like quick hammer blows.

In debate he showed a brilliant, quick intellect and a devastating logic; but he sought (says Élie Bois) 'to master, not to charm', and this with his natural assertiveness and love of battle did not endear him to other politicians of the Third Republic, especially to Daladier, who loathed him. Hard-working and intensely patriotic, Reynaud had never been afraid to swim against the current. From the earliest days he had warned France about Hitler's designs, in opposition to the Flandins, Lavals and Bonnets, and it was he who had gone against official French military doctrine by taking up the views of de Gaulle. As Minister of Finance in 1938, he had achieved remarkable success in reordering France's economy after the ravages of the Popular Front; but his tough measures had gained him many more enemies. From September 1939 he had pledged himself to total war against Hitler, though by the time he came to power it was a bit late, in so far as Hitler was himself on the brink of unleashing total war against France.

As the small voice in the French wilderness, Reynaud repre-sented the equivalent of Churchill, whom he hugely admired; but unfortunately he possessed neither the essential grandeur nor the support. He also was too much a product of the Third Republic, had played the game of musical chairs to its limit, manoeuvring and counter-manoeuvring. More than this, because of the loneliness of the positions he adopted as well as his combative manner, in the Assembly he was a maverick; sitting in the centre, he possessed no party of his own, few intimates, and his judgement in choosing his political 'friends' was to prove far from impeccable. Thus, in contrast to the great *carte blanche* given to Churchill on his accession to power, Reynaud from the start was forced to compromise and tight-rope-walk in his formation of a government.

But by far the heaviest burden Paul Reynaud had to bear was his mistress, Madame Hélène de Portes. Ambitious, busy women have traditionally exercised a powerful influence be-hind the scenes of French politics. At the end of the 1930s, there were three who had dominated the stage of the Third Republic. There was Madame Bonnet, nicknamed 'Madame *soutien-Georges*'; the Marquise de Crussol, a handsome and youthful-looking blonde who was Daladier's Egeria and whom the punsters christened '*la sardine qui s'est crue sole*', on account of the family's sardine-canning business; and Reynaud's Comtesse Hélène de Portes, the most powerful of them all and regarded as almost too sinister to be granted a sobriquet, although the wits occasionally referred to her, aptly as 'the side door' – '*la porte à côté*'.

The extraordinary thing about Hélène de Portes is that, of the countless people who knew her, none can satisfactorily explain wherein lay her allure. The practised eye of General Spears describes her as having 'very good feet and ankles, but her complexion was sallow. Of medium height, she was dark, her curly hair, brushed upwards, looked untidy ... Her mouth was big and the voice that issued from it was unharmonious.' Spears thought she dressed fashionably, but lacked 'the attractiveness so often found in Parisiennes, that of being *bien soignée*'. Élie Bois, less vitriolic than most, observed in her a physical attribute which perhaps compensated for her lack of traditional beauty: 'Her way of walking, quick of step, disclosed that the suppleness of her limbs and the agility of her whole body were maintained by physical exercise.' But he thought her 'ardent and ruthless in every way ... a match for others at the game of secret slander'. However, he added, 'she preferred direct attack, haughty, and even violent, for thereby her will to dominate could be more surely exercised'. Giving a woman's view of Hélène de Portes, Clare Boothe saw her as 'a dark, homely, talkative little woman, in her late forties. She looked as much like a *Hausfrau* as a French *maîtresse* can. She was patriotic, energetic; she had many friends and a lot of notions about everything.' But to regard her as 'the Du Barry of France' was, she thought, as wide of the mark as calling 'Mrs Eleanor Roosevelt the Cleopatra of the New Deal!'

What, then, was the secret of her hold over Reynaud? Most probably it resided in his small stature. As a Frenchman remarked to Harold Nicolson in 1941, 'she made him feel tall and grand and powerful. Had Reynaud been three inches taller, the history of the world might have been changed.' He needed and depended upon his Hélène, and thrived upon her flattery; she in her turn, dedicated to seeing her hero reach the top of the political ladder, sustained him and goaded him in his own strong ambitions. Their relationship, as someone once remarked, was 'far more like Diana clinging to her charger than Venus clutching her prey'.

In the aftermath of France's defeat, Hélène de Portes came to be regarded by many as an out-and-out Fifth Columnist. Certainly before the war her famous salon had been frequently visited by Otto Abetz and members of the *Comité France-Allemagne*; she was never a 'hard' like Reynaud, and she was strongly anti-British, a tendency which increased as the war went progressively worse for France from 10 May onwards. But in retrospect it seems fair to judge that she was no more of a 'Fifth Columnist' than most of the patriotic but self-interested *haute bourgeoisie* whose shibboleth under the Popular Front had been 'Rather Hitler than Blum!' Perhaps the most baneful feature of her relationship with Paul Reynaud was that she held him totally her prisoner, and chivvied him relentlessly until he was simply worn out. Together they lived in Reynaud's bachelor flat near the Assembly, where much business of state was transacted. She was constantly intervening and interfering, and even in his office Reynaud was never immune from her endless telephone calls. On at least one occasion Madame de Portes was to be found actually seated at his desk, presiding over a gathering of generals, deputies and government officials. Once when André Maurois criticized a political appointment made by his friend, Reynaud admitted: 'It was not my choice, it was hers.' Maurois replied: 'That is no excuse.' 'Ah,' sighed Reynaud, 'you don't know what a man who has been hard at work all day will put up with to make sure of an evening's peace.'

Another aspect of Madame de Portes's unfortunate influence behind the scenes was the fact that she was at daggers drawn with the Marquise de Crussol, Daladier's champion. The rivalry of these women injected poison into the already bad relations between the two most powerful leaders of war-time France. From about January, Hélène de Portes had begun to campaign for Reynaud to oust Daladier, in the clumsiest fashion, filling the salons of Paris with stories of Daladier's lethargy. This gossip the faithful Marquise promptly passed back to Daladier, duly magnified, until the rift between him and Reynaud became almost intolerable. To Maurois, Reynaud confided grimly: 'I believe he desires the victory of France, but he desires my defeat even more.' Of this feud, Churchill was to comment to Spears in despair. 'What will centuries to come say if we lost this war through lack of understanding?'

Reynaud Saddled with Gamelin

The tragedy for France was that Reynaud, the lone operator with no political machine behind him, could not survive without the backing of Daladier in his Cabinet. On the very first day of the new Government, Reynaud was confronted with a vote of confidence. He scraped by with only one vote, so precarious was the balance of the Government about to face Hitler's onslaught. Reynaud wanted to take over the Ministry of National Defence from Daladier, but he had to renounce it because of his need for his enemy's support; he wanted to sack Gamelin, but could not, because Gamelin was Daladier's man; he wanted to bring in Colonel de Gaulle as Secretary to the War Cabinet, but de Gaulle would not serve with Daladier and preferred to return to his tanks.[5] Paul Baudouin, a director of the Bank of Indo-China, youngish, good-looking, but a 'soft' and a favoured protégé of Hélène de Portes, got the job instead. Bonnet was sacked at last, but later, as part of his complex balancing act, Reynaud was constrained to bring in two extreme right-wingers, Marin and Ybarnegaray. The appointment of the latter, a member of Colonel de la Rocque's *Croix de Feu*, was roughly the same as if Churchill had taken Oswald

5. De Gaulle was then commanding a tank brigade dispersed behind the Maginot Line. At the end of January he had re-entered the limelight by circulating to political and military leaders a courageous memorandum in which he warned of the dangers of the Germans smashing through the French defences with an overwhelming mechanical force. The official, complacent response was that France 'was not Poland'. There is a curious historical parallel between Colonel de Gaulle's memorandum and one which gained disbelief and disfavour for another colonel, Émile Driant, when he warned Joffre of the impending attack on Verdun in 1916.

Mosley into his Cabinet. Daladier himself grumbled to Élie Bois: 'I ought not to have entered this Government. I was tired, worn out ... I must get out of it at the first opportunity.'

It was typical of how self-interest continued to prevail in a France perched on the very brink of disaster. The nation at large was all too discouragingly aware of the 'swamp of personal jealousies and ministerial appetites' in Paris. At the front, Major Barlone spoke for many soldiers when he wrote in his diary of the new Government: 'People see a schemer and a thief in every politician ... Our enemies do not waste their time over Parliamentary manoeuvres ... Spring is now here, the time of trial is probably at hand, and look what a Government we have!'

Yet for all the political ligaments binding him and restricting his movements, Reynaud himself, with his little man's combativeness, came to power just as dedicated to waging war with a fresh bellicosity as Clemenceau had been. One of his first acts was to go to London to sign, on 28 March, a joint declaration with the British, pledging that neither country would conclude a separate peace without the agreement of the other, an undertaking to which Daladier had long been reluctant to commit himself.[6] Then, on 12 April, Reynaud, who had been infuriated by Gamelin's showing over Norway, determined to precipitate a crisis here. To Baudouin he remarked: 'It would be criminal to leave this nerveless philosopher at the head of the French Army.' He was, he said, 'hesitating between General Georges and General Weygand'. But in the Cabinet, Daladier immediately ranged himself behind Gamelin, and threatened to resign himself if there were any change. Reynaud was stymied. Baudouin claims he came out of the meeting 'thunderstruck by the pitiful spectacle of the Prime Minister's impotence to break the political chains which bound him'. At a Cabinet Meeting on 23 April, Reynaud once again remained silent. On the 27th, Reynaud told Baudouin that the time for procrastination was over; he would take action within the next two or three days. But President Lebrun, whose whole-hearted

6. This declaration was later to be a source of enduring bitterness between Britain and France.

support would be indispensable to Reynaud, merely passed him
a message, telling him to 'be patient. Time will settle many
things.' Indeed it would. Then on 28 April, Reynaud collapsed
with influenza. He was confined to his bed for a week, and
Gamelin was saved a second time. On returning to his office,
still shaky, Reynaud now prepared for a final offensive against
his commander-in-chief.

Notices went out on the evening of 8 May for a Cabinet
meeting the next morning. Reynaud arrived with a bulky file,
from which he read for two hours. According to Élie Bois, his
colleagues, many of whom had not seen him for a fortnight,
'found him much altered, thinner, feverish of eye, unsteady of
voice'. He closed with a warning that France, if she persisted
in the errors which had encompassed the Norwegian operation,
would almost certainly lose the war. Gamelin could not be left
in charge. There followed a painful two-minute silence before
Lamoureux, the Minister of Finance, rallied to Reynaud.
Daladier counter-attacked vigorously. Reynaud wound up the
session by stating that, in view of the opposition, he considered
the Government as having resigned and would inform the
President accordingly. All that afternoon of the 9th discussions
went on at the Élysée. The next day the Germans attacked. A
third respite was granted Gamelin.

Meanwhile, in London, in the midst of questions about such
grave matters as Kentish sheep being frightened by aircraft,
Scottish hotels over-charging for coffee and the advertising of
patent medicines in stamp books, the Commons was concluding its great debate on Norway. Chamberlain was finished. On
10 May, just as Hitler's Panzers were plunging into Holland
and Belgium, Churchill became Prime Minister. In those
lapidary words, he remarked: 'I was conscious of a profound
sense of relief. At last I had the authority to give directions
over the whole scene. I felt as if I were walking with destiny . . .'
Britain had at last found her war leader, and he embarked
upon his task with the undivided support of parliamentarians;
but there were many government matters concerning the conduct of war which were strange to him and would necessarily
and perilously remain outside his grasp for some time. How

different though, was the scene in France on 10 May. Indubitably, time had 'settled' matters, but not in the way Lebrun might have hoped. Here was a government in the throes of dissolution, a commander-in-chief under suspended sentence.

The Opposing Forces: Tanks

For employment in *Sichelschnitt*, by May Hitler could count upon 136 out of the Army's 157 divisions, of which no more than a third qualified as first-rate offensive material. Against this, France's North-East Front was now held by 94 French divisions of mixed value,[7] plus 10 British, augmented by a further 22 Belgian divisions and 10 Dutch (though, despite Gamelin's hopes, these latter were able to exert a minimal influence in the battle) – a total also of 136, so that in numbers alone the Germans did not possess the kind of overwhelming superiority which the Allies required to crush the Wehrmacht later in the war.

In the crucial matter of armour, figures have varied wildly; on 10 May, the French *Deuxième Bureau* estimated that the Germans had 7,000 to 7,500 tanks, a vastly inflated figure which came to be extensively used in France by way of excuse for what was to follow. According to Guderian, Germany's ten Panzer divisions should have had 2,800 tanks, but in reality had only 2,200; as a reliable figure based on German archives, one could, however, accept a total of just over 2,400 and well under 3,000.[8] For the number of Franco-British tanks available to the North-East Front, Gamelin himself gives a total of 3,432 modern vehicles, while Colonel Goutard, a generally trustworthy source, puts the Allied total 'in the region of 3,000', and the most recent estimate (by General de Cossé Brissac,

7. Owing to the blood-letting of 1914–18 and the attendant fall in the birth-rate, France had been able to mobilize far fewer men in 1940 than in 1914; the difference was most noticeable in the fact that whereas in 1914 France had 1,250,000 men between the ages of twenty and twenty-five, in 1940 she had only 600,000 in this vital age-group.

8. This wide discrepancy arises from the exact numbers of the obsolescent Mark I and Mark II tanks which the German Army 'retired' during the winter of 1939–40.

former head of the French Army's *Service Historique*) calculates the French total alone at '3,100 of which 2,285 were modern'. Thus, in overall tank numbers, the French and British jointly were actually superior.

Nor in quality of tanks was the gulf between the Wehrmacht and the Allies quite so wide as it had been two years previously. The mainstay of the German Panzer divisions was the light Mark II tank, which carried only a 20-mm. cannon; more than 1,400, or over half the total Panzers, were Marks I or II, while there were only 349 of the medium Mark III tanks, which carried a 37-mm. gun, and only 278 of the new 24-ton Mark IV, carrying a low-velocity 75-mm. gun. Against this, the French possessed their new, heavy (33-ton) 'B' tank – possibly the best of any nation in 1940 – and the fast, medium (20-ton) 'Somua'. The 'B' tank mounted a 47-mm. gun in a revolving turret and a 75-mm. mounted in the hull,[9] and had armour thicker than any German tank; the 'Somua' also mounted the high-velocity 47-mm. gun, with better penetrative power than any other gun of the period, and the numbers of these two tanks, despite all the delays in French production, totalled 800, or more than the Marks III and IV possessed by the Germans. (In addition, the 100 British infantry tanks in France were also more heavily armoured than their German counterparts, and their 2-pounder gun more potent than the Germans' 37-mm.) The defects of the 'Somua' and 'B' tanks were that their turrets were operated by one overworked commander-loader-gunner, compared with the two- or three-man turrets of the British and Germans; the 75-mm. of the 'B' tank (fired and aimed by the driver) could only be pointed laterally by moving the tank itself; and French gun-sights were inferior. The other modern models of tank principally employed by the French were the R.35 (Renault, model 1935) and the H.35 (Hotchkiss, model 1935), still mounting an old-fashioned, stubby 37-mm. gun that was useless against armour.

But the gravest defects of the French tanks still lay, as has been mentioned earlier, in their poor operating range and the fact that four-fifths of them carried no radio. Thus was their

9. In this design, it was a kind of stepfather to the American 'Grant' tank.

mobility badly impaired. Still weightier than any technical advantage, however, was the superiority of the German Panzer crews in training and doctrine. During the *Anschluss* of 1938, many German tanks[10] had broken down on the way to Austria and there was chaos on the roads. In the meantime, however, Hitler had had two years and two campaigns – Czechoslovakia and Poland – in which to put this right. He had not wasted his opportunities. Finally, worst of all, of course, was the way in which the French tanks were scattered: 700 to 800 in the cavalry divisions or D.L.M.s, 1,500 to 1,700 dispersed in independent battalions under the infantry. The remainder belonged to the three new armoured divisions, only formed in 1940,[11] and each contained just half as many tanks as the ten powerful Panzer divisions into which was concentrated all the German armour.

In anti-tank weapons, the German 37-mm. gunners would be hard pressed to make an impression on the heavier French tanks. But the much superior French 47-mm. was in such short supply that only sixteen divisions possessed any at all; the few that existed were drawn by fifteen-year-old converted tractors, but the ammunition was carried in trucks, so that the guns could move across country but not their ammunition. The older 25-mm. lacked punch, weighed half a ton and depended largely on horse transport. It too was short in numbers, with Corap's Ninth Army (which would need them most desperately) possessing only half of the established number of 25-mms. The situation in anti-tank mines was even worse; by some extraordinary omission, not one had been ordered in France before the war, and by May 1940 they were just beginning to reach the front-line forces. In artillery, France was numerically superior, with 11,200 guns to 7,710. But still as reliant upon the horse, so pathetically vulnerable from the air, as it had been in 1918, the French artillery was equipped with none of the self-propelled guns to be found in every German Panzer division.

10. Jodl claimed 70 per cent, though Guderian denies the number of breakdowns was even 'as high as 30 per cent'.

11. The 4th Armoured, whose command was later given to de Gaulle, was actually in process of formation when the Germans struck.

Aircraft

In anti-aircraft weapons, France's position was particularly deplorable. According to General Roton, 'on 10 May we possessed 17 guns of 90-mm. calibre'. Of light anti-aircraft, so vital in defence against dive-bombers, only 22 French divisions were equipped with the 20-mm. Oerlikon, and their allocation was a mere twelve pieces each; 13 other divisions had the new French 25-mm. anti-aircraft gun (six each), but these had only begun to arrive at the end of April, hardly time enough to give the crews adequate training. There were 39 batteries kept in reserve at Army level; otherwise the remainder of France's anti-aircraft defence was made up of 75-mms. left over from 1918. In contrast, against a total of just over 1,500 weapons, the Germans could mount 2,600 of the powerful 88-mm., and 6,700 light flak with which each Panzer and motorized division was plentifully endowed.

It was of course in the air that the most blatant inferiority of the Allies lay. By the spring of 1940, the Luftwaffe stood nearly at its peak. Despite the efforts of Raoul Dautry, in April the French aircraft industry was still only producing sixty planes a month,[12] the same quantity it had produced during September 1939. The relative merits of the opposing aircraft have already been discussed; in numbers the balance was now as follows:

	Germany[13]	France[13]	Britain (in France)[14]
Bombers	1,400	150–175	220
Dive-bombers	342	54	0
Fighters	1,000	700	130
Reconnaissance and scout planes	500	350–400	50

12. Although this was the month that, for the first time, British aircraft production actually surpassed Germany's.

13. These are to some extent approximate figures, as there remain considerable discrepancies over the number of German and French machines actually in line on 10 May. One more recent estimate puts the total of French single-seat fighters in line on that day at no more than 542, of which only half were Morane-Saulniers 406, and only 36 France's newest, and best, fighter, the Dewoitine 520.

14. Excluding planes based in Britain but used in France.

The French total was thus approximately 1,200, and the British deployed something over 600 in France, if one also took into account the aircraft of Bomber Command which could intervene in the battle. But according to General d'Astier de la Vigerie, who commanded the *Zone d'Opérations Aériennes Nord* (Z.O.A.N.), because of the French system of dispersal, his vital *Zone*, supporting Billotte's No. 1 Army Group, could only count on a total of 746 aircraft. Against this, Goering would be able to deploy 3,000–3,500 planes out of a grand total of 5,000, the remainder (including the Ju-52 transports) being kept in Norway or in reserve in Germany. What the Wehrmacht lacked in guns on the ground was more than made up for by its 'flying artillery'. In mobility and training, the Luftwaffe, with its experience in Spain and Poland, also had an incalculable advantage.

The French on the Meuse

The French forces which specifically would bear the weight of the German offensive, of Rundstedt's forty-five divisions spearheaded by those seven Panzers, were the Ninth Army of General Corap and the Second Army of General Huntziger.

As already noted, the function of the Ninth Army under Gamelin's 'Dyle–Breda Plan' was to wheel forward upon its pivot north of Sedan to hold the Belgian section of the Meuse running from Namur southwards, which would involve an advance of up to forty-five miles. The front Corap was expected to hold spanned approximately fifty air miles; but in fact, taking into account the sinuous twists and turns of the Meuse, it amounted to considerably more than this. For this task, he had only nine and a half divisions. There were two Light Cavalry Divisions (the 1st and 4th), plus the 3rd Spahi Brigade, a mixture of horses and light armour that could in no way stand up to a German Panzer division; these, acting as a reconnaissance screen, were to push into the Ardennes across the Meuse and absorb the first shock of a German attack while the infantry were taking up position along the Meuse.

Of Corap's seven infantry divisions holding this key sector of the front, only two, the 5th Motorized and 4th North African, were regulars; two (the 18th and 22nd) were 'A' series, which meant that only 23 per cent of their officers, 17 per cent of the N.C.O.s and 2 per cent of the men were regulars, the remainder reservists; two others (the 61st and 53rd) were 'B' series, which were composed almost exclusively of reservists (and the oldest reservists at that – men of forty unkindly nicknamed 'crocodiles' by the rest of the Army) commanded by generals called back from retirement; finally, one (the 102nd) was a fortress division of the kind to be found embedded in the Maginot Line, severely limited in its mobility.

Corap's mixed bag of an army comprised largely Normans and Bretons (good fighters, but very conscious of the past tendency of French commanders to commit them where other softer, more *meridional* troops might fail), men from the Loire and colonials from North Africa, Indo-China and Madagascar. Altogether, they had certainly not made a good impression on Lieutenant-General Alan Brooke, when he had attended an Armistice Day parade with Corap in November 1939. Beneath a monument on which was inscribed *'Ici triompha par sa ténacité le Poilu!'*, Brooke watched Corap's guard of honour march past:

> I can still see those troops now. Seldom have I seen anything more slovenly and badly turned out. Men unshaven, horses ungroomed, clothes and saddlery that did not fit, vehicles dirty, and complete lack of pride in themselves or their units. What shook me most, however, was the look in the men's faces, disgruntled and insubordinate looks, and, although ordered to give 'Eyes Left,' hardly a man bothered to do so. After the ceremony was over Corap invited me to visit some of his defences in the Forêt de St Michel. There we found a half-constructed and very poor anti-tank ditch with no defences to cover it. By way of conversation I said that I supposed he would cover this ditch with the fire from anti-tank pill-boxes. This question received the reply: *'Ah bah! on va les faire plus tard – allons, on va déjeuner!'*

The bitter, idle winter had certainly brought little improvement, while of the whole French front there was probably no other sector less densely held than Corap's. On a visit to the

Ninth Army, André Maurois was 'struck by their lack of numbers. Returning to Vervins, I had the feeling of traversing an abandoned country.'

At Dom-le-Mesnil, on the confluence of the Meuse and the Ardennes Canal about five miles downstream from Sedan, lay the boundary of the Ninth and Second Armies. General Huntziger's Second Army, whose role under the 'Dyle Plan' did not entail any advance into Belgium, consisted of only two army corps (plus a cavalry screen similar to Corap's).

It is, however, X Corps (General Grandsard) which principally concerns this story, as his was the one to be attacked by Guderian's Panzer spearhead at Sedan. To guard against an outflanking attack on the Maginot Line, Huntziger (disastrously) had deployed his best divisions on the right and his poorest on the left immediately behind Sedan, where they linked hands with Corap's indifferent forces. Grandsard's right wing was held by the regular 3rd North African Division, which would be almost left out of the crucial phase of the battle, while his left was held by the 55th Infantry Division, another 'B' series unit, and a poor one at that. Behind, in reserve, stood the 71st – also a 'B' division belonging to X Corps.

Quite early in the war, Huntziger, talking in confidence to an American volunteer ambulance driver, Florence Conrad, admitted that the poor morale of his troops was worrying him. Of the 55th and 71st Divisions, General Grandsard himself says:

. . . cases of ill-will were rare, but the ardour for work, for training and the desire to fight, were even rarer. Nonchalance was general; it was accompanied by the feeling that France could not be beaten, that Germany would be beaten without battle . . . the men are flabby and heavy . . . In the artillery the men are older, the training is mediocre . . .

The 55th (General Lafontaine), recruited in the region of Bourges, has been described as a 'poor relation' in terms of equipment;[15] it was particularly short in modern anti-aircraft

15. The best equipment having been siphoned off for the Seventh and First Armies in the north.

weapons. Of its 450 officers, only 20 were regulars, and this
included only the colonel of each infantry regiment, and 3 out
of 50 gunner officers. The 71st, recruited in Paris (including
some of the more red-tainted suburbs), was probably even more
mediocre than the 55th. On 10 May, owing to leave, sickness
and other causes, it could muster no more than 10,000 men out
of its normal establishment of 17,000, while (according to
General Ruby) its commander, General Baudet, 'brilliant once,
but now physically enfeebled, did not inspire confidence either
among his troops or their leaders. His replacement was a matter
of days.'

Thus three third-rate 'B' divisions, the 55th, the 71st and
Corap's 53rd, were left guarding the fateful sector of Sedan. It
was, as Gamelin mildly admits in his memoirs, a 'dangerous'
thing to do – and a heaven-sent gift for Guderian.

Football and Roses

Of the general state of French training and defence preparations during the bitter winter of the 'Phoney War', Churchill
comments how

visitors to the French front were often struck by the prevailing
atmosphere of calm aloofness, by the seemingly poor quality of
the work in hand, by the lack of visible activity of any kind. The
emptiness of the roads behind the line was in great contrast to the
continual coming and going which extended for miles behind the
British sector . . .[16]

This was an impression also shared by many Frenchmen,
soldiers and civilians. Instead of ardently studying and exercising upon the sober lessons of Poland, too many French troops
were employed in blancoing the kerbs and steps of their barracks, playing organized football, growing roses to embellish
the glacis of the Maginot forts, and, as spring came, tilling the
fields, by way of dispelling boredom. Writing to Simone de

16. It should not be forgotten, however, that the British Secretary of State
for War, Leslie Hore-Belisha, was sacked (in January) for criticizing the
poverty of the B.E.F. defence works.

Beauvoir from the front, Jean-Paul Sartre described his daily contribution to the war effort in terms that represented the futility shared by countless other French soldiers:

My work here consists of sending up balloons and then watching them through a pair of field glasses; this is called 'making a meteorological observation'. Afterwards I phone the battery artillery officers and tell them the wind direction; what they do with this information is their affair. The young ones make some use of the intelligence reports; the old school just shove them straight in the wastepaper basket . . . Since there isn't any shooting, either course is equally effective . . .

At Arras, André Maurois, on observing Territorials engaged in planting kitchen gardens and raising rabbits and pigs, inquired why they could not have been set to work fortifying the River Scarpe.[17] He was told 'The enemy will never advance that far. You are a defeatist!' Hans Habe, an Austrian refugee who had joined up in a regiment that would later be thrown into the Battle of Sedan, recalled the futility of training with hopelessly rusted rifles on a beach near Perpignan: '. . . hardly an ideal drill ground. At every step you sank up to your ankles in sand; it was impossible to set up a single machine-gun or dig a single trench.' The rare tank exercises had a habit of grinding to a halt, because the *Intendance* had not provided sufficient petrol in advance. Gamelin's G.Q.G. would issue instructions nineteen pages long on the conduct of patrol actions, while officers at the front wondered why on earth it was not holding exercises to simulate dive-bomber attacks, so that the troops could be made to realize that safety lay, not in running about in a panic, but in staying put in fox-holes and weapon-slits. And during all these months of Phoney War wasted by the French, on the German side second-, third- and fourth-line divisions were being transformed from what was described as 'an armed rabble' into fully operational units.

With Corap's and Huntziger's mediocre divisions protecting the Meuse – those who could most have benefited from intensive training – the picture was particularly depressing. The

17. Which the Panzers were to reach by the eleventh day of the offensive.

trouble was that the urgent need both for training of the reservists and for work on the deficient fortifications stood in direct conflict with each other. Four out of every five divisions were required in defending and working on the line all the time, so that on average only half a day per week could be devoted to firing practice and training, while after each of the numerous false alarms, training and works had been interrupted for five to six days. The Arctic weather conditions had also had their effect; Grandsard noted that it was not possible until the beginning of March to send two of his infantry regiments to the rear for three weeks' training. Instructors tended to be inexperienced, and, commenting on the 'general apathy' of the Second Army's 'B' divisions, General Ruby remarks that 'every exercise was considered as a vexation, all work as a fatigue. After several months of stagnation, nobody believed any more in the war . . .'

In France it has always been held against Pétain that, in March 1934, he was the one to declare the Ardennes 'impenetrable' (though why the French General Staff should have persisted in unquestioningly accepting this thesis is another matter!); but Pétain's rider, 'provided special dispositions are effected there', tends to be forgotten. By 10 May, just what 'special dispositions' had the men of the Second and Ninth Armies, 'soldiers become navvies', achieved? Some French staff officer had indeed suggested that the forest roads leading through the Ardennes towards the French frontier be blocked by the simple expedient of felling thousands of trees. But this had been rejected. Why? Because these roads had to be kept clear for the advance of the French cavalry screen. At Sedan itself, General Grandsard tells us, the Meuse at the beginning of the war had been guarded by only some forty bunkers of 'type Barbeyrac'. Carrying either two machine-guns, or a small anti-tank weapon and one machine-gun, these could stand up to nothing heavier than a 105-mm. shell. There were no concrete installations for command posts or for artillery positions. Not until 25 November was a first programme launched to double the number of bunkers. Work began only on 5 December, and by 10 January no more than a fifth of the 45,000 tons of material required had actually arrived. Then, too, the terrible cold rendered the pouring of concrete almost impossible, so that virtually two months of the winter programme had to be written off; and to add to its residual disgruntlement, the 71st Division was forced to remake over ten miles of slit trenches which winter had wrecked.

But why the delay in starting this urgent programme? Grandsard criticizes the idleness and softness of his men, and the lack of authority of the junior officers; but the most injurious factor seems to have lain in the protracted inability of Billotte and his army commanders to agree upon a standard type of fortification.

Meanwhile, in early March, Gamelin had received a prophetic letter from a Deputy, Pierre Taittinger, who had just completed a parliamentary inspection of the line. The defences at Sedan so shocked Taittinger and his colleagues that they foresaw it as a sector 'of misfortune for our forces'. Gamelin responded by reinforcing Givet, fifty miles down the Meuse, with a solitary battalion,[18] and ordained the construction of a line of *maisons fortes*, protecting Sedan midway between the Belgian frontier and the right bank of the Meuse. A *maison forte* was a small semi-disguised block of masonry with a thick layer of concrete in the ceiling; above was a superstructure providing living accommodation for its garrison of four to five men. They were supposed to resist any bombardment, but in fact one Stuka bomb or even a direct hit from a big German self-propelled gun would be sufficient to blow them apart. The garrisons of the *maisons fortes* tended to be selected from the 'undesirables' – grumblers and men under suspended sentence. It was a formula that hardly spoke for success; moreover, by 10 May, the right-bank line covering the Sedan 'bridgehead' was far from completed – as Rundstedt's keen-eyed photographic expert, Major von Stiotta, had spotted.

On 11 April, Huntziger, more anxious than ever about the state of the Sedan defences, begged Gamelin to send him four reserve divisions to speed the work. His request was refused.

18. Compared, by General Beaufre, to Marshal Bazaine 'laying one cannon at St Privat' in 1870.

Thus, by 10 May, only 54 out of 100 bunkers had been completed, representing an increase in density of from three to six per kilometre.[19] But, worst of all, most of those completed had still not received their steel doors or the armoured shields protecting the weapons embrasures. The latter were left inadequately protected by sandbags, gaping Achilles' heels for Guderian's high-velocity tank cannon to seek out; and the same deficiency applied to bunkers built on Corap's front.[20] On the vital heights behind Sedan, only one casemate mounting two 75-mm. guns – that at Bellevue – was ready when battle began. The standard of construction of many of the Meuse works also seems to have been deplorable. Sarraz-Bournet, a major on Gamelin's *Deuxième Bureau*, was appalled to discover that some new bunkers built by civilian contractors did not even have embrasures that overlooked the Meuse: 'Was this sabotage, or was it simple forgetfulness?' Near Givet, he found barbed-wire entanglements of which the stakes were so poorly planted in the ground that they hardly held: 'Nobody had ever taught the officer concerned to lay out wire; no senior officer of his unit had come to supervise his work . . .' On the Belgian frontier, Major Barlone recorded inspecting an anti-tank ditch so unimpressive that 'a quarter of an hour's bombardment and the earth would crumble away and would leave free passage, I fear, to any armoured vehicle'. To back up these inadequate anti-tank ditches, there were of course mines. General Ruby reckons, however, that Huntziger's Second Army would have required 100,000; it was allocated only 16,000. To make matters worse, by March it was discovered that those already laid were suffering from humidity, so they were lifted and stored in a dry place, and Ruby cannot swear that they were replaced by 10 May.

Little enough effort seems to have been made to camouflage or conceal the new construction work. By the beginning of

19. By comparison, Hitler's despised Siegfried Line could boast a density of between twenty and thirty.

20. Despite the fact that, as previously noted, G.Q.G. had been fully informed of what had happened to the Polish bunkers when attacked by the Panzers.

May, Grandsard admits that on his corps front 'the building zones had not been cleared up and remained clearly visible to aviation, and sometimes the mass of material even hindered fields of fire'. Marcel Lerecouvreux, serving with Huntziger's cavalry, recalls being shocked by the lack of security surrounding the defence works at Sedan; on Sundays the soldiers were frequently visited by young women whom they 'did not appear to have known for long'. How easy it would have been, he reflected, for the Germans to infiltrate among these ladies agents crossing over the open Belgian frontier only a few miles distant!

The 'Impenetrable' Ardennes

The success of any French defence along the Meuse would obviously depend to an important extent upon Belgian intentions for holding the Ardennes. The Belgians in fact had entrusted this large sector to no more than seven battalions of Chasseurs Ardennais, almost without reserves, which made the prospects of manning any 'continuous front', let alone any defence in depth, quite impossible. Their orders were, on being attacked in force, to destroy communications and then withdraw northwards (i.e. uncovering the French positions on the Meuse), so as to link up with the main body of the Belgian Army. Of the fortifications on the Liège–Arlon line, Paul Reynaud quotes a Belgian general as having remarked: 'I piss on it, and I pass by!' The Belgian strategy was perfectly clear and intelligible; they did not reckon to have sufficient forces to protect their whole country, so they would concentrate on defending the centres of population and industry in the north, rather than the underpopulated wilderness of the Ardennes southwards of Liège. They hoped that the French cavalry would arrive in time and strength enough to secure the Ardennes. Citing the Belgian refusal, after 1936, to discuss their defence plans with the French High Command, French writers have blamed the 'surprise' at Sedan partially upon the Belgians, for not revealing that it was their intention to 'vanish' in the Ardennes. But the French *Deuxième Bureau* must have had a good idea of what the Belgian plan was, and one Belgian general, Wanty, goes so far as to claim that the whole French High Command from Gamelin down was fully aware of it.

What of the actual terrain across which Rundstedt's mighty mechanized phalanx was to advance, described by Petrarch six centuries previously as 'the savage and inhospitable forests from which warriors and arms emerge at great risk'? In August 1914, General Lanrezac of the French Fifth Army had warned the army commander on his right, de Langle de Cary, of the dangers which would confront his impending attack in the Ardennes: 'All this country is eminently suitable for the defensive and for ambushes ... you will not enter into this region, and if you do you will not return from it.' Langle plunged in, was ambushed, and reeled back with heavy losses. Although between the sixteenth and eighteenth centuries no fewer than ten successful military operations had been carried out in the 'inhospitable' Ardennes, it was Langle's unfortunate experience that made the most indelible impression upon the post-war French High Command, adorning the Ardennes with its reputation of being impenetrable.

There are indeed parts of the Ardennes which, extremely rugged, could constrict the passage of a large and cumbersome army. On stretches of the Meuse, as between Charleville and Givet, the approaches are protected from the east by sheer and rocky cliffs. At Dinant the river can be reached only through wooded, twisting gorges difficult for tanks to negotiate and easily blocked by resolute demolition teams. Sedan itself is protected by dense woods and a vulnerable road that winds for three to four miles up the gorge of the Semois from picturesque Bouillon, and all its eastern approaches are superbly overlooked from the Marfée heights west of the river, providing both a view and an observation point on which it would be hard to improve. But once up on the high plateau of the Ardennes, much of the landscape provides ideal tank country. The forests are interspersed with large clearings of rolling pasturage; the triangle Arlon–Bastogne–Neufchâteau, through which would run Guderian's main approach route beyond the Luxembourg frontier, is generally flat, wide-open country. Even the minor roads are good and well surfaced; nor was it generally true to say, as Gamelin claims in his memoirs, that the terrain 'did not permit infantry and tanks to deploy from the roads'. Even in the magnificent forests of oak and beech and fir where, in May, the wild raspberries are pushing up bright green shoots and the broom bursting into saffron explosions, there are numerous tracks cutting through them, readily viable to armoured vehicles. In fact, far from being a hindrance, here the thick boscage provides superb natural camouflage from the air, so that whole Panzer divisions could easily lose themselves to the enemy's sight, effecting a modern variant of Birnam Wood come to Dunsinane. To be sure, there are ravines and natural barriers such as the meandering River Semois, but none of any value unless backed by a powerful, organized defence. As Liddell Hart has remarked, all natural obstacles are more readily surmountable than those of human resistance.

Even allowing for the distortions of hindsight, after one has actually explored the terrain, it is hard to comprehend how anyone (except perhaps a *Deuxième Bureau* officer who had never set foot outside the Crillon Bar) could possibly have deemed the Ardennes 'impenetrable' for a modern army. It becomes still more extraordinary when one learns that, in 1938, manoeuvres were actually conducted under General Prételat (then commander designate of the Second Army) which *exactly paralleled* the German attack of May 1940. Hit by an imaginary seven German divisions, four of them motorized plus two tank brigades, debouching from the Ardennes, the French 'defence' in these manoeuvres was battered beyond possibility of re-establishing itself. The results were so decisive that at least one senior commander begged that they never be published, lest they 'upset the troops'. Studying the manoeuvres from the Citadel of Verdun, amid the opiate memories of those past miracles wrought by the French Army on the defensive, Gamelin had simply observed that adequate reinforcements would have been available in time for the enemy blow to be parried. Even General Ironside, the British C.I.G.S. who was hardly an outstanding military thinker, had predicted as early as October 1939 that the Ardennes might be selected by the

Germans as the sector for their main attack. It remains to be
explained why, despite the lessons of the Polish campaign,
despite admonitions by de Gaulle and by Taittinger, and despite
the repeated warnings leaking out about Hitler's intentions
during the spring of 1940, Gamelin appeared to remain blind
to the danger lurking in the dark woods of the Ardennes.

Was Gamelin Blind?

In 1940, one of the principal arms of military Intelligence was
aerial reconnaissance, and we have already seen what use the
Germans made of it to reveal the state of readiness of the
Meuse defences. Why were the Allied air forces, then, apparently unable to observe the massive concentrations of German
armour pointing towards the Ardennes? Every appeal made by
Air Marshal Barratt for permission to carry out high-altitude
reconnaissance flights across Belgium was turned down on
political grounds; needless to say, the Germans were not similarly impeded and are reported (by the Belgians) to have carried
out some five hundred flights in the eight months preceding
May 1940. But the French Air Force, flying north from Alsace-
Lorraine, could easily have reconnoitred the Eiffel and the vital
communications across the Rhine. Their failure to do so has
been variously attributed (by the French) to the inferiority of
their aircraft and the bad weather conditions of the winter of
1939–40.[21] After the loss of several planes, at the end of
September 1939 the Bloch 131s were withdrawn from daylight
operations and put on night work only, the Bréguet and Potez
reconnaissance planes were instructed to operate only 'behind
battery positions', and the Mureaux were permitted to 'approach between one and two kilometres from the lines, on condition that they operated in patrols of two'. General Ruby
writes that the French reconnaissance planes 'could not pass
over our lines except under fear of death'. Less charitably, Air
Marshal Barratt, who from the very first had been appalled at
the apathy and defeatism that he found in the French Air

21. Note, though, that the weather did not appear to halt Luftwaffe
operations.

Force, declared that their reconnaissance teams simply 'would not leave the floor, often they gave the *excuse* that the weather was too bad'. The fact is that, during the crucial month of April, only four French aircraft were lost through enemy action, hardly an excessively high price to have paid when one considers the mortal danger then confronting France.

Despite the shortcomings, however, of French aerial reconnaissance, G.Q.G.'s *Deuxième Bureau* had managed to acquire a remarkably accurate picture of the German order of battle – more complete perhaps even than the breakdown of the French forces prepared by the O.K.H.'s 'Foreign Armies West'. Already in March it had become aware of the German concentrations building up near Trier and in the area between the Rhine and Moselle; towards the end of March it reported that German Intelligence had suddenly begun inquiring about road conditions along the Sedan–Abbeville axis; a month later it knew the location of all the German Panzers, as well as of the three motorized divisions. From this massive accumulation facing the Ardennes – which, to shift elsewhere, would have required a major military operation – the French High Command should certainly have been entitled to suppose (and *know* beyond a shadow of a doubt, if it had studied Guderian's *Achtung – Panzer!*) in which direction the centre of gravity of an attack might be aimed. A Swiss military historian, Eddy Bauer, tells us that Swiss Intelligence had observed the construction of eight military bridges across the Rhine between Bonn and Bingen, and had deduced from this that the main thrust could not be coming in the north, or south through the Maginot Line; he claims that these facts were also known to the French. Probably on the basis of this Swiss Intelligence work, the French Military Attaché in Berne informed G.Q.G. on 30 April that the Germans were going to attack between 8 and 10 May, with Sedan as 'principal axis of the movement'.

All this various information was duly passed to Gamelin, but he remained sceptical; among other things, to the bitter end he insisted that the Germans were holding twice as many troops in Army Group 'C', opposite the Maginot Line, as his Intelligence experts stated, and that the O.K.H. was keeping forty-five – instead of twenty – divisions in reserve.

The blindness of Gamelin – and, for that matter, of Georges, Billotte and the weight of French generaldom – lay partly in the genuine belief that the defences at Sedan were adequate, based upon that ineradicable, mystical self-assurance of the invincibility, *in extremis*, of the French Army. But one must also take cognizance of the effectiveness of German deception measures, which were all part of the final *Sichelschnitt* plan. From February onwards, Admiral Canaris's Abwehr was deliberately spreading reports in neutral countries telling of war-weariness in Germany, and of how the Army would be incapable of sustaining a major offensive against the Allies;[22] less than a month before *Sichelschnitt* began, the German Military Attaché in Brussels was heard to discount any attack 'in depth', on grounds that 'we would have an initial success, but that would lead to nothing'. German 'travellers', beautiful women in night-clubs, indiscreetly talked about a German offensive coming along the old Schlieffen route. But the most highly organized deception plan was that carried out by Leeb's Army Group 'C'. Few officers in that group were even aware that it was a 'deception'; up to the last it was widely believed that they would be involved in an offensive at the southern end of the line, combined with much talk about Italy coming into the war and lending twenty divisions for such an attack. Around 20 April, the *Deuxième Bureau* picked up a speech by Goering in which he declared that the Maginot Line was going to be attacked at two points between 5 and 15 May and that the Germans were prepared to lose 500,000 men and 80 per cent of the Luftwaffe in pursuit of success. This mass of conflicting evidence relayed by the *Deuxième Bureau* was undoubtedly confusing to Gamelin, who could never shake from his mind the possibility of a serious enemy effort being made against the Maginot Line, or even one outflanking it via Switzerland. But the fact is that it was the latest reports, particularly that emanating from the French Military Attaché in Berne, which should have been believed.

As May brought the unleashing of *Sichelschnitt* ever closer,

22. Possibly his single most helpful contribution to Hitler during the war.

some remarkable warnings came out of Germany itself, the most accurate of which were received by the Dutch. Colonel Hans Oster, a senior officer in the Abwehr itself and one of the most active and courageous members of the German 'resistance',[23] was an intimate friend of Colonel Sas, the Dutch Military Attaché in Berlin. Four times between November and 10 May he provided Sas with precise warnings of Hitler's offensive plans; but the Dutch were mistrustful – partly because of the past false alarms, partly because they ardently *wanted* to believe that they would not be attacked. On 3 April, Oster had warned Sas (correctly) of the Norwegian operation; now, on 3 May, he told Oster that Holland was imminently to be attacked. The Dutch informed the Belgians, and took some measures to alert their Army. Sas would meet Oster once again, on the evening of 9 May.

On the Brink

Seldom had there been a more marvellous spring (though few cared to remember that it was just the same wonderful weather, 'Goering's weather', as had accompanied the rape of Poland the previous September). Parisians lingered in the pavement cafés, listening to the strains of *J'Attendrai* and dreaming nostalgically of last year's holidays. Clare Boothe went into raptures at how

chestnuts burst into leaf on the lovely avenues of Paris, sunlight danced off the opalescent grey buildings, and the gold and grey sunsets, glimpsed through the soaring Arc de Triomphe at the end of the long splendid vista of the Champs-Élysées, brought a catch of pain and pleasure in your throat.

There were art shows in the Grand Palais, racing at Auteuil, and soccer matches between Tommies and *poilus* in the suburbs. 'The shop windows of van Cleef and Arpels and Mauboussin and Cartier sparkled with great jewels in the sunlight,' she recalled. 'And lots of people bought them ...' The Ritz, as usual, was 'crowded with lovely ladies wearing simple dresses

23. Oster was executed in the aftermath of the July 1944 bomb plot.

or the smart uniforms of the *Union des Femmes de France* service'. There was also a wealthy Mrs Corrigan who wore a uniform of her own design, embroidered with her motto 'Bien
Venu!' There were meatless days, sugarless days, liquorless
days, no more luxury chocolates and the *pâtisseries* closed three
days a week, but none of this made too much difference to
Parisian gastronomy. On 2 May, says Fabre-Luce, 'Parisian
society gave its last party. It was a charity gala at the Marigny
Theatre . . .' The front seats were occupied by such dethroned
monarchs as the Duke of Windsor and King Zog of Albania.
About the same time, André Maurois found the Academy
peaceably working away on its eternal dictionary:

. . . the definition of the word *aile* led to a passage of arms between Abel Bonnard and Georges Duhamel. The previous edition
had called a wing 'a muscle'. 'It's perfectly ridiculous,' said Bonnard. 'A wing is a limb.' 'On the contrary,' said Dr Duhamel, 'a
wing is a muscle. What you eat in the wing of a chicken is the
muscle, no more and no less . . .'

And so the argument continued. Could anything, one might
have wondered, could anything alter the basic facts of French
life?

But underneath this veneer of 'business as usual', reality was
still all too evident to the discerning. Pierre Mendès-France,
returning on leave from Syria at the beginning of May, was
shocked at what he found:

Everyone, civilian and military, thought only of organizing his
personal life as well as possible in order to get through this seemingly indefinite period without too much risk, loss or discomfort
. . . One heard only of recreation for the Army, sport for the
Army, art and music for the Army, theatrical shows for the Army,
and so on . . .

(Meanwhile, in England Lady Astor had caused a stir in the
Commons by inquiring about the number of licensed French
brothels at the front.) Since January the amount of leave given
the French Army had been vastly augmented. In fact, on 7
May, Gamelin had actually restored normal leave throughout
the Army. Major Sarraz-Bournet of the *Deuxième Bureau*

recounts that 'Despite the warnings of Colonel Gauché, leave at the beginning of May had not been suspended, even at the *Grand Quartier Général*. I had myself gone off on the eve of Whitsun to go and spend a few days of a brief leave in the Dauphiné ...' But better leave conditions had certainly done little to boost morale. Sarraz-Bournet (whose job was to control postal censorship) detected a belief widespread in the Army by the spring of 1940 that the war would end 'without battle, by a diplomatic arrangement between the interested Governments ... nothing could have been worse for morale', while Major Barlone from Blanchard's élite First Army wrote in his diary on 30 April: 'The General advises us to look after the morale of our men; we must give them some distraction. The postal censorship shows that the men are fed up ...' Nevertheless, despite all the manifestly disturbing symptoms within the Army, at the beginning of May, General Billotte could still tell some of his corps commanders who had complained to him about arms deficiencies: 'Why bother yourselves? Nothing will happen before 1941!'

In Germany, rationing had cut food consumption to some 75 per cent of the pre-war average, but nobody was hungry. Over the winter, Joseph Harsch of the *Christian Science Monitor* remarked, Berliners had been kept 'in good humour' by a variety of 'Japanese tumblers, Italian aerial artistes, Hungarian folk orchestras and clever Viennese skits, often at the expense of the Party great'. After eight months during which they had not been attacked by the Allies, and particularly after the successes of the Norwegian campaign, German nerves were much restored. But still it was hard to find actual enthusiasm for the war. On Easter Sunday (24 March) William Shirer thought the faces of the Berliners 'looked blank. Obviously they do not like the war, but they will do what they're told. Die, for instance ...' On 19 April, the eve of Hitler's fifty-first birthday, Shirer found only some seventy-five people outside the Chancellery waiting for a glimpse of their Führer, whereas in other years 'there were ten thousand'. On 1 May, Shirer once again visited the Rhine front: 'all was quiet ... Not a single airplane could be seen in the skies.' His diary continues:

May 7. For three or four days now the German newspapers
have been carrying on a terrific campaign to convince somebody
that the Allies, having failed in Norway, are about to become
'aggressors' in some other part of Europe . . . Where is Germany
going in next? I'm suspicious of Holland, partly because it's the
one place not specifically mentioned in this propaganda campaign . . .

May 8. Could not help noticing a feeling of tension in the
Wilhelmstrasse to-day. Something is up, but we don't know
what . . .

May 9. Headlines increased in size to-night 'BRITAIN PLOTS
TO SPREAD THE WAR' they roar . . . it may well be, as many
people over here think, that the war will be fought and decided
before the summer is over. People somehow seem to feel that the
Whitsuntide holidays this week-end will be the last holidays
Europe will observe for some time.

At last, Hitler's Panzers were ready to roll. On 7 May he had
allowed Goering to extract one last postponement, on account
of the weather, from him – 'but not a day longer'. Then, on the
evening of 9 May, the Luftwaffe announced that 'the weather
on 10 May will be good'. Like the bearer of good tidings to
some oriental despot of bygone years, the head of the Meteorological Service earned a gold watch for his favourable report.
Inside the Chancellery and at both O.K.W. and O.K.H. headquarters, however, extreme nervousness prevailed. On the 9th,
Halder recorded anxiety aroused by 'alarming reports' from
Yugoslavia, purporting that French and British tanks had
landed there. Nevertheless, that evening Hitler and his entourage embarked on the 'Führer Special' from a small railway
station near Berlin, heading north. Only after dark would it
turn westwards, to bring Hitler to his specially prepared battle
H.Q. at Münstereifel, midway between Bonn and the Belgian
Ardennes. That night, at 2100 hours,[24] the O.K.W. transmitted
the codeword 'Danzig' to all the formations waiting expectantly
behind the western frontiers of the Reich, signifying that the
great offensive was to begin at 0535 hours the next morning. In
Berlin, Colonel Sas met his friend, Hans Oster, again – for the
last time. Oster remarked that, as there had been so many post-

24. German time, i.e. one hour ahead of French time.

ponements, it could just happen again; but if, by 2130, no counter-order were given, 'then this is finally it'. At 2130 the two colonels went to O.K.W. headquarters. Sas waited outside in the darkness. When Oster rejoined him, he told Sas that there had been no counter-order: 'The swine has gone off to the West Front ... Let's hope that we'll meet again after the war.' Using a prearranged code, Sas then telephoned The Hague. An hour and a half later he was rung back by the Dutch Chief of Intelligence, who said, doubtingly, 'I have just received the very bad news about the operation on your wife. Have you now spoken to all the doctors?' Sas, much vexed, replied, 'I don't understand why you bother me now under these circumstances. You know now. Nothing can be done any more about this operation. I have spoken to all the doctors.' He ended (though it seems extraordinary that German security should have allowed such a conversation to pass in clear down the telephone line): 'Tomorrow morning, at dawn, it takes place.' At three o'clock on the morning of the 10th, belatedly, the Dutch blew up the first of their frontier bridges.

In London, as 9 May, the 250th day of the war, came to a close, Neville Chamberlain had resigned; in Paris, Paul Reynaud had offered his resignation to President Lebrun, because Daladier would not let him sack Gamelin. Near Nîmes, Janet Teissier du Cros, a Scotswoman waiting for her French husband to come home on leave, read joyfully in a newspaper she picked up late on the night of the 9th: '*Détente en Holland*'. 'The cock-eyed war was going to last long enough to allow François to enjoy his leave,' she thought. 'Nothing else mattered ...' Nearer the front, the staff officers of General Huntziger's Second Army H.Q. had spent an agreeable evening watching a play performed by the *Théâtre aux Armées* at Vouziers. Gontaut-Biron, a mechanized Dragoon from the Third Army's 3rd Light Cavalry Division, which was to push into Luxembourg if the Germans attacked, recalled that his evening had been 'very gay ... We played bridge very late into the night. We had no fears about anything, we had been so often told that we would be warned at least twenty-four hours in advance by our Intelligence Service. Towards eleven o'clock in the even-

ing we separated, and went back to our respective quarters ...'
That same day, her acute journalistic instinct had persuaded
Clare Boothe to fly to Amsterdam: 'Motoring from Amsterdam to the Hague,' she recalled, 'you couldn't have told there
was a crisis, except in the wonderful tulip fields, which had
reached their maximum bloom and were about to wither.' She
reached Brussels that night, where she stayed with the American Ambassador, Cudahy. He told her: ' "I've been on the
telephone night and day. But now" – his voice sounded
strangely dubious, as though he himself did not quite believe it
– "it's over, thank God. The King has reinstated all his appoint-
ments for the week-end ..." ' Near Metz, on that last day of
the Phoney War, the Inspector-General of Artillery, General
Boris, had comforted artillery commanders of the Third Army
by telling them of the modern guns that would be ready 'next
spring'.

The following morning, Friday 10 May, on a tour of inspection of the sector, General Boris heard explosions: 'Is that a
manoeuvre?' he inquired. '*Mon général*, it's the German offensive,' came the reply. In Brussels, Clare Boothe was woken up
by a maid shaking her: ' "Wake up! The Germans are coming
again!" '

So the scene opens on the confrontation of the century, of
which the Great War – the Marne, Verdun, the Somme, Pas-
schendaele and Amiens – was perhaps but a thunderous overture. On one side, France, a nation divided and with little heart
for war, led by a Premier weakened by influenza and his mistress, who had offered his resignation, and by a Generalissimo
under suspended sentence; guarded by an Army whose morale
was to say the least patchy, weak in numbers and equipment,
guided by outdated doctrine and commanded by mediocre
leaders, and by an Air Force outclassed in every respect; and
supported by a solitary ally who could still only contribute a
handful of divisions to the coming battle. On the other side, a
revolutionary Germany led by a daemonic prophet possessed of
total self-assurance, but supported by professional soldiers
many of them nervous, hostile and not sharing their Führer's
certainty of success; equipped with a superlative war machine,

but with relatively far fewer élite divisions than the Kaiser's army which had lumbered into Belgium a generation earlier; and marching to one of the most brilliant war plans of all time – but one so risky that any serious setback to it, any breaking of the steel cutting-edge of Guderian's Panzers, could but end in another calamitous defeat for Germany.

Part Two

Chapter 9

The Crocus Blossoms

10 May

'When the crocus blossoms,' hiss the women in Berlin,
'He will press the button, and the battle will begin.
When the crocus blossoms, up the German knights will go,
 And flame and fume and filthiness will terminate the foe . . .
When the crocus blossoms, not a neutral will remain.'
 A. P. HERBERT, 'Spring Song'

The Germans Move

From the Eifel Mountains on the night of 9 May, a forty-eight-year-old major-general, Erwin Rommel, commanding the 7th Panzer Division which he had taken over less than three months previously, dashed off a brief note to his wife:

Dearest Lu,
 We're packing up at last. Let's hope not in vain. You'll get all the news for the next few days from the papers. Don't worry yourself. Everything will go all right.

All over western Germany, and far behind the Rhine, there were similar scenes of rapid 'packing up' and the writing of last letters. The élite Grossdeutschland Regiment, which was to play a key role in the coming battle, received a terse order from its commander, Lieutenant-Colonel Graf von Schwerin: 'Forward against the enemy! *Mit Gott! Es lebe der Führer!*' On returning from manoeuvres, Werner Flack, wireless sergeant in a horse-drawn unit that had fought in Poland, and who was hoping to get a day's pass to enjoy the gorgeous spring weather at Bingen-am-Rhein, was told by his *Feldwebel* that afternoon that the company was to move again in four hours' time. More manoeuvres? On reaching the wireless office, he found a type-written slip bearing the unit's action frequencies. Now knowing that it was the real thing, he recalled that 'The warmth and brilliance of the day was stunningly oppressive. But I saw neither the mountains nor the flowers, neither the meadows nor the sunshine. I simply pushed the sheet with the action frequencies on it into the Command folder.'

The conditions of secrecy and speed which Hitler had imposed after the Mechelen Incident were superbly fulfilled. Even commanders of units in the van of attack were kept ignorant of its timing until the last possible minute. On the afternoon of 7 May, for instance, Oskar Reile, an Abwehr officer stationed in Trier and charged with the important task of controlling undercover agents in Luxembourg, had asked for, and been granted, a few days' leave. His superior had requested him to stay in the neighbourhood, but added, 'As far as I can see, nothing special will happen in the next few days.' It was only on the afternoon of 9 May that Reile was recalled from his leave. Captain Graf von Kielmansegg,[1] the second staff officer at H.Q. of the 1st Panzer Division, which was to spearhead the attack on Sedan, noted that when they received their orders at lunchtime on the 9th, 'the division's officers were completely unprepared for the news'. Some had already left on Whitsun leave. Without them, the 1st Panzer departed from its quarters that night, driving with lights extinguished up the winding roads of the Eifel. One of the tankmen wrote:

With every hour that goes by, it becomes more lively on the approach roads, more and more troops quartered here in the Eifel are getting underway. We overtake marching, riding and driving columns. The noise of the motors gets on one's nerves in this night of uncertainty. The drivers must exert the utmost powers of vision, so as not to end up in the roadside ditches. It's pitch dark . . . Now we realize why we came here so often to carry out peace-time operations.

At 0430 [2] the 1st Panzer, bearing General Guderian with it, crossed the Luxembourg frontier near Vianden, where that famous propagandist of an earlier Franco–German war, Victor Hugo, had spent his declining years. But Guderian's men were

1. Later he became General, and Commander of Central Forces, NATO.
2. French time, which, together with British time, was one hour behind German time. French times are given throughout the rest of the narrative.

not the first Germans to enter the Grand Duchy; on previous days an unprecedented number of 'tourists' on bicycles and motor-cycles had been checked through by the unsuspecting frontier guards. Dispatched by the Abwehr, their role was to dislocate telephone communications, and prevent the Luxembourgers from destroying vital road junctions. Further to the north, Rommel and his 7th Panzer were swarming across the Belgian frontier, heading for Dinant on the Meuse, sixty-five miles away. Still further north, along the Dutch frontier facing Maastricht, German stormtroopers had nestled right up to the Dutch customs post. As the first light of dawn came up, the Dutch could hear the rumble of approaching tanks; the tension grew unbearable, but still the frontier guards continued to stroll quietly up and down, apparently noticing nothing. Then the rumbling grew louder and louder as squadron after squadron of Ju-52s, containing the whole of the German 22nd Airborne Division, plus some 4,000 paratroopers, passed overhead. Meanwhile, over the German radio that dawn came the usual martial music and the first news of the day's sporting events.

The Luftwaffe Attacks

The Luftwaffe bomber crews too had not been warned of the imminent offensive. Roused out of their beds during the early hours of 10 May, while it was still dark, they were ordered to attend briefings at fifteen minutes' notice. There was no time even to shave. Shortly before sunrise, every available aircraft left its field. Ranging far out, they laid mines off the Dutch and British coasts, struck at airfields in Holland, Belgium and France, and bombed road and railway centres deep in France. At Abbeville, a sugar warehouse was set on fire; burning for several days it produced rivers of treacle, which the inhabitants did not allow to go to waste. At the R.A.F. airfield of Conde-Vraux south of Rheims, Dorniers ('Flying Pencils') destroyed six of 114 Squadron's eighteen Blenheim bombers, all neatly lined up in a row, and rendered the remaining twelve unserviceable, though otherwise the R.A.F. were fortunate enough to sustain little serious damage on the ground that day. Altogether nearly fifty French airfields, in General d'Astier's Z.O.A.N. and behind Paris, were attacked that day. General d'Astier himself claims that all the fields were quickly restored, and that only four planes were destroyed and another thirty damaged. Three Heinkel 111s setting out to bomb Dijon strayed, and bombed the German city of Freiburg-im-Breisgau by mistake, killing fifty-seven civilians, including twenty-two children.[3]

It was against little Holland, however, that the main weight of Goering's fury was turned on the 10th. Flying over the Dutch pastures that morning, Theo Osterkamp, a fighter ace who had won the Pour le Mérite (Germany's highest decoration) in the First War, thought to himself how peaceful it all seemed:

. . . children playing by the stream, a white dog jumps around them barking, and they wave and laugh and are happy. How crazy! Why is this lovely peaceful land suddenly 'enemy territory'? . . . Why will those girls with rakes in their hands be threatening and screaming tomorrow, instead of waving with their coloured handkerchiefs and laughing?

The answer was not hard to arrive at, as at the same moment less idyllically-minded young Germans were already machine-gunning the streets of The Hague. Curving out into the North Sea so as to take the Dutch by surprise (not unlike the Israeli fighter-bombers of June 1967), the Heinkel 111s hammered the airfields at Amsterdam–Schiphol, Bergen op Zoom, and Rotterdam–Waalhaven. At Waalhaven bombs killed a large number of Dutch soldiers who, despite Colonel Sas's warning, and the ensuing alert, had been allowed to 'sleep on' in vulnerable hangars. Most of the few planes of the Dutch Air Force were wiped out. After the bombing and strafing came the paratroops and German airborne forces in what was to be the first major attempt in history to occupy and conquer a nation from the air.

3. Hitler immediately claimed that the bombers had been Allied, thereby providing himself with an admirable *quid pro quo* to excuse the launching of terror raids against Allied – as well as Belgian and Dutch – civilian centres. Goebbels's propaganda machine kept up the story of the Allied atrocity against Freiburg throughout the war, and it was not until several years afterwards that the whole truth was revealed.

With the main visible effort of the Luftwaffe concentrated over Holland, there was nothing here that might betray to Allied Intelligence the true direction of *Sichelschnitt*. Meanwhile, over the Panzers creeping slowly along the densely-packed roads of the Eifel and into the Ardennes, an immense fighter umbrella flew cover against any Allied 'spy' planes that might attempt to intrude. But few did.

To the vigilant Luftwaffe patrolling above, the roads leading towards Sedan and the Meuse presented the spectacle of a lifetime. Nose to bumper was the greatest concentration of tanks – between 1,200 and 1,500 of them – yet seen in war. Kleist's massive Armoured Group was moving forward in three blocks, one densely closed up behind the other. 'Like a giant phalanx,' remarked General von Blumentritt, Rundstedt's Chief of Operations, 'they stretched back for a hundred miles, the rear rank lying fifty miles to the *east* of the Rhine. Had this mass formation of Panzers been placed in single file, the tail-end would have been in Königsberg, in East Prussia, and the head of the column in Trier.' First came the tanks and the motorized infantry shock-troops; then the heavy supply echelons; and finally, far beyond the Rhine, singing lustily and marching against each other as if in competition, the infantry regiments whose job would be to hold and consolidate the ground conquered by the Panzers. It would be another two days before they would even reach the frontier. Occasionally the columns would be halted by a single vehicle breaking down. But such halts were rare; the moment a tank or a car showed signs of stalling, it was ruthlessly pushed off the road. Uneasily, the Panzer commanders, aware of what a superb target the dense, crawling columns presented, gazed up to the skies; but there they saw only the reassuring black crosses of the Luftwaffe.

Guderian

The passage of Guderian's column through Luxembourg took place smoothly and peacefully. *Feldwebel* Schwappacher of the Grossdeutschland Regiment, which was leading the Panzers across the Ardennes, recorded how the outlines of the last houses in the frontier town of Echternach

appear and fade in the early morning mists . . . An old grand-mother greets us happily and gives us her blessings for the forth-coming battle . . . The Luxembourgers try to blow up the bridge over the Sauer; it only half succeeded, so that our engineers were immediately able to put it back in order by using a few boards . . .

Other German soldiers were astonished to see farmers in the fields continuing to plough and barely raising their heads as the Panzers rumbled past. The 'tourists' of Admiral Canaris had performed their tasks well; there were few hold-ups caused by demolitions, while on the main Trier–Luxembourg road the advancing columns found several stretches that had been mined, but not detonated. The German engineers carried wooden ramps with them, specially designed to fit over the paltry Luxembourg tank obstacles, so that the Panzers could roll across them with the minimum delay. Backing up the Abwehr 'tourists' was the first of Hitler's 'special operations' brain-children. A detachment of 125 volunteers, commanded by Lieutenant Hedderich, had been landed before dawn by twenty-five Fieseler Storchs near Esch-sur-Alzette on the Franco-Luxembourg border with the task of holding this vital communication centre until Guderian's main force arrived. After halting and turning about a number of Luxembourg workers cycling to collect their Friday pay-packets, Hedderich's group were accosted by a bewildered but amicable gendarme who informed them that they were 'on neutral territory', and ordered them to leave it. He was quietly arrested. Narrowly missing the present Grand-Duke, Jean, who happened to be passing in a car, the Germans then settled down to wait for Guderian. By 0900 that morning the forward elements of the 1st Panzer had already reached the Belgian frontier after traversing the whole of Luxembourg. Hardly a shot had been fired; total Luxembourg casualties amounted to six gendarmes and one soldier wounded, seventy-five captured, none killed.

Rommel

Out beyond the right flank of Kleist's Armoured Group, the 5th Panzer reported that its first tank to cross the Belgian frontier had bravely managed to shoot up a group of unprepared Belgian infantrymen, lolling about on a frontier bridge. Later that morning the 5th was attacked by two enemy bombers, which dropped their bombs aimlessly in the woods. One was shot down by the German light flak, and a parachute opened. Just south of the 5th Panzer, Rommel was encountering elaborate obstructions prepared by the Belgians:

All roads and forest tracks had been permanently barricaded and deep craters blown in the main roads. But most of the road blocks were undefended by the Belgians, and it was thus in only a few places that my division was held up for any length of time. Many of the blocks could be by-passed by moving across country or over side roads. Elsewhere, all troops quickly set to work to deal with the obstructions and soon had the road clear.

Nevertheless, the Belgian frontier works, undefended as they were, proved sufficient to slow Rommel's advance down to six kilometres in three hours, a first setback which made the impatient Rommel distinctly nervous. Much of the Belgian demolition work had certainly been effected with consummate skill: bridges so well dynamited that their remains provided little of use for emergency bridges; roads blown up with charges dug so deep into their foundations as to make them completely impassable. At Martelange, just inside the Belgian frontier from Luxembourg, minefields and a destroyed river bridge presented the 1st Panzer with its first minor check, forcing it to postpone its attack on the Belgian main line of resistance until the following day. But, obeying their orders to the letter, the Belgian Chasseurs Ardennais, having completed their demolitions, withdrew from the scene. How much more the delicately balanced German timetable might have been thrown out of gear, even on the first day, if those frontier obstructions could have been supported by resolute covering fire! Here was perhaps the first of the painful consequences of Belgium's return to neutrality of 1936.

Operation 'Niwi'

So far the most demonstrative sequences in the land fighting on 10 May had followed from Hitler's airborne 'special operations', the first time that these had ever been employed in warfare on so large a scale. Lieutenant Hedderich's airborne commando dropped outside Esch in Luxembourg has already been mentioned, but further north in the Belgian Ardennes a more ambitious endeavour, Operation 'Niwi', was also under way. 'Niwi', so named because of the two villages concerned, involved a landing of some 400 men of the Grossdeutschland at Nives and Witry in the Belgian Ardennes, roughly midway between Neufchâteau, and the frontier towns of Bastogne and Martelange. Neufchâteau, sitting on a very commanding height with roads radiating out of it in all directions, was potentially a most important defensive position, and its rapid capture was also essential to Guderian's advance upon Sedan. Dispatched in two groups aboard ninety-eight of the light Fieseler Storchs, 'Niwi's' instructions were to keep open the roads running eastwards from Neufchâteau, impede the passage of enemy reinforcements through Neufchâteau, and aid the progress of Guderian's XIX Corps by attacking the Belgian frontier position from the rear. The Witry group, under the 'Niwi' commander, Lieutenant-Colonel Garski, landed according to schedule, but Captain Krüger's group heading for Nives was beset with the errors that so often plague airborne operations.

A sergeant with Krüger describes how 'soon after take-off we lost sight of the other Storchs flying with us . . . on the roads there is the endless worm of the Army stretching out. People wave to us . . . we land in Belgium on a meadow. It's the wrong place, and with loud curses from us the three machines take off again.' The pilots then spotted a Storch burning on the ground, and landed near it: 'there is a terrible muddle. The ammunition is taken into a near-by wood, the road barricaded.' Stunned Belgian passers-by told the lost detachment that they had landed near the village of Léglise, about nine miles from Nives and on the wrong side of Garski's group. 'Our defence measures are strengthened, machine-guns put in position . . . we requisition civilian cars . . . then suddenly our runner, Preusch, arrives with a bicycle; he has landed with the captain some two kilometres away.' They joined up with Krüger's group, but not with Garski and the rèst of the battalion until the afternoon. There was some sharp fighting against the Chasseurs Ardennais for possession of Witry, which finally fell at 1300 hours, at a cost of nineteen German casualties. A short time later contact was made with the advanced elements of the 1st Panzer. The approaches to Neufchâteau were open.

'Brandenburgers'

Although Operations 'Hedderich' and 'Niwi' were more fundamental, tactically, to the success of *Sichelschnitt*, events up in the north were certainly more colourful and eye-catching. Holland, with her small, weak Army,[4] based her defence upon the flooding of large areas and the destruction of bridges over the numerous canals. It was to forestall this that Hitler decided to strike swiftly, from behind. By the end of 10 May, General Student's airborne troops had succeeded in capturing the three key airfields of Ockenburg, Ypenburg, and Valkenburg which ring The Hague, though they had suffered setbacks and severe losses. They had also seized the important bridges over the Maas estuary (the Dutch extension of the Meuse) at Dordrecht and Moerdijk, and destroyed 62 of the Dutch Air Force's 125 planes. Meanwhile, to open up Holland to Bock's Panzers and infantry moving in from the east, some ruses had been resorted to that were particularly dear to Hitler's heart. As early as November 1939 he had first mooted the idea of seizing the vital Maas bridges by commandos dressed in Dutch uniforms. Canaris, although allegedly disapproving of the operation as being unethical, had provided the necessary uniforms. Their theft did not go unnoticed in Holland, where a newspaper even caricatured the uniform-loving Goering disguised as a Dutch tram-conductor, but otherwise the phlegmatic Dutch were not disposed to let their suspicions be aroused. The troops for

4. In 1940 Holland, with a larger population, had an Army of only 250,000 men, compared to Belgium's 700,000.

this cloak-and-dagger role originated from a body with the cover name of *Bau- und Lehrkompanie Brandenburg*,[5] or 'Brandenburgers' as they were more commonly christened, which was to grow from a company to a battalion and later to a division during the course of the war. The 'Brandenburgers' had first been thought up at the time of the Czech crisis by Captain Theodor von Hippel, who had fought in Lettow-Vorbeck's brilliant guerilla campaign behind the British lines in East Africa in the First War. They were to infiltrate behind the Czech lines to link up with Sudeten 'patriots'. Thanks to Chamberlain, their services were never required. In October 1939, however, Canaris had instructed Hippel to set up the *Bau- und Lehrkompanie*, and their first service had been the capture intact of Danish bridges over the Belts.

The attempt on the Dutch bridges at Maastricht ended in dismal failure. There was a confused shoot-up, in which the leader of the bogus Dutchmen, Lieutenant Hocke, was killed; it was impossible to remove the explosive charges, and all three bridges blew up in the face of the waiting Panzers. When Canaris's Abwehr delegate arrived outside Maastricht, he found a depressing sight of mile upon mile of Panzers and vehicles jamming the roads, and it was not until mid-morning that an assault bridge could be thrown across the Maas. A similar fiasco took place at Arnhem where the 'Brandenburgers', to make up for their shortage of Dutch uniforms, utilized outlandish cardboard helmets and were immediately spotted. But at Gennep they were triumphant; under Lieutenant Walther three Dutch 'Fifth Columnists' dressed as policemen marched up to the bridge with a posse of 'captured' German P.O.W.s, fully equipped with machine-pistols and grenades under their Army overcoats, and succeeded in securing the bridge from the surprised defenders. Walther's seizure of the bridge at Gennep had important enough consequences;

5. 'Construction and Training Company'. Quite by coincidence, the Germans who had pulled off without loss the greatest *coup de main* of the First War, the capture of Verdun's Fort Douaumont, the world's most powerful fortification, were also 'Brandenburgers', in that they came from III Brandenburg Corps.

across it the 9th Panzer Division rushed to interpose itself between the Dutch Army and General Giraud's Seventh Army, to forestall Gamelin's 'Breda Variant'; while at the same time General von Reichenau was able to divert northwards to Gennep some of the units of his Sixth Army bogged down before Maastricht. The *Blitzkrieg* rolled into Holland.

Meanwhile, it was also the 'Brandenburgers' who were charged with securing some twenty-four objectives in Belgium, including bridges and viaducts and the tracing-out of minefields which had previously been reported by German agents. At St Vith, on Rommel's route to Dinant, Captain Rudloff, who had been studying the habits of the Belgian frontier guards minutely over the previous weeks, was particularly successful. There had been some wild shooting in the railway station, during which a locomotive managed to take off to give the warning; but otherwise three out of four of St Vith's bridges fell intact into German hands. For their achievements, 3 Company of the 'Brandenburgers' received no fewer than ninety-two Iron Crosses.

Eben Emael

But the single most striking episode of 10 May was undoubtedly the capture of the Belgian Fort Eben Emael. The nearest equivalent in 1940 to Verdun's Fort Douaumont of 1916, Eben Emael was the northernmost fortification guarding Liège and the linchpin of the Albert Canal position, along which Gamelin anticipated the Belgians could hold the Germans at bay for five days, until the French and B.E.F. could be established, a calculation that formed the whole basis of the Allied Dyle–Breda Plan. It was also a vital factor of Hitler's *Sichelschnitt* that such a delay in the north should not occur, for until the powerful mechanized forces belonging to the French First Army were inextricably engaged by frontal attack there, there would always exist the grave danger that they could be diverted to strike the vulnerable northern flank of the main German breakthrough at Sedan. Therefore, for both sides, a very great deal depended on Eben Emael.

Completed as recently as 1935, the fort measured some 900 yards by 700, and was protected by an enormous cutting which fell 120 feet, sheer and unassailable, into the Albert Canal. In various single and double turrets, it mounted nearly a dozen pieces of artillery from 75-mms. to 120-mms., as well as numerous light cannon and machine-guns, and safely underground it contained a full battalion of troops. No single fort of the Maginot Line was as powerful. But like all fixed, unmanoeuvrable and supposedly invincible strongholds, it had its Achilles' heel: it possessed virtually no anti-aircraft defences, and the actual surface of the fort itself was unmined.

The mission of capturing Eben Emael was entrusted to the 'Koch Storm Detachment', consisting entirely of volunteer sappers, who, under Captain Koch, had been trained at Hildesheim in the most rigid secrecy since November 1939. Its members had been allowed no leave, were forbidden to mix with men of other units and had been sworn to secrecy under pain of death. Initially they had practised their attack on models, and later on bunkers of the Czechs' Sudeten fortress system, so that by May they knew every detail of Eben Emael in their sleep – except its name. At 0330 on 10 May, while it was still dark, they took off from Cologne in eleven large gliders, each carrying seven to eight men and towed by a Ju-52. The gliders were piloted by some of the star German pilots of peace-time gliding competitions – a sport at which Germany, on account of the Versailles limitations, had long excelled – including the former world champion, Sergeant Bräutigam. The reason for employing gliders was simple: in the dusk, they could cover the thirteen odd miles across the frontier unheard and unseen, and could land on top of the fort itself within twenty yards of a given spot. The superbly precise timing allowed them to land on Eben Emael just five minutes before the bulk of the Wehrmacht crossed the frontier. After circling to gain height, the Ju-52s followed a line of beacons to Aachen where they cast off the gliders from a height of 8,000 feet. They flew on, dropping quantities of parachute 'dummies' stuffed with fire-crackers, to confuse the Belgian defenders. At Eben Emael, the Belgian sentries heard

Dutch anti-aircraft fire over the Maastricht appendix, but heard or saw nothing else, until suddenly, like great black birds that seemed to hang almost motionless in the air, the gliders were on top of them.

For all its minute planning, however, the operation nearly failed when the tow-ropes of two of the gliders snapped, including the one containing the expedition commander, Lieutenant Rudolf Witzig, himself. One landed near Düren, midway between Aachen and Cologne, and its disgruntled members were forced to join up on foot with the advancing ground forces. Witzig landed in a field not far from Cologne; with commendable energy, he prepared a field by chopping down willow hedges and called up another Ju-52 to tow him off. He arrived safely at Eben Emael to find that, no doubt as a by-product of the superb training they had undergone, his Sergeant-Major, Wenzel, already had the situation well in hand, having landed unopposed plumb on top of the fort. Swiftly the German engineers blasted the thick steel carapaces which protected the subterranean gun turrets, using (for the first time) powerful hollow charges. One by one Eben Emael's turrets and gun casemates were knocked out in this fashion; the heavy twin 120-mm. turret, whose armour proved too thick for the hollow charges, was dispatched by the simple device of poking explosive charges down the barrels. Some time was wasted on two turrets which proved to be dummies, but by the time Lieutenant Witzig reached Eben Emael the mighty fort had been blinded and its teeth drawn. Near-by Belgian artillery opened heavy fire on the Germans on the fort glacis, but no really dangerous counter-attack had been mounted by the battalion-strong infantry garrison, nor any mines or other obstacles encountered. Witzig now entered the fort to clean up inside. Meanwhile, other detachments of Koch's glider-borne engineers had seized two near-by bridges over the Albert Canal. All through the night of 10–11 May the garrison of Eben Emael held out, while Belgian infantry from outside the fort attempted to dislodge the Germans. The situation for Witzig's eighty-five men was becoming precarious when, at 0600 hours on the 11th, they were relieved by the

advance troops of Reichenau's Sixth Army. Six hours later
Eben Emael surrendered, and 1,100 men were taken prisoner.
In the fighting the Belgians lost 23 killed and 59 wounded;
Witzig, 6 dead and 15 wounded. Hitler promptly awarded
Koch and Witzig [6] (then only twenty-four) the Ritterkreuz,
one of Germany's highest decorations.

Of all the successes of 10 May, none pleased Hitler more
than the capture of Eben Emael. His pleasure was indeed
justified. It was undoubtedly one of the boldest *coups* of war,
more brilliant even than the seizure of Fort Douaumont in
1916, which fell virtually by accident. Its capture meant that
within thirty hours the Germans had already breached the
Albert Canal line and thrown into jeopardy the whole of
Gamelin's strategy. But, as already noted, this tactical success
only concerned the secondary part of the German plan. Of
still greater importance was the psychological impact of the
sudden collapse of Eben Emael. Cunningly, Goebbels's propaganda machine, suppressing all mention of Witzig's hollow
charges, made mysterious capital by referring to a 'new
method of attack'. The refrain was promptly taken up in the
Allied camp and dark rumours circulated about secret
weapons, such as nerve gases. Even a year later an American
magazine was claiming that Eben Emael had been blown up
by Germans who in peace-time had grown chicory in nearby
caves, which they treacherously filled with explosives! Coming so soon after Hitler's extraordinary successes in Norway,
talk about 'secret weapons' at Eben Emael left a nasty feeling
in the pit of French stomachs; if the Germans could deal thus
with the world's strongest single fort, what would be the fate
of the impregnable Maginot Line? Eyes became nervously
diverted there – eyes that should have been fixed in gaze upon
the danger hourly mounting in the Ardennes. Meanwhile, the
employment of the handful of 'Brandenburgers' disguised in
Dutch uniforms was itself to achieve a major success of
psychological warfare for Hitler. Like wildfire, the rumours of
ubiquitous Fifth Columnists – nuns in hobnailed boots, priests

6. After the war Witzig rejoined the Army and ended his career commanding a wing of the Engineer School of the Bundeswehr.

with machine-pistols under their *soutanes* – spread through Holland, and then into Belgium and France, carrying paralysis and demoralization in their wake like the germs of a deadly plague.

The Allies Move

In London, at 6 a.m. on the morning of the German attack, Sir Samuel Hoare visited Churchill – still waiting to be summoned by the King to form a government – at the Admiralty. He was smoking a cigar and eating fried eggs and bacon as if nothing serious had occurred. Two hours later the War Cabinet met to discuss events on the Continent, and Churchill with supreme calmness insisted that the Cabinet listen to a report he wanted to make on a 'homing A.A. fuse'. The Cabinet listened. ('We are impossible!' exclaimed General Ironside.)

On hearing the news in Paris, Paul Reynaud swiftly agreed with President Lebrun that it was no time for the Government to fall, and withdrew his letter of resignation. Equally, he agreed that it was now inopportune to switch commanders-in-chief, and to Gamelin he addressed a brief conciliatory note: '*Mon général*, the battle is engaged. Only one thing matters; to win it. We shall all work for this end together, with a single heart.' Speaking to the nation over the radio, he declared bravely, 'The French Army has drawn its sword; France is gathering herself', and then pleaded for national unity in the coming crisis. Privately he expressed concern about the projected Allied advance into Belgium; to Baudouin he admitted: 'I am disturbed. We shall see what Gamelin is worth.'

At Vincennes, from 0100 onwards, G.Q.G. had been kept in a state of alert by reports from Luxembourg of suspicious German troop movements. Then at 0505 hours, the sirens had begun to wail. Warned of the German attack by his *chef de cabinet*, Colonel Petitbon, Gamelin came down to his office. According to one of his staff, 'his face revealed no apparent emotion, no interior disquiet'. Toward 0700 Gamelin gave the order for the Dyle–Breda Plan to get under way. Captain André Beaufre, visiting Vincennes from General Doumenc's G.H.Q. staff, saw Gamelin

pacing up and down the corridor of the barracks, humming audibly with a martial air . . . It has been said since that he had foreseen defeat, but I can scarcely believe that this was his state of mind at that moment.

The Secretary-General of the Department of War was later heard to remark:

If you had seen, as I have done this morning, the broad smile of General Gamelin when he told me the direction of the enemy attack, you would feel no uneasiness. The Germans have provided him with just the opportunity which he was awaiting.

To the men under his command he drafted an Order of the Day, ending symbolically with a reiteration of Pétain's immortal words at Verdun: '*Nous les aurons!*' But somehow the message seemed banal and lacked the C.-in-C.'s customary fluent ease. After a hasty breakfast, Gamelin drove to General Georges's H.Q. at La Ferté. There he heard a report sent from a French colonel attached to the King of the Belgians that 'a rather serious incident has occurred at Fort Eben Emael'. Otherwise the impression given by the news for the remainder of that day, as it reached G.Q.G., seemed 'favourable'.

Up at the front, Lieutenant Jamet's comment in his diary on hearing of the German attack was simply. 'So it's war at last?', and it was a reaction widely shared among the soldiers of No. 1 Army Group as they prepared to move into Belgium. As the eight months of Phoney War ended, apprehension was not entirely unmixed with relief. On receiving his orders to march up to the Dyle Line, Lieutenant-General Alan Brooke of the B.E.F.'s II Corps recorded that 'it was hard to believe on a glorious spring day, with all nature looking its best, that we were taking the first step towards . . . one of the greatest battles of history'. General Prioux of the French Cavalry Corps noted with pride the admirable route discipline of his units, and their encouraging lack of mechanical breakdowns. The air-liaison colonel accompanying him also expressed admiration, but added apologetically how sad it made him to see such fine men and equipment granted such miserable air cover. That night, after a smooth advance of seventy-five to ninety-five miles, Prioux's corps reached the Dyle Line according to schedule. But he was horrified to find there a complete absence of any defensive work, such as he had been led to believe the Belgians had promised.

Ninth Army

On General Corap's Ninth Army front, the infantry divisions marched forward as planned to line up along the Belgian sector of the Meuse, while the cavalry screen fanned out ahead of them into the Ardennes. Lieutenant Georges Kosak of the 4th D.C.L. recalled their rapidly altering reception as they entered Belgium on the morning of the 10th:

At first we pass through several small villages where the people did not seem to be informed about events; then important centres where the population mass on the sidewalks and at the windows greeting us frenziedly. French flags and garlands were hung from all windows. Women have their arms full of flowers, and their aprons full of packets of cigarettes, sweets and chocolates . . . It is very moving. Our hearts beat; an immense pride overcomes us . . .

On crossing the Meuse, like General Alan Brooke, Kosak found it hard to believe that the battle had really begun: 'everything is so gay and sunny'. But on reaching the small town of Ciney, just forty-five air miles from the German frontier and towards which Rommel's Panzers were already advancing,

a strange feeling comes over us; the streets are quiet and silent, the shutters are closed, and a few curious onlookers watch us pass without showing any emotion . . . the atmosphere is indifferent, if not hostile; our men have become watchful and serious. After Ciney, no longer any songs, no longer any laughter . . .

The advance of Corap's infantry progressed somewhat less

smoothly. Inexcusably, General Martin's XI Corps seems to have been taken by surprise. The 22nd Division had a number of battalions absent on exercises; in order to regroup themselves, some had to march twelve miles on foot, thus losing nearly twenty-four hours. The 18th Division, which had to cover over fifty-five miles in order to reach its positions around Dinant (compared with the seventy-five miles facing Rommel), could only rush up two battalions by truck on the first day. The rest of the 18th would not be in position until 14 May; but then it was reckoned that the enemy could not possibly reach the Meuse until the morning of the 16th at the earliest. Meanwhile, on leaving its frontier positions, XI Corps was ordered to lock up all bunkers there and hand the keys to the staff of the 53rd Division. But this division, held in reserve by Corap, was subsequently moved southwards. The bunkers were to remain locked, and inaccessible.

Second Army

Although the cavalry divisions of the Ninth and Second Armies were supposed to work closely together, in fact liaison between them was extremely poor from the beginning. On Huntzigers Second Army front, the cavalry screen at once advanced far ahead of Corap's, and it was on this sector that the first direct confrontation of the Battle of France between French and German troops took place. Covering the Arlon gap, the advance guard of the 2nd D.C.L. came up against reconnaissance troops of Guderian's left-hand Panzer division near Habay-la-Neuve (about eight miles north-west of Arlon) at 0900 hours on the 10th. There was confused fighting in the area, during which a German regimental commander, Lieutenant-Colonel Ehermann, was killed. At Étalle, a French detachment had its 25-mm. anti-tank gun destroyed the moment it was put into action; it was encircled and crushed after a brief street fight with the Grossdeutschland Regiment. 'To our right, a group of French marching into position in a field of clover,' a German rifleman of the Grossdeutschland wrote of this first encounter.

They look at us in astonishment; we ourselves don't exactly look at them cheerfully – are we to shoot? . . . Major Föst gives the order to fire! . . . One of the French somersaults in the clover, the first dead man, who looks completely white. Dead! . . . something cold grips us around the heart. We will have to get used to that yet . . .

There was more shooting around Étalle, during which Major Föst, a veteran of 1914–18, was killed and several men wounded. Because of their immobility, the 2nd D.L.C. was unable to bring up its 105-mm. guns in time to give support, and by mid-afternoon it was forced to abandon Arlon. By nightfall, scattered over far too wide an area and badly shaken by its first engagements, the 2nd D.L.C. had fallen back on the River Semois, the last serious barrier in the southern Ardennes beyond the French frontier.

Meanwhile, at about the same time, on the right of the 2nd D.L.C., the 3rd D.L.C. (belonging to General Condé's Third Army), passing the Luxembourg grand-ducal family on its flight westward, had fought a sharp engagement at Esch against Lieutenant Hedderich's group, which it at first erroneously reported as 'Fifth Columnists'. By 0900 hours, a French machine-gun carrier and a tank having been blown up by land-mines, the 3rd D.L.C. decided it could not force Hedderich's hastily constructed barriers, and sent its H.35 tanks to try to block the roads entering Esch from the north and east. A French dragoon, Captain Gontaut-Biron, describes how the tanks were brought under fire by

very numerous anti-tank guns . . . while the enemy artillery pinned us down on the positions we had acquired . . . the enemy was there before us with very superior forces, and greatly helped by numerous formations of the Fifth Column in Esch-sur-Alzette which continued to fire on all isolated men . . .

In fact, Hedderich's ninety men, plus the light forward ground elements that came to reinforce them, were heavily outnumbered throughout the day. Nevertheless that evening the French withdrew from Esch, their withdrawal acutely complicated by some 25,000 desperate civilians attempting to escape down the only route towards the French frontier. It was the first of such experiences with uncontrollably panicking refugees that were to bedevil the French Army for the rest of the campaign.

On Huntziger's left, the 5th D.L.C. had the task of covering the open country in the area Neufchâteau–Libramont–Bastogne. It was through here that the route of Guderian's main force lay, but because of the hold-ups inflicted by the Belgian demolitions at Martelange, the 5th D.L.C. was able to fulfil its objective for the 10th without any serious fighting. Meanwhile that day General Huntziger himself had driven up to Bouillon, the ravishing Crusader fortress on the Semois, to inform himself of the situation in the Ardennes. He was somewhat surprised by the Belgian mayor who, when requested that one of Bouillon's hotels be turned into a field hospital, replied in astonishment: 'But, *mon général*, Bouillon is a summer resort, our hotels are reserved for tourists.' Nevertheless, General Ruby tells us that Huntziger returned to his H.Q. at Senuc 'in general satisfied with the course of the day'. That night, however, aerial reconnaissance reports reached Senuc which identified two large mechanized masses of the enemy crossing into the Ardennes, apparently menacing both Sedan and Carignan to the south-east.

By the evening of 10 May, General Kayaert's Belgian Chasseurs Ardennais in front of Huntziger, in obedience to their instructions, had withdrawn northwards, leaving a vacuum between the French cavalry and Guderian's Panzers. Only on Corap's front did they stay to fight a bitter action, thereby inflicting upon Rommel his first setback of the campaign. That night he had intended to reach the River Ourthe, but just as night was falling he was held up by a spirited defence at Chabrehez, some twelve miles inside the Belgian frontier and about the same from the Ourthe. Here part of the 3rd Regiment of Chasseurs Ardennais was dug in in well-sited fieldworks, amid heavily contoured country ideally suited for the defence. Though they had no anti-tank weapons, the Belgians courageously kept up a disturbingly accurate fire on Rommel's 7th Motorcycle Battalion. Frustrated, Rommel was forced to abandon his aim of reaching the Ourthe that night, and Corap's cavalry were granted a respite to move up behind the river without meeting the Germans that day.

Allied Air Effort

The Luftwaffe's early-morning attacks on air bases in France on 10 May had been followed by a dismal tardiness to mount any riposte in the air on the part of the Allies, and damage done to airfields was by no means the chief cause of this. We are told, for instance, that the powerful *Groupe d'Assaut* I/54, equipped with Bréguet attack-bombers and located in a well-placed base midway between Paris and Châlons-sur-Marne, received no instructions until midday on the 10th. Then a written order arrived, earmarking it for operations over northern Belgium and shifting it to Montdidier. But no movement order arrived until the following day, with the result that *Groupe* I/54 was not in action until the 12th. Almost the whole of the fighter strength of General d'Astier's Z.O.A.N., plus strong support from R.A.F. Hurricanes based in England, had been ordered by General Gamelin, who was still obsessed with the importance of his left-flank movement, to cover General Giraud's Seventh Army racing up to Breda, while only two French fighter *groupes*, totalling thirty-seven planes, were dispatched for the support of the Ninth and second Armies.

In their joint air H.Q. at Chauny, General d'Astier and Air Marshal Barratt had spent the morning fretting with frustration. At 0800 they had received the following order from G.Q.G.: 'Air limited to fighters and reconnaissance.' This meant that, during the very hours when the massed German columns crowding the Ardennes roads would be most vulnerable to it, they were immune from air attack. It was not until 1100 that the Allied air commanders received authority to bomb enemy columns (first priority) and airfields (second priority), and even this authorization contained a rider added by General Georges: 'At all costs avoid bombing built-up areas.' Motivated by the deep French dread of Luftwaffe reprisals, and predicated by Gamelin's utterly unrealistic hopes that a 'bombing war' could somehow be avoided, it meant that Allied pilots were hamstrung by their inability to bomb the Panzers as they were passing through, or halted in, the innumerable hamlets on their route.

Overcome by impatience at the lethargy of the French Air Force, Air Marshal Barratt finally took matters in to his own hands and independently ordered a first flight of Fairey Battle bombers to attack Guderian's columns advancing through Luxembourg. Barratt's Battles were the only bombers to strike there that day. Attacking without fighter support at very low altitudes, the Battles were met by a hurricane of fire from the German light flak on the ground, and pounced upon by hovering Me-109s. Immediately the Battle revealed its extreme vulnerability to attack from below, which was to prove tragically costly later at Sedan. Of the first eight Battles to attack, three were immediately shot down. More returned to make low-altitude runs that afternoon, and of thirty-two Battles dispatched that day, thirteen were destroyed and all the remaining nineteen damaged.

That night a massive Franco-British operation, in which Bomber Command was to participate from Britain, was also torpedoed by General Georges's veto. Eventually, attacks were limited to the R.A.F. bombing three airfields in Holland and a few French Amiots scattering bombs on German airfields and roads west of the Rhine. By the end of the 10th Air Marshal Barratt's temper was barely under control, his view of his apparently torpid ally all but unprintable.

Hitler Weeps for Joy

As 10 May drew to a close, behind the scenes on the German side Hitler was well satisfied with the day's events. As his train had arived at his *Felsennest* [7] in the Eifel that morning, the Luftwaffe had been roaring overhead, going and returning on its sorties to destroy Allied air bases. When later the

7. Literally 'crag's nest'. Hitler had a passion for giving his headquarters gothically romantic names.

O.K.W. Intelligence informed him that Gamelin had already reacted to the 'matador's cloak' in the hoped-for fashion by rushing into Belgium, Hitler, after a sleepless night, was enraptured:

I could have wept for joy; they'd fallen into the trap! It had been a clever piece of work to attack Liège. How lovely *Felsennest* was! The birds in the morning, the view over the road up which the columns were advancing, the squadrons of planes overhead. There, I knew just what I was doing!

In his diary that night, General Halder commented succinctly on the advance of Kleist's Armoured Group: 'Very good marching achievements.'

Closer to the front, however, opinions were not quite so sanguine. In the Ardennes, despite the feebleness of the enemy reaction, there had been worrying bottlenecks and traffic snarl-ups, and only the superb organization and route discipline had prevented real chaos on the overloaded roads. What might have happened if Kleist's Panzers had not had behind them the indispensable experience of the Austrian and Czech approach marches, and the Polish campaign, and if the Allies had attacked relentlessly from the air, surpasses the imagination. As it was, Rommel's hold-up at Chabrehez meant that Hoth's Panzer Corps on the northern flank of the thrust had failed to attain the day's objective; while in the south, the Belgian frontier demolitions had caused the impetuous Guderian to fall behind schedule. And every minute counted! In fact, at Kleist's H.Q. that night serious fears were expressed that the delays might have sufficed to give the French a good chance of regaining their balance. There had also been a first tactical disagreement between Kleist and Guderian. Taking an exaggerated view of the threat presented to his southern flank by the efforts of the French 2nd D.L.C., Kleist ordered the 10th Panzer to swing off course and move on Longwy instead of Sedan. Infuriated, Guderian demanded that the order be withdrawn, expostulating that 'the detachment of one-third of my force to meet the hypothetical threat of enemy cavalry would endanger the success of the Meuse crossing and therefore of the whole operation'. Guderian won, but Kleist remained anxious.

Thus, at the end of the first day, one finds a curious inversion of moods: in Gamelin's G.Q.G., complacent optimism; in Kleist's battle H.Q., nervous pessimism.

Chapter 10

Through the Ardennes

11 May

Soldiers of the West Front! The hour of the most decisive battle of the future of the German nation has come.

For three hundred years it was the aim of British and French Governments to hinder every workable consolidation of Europe, and above all to keep Germany in weakness and impotence . . .

Soldiers of the West Front! With this, the hour has come for you.

The battle which is beginning today will decide the fate of the German nation for the next thousand years.

Do your duty . . .

ADOLF HITLER, Order of the Day, 10 May 1940

Rommel

As soon as day broke on Saturday, 11 May, the Panzers were once again on the move everywhere. Rommel, having concentrated and reorganized his forces during the night, swiftly smashed the courageous resistance of the Chasseurs Ardennais at Chabrehez. By the end of the morning, leading elements of his 7th Panzer had already reached the River Ourthe, the objective that had been denied him the previous night. On the other side of the river, parts of the French 4th D.L.C. had arrived. At Hotton, Lieutenant Georges Kosak's sapper company had been detailed to demolish a bridge which had been inefficiently blown by the Belgians, his job greatly complicated by the masses of Belgian refugees streaming across it. At 1345 he finally succeeded in clearing the bridge, and detonated charges under it, just at the very moment when the first of Rommel's armoured cars appeared on the opposite bank. Kosak then withdrew to Marche, some five miles behind the river. The French cavalry made no attempt to cover the destroyed bridges on the Ourthe, and within a matter of hours the German engineers had thrown pontoons across the undefended river.

Appearing with unexpected suddenness on the other side of the Ourthe, Rommel's Panzers struck their first blow savagely at the dispersed French cavalry. At Marche, Lieutenant Kosak and his troop were surprised by machine-gun fire from a German armoured car. He leaped into a small French car and tried to make off:

. . . all of a sudden, a grey-green mass bars the road; with all my concerted strength, I brake, my hands clutching the wheel; the tyres make a noise like a large electric saw cutting wood; I swerve to the left. A quite brutal shock stops the car . . . the enemy armoured car manoeuvres; it is lying sideways on across the road, trying to turn about.

Kosak then managed to reverse and swing behind some buildings, a second before the Germans opened fire. Outside Marche, he regathered his troop, and reckoning that escape seemed impossible, decided to take up a defensive position. The sappers buried a few mines and took over. A group of German armoured cars approached. The first one blew up with a devastating explosion on one of Kosak's mines, which also knocked out a second vehicle. Benefiting from the ensuing disarray of the enemy, Kosak miraculously managed to escape to Ciney, where only the previous day he had experienced that 'strange feeling' on moving up through the first shuttered and frightened Belgian town. Here, less than ten miles from Dinant and the Meuse, the divisional commander, General Barbe, interviewed Kosak and declared 'I am pleased with you.'

Throughout the day there was confused fighting on Rommel's axis similar to that reported by Kosak. At times the tanks of the 4th D.L.C. attacked strongly, but their Renaults and Hotchkisses were both outnumbered and outclassed. Rommel's own account of the day's action describes how 'prompt opening fire on our part led to a hasty French retreat'. On this first day of battle with the French he discovered 'again and again that in encounter actions, the day goes to the side that is the first to plaster its opponent with fire. The man who lies low and awaits developments usually comes off second best.' His Panzers thus advanced, spraying the woods on either side of the roads promiscuously with machine-gun and cannon fire. Into these woods the French cavalry, horses and tanks mixed up with one another, scattered in disorder. By the evening of the 11th, Rommel was in fine fettle, having more than made up for the setbacks of the previous day. To his wife, he dashed off a second quick note:

Dearest Lu,

I've come up for breath for the first time today and have a moment to write. Everything wonderful so far. Am way ahead of my neighbours. I'm completely hoarse from orders and shouting. Had a bare three hours' sleep and an occasional meal. Otherwise I'm absolutely fine. Make do with this, please, I'm too tired for more.

The outstripped 'neighbours' to whom Rommel refers consisted chiefly of the 5th Panzer division on his right. Not led with Rommel's élan, the 5th had become tangled up on the Ardennes roads and lagged badly behind. From the 11th onwards, it would never quite catch up, and Rommel would seize all the limelight on the right flank of the breakthrough thrust.

Reinhardt

On Rommel's left, Reinhardt's corps, consisting of the 8th and 6th Panzers who were to advance through Bastogne to Monthermé on the Meuse, also had their problems. Reinhardt had actually set off after Guderian, so as to make room for XIX Panzer Corps on the saturated and tortuous roads of the Ardennes. But in the afternoon the 6th found its route blocked by elements of Guderian's 2nd Panzer which had strayed too far to the north. At 1520 orders were given for it to hold fast until the muddle was sorted out. Finally, the 2nd Panzer had to cede this route to the 6th; later it was also deprived by Guderian of another on the right of its axis, a factor that was to delay the division's appearance at Sedan

on the critical day. In its approach march, the 1st Panzer too
had suffered inconvenience by being 'squeezed' by the 10th
Panzer on its left. Here Guderian appears to have been at
least partly to blame; over-reacting against Kleist's rescinded
order for the 10th to swing southwards, at 0100 on the morning of the 11th he had instructed it to aim for the River
Semois at Cugnon, several miles further north than Floren-
ville where it was originally directed. Back at O.K.H. headquarters, Halder noted in his diary that Brauchitsch, the Army
C.-in-C., wanted 'to put pressure on Army Group 'A' (they
report that route difficulties have been very great on account
of numerous road destructions!)'. Had it not been for the
apparently almost miraculous efforts of the mechanized engineers, who seemed to have been everywhere at the right
moment, destroying Belgian anti-tank obstacles, replacing
bridges, and constructing road detours, the hold-ups would
undoubtedly have been far graver that day. As it was, the
tank commanders cursed at the tangles and delays as their
engines overheated, growled at the military police trying
frantically to unsnarl the vast columns and continually threw
nervous glances upwards into the dazzling clear blue sky.
What fantastic targets these mile-long traffic jams offered the
enemy air forces! How could they miss such an opportunity!

Guderian

On Guderian's front, the principal action on the 11th was
fought by the 1st Panzer. Having moved his tanks up in
strength to the positions just east of Neufchâteau that had
been seized the previous day by 'Operation Niwi', the divisional commander, General Kirchner, now swept aside the
few remnants of the Chasseurs Ardennais in order to strike
forcefully at the French 5th D.L.C. Near Suxy, south of Neufchâteau, some thirty tanks bearing the white oak-leaf em-
blem of the 1st Panzer broke through the French positions
and swiftly surrounded a battery of 105-mm, field-guns. These
were modern weapons, but they were completely unsuited for
combating armour. The whole battery was swiftly destroyed,

a first unpleasant foretaste of what was to await the defenders on the other side of the Meuse. Shaken, General Chanoine, the commander of the 5th D.L.C., ordered the *groupement* forming his right wing to fall back on the Semois. Meanwhile, north of Neufchâteau, his left wing was also being hard pressed, and during the course of the day Chanoine received Huntziger's permission to withdraw his whole division across the Semois. But, insisted Huntziger, the Semois must be held at all costs, and to bolster the line there, he expedited a battalion of the 295th Infantry Regiment, borrowed from one of General Grandsard's 'B' divisions, the 55th – which was holding the key sector at Sedan.

To the right of the 5th D.L.C., the 2nd, licking its wounds from the previous day, was left relatively alone. The explanation for the failure of the 10th Panzer to resume its attack seems to lie in the confusion caused over its change of axis and the resulting bottlenecks, but this apparent switching of enemy emphasis from the 2nd D.L.C. front to the 5th resulted in adding to the bafflement of Huntziger. Was Guderian's main effort aimed at Carignan and the northern anchor of the Maginot Line, as it might have seemed on the 10th, or now at Sedan? On its right, the 2nd D.L.C. was left somewhat in the air by the withdrawal on the evening of the 10th of the Third Army's cavalry screen (the 3rd D.L.C.), which, abandoning Esch, fell back across the Franco-Luxembourg frontier. Much more serious, however, was the threat presenting itself to the other flank of Huntziger's cavalry detachments. To the left of the hard-hit 5th D.L.C. lay the 3rd Spahi Brigade, an élite North African unit under the command of General Corap's Ninth Army. Its role was to ensure liaison between the cavalry screens of the two armies. Because of the lagging behind of the 6th Panzer, in whose approximate path the Spahis stood, they were attacked on neither the 10th nor the 11th. Nevertheless, on learning of the 5th D.L.C.'s withdrawal, the Spahi commander, Colonel Marc, pulled his brigade back across the Semois even more precipitately – the consequences of which were to be particularly unfortunate the following day.

Thus as 11 May ended, the situation of Huntziger's cavalry was as follows: the 2nd D.L.C. was still capable of resistance, but the 5th was battered and was left holding a twenty-mile front on which two of the most powerful German Panzer divisions (the 1st and 2nd) were advancing. Both flanks of Huntziger's cavalry screen were in the air, and the whole of it had withdrawn across the Semois. Here was the last natural barrier between the French frontier – and Sedan. It was not much of a barrier! On staff officers' maps, the Semois may look imposing; along its upper reaches it is in fact little more than a very pretty trout stream, not unlike Hampshire's River Itchen, meandering in countless loops through water meadows and wooded banks. In many places it is shallow enough to wade across; in others, narrow enough for a not particularly expert thrower to land a hand-grenade on the far side. Its numerous convolutions would make it hard for an extended defence force to prevent a determined and numerous enemy infiltrating across it. The principal route over the Semois, and the one heading directly for Sedan, lay through Bouillon. Here the physical features for a resolute defence – dominating heights and clearly observable approach roads from which Panzers could not easily deploy – were more promising. But it was clear that Bouillon would be the scene of Guderian's major effort for the 12th. Nevertheless, an extraordinary atmosphere of business-as-usual still prevailed there.

Like Rommel's 7th Panzer, Kirchner's 1st was now leading both its neighbours. Heading west from Neufchâteau until it had reached the important road junction of Fays-les-Veneurs, it had then swung southwards to face for the first time towards Bouillon and, beyond it, Sedan. By nightfall on the 11th, the leading tanks of the 1st Panzer Regiment had actually reached the Semois at Bouillon. Immediately they came under heavy anti-tank fire from the far bank, which knocked out a tank. An undestroyed stone bridge was then discovered, but just as the Panzers were about to cross it the French blew it up. Captain von Kress managed to cross by a ford discovered by regimental reconnaissance, but shortly afterwards he was bombed in error by twenty-five Stukas. The 1st Panzer Regiment was withdrawn, and it was decided to resume the attack the next morning, using the division's motorized infantry.

During the 11th, the vast majority of the men marching with and behind Kleist's armoured phalanx had still not caught a glimpse of the enemy, a factor which lent to the campaign in the Ardennes a certain phantom quality. From time to time, Guderian himself had spotted French reconnaissance vehicles flitting silently through the trees of the Ardennes Forest, in retreat, without apparently either side opening fire. A young sapper lieutenant, Karl-Heinz Mende, wrote home in amazement at advancing through country 'as fruitful and beautiful as the German landscape', but empty and abandoned – 'We are not fighting for this land, we are simply swamping it' – and the whole campaign so far had reminded him of a well-conducted sand-table exercise. Indeed, as General von Blumentritt told Liddell Hart after the war, it 'was not really an operation, in the tactical sense, but an approach march. In making the plan we had reckoned it unlikely that we should meet any serious resistance before reaching the Meuse.' In the first two days of the Ardennes campaign, the German appreciation so far had certainly held good; resistance met had been only 'weak opposition, and easily brushed aside. . . The main problem was not tactical but administrative.' That night Guderian with his highly mobile corps H.Q. took up quarters at Neufchâteau in a much happier frame of mind. The approach march still presented its 'administrative problems', but with the exception of the 2nd Panzer, which continued to lag behind, the whole Panzer Corps had more than recovered the time lost on the 10th. Back at O.K.H., Halder recorded a visit from the Führer, lasting from 1640 until 1900 hours, and during which there had been 'rejoicing over the success'; on the French side of the lines, there was still 'no sign of any major railway movements anywhere. Enemy air force astonishingly restrained.' But in a qualifying and significantly cautious note he added that there was 'expectation of [enemy] attack from the south'.

Air War

In the air, the Luftwaffe continued its strategic bombing of Allied airfields and communication centres, though with no greater intensity than on the previous day. According to General d'Astier, only three French planes were destroyed and one landing-strip put out of action. Tactically, the main German air effort was concentrated upon the annihilation of the Dutch forces in the north. Over the Ardennes, the protective fighter cover remained dense, and the Panzers appear to have had as much air support as they required. Lieutenant-Colonel Soldan, a Wehrmacht chronicler, states that Luftwaffe co-operation was 'most admirable' during critical moments of that day:

Planes, watching the situation from above, promptly recognized any position where help was needed. Dive-bombers flung themselves on the enemy and opened the way for the countless vehicles whose motors were making a terrible noise as they laboured through this forest region of hills and mountains.

But otherwise the Luftwaffe still adroitly avoided any intensification of activity over the Dinant–Sedan area that might have given away the *Sichelschnitt* objectives. Meanwhile, on the 11th the Allied air forces undertook one single operation against those miles of irresistible targets worming through the Ardennes. The R.A.F. official history relates:

Eight Battles of Nos. 88 and 218 Squadrons were ordered to deliver a low-level attack on a column in German territory moving up towards the Luxembourg border. Whether they managed to reach their target area is doubtful. The only pilot to return saw three of his companions succumb to ground fire in the Ardennes.

Again, the French Air Force took no part.

At the other end of the battlefront, with similar ineffectiveness and high losses, a squadron of Belgian Battle bombers attacked the captured Maastricht and Albert Canal bridges, carrying 50-kg. bombs which were ludicrously small for the task. Ten out of fifteen planes were shot down. The attacks were followed up by R.A.F. Blenheims; on one mission, five out of six were destroyed by flak. It was not until the end of the morning of the 11th that General Georges's restrictions on the bombing of built-up areas by the French Air Force was lifted. At 1630 Gamelin himself telephoned d'Astier, ordering him to 'put everything to work to slow up the German columns in the direction of Maastricht, Tongres, Gembloux, and not to hesitate to bomb towns and villages in order to obtain the required result'. But much irreplaceable time had been lost, and in any case Gamelin was concentrating his limited air resources in the wrong place – as indeed the *Sichelschnitt* planners had intended that he should.

The Allies in Belgium

On 11th May, General d'Astier noted that Giraud's Seventh Army in its dash towards Breda 'is not being troubled' by the Luftwaffe. In view of the merciless pounding that was being inflicted upon the poor Dutch, was there not something curious in the apparently blind eye the Luftwaffe was turning upon Giraud? The B.E.F. had experienced a similarly quiet time in its advance to the Dyle Line position. With it went a certain 'Kim' Philby, representing *The Times*, who, showing an astuteness which would later bring untold advantage to another employer, remarked apprehensively to an American colleague, Drew Middleton: 'It went too damn well. With all that air power why didn't he bother us? What is he up to?'[1]

The B.E.F. advance – apart from the one incident on the 10th when an officious Belgian frontier guard had tried to halt the passage of Major-General Bernard Montgomery's 3rd Division because it did not possess the necessary permits – had indeed proceeded with exemplary smoothness. To many of its older members who had fought in Belgium once before, there was an uncanny quality about that advance: 'It was almost,' wrote Drew Middleton, 'as if they were retracing steps taken in a dream. They saw again faces of friends long dead and

1. Philby's remark was recorded, long before he came to fame, by Middleton in *Our Share of Night*, published in 1946.

heard the half-remembered names of towns and villages.' But
the Tommies were in excellent spirits; passing them on the
road back to Paris from Brussels, Clare Boothe 'remembered
how everybody had remarked that it was funny the soldiers
didn't sing in this war. Well, these soldiers were singing . . .
they stuck up their thumbs in the new gesture they had, which
meant "O.K., everything's fine," and winked and blew cheerful kisses . . .' By the evening of 11 May, the B.E.F. was well
dug in on its appointed sector along the Dyle, from Louvain
to Wavre, and although the river here was in fact little more
than a wide stream, the British position was a relatively strong
one.

The French First Army of General Blanchard, earmarked
to fill the 'Gembloux Gap' between the B.E.F. and Corap's
Ninth Army, was not so well off. Moving up from Valenciennes, Major Barlone sombrely noted meeting Belgian refugees racing towards France from the Liège area: 'The news
these people bring is pessimistic . . . Treachery and the Fifth
Column are the sole topics of conversation.' On reaching
Gembloux, General Prioux of the crack Cavalry Corps was
'dumbfounded' to discover how little the Belgians had done
to fortify this vital area; it seemed a completely open plain
offering itself to the German Panzers. Meanwhile, a staff captain had brought him grave news from Liège; mighty Eben
Emael had fallen, and the Germans were already flooding
across the Albert Canal line. By the afternoon the Germans
were in Tongres and reaching out to Waremme some six
miles west of Liège, thus threatening it from the river. At this
rate, Prioux reckoned that his corps would never have time to
establish itself before the enemy was on top of it. Early that
afternoon he reported to Blanchard that 'in view of the feeble
Belgian resistance and superiority of the enemy aviation, the
Dyle Manoeuvre appears to be difficult to execute and it
would seem to be preferable to resort to the Escaut Manoeuvre'. Blanchard passed this on to Billotte, attaching his
own recommendation. Billotte, always the staunchest supporter of the Dyle–Breda Plan among the French hierarchy, was
shocked. Visiting Prioux that night in person, Billotte told

him that the Dyle Plan could not possibly be put into reverse; he would speed up the advance of the bulk of the first Army, but meanwhile Prioux would have to hold fast until D+5, 14 May.

Holland

In Holland, the defences were crumbling at a terrifying speed. Rumours of Fifth Column treachery were multiplying: hand-grenades were reported to have been filled with sand instead of explosive, bunkers crumbled because the concrete had been 'cut', children were 'poisoned' by chocolates dropped from the air. Panic was everywhere. The Dutch Army was still valiantly attacking the pockets held by General Student's airborne troops, but the Dutch Air Force had been all but wiped out, and the 9th Panzer Division had now got its tanks across the Maas (via the bridge at Gennep captured by the 'Branden-burgers') and was rapidly striking westwards, towards Rotterdam. The advance guard of Giraud's mechanized divisions reached its destination at Breda, only to find that the Dutch Army to whom it had come to 'extend an arm' had been forced to withdraw northwards covering Rotterdam. By lunchtime on the 11th Giraud had run into the 9th Panzer, in the vicinity of Tilburg. Shaken by this unexpected encounter, his armour turned about, falling back in the direction of Antwerp, now savagely strafed and bombed by low-flying German planes. Thus within thirty-six hours of the opening of battle, Gamelin's 'Breda Variant', upon which was wagered his irreplaceable mobile reserve, had already been rendered null and void.

French High Command

Back at Vincennes, Gamelin's eyes were still kept riveted upon the north by the crescendo of events there. In London, General Spears was told by the French Military Attaché (on the 11th and again on the 12th) that G.Q.G. was convinced that the Germans were making their main effort between

Maastricht and Liège, while, on the 11th, the *Times* Military
Correspondent (obviously also fed by a similar *tuyau* from
Vincennes) declaimed confidently that 'This time at least
there has been no strategic surprise.' General Ironside recorded sanguinely in his diary: '...we shall have saved the
Belgian Army. On the whole the advantage is with us. A
really hard fight all this summer . . .' To outer commands
such as General Weygand's in Syria, French G.Q.G. concluded its summary that day: 'The Allied manoeuvre is
developing favourably.' If there was any diminution of Gamelin's optimism that day, it lay in disappointment at the rapid
disintegration of Dutch resistance and at the unexpectedly
poor quality of the Belgian defence preparations. As Gamelin
admits in his memoirs, during the first three days of the battle
'I was above all preoccupied with Holland.'

Yet the indications were mounting steadily that something
serious was also afoot in the Ardennes. Already by the morning of the 11th, both French and R.A.F. reconnaissance reports had contained such items as 'numerous columns on the
road from Euskirchen to Prüm and on the Belgian road network to the west of Luxembourg,' the unloading of tanks
north of Neufchâteau, and considerable motorized forces deploying towards Arlon, while in his midday bulletin General
d'Astier stated: 'The enemy seems to be preparing an energetic action in the general direction of Givet.' [2] It was the
actual numbers of the Panzer divisions operating in the Ardennes that continued to elude G.Q.G.'s *Deuxième Bureau* in
composing its enemy order of battle. The effectiveness of the
German fighter umbrella against reconnaissance intruders,
and the leafy natural camouflage of those 'impenetrable'
forests into which whole divisions could melt without trace
from one hour to another, all conspired to this end, while the
forcefulness with which Bock was brandishing the 'matador's
cloak' north of Liège certainly suggested that more than just
a quarter of the German Panzer strength might be deployed
there.

Nevertheless, it would not be true to say that, even as early

2. About ten air miles up the Meuse from Dinant. See Map 3.

as 11 May, the French High Command had received no warnings of the danger in the Ardennes, or that they were not reacting to these warnings. On that afternoon, General Georges issued an Instruction No. 12 in which he 'foresaw' the need to 'push up on to the second position behind Sedan the 2nd and 3rd Armoured Divisions, the 3rd Motorized and the 14th, 36th and 87th Infantry Divisions', all belonging to the general reserve. The orders for the transportation of these units would be passed on between the 11th and 13th; but as events were soon to prove, they would come too late.

During the afternoon of the 11th, Gamelin visited General Georges at his headquarters of Les Bondons. The previous day he had, on his own initiative, delegated to Georges powers to deal directly with King Leopold as Commander-in-Chief of the Belgian Army. Now he was astonished to discover that Georges in his turn had sub-delegated these powers to Billotte, to whom he also wanted to pass his 'powers of co-ordination' over Lord Gort's B.E.F. It was, said Gamelin crossly, 'an abdication', yet he did nothing to attempt to alter his subordinate's decision. When he returned to Vincennes that evening the tangle of the Allied command network had in no way been simplified, nor were relations between Gamelin and Georges any friendlier.

Chapter 11

On the Meuse

12 May

The Germans announce that one of the forts of Liège is in their hands. Even if this claim is true, its significance is diminished by the announcement that a captain and a lieutenant have been decorated for it. That would indicate that . . . the fort was only a bunker or a small pill-box.

New York Herald Tribune, 12 May

DESPAIR IN BERLIN
Sunday Chronicle, 12 May

The attack of the German Wehrmacht in the west made good progress on 12 May.

Wehrmacht communiqué 13 May

The Low Countries

Allied newspapers on the morning of Whit Sunday, 12 May, generally gave the impression that the German offensive had been stemmed by the Dutch and Belgians – as indeed, according to Gamelin's plans, it should have been. But in fact by that morning the situation in Holland was already desperate, and in the course of the next twenty-four hours it became hopeless. In the extreme north, the German ground troops reached the eastern shore of the Zuyder Zee; in the centre, advancing beyond Arnhem, which the airborne troops had captured on the first day, they broke through the Grebbe Line at Rhenen after some hard fighting, whence the very heart of the country could be threatened; in the south, the 9th Panzer was pushing towards the great bridge over the Maas estuary at Moerdijk, to link up with the German paratroopers still holding it. By the evening of the 12th, Moerdijk was captured and with it vanished all hope of assistance from Giraud's Seventh Army. Holland was cut in two and the Dutch Army, though it continued to fight on with bitter desperation, was left with no

option but to retreat into *Vesting Holland*, the area containing
the main cities, The Hague, Rotterdam, Utrecht and Amsterdam, with their backs to the sea. Only one airworthy bomber,
a Fokker, was left to the Dutch Air Force, and this was shot
down over Moerdijk the following day. General Giraud's fine
mechanized units found themselves in a menacing predicament: heavily hit both by Stukas and German armour, their
right flank was increasingly threatened by the 9th Panzer, ammunition was running short, and many of their tanks were still
moving up through Belgium on flat-cars. Losses had been
heavy. Giraud decided to withdraw from all but a tiny corner
of Dutch soil, and try to hold a line from Bergen op Zoom to
the Turnhout Canal, covering Antwerp.

After General Prioux's alarming account of the state of the
Dyle Line on the 11th, Billotte had ordered Blanchard's First
Army to speed up its advance so that it would be established in
position twenty-four hours earlier than previously stipulated,
on the 14th instead of the 15th. Moving by day instead of during the short May nights, the French mechanized columns now
came under systematic Luftwaffe attack for the first time. In
the forced marches necessitated by this acceleration of the
timetable, much of the artillery was left behind. Meanwhile,
during the morning of the 12th the Belgian Army was in full
retreat from the Albert Line and attempting to take up position
on the line Antwerp–Malines–Louvain, linking up with the
B.E.F. on its right. The Belgian withdrawal in turn exposed the
forward elements of General Prioux's Cavalry Corps to attack
from the armour of General Hoeppner's XVI Panzer Corps. In
the general area of Hannut, roughly midway between Liege
and the Dyle, preliminary blows were now exchanged in the
first major tank battle between the French and Germans. On
that opening day Prioux's tanks gave a good account of themselves. The armoured forces of both sides were over-extended,
and the German infantry were moving up so slowly behind that
the harassed Belgian command was given a badly needed
breather in which to effect its withdrawal without precipitating
a real crisis. By the evening of the 12th, Prioux's armoured
screen was still clinging to its forward positions, though

precariously. The day's fighting had been indecisive, but it seemed to show that, on anything like equal terms, French armour could hold its own against the German Panzers. From army, army group, and back to Gamelin at G.Q.G., Prioux was showered with flattering praise for these first – alas premature – results. But by the end of the 12th no more than two-thirds of the First Army had reached the Dyle, and it looked as if the main weight of Hoeppner's two Panzer divisions might hit Prioux on the morrow.

The B.E.F., entrenched along the Dyle from Louvain to Wavre, enjoyed another quiet day. That afternoon, Gort's Chief of Staff, General Sir Henry Pownall, attended what the British official historian describes as 'a momentous meeting', at the Château de Casteau, near Mons of 1914 fame. Present were King Leopold and his chief military adviser, General van Overstraeten, Daladier (still Minister of National Defence), Georges and Billotte. Under pressure of this first crisis confronting the three embattled allies, all now agreed to General Georges's earlier proposal that Billotte act as his 'delegate' to 'co-ordinate the actions of the Allied forces in Belgian territory'. One of the first practical results of the Casteau conference was to resolve the defence of Louvain, which, since 10 May, as one further consequence of the poor liaison with the Belgians before the offensive began, had been duplicated by both a British and Belgian division; the sector was now handed to the B.E.F. In effect, however, the terms of reference within the Allied command remained vague, and with Billotte increasingly overwhelmed by the responsibilities heaped upon him by his large command, he was to have little time for 'co-ordinating' the Belgians and the B.E.F. with the French forces. Henceforth, Gort for one would have to carry on virtually without directives from above, a neglect that was to have its repercussions at a critical stage in the battle ten days later.

The skies on that brilliantly sunny Whit Sunday once again saw the main Allied air effort concentrated in the north. It was the Maastricht bridges and the stretch of road leading from them through Tongres that attracted particular attention. Here Hoeppner's Panzers were pouring towards the Dyle Line, presenting (apparently) far more threatening and obvious targets than the many times larger force 'lost' in the Ardennes. At 0600 on the 12th, Billotte called upon French Fighter Command to lend all its support that day to flying cover for the bombers attacking the Maastricht bridgehead. According to General d'Astier, the French bomber squadrons were still not yet ready for action. The crack 'ground-level' attack unit, *Groupe* I/54, for instance, which had been ordered to shift bases on 10 May, had been lacking some vital bomb-release accessories right up to the night of the 11th–12th, when these had actually been fetched by truck from the factory itself. Therefore, on the morning of the 12th, Astier was forced to call again on the R.A.F. to shoulder the main burden against Maastricht. Out of nine Blenheims bombing columns between Tongres and the Maastricht Bridges, seven were shot down by Messerschmitts.

By midday on the 12th, *Groupe* I/54 was at last ready for its first action. Flying with its leading flight of six Bréguets, Sergeant-Gunner Conill gives a graphic account of a low-level attack on an enemy column at Tongres that typified the experience of many Allied bomber crews during these May days. On approaching Liège, Conill's formation was ordered to dive to zero altitude:

In front of us the Major flew his Bréguet with incredible daring, skimming the roof-tops, brushing the trees, jumping obstacles. A grand game! . . . The roofs of Tongres rose up in front of us . . . A main road was there, the one we were looking for, flanked by trees and ditches. And what a sight! Hundreds and hundreds of vehicles rolling towards France, following each other at short intervals, mobile, and travelling fast. A lovely target! . . . at 350 [kilometres] an hour, right down the axis of the road, flying at tree top level, the Major attacked . . . Suddenly white and blue flashes sprang up underneath us and there was a hell-like outburst of fire and steel and flames, which grew bigger. I saw clearly the bursts of small-calibre shells climbing towards us by the thousand. Each one of us felt they were aimed at him personally . . .

Ahead, Sergeant Conill could see the German flak ripping into the Major's plane; suddenly it 'tipped on one wing', tore through some poplar branches, 'and crashed in the midst of the German troops, right on the road'. Conill then turned to see his wing-man plunging earthwards in flames. Undismayed, however, the pilot of Conill's plane, Lieutenant Blondy, managed to drop his bombs squarely among a group of lorry-borne infantry, before his Bréguet too was riddled with flak. On one engine the Bréguet limped back to make a belly-landing in a French field. The plane was a write-off, but none of the other five planes of the flight returned.

The effectiveness of the 20-mm. and 37-mm. flak, and the speed with which the Germans had managed both to bring up and mass these weapons around important passages, provided a singularly disagreeable shock to the French Air Force that day. The severe losses (eight out of eighteen planes in all) suffered by *Groupe* I/54 was also to bring a virtual end to the ground-level attack technique. That evening a dozen Léo bombers from *Groupement* 6 again attacked the Tongres road network, but this time prudently from an altitude of 2,500 feet, while the flak still forced them to take such evasive action that accuracy suffered badly. All the Léos returned, though none was undamaged. Meanwhile, during the afternoon, Air Marshal Barratt, under constant pressure from Billotte and fully realizing how suicidal future attacks on the well-guarded Maastricht bridgehead would be, took the exceptional step of calling for a volunteer effort from No. 12 'Battle' Squadron. The whole squadron, well nicknamed the 'Dirty Dozen', volunteered. Under a strong cover of Hurricanes, five 'Battles' went out. Only one crippled plane was brought back, after the pilot had ordered his crew to bale out; the other four were never seen again. Flying-Officer Garland and Sergeant Gray in the leading aircraft were posthumously awarded the V.C., the first to be awarded in the campaign. One truss of the Veldwezelt bridge was knocked down. Pulled out of the burning wreck of his plane, one of the survivors was told by his German captors:

You British are mad. We capture the bridge early Friday morning. You give us all Friday and Saturday to get our flak guns up in circles all round the bridge, and then on Sunday, when all is ready, you come along with three aircraft and try to blow the thing up.

It was not an unreasonable judgement.

According to General d'Astier, altogether that day R.A.F. bombers made 140 sorties and lost twenty-four planes, while French bombers flew only thirty sorties, losing nine planes. French fighters flew about 200 sorties, losing six planes and claiming twenty-six of the enemy, while with its 124 Me-109s that had pounced upon the Maastricht Blenheims, the German Fighter Group 27 alone chalked up as many as 340 sorties that day, losing four planes for a claimed twenty-eight. As regards the results achieved by the sacrificial Allied efforts against Maastricht, the war diary of Hoeppner's XVI Panzer Corps admits that it caused 'considerable delays'. But at what a cost! And why were the Allied air forces continuing to waste their precious substance upon this purely secondary threat?

In his reconnaissance report for the 12th, d'Astier once again emphasized the German effort in the Ardennes: 'Considerable motorized and armoured forces are on the march towards the Meuse round Dinant, Givet, and Bouillon, coming respectively from Marche and Neufchâteau.' Ominously he noted the substantial amount of bridging equipment being carried by the German columns, and concluded: 'One can assume a very serious enemy effort in the direction of the Meuse.' But, to his amazement, by midday on the 12th Billotte was still allocating priority for air operations to the Maastricht area, though he now switched second priority from the battered 7th Army and the untroubled B.E.F. to support of Huntziger. At 1600 hours, says d'Astier, General Georges intervened to grant first priority to Huntziger. Billotte, having moved into a battle H.Q. behind the French First Army, had his eyes fixed upon this sector of the front, and was astounded. Resuming his former tack he declared: 'Two-thirds of the air effort in support of the First Army, one-third in support of Second Army.' To some extent, Billotte can be exculpated by the surprising fact that Huntziger himself, although informed of the bomber support earmarked for his Second Army, apparently made no appeal for it to General d'Astier at all that day. It was purely on his own initiative, based on the reconnaissance reports, that d'Astier requested fifty British aircraft to bomb the Neufchâteau and

Gouillon areas on the evening of the 12th, from which another eighteen bombers failed to return.

Guderian: Across the Semois

During the night of the 11th–12th, Guderian had swiftly exploited the precipitate withdrawal made by Corap's 3rd Spahi Brigade across the Semois the previous day. The motor-cycle battalion of the 1st Panzer, deployed on the right of the division, got over the river at Mouzaive under cover of darkness, establishing itself in force on the other side before the defenders could react. Less than five air miles from Bouillon, the mainstay of the French defence along the Semois, the Mouzaive bridgehead gave the attackers an immediate and powerful advantage as dawn broke on the 12th. By 0600 Guderian had tanks across at Mouzaive, and the left flank of Huntziger's 5th D.L.C., not forewarned of the Spahis' withdrawal, was now already threatened. At Bouillon itself, men of Lieutenant-Colonel Balck's 1st Rifle Regiment, who were later to cover themselves with glory on the far side of the Meuse, infiltrated down through steep and densely wooded banks until they reached a ford across the Semois which the reconnaissance unit had located the previous night. Within a short space of time they had carried their objectives, and the first tanks were rolling across the ford, their passage aided by the fact that the dry spring had considerably reduced the level of the Semois.

As usual, Guderian was up in the cockpit that morning, watching Balck's river crossing. After he had satisfied himself with the immediate building of a new bridge by the divisional engineers, he followed the tanks across the Semois, up the steep gorge towards Sedan. 'But mined roads compelled me to return to Bouillon. Here, in the southern part of the town,' Guderian admitted, 'I experienced an enemy air attack for the first time; they were after 1st Panzer Division's bridge. Luckily the bridge remained undamaged, but a few houses were set on fire.' In his command vehicle, Guderian then drove to the Cugnon–Herbeumont sector, where his 10th Panzer Division was engaged in crossing the Semois. This he found 'an impressive sight', and he returned 'without anxiety' to Bouillon, where his staff had set up corps H.Q. in the Hôtel Panorama, well named on account of its splendid view over the Semois. In an alcove heavily decorated with trophies of *la chasse*, Guderian went to work, planning the next stage of the advance.

Suddenly there was a series of explosions in rapid succession; another air attack. As though that were not enough, an engineer supply column, carrying fuses, explosives, mines and hand-grenades, caught fire and there was one detonation after another. A boar's head, attached to the wall immediately above my desk, broke loose and missed me by a hair's breadth; the other trophies came tumbling down and the fine window in front of which I was seated was smashed to smithereens and splinters of glass whistled about my ears . . .

After this narrow escape, which might so easily have altered the course of the coming battle, Guderian moved his H.Q. back out of Bouillon. Once again he was bombed, and once again forced to move, this time to the delightful small village of Noirefontaine, on the Ardennes plateau three miles north of Bouillon.

Throughout the day Allied bombardment of the Bouillon bridgehead continued. From Torcy, ten miles away on the Meuse near Sedan, French 'long 155s' lobbed in shells with sufficient accuracy to make the German engineers' bridge-building a highly dangerous occupation. Rather less accurately, R.A.F. Battle bombers, such as those that had nearly hit Guderian in the Hôtel Panorama, made repeated runs on the bridges down the narrow, twisting valley. As noted earlier, eighteen out of fifty did not return. But things did not go all the Luftwaffe's way; five American-made Curtiss fighters belonging to *Groupe* I/5 – the *Cigognes* squadron to whom had passed the mantle of the legendary Guynemer of 1914–18 fame – pounced upon twelve Stukas returning from a bombing mission between Bouillon and Sedan. All were shot down, at no cost to the *Cigognes*, who then attacked a second wave of Stukas coming in to bomb. Several more were shot down, and the rest put to flight. The two encounters demonstrated clearly the vulnerability of the dreaded Stuka; but alas, it was a lesson from which little benefit would be drawn.

Despite this Allied effort, by mid-morning the 1st Panzer had established a sizeable bridgehead over the Semois and was thrusting down the road to Sedan, by the signposts now just eighteen kilometres distant. While Britons were reading their morning newspapers, the first of Guderian's tanks was leaving Belgium behind it and crossing into France. As they burst out of the 'inhospitable' Ardennes which had concealed and sheltered them for the past two and a half days, the Panzers could make out in the distant haze the Frénois heights beyond the Meuse, where, seventy summers ago, the King of Prussia and Bismarck had stood as German soldiers closed in to win that first Battle of Sedan.

Second Army

When Huntziger had realized, early that morning, that the threat to the rear of the 5th D.L.C. by the Panzer crossing at Mouzaive rendered any defence at Bouillon impossible, he ordered the cavalry to fall back on the line of the *maisons fortes*, which had been constructed that winter between Sedan and the frontier. But the withdrawal of the infantry battalion of the 295th Regiment, sent up from the 55th Division to bolster the Bouillon defences only the previous day, did not go smoothly. Its motor transport appears to have vanished and, according to General Ruby, this battalion of 'B class' reservists

scattered in the woods, and cut off from its route, lost its C.O., Major Clausener, as well as the major part of its effectives; only three hundred demoralized men were seen again, crying 'treachery' against the cavalry, and devoid of any value for the actions of the following days.

It was an ominous indication of what might happen when a 'B' division was really hit hard by the German Panzers or Stukas.

Meanwhile, further to the right on the sector of the 2nd D.L.C., Marcel Lerecouvreux paints a similarly depressing picture. With the 10th Panzer now thrusting across its front on the general axis Herbeumont–Sedan, the 2nd D.L.C. had enjoyed a relatively calm morning, but that afternoon Lerecouvreux, back at divisional H.Q. well behind the Semois, was astonished to hear the sound of small-arms fire close at hand. He learned that the neighbouring divisions were already pulling back across the River Chiers in retreat. Hastily, divisional H.Q. was packed up, with the French artillery firing over its head. Lerecouvreux noted that some of the division 'wept at having to leave entrenchments which they had built with their own hands, where they had hoped to halt the enemy and which now served no purpose'; nevertheless the cavalry, though fatigued after three days' combat, withdrew in good order. But it was not so with all units; at Margut, a crossing point on the Chiers, 'during the two days that had passed since the departure of the civil population, there had been many depredations and pillages committed by the non-combatant troops, and the wine ran down into the gutter from barrels which had been smashed open'. There was much drunkenness, leading to a particularly disgraceful incident that night:

. . . a soldier, manifestly drunk, approached a platoon of the 18th Chasseurs who were halting at Margut after the battle, before regaining their regrouping area, and without any motive killed an unfortunate Chasseur with a bullet square in the chest. Taking advantage of the general surprise, the murderer disappeared before he could be arrested.

Lerecouvreux also mentions the rout of a battalion of colonial infantry that day.

Guderian at Sedan

For the retreating French, the halt on the line of the *maisons fortes* was far shorter than anticipated. By 1400 hours, tanks of the 1st Panzer, curling round behind the back of the 5th D.L.C. via Fleigneux and St Menges, forced it to abandon hope of standing there, and to fall back on the Sedan bridgehead. Relentlessly the Panzers pursued them. Although Gamelin's orders were to hold the city of Sedan (the greater part of which lies on the Ardennes side of the Meuse) 'at all costs', within another four hours the cavalry had yielded it and retreated across the Meuse, leaving the Germans to occupy Sedan virtually unopposed. Well before dusk the forward tanks of the 1st Panzer were in the city. Sedan! The name that the visionary mind of Hitler had first spewed out, quite casually, the previous October; a small provincial French centre of some 13,000 inhabitants, a little less than that of Verdun in 1916, but what magical connotations it held for German minds! The birthplace of Turenne, a castigator of Teutons in a past era, in 1870 it had witnessed France's great humiliation and the ascendant Prussia's greatest triumph: the unconditional surrender of Emperor Napoleon III and 100,000 men to Moltke the Elder, a surrender that had forever altered the course of European history.

Now Guderian's advance guard entered a dead city. The streets were unnaturally empty and deserted. A few French stragglers, detached from the retreating cavalry, opened up desultory fire from rifle and machine-gun nests, but were rapidly silenced. As the German infantry and engineers groped their way towards the Meuse, heavy artillery fire descended on them from the other side of the river, and suddenly there was a tremendous roar as a bridge blew up. One after another the Sedan bridges erupted until not one was standing – although, in the heat of the moment, Paul Reynaud was later to claim that some had been left intact, by 'treachery'.

As night fell, the 1st Panzer had reached the glittering Meuse in force. General Kirchner, the divisional commander, set up his H.Q. just a mile or two north of Illy, the scene of the French General Gallifet's last desperate cavalry charge in 1870, which had so excited the admiration and compassion of the watching King of Prussia. On the left, the 10th Panzer had also reached the Meuse in the area of Bazeilles, where another savage battle had been fought during the war of 1870. Only the 2nd, whose delays on the previous day had been compounded with a difficult crossing of the Semois, bad roads and more interference with its itinerary from other units, was still

On the Meuse 293

hanging badly behind – much to Guderian's annoyance and concern.

Reinhardt

On Reinhardt's XLI Corps sector, where the principal objective was Monthermé on the confluence of the Meuse and the Semois, the 6th and 8th Panzers were still making only slow progress. The reason for this was the continued confusion on their routes of advance; it was not only with Guderian's 2nd Panzer that the traffic tangles had occurred, but also with elements of some of Rundstedt's leading infantry divisions that were now beginning to press in from behind on to the already cluttered Ardennes road network. By the late afternoon of the 12th, the War Diary of the 6th Panzer admits that even radio communication could no longer provide any clear picture as to just where its various units had got to. Fortunately for Reinhardt, his straggling columns were again not attacked from the air, nor did they encounter any ground resistance that day. It was as if they were advancing into open air. The corp's aerial reconnaissance that afternoon could find no enemy formations east of the Meuse, and the War Diary of the 6th tersely records the capture of 'only one drunken French soldier'. By nightfall the advance formations of the 6th Panzer, accompanied by its commander, General Kempf, had crossed the French frontier north-east of Monthermé and stood almost on the edge of the Ardennes escarpment where it falls with dramatic suddenness down to the Meuse. But the continued, mystifying absence of the enemy was distinctly unnerving: 'Either the French have taken leave of their senses,' observed a Sergeant Sievert with a storm detachment of the 6th Panzer, 'and really don't know that we are just about to reach the Meuse – or they are preparing something particularly devilish for us.'

Ninth Army: Cavalry Withdraws

On the French side, however, the reason for this apparent vacuum was depressingly simple. Surprised to discover that, by the night of the 11th, the 3rd Spahi Brigade constituting the right wing of his cavalry screen had pulled back as far as Mézières on the wrong side of the Meuse, Corap had promptly ordered it to turn about and reoccupy its positions along the Semois. But, as already seen, events had moved far too quickly. Guderian's Panzers had got across the Semois before the main body of the Spahis had even left Mézières on their return trip. Corap now realized that this flank of his cavalry was completely exposed; at the same time he had received an aerial reconnaissance report that morning which described a fifteen-mile-long enemy motorized column moving towards Marche, on the way to Dinant. A column this length could denote only one thing – a Panzer division.[1] Concerned at the poor state of the defences covering Dinant, owing to the tardy approach march of his infantry, Corap had decided to order his entire cavalry screen to fall back and take up positions along the west side of the Meuse. By 1600 hours on the 12th the order had been carried out, and all Meuse bridges on the Ninth Army front, from Dinant to the River Bar, were destroyed.

The French cavalry action was now over, having lasted just two and a half days, instead of the five upon which the French High Command had counted when it had calculated that the Germans could not possibly mount any crossing of the Meuse before the ninth day of the campaign. Despite the disarray into which the French cavalry units had been thrown, losses on both sides had been light.

In the sector facing Reinhardt, Corap's cavalry had disengaged themselves without hindrance. It was a different story, however, opposite Rommel's fast-thrusting 7th Panzer, and it was here that the most significant and decisive event of 12 May occurred. Lieutenant Georges Kosak describes the withdrawal across the Meuse north of Dinant of his badly battered division, the 4th D.L.C.:

Towards midday, groups of unsaddled horses returned, followed on foot by several wounded cavalrymen who had been bandaged as well as possible; others held themselves in the saddle by a

---

1. In fact, it was of course Rommel.

miracle for the honour of being cavalrymen. The saddles and the harnesses were all covered with blood. Most of the animals limped; others, badly wounded, just got as far as us in order to die, at the end of their strength; others had to be shot to bring an end to their sufferings . . .

Pursuing hotly behind them came Rommel. By 1130 hours his 25th Panzer Regiment under Colonel Rothenburg [2] had captured Ciney and Leignon, just ten miles from Dinant. Although the narrow gorges from Ciney down to Dinant should have been easy to block and difficult to clear, by early afternoon the first German reconnaissance armoured cars were rolling down to the banks of the Meuse itself. Sitting in a pill-box that guarded the western end of the railway bridge at Houx [3] (destroyed earlier that afternoon), Private Darche of the Chasseurs Ardennais heard the noise of their motors. It was about half past four. A few minutes later an enemy armoured car reached the other end of the bridge, little more than a hundred yards from Darche. He fired his anti-tank rifle at it, missing with his first shot, but stopping it dead with the second. Machine-gun fire from the pill-box also scattered some lorry-borne infantry imprudently debussing on the Meuse. Then Darche was killed by another armoured car firing shells straight into the gun embrasure. The survivors were forced to evacuate the pill-box, but for the time being they had imposed greater wariness upon the approaching Germans.

Rommel

Rommel's 7th Panzer, converted from a 'light' division, contained only one tank regiment instead of the two allotted to the standard Panzer divisions. Then, at midday on the 12th, he received a valuable reinforcement. This was Colonel Werner's 31st Panzer Regiment, which belonged to the lagging 5th Panzer Division but which Hoth, the corps commander, now temporarily transferred to Rommel to back up the latter's

2. Later killed in Russia.
3. Midway between Dinant and Yvoir, and about two and a half miles from each. See Maps 3 and 4a.

already encouraging success. Werner's regiment was already well ahead of the rest of the division, and under Rommel's guidance, after some sharp encounters with the rearguard of the French 4th D.L.C. near Ciney, it now surged down to the Meuse at Yvoir late that afternoon. The last French vehicles were just crossing the bridge, and Werner's armoured cars immediately tried to rush the bridge before it was destroyed. In a bunker on the other side of the river a gallant Belgian sapper, Lieutenant de Wispelaere, pressed the demolition plunger. Nothing happened. One of the German armoured cars was already moving up the incline towards the bridge. Under heavy fire, an anti-tank gun under de Wispelaere's command brought it to a halt, belching smoke, actually on the bridge itself. But its commander, clad in a black leather jacket, climbed out of the stricken vehicle and started running towards where the explosive charges were located, a large pair of pliers in his hand. He was felled by de Wispelaere's group, while another shot from the anti-tank gun knocked out a second armoured car attempting to follow its precursor on to the bridge. With extreme courage, de Wispelaere now darted out into the open to ignite the demolition charges by hand, under heavy enemy fire. Miraculously he managed to light the fuse; but as he stood up to run for the shelter of the bunker, he was struck by a shell, and killed outright. Almost simultaneously the bridge erupted; according to a German account 'a huge plume of flame leaped into the air. There was a crash like thunder. Bits of steel, stone blocks fly high into the air, and with them the two armoured cars . . .' Now the last of the Meuse bridges was down. But was it the last?

By nightfall on the 12th, Rommel's motorized infantry brigade had moved up and were firmly in control of the east bank of the Meuse between Dinant and Houx. Because of the sharpness of the reaction they had encountered earlier from pillboxes like Darche's on the west bank, the leading reconnaissance detachments had carried out no more than a cursory examination of the river itself. But at Houx that afternoon they had spotted what looked like an ancient weir, connecting with a narrow island in midstream, which, unaccountably, it seemed

the defenders had neglected to destroy. Under cover of darkness, and further aided by a low mist clinging to the river bed,
Rommel's foot patrols now explored the weir and reported it
viable. Immediately the infantry commander, Colonel Furst,
ordered the divisional motor-cycle battalion to infiltrate across
it on foot. A divisional chronicle gives an impressionistic
account of the crossing:

They grope their way out of the woods, and in one single rush
are fifty yards beyond the trees. Panting, they lie down in the
shell-holes . . . Onwards! They don't shoot, they don't want to
bring the enemy fire down on themselves . . . Star rockets are fired
above. Their light seems to last forever, like the rays of a huge
searchlight, covering the countryside far and wide with a deadly
brightness . . . At last, after what seems an eternity, their groping
fingers reach the leaves and branches on the bank. In front of
them runs the river. The first phase has been achieved.

The Germans reach the

thin spine with many gaps in it which comprises the old unprotected and weather-worn stone weir . . . Right and left machine-
guns take up position. They give covering fire . . . The first assault
troops do gymnastics, one behind the other, with a distance in
between them, on the fragile framework of the weir. Like tight-
rope walkers they balance their way forwards.

The enemy did not react, and the long thin island turned out
to be untenanted. Rommel's motor-cyclists made their way
stealthily through its scrub and bushes, until they discovered on
its far side a lock gate, equally intact. They crossed this, and
taking advantage of the hubbub and confusion of the night
firing, they swiftly dug themselves in. Pinned under a cross-fire
from German and French machine-guns, with friendly bullets
ricocheting disagreeably off the railway line that ran along the
west side of the river, the motor-cyclists clung to a precarious
foothold. Packet by packet they were reinforced until several
companies were across, and still, strangely enough, no serious
attempt was made to dislodge them. Shortly after midnight on
12 May, less than three days after the campaign had begun,

German soldiers were actually established on the west side of the Meuse. And it had cost Rommel that day the lives of no more than three officers, six N.C.O.s and fifteen men.

Rommel's easy initial crossing resulted from an unusual combination of circumstances. By sheer luck, at Houx he had struck a particularly sensitive point in the Meuse defences. The lock and the weir had expressly not been destroyed because it was feared (not unreasonably) that, with the exceptionally dry season, their destruction would so lower the level of the Meuse that it might actually be fordable in certain places. Yet the banks of the island were fringed with high trees so that the Germans could cross concealed from the defenders on the west bank, while on that side the road and railway, both running along the river, further impeded the defenders' field of fire. Westwards from Houx, the terrain climbs gently towards Anthée and Philippeville on the open plateau beyond, offering a very enticing axis of penetration for armour. Houx was therefore, from all points of view, a danger area not lightly to be ignored, and it might have been assumed that its defence would have assumed particular priority. This was not so, however.

The French at Houx

To compound the misfortunes of the sector, the German crossing point happened to fall right on the boundary between General Bouffet's II Corps and General Martin's XI Corps. Bouffet's solitary division, the 5th Motorized, which formed the left flank of Corap's army, on account of its mobility had already arrived and was more or less in position by the 12th; but its neighbour to the right in Martin's sector, the 18th Infantry Division (an 'A' class unit), had only managed to get six of its battalions and a portion of its artillery into line. In fact, according to Corap's original plans, the 18th was not scheduled to be entirely in position until D+5, or 14 May. As a result, its companies were so thinly spread out along the Meuse that they could not hope to keep their whole front covered, and after the more than fifty miles they had had to cover by forced marches from the French frontier, the 'A' class reservists were thoroughly exhausted. Already on the 11th, General Martin had expressed disquiet about the Houx area and had obtained permission to plug the gaps in his defence with the retreating remnants of the 1st D.L.C. But by now the value of the chastened cavalry was not great, and what little it possessed was thrown away by dispersing it among the infantry. There was added confusion caused by a conflict in seniority between the colonels commanding the cavalry regiments and the lieutenant-colonels of the infantry.

To give further teeth to the defences opposite Houx, Martin had also asked the 5th Motorized Division to transfer one of its battalions to the 18th, until such time as all that division's effectives could be in line. Although the unit concerned, the 2nd Battalion of the 39th Infantry Regiment, received its orders on the 11th, it did not reach its new position until 1600 hours on the following day; thus, at the time of Rommel's arrival on the other side of the Meuse, it was just in the process of taking over from the 66th Regiment. Observing that the river bank was already exposed to fire from Rommel's advance guard on the east side, the newly arrived battalion had shown no predilection to send outposts down there. Instead, the 39th had sat on the high ground west of the river, whence it was impossible to cover the Isle of Houx, or its approaches, and it remained there even after darkness had removed the excuse of enemy fire. This error was a radical contravention of Corap's orders (No. 12 of 22 April), which stated explicitly that the main defence must be carried forward down to the water's edge. Here was perhaps one first practical consequence of the poor discipline of the French Ninth Army on which General Brooke had commented the previous autumn.

It was 0100 [4] on the morning of 13 May when General Boucher, commanding the 5th Motorized Division, learned that a German detachment had crossed the Meuse. But General Martin, the senior commander most concerned, did not receive the news until 0400. As a further example of the lethal sluggishness of French communications, Martin found it quite impossible to get through on the telephone to Corap. Thus, Martin

4. i.e. roughly two hours after the actual crossing.

was forced to co-ordinate plans for a localized counter-attack laterally with Boucher; a wider consequence was that nobody from the army commander, Corap, upwards was aware of the extent of the threat at Houx until late on the 13th, by which time a much greater danger was already revealing itself at Sedan.

French High Command

At the top echelons of the French High Command, despite the repeated warnings of aerial reconnaissance and the fragmentary items of bad news from the cavalry, the day passed once again in a general atmosphere of optimism, and without any specific alarm at the turn of events in the Ardennes. Attention was concentrated on the tank battle in the Gembloux Gap, which (as General Georges later admitted) the French High Command continued to regard as a greater danger to the Allied front than Sedan – because this was the way the Germans had come in 1914. In Government circles the talk was all about 'Fifth Columnists' and parachutists; Alexander Werth, a British correspondent, recalls one of Reynaud's chief spokesmen at the Quai d'Orsay, Duroc, telling him reassuringly that Sunday: 'After all, if the Germans have to resort to tricks like dressing up their soldiers in foreign uniforms – well, then they can't feel so very strong. It makes me confident they'll still lose the war.' On the 12th, Gamelin is to be found suggesting to General Georges that the cavalry screen withdrawing from the Ardennes now be sent to the rear in readiness to round up German parachutists; then he changed his mind and suggested it should be sent northwards to back up Blanchard's First Army – both proposals only serving to illustrate just how badly out of touch the Generalissimo was, at his radio-less G.Q.G. Gamelin admits that he was 'above all devoted to dealing with matters of overall organization'. These appear to have included all sorts of minor details concerning tactical defence against tanks in northern Belgium, and warnings to the Maginot Line of the technique employed by the Germans to capture Eben Emael. He complains at the poverty of the intelligence reaching him from the

Ardennes sector, but went to bed that night contented by the evening's situation report from General Georges, which stated: 'The defence now seems well assured on the whole front of the river [Meuse].'

At General Georges's headquarters at La Ferté, his Chief of Staff, General Roton, records the receipt at 1500 hours on the 12th of 'a very alarming report' from Huntziger's Second Army. The cavalry had suffered 'very severe losses' (something of an exaggeration), and Huntziger was calling for a fresh division to replace the 71st, which Grandsard (commanding X Corps) was having to insert into the line south of Sedan. Georges was away in the north, and in his absence Roton took the initiative to order the movement 'immediately' of three of the five divisions from the general reserve which Georges had earmarked for the Sedan sector the previous day: the 3rd Armoured,[5] the 3rd Motorized and the 14th Infantry Divisions. These were also among the best in the French Army. But at 1700 hours, surprisingly enough, a 'more reassuring' message came through from Huntziger's Chief of Staff: 'Calm had returned to the front', says Roton. 'He estimated that there was no urgency to push the 3rd Motorized as far as Stonne. But I held to my point of view; this division was to arrive punctually on 14 May at the battlefield of Sedan.' This would be, however, at least one critical day too late. Meanwhile nothing further was done for the more immediately threatened Corap.[6]

Huntziger's *Orders to the Second Army*

With nightfall, it was abundantly clear to the French Second Army that they were going to be attacked in earnest the following day. All night long the troops opposite Sedan could hear the growl of German tanks moving up on the other side of the Meuse, and any pretence of secrecy or camouflage now

5. Note that the 2nd Armoured dropped temporarily out of sight; next day it was dispatched to the First Army.

6. It should also be noted that, by 12 May, Georges had already oriented several more of his reserve divisions – including both the 1st and 2nd Armoured, towards northern Belgium – away from the main threat.

appeared to be abandoned. Night reconnaissance flights reported vast motorized columns, moving with headlamps full on in flagrant contempt of the Allied air forces, along all the roads leading to the Meuse south of Namur, and heaviest of all was the traffic heading towards Sedan. That day the 1st Panzer Division had been positively identified, and while even from the garbled reports of the French cavalry screen it was obvious that this was not the only one converging on Sedan, the fact that the 1st Panzer was known to be the pride of Hitler's armoured formation must have clearly suggested to Huntziger the scale of the pending attack.

Huntziger himself was rated to be perhaps the most brilliant intellect among the senior commanders of the French Army. Half Alsatian and half Breton, on leaving St Cyr in 1901 his first choice was to join the Marines. After taking part in pre-1914 colonial wars in Madagascar and Indo-China, he commanded a battalion during the First War, ending it with the rank of lieutenant-colonel as Marshal Franchet d'Esperey's Chief of Operations in Salonika. By 1938 he was appointed to the *Conseil Supérieur de la Guerre* (Supreme War Council), having already commanded the French forces in Syria as one of the youngest army commanders on record. On taking over the Second Army, he was still well under sixty (which, by the standards of 1940, was youthful), a trimly elegant, alert and vigorous figure. His cold blue eyes gave away a certain tendency to be remote in his dealings with subordinates, but most of them agreed upon his 'dazzling intelligence' as a theoretician, and he was generally regarded in the French Army as the likeliest successor to Gamelin.

Perhaps the most fundamental truth about Huntziger, like so many of his contemporaries of 1940, however, is to be found in the concluding words of his Order of the Day of the night of 12 May, warning the Second Army of the coming battle on the Sedan 'position of resistance':

Every portion of terrain upon which the enemy may have set foot must be retaken from him.

The honour of leaders at all levels is at stake in preserving the integrity of the position, without regard to casualties.

No *défaillance* will be tolerated.

On the Maginot Line, we shall defend the sacred soil of the nation.

I am sure of the Second Army.

Resounding, courageous and inspiring words, but they were those of a past war, redolent of the resolute but rigid linear defence at Verdun. They revealed that Huntziger's thinking, for all his intellectual power, remained rooted in the victory of 1918. The French General Staff, basing its judgements on its own capabilities, knew that it could not execute a full-scale crossing of the Meuse before 18 May; therefore, q.e.d., the Germans could not either. And by the evening of 12 May, Huntziger equally still seems only to have half believed, despite all the signs, in the imminence of the danger confronting him.

Symptomatic of that fatal leisureliness with which his Second Army (or, for that matter, Corap's Ninth) carried out its final preparations was the manner in which the 71st Division was being brought up into the line. Up till March, this Parisian-recruited 'B' division, probably the poorest of all Huntziger's units, had been holding a sector on the Meuse at Mouzon, but since then it had been undergoing badly-needed training in the Vouziers area. On 10 May, Huntziger had ordered it to resume its position on the Meuse, between the 55th and 3rd North African Divisions, but he appears to have failed to impart to his subordinates any particular sense of urgency for this transfer. General Grandsard, to whose X Corps the 71st belonged, claims in his apologia that by the night of the 12th he still had no idea of the strength of the German force approaching Sedan, details of air and cavalry reconnaissance intelligence not having filtered down to him, and his appreciation that night was that the enemy could not attack with any likelihood of success on the 13th. (He adds that of course he knew all about the German Stukas, but had complete faith in the French Air Force to keep them at bay.) But Grandsard blames Huntziger for having stationed the 71st so far away from the line on 10 May: 'To demand an infantry division to march on foot,' says Grandsard, 'some sixty kilometres in two short May nights (six hours approximately each night), plus a relief, is to demand the impossible.'[7] On the afternoon of the 12th, the commander of the 71st Division, the elderly and ailing General Baudet, requested Grandsard for a time extension. Grandsard refused. On moving into line, General Baudet found that his command post had not been set up, while the divisional telephone exchange was linked with only light temporary cables, many of which were not even buried. Meanwhile, to make way for the entry into line of the 71st, General Lafontaine's 55th Division was also in the process of extensively reorganizing itself. Altogether, Grandsard reckoned that the earliest date by which the whole of his corps could possibly be in position was the 13th; but in fact, General Ruby tells us, General Lafontaine was not planning to complete *his* dispositions before the *night* of 13–14 May.

In terms of artillery, Grandsard's position by the night of 12 May was somewhat rosier – on paper. Early on the morning of the 12th, Huntziger had ordered up two additional regiments to support Grandsard, while the 55th Division, though short on machine-guns and anti-tank weapons, had twice the normal establishment of artillery, with some 140 guns supporting its front. Without apparently informing Grandsard, however, the commander of the long-range 155-mm. regiment had pulled back the battery at Torcy, which had been shelling the Bouillon crossing points so effectively, after it had run out of ammunition. To his annoyance, Grandsard discovered that evening that he could no longer maintain interdiction on the German approach routes.

Thus as 12 May drew to a close, the overall picture on Grandsard's X Corps front was not an encouraging one. Some of the artillery was still digging itself in, while other reinforcement batteries would not arrive before dawn. Of the infantry, the elderly reservists of the 71st were thoroughly fatigued from their two nights of forced marching, and had little time to acclimatize themselves to their new positions; the 55th was also still moving house, while this already weak unit had virtually

7. Again, this was thinking in 1914–18 terms; it need hardly be remarked that the German infantry divisions of 1940 would not have found such a march beyond their powers, even on foot.

lost one of the battalions of its 295th Regiment. Chewed up on the River Semois, the remnants straggling back across the Meuse hardly aspired to *encourager les autres* with their dismal narratives. Altogether, Grandsard's X Corps was hardly an imposing force to put up against the élite of the German Panzers. The big question to be answered on 13 May was, would the reinforcements ordered by General Georges reach the field in time? Or would Guderian be able to beat them to it by bringing up enough of his corps to effect a river crossing in strength? Behind this, still more was at issue – the training and philosophy of a whole generation – and beyond that a whole trend of history dating back to the first Sedan in 1870.

German High Command

Would Guderian be able to cross the Meuse on the 13th? During the 12th, Hitler had sent his chief adjutant, Colonel Schmundt, to the battle H.Q. of Kleist's Armoured Group to ask Kleist whether he intended to attempt an immediate crossing, or to wait until the main body of the infantry arrived. The question reflected the German High Command's nervousness, still lurking just below the surface, about the audacity of the Manstein–*Sichelschnitt* Plan. Kleist, encouraged by the results of the previous three days and by Intelligence reports indicating that the French had not yet begun shifting any major reserves behind the Sedan sector, replied that he preferred to 'attack at once, without wasting time', so as to hit the French before they could regain their breath. A Fieseler Storch was dispatched to fly Guderian from Bouillon to Kleist's H.Q. There he received orders for his corps to attack across the river at 1500 hours the next day. For the first time, the ever-eager Guderian demurred; the 1st and 10th Panzers would be in position on time, but not the 2nd which was still hung up along the Semois; the *Sturmpionieren*, upon whom the vital task of throwing bridges across the river would depend, were weary from their labours in the Ardennes; and Guderian himself, though he does not mention it in his memoirs, may well have been somewhat shaken from his own two close escapes that

day from Allied bombers. He questioned the wisdom of moving with only two-thirds of his corps available. But Kleist was
adamant, and Guderian says: 'I felt obliged to admit that there
were probably advantages in thrusting forward immediately.'
He was, however, much more discountenanced by Kleist's
alteration in the air plan for the 13th. Guderian had previously
agreed with General Loerzer of the Luftwaffe that the crossing at Sedan should be given 'continuous support' throughout
the operation, in order to keep the heads of the enemy gunners
permanently down. Now Kleist ordered 'a mass bombing attack,
to be co-ordinated with the beginning of the artillery preparation'. Guderian claimed that his 'whole attack plan was thus
placed in jeopardy', but again Kleist insisted. In evident ill-
humour, Guderian flew back to his H.Q.

On the way there was very nearly a repeat of the Mechelen
Incident, which might have had much graver consequences for
the Germans. The inexperienced young pilot of the Fieseler
Storch could not find XIX Corps landing strip 'in the fading
light, and the next thing I knew', says Guderian, 'we were on
the other side of the Meuse, flying in a slow and unarmed plane
over the French positions. An unpleasant moment. I gave my
pilot emphatic orders to turn north ... we just made it.'

Safely back at corps H.Q., Guderian got to work on drawing
up his orders for the next day. In an interesting revelation of
just how thorough German training for this momentous operation had been since the redrafting of *Fall Gelb* three months
previously, Guderian states:

In view of the very short time at our disposal, we were forced to
take the orders used in the war games at Koblenz from our files
and, after changing the dates and times, issue these as the orders
for the attack. They were perfectly fitted to the reality of the
situation. The only change that had to be made was that at Koblenz we had imagined the attack going in at 0900 instead of 1500
hours.

Yet while all eyes of the German High Command were
focused upon the Meuse crossing being prepared by Guderian,
no one was aware that to the north Major-General Rommel,

allotted only the secondary role of providing flanking cover to the main thrust, already had a toe-hold on the far side of the river and was indeed about to develop a major offensive of his own.

Chapter 12

The Crossing

13 May

It seems that the Germans are not interested in France this time . . .
   New York Journal American, 13 May

'*La description d'une bataille devrait être une leçon de Moral.*'
JOSEPH JOUBERT

Rommel Emerges

On the eve of an adventure which would launch a reputation ultimately more familiar to the world at large than that of any other German general of the Second World War, Erwin Rommel was a name completely unknown outside the Army even at home, and little enough known inside it. He came from a simple middle-class family of moderate means, with no military tradition; both his father and grandfather had been schoolteachers. Rommel was a Württemberger, a race more renowned for its solidity and shrewd thriftiness than for any martial attributes. Aged forty-eight in 1940, he had been commissioned in 1912, with not particularly brilliant marks, into a not particularly brilliant line regiment. He appears to have made an early impact as a meticulous regimental officer, intolerant of anything slipshod, but – as his British biographer, Desmond Young, remarks – he was one of those soldiers who only 'find in war the one occupation to which they are perfectly adapted'. It was on the southern fringe of those fateful Ardennes, near Longwy, that Lieutenant Rommel had his first opportunity three weeks after the war broke out in 1914. With only three men and suffering painfully from food poisoning, he ran into some fifteen to twenty French troops; instead of calling up the rest of his platoon Rommel immediately opened fire and, taken by surprise, the enemy scattered. Five months later, after recovering from a thigh wound, Rommel won the Iron Cross by crawling with his platoon through barbed wire into the middle of the main French position, knocking out four block-houses and then withdrawing with light losses before the defence could make an effective riposte. Although this was only a small-scale action, it was as characteristic of Rommel's expertise in the tactics of infiltration – which, as a senior com-mander, he was to bring to a supreme art – as it was of his nerveless audacity. Later in 1915 Rommel's skill at this kind of operation gained him transfer to a newly-created mountain battalion, designed to perform special tasks in 'battle groups', the commanders of which were granted a freedom of action far in excess of their rank. In the brief Roumanian campaign of 1916–17, Rommel carried out some almost incredible exploits, often with up to a whole battalion under his control, although he was still no more than a 1st lieutenant.

But the real summit of his First War career came during the Battle of Caporetto in October 1917, against the nation that would fight under his command in the Western Desert twenty-five years later. Penetrating the Italian lines at dawn, Rommel first surprised an enemy gun battery without a shot being fired. Then, diving still deeper behind the enemy positions, he sur-prised from the rear a counter-attacking Italian battalion. That too surrendered. After this success, Rommel was reinforced to a total of six companies and now took up position astride an important supply road well behind the enemy lines. Here he succeeded in capturing the best part of a brigade of crack Bersaglieri moving up towards the front. After fifty hours con-stantly on the move, he returned with the astonishing bag of 150 Italian officers, 9,000 men and 81 guns. For his feat, he was promoted captain and awarded the Pour le Mérite, the equivalent of the Victoria Cross when given to a junior officer.

After the First War, Rommel became a natural candidate for the élite cadres of Seeckt's tiny Reichswehr. Promoted major in 1933, he chose to remain with his mountain troops as a regimental officer until two years later, when he was appointed instructor at the Potsdam War Academy, with the rank of lieutenant-colonel. During that time he was also assigned on special attachment to the Hitler Youth, but this ended after a short while when Rommel fell foul of their leader, the arrogant Baldur von Schirach. After three years at Potsdam, he was then sent to command the War Academy at Wiener Neustadt. He was by this time a full colonel, which, considering the huge expansion of the Wehrmacht, did not in any way denote a meteoric career. But he had neither connections with any of the great military clans, nor affiliations with the Party. His relationship with the Nazi machine in pre-war days was, in fact, not dissimilar to Guderian's; never remotely a Party man, he admired Hitler as a technician, and was responsive both to his kindred dynamism and receptiveness to unorthodox ideas. It was in 1938 that Rommel first caught Hitler's eye after publication of a simple but admirably clear textbook on infantry tactics, based on his own personal experiences from the First War and called *Infanterie Greift An* ('The Infantry Attacks'). At the time of the occupation of the Sudetenland, he was selected to command the battalion entrusted with Hitler's personal safety. On the outbreak of war the following year, Rommel was promoted major-general and, as Headquarters Commandant, again made responsible for guarding Hitler during the Polish campaign. He chafed at having no operational command, found himself antipathetic to the Party potentates like Martin Bormann, but was fascinated by the front-row view his job gave him of the campaign and its techniques. When it was over he asked Hitler for command of a Panzer division, by way of reward for past services. This was granted. On 15 February, Rommel arrived at Bad Godesberg to take over the 7th, one of the four 'light' divisions [1] to be converted into Panzers that winter. Weaker than the original Panzer division, the 7th had three instead of four tank battalions, 218 instead of 276 tanks, and over half of these were Czech-made light-medium T-38s.

It was quite one of Rommel's most astonishing achievements that, in middle age, after a lifetime spent with the infantry and without any experience whatever of armour or mechanized

---

1. Mixed divisions, roughly comparable to the French D.L.M.s, consisting of two rifle regiments and only one tank detachment. The Polish campaign proved them to be unsatisfactory.

forces, he should within three short months not only have been able to master the technique, but also to so mould a new unit that it would become perhaps the most consistently successful of all the Panzer divisions employed in France – and this despite the relative lightness of its armoured contingent. There were indeed those among his critics who considered that he never really understood the principles of armoured warfare. Again and again, he handled his large bodies of tanks very much as he had led those few raiding companies on their deep penetrations behind the Italian lines, with a bold unorthodoxy that sometimes shocked the purists. Often he had miraculous luck. Even more than Guderian, he was a commander whose constant closeness to the front provided him with an instant grasp of events.

Rommel's Opponent

The unhappy French commander against whose army Rommel would strike the first hard blow on 13 May, General Corap, was perhaps as representative of the median of the old-style French officer as Rommel was of the élite of the new, revolutionary Wehrmacht. Sixty-two in 1940, Corap was a Norman who had passed out top of his class in St Cyr in 1898. Joining the Algerian *Tirailleurs*, he spent most of his career on colonial operations in North Africa. A captain in 1914, he was appointed to Foch's staff the following year and in 1918 switched to Pétain's, ending the war as a lieutenant-colonel. Afterwards he returned to Morocco, where in 1926 he achieved the summit of his career by capturing the famous rebel, Abd-el-Krim. He was what in the French Army was called a typical *baroudeur*, an old sweat from North Africa, and this largely conditioned his thinking. André Maurois remarks of him: 'His conversation was very interesting, but one felt his attention was directed entirely toward the past. He told me how, at the time of Fashoda, he had been mobilized against England as a young second lieutenant ...' Corap is described by Maurois as being 'a timid man, held in high esteem by his superiors, unmilitary in appearance, and running to fat around the middle. He had trouble getting into a car ...' In contrast to the elegant, slim and aloof Huntziger, Corap had a certain vulgar, fat man's geniality that made him well liked by the troops, although politically he was known to have a particularly violent antipathy towards the Popular Front. But even more than Huntziger, his military education had ceased with 1918, and he was totally ignorant of mechanized warfare; above all, he had not the faintest idea of just how quickly an opponent like Rommel could move in 1940.

Rommel Crosses the Meuse

At 0300 on the 13th, Rommel with his A.D.C., Captain Schraepler, drove down to Dinant to find out what was going on. There he found shells falling from the French artillery on the other side of the Meuse, and a number of knocked-out tanks lying about in the streets leading down to the river. Enemy fire made it impossible for him to go any further in his conspicuous command vehicle, so he and Schraepler clambered on foot down to the river. Here his 6th Rifle Regiment was about to cross to the other bank in rubber assault boats, to reinforce the foothold made during the night by the motor-cycle battalion. From here on, Rommel's own account remains probably the best and clearest of the day's events. The riflemen, says Rommel, were

being badly held up by heavy artillery fire and by the extremely troublesome small arms fire of French troops installed among the rocks on the west bank.

The situation when I arrived was none too pleasant. Our boats were being destroyed one after the other by the French flanking fire, and the crossing eventually came to a standstill. The enemy infantry were so well concealed that they were impossible to locate even after a long search through glasses. Again and again they directed their fire into the area in which I and my companions – the commanders of the Rifle Brigade and the Engineer Battalion – were lying.

The early-morning mist, which had provided such invaluable cover for the motor-cyclists in their crossing at Houx, was meanwhile dissipating. A smoke-screen was desperately needed with which to render innocuous the searing fire of the enemy infantry:

But we had no smoke unit. So I now gave orders for a number of houses in the valley to be set alight in order to supply the smoke we lacked.

Minute by minute the enemy fire grew more unpleasant. From up river a damaged rubber boat came drifting down to us with a badly wounded man clinging to it, shouting and screaming for help – the poor fellow was near to drowning. But there was no help for him here, the enemy fire was too heavy.

At this point Rommel turned his attention northwards to Houx, where the motor-cyclists were clinging precariously to their gains of the previous night. Most of the battalion had now reached the west bank, but the French resistance was mounting. Shortly after crossing, the commander of No. 1 Company, Captain Heilbronn, was wounded; then the Battalion Adjutant, Senior Lieutenant Pflug, and another subaltern were killed. Leading two companies himself, the Battalion Commander, Major Steinkeller, pushed up inland on to high ground after a brief struggle, taking the small hamlet of La Grange. But by mid-morning all contact with the east bank of the river had been effectively severed, there were still enemy pockets of resistance behind and heavy gunfire was coming down on the crossing area; the motor-cyclists had not yet been able to bring over any anti-tank guns, and in the event of any early French counter-attack accompanied by tanks, their position would of necessity be extremely perilous.

Not particularly happy, Rommel now drove south in a Mark IV tank to the 7th Rifle Regiment which, under Colonel von Bismarck,[2] was trying to cross the Meuse opposite Bouvignes, about two miles south of Houx. On the way, he came under fire again several times from the west bank, and shell splinters wounded Schraepler in the arm. Bismarck had already managed to get a company across the river; but, says Rommel,

2. Later killed at the Battle of Alam Halfa in the desert, while again serving under Rommel.

the enemy fire had then become so heavy that their crossing equipment had been shot to pieces and the crossing had had to be halted. Large numbers of wounded were receiving treatment in a house close beside the demolished bridge. As at the northern crossing point, there was nothing to be seen of the enemy who were preventing the crossing . . .

Rommel decided that there was no hope of getting any more men over the Meuse without bringing right down to the river bank 'powerful artillery and tank support to deal with the enemy nests'. To effect this, he drove back to divisional H.Q., where he found both his corps commander, Hoth, and the commander of the 4th Army, Kluge, following his progress with interest. Then he returned to the Meuse, to Leffé on the northern outskirts of Dinant, so as 'to get the crossing moving there'. At Leffé, Rommel continues:

we found a number of rubber boats, all more or less badly damaged by enemy fire, lying in the street where our men had left them. Eventually, after being bombed on the way by our own air-craft, we arrived at the river . . . The crossing had now come to a complete standstill, with the officers badly shaken by the casualties which their men had suffered. On the opposite bank we could see several men of the company which was already across, among them many wounded . . . The officers reported that nobody dared show himself outside cover, as the enemy opened fire immediately on anyone they spotted.

The Mark IV tanks [3] called for by Rommel began to arrive, and Captain König of the 25th Panzer Regiment takes up the story:

Only half the tanks reach the edge of the Meuse, the rest remain with tracks that have been thrown off and other damage, some-where on the slope. On the Meuse all hell is let loose – the enemy defends himself from a mass of bunkers and provisional battle positions – every house on the other side of the bank is equipped to assist the defence. Concentrated fire is coming down on the positions of our engineers, and the Meuse water is whipped up by constant artillery and mortar-shell explosions.

---

3. The whole 7th Panzer in fact possessed only some two dozen of the new Mark IV tank with its heavy 75-mm. gun.

The tanks cruised slowly along the river road, with their turrets traversed at 90 degrees, firing at little more than one hundred yards' range directly into the French bunkers and machine-gun nests on the opposite bank.

The fire of the Panzer guns [continues König], the 75-mm. shells as well as the well-scattered 20-mm. quick-firing cannon, soon show an effect . . . the companies shoot almost as if they were in training, and no recognized target, no suspicious movement of the enemy, remains unnoticed. The enemy fire begins to slacken noticeably, but nevertheless the crossing of the first storm boats, the engineers, remains a hard task, a task from which many don't come back. In impotent rage, the tank crews watch boats torn to pieces by direct hits . . .

One particularly troublesome pill-box [4] was engaged by Lieutenant Hanke,[5] who, after firing several rounds, knocked it out.

Under cover of the tanks' gunfire, the crossings slowly got under way again, and a cable ferry using several large pontoons was started up. During these operations, according to Captain König, 'General Rommel is everywhere. He is with the engineers, he leaps on to a Mark IV tank in order to give it the target himself. He is no easy chief for his staff . . .' To whip up the flagging zeal of his obviously badly shaken riflemen, Rommel seems to have returned to a previous incarnation that morning, and to have acted more like the junior officer leading his raiding parties behind the Italian lines at Caporetto than a divisional commander. He states:

I now took over personal command of the 2nd Battalion of the 7th Rifle Regiment and for some time directed operations myself.

With Lieutenant Most [6] I crossed the Meuse in one of the first

---

4. Many of which, it will be remembered, had never received the vital armour plates protecting their embrasures.

5. Hanke, according to Rommel's son, Manfred, was an out-and-out Nazi highly unpopular with the other officers. He ended the war as Gauleiter of Silesia, and conducted the last-ditch defence of Breslau. When the devastated city finally capitulated to the Russians, Hanke disappeared in a plane and has never been heard of since.

6. Successor to the wounded Schraepler.

316   To Lose a Battle

boats and at once joined the company which had been across since
early morning. From the company command post we could see
Companies Enkefort and Lichter were making rapid progress.

I then moved up north along a deep gully to Company Enkefort.
As we arrived an alarm came in: 'Enemy tanks in front.' The
company had no anti-tank weapons, and I therefore gave orders
for small arms fire to be opened on the tanks as quickly as
possible.

From this there arose the *belle légende*, long attributed to
Rommel, that he told his hard-pressed infantry to fire their
Very pistols at the French tanks, to simulate the tracer effect
of anti-tank shells. Whether true or not, the result was indis-
putable and the tanks withdrew, while Rommel reported that
'large numbers of French stragglers came through the bushes
and slowly laid down their arms'.

It was now about midday, and things were beginning to look
a bit better for Rommel. With Lieutenant Most, he returned
once more to the east bank, driving north with a tank and a
signals vehicle to where the 6th Rifle Regiment were supporting the beleaguered motor-cycle battalion. Here the crossing
was 'in full swing', and Rommel was told that already twenty
badly-needed anti-tank guns had been forded across the river.

A company of the engineer battalion was busily engaged in building 8-ton pontoons, but I stopped them and told them to build the
16-ton type. I aimed to get part of the Panzer Regiment across as
quickly as possible. As soon as the first pontoon was ready I took
my 8-wheeled signals vehicle across.

The waiting Panzer crews, their vehicles under cover just off
the river, watched impatiently as the sweating engineers
struggled away under a broiling midday sun. Several times the
pontoons were hit, at least one of them actually sinking to
the bottom of the river with a tank on it, and the Engineer
battalion commander was killed, together with a number of
his men.

At this point in the consolidation of the bridgehead, Rommel
seems momentarily to have been struck with an excess of
optimism. According to 7th Panzer's official history, in the late

afternoon he summoned three subalterns commanding his light
tank detachments and told them: '*Meine Herren!* The enemy
is in full retreat. We shall follow up immediately, and even
today we shall reach X-locality eighteen kilometres west of
Dinant!' But work on the ferries was further delayed by French
interdiction fire, and it was not until twilight that the first of
these tank detachments was able to cross, so that Rommel had
to drop any intention of breaking out of the bridgehead in
favour of consolidation.

Meanwhile, according to Rommel, 'the enemy had launched
a heavy attack, and the fire of their tanks could be heard
approaching the ridge of the Meuse bank'. Rommel crossed
the Meuse again, heading towards the firing. Arriving at the
infantry brigade H.Q. now established there,

I found the situation looking decidedly unhealthy. The Commander
of the 7th Motor-cycle Battalion had been wounded,[7] his adjutant
killed, and a powerful French counter-attack had severely mauled
our men in Grange. There was a danger that enemy tanks might
penetrate into the Meuse valley itself.

Leaving my signals lorry on the west bank, I crossed the river
again and gave orders for first the Panzer Company, and then the
Panzer Regiment, to be ferried across during the night. However,
ferrying tanks across the 120-yards-wide river by night was a slow
job, and by morning there were still only fifteen tanks on the
west bank, an alarmingly small number.

This 'powerful French counter-attack'[8] was in fact an exaggeration, and it remains to be seen just what in fact the French
reaction amounted to on this critical day.

Corap Reacts

The sparsity and incompleteness of French accounts of the
fighting exemplify the confusion enveloping this and the

7. Rommel's total losses that day were five officers, seven N.C.O.s and
forty-nine men killed, plus a considerable number of wounded.

8. The fact that Rommel considered it 'powerful' is in itself indicative of
just how precarious his position on the west bank was, and what might have
been achieved by any really resolute French riposte.

succeeding days, not only opposite Rommel but everywhere else where the Germans managed to cross the Meuse. Yet it is clear from Rommel's version alone that the Belgian Chasseurs Ardennais manning the pill-boxes and bunkers down on the Meuse, as well as the men of the French 66th Regiment plugging the intervals, fought hard and well throughout the 13th. By the end of the day, there were still pockets holding out behind the German bridgehead, but their resources in supporting arms were very inadequate; the 66th was far too thinly spread out along the river and was already much fatigued by its approach march before the attack began. A relieving force was urgently needed.

During the 13th, the situation immediately behind the threatened area seems to have been worse even than down on the river itself, a phenomenon to be repeated, with interest, later at Sedan. As every available plane was being committed to support Guderian that day, the tactical air strikes on Rommel's front had been strictly limited, and they could at most have been only partly responsible for the chaos which was to exert so disastrous an influence in the mounting of the French counter-attacks. General Boucher, commanding the 5th Motorized Division, had, as already noted, first learned of the Houx crossing at one o'clock that morning. Five hours later, although his battle H.Q. was less than ten miles removed from the scene of the action, he discovered that all liaison with the battalion of the 39th Regiment which he had loaned to his neighbour had somehow been broken. To restore contact, he pushed forward a squadron of motor-cyclists and two troops of machine-gun carriers from divisional reconnaissance, probably the same that were repulsed by the small-arms fire and 'Very pistols' brought to bear by Rommel himself that morning. At 1000 hours, Boucher now decided to throw in an infantry attack on Haut-le-Wastia executed by one battalion of the 129th Regiment. H-Hour was to be 1300 hours, but the battalion did not begin to move until 1400 hours and was then almost immediately dispersed by enemy aircraft. A crack regiment of Motorized Dragoons under command of II Corps was then ordered to take over the task, but when this regiment said it could not arrive at the start-line until 2000 hours, the operation was postponed until the following morning. This was the extent of the effort mounted on the 13th from II Corps's sector north of the Houx bridgehead – by some of the best units to be found in the whole of Corap's Ninth Army.[9]

Between 18th Division H.Q. and its various regiments (the 66th, 77th and 125th) communications became extremely poor in the course of the morning. General Doumenc notes: '... lines are cut. They had ceased with the 77th, and could not be re-established with the 125th. The radio did not function. There were no more motor-cycles.' General Martin, having received no news of the crossing, although his XI Corps H.Q. lay less than fifteen miles from Houx, visited the 18th Division early that afternoon, where he called up the colonel of the 39th Regiment, which did not seem so far to have particularly distinguished itself. The colonel, in some agitation, told him that he had only just managed to escape from a group of German scouts whom he had met, in his staff car, on a railway bridge at Sosoye – eight miles west of the Meuse. Martin then ordered the 39th to prepare a counter-attack aimed at recapturing Surinvaux Wood and throwing all the enemy troops on the west bank back into the Meuse. The operation would be supported by three artillery groups and a squadron of tanks; H-Hour was to be 1930. Meanwhile, the battered 66th Regiment had 'begun to show signs of exhaustion', says General Doumenc, and 'little was known of the rest of the division. The 77th [10] appeared to have fled. Of the 125th [10] nothing was known ...' All this had been achieved by Rommel's dozen-odd infantry companies, unsupported by any heavy weapons on the west side of the Meuse.

9. The sluggishness and lack of punch with which these first ripostes were executed characterized almost all the French counter-attacks subsequently carried out at various levels; in contrast, right through to the last days of the war, the art of the counter-attack was something in which the German Army was particularly skilled. As many American and British veterans will testify, the German capacity to hit back with an instant and weighted blow with whatever forces happened to be at hand was often little short of miraculous.

10. Like the 66th Regiment, both were 'A' series reservist units.

Then, at 1830 hours, just one hour before Martin's counter-attack was due to go in, according to General Doumenc:

the Colonel of the 39th Infantry Regiment communicated by tele-phone that he would not be ready at the appointed hour. H-Hour was fixed for 2000 hours. At 1945 he reported once again that the attack could not take place at 2000 hours. Thus it happened that, alone, the squadron of tanks moved forward to the Bois de la Grange; the tanks swept all that they found in front of them, and brought back eight prisoners as night was falling.

Realizing that there was no infantry following them to con-solidate on the captured ground, the tanks then withdrew.

Thus ended the sum effort of Corap's Ninth Army on 13 May against the malignant, mortal tumour swelling in its side – one 'hit-and-run' raid by a squadron of unsupported tanks. A golden opportunity to wipe out Rommel's bridgehead and inflict a severe reverse upon him had been lost. All that day, events had been balanced upon a knife's edge – much more finely balanced, indeed, than was apparent to the French defenders at the time. Without Rommel's personal leadership on the one side, with just a little more determination on the other, the story might have been different. Presumably Rom-mel would have made a fresh attempt at crossing the river on the 14th or the 15th; but as his subsequent career after the tide of war had begun to flow against Germany showed, he was a commander exhilarated by success but easily dejected by adversity. If his motor-cyclists and riflemen had been pushed back into the Meuse on the 13th, the reverse might well have seriously blunted the cutting-edge of the 7th Panzer, but indisputably it would have gained for Corap at least some of the commodity which the French Army was to need most desperately throughout the campaign – *time*. Even through the night of the 13th and the early morning of the 14th, Rom-mel's position remained extremely critical. His bridgehead was only a couple of miles deep and perhaps three wide; pockets of resistance were still holding out in its rear, and it was by no means certain that he could get his tanks across in sufficient strength before a concerted attack by French armour might overrun it completely. As the night dragged on, the waiting Panzer crews listened impatiently to the sappers hammering away at their bridge, which had been slightly damaged in an enemy bombing raid the previous evening.

At lunchtime on the 13th, the first news of Rommel's crossing was transmitted to Gamelin by General Georges's headquarters, in a brief signal which added simply 'a battalion had been knocked about'. Colonel Minart at G.Q.G. tells that the news created 'a lively emotion'. A short time later, G.Q.G. was informed that a counter-attack with tanks was in process. Now, at last, all attention was concentrated on what was happening on the Meuse, says Minart:

but two long hours went by without our being able to know if the announced counter-attack had succeeded and if the Germans had been thrown back on to the right bank of the river. Various rumours, unchecked, began to reach as far as Vincennes. The Germans were supposed to be at Mézières. Anxious about being incorrectly informed, General Gamelin, at two various attempts (1400 and 1415 hours) telephoned – the only time – direct to Ninth Army. General Thierry d'Argenlieu,[11] Chief of Staff to Corap's Army, replied with his usual calm: 'Nothing to report at Mézières; we are surveying the region at Monthermé. The incident at Houx is in hand; General Martin is on the spot with General Duffet.' [12]

After this report, some hours elapsed without any further news from the Ninth Army. Then suddenly, at 1615 hours, a first smattering of ill tidings came through about Huntziger's Second Army. At 2125 hours that night, General Georges rang through to tell Gamelin tersely that there had been *'un pépin assez sérieux'* ('a rather serious pin-prick') at Sedan. It was the understatement of the century.

Guderian's Panzers

That morning at 0715 hours Guderian had issued his final orders for the crossing operation in the afternoon. It would

11. D'Argenlieu was killed a few days later.
12. Duffet was commander of the 18th Division.

have the support, he promised in only a modest exaggeration, of 'almost the whole German Air Force'. The French defences would be smashed 'by means of uninterrupted attacks lasting for eight hours'. At 1500 hours, his XIX Panzer Corps would effect crossings on either side of Sedan, between the mouth of the River Bar [13] and Bazeilles. If it arrived in time, the 2nd Panzer would form the right flank of the assault, crossing the Meuse at Donchery. In the centre, the 1st Panzer would strike at Glaire, on the root of the Iges peninsula formed by a sharp loop in the Meuse, and Torcy on the northern outskirts of Sedan. The 10th was to cross south of Sedan, securing the left flank with the capture of the high ground running along the west bank of the Meuse above Pont Maugis.

But the main effort of the day was to be made by General Kirchner's 1st Panzer. The task prescribed for it by Guderian was to mop up inside the Iges peninsula and push forward to the Bellevue–Torcy road, then to attack the dominating Bois de la Marfée heights, the anchor of the whole French position at Sedan, and finally to establish itself on a line from Chéhéry [14] to Chaumont. For this task the division would be reinforced by the Grossdeutschland Regiment, transferred from the strength of 10th Panzer; an entire battalion of *Sturmpionieren* (assault engineers); and the heavy artillery battalions belonging to each of its sister divisions. A tremendous concentration of firepower could thus be brought to bear on 1st Panzer's front of less than two miles in width, but the success or failure of the day would in the final analysis depend upon the three rifle battalions of Lieutenant-Colonel Hermann Balck's 1st Rifle Regiment, the four of Lieutenant-Colonel Graf von Schwerin's Grossdeutschland, and the various *Sturmpionieren* companies. As with Rommel at Dinant, there would be no question of tank support on the west bank until the infantry had secured the bridgehead.

To provide his Panzer Corps with further encouragement, Guderian added the information that the other two Panzers in

13. It is to be recalled that this also marked the hinge between the French Ninth and Second Armies.
14. Note the two different, closely situated place-names over which confusion was later to arise: Chéhéry and Chémery.

Kleist's group, Reinhardt's 6th and 8th, would also be crossing the Meuse that day, in the Monthermé and Nouzonville areas. Meanwhile, behind Guderian, Wietersheim's XIV Motorized Corps would be assembling, ready to support and exploit their success.

The Battle for Sedan

An intense, nervous hubbub surrounds that morning, mingled with a new wariness. From contemporary German news-films one has glimpses of the assault troops covering on foot the last few kilometres of the approach march down to the Meuse: tough, bronzed, enormously fit young men striding in shirt-sleeve order through meadows knee-high with lush grass and spring flowers, brimming over with arrogant self confidence. The sun beats down on them. On the way they pass innumerable heavy weapons destined to help get them across the river. Everywhere the crews are breaking off branches of trees to camouflage their vehicles. Overhead there is a steady, comforting drone of friendly aeroplanes. Inevitably there are moments of confusion; there is still the residue of the traffic tangles in the Ardennes to be sorted out, separated units to be reunited. Sergeant Prümers, with a signals unit of the 1st Panzer, recalls being ordered the previous day to prepare an assault pack, because 'for two days we would no longer see the transport'. At midnight his unit began to move. In the pitch darkness,

we observed radio silence, so as not to betray ourselves. When we come upon a long transport column, there are hold-ups in the darkness, and suddenly we lose contact. We overtake, and find ourselves on the edge of a huge bomb crater; we attempt to take the road to the right; this too is filled with vehicles, and nobody knows where the Regimental Staff has gone. So we wander about until morning, before we finally come upon Rifle Brigade H.Q. . . .

Then the enemy artillery began to open up: 'The French are shooting at every single vehicle, even motor-cyclist signallers. Shot upon shot . . .' Voicing the thoughts of hundreds of young Germans that day, Prümers wondered nervously: 'What on earth will it be like on the other side?'

As the morning went on, General Kirchner several times informed Guderian that the enemy gunfire was rendering his own movements practically impossible, warning him that the crossing could only succeed if the Luftwaffe knocked out the French artillery. Yet on the whole the French interdiction fire that morning was sporadic and not outstandingly accurate, although to some of the Panzer crews it seemed almost impossible that any single enemy shell could fail to hit a target. Tanks and soft vehicles were cramming into every gulley and hollow leading to the river; the Fond de Givonne, a long open valley of fertile farms and orchards that runs down to Bazeilles on the Meuse, and is partially concealed from the west bank, held the main body of Guderian's armour in one of the most formidable concentrations of mechanized might ever assembled. With tracks almost touching, the deafening roar of their motors was audible well beyond the French front-line positions on the other side of the Meuse. Using the houses along the river as cover, gunners of the light artillery and flak worked their weapons forward into their firing positions. Engineers, panting under the weight of the heavy rubber assault boats, struggled with them to the dead ground nearest the river, which they aimed to reach in one bound as soon as the signal to attack was given. With the brilliant sunlight shining in their eyes, in many places the assault teams could not make out the individual French strongpoints just sixty, eighty or a hundred yards across the sleek, silver ribbon of water. But from almost all angles, they could gaze up apprehensively at the imposing heights of La Marfée which seemed to dominate the battlefield in every direction. How could anything approach this imposing redoubt and remain unseen or undestroyed?

From La Marfée, the French observers' view of Guderian's line-up was indeed superb. Over the whole of his corps frontage, from first light onwards, says General Grandsard, they could see 'the enemy emerging from the forest . . . the deployment is general; everywhere observation points report an almost uninterrupted descent of infantrymen, of vehicles either armoured or motorized'. To the gunners there poured in signals pin-pointing 'at least 200 tanks in the St Menges area ... another 200 in the outskirts and centre of Sedan'. What targets! 'What an opportunity,' wrote a French military critic, General Menu, 'for the artillery to rain down those "hammer blows", to practise those "sweeping concentrations" which constitute, in the manipulation of firepower, the high point of the five hundred very scientific pages of the "General Instruction on Artillery Fire"!' But the French guns 'hammering' Guderian's tank concentrations on the morning of the 13th limited their fire to thirty rounds apiece. Why? Grandsard explains that he was anxious 'to spare ammunition' (though at Sedan within the next few days large dumps of shells were to fall, unexpended, into German hands). Despite all the evidence of this rapid build-up of enemy might on the opposite bank, Grandsard for one still seems to have been clinging, even on the morning of the 13th, to the archaic belief that Guderian could not attempt a river crossing that day. To General Lafontaine of the 55th Division he declared reassuringly: 'The enemy would be unable to do anything for four to six days, as it would take them this long to bring up heavy artillery and ammunition and to position them.'

Strictly speaking, and by all the canons of conventional 1918 warfare, Grandsard's appreciation was correct. On the 13th, Guderian would only be able to bring up a fraction of the heavy artillery available to the defenders, and, according to Kleist, his guns were rationed to 'only fifty rounds *per battery*', as a result of the ammunition columns being delayed by the road congestion in the Ardennes. This was indeed a problem which Guderian had foreseen when he wrote *Achtung – Panzer!* four years previously, but in the meantime the artillery had been substituted by a powerful air weapon, and it is typical of the unreal world in which the French commanders existed that, by 13 May 1940, Grandsard should not have been capable of envisaging the part that the Luftwaffe would play in a Meuse crossing.

The Luftwaffe Attacks

For the massive air support promised that day, the Luftwaffe had allocated the whole of Lieutenant-General Bruno Loerzer's *Fliegerkorps* II, one of the principal components of the Third Air Fleet, commanded by General Hugo Sperrle, plus Major-General Wolfram von Richthofen's *Fliegerkorps* VIII, borrowed from Kesselring's Second Air Fleet operating in the north. Kesselring and Sperrle (later promoted Field-Marshals for their work during the French campaign) were both regular, Army officers who had transferred to the Luftwaffe in the 1930s, while Kesselring, an artillery man, had only learned to fly when he was forty-eight. Sperrle, a vast brooding figure, had, however, gained invaluable experience as first commander of the Condor Legion in Spain. Loerzer was what was known as 'an old eagle', who, claiming forty-four victories, had tied for seventh place in the German list of First War aces. Freiherr von Richthofen, cousin of the famous 'Red Knight' and who had also been a junior member of his 'Flying Circus' in the First War, had succeeded Sperrle in the Condor Legion, establishing a reputation as the Luftwaffe's outstanding expert on 'close support' tactics. It was his Stukas particularly that were to make their mark at Sedan. Between them, Loerzer and Richthofen disposed of nearly 1,500 aircraft,[15] roughly equivalent to the combined British and French total available air strengths in France. Certainly by 1940 standards, it was a staggering concentration of air power to be brought to bear on just a few miles of front.[16]

At 0700 hours, Loerzer's level bombers, mostly Dornier 17 'Flying Pencils', started bombing the French positions. But these were 'harassing attacks', hardly heavier than the raids of the previous days. The bombing continued for four hours, gradually mounting in intensity. It was particularly the com-

15. In the Luftwaffe of 1940, the basic unit was the *Staffel*, comparable to an R.A.F. squadron and containing 10–12 planes; three *Staffeln* comprised a *Gruppe*, equivalent to an R.A.F. wing; three *Gruppen* made up a *Geschwader*, which consisted of approximately 120 planes. Then came the *Fliegerkorps*, constituted of *Geschwader* of different types of aircraft. The two Air Fleets deployed in the West between them contained five *Fliegerkorps*.

16. Though in terms of weight of explosive delivered, it was still probably eclipsed by the German artillery bombardment on the opening day of the Battle of Verdun in February 1916.

munication links of the defenders that were hit by this preliminary 'softening-up'. Grandsard stated that his artillery fire plan was greatly hindered by repeated breaks in telephone lines, and as the morning progressed, its fire began to slacken. Visiting the H.Q. of General Baudet's newly arrived 71st Division, Grandsard found that the makeshift divisional telephone exchange had been destroyed, and that Baudet, still disgruntled at the accelerated movement into line of his division, had already 'been affected by this bombardment'. Grandsard says he tried to 'comfort' Baudet, telling him too that 'it did not seem the enemy would be able to attack on the 13th with important forces'. Meanwhile, General Lafontaine of the 55th Division was complaining to Grandsard that he was being bombed without any intervention from Allied aircraft, and this was of course shaking the morale of his soldiers. Grandsard promptly passed on these views to Huntziger, coupled with a plea for immediate air cover; but according to Grandsard, Huntziger gave a most 'unsatisfactory' response: 'They must receive a baptism of fire.'

The total failure of both Allied air forces at Sedan on 13 May is one of the more extraordinary, in some ways inexplicable, features of the whole battle. If any simple, general explanation is to be found, it must lie in the dreadful quagmire of liason links between the various French ground armies and combat units of the Air Force. As far as bombing missions to break up the German concentrations east of the Meuse were concerned, General d'Astier tells us that at 0940 hours on the 13th, he was at last asked by Billotte to allot priority to air support for the Second Army. But he claims that he was given no inkling of the imminence of a German river-crossing attempt, Billotte speaking only in vague terms of 'the next two or three days'. It was not until midday that the Second Army reported tank concentrations near Givonne, and it added that for the moment it did not require intervention by bombers as its artillery 'was engaging these targets'. Thus, in the stereotyped mind of the French artilleryman, simultaneous aerial bombing could only upset his observation. (Meanwhile Billotte, reporting Rommel's crossing at Houx, also refused air support on the grounds that armour had already been sent for – the sequel to which has been recounted.)

What about the British? In the absence of any desperate plea for assistance from General Georges, Barratt's Advanced Air Striking Force (A.A.S.F.) spent the 13th licking its wounds. They were painful. For the previous three days, the rate of loss had amounted to 40 per cent of all sorties on the 10th, 100 per cent on the 11th, and 62 per cent on the 12th. By the evening of 12 May, the A.A.S.F.'s total of 135 serviceable bombers had dwindled to 72, and perhaps not surprisingly Barratt had received a signal from the Chief of the Air Staff in London expressing concern at his heavy losses, and warning 'we cannot continue indefinitely at this rate of intensity ... If we expend all our efforts in the early stages of the battle we shall not be able to operate effectively when the really critical phase comes.' It would be hard to conceive of a more 'critical' day than 13 May; nevertheless, with this *caveat* of the previous night, Barratt made no call on his Blenheims, and the Battles restricted themselves to blocking a crossroads near Breda, in Holland.

As for Allied fighter cover over Sedan, General Ruby, who was then at Huntziger's H.Q., claims that all Grandsard's requests were immediately passed on to the air command, but the latter's 'appalling organization' somehow swallowed them up. General d'Astier states that his fighters in fact made 250 sorties that day between the Ninth and Second Army fronts, shooting down twenty-one enemy planes for the loss of twelve; but this was a mere drop in the bucket compared with the turn-out of the Luftwaffe. Typical of what the French fighters were up against was this entry in a squadron diary: 'Between 10 and 11 o'clock, a three-plane patrol flying over the area Carignan–Sedan runs into 50 enemy bombers protected by 80 Messerschmitts. Free-for-all in which Lieutenant Wrana is shot down ...' Against this kind of competition, the French Curtisses – 60 m.p.h. slower than the Me-109s – were at a grave if not hopeless disadvantage. Nevertheless, considering the seriousness of the threat on the 13th, one does get the impression that the French fighter squadrons, whose pilots were already short on sleep, did not press home their attacks with every ounce of vigour.

At midday the intensity of the bombing rose sharply, with the Luftwaffe sending over hundreds of planes in dense formations. Sergeant Prümers of the 1st Panzer, still being heavily shelled by the enemy artillery, was among those to watch with awful fascination the first appearance of Richthofen's Stukas:

Three, six, nine, oh, behind them still more, and further to right aircraft, and still more aircraft, a quick look in the binoculars – Stukas! And what we are about to see during the next twenty minutes is one of the most powerful impressions of this war. Squadron upon squadron rise to a great height, break into line ahead (*Reihenformation*) and there, there the first machines hurtle perpendicularly down, followed by the second, third – ten, twelve aeroplanes are there. Simultaneously, like some bird of prey, they fall upon their victim and then release their load of bombs on the target. We can see the bombs very clearly. It becomes a regular rain of bombs that whistle down on Sedan and the bunker positions. Each time the explosion is overwhelming, the noise deafening. Everything becomes blended together; along with the howling sirens of the Stukas in their dives, the bombs whistle and crack and burst. A huge blow of annihilation strikes the enemy, and still more squadrons arrive, rise to a great height, and then come down on the same target. We stand and watch what is happening as if hypnotized; down below all hell is let loose! At the same time we are full of confidence . . . and suddenly we notice that the enemy artillery no longer shoots . . . while the last squadron of Stukas is still attacking, we receive our marching orders . . .

The Stukas operated in three groups, each of about forty planes; the first coming in at about 5,000 feet, would attack with two or three planes at a time while the second group hovered watchfully at 12,000 feet, looking for the targets missed by the first group and then – after that had expended its bombs – moving in in turn; the third group operated in isolation, picking out single or moving targets. After the Stuka waves, the Dorniers would resume their work; then more Stukas. Around them buzzed the Me-109s and the heavier

Me-110 'destroyers', pouncing on any slower French fighter that attempted to get at the vulnerable Stukas.

Watching the steady procession of the bomber formations, Guderian suddenly realized that the Luftwaffe was carrying out the tactics he and Loerzer had agreed upon, not the massive, once-for-all bombardment dictated by Kleist. Though puzzled, Guderian 'sighed with relief'. When the day was over he questioned Loerzer; shrugging his shoulders, the First War ace explained that Kleist's change of orders had arrived 'well, let's say, too late. They would have muddled the *Geschwader*. So I didn't pass them on!'

The Stukas kept on coming in. Down they screamed, sirens howling, loosing their solitary 550-lb bomb upon the thin-skinned French pill-boxes, on the infantry crouching exposed in their trenches, and on the gun crews. It was against the French artillery positions in their poorly concealed and shallow gunpits that the rage of the Stukas was particularly concentrated, and among these it was the new reinforcements arrived the previous night, with insufficient time to dig themselves in, who suffered most. The explosive force of the heavy bombs literally turned batteries upside down, wrecked guns and filled the working parts of anti-aircraft machine-guns with earth and grit. Observers in concrete bunkers were blinded by dust and smoke, and everywhere telephone lines were ruptured. The noise was terrifying.[17] Grandsard's reservists had the impression that each plane was about 'to land right on top of him', that it simply could not miss. In some uncanny way, the German pilots seemed to know exactly where every gun and bunker lay. Nowhere was one out of sight, nowhere out of range of this dreadful weapon.

Yet owing to the inaccuracy of the Stukas, casualties were in fact not great. But as an instrument of terror it was far more effective than the Kaiser's 'secret weapon' of 1914, the

17. It was perhaps the noise that constantly seemed the most unnerving feature of the Stuka attack. In Florence Conrad's field ambulance, the French wounded kept repeating: 'The noise, the horrible noise! . . . You feel the bomb coming, even if it falls 50 or 100 yards away. You throw yourself to the ground, certain of being blown into thirty pieces. And when you realize it was only a miss, the noise of this shrieking *vous casse les pattes . . .*'

'Big Bertha' shells that had plunged down on the Belgian forts; more effective than the gas attack at Ypres; more than the first appearance of flame-throwers, or even the tank. This was a new dimension of war for which not even tough regulars had been prepared, and Grandsard's men were flabby civilians whose morale was not conspicuously high, and who had received absolutely no training in how to cope with dive-bombing. For what ensued they could not entirely be blamed. Says General Ruby:

The gunners stopped firing and went to ground, the infantry cowered in their trenches, dazed by the crash of bombs and the shriek of the dive-bombers; they had not developed the instinctive reaction of running to their anti-aircraft guns and firing back. Their only concern was to keep their heads well down. Five hours of this nightmare was enough to shatter their nerves, and they became incapable of reacting against the enemy infantry . . .

To add to their demoralization, over their heads they could see no sign of any Allied planes coming to their assistance. Plea after plea from the 55th Division went apparently unanswered.

Seen from the German side of the river, the whole of the west bank had disappeared in a blanket of smoke. Even at a distance the waiting Germans suffered disagreeably from the tremendously high pressure caused by the bomb blasts. In awe, they wondered how anything could possibly survive such an inferno. Then, half an hour before H-Hour, Guderian's artillery joined in the hideous fugue with a short but ferocious barrage. Meanwhile, taking advantage of the stunning effect of the Stukas, the flak gunners moved their weapons out of cover, manhandling them right down almost to the very river's edge to engage with flat trajectory fire the French bunkers just across the river. At this close range, the twin-barrelled 20-mm. and 37-mm. automatic cannon swiftly sought out the bunker slits and gun embrasures. Against those bunkers where the protective armour had not arrived, the consequences were deadly, though much less so with those that were properly equipped. But the most lethal work was affected by a piece that was later to achieve renown as the most feared anti-tank gun on any side – possibly, with the Russian T.34 tank, as the most successful single weapon of the whole war. This was the German '88'. Designed by Krupp as the Wehrmacht's standard heavy anti-aircraft gun, it was a direct descendant [18] of the weapon hastily produced (also by Krupp) in 1870 to shoot down the French balloons escaping from besieged Paris. The 88-mm. imparted a very high muzzle velocity, and therefore, at close ranges, tremendous hitting and penetrating power. The '88' had been tried out experimentally in the early part of 1939, firing at close range into the embrasures of the French-designed bunkers among the Czechs' 'Little Maginot Line', supposedly at Hitler's own instance. The results were devastating, and it is worth noting that (according to General Menu) they were reported upon in detail by the then French Military Attaché in Prague. The first combat employment of the '88' in a horizontal role, however, occurred purely by accident; during the Polish campaign, an isolated flak unit had been attacked by surprise by Polish cavalry and, in the emergency, brought their '88s' to bear, firing them over open sights. The success achieved surprised even the Germans. Suddenly new possibilities presented themselves. Now at Sedan, the French bunkers designed to stand up to the oblique fire of guns of all calibres up to 210 mm. proved desperately vulnerable to the direct fire of the '88s', limited in number as they were. One by one the guns in the bunkers were smashed, their crews blinded by splinters, or horribly mutilated by shells exploding within the confined space of the bunkers; or else simply forced by the torrent of light flak fire to abandon guard at the embrasures.

Sedan: the Fatal Moment

Abruptly, at 1500 hours, the Stuka bombardment lifted, shifting to targets further behind the Meuse. Though few of the soldiers confronting each other across this narrow strip of water can have had time to reflect upon it, the moment of crisis in the whole battle had arrived. Here was the culminating point of all the elaborate plans of *Sichelschnitt* – indeed, of Hitler's very

18. It was also the antecedent in design of most present-day tank guns.

aspirations to become the founder of a 'Thousand-Year Reich'. If the crossings at Sedan were to fail, if Guderian's spearhead were to be smashed, who could foretell what future would lie ahead for Germany? It was the crisis for France, for Western civilization, and it would come to be regarded as one of the critical moments of the twentieth century. At such a moment, suddenly the great, complex stratagems of both sides, in which armies are moved about like chess pieces, become reduced to the isolated actions of one or two men. Like the adage of the nail, the horse and the rider, the success or failure of such lone combats leads to the success or failure of a platoon, from a platoon to a company, a company to a regiment, and so on until the whole battlefield is in flux and the day is decided.

At Sedan, events move with such brutal speed that the historian is left floundering – as blinded by the all-obscuring smoke of the Stuka bombs as the French defenders. Unlike the leisurely four months of siege warfare around Paris in 1870, or the ten months of static warfare at Verdun in 1916, minutely and superbly recorded at every level, the decisive acts at Sedan pass in confused, unchronicled minutes, or even seconds. On the French side, there would be but little time to enter up the regimental diaries; whole pages of the story that day have disappeared for ever with the participants. Others are, alas, so shaming to French *amour propre* that, like the details of the mutinies of 1917, they will probably lie forever hidden from sight in the archives contained in the gloomy dungeons at Vincennes. Even on the German side, where headquarters units were not destroyed or dispersed, the pressure of events resulted in an unfortunate lack of cohesive reports on the course of the battle. Thus one is forced to build up a picture of the day upon snatches and fragments of small, scattered scenes, and to rely to a large extent upon the German accounts, with their occasional distortions imposed by National Socialist bombast.

10th Panzer

Even before the smoke from the last Stuka bombs had cleared, the attackers were appearing everywhere on the river in their inflated rubber dinghies.[19] There were many casualties among the first wave. To the survivors, the sixty-yard crossing seemed to last interminably. On the left of Guderian's corps, the 10th Panzer, crossing 'according to the last war-game at Bernkastel' (on the Moselle), made a bad start. The boats for the right-hand group, composed of the 86th Rifle Regiment, reached the water's edge too late for it to take full advantage of the Stuka bombardment. On its left, the 69th reported (at 1600 hours) to Lieutenant-General Schaal, the divisional commander, that it could not move on account of heavy flanking shell fire from guns [20] apparently left untouched by the Luftwaffe, which rained down upon it in the flat, exposed meadows bordering the Meuse near Bazeilles. Out of some fifty small rubber dinghies, all but two had been shot up. A vivid account is provided by Sergeant Schulze of the 69th. His platoon had come under heavy artillery fire at Givonne that morning, and after being ordered to 'dig in' for the first time during the campaign, it had been particularly gratified to see the first Stukas come shrieking down on the enemy guns. At H-Hour, Schulze's team began to work its way through the village of Balan:

A large meadow lies in front of us. On a hill about 800 yards away, the enemy is dug in [on the far side of the Meuse]. To begin with we move forward well; the meadow is wet, finally we are wading up to our calves through the water, here and there shots fly over our heads. Barbed wire is cut through, and we move on ahead. In the next second everything breaks loose. Machine-gun bursts whistle over us, there are strikes before, near and behind us. The enemy is shooting well. Under this fire it is impossible for anybody to get forward. The least movement . . . brings the fire down anew. We are lying in the water, we hug the ground very close, and are delighted when a particularly high grass hummock keeps us out of sight of the enemy. To the left of us some of our own troops are going back, but for us any movement is impossible. About 300 to 400 metres further to the right is *Ober-*

---

19. At the Riom Trial, French Army witnesses claimed, surprisingly, that the use of these boats 'came to us as a great surprise'.

20. Belonging to Grandsard's 71st Division.

feldwebel S.P. with his platoon. The men have already got to within 80 yards of the river . . .

The enemy artillery, whose shots hitherto have fallen far behind Balan, have adjusted their fire forwards, and now it is very close behind the attackers. Enemy infantry in front of us, behind a separating river, artillery bombardment behind us, here it is impossible to move either forwards or backwards. Unexpectedly, over to the right appear engineers, men hard as iron, who bring up assault boats. There *Oberfeldwebel* S.P. decides to risk it with the engineers. He had three of his men spring forward and leap into one of the boats. In a second the boats are in the water . . . they are on their way to the safe shore. The second boat follows with reinforcements and the Battalion Adjutant, Lieutenant M. By the time a third boat is about to enter the water, the artillery has adjusted its fire so far towards the Meuse that the assault boat is destroyed. The engineers fall. But a small group of ten to twelve men has made it. The first on the other side of the Meuse. They lie close up against an enemy bunker. What are they to do? If there is any French counter-thrust they are lost.

From the Balan side of the river, Schulze then observed that the enemy bunker appeared to be knocked out, having received a direct hit from a German gun a short time previously. A German officer was seen to disappear behind the bunker:

soon he comes back with five prisoners, the bunker was still occupied – then they lay out white sheets, because from the other side, our own troops are often still firing; they have no idea that our own people are already over there. Meanwhile hours pass by; while *Oberfeldwebel* S.P. has crossed the Meuse, the company is stuck in the water, pinned down by the enemy fire.

Schulze's platoon falls back on Balan that evening, and is told to stand by as reinforcements:

The enemy artillery shoots on Balan. We are sitting in our wet uniforms in safe cellars. There was no thought of sleep, for the evenings are bitterly cold. Teeth chatter and limbs tremble.

As far as Schulze's immediate front was concerned, by nightfall on the 13th the prospects did not look brilliant. That the 10th Panzer obtained a foothold on the opposite bank at all that day seems to have depended largely on the initiative of individual detachment leaders of the assault engineers such as *Feldwebel* Rubarth. Specially equipped with explosive charges for knocking out bunkers which had survived the Stukas and flak, Rubarth and his section of eleven men assembled their gear in the private park of a mansion near Balan. Across the wide stretch of open meadow where Schulze had been pinned down, Rubarth could clearly recognize the enemy strongpoints on the river at Wadelincourt; but he noted 'the terrain is extremely unfavourable for an attack'. Moving down to the Meuse over this dangerously exposed ground as H-Hour arrived, Rubarth records:

Immediately we were met by strong machine-gun fire. There are casualties. With my detachment I reach the bank of the Meuse under cover of a row of trees and a sports-ground.

He appears to have had available only two small rubber dinghies designed to carry no more than three men. Cramming four into each, however, Rubarth paddled out under a hail of fire, into the sixty-yard wide river. Because of the extra weight, plus their heavy equipment of wire-cutters, grenades and hollow charges, the water came perilously close to the gunwales of Rubarth's dinghy. He ordered his men to throw out all unnecessary ballast, entrenching tools included, remarking grimly: 'No digging in for us – either we get through, or that's the end.' To upset the defenders' aim during their crossing, the *Feldwebel* ordered his driver, Corporal Podszus, to blaze away with a machine-gun into the weapon slits of a particularly menacing-looking bunker immediately to their front, using another man's shoulder to steady his aim in the wildly unstable dinghy. On landing (near Wadelincourt), Rubarth speedily finished off this bunker. His own story continues:

The enemy artillery is now laying down heavy artillery fire on our crossing. Crawling past the next bunker in dead ground out of reach of its guns, the section attacked it from the rear. I made use of an explosive charge. In the next second part of the rear bunker wall is ripped out by the power of the explosion. We utilize the opportunity to reduce the occupants of the bunker with hand-grenades. After a brief fight they appear with white flags, and a few seconds later our Swastika flag flies over the bunker. From the other bank the sound of loud cheers from our comrades comes over to us. Thus encouraged we fling ourselves at two further field-works we had spotted some 100 metres half left of us. To get to them we have to go through a patch of swamp where part of the time we stand up to our thighs in water. With reckless audacity Corporal Bräutigam alone attacks the left bunker and through a clever action captures the occupants. Together with Sergeant Theophel and Corporals Podszus and Monk, I take the second bunker. Thus the first line of bunkers immediately behind the Meuse is broken through over a stretch of some 300 metres.

The facility with which Rubarth and his few men succeeded in knocking out this row of bunkers, one after the other, suggests the state to which the French defenders had already been reduced. What were the 'interval troops' entrusted with guarding the vulnerable flanks of these important bastions doing? There is virtually no mention of them in Rubarth's accounts; where were they? All was clearly not well with the river defences at Wadelincourt.

Rubarth's own account continues with his detachment pushing forward to the railway embankment a hundred yards or so from the river bank. Here, for the first time, he came under such strong fire 'that temporarily we have to seek cover'. Taking stock of the situation, Rubarth ascertained that the other dinghy bringing his section across the river had been hit in midstream, its occupants presumably killed. Thus

with one sergeant, four men and the group of infantry which were covering our right flank, I am alone on the far side of the river. Moreover, our ammunition is exhausted, so that we cannot continue our attack. In order to bring up reinforcements and ammunition, I go back to the crossing place and discover that the crossing operation has been interrupted by very heavy enemy fire. The dinghies are partly deflated or shot to pieces. Four men of my detachment have been killed there. My company commander, who is still on the other side of the river and has watched the course of the battle, immediately orders the bringing-up of new dinghies and appoints new crews.

While waiting for these reinforcements under the blazing sun, Rubarth's Corporal Bräutigam, who spoke French, ordered one of the prisoners to go back into his bunker and get something to drink. He returned with a bottle of wine. During the interval the Wadelincourt defenders suddenly rallied and launched a surprise attack on Rubarth. They were beaten off, but Bräutigam was killed, and Corporals Monk and Podszus wounded. Shortly after this critical moment, an infantry group arrives, and Rubarth joins up with it. With fresh reinforcements of assault engineers reaching him at last from the east bank, he then goes on to blast a gap in the second line of bunkers. By nightfall, exhausted and having lost six dead and three wounded out of his original eleven men, Rubarth, together with riflemen of the 86th Regiment, had reached his objective on the heights above Wadelincourt. For his achievements Rubarth was immediately awarded the Ritterkreuz, and a lieutenant's commission.

Thus, by dusk, the 10th Panzer had a firm but small toehold on the west bank, between Wadelincourt and Pont Maugis.

1st Panzer
With the tremendous concentration of firepower supporting it, the 1st Panzer was having a somewhat easier time. On its left flank, the job of clearing the western suburbs of Sedan and then rushing the La Marfée heights fell to the Grossdeutschland Regiment. One of the élite fighting units of Nazi Germany, the Grossdeutschland could trace its origins in the 1870s as the Berlin 'Guard Regiment'. In the turbulent 1920s it was employed to put down any attempted *putsches* in the capital, while in more peaceful times its principal function was to march three times a week, with bands thundering out *Deutschland über Alles*, to change the guard at the Brandenburger Tor, and to provide guards of honour for such visiting dignitaries as Ciano of Italy and Horthy of Hungary. Just three months before war began, Hitler had issued a proclamation changing the regiment's name to Grossdeutschland as a martial symbol of the unity of all Germans within the new Reich. Officers of the Regiment Grossdeutschland (which later in the war was expan-

ded to a division, and eventually to an army corps) were specially selected from the rest of the Army. As with the British Brigade of Guards, the men had to be over a certain height, and the regiment always fought as a separate unit, its name proudly emblazoned on the sleeves of its members. Regarded as an élite force set aside for especially tough operations, the Grossdeutschland had been earmarked by Guderian ever since February for the role of smashing a hole in the French lines through which the Panzers could then pour. At that time Guderian had evidently made some disparaging remarks about infantry who 'slept instead of advancing at night', to which the regimental commander, Lieutenant-Colonel Graf von Schwerin, rose testily, betting Guderian a case of champagne that this would not happen with the Grossdeutschland. All through April it had undergone rugged toughening-up exercises: marching on short rations, river crossings on the Moselle, and night attacks.

At midday on the 13th, the shock troops of the Grossdeutschland had been issued with their iron rations, their field-flasks filled with coffee, and weapons inspected. Then Colonel von Schwerin had arrived, jauntily carrying a stick, and the regiment had set off through Floing less than a mile from the appointed crossing area. Senior Lieutenant von Courbiere, commanding No. 6 Company, which was to be second over the river, was struck by the unnatural stillness at Floing: 'Not a shot falls, the inhabitants have fled, dogs and cats roam through the streets whose destroyed houses bear witness to the fearful force of this war.' Apprehensively, he wondered whether the silence of the French guns meant that they 'had already been hit so hard, or are they just waiting for the moment we get moving to cross the river?' Then, as his company reached the cloth factory, with its blue-tinted black-out windows overlooking the river, where it was to embark,

at last the French recognize the danger threatening them, and begin to fight back, without worrying about the bombs exploding around them. The engineers bring up their assault boats, but they cannot reach the river. Despite our covering fire the enemy can watch all movements out of his bunkers and hits back at us.

Assault guns roll up, but even their shells can do nothing against the concrete and iron. Valuable time is lost, until finally a heavy 88-mm. flak silences the enemy. Once again the assault boats are brought up, but this attempt also brings down enemy fire. The young lieutenant of the 7th Company, Lieutenant Graf Medem, and two engineers are killed. The wounded are brought back – once again a heavy flak is brought into action. Under its protection the first sections of the leading (No. 7) company cross the Meuse. The crossing has succeeded! Swiftly, as we had already practised in the winter, 6th Company follows.

A little over two miles ahead, Courbiere could clearly make out the forward slopes of La Marfée. The Stukas were still hurling their bombs into the fortifications on top of it, often apparently only a 'hair's breadth' from the leading attackers. Approaching the main Sedan–Donchery highway, Courbiere saw the first French appear, with their hands up. At the same time, No. 7 Company on his right was coming under heavy fire from several bunkers along the road:

A quick reconnaissance shows that a large bunker with six weapon slits some 200 yards south of the road, on the edge of a vegetable garden, offers good prospects of approach . . . after a short fight the bunker is reached by a sergeant and two men. The enemy are smoked out by hand-grenades; they are completely vanquished; they come out. Their faces reveal the psychological strain of this fighting. Close to each other they stand with their backs to their bunker and raise their hands; 'Tirez!' they cry . . .

Courbiere's company then cleaned out a second bunker, and an anti-tank position concealed in a barn. Here to their delight they discovered a cache of soda-water bottles with which they slaked their thirst in the sultry heat of the late afternoon; after a short rest, they were even more delighted to make contact with elements of Lieutenant-Colonel Balck's 1st Rifle Regiment, which had also successfully crossed the Meuse. It was now about 5 p.m. After some savage hand-to-hand fighting, just as daylight was fading Courbiere's company reached their objective atop Height 247, not far from where Moltke had directed the first battle of Sedan seventy years previously.

Together with the Grossdeutschland, it was the 1st Rifle Regiment [21] that was to play so important a role in the early phases of the breakthrough at Sedan. Its commander, Lieutenant-Colonel Balck, came of a long military line; as an officer of the 'King's German Legion', his great-grandfather had served on Wellington's staff during the Peninsular War; his grandfather had served in the Argyll and Sutherland Highlanders, while his father had been a personal friend of General Sir Ian Hamilton of Gallipoli fame. Himself a tough frontline soldier who had gone through Verdun and been wounded five times during the First war, Balck was a most forceful personality (Chester Wilmot rates him, perhaps too harshly, as 'a notorious optimist with a reputation for ruthless aggression', while the American official history, *The Lorraine Campaign*, portrays him as a swashbuckling martinet), and there were certainly not many Second World War commanders who could exact more from their troops. After Sedan, Balck's hitherto slow rise was vastly accelerated, and there were few campaigns from which he was absent: a divisional, then a corps commander in Russia; an army commander in Poland and Hungary; finally, as a full general, an army group commander in the later stages of the retreat from France. On the 13th and the next two days his qualities as a leader undoubtedly contributed most significantly to Guderian's success.

Balck's orders for 13 May were to cross in the Glaire–Gaulier area, in the tracks of the Grossdeutschland, push up on to the northern slopes of La Marfée, then swing round it to thrust along the main road running southwards from Sedan to Vouziers. The Grossdeutschland having borne the brunt of the fighting, Balck's riflemen had perhaps the easiest time of any of the German assault units that day. According to Guderian, watching at Floing and chafing with impatience to get over the Meuse himself, their crossing developed

as though it were being carried out on manoeuvres. The French artillery was almost paralysed by the unceasing threat of attack by Stukas and bombers. The concrete works along the Meuse had been put out of action by our anti-tank and anti-aircraft artillery,

21. The motorized infantry belonging to the 1st Panzer Division.

and the enemy machine-gunners were forced to keep down by the fire of our heavy weapons and artillery. Despite the completely open nature of ground, our casualties remained light.

Balck himself, who had the impression that the French gunners had already begun to desert their batteries, noted that the cessation in French artillery fire had a remarkable effect on the morale of his riflemen: 'A few minutes before, everyone was seeking refuge in slit trenches, but now nobody thought of taking cover. It was impossible to hold the men ...' An hour and a half after H-Hour, Balck with the leading elements of his regiment had reached the railway line running from Sedan to Donchery; another hour (1730 hours), and he had beaten his way through to the main road lying parallel to it, thus breaking into the main French line of defences. Meanwhile, the division's motor-cycle battalion which had crossed over the Meuse loop at Iges had cleaned up the whole Iges peninsula, rejoining Balck on the banks of the canal that traverses its root. By 1930 hours, the 1st Panzer had elements of six battalions established in a substantial bridgehead. A large part of the all-important La Marfée heights, crowned by pine woods, First War cemeteries, and a monument to a French infantry regiment which, in August 1914, threw back the Germans on the Meuse by a *contre-attaque à la bayonnette*, had already fallen into their hands.

On the west bank of the Meuse, however, Guderian still had no tanks, anti-tank guns or artillery. Like Rommel to the north, he faced an anxious night during which the French might prepare an armoured riposte to crush his unprotected infantry before the first Panzers could be pushed across the river. Every priority was now devoted to rushing the construction of ferries and bridges. While the east bank was still under machine-gun fire from the bunkers opposite, Lieutenant Grubnau, commanding a special bridging company of the engineers, had already reconnoitred 'a completely level field with firm dry ground and good approaches to the river bank ... But there is no cover.' It was close to the cloth factory at Gaulier, under cover of which the engineers assembled their heavy equipment. The Meuse is here approximately seventy yards wide. Although some of Grubnau's transport had been held up in the Ardennes, by 1630 hours, while Balck's riflemen were still struggling across in their assault boats, work was already beginning on the first pontoon bridge. 'The engineers leap from their vehicles and unload the pontoon trucks,' recorded Grubnau, adding in surprise at the lack of anti-tank obstacles:

It is astonishing how easily heavy bridge-building could be carried out today. An enemy bombing attack causes everyone to take refuge in the little cover that is at hand. Our nine light machine-guns fire . . . the bombs fall far from us. With undiminished strength the construction continues. Now enemy artillery fire begins. The enemy artillery plane is, however, driven off by our fighter cover . . . It seems that the French are expecting our bridge to be built at another place . . . shells fall fifty yards from us . . . fortunately, the village of Glaire hinders any observed fire.

Throughout the afternoon, the young sappers, half-naked and their steel helmets cast aside in the torrid heat, worked away at the bridge in almost casual detachment despite the intermittent rain of shot and shell. In the record time of thirty-eight minutes, Grubnau's men had the first light ferry operating; shortly before midnight a sixteen-ton bridge was ready, with a tremendous concentration of armour queuing up behind it on the east bank.

2nd Panzer

On its right hand, the performance of the 2nd Panzer stood out in even sharper contrast to the successes registered by the 1st than did the limited progress of the 10th on the left flank. Guderian's old division, the 2nd Panzer, had taken part in the march into Austria in 1938 and, remaining as part of the garrison troops of Vienna, had become known in the Wehrmacht as the 'Vienna Division'. Its formations contained a large number of Austrians and Bavarians. Led by Lieutenant-General Rudolf Veiel, its commander since the *Anschluss*, the 'Vienna Division' had spearheaded the occupation of the Sudetenland, and during the Polish campaign had thrust into Poland on the southern flank, via Czechoslovakia. Its limited contribution to the crossings on the 13th was expected; the night before, Guderian had warned Kleist that the 2nd, still bogged down on the Semois, would not be in position on the Meuse at H-Hour, and in any case it had forfeited its heavy artillery support to the 1st. When it did get over the Meuse (at Donchery), its orders from Guderian were fairly ambitious; after seizing the high ground behind Donchery it 'will then swing immediately west-ward, will cross the Ardennes Canal to the Bar bed inclusive, and will roll up the enemy defences along the Meuse'. On the higher strategic plane, the role of the 2nd Panzer would assume great significance, for it would be the formation to force the hinge between the two French armies of Huntziger and Corap.

Against expectations, on the morning of the 13th the 2nd made surprisingly rapid progress and by mid-afternoon some of its elements were already reaching Donchery, a gloomy small Meuse village straddling the river roughly two miles downstream from Sedan, where at a humble weaver's house in 1870 Bismarck had first met Louis-Napoleon to discuss the terms of the French capitulation. As soon as the first German tanks deployed down into the river valley, they were met by a storm of artillery fire. The French observation from the over-looking hills was excellent, while with the sinking sun now glistening brilliantly behind the Meuse the Panzers found it extremely difficult to pin-point the well-camouflaged French positions. The tanks fanned out, slowly groping their way into the abandoned portions of Donchery lying on the east bank. Pinned down under the heavy fire, the *Sturmpionieren* per-suaded the tank crews to carry them and their rubber dinghies down to the river on the backs of the tanks. Corporal Frömmel, with a squadron of tanks, describes how, under fire from a French anti-tank gun sited in a superbly covered position,

The engineers leap off and attempt under this hail of fire to get their boat to the Meuse. There are only a few metres separating them from the bank, and yet each step means hell. The tank shoots with all its guns, it attempts to give fire cover to the deter-minedly working engineers. The boat is already in the water, its paddles cutting deep into it. Like a shower, a machine-gun bursts from the bunker and falls on this single boat. All around it the water springs up high, and several brave engineers are killed. It is impossible! Back! They come back to the bank, and attempt to find cover in the deep grass. The same fate occurs several minutes later to men whose inflatable dinghy has been brought down by three further tanks to this death-dealing river.

A company commander of the engineers, Lieutenant Zimmermann, is seriously wounded in midstream and barely manages to struggle back to the bank. Here several more German wounded lie in agony in the grass, still under French machine-gun fire. Tanks carry them back to safety behind a railway embankment. In the growing twilight a murderous duel goes on between the tanks and the French bunkers across the Meuse. Tracer shells whizz back and forth like fireworks. Says Sergeant-Major Keddig:

We fired off shell after shell, always at the recognized bunkers, to try and silence them. It became unbearably hot inside the tank's turret, which was filled with powder smoke. A beautiful summer evening lay across the countryside. But the firing of the French artillery continued with undiminished violence. We couldn't dream of opening any of the tank's hatches.

Despite the French artillery and anti-tank fire, few of the Panzers appear to have been knocked out. Finally, one of the bunkers is silenced and a white flag is spotted. The first *Sturmpionieren* dinghy makes a safe crossing, and shortly afterwards triumphant white Very lights arc up from the enemy bank.

Their ammunition exhausted, the tanks withdraw after nightfall. Greatly aided by the hole driven in the centre of the French lines by Balck and the Grossdeutschland, the 2nd Panzer too had gained a foothold over the Meuse. Hurrying back and forth across the river that night with reinforcements, one of its infantry officers noted in the moonlight, among the destroyed enemy bunkers and the huge Stuka craters, the extraordinary number of incomplete fortifications:

The wooden scaffolding still stands there, the foundations have not yet been dug. Astonishing these Frenchmen! They have had now nearly twenty years to build their lines of defence . . .

Sedan: the French View

As noted earlier, the French view of what happened down on the Meuse on the 13th is perforce scanty and confused. It was General Lafontaine's 55th Division which, almost exclusively, had borne the brunt of Guderian's attack. Undoubtedly, most of the odds were against it from the start. Its elderly, poorly trained reservists were in no way a match for the best troops in the German Army, backed by pulverizing air power; they were caught partly moving house, and one battalion had already been mauled almost to death on the Semois. On the other hand, the 55th had very strong artillery support and a fabulous natural position in the shape of La Marfée. Here and there the men of the 55th fought back with gallant, unsung heroism, and Captain von Kielmansegg, on the staff of the 1st Panzer, himself pays tribute to the 'numerous bunkers which defended themselves desperately'. But out in the open the French infantry seem to have melted away under the aerial onslaught, and by and large most French military historians concur with the summing-up of Colonel Goutard, one of the most outspokenly objective among them, that 'in general, resistance was very feeble'.

The news reaching divisional and corps headquarters was fragmentary. At 1710 hours, one of the first reports received by Grandsard from the 55th Division stated tersely: 'The Meuse has been crossed by some forty men [22] at reference 1572 south of Wadelincourt. A barrage has been opened up. Donchery occupied by a battalion and a half of infantry. Divisional artilleries firing.' It added ominously: 'No longer any contact with the infantry regiment on the left.' At that moment, General Huntziger had himself arrived at Grandsard's command post, commenting calmly on the numbers of enemy reported crossing at Wadelincourt: 'There will be just that number of prisoners.' Huntziger did not intervene in the battle, says Grandsard, leaving him to cope with the situation. Grandsard explains that his first appreciation was that 'nothing was lost, provided that the position of resistance defended itself, and

22. Presumably Rubarth and company.

provided that orders given to reserves were executed'. However, he continues:

The hours that followed were to give a cruel disappointment to the hopes of the Commander of X Corps. From 1800 to 1900 hours approximately, the situation evolved with a disconcerting rapidity towards catastrophe.

At 1830 hours there came a most disquieting report from the commander of a battery of guns at Chaumont that enemy *tanks* had been spotted in the La Marfée area. This was followed up a quarter of an hour later by an item that was even more disturbing. According to Grandsard:

the colonel [Dourzal] commanding Group B of the Corps Heavy Artillery at Bulson reported to the colonel [Poncelet] commanding the Corps Heavy Artillery that violent fighting had broken out 400–500 metres from his command post and he was requesting orders to withdraw; on a request for details from his chief, he confirmed that there were definitely German machine-guns and that he would be encircled within five minutes; he received from his chief the authority to withdraw.

At more or less the same time, Colonel Poncelet also evacuated his command post back at Flaba, well behind Bulson and over five miles from the nearest Germans, while giving the order for the heavy batteries under his command to withdraw. (It should be noted here that not one German tank reached the west side of the Meuse until the following morning, and that no German infantrymen reached anywhere near Bulson that night.) Yet Poncelet was heard (according to General Ruby) to declare that 'the German tanks were arriving as he left his command post at Flaba'. Both these gunner colonels, General Ruby comments scathingly, 'bear a particularly grave responsibility' for the panic which was to follow. No one, it transpires incredibly enough, seems to have made any attempt to verify these alarmist reports, including Grandsard himself, although later that night he ordered the panicky colonels back to their command posts. Colonel Poncelet, apparently shattered by what had happened at Sedan, fell into a deep depression and committed suicide twelve days later.

Meanwhile, about three hours after the first crossings had taken place, General Lafontaine of the 55th Division was taking stock of the situation at his command post at Fond-Dagot, just behind Bulson, with a certain calmness. The bombing had ceased; he had established liaison with the 53rd Division belonging to Corap on his right; and he had dispatched a battalion to reinforce La Marfée (which would in fact succeed in checking the German advance there until dawn the next day). Then, suddenly, says General Ruby,

A wave of terrified fugitives, gunners and infantry, in transport, on foot, many without arms but dragging their kitbags, swept down the Bulson road. 'The tanks are at Bulson!' they cried. Some were firing their rifles like madmen. General Lafontaine and his officers ran in front of them, tried to reason with them, made them put their lorries across the road . . . Officers were among the deserters. Gunners, especially from the corps's heavy artillery, and infantry soldiers from the 55th Division, were mixed together, terror-stricken and in the grip of mass hysteria. All these men claimed actually to have seen tanks at Bulson and Chaumont! Much worse, commanders at all levels pretended having received orders to withdraw, but were quite unable to show them or even to say exactly where the orders had come from. Panic brooked no delay; command posts emptied like magic.[23]

There is no doubt that the real collapse at Sedan began with the gunners. Ever since Napoleon, in the French Army the artillery has always occupied a far more exalted position than in other armies. During the First War it became almost axiomatic that, so long as the artillery 'held', the infantry would hold. But when the guns fell silent, the infantry would give up. By a strange coincidence, the first German success on the opening day of the Battle of Verdun had also come when they broke a second-line Territorial unit of elderly pépères, comparable to the 'B' divisions of 1940. But in contrast the

23. The 'Panzers at Bulson' were in fact almost certainly their own tanks, belonging to Grandsard's reserve tank battalions. One more ingenious variation of the story, recounted to Madame Conrad at her Field Service Unit by fugitives several days later, was that the wicked Boche had confused the defenders by utilizing Renault tanks captured in Poland!

French artillery at Verdun had stood its ground, and the hole had been plugged by counter-attacking infantry, though at terrible cost. Why had the French gunners at Sedan not been able to 'endure' as their fathers had? Undoubtedly the mass onslaught of the Stukas that afternoon had been a horrifying experience, difficult to recapture at this range in time; but was not the terrible hammering of the German 210s and 150s at Verdun, prolonged over an infinitely longer period, just as injurious – if not more so – to human nerves? And had not the Polish artillerymen in 1939, though fighting at even greater material disadvantage, stood by their guns under Stuka attack until they were literally pulverized? But the Poles were fighting for their very existence; and, in May 1940, what were the Frenchmen of the Third Republic fighting for? In attempting to isolate the reasons for the breaking of the Sedan gunners, one comes face to face once again with the twenty-four corrosive years separating the *poilus* of Verdun from the men of Sedan; here is the terrible harvest of those years of mutual mistrust, disunity, despair at the losses of 1914–18, *je-m'en-foutisme* and defeatism in France.

Paradoxically, there were still determined and courageous pockets of French infantry continuing to hold out *in front of* the artillery, while the commanders of the latter were pulling out. But when the word got round that the gunners had deserted their guns, panic and all its repercussions spread like a vast ugly oil-slick. There semed to be no stopping the fugitives of the 55th Division, or the escalation of the rumours they carried. As far back as Vouziers, the Second Army Provost-Marshal, Colonel Serin, called in two companies of Gardes Mobiles in an attempt to 'canalize' the flood. Yet still, according to General Ruby, the fugitives managed to reach Rheims before they could be rounded up – having in the meanwhile 'pillaged from top to bottom Ste Menehould and Vouziers'. Even Huntziger's H.Q. at Senuc was not immune to this tide of panic: 'Towards 2100 hours,' says General Ruby, 'two sapper officers presented themselves to the General; much affected, they testified to having seen German tanks at Vendresse. Coldly, General Huntziger called them liars. They had taken our 7th Tank Battalion for a Panzer unit!' Still further afield, Jean Muray, at a village where his division was in reserve behind Corap's front, thirty-five miles from Sedan, met men from Sedan the very next morning, bearing terrible tales: 'They had seen it; the scattering of French divisions. The pulverizing of a whole army . . . the courage of some, the cowardice of others . . .' Roland Dorgelès, the famous novelist, tells of ten gunners and a medical officer fleeing from Sedan in a truck who were stopped at Auxerre, in the middle of France, six days after the débâcle; interrogated about his departure from the front, the officer replied, 'But, *mon capitaine*, bombs were falling . . .!' In the ensuing days, wretched tales like this could be multiplied a thousandfold.

Closer to the front at Sedan, however, the consequences of this wave of panic were much more immediately disastrous. Never pausing to check the rumour that 'the Panzers are at Bulson!', General Lafontaine requested Grandsard to be allowed to move his command post back to Chémery. Grandsard said he must decide what was best. Lafontaine did. Half in transport, half on foot, his headquarters hastily retired. This in itself, according to Grandsard, had a baneful effect; officers presenting themselves for orders at Lafontaine's former command post during the night found it abandoned, and 'deduced a definitive withdrawal on the part of the 55th Division. They saw therein an argument for their own pride.' [24] At Chémery, General Ruby tells us, Lafontaine

fell into the middle of unimaginable chaos; the flood of fugitives traverses the village without pause; all the echelons of the division,

24. In the wake of Sedan, the quest for 'an argument for their own pride' seems to have been carried out at all levels. General Lafontaine himself, in a report to Gamelin dated 18 May, attempts to utilize the old, untenable bogey (about which more will be said) of the German Fifth Column: 'one must note the almost certain presence,' he declares, 'of doubtful characters, certainly of parachutists charged with a definite mission to fulfil, who transmitted the orders for withdrawal . . .' As with so many major French débâcles throughout history, there has to be somewhere a 'traitor' or an enemy agent – '*Nous sommes trahis*!' Needless to say, no hard evidence has ever been produced for this 'Fifth Column' activity at Sedan.

accumulated in this region – fighting units, regimental H.Q.s, supply columns, vehicle parks . . . – all are heading for the south, swelled by stragglers; as if by magic, their officers have naturally received a mysterious order to withdraw. Barriers established by the military police are swept aside.

Amid this scene of anarchy, with *ad hoc* lines of communication even worse than those at Bulson, so badly disrupted by the German bombing, Lafontaine was attempting to organize a counter-attack. But the commander of his principal reserve formation, Lieutenant-Colonel Labarthe of the 213th Infantry Regiment, depressed by the effect the prevailing atmosphere was having upon his men, kept mumbling to him, '*Surtout, pas de contre-attaque!*'

Next, the impact of the panic on the 55th's front swiftly made itself felt upon its sister 'B' division, the 71st, which, although still slowly moving up into line, had suffered little during the day's fighting. Almost immediately after receiving the first news of the purported enemy tanks being at Chaumont and Bulson, Grandsard had relayed it to General Baudet, requesting him to make the necessary dispositions. Baudet at once decided to pull *his* freshly established command post at Raucourt back three or four miles, taking with him the commander of the divisional artillery. This withdrawal of the division's chief gunner had its attendant repercussions on the various batteries; in the absence of authority, the personnel of some dispersed in the woods, where they wandered all night, only returning ('naturally, incomplete', says Ruby) to their guns in the morning; others, on notional orders, destroyed their weapons and headed for the rear. All too few were the battery commanders who, like Major Benedetti of the 363rd Regiment, actually man-handled their guns forward during the night, against the demoralizing flood tide of fugitives. On the 71st Division's front, says General Ruby, already 'three groups of 75s out of four had been abandoned by their crews . . . four out of six groups of the heavy artillery'. These were the guns which had halted the German crossings at Wadelincourt by their flanking fire. The prospects for the 71st, if attacked the following day, were hardly auspicious.

Sedan: the French Counter-attack

We have seen the results of the first French counter-attacks mounted against Rommel's bridgehead at Dinant. What was being prepared to repulse Guderian's at Sedan? Under his command Grandsard had in reserve two tank battalions, the 4th and the 7th, and two infantry regiments, the 205th and the 213th, the latter led by the reluctant Lieutenant-Colonel Labarthe. Behind them, the powerful units ordered up by General Georges, the 3rd Armoured and the 3rd Motorized Division, were now arriving to be placed under Huntziger's control. Grandsard had put all four of his reserve units at Lafontaine's disposal, and at 0130 hours on the morning of the 14th the harassed Lafontaine ordered them to carry out a two-pronged dawn counter-attack. If the operation had been executed as planned, before Guderian's armour had begun to reach the west side of the river, and before the Luftwaffe returned, it would have had a good chance of success; and even if it had not overrun Guderian's soft-skinned riflemen, it would at least have gained valuable time for Huntziger to swing his main punch.[25] But, in the event, not one unit was ready to attack on time. Lieutenant-Colonel Labarthe managed to persuade Lafontaine that, in view of the uncertain morale of the 213th Regiment, it would be too risky to undertake a night march through all that calamity-crying débris reeling back from the front; the 7th Tanks, detailed to accompany it, claimed never to have got the order in time. The 205th Regiment (belonging to the 71st Division) was held up in the approach march by lorry-borne fugitives crying 'Infantrymen, don't go forward! The Boches are there!', and finally received orders from a dispatch-rider to halt ('From whom came this counter-order?' queries General Ruby); while its

25. 'If the ill-starred French had not been still dogged by misfortune,' commented Captain von Kielmansegg, giving a German view of this missed opportunity, 'they would have made a spirited counter-attack to remove while it was still small the bulge which had developed in their lines and destroyed all the German units on their side of the Meuse before they could be reinforced.'

supporting tank battalion, the 4th, having been met by one of Grandsard's own staff captains at about 2100 and told that there were Panzers at Chaumont, decided to camp down for the night, never meeting up with the infantry from the 205th until morning. There was, says Grandsard with admirable restraint, 'too great a facility to interpret an order than to execute it as received; too great a facility to modify under the pretext of initiative, when confronted by unchecked information'. As a result, instead of getting off the ground at 0400 hours, Grandsard's counter-attack would not start until three hours later. By then, the whole picture in the German bridge-head would have changed. In essence, the story was much the same as at Dinant. The French Army had forfeited its second big opportunity of the campaign.

As night fell, Lieutenant-Colonel Balck, sitting comfortably on his objective just beyond Frénois, became aware of the fading away of French gunfire. An inkling of what was going on among the enemy gunners seems to have occurred to him. His riflemen were dog-tired from the day's exertions, but, infusing his own energy into them in a notable feat of personal leadership, he rallied them and got them on their feet again. Bullying and driving, Balck led the weary regiment in a five-mile night march towards the south, so that by dawn, without opposition, they had reached Chéhéry, thereby at one bound doubling the depth of the bridgehead. On the left flank, night-fall and the diminution of the flanking fire from the 71st Division enabled the stalled rifle battalions of the 10th Panzer to get across the Meuse. Creeping from one bomb crater to another, 'ideal positions' thrown up by the Stukas, Sergeant Schulze noted how many bunkers seemed to have been abandoned by their occupants. Swiftly the divisional engineers began construction on a bridge for the 10th Panzer, just south of Sedan. On the 1st Panzer front Guderian, who had already crossed the river closely on the heels of Balck's riflemen, stood by watching anxiously as Lieutenant Grubnau's men put the finishing touches to their bridge at Gaulier. The regimental historian of the Grossdeutschland notes that 'the noise of

fighting had almost stopped; only occasionally there was one
shot, otherwise silence – the enemy is beaten!' Shortly before
midnight, the pontoon bridge was ready, and

we roll slowly over on to the other bank, turn sharply to the right
and follow the road running along the Meuse some thousand
yards to the small village of Villette. A crater-like Stuka bomb
hole forces us out on to the fields . . . around us are burning
houses, shimmering with heat.

As the first Panzers rumbled into the Sedan bridgehead, it
measured some three miles wide by four to six miles deep at
the point where Balck had completed his night march.
'Pleased and proud with what I had seen', Guderian returned
to his H.Q. at La Chapelle to prepare operational orders for
the 14th. It was, he felt, clear that this day would 'bring a
decision'. At the same time, he could not resist sending off a
telegram to General Busch, the commander of the Sixteenth
Army, who, at that meeting with Hitler, had told Guderian
he would never get across the Meuse.

Reinhard's Difficulties

If on both wings of the *Sichelschnitt* thrust – at Dinant and
Sedan – the results on the 13th left little to be desired (from
the German point of view), the same could hardly be said of
the centre. Here, at Monthermé, Reinhardt's XLI Corps was
badly stuck, and would remain so for the next two days. The
story of Reinhardt's difficulties makes an interesting comparison with the easy successes of Rommel and Guderian, though
it was not really his fault. The terrain around Monthermé
is some of the ruggedest in the Ardennes; the approach roads,
on which Reinhardt's supply columns had become so badly
entangled with those of Guderian's 2nd Panzer on the previous days, are few and poor. The defenders, unlike the troops
of Corap's northern wing at Dinant, who had had to take up
unfamiliar positions after a sixty-mile march into Belgium,
were on French territory and had been dug in there since the
beginning of the war; also, in contrast to Huntziger's troops

at Sedan, they were not 'B' reservists, but regulars of the 102nd Fortress Division. With its main weight concentrated on Sedan, the Luftwaffe could lend only relatively small support to Reinhardt, and against the well-prepared French positions in this heavily wooded country its bombs had but limited effect. In fact, the Germans seem to have suffered almost as much as the French, when Stukas mistakenly attacked a detachment of the 6th Panzer, knocking out several guns and vehicles and killing eleven personnel. On the other hand Corap, judging the Charleville–Mézières gap to be the most vulnerable portion of this sector, had located most of the available artillery there, leaving the defence of Monthermé largely to the 42nd half-brigade of colonial machine-gunners, a number of them Indo-Chinese.

During the morning of the 13th, the advanced elements of General Kempf's 6th Panzer cleared the parts of Monthermé lying on the right bank of the Meuse. Kempf himself arrived at the Roche-à-Sept-Heures, a famous tourist halt overlooking the town a mile to the north, to plan his attack. Around him stretched one of the most memorable panoramas of the whole Ardennes. Below, the heights dived almost perpendicularly through great slabs of slippery rock and treacherous shale, broken with belts of thick forest, down to the Meuse several hundred feet beneath. Beyond the river, he could see the whole Monthermé isthmus protruding from its narrow base like a swollen thumb (the Germans promptly nicknamed it the 'bread-roll') into the folds of the Meuse and rising to heights quite as dominating as the Roche-à-Sept-Heures – a superb natural defensive position. In the Meuse at his feet, faster flowing and wider than at Sedan, lay the half-submerged trusses of the destroyed road bridge. It was by no means an ideal place for a major river crossing, though Kempf was agreeably surprised at the astonishing resemblance to the Lahn in Germany where the division had been posted to carry out its preparatory training for *Sichelschnitt*. He ordered his 4th Rifle Regiment to prepare for an immediate attempt, deploying, like Rommel at Dinant, all his available Mark III and Mark IV tanks to provide close covering fire.

Painfully the riflemen scrabbled, stumbled and slid down the steep slope with their weighty machine-guns, mortars and ammunition boxes. Small avalanches of loose stones started up from beneath their boots, and there were many painful falls. The valley, however, was filled with a welcome pall of smoke, and gratefully they noted the sparsity of the French artillery fire. On reaching the level of the river, there was an uneasy silence during which the riflemen could distinctly hear the asthmatic sounds of the foot-pumps inflating the rubber assault dinghies under the cover of dead ground. Just across the river they could read the signs of *'Café'* or *'Boucherie'* on the riverside buildings, but there was no sign of life from the enemy. The moment the first team reached the water with their dinghy, however, devastating machine-gun fire opened up. Several men were wounded, the remainder dropped the boat and ran for shelter. The next team was also shot up, and it was difficult in the smoke and confusion to pinpoint just where the fire was coming from. At last a bunker was located carefully camouflaged underneath a terrace café, where in happier times tourists had sat and gazed out over the Meuse. Tanks were brought to bear on the café, and under cover of smoke from a burning coal barge, more assault teams were launched. They noted that the tanks had reduced the bunker beneath the café to a gaping hole; meanwhile it was also discovered that dinghies launched upstream and carried away by the current were jamming into the spans of the demolished bridge, where they appeared to be covered from fire by the remaining French bunkers. Swiftly the engineers capitalized on this discovery and brought up planks and more dinghies, creating a rickety footbridge lashed to the remnants of the bridge. In the twilight, the remainder of one of the rifle battalions made its way across the bridge, establishing by midnight a small bridgehead on the Monthermé peninsula. But there was no question here of French resistance being broken, and Kempf's riflemen, tired and having suffered distressing casualties, were forced to dig in defensively, under heavy fire from the French-held heights, and with little prospect of getting their tanks across the Meuse the next morning.

Holland: a Matter of Hours

For all the new, menacing fury of the fighting on the Meuse, developments in northern Belgium and Holland were not without gravity on the 13th. The Dutch had reached a point where it was clearly only a matter of hours before the end came. The 9th Panzer was hammering its way towards the outskirts of Rotterdam. Yet still the Dutch fought back, and by the evening an exasperated General von Küchler (commander of the Eighteenth Army) was issuing orders for his forces 'to break the resistance in Rotterdam with all means'. Meanwhile, Giraud's Seventh Army had retired more or less out of harm's way towards the estuary of the Scheldt. Further south, the main body of the Belgian Army had made its way back behind the Dyle Line, and on the B.E.F. front Lord Gort could once again state that 'No event of major importance occurred during the day.'

It was General Prioux's Cavalry Corps which, still standing ahead of Blanchard's First Army, bore the main burden of the fighting in northern Belgium. What had been armoured skirmishes on the 12th had turned into the first full-scale tank-versus-tank battle of the campaign. Adroitly supported by Stukas, powerful concentrations of tanks from both the 3rd and 4th Panzer Divisions hammered at Prioux's two Light Mechanized Divisions. All day the battle had seethed like a cauldron around Merdorp, a village just west of Hannut and a few miles from Marlborough's battlefield of Ramillies. Although contemporary German accounts admit to few losses on their side, it is clear that they were much disconcerted at first by the 'unbelievable' armour of the medium Somuas, which could stand more than one hit by all but the heaviest German tank cannon. Then the German Panzer commanders began to detect an Achilles' heel in French gunnery, in so far as the French tanks consistently seemed to fire short and at a slower rate than their own. So the Germans closed the range whenever possible. But, according to a German Panzer officer who was there, they learned a far more basic lesson about French armoured techniques that day at Merdorp –

'their lack of manoeuvrability and the fact that they fight single and in loose formation, not all together under one command. They cannot take advantage of strength and number.' Never again in the campaign would French tanks fight on such closely equal terms with the enemy; at Merdorp they fought with tenacity and courage, but too often in penny packets that were repeatedly outmanoeuvred, and it was the Panzers which, at the end of the day, held the field. That night Prioux drew his tanks back behind the Belgian anti-tank obstacle at Perwez. Both sides had suffered heavy losses,[26] but the French losses were to have much more far-reaching consequences on the overall strategic position.

The Allies: Tears and Ignorance

As this eventful Whit Monday came to a close, at the upper echelons of the French High Command, General Georges for one seems at last to have been awakened as to what was at stake on the Upper Meuse. Early that morning, Captain Beaufre recalls drawing in on General Doumenc's situation map a large arrow, denoting that the main German effort was being made 'not in Belgium, but on the axis Luxembourg–Mézières'. He claims that Georges's *Deuxième Bureau* had arrived simultaneously at the same conclusion, but had dismissed it on the grounds of the 'defensive value of our position' at Sedan. During the day, dispatch-riders rushed back and forth between Doumenc's G.H.Q. at Montry and Georges's at La Ferté, bearing a flood of reports. Then, late that evening, Beaufre informs us that he was awoken by a telephone call from General Georges, asking him to 'tell General Doumenc to come at once!' Accompanied by Beaufre, Doumenc arrived at La Ferté at about 0300. Georges's staff officers were clustered together in the *grand salon* of Les Bondons, which had been transformed into a map room. The lights were low; in the rest of the villa they were extinguished.

26. The Germans claim to have knocked out 30 Somuas and 70 Hotchkiss H-35s.

At the telephone, Major Navereau repeats in a soft voice the information he is receiving. The others are silent. General Roton, the Chief of Staff, is slumped in an armchair. The atmosphere is that of a family keeping vigil over a dead member. Georges rises briskly and comes up to Doumenc. He is terribly pale. 'Our front has been pushed in at Sedan! There have been some failures (*défaillances*) . . .' He falls into an armchair and a sob silences him.

It was the first man that I had seen weep in this battle. I was to see many others, alas. It made a dreadful impression on me.

Doumenc, says Beaufre, did his best to comfort the C.-in-C. There were collapses like this in all wars, he said reassuringly. 'Come, let's look at the map. We'll see what can be done.'

Gamelin, meanwhile, and beyond him the French and British Governments, remained blissfully unaware of Georges's state of mind, cushioned from the full gravity of the situation by sheer lack of Intelligence. After General Georges's first lustrous communication, warning of the 'rather serious pin-prick' at Sedan, Gamelin's last news that night from Sedan, via Georges, announced that the Second Army was 'holding' and concluded, superbly: 'Here we are calm . . .' Baudouin, the Secretary to Reynaud's new War Cabinet, declares that after three vain attempts on 12 May to gain accurate information from G.Q.G., Colonel Villelume, the Cabinet's Military Liaison Officer, succeeded in bringing in the news at about 1800 on the 13th that 'Our advance guards had been violently thrown back in the Ardennes.' Finally, from the depths of his isolated *Thébaïde*, Gamelin issued the following somewhat meaningless Order of the Day to the French forces at large:

The onslaught of the mechanical and motorized forces of the enemy must now be faced. The hour has come to fight in depth [27] on the positions appointed by the High Command. One is no longer entitled to retire. If the enemy makes a local breach, it must not only be sealed off but counter-attacked and retaken.

---

27. The last thing for which the 'continuous front' philosophy was in fact designed!

In London, the British G.I.G.S., Ironside, summed up his day
in his diary:

There is yet no sight of the Germans having done anything except
move forward their mechanized columns under cover of intense
air activity.

Chapter 13

Consolidating the Bridgeheads

14 May

In the area south of the line Liège–Namur our troops have left the Ardennes behind them and reached the Meuse between Namur and Givet with their advance guard ... Under the protection of German fighter, Stuka and 'destroyer' units, which attacked non-stop, and with a shattering effect, it was also possible to cross the Meuse on French territory.

Wehrmacht communiqué, 14 May

In general it may be said that the Germans have not yet made contact with the bulk of the French and British forces, except possibly in the Longwy area, where they are said to be challenging the underground hill fortresses of the Maginot Line.

The Times, 15 May

Onhaye: Rommel Attacks

For the Germans, 14 May was a day devoted to consolidating their bridgeheads over the Meuse, in preparation for the great armoured breakthrough across northern France; for the French, a day of building up major counter-strokes against the two German bulges.

At Dinant, it did not seem to begin under the most brilliant of auspices for Rommel. The dawn attack (postponed from the previous night) by a battalion of Motorized Dragoons (the 14th) from General Boucher's 5th Division succeeded in capturing the village of Haut-le-Wastia and some forty of Rommel's motor-cyclists. Not pressing their advantage, however, the French had then withdrawn to a 'line of containment' fixed by Corap. On the other side of the bridgehead, Colonel von Bismarck signalled that under cover of darkness his 7th Rifle Regiment had pushed up to Onhaye, three miles down the main road west of Dinant. It had overrun enemy positions there, but was being engaged by powerful forces. Rommel rushed back and forth, positioning his anti-tank guns, and urging on the tanks which were just beginning to cross the barely completed pontoons, but with what seemed like agonizing slowness. Suddenly Rommel received a wireless message from Bismarck stating that his regiment was 'encircled'. Thereupon Rommel decided 'to go to his assistance immediately with every available tank'. By 0800 hours, his 25th Panzer Regiment, under the command of Colonel Rothenburg, had succeeded in assembling just thirty tanks on the west bank. All of these now moved up behind Bismarck, but encountered no opposition. Says Rommel: 'It transpired that von Bismarck had actually radioed "arrived" instead of "encircled"'! [1]

With five tanks providing mobile support fire, Bismarck's riflemen now carried out a flanking attack to seize Onhaye from the rear. From Dinant the main road climbs steeply through woods to Onhaye, but once Onhaye is passed you stand on the height of land, with flat open country ideal for armoured deployment, leading westwards to Philippeville, and beyond it the featureless plains of northern France. Thus the securing of Onhaye (which had been the object of a special exercise conducted by Rommel at Bad Godesberg) was of paramount importance to the break-out phase of the 7th Panzer's advance. To keep a tight control over the action, Rommel mounted himself in a Mark III tank and followed closely behind Colonel Rothenburg. This typical audacity nearly brought an end to his career. Approaching the corner of Onhaye wood,

suddenly we came under heavy artillery and anti-tank gunfire from the west. Shells landed all round us and my tank received two hits one after the other, the first on the upper edge of the turret and the second in the periscope.

The driver promptly opened the throttle wide and drove straight into the nearest bushes. He had only gone a few yards, however, when the tank slid down a steep slope on the western edge of the wood and finally stopped, canted over on its side, in such a position that the enemy, whose guns were in position about 500 yards away on the edge of the next wood, could not fail to see it. I had

1. *Eingetroffen* instead of *eingeschlossen*.

been wounded in the right cheek by a small splinter from the shell which had landed in the periscope. It was not serious, though it bled a great deal.

I tried to swing the turret round so as to bring our 37 mm. gun to bear on the enemy in the opposite wood, but with the heavy slant of the tank it was immovable.

The French battery now opened rapid fire on our wood and at any moment we could expect their fire to be aimed at our tank, which was in full view. I therefore decided to abandon it as fast as I could, taking the crew with me. At that moment the subaltern in command of the tanks escorting the infantry reported himself seriously wounded, with the words: 'Herr General, my left arm has been shot off.' We clambered up through the sandy pit, shells crashing and splintering all round.

Just ahead of him, Rommel was shocked to see Rothenburg's tank 'with flames pouring out of the rear'.

The adjutant of the Panzer Regiment had also left his tank. I thought at first that the command tank had been set alight by a hit in the petrol tank and was extremely worried for Colonel Rothenburg's safety. However, it turned out to be only the smoke candles that had caught alight, the smoke from which now served us very well . . . It was only the involuntary smoke-screen laid by this tank that prevented the enemy from shooting up any more of our vehicles.

Meanwhile, Rommel's own armoured signals vehicle pushed into the wood where it too was immobilized with a shot in the engine. Rommel got away from the fracas, though his biographer, Desmond Young, claims that he narrowly escaped being captured by French native troops.[2] He then ordered Stuka strikes to liquidate the troublesome French gun positions. Later his riflemen winkled out a courageous French gunner captain from the cellar of a half-destroyed house, where, 'smoking cigarettes and drinking red wine, on a sofa', he had remained to telephone observations to his battery as the German columns marched past his refuge. His capture did not immediately silence the French guns, but thenceforth their fire fell wildly all over the place. However, on account

2. From the newly arrived 4th North African Division.

of the morning's setback, it was not until evening that Rommel could lay hands on his vital assembly area at Onhaye.

Onhaye: French Counter-attacks

On the French side, there was more fatal procrastination in the dispatch of reserves to counter-attack Rommel's bridgehead. The most powerful piece that General Georges could bring into play – in fact one of the most powerful pieces on the whole French chessboard – was the 1st Armoured Division. Originally earmarked by Gamelin to back up the Dyle Manoeuvre, on 11 May the 1st Armoured had been sent to Charleroi to be at the disposal of Blanchard's First Army, with the specific object of covering the Gembloux Gap. Commanded by General Bruneau, the 1st Armoured contained only 150 tanks, compared with Rommel's 228, but half of these were the excellent heavy 'B' model. On the other hand, it possessed no armoured liaison cars, it lacked signals units, and among the tanks which were equipped with radios it was found that the accumulators were inadequate to maintain transmission over any length of time. Fear of the Luftwaffe forced the division to make its approach march to Charleroi by night, which, in the short May nights, would have required four stages to cover 130 kilometres.[3] Then, following the rapidity of the German progress, it was decided to reduce the stages to two, the second being carried out by daylight; finally, a third decision prescribed that Bruneau reach Charleroi in one hop. Much confusion resulted. In fact, German bombing of the railways delayed the division's arrival by eighteen hours, and as soon as Bruneau had established his command post at Lambusart (near Charleroi) on the night of 12 May he received a request from the local corps commander to help him round up parachutists reported in his region. Wisely, Bruneau refused.

All through the 13th the 1st Armoured remained inactive there, less than twenty-five miles from where Rommel's bridgehead was developing. That day General Georges had

3. Not much faster than the rate of advance of the Panzers through France.

promised it to Corap, but Billotte, alarmed by the course of the fierce tank battle in which Prioux's Cavalry Corps had become engaged in front of the sensitive Gembloux Gap, and still disinclined to accept that the main German thrust was materializing in the south, continued to hesitate. Only at midnight on the 13th did Bruneau receive preliminary instructions preparing the 1st Armoured to strike south in order to aid General Martin's XI Corps. Then another twelve hours were frittered away by muddled staff work, until, at 1300 hours on the 14th, it was ordered to move to the Florennes area just over twenty miles to the south. But 'It took them a long time to reach their positions,' wrote Colonel Bardies, 'for the roads were cluttered with fleeing troops and civilians. . . It took the armoured division seven hours to cover those twenty miles. It was short of petrol. It would be unable to fight that day.' One battalion lost its way, and it was not until after midnight that Bruneau had three battalions of tanks in the Florennes assembly area; meanwhile, mistakenly, he had relegated his petrol trucks to the rear of the divisional column, and thus it semed doubtful whether the 1st Armoured would even be in a fit state to attack early on the morning of the 15th.

By this time, the whole picture would have altered radically. How different things might have been if it could have hit Rommel on the 13th, when only his infantry were across the Meuse, or even on the morning of the 14th when Rommel was still being vigorously resisted around Onhaye.

The other major force at Corap's immediate disposal for a counter-attack against Rommel was General Sancelme's 4th North African Division, which had been standing by in reserve. A tough regular unit comprised of Zouaves and Algerian *Tirailleurs* – many of whose kinsmen would be fighting against France less than two decades later – and constituting the finest division [4] in the Ninth Army, it should

4. As will be seen on subsequent occasions, it was frequently the French North African and colonial units which put up the best resistance in 1940. On the other side, German troops inoculated with Nazi racial doctrines are repeatedly to be found protesting at the 'shame' of the *Herrenvolk* having to fight against inferior 'nigger-people' in France.

ideally have been employed in a forceful attack co-ordinated with the 1st Armoured. Corap, however, true to the 1918 doctrine of 'containment', immediately cast it in a defensive role, to hold the line at Onhaye. Fighting splendidly, it had been the *Tirailleurs* forming its advanced elements which had administered the check to Rommel here during the morning of the 14th, but the defensive tone of Corap's order did not have an encouraging effect on the hard-pressed remnants of his 18th Division. The news from its left flank, opposite Rommel's original crossing place at Houx, was particularly bad. Here the battalion of the 39th Regiment detailed off to attack Surinvaux Wood at dawn had stumbled into it too early during the night. At daybreak it was swiftly rounded up by the Germans, supported with tanks. Then, fighting gallantly, the remains of the 66th Regiment were submerged. After which, says General Doumenc,

the whole line ebbed back and attempted, without much success, to anchor itself to the Anthée–Sosoye defence line. The Luftwaffe raged relentlessly around the sector; communications were cut, orders could not be passed; it became impossible to control the battle.

Corap in Trouble

Control was not aided by Corap's own movements that day. Having found that his H.Q. at Vervins was too far from the battlefield to keep abreast of events, in the morning he had moved up to General Martin's command post at Florennes and had then spent the rest of the day visiting the various divisional command posts. Liaison officers urgently requiring instructions for orienting the 1st Armoured and the 4th North African Divisions found it difficult to locate him. What Corap saw and learned that day depressed him in the extreme. In addition to Rommel's bridgehead, a German infantry division was getting across the Meuse at Yvoir, to the north of Dinant. Worse still, another infantry division had partly overrun the southerly division (the 22nd) of General Martin's corps, which was holding the line near Givet. As bad luck would have it, the divisional commander, General Hassler, had been injured in a car accident the previous month and did not return to his division until 15 May. Losing his head, Hassler's Chief of Staff ordered the 22nd Division to abandon the strongpoint guarding Givet and fall back some six miles behind the river. Furious, Corap threatened him with a court martial and formally ordered him to counter-attack. But it was too late; as Colonel Goutard acidly comments, 'Here was another division which disintegrated at the first blow.'

Everywhere Corap found indications that morale was flagging, and especially among the 'A' reservists of the 18th Division which had so far absorbed the hardest blows from Rommel. Officers seemed to be giving up all too readily. To the Ninth Army at large he addressed an exhortatory signal with the following words:

Some *défaillances* have occurred at certain points . . . At this moment, when the destiny of France is in the balance, no weakness will be tolerated. At all levels, leaders have the duty to set the example, and if necessary force obedience! Pitiless sanctions will fall upon any leaders who fail.

By evening Rommel had succeeded in wresting Onhaye from the North Africans. Although they were still fighting back hard, at 1900 hours General Martin, concerned at the shaky position of both his 18th and 22nd Divisions and their poor state of morale, gave order for the whole corps to fall back behind a 'barrier' line running through Florennes. Moving up to the front that evening, the 13th Zouaves, the reserve regiment of the 4th North African Division, was astonished to pass Martin and his H.Q. heading in the opposite direction. The Zouaves had begun to move up from their positions on the Belgian frontier on 10 May, repeatedly attacked by German bombers and Stukas, and during the night of the 13th they had circuited the burning town of Philippeville. Now, still not having seen the enemy, they were 'thrown into the ditches alongside the road, and remained there immobilized for more than three hours, watching without comprehension', as the H.Q. of XI Corps, accompanied by a flotsam of fighting troops, withdrew through them. Hard upon its heels came Colonel Rothenburg's Panzers, who by nightfall on the 14th had pushed down the Philippeville road as far as Anthée. Rommel's bridgehead was now over seven miles deep – at a total cost of three officers, seven N.C.O.s and forty-one men killed that day. The tanks of both Rommel's division and those of Colonel Werner's from the 5th Panzer, which were still at his disposal, were flowing into the bridgehead with ever-increasing speed, despite Allied air attacks on the pontoons, and all was now set for the break-out phase. In this, Rommel was still one jump ahead of Guderian at Sedan.

About the only comfort that Corap, the portly old colonial soldier, could find on his front that day was the continued resistance that the colonial machine-gunners of the 102nd Fortress Division were putting up at Monthermé. Here General Kempf's 6th Panzer was not having an easy time. During the early hours of the morning, accurate French artillery fire had destroyed the footbridge made up of rubber dinghies. The riflemen clinging to the west bank of the Monthermé isthmus had been repeatedly counter-attacked, and were much hampered by the non-arrival of the divisional heavy artillery, still held up in the Ardennes traffic blocks. With heavy losses, Colonel von Ravenstein's riflemen managed to push up on to Height 325 during the morning, but by midday Kempf was forced to tell his corps commander, Reinhardt, that he saw little prospect of any further progress that day. There was certainly no question of building a heavy pontoon bridge to get the tanks across. All through the day and the following night the French gunfire kept up. But the few heavy weapons available to the defenders were slow-firing, First War models of the 'long' 155, which with their flat trajectory had difficulty in hitting the Germans on the steep reverse slopes of the Monthermé isthmus. To help them, Corap sent up a group of sixty year old 220-mm. howitzers. At midnight these were found by the commander of the 42nd Half-Brigade abandoned on the road by their personnel, presumably after being attacked by the Luftwaffe. That same evening a solitary 47-mm. anti-tank gun was also sent up to

Monthermé; according to General Menu, it too was discovered by the enemy the following day, abandoned by its
crew without having fired a single shot.

German Infantry Reach the Meuse

Despite the continued agglomeration of traffic in the Ardennes, the first of Rundstedt's infantry divisions, which were
to play a vital role in 'lining' the corridor of the Panzer breakthrough, had now reached the Meuse. On the 14th, three of
them established crossings on either side of Rommel's bridgehead, while two divisions of General Haase's III Corps,[5] the
3rd and 23rd, fought their way down to the Meuse at Nouzonville, roughly midway between Monthermé and Charleville–Mézières. One of the subalterns of the 23rd Division was
Axel von dem Bussche, a twenty-one-year-old regular who
was later to become distinguished for his participation in
various bomb plots against Hitler. So far, the march through
the Ardennes had seemed like a jolly picnic, and, until the
commanding officer had berated them for unmartial practices,
his footsore men had taken to wheeling their weapons along
in commandeered prams. Then, fighting his way down to the
Meuse, von dem Bussche, his arm raised in the act of lobbing
a grenade into a French position, saw a frightened Annamite
face taking aim at close range. The bullet removed his right
thumb, and for him the campaign was over.

Lieutenant Karl-Heinz Mende of the Engineers had shared
similar experiences of the campaign so far. Still not having
seen a shot fired, he recalled how when passing a customs
house on the French frontier that morning his men had acquired a rubber stamp marked 'Douane Française, 9 Mai
1940', which they adjusted to the right date, and frivolously
stamped their letters home with it. One even tattooed his
breast with it. There was an occasional sound of gunfire in the
distance, but that was all. Then suddenly Mende's unit was
plunged into the inferno. In spite of repeated Stuka attacks on

5. Its immediate forebear, III Brandenburg Corps of 1914–18, had pulled
off the remarkable *coup* of capturing Verdun's Fort Douaumont.

Nouzonville, the French 102nd Fortress Division fought back tenaciously from well-hidden positions, and it was only on the third attempt that his division got across the river. Later Mende wrote home describing this first confrontation with war in more pensive terms, which perhaps typified the emotions of many a young German during those days:

We have it behind us . . . after everything that I have experienced I do not know whether I have become richer or poorer and whether the experience of such things is the true new value of this campaign. I only know one thing – and I have also found this conviction among brave comrades: the worst thing in battle is not the danger, which stands burning before one's eyes; the worst feeling is nervousness about success.

After the crossing had succeeded,

I cannot say that we were worried or uncertain, we simply had no feeling left in us. That was the mood of the battle. And only, when in front of us an infantryman who was hit collapsed and a dead comrade lay nearby, did there awake a piece of the old feeling and we thought for one second how dangerous it all was and that we were after all human beings of flesh and blood.

By the end of the 14th, however, it was not the crossings at Monthermé and Nouzonville that were most endangering Corap's right flank, but the change in direction of Guderian's thrust. To study this, one now has to return to the scene at Sedan.

The French: a Mission of Sacrifice

As an indication of just how well according to plan *Sichelschnitt* was going, the main directive contained in Guderian's brief orders for the 14th read: 'The divisions will capture their objectives according to the map exercise.' By dawn a substantial number of the 1st Panzer's tanks had already trundled across Lieutenant Grubnau's bridge. The concentration of vehicles queueing up on the east bank was so enormous that it was quite impossible for anything to move in the opposite direction. Thus, noted Grubnau, the cloth factory from which the first crossings had been launched on the 13th had been transformed into a field hospital in which all the German wounded, plus two hundred French were being tended. The 1st Panzer tanks immediately headed towards Chéhéry (where Colonel Balck was sitting somewhat precariously) and Bulson. These happened to be the same axes along which General Lafontaine's two counter-attacking groups, each consisting of an infantry group and a battalion of support tanks, were advancing. The first head-on collision between Guderian and the French armour was now imminent. But on top of all the delays of the previous night, the two groups still proved incapable of co-ordinating with one another. The right-hand group (comprised of the 4th Tank Battalion and the 205th Infantry Regiment of the 71st Division) were still not ready for action. So only the 7th Tanks and Lieutenant-Colonel Labarthe's 213th Infantry Regiment went, piecemeal, into battle. Still complaining about the state of his regiment, Labarthe begged to be allowed to adopt a defensive position in the villages of Chémery and Maisoncelle. But he was overruled by Lafontaine (backed by Grandsard), and finally set forth at 0700 hours, muttering '*C'est une mission de sacrifice!*' The 213th carried with it not one anti-tank weapon, artillery support was doubtful, and the 7th Tanks was equipped only with the light F.C.M. infantry model mounting an obsolete 37-mm. gun with little penetrating power. Nevertheless, the battle started well enough for the French armour. Near Chéhéry they came upon vehicles of the 1st Panzer that were refuelling and a savage encounter at short range ensued, in which the two leading German tanks were knocked out and the commander of the 1st Panzer Brigade, Colonel Keltsch, severely wounded.

Even the German accounts admit that this was an ugly moment for them, and it leads one to speculate what havoc the 4th and 7th Tanks might have inflicted on Balck's soft-skinned infantry had they only been able to attack a few hours earlier. With that mixture of optimism and misinformation still prevalent in the French High Command, half an hour later General Georges was reporting to Gamelin that 'the breach at Sedan has been contained and a counter-attack with strong formations was carried out at 4.30 a.m.'. Shortly afterwards, the tide of battle was already turning against 7th Tanks. With extreme courage, a nearby German *Sturm-pionier* battalion flung itself on the French tanks, hurling hollow charges between the tracks and under the motors; during this attack the commander, Lieutenant-Colonel Mahler, lost his life. The French tanks seemed hesitant to press their advantage. As in the armoured battle in northern Belgium at Merdorp, they were seen to be manoeuvred slowly and clumsily by their commanders. While the few German anti-tank guns that had reached the battle-line (plus two '88s') held the 7th Tanks at bay, with customary speed the 1st Panzer prepared a smashing counter-blow. Towards 0830 hours, a mass of Panzers struck in the area of Connage (midway between Chéhéry and Chémery), accounting for eleven out of the fifteen F.C.M.s. there. A similar fate overtook the French tank companies deployed on the dominating high ground at Bulson. Now it could be said with truth that 'The Panzers are at Bulson'. The 7th Tanks reeled back, having lost more than half of their machines on much the same ground where the French *cuirassiers* had sacrificed themselves at the 1870 Battle of Sedan. German armour hooking left from Chémery then tore into the flank of the unprotected 213th Infantry Regiment. Its commander, the reluctant Labarthe, was wounded and taken prisoner, while the broken remnants of his regiment streamed back to the 55th Division's second line of defence at Mont-Dieu.

It was about 2130 when General Lafontaine heard of the failure of his counter-attack. Under the circumstances, he considered it pointless to throw in the right-hand combat group. Instead he ordered it to fall back behind Raucourt, the 4th Tank Battalion dispersing without ever having been engaged that day. This, says General Ruby, 'marked the end of the 55th Division'. Some three hours later, an exhausted and saddened Lafontaine, alone with his H.Q. staff, reported to Grandsard's Corps H.Q. Two days later he was officially removed from command of a division that no longer existed.

The 71st, though still not attacked, was not long to survive its sister 'B' division. Poor General Baudet, ill and overdue for retirement, who had been told by Grandsard only the previous morning 'the enemy cannot possibly attack today with forces of any size', had wandered about all night in a state of bemusement, from his own command post to that of his right-hand neighbour, the 3rd North African Division, and to Grandsard's H.Q. During the night he moved his own command post from Raucourt back to La Bagnolle, and once again in the morning to Sommauthe, seven miles further south. Thus, at a moment when the 10th Panzer was beginning to press in from Pont Maugis and Thélonne, and grim reports were percolating through about the fate of the 55th, General Baudet had lost all contact with his troops. There were cries of 'Tanks to the rear and to the left!', and, says General Menu,

This cry re-echoed from group to group, from section to section. Riflemen and machine-gunners got up and fled, taking with them in their flight those of the artillerymen who had not already beaten them to it, mingled with elements flooding backwards from the neighbouring sector . . . by 1400 hours there was no one any longer in position.

Except for the 205th Regiment, earmarked for Lafontaine's counter-attack *manquée*, which continued to hold out bravely around Raucourt, the 71st Division, with no one visibly in command, just disintegrated. By the evening of the 14th it had, in the acid words of General Ruby, 'literally faded away at the mere threat of the enemy'. Baudet's head too fell into the basket, along with Lafontaine's.

The contagion of fear seems also to have spread to Grandsard's X Corps H.Q. during the morning of the 14th. Its chief Signals officer, who (according to Grandsard) 'since the previous day had shown a regrettable agitation and nervousness', had evacuated the H.Q. telephone exchange without any orders: 'When, towards midday, I wanted to call up Army

once again, the exchange no longer replied. Going down to it,
I discovered that it had been completely taken apart!' By
nightfall, Grandsard himself possessed only the empty husk
of a command. All that remained of his corps artillery were
one 105-mm. and one 155-mm. gun which had been in the
repair shop, and his one intact division, the 3rd North
African, was tranferred by Huntziger to XVIII Corps. The
remaining fragments of X Corps were then placed at the disposal of General Flavigny, commander of the newly constituted XXI Corps, which, with the 3rd Armoured and 3rd
Motorized Divisions, was hastening up towards the Sedan
bulge. With this Grandsard's X Corps and its hapless 'B' divisions disappear from the story, to be replaced by the first of a
steady flow of new names and new units.

Guderian Swings West

On the morning of the 14th, Sergeant Schulze with the riflemen of the 10th Panzer, who had such a hard time crossing
the Meuse the previous day, reached the heights above
Thélonne once tenanted by the 55th Division. 'We found
their artillery positions left as if they had fled. Some of the
guns were still loaded; the enemy had not had time to render
the weapons unserviceable.' The size of the hole which had
been rent in the French defences was also immediately apparent to the German field commanders. During the morning
Guderian had again driven across the Meuse to the front of
the bridgehead, passing thousands of French prisoners on the
way, and had been present while General Kirchner gave the
1st Panzer his orders for warding off the French tank attacks.
Shortly after leaving Kirchner, the 1st Panzer concentrations
at Chémery had been attacked with heavy losses by Stukas,
unaware that their own troops had advanced so far. Meanwhile, since early morning there had been reports from Luftwaffe Intelligence of hectic transport movements from Verdun,
Metz and Soissons towards Sedan, despite heavy bombing of
road and rail networks. It deduced that 'movement up by rail-

road of the French Army reserve is apparently beginning'.[6]
Going back to the Meuse bridge, Guderian ordered the tank
brigade of the 2nd Panzer to hasten across the river immediately behind the 1st, so as to be in a position to meet the main
French counter-thrust. The principal task of the 1st Panzer and
the Grossdeutschland Regiment must be to secure with all
urgency the vital high ground at Stonne which commanded the
whole Sedan bridgehead. Then, by early afternoon, the breaking-up of Lafontaine's counter-attack and the lack of any other
immediate French threat made the weakness of the whole
enemy position apparent to Guderian. He returned once more
to the 1st Panzer, which was now facing south on the line
Chémery–Maisoncelle, to put a most important question to
General Kirchner:

I asked him whether his entire division could be turned westwards
or whether a flank guard should be left facing south on the east
bank of the Ardennes Canal.

By way of reply, Kirchner's senior staff officer, Major Wenck,
promptly   interjected   Guderian's   own   favourite   slogan,
'*Klotzen, nicht Kleckern.*'[7] 'That', says Guderian, 'really answered my question.' He immediately issued orders for the 1st
and 2nd Panzers 'to change direction with all their forces, to
cross the Ardennes Canal and to head west with the objective
of breaking clear through the French defences'. To Kirchner,
Guderian supplemented his orders with the dramatic words:
'For the right wheel, road map Rethel!' Driving back to
corps H.Q. on the east bank of the Meuse to prepare his detailed orders for the 15th, Guderian paused on the heights
above Donchery, and, 'as I looked at the ground we had come
over, the success of our attack struck me as almost a miracle'.

Guderian's order was perhaps the most significant event of
the campaign to date, and with it was introduced a third,
decisive phase. The first phase had been the tricky approach

6. These reserves would have been principally the 3rd Armoured and 3rd
Motorized Divisions.
7. Literally, 'Wallop them, don't tap them', i.e. strike as a whole and don't
disperse the effort.

march through the Ardennes, with its accompanying deception of the 'matador's cloak' operating to the north; the
second, the crossing at Sedan and the constitution of a bridgehead. Now, by facing westwards, Guderian was poised in
readiness for the dash to the Channel which would cut in two
the Allied armies. The Battle of Sedan was over, and the
Battle of France about to begin, bringing with it a complete
change in the character of the campaign. By swinging right-
handed across the Ardennes Canal – forming as it did the
hinge between the French Second and Ninth Armies –
Guderian was also altering the immediate tactical situation,
gravely to the detriment of his opponents. His back turned
upon the battered Huntziger, he would now be striking at
the southern flank of Corap's Ninth Army, already in such
disarray where it faced Rommel in the north. But Guderian
was undoubtedly taking a colossal risk by offering his southern
flank to the major counter-thrust by those reinforcements
that Intelligence had warned were on their way. This flank,
of which Stonne was the keystone, was to be guarded only by
the Grossdeutschland and the 10th Panzer. But the Grossdeutschland had already suffered considerable losses, and it
would still be some time before the tanks of the 10th could
intervene effectively. Would they be able to hold until the consolidating infantry reinforcements, still marching up through
the Ardennes, could arrive? Meanwhile, there was yet a
second contingent source of worry confronting Guderian:
would the Allied air forces be able to destroy the pontoon
bridges across the Meuse, those tenuous lifelines on which
everything depended?

Allies bomb Sedan

Towards midday on the 14th, Rundstedt, the Army Group
Commander, had himself arrived at Sedan to examine the
situation. Guderian reported to him 'in the very middle of the
bridge, while an air raid was actually in progress. He asked
drily: "Is it always like this here?" I could reply with a clear
conscience that it was.'

Throughout the 14th, French and British bombers attacked the Sedan bridges with a reckless courage that impressed even the German flak gunners. The news of Rommel's and Guderian's crossing of the Meuse had reached Air Marshal Barratt on the night of the 13th. Accordingly Barratt, although it had already lost a quarter of its bombers, had warned the A.A.S.F. to be ready to throw in its full strength the next day, but also to prepare plans for retirement. Shortly after daybreak, ten Battles from Nos. 103 and 150 Squadrons took off for Sedan on two separate missions. Catching the German flak by surprise in the early-morning mist and encountering no Messerschmitts, they returned without loss; but, with their light-weight bombs, they caused only small damage to the pontoons, which was speedily repaired. It was then Barratt's intention to switch to Rommel's bridges at Dinant, but following the failure of Lafontaine's counter-attacks, General Billotte made an urgent 'victory or defeat' appeal to him for all available Allied bombers to be thrown in at Sedan. At mid-morning, it became the turn of the French Air Force, which could only scrape together the pitifully small total of twenty-eight bombers. First of all eight Bréguets from *Groupement d'Assaut* 18, escorted by fighters, attacked troop concentrations on the west bank. Heeding the disastrous losses from the ground-level attacks earlier in the campaign, they flew in at over 2,500 feet; this confused the German flak gunners but it did not make for accuracy. Five of the Bréguets were hit, but only one came down – behind the French lines. Next, shortly after noon, thirteen lumbering and elderly Amiots and six Léos attacked the outskirts of Sedan. Five of the French bombers were shot down, and by evening on the 14th *Groupe* I/12 had only one serviceable machine; consequently, the French air command called off its remaining operations for the day.

In the afternoon, Barratt's A.A.S.F. returned, throwing in every available Blenheim and Battle. Like the French, the British made the mistake of attacking in small packets; and, in any case, as had already been proved in the north, the slow and under-armed Battles were horribly vulnerable both to

enemy ground fire and Messerschmitts.[8] By now the German
defences were thoroughly prepared. Against an impressive
escort of 250 Allied fighters, Loerzer and Richthofen fielded
814 machines; the German flyers called it 'fighters' day'. But
in truth the day belonged at least as much to Guderian's light
flak teams. With that extraordinary organizational brilliance
which characterized the whole Sedan operation, Guderian had
somehow disentangled his flak batteries from the columns still
stretching across the Ardennes and rushed them forward so
that they now ringed the pontoon bridges with an imposing
concentration of firepower. Captain von Kielmansegg stood
watching near the 1st Panzer bridge at Gaulier:

the summer landscape with the quietly flowing river, the light
green of the meadows bordered by the darker summits of the more
distant heights, spanned by a brilliantly blue sky, is filled with the
racket of war. For hours at a time, the dull explosions of the
bombs, the quick tack-tack of the machine-guns, the different
notes, and the various effects of the separate flak calibres, mingles
with the droning of the aircraft motors and the roar of the divisions passing over the bridges unimpeded. The flak soldiers serve
their guns with rolled up shirt-sleeves, covered in sweat, and carry
out their defensive role with almost sporting ambition, encouraged
by the spectators occasionally coming up from the ranks of the
troops waiting at the crossing. Again and again an enemy aircraft
crashes out of the sky, dragging a long black plume of smoke
behind it, which after the crash of the succeeding explosion
remains for some time perpendicular in the warm air. Occasionally
from the falling machines one or two white parachutes release
themselves and float slowly to earth . . . in the short time that I
am at the bridge, barely an hour, eleven planes alone were brought
down.

For the R.A.F. the Meuse that day was an unimaginable hell,
a real Valley of Death from which few returned. In it, the
targets they had to hit were mere threads sixty yards long by
a few feet wide, and more than one German writer testifies to
the 'unbelievable bravery' with which the hopelessly out-

8. Against fighter attack from the rear the Battles (designed in 1933) had
only one flexibly mounted Lewis gun, roughly the same armament as that
carried by the aircraft of 1914–18.

classed Battles pressed home their attacks. No. 12 Squadron –
the 'Dirty Dozen' which had already suffered so heavily at
Maastricht – lost four out of its remaining five planes; No.
150 Squadron, four out of four. Altogether, out of seventy-
one bombers engaged, forty did not return. As the R.A.F.
official history soberly remarks, 'No higher rate of loss in an
operation of comparable size has ever been experienced by
the Royal Air Force.'

That evening twenty-eight Blenheims from Bomber Command continued the attacks; they lost a quarter of their numbers. The Germans later claimed to have shot down two
hundred Allied planes, bombers and fighters; Guderian's flak –
the commander of which, Colonel von Hippel, was decorated
with the Ritterkreuz for his work that day – was said to have
accounted alone for 112 aircraft. These claims were certainly
exaggerated,[9] but the losses were high enough to break the
back of the Allied tactical bombing potential. The Luftwaffe
too had suffered fairly heavy casualties, including the death
of two of its most senior combat leaders, Major-General von
Stutterheim and Colonel Schwartzkopf, the Stuka ace. The
constant bombing attacks had undoubtedly shaken German
nerves, and an entry in XIX Panzer Corp's War Diary for
that evening notes that 'The completion of the military bridge
at Donchery had not yet been carried out owing to heavy
flanking artillery fire and long bombing attacks on the bridging points . . . Our fighter cover is inadequate.' But the
bridges had not yet been destroyed; the procession of
Guderian's armour and supplies across the Meuse had been
briefly delayed, but not halted. Thus it was a grotesque piece
of wishful thinking on the part of General Georges to inform
Barratt in the evening that the air attacks had enabled Huntziger to 'contain' the bridgehead, and to add a prediction that
the 'centre of interest' would shift next day to Dinant. As it
was, that black day marked the supreme effort of the Allied
bomber forces, an effort that could never again be repeated –
and it had failed in its objective.

9. Total French and British losses from the Sedan action on 14 May were
probably nearer ninety.

The heroic sacrifice of Barratt's Battle squadrons had certainly not halted the impetus of the crucial right-wheel by the 1st and 2nd Panzers. During the morning, even before Guderian's momentous decision, the forceful Colonel Balck had already seized a crossing point over the River Bar and the closely parallel Ardennes Canal near Omicourt, against light resistance. All the way down to its confluence with the Meuse, the Bar valley is very wide and open, and there are no natural defensive positions comparable to the La Marfée heights to the east, now lost to the French. The Bar itself is no more than what is sometimes described in France as a *pipi du chat*, thirty feet wide in most places, and the bridges over it appear not to have been destroyed. Westwards from the Bar, the country transforms itself rapidly into the great monotonous plain of northern France, stretching all the way to the Channel, with no serious defensive feature until the River Oise just short of St Quentin. Swiftly the tanks of the 1st and 2nd Panzer began pushing over the Bar crossing places secured for them by Balck's riflemen. Shortly after midday, there was a third French tank attack, coming up from the south-west, against the 1st Panzer, which had to refurnish its tanks with ammunition right up in the firing line. But by 3 p.m. there was a noticeable slackening in the French resistance southwest of the Bar. At least in this direction, the audacity of Guderian's right-wheel seemed justified so far.

French Reinforcements to Sedan

On the French side, the forces sent by Huntziger (on the night of the13th) to hold the Bar consisted of the 5th D.L.C. and the 1st Cavalry Brigade – both badly knocked about during the early skirmishes in the Ardennes – under command of General Chanoine. To link up with them, on the Second and Ninth Army hinge, General Corap had dispatched Colonel Marc's 3rd Spahi Brigade, which had retired with such disastrous precipitancy from the Semois, and the 53rd Division. But owing to a series of typical counter-orders which had sent the 53rd chasing around in circles all night, only the Spahis and

Chanoine's group were in position that morning, and it was upon them that the weight of Guderian's right-wheel had fallen.

Commanded by General Etchberrigaray, the 53rd was the third of those 'B' divisions so disastrously located around Sedan at the time of the German attack. It had spent the winter building the fortifications in the north, and the early spring working on farms outside Paris. Constituting Corap's reserve for his right-hand sector, on 12 May the 53rd had been ordered to back up General Libaud's XLI Corps, between Mézières and the Bar. At 2100 hours on the 13th, Corap warned Libaud that contact had been lost with the Second Army at Sedan, and therefore the 53rd Division should be sent to hold the Bar, facing east. Then, three-quarters of an hour later, when the 53rd was already under way, Libaud received another message from Corap, announcing (for no very clear reason) that the situation had become less critical and that the 53rd was to resume its position facing *north*, i.e. in support of the Ninth Army, anticipating a threat coming via Mézières. At 2230 hours, Libaud re-transmitted this latest order to General Etchberrigaray, but on his way the liaison officer carrying it received another counter-order direct from Corap, instructing the 53rd once again to deploy along the Bar. Meanwhile, to add to its sense of insecurity, the division in its peregrinations was soon running into those demoralizing fugitives encountered by other reinforcements on that night of 13 May. Says General Doumenc:

elements of our own artillery passed with their trucks but without any guns. Their officers declared that there was no longer any infantry in front of them; that the Germans had crossed the Meuse near Donchery, that they were already on the Ardennes Canal.

In this nocturnal confusion, General Etchberrigaray had the greatest difficulty in catching up with his troops to marshal them. By morning the 53rd Division was so dispersed that it would be unable to reach the Bar in time to be of any use during the 14th. Thus neither in its quality nor its location was it exactly the ideal formation with which to bar the vital gateway between Huntziger and Corap against the all-out on-slaught Guderian was about to mount.

After some hard fighting, in which the French cavalry put up a splendid resistance, by nightfall on the 14th Colonel Balck's riflemen, still at the apex of Guderian's thrust, had reached their objective at Singly. Their losses had by no means been light; Balck had lost a large number of his officers and riflemen, while only three-quarters of the 1st Panzer's tanks were still fit for action. But the division had already captured 3,000 prisoners and twenty-eight guns, and had knocked out some fifty French tanks. During the night, the 1st and 2nd Panzer brought all their tanks across the Bar in readiness for the big push westwards on the 15th.

Grossdeutschland at Stonne

On the other side of Guderian's bridgehead, Sergeant-Major Rubarth and his exhausted Engineers had been overjoyed to see the first of the 10th Panzer's tanks coming through the morning mist, after an anxious night. But during the day a combination of flanking French artillery fire, R.A.F. bomb damage to the pontoons and various technical difficulties had delayed crossings still more than in the 1st and 2nd Panzer sectors. Consequently, the 10th would not be able to lend its full weight to the vital, defensive role allotted it in Guderian's right-wheel until the 15th. Meanwhile it was up to the Gross-deutschland, now detached from the 1st Panzer and returned once more to the 10th, to secure the key heights around Stonne, some twelve miles south of Sedan, against the enemy's anticipated major counter-attack. Moving up towards Stonne, the Grossdeutschland was strafed by French Moranes. The war diarist of the 15th Company watched with detached curiosity as the Moranes released two bombs on it:

Helplessly we shoot back with our weapons! We look at each other. Where is the explosion? Somebody cries 'It's a dud.' Corporal Waldemar Kiedrowski from Essen . . . leaps out of the ditch on to one of the duds . . . Kiedrowski throws it on to the street –

the bomb blows up! There is nothing left of Corporal Kiedrow-ski! Corporal Schieg loses a leg – further behind us the Morane crashes, a victim to our machine-guns – Kiedrowski is our first dead. Nobody can find him, nobody can bury him!

And what of the counter-attack by the Second Army, to be launched with the powerful units that General Georges had dispatched to it? In the carefully measured words of General Ruby, such a thrust against the flank of Guderian's bridge-head, at a moment when the main weight of the Panzers was performing its 90-degree turn, leaving the flank to be guarded by the infantry of the Grossdeutschland, would probably have gained on the evening of 14 May, 'a fine local success, the repercussions of which . . . would have been felt beyond the boundaries of the [Second] Army'.

3rd Armoured at Stonne

General Brocard's 3rd Armoured Division, together with its sisters, the 1st and 2nd, constituted one of the rooks of the French chessboard; they were the most powerful pieces that General Georges had to play. It had two battalions of new Hotchkiss H-39s, and although fewer in overall numbers, these should have been a match for the extended 10th Panzer, half of whose tanks were light Marks I and II which were not designed for tank versus tank engagements. Its morale was excellent; on the other hand, it was such a newly constituted division that its battalions had only started divisional training on 1 May, and some of its tank engines were not yet properly run-in. The 3rd Motorized Infantry Division (under General Bertin-Boussu) was also a first-rate unit, at the peak of its training. When the 3rd Armoured received its movement orders on the afternoon of 12 May it had been in training north of Rheims, some forty miles away, and it was then generally believed that the division was being transferred to another training area, not that it was going to be pitched into battle. Though not actually bombed on its approach march by the Luftwaffe, the 3rd Armoured encountered many delays resulting from bomb damage, and it lacked engineers or sappers to put the roads in order. The heavy 'B' tanks had had difficulty crossing the Aisne, while at one place the encumberment caused by refugees and military fugitives was such that they were compelled to force a passage by crushing cars that obstructed their way.

What the reinforcements moving up to Sedan ran into on the roads is graphically described by Marcel Lerecouvreux.[10] Well behind the front, bridges and telephone exchanges were discovered to have been destroyed with precipitate haste, on 'superior orders' – the origins of which were never traced, but were later wildly attributed to the 'Fifth Column'. Meanwhile, fresh bands of fugitives were arriving the whole time:

One squadron of the 5th Cuirassiers discovered a sergeant-major who had torn off his badges of rank, so as to take flight more easily, both from the enemy and from his own responsibilities; later a lieutenant of the divisional anti-tank battery reported fugitives among whom were found two lieutenants who had similarly degraded themselves; he made this troop turn about under threat of his sub-machine gun. All these cowards were causing terrifying rumours to run around, notably about the aerial bombardments to which they had been subjected, and about the avalanche of tanks which was closely pursuing them . . . One had to seek proper justification for the rout . . . The fugitives said that they had been pursued by formidable masses of tanks (some spoke of 400, others of 500, or even 5,000!).

Such panic-spreading tales, Lerecouvreux goes on to explain, 'were probably one of the causes that had made excessively nervous commanders carry out the hasty demolitions which had taken place behind us'.

Closer to the front, the rumours had caused the wholesale disappearance of a battalion of sappers charged with organizing the defences of the village of Vaux; while, in the confusion, some French units, 'reacting to mutual suspicions had machine-gunned and fired at each other with rifles; near Raucourt in particular two battalions had thus inflicted upon

10. His unit, the 2nd D.L.C., having regrouped after its withdrawal from the Ardennes, was due to attack on the right of Flavigny's group, comprising the 3rd Armoured and the 3rd D.L.M.

each other some fairly serious losses'. At Sommauthe on the way towards Stonne there were scenes of chaos and pillage where 'vehicles lay about on the side of the road, smashed during the precipitate retreat without this even being the work of the enemy, and left by their drivers who had completely lost their heads'. Here were also some abandoned horse-drawn artillery, one gun of which was still harnessed to its dejected horses, standing in the middle of a small stream. Despite the haste of their flight, the fugitives had nevertheless found time to pillage everything, even the medical stores. 'The spectacle of all this débris, which inscribed our defeat upon the ground,' says Lerecouvreux, 'was lamentable and it gripped my heart.'

For all the delays and degrading panic it had experienced on the approach march, the 3rd Armoured reached its assembly area behind Stonne at 0600 on the 14th, full of spirit and eager to have a go at the enemy. General Brocard promptly reported to Second Army H.Q. at Senuc, where he met the commander of the newly constituted XXI Corps,[11] General Flavigny, who handed him his orders. XXI Corps was to

(a) Take up positions along the second line to the east of the Bar ... and contain the bottom of the pocket created by the enemy ...
(b) Having contained the enemy, counter-attack at the earliest in the direction of Maisoncelle–Bulson–Sedan ...

Specifically, the 3rd Armoured was to hasten its refuelling and attack in co-ordination with the 3rd Motorized, 'as soon as possible', towards Bulson with the object of 'throwing the enemy back across the Meuse'. But, as Colonel Goutard points out, the two terms of 'containment' (that old stand-by from 1918) and 'counter-attack' in Flavigny's orders were contradictory:

Containment is defensive and demands linear dispersion along a front; counter-attack is offensive and requires concentration in depth at one point ... How could one group fulfil these contradictory missions simultaneously, or even one after the other? And

11. Comprising the 3rd Armoured, 3rd Motorized and 5th Cavalry Divisions and the 1st Cavalry Brigade.

when containment has been effected, the opportunity for counter-attack would be over; it would be too late. It was obvious that, with our mania for an unbroken front, the containing mission would have priority.

Flavigny's orders ended ominously: 'The time of the counter-attack will be fixed later.' Brocard then brought to Flavigny's attention the state of his division after its night march of a full thirty miles. He did not think it would be ready to attack for some ten hours. (How closely this resembled the story of the 1st Armoured Division at Dinant!) Rejecting Brocard's suggestion that H-Hour be fixed for 1600, Flavigny told him by word of mouth to attack at 1100. But Brocard seems to have been tardy in issuing his orders, while refuelling proceeded with painful slowness, so that the 3rd Armoured was not ready to set off for its start-line before 1300 hours. Even then, its progress was impeded by the results of bombing and more waves of fugitives to such an extent that the division was not in fact deployed for attack until 1600. Meanwhile, the 3rd Motorized Division had experienced still worse hold-ups on its approach march, and instead of reaching the battle area on the morning of the 14th, by 1600 it was able to support the 3rd Armoured with only three reconnaissance groups. But there yet remained four hours of daylight left for the counter-attack, and, says General Ruby, 'the tank crews were champing at the bit in their eagerness'.

By this time, however, the speed with which the battlefront was changing had made its impression on General Flavigny. He was now alone at Senuc; Huntziger, fearing Second Army H.Q. to be threatened by the enemy, had moved it back to Verdun. Himself an old tank man, Flavigny (according to General Ruby) also seems to have begun to entertain doubts as to the technical qualities of Brocard's division, with its limited training. Whatever the combination of his motives, at 1530 Flavigny made a fateful decision. He would abandon the attack part of his orders in favour of that 1918 principle of 'containment first'. 'The most important thing,' he said, 'was to ensure the safety of the second line'.

In consequence, the 3rd Armoured was ordered to disperse

itself defensively over a front of some twelve miles, from Omont west of the Bar to Stonne. On all tracks and potential corridors of penetration it was to form 'corks', each comprised one 'B' and two H-39 tanks. During the night this powerful, modern unit was thus broken up into a series of penny packets. 'From then on,' says Colonel Goutard, 'there was a line, a few tanks but no 3rd Armoured Division. The steel lance was buried for ever, and so was the counterattack.' The best – and last – opportunity of administering a severe check to Guderian before he burst out of his bridgehead had been thrown away. It was a tragic error of judgement.

The Generals: Georges and Huntziger

On 13 May General Georges, in order to relieve the already overburdened Billotte from responsibility for the fighting at Sedan as well, had transferred the Second Army from No. 1 Army Group to his direct control. Thus it was to Georges that Huntziger had to report back on the 14th. Although his headquarters attempted to fob British correspondents off with the bland statement that 'we are withdrawing our advance posts, as has always been our intention', Huntziger warned Georges that morning that some of his troops were not holding, 'that men had been seen emerging from block-houses with uplifted arms and that he had given orders to open fire on them'.

Huntziger's references to Flavigny's counter-attack seem, however, to have been so discreet as to be almost evasive. At 1900, his Chief of Staff told Georges that it had been unable to begin 'for technical reasons'. Half an hour later Huntziger was on the telephone himself, claiming with ill-founded optimism that 'the enemy advance has been contained by Flavigny's *groupement* between the Ardennes Canal and the Meuse'.[12] Georges, obviously much vexed by Huntziger's procrastination but at the same time still only partially aware of the full gravity of the situation at Sedan, replied sharply:

12. This was duly passed on to Gamelin, with the addition of a little extra saccharine at Les Bondons.

The 3rd Armoured Division was put at your disposal in order to counter-attack at Sedan. Tomorrow, therefore, you must vigorously pursue the operation so well started (*sic*!) today by pushing on as far as you can towards the Meuse, and consolidation with the infantry the terrain conquered by the tanks. This is the only way to gain a supremacy over the enemy and to paralyse his whole advance to the west and south.

By the end of the 14th, Huntziger was in fact far from feeling the optimism which he attempted to impart in his messages to Georges. To one of his officers he remarked sadly: 'I shall always be *le vaincu de Sedan*.' In his depression at the buffeting his army had received he now made a miscalculation on an even graver scale than Flavigny's halting of the counter-attack and dispersal of the 3rd Armoured. Reacting in a manner typical of the epoch in which the Maginot Line had come to be regarded as the be-all and end-all of French military policy, Huntziger concluded that Guderian's thrust was aimed principally at outflanking the Maginot Line and then rolling it up from the north. Thus he decided to meet this notional threat by pivoting on his right heel which was planted where the Line ended near Longwy, and swinging back the centre of his army from its position astride the Meuse at Mouzon to one further back at Inor. In effect, this would mean the relinquishment without fighting of over 130 bunkers along the Meuse, and the expansion of the four mile wide Donchery–Wadelincourt pocket into a large breach more than fifteen miles across. It also meant that the 10th Panzer crossing-point could no longer be brought under interdiction fire by Huntziger's flank artillery, which in turn critically reduced the prospect of any counter-attack that might be launched on the 15th. But worst of all, Huntziger's decision meant that the Second Army would in fact be *pulling away* from the Ninth, thereby increasing the gap through which Guderian was planning to burst.

The Generals: Guderian and Kleist

At his H.Q. near La Chapelle that night Guderian was drafting his orders for the break-out by the 1st and 2nd Panzers the next day. In one hop of over twenty miles they were to 'reach as primary objective the line Wasigny-Rethel', while the corps reconnaissance was to probe as far ahead as Montcornet. These orders immediately provoked another heated disagreement between Guderian and his superior, Kleist. Having studied the Intelligence reports on the movement of Flavigny's reinforcements towards Stonne, Kleist – just that much further removed from battlefield realities than Guderian – had become extremely nervous for the safety of that southern flank. It was an anxiety that would plague the German senior commanders repeatedly from this day on, as indeed it had during the planning stages of *Sichelschnitt*. Kleist and other German officers of his generation could not help but be haunted by memories of how, in 1914, victory had been snatched from them on the Marne after Kluck had wheeled inwards prematurely, thereby exposing his flank to Galliéni's counter-attack out of Paris.[13] Instead of pushing on to Rethel, Kleist now told Guderian that he would prefer to halt and consolidate on the line Montigny–Bouvellemont, just a mile or two beyond where the Panzers had come to rest that same night. Guderian was furious. According to XIX Corps's War Diary, he 'bitterly criticized this plan which throws away the victory'. After some forceful argument, Guderian won, and his orders for the 15th were issued as intended. But if any additional justification was required for Flavigny launching his counter-attack on the 14th, this hesitancy revealed by Kleist certainly seems to provide it.

Terror at Rotterdam

Holland was at her last gasp. During the morning of the 14th negotiations for a cease-fire had begun between Dutch and German representatives outside Rotterdam. Meanwhile the

13. Another factor was the serious shortage of fuel threatening the Panzers at this stage in the campaign. To an important extent the planning of *Sichelschnitt* had been predicated on the German ability to supplement its own reserves from captured enemy supplies.

Luftwaffe was preparing a 'terror' blow against the city in case the Dutch there continued to resist. At 1400 hours, sixty He-111s bombed the old centre of the city for twenty minutes, utterly unopposed, as the Dutch Air Force had been annihilated. The Germans have since claimed that efforts were made to call off the raid, but the planes, already airborne, never received the signals. Whatever the explanation, it was a brutal act which shocked world opinion at the time. Just under 900 people were killed, but in the terror of the moment the Dutch Foreign Minister put the figure at 30,000, an exaggeration which in itself only added to the paralysing alarm felt in France at the apparently invincible ferocity of the German war machine. Shortly before 10 o'clock that night, Parisians listening to their radios heard Holland announce the news of her capitulation.

Tank Battle in the Gembloux Gap

On the front in northern Belgium, the B.E.F. had faced its first serious challenge on the 14th. Bock's forces attempted to take Louvain, but were repulsed by a fierce barrage from the 60-pounders of Montgomery's 3rd Division. But it was further south, on the French First Army's front, that the heaviest fighting again took place. The previous night Prioux's Cavalry Corps had withdrawn, after the savage tank battles of that day, behind the Belgian anti-tank obstacle running south of Perwez. Shortly after dawn on the 13th, Hoeppner's Panzers began to smash through it, supported by powerful concentrations of artillery. They succeeded in forcing a 200-foot breach, but by throwing in every gun, tank and soldier Prioux managed to push them back. By late afternoon Blanchard's First Army had at last established itself in position in the Gembloux Gap. The role of the Cavalry Corps was now fulfilled, and in the late afternoon it was pulled back for reorganization in the rear of Blanchard's main line. The first great tank battle of the campaign was over. In Paris the papers claimed victory, and indeed Prioux's tank crews had fought with fiercest determination – something very different from the performance already evinced on the French Second and Ninth Army fronts. But Prioux's losses had been appallingly heavy: one-third of the new medium Somuas and two-thirds of the Hotchkisses had been knocked out, with some units losing up to 60 per cent of their effectives. The strategic impact of this on the course of the battle as a whole was not to be under-estimated. That night Gamelin was contemplating the concentration of all armoured and motorized forces on the right of the First Army so as to attack the northern flank of the Ardennes breakthrough. The crippling of the élite Cavalry Corps now rendered this proposition hardly feasible.

Gamelin Ill-informed

Back at G.Q.G., Gamelin's light had been observed burning well after midnight on the 13th–14th. The next morning he visited Georges's H.Q. at La Ferté, and again in the afternoon. In his memoirs he says that his 'presence there was necessary from the point of view of morale'. Georges had evidently not recovered from the breakdown which Beaufre had witnessed the previous night – no doubt exacerbated by the debilitating effects of his old wound. However shocked he was by what he saw at Les Bondons, Gamelin nevertheless also admits elsewhere that, at the time, the situation at Sedan seemed to him less grave than it really was. For this Huntziger's over-optimistic reports, to which General Georges had added his own rose-tinted glaze, are to be blamed. At 0730 hours, Georges had fed the following misleading fragments of information to the Generalissimo:

Ninth Army: The counter-attack at Houx did not succeed, the infantry not having followed the tanks . . . Second Army: The breach at Sedan has been plugged on the halt line . . . Counter-attack with serious forces was unleashed this morning at 0430 hours . . .

At 1030 hours, fuller reports gave G.Q.G. the impression that the Second Army was 'in hand and that the troops are holding'. Then a couple of hours later, Captain Beaufre telephoned some rather more disquieting news: 'Panic, with the 5th Light Cavalry Division. The Germans are at Omicourt, on the Bar Canal . . . 'At 1625, Gamelin heard the first news that Rommel had got his tanks across the Meuse. Late that evening he received a disagreeable *canard* (part of the Germans' skilful deception plan) about an imminent enemy attack through Switzerland; Goebbels was reported as having declared that 'within twice twenty-four hours there will no longer be any neutral states in Europe'. Could it indeed be, for all its apparent force, that the attack at Sedan was *not* in fact the main German effort? The Wehrmacht communiqué of the 14th certainly still continued to make no great capital out of the Meuse crossings. Were the Germans perhaps keeping up their sleeves a flanking attack on the Maginot Line from the Swiss end as well? Obviously, one had to remain cautious about moving reinforcements from behind the Line. The day ended for Gamelin with a last unrealistic report about Sedan from Les Bondons:

Not much has changed since the last report. Still some small infiltrations in the area of Mézières–Charleville. There has not been any counter-attack at Sedan, but violent aerial bombardment and blocking action. The German advance appears to be blocked . . . All the prisoners indicate the fatigue of the German troops.

Says Colonel Bardies acidly of Georges's optimism:

It aimed at nothing but minimizing the setbacks, at reassuring General Gamelin, and above him the Government, and above the Government, public opinion ... one has the impression that G.Q.G. did not yet believe in a disaster, and as a result did not envisage any means of major scope to counteract it.

For all the reassuring noises emanating from La Ferté and Vincennes, there were those in Paris who on the 14th already sensed that all was not well at the front. Alexander Werth of the *Manchester Guardian* noted in his diary: 'Gloom at the office ... The parachutist who descended on Paris yesterday was only a deflated sausage balloon.' Paul Baudouin, the Secretary to Reynaud's War Cabinet, relates how he had just been to a lunch in honour of the Prime Minister and the Foreign Minister of Luxembourg and of the Belgian Foreign and Finance Ministers, and I was just coming out when Colonel Villelume said that he wanted to speak to me urgently. At that moment I was walking on the big lawn of the Quai d'Orsay in glorious sunshine, but a chill came over me ... The news was very bad; Huntziger's Army had been violently attacked and some fortifications in the Sedan district had been lost. We felt that the situation had suddenly become tragic.

A meeting of the War Cabinet was convened at the Élysée that afternoon at which Gamelin confirmed that the news was bad. (But just how bad he did not say, for the simple reason that he did not know.) He admitted he was 'surprised', but externally continued to show every sign of Joffrian sang-froid.

In London, the British Government also remained oblivious of the full gravity of events.

Chapter 14

The Break-Out

15 May

If our tanks are distinctly superior to those of the enemy, our fighters dominate perhaps even more the enemy air force.

Le Temps, 16 May

Responsible circles lay stress on the fact that north of Sedan, inclusive, a war of movement is in progress, and the conflict must therefore inevitably sway to and fro until the main bodies get to grips and a continuous front is established . . . Under a seemingly endless torrent of bombs, backed up by artillery barrage from the French forces, the Germans wavered and then began to fall back. They found the roads to their rear choked and blocked in many places by wrecked and overturned lorries, tanks, armoured cars, and supply transport.

The Times, 16 May

Upon the crossing of the Meuse in the area of Sedan, with the closest co-operation of the Luftwaffe, the protective wall of France − the Maginot Line − has been broken in its extension to the north-west.

Wehrmacht communiqué, 15 May

Corap: Another Terrible Day

14 May had been a terrible day for General Corap. What the incessant bombing by the Luftwaffe, which had concentrated its attention on the Ninth Army that day, had done to the morale of his battered divisions made a deep impression upon him. But most of all he was concerned at the growth of Rommel's pocket west of Dinant; and now Guderian was slicing deep into his other flank. Late that night he took a fatal decision, and at 0200 on the 15th he was telephoning Billotte to report that he intended to abandon the whole line of the Meuse. He proposed withdrawing the Ninth Army behind the French frontier positions which they had left just five days earlier in fulfilment of the Dyle Plan. Billotte raised no objec-

tion in principle, but instructed Corap to 'establish an intermediate stop-line on the line of Walcourt–Mariembourg–
Rocroi–Signy-l'Abbaye' – roughly along the main road running
north to south from Charleroi to Rethel. But Billotte's 'intermediate line' existed solely on paper, and in the chaos of communications inside the Ninth Army this order marked the
beginning of its disintegration. Some of Corap's units only
received orders to halt on the barrier position which General
Martin had been trying to establish behind Florennes the
previous evening; others duly pulled back to the 'intermediate
line'. Some were unable to move at all; others, receiving no
orders, simply disbanded and straggled westwards of their own
accord. In a state of high emotion, Corap telephoned General
d'Astier begging for air support at dawn to cover his withdrawal. Although his orders were to devote all forces to Huntziger's front, d'Astier said he would see what he could do; but
Corap was even unable to tell him precisely where his own
front lay.

Such was the situation at Army level as dawn broke on the
15th. In effect, Huntziger the previous evening had opened one
sluice-gate; Corap was now opening the other. Through the pair
of them the flood was about to burst into France.

Rommel Strikes Again

Opposite Rommel's bridgehead, the 'stop-line' decreed by
Corap ran close by Philippeville, some twelve miles from where
Rommel had come to a halt on the 14th. But his orders to the
7th Panzer for the 15th were to 'thrust straight through in one
stride' to the Cerfontaine area, eight miles to the *west* of
Philippeville. Rommel himself intended to ride with Rothenburg's tanks so as to direct operations from up forward, leaving divisional H.Q. in the hands of his senior staff officer, the
extremely able Major Heidkaemper who was to end the war as
a lieutenant-general. Guarding his right flank, but still slightly
behind, came Colonel Werner's tanks from the 5th Panzer. At
about 0800 hours a Luftwaffe liaison officer informed Rommel
that Stuka support would be available for the 7th Panzer that

day. Rommel called for them to go into action immediately just ahead of his tanks, which were already beginning to move forward. Within the next hour they came up against General Bruneau's 1st Armoured Division, positioned near Flavion, in what Rommel describes as a 'brief engagement'.

On reaching its concentration area late on the night of the 14th, Bruneau's tank battalions had adopted a defensive stance of 'rassemblement gardé' while waiting for the arrival of the fuel tankers which Bruneau had mistakenly placed at the rear of his column. Agonizingly the hours ticked by and still the tankers, held up by the appalling chaos on the roads, did not arrive. Finally, Bruneau had told General Martin that he could not possibly attack at dawn, as prescribed by XI Corps. Re-fuelling, he now reckoned, would only be complete by the end of the morning. Accordingly, he sent back his artillery, deploying one lone battery out of six in support of his immobilized armour.[1] Soon after dawn, Bruneau learned that his units were being heavily dive-bombed. Then at 0830 hours his two battalions of heavy 'B' tanks were caught by a dense concentration of Rommel's Panzers just as they were refuelling. A confused action ensued at close range. One French squadron managed to counter-attack, inflicting noteworthy losses. Once again the Germans discovered that their 37-mm. guns could not penetrate the massive 'B' tanks, and that their best bet lay in shooting off the tracks. But many of these superb instruments, tragically immobilized like hobbled elephants by their lack of fuel, simply had to be set on fire in haste by their own crews.

With that magical feeling for the situation which characterized all his movements, Rommel then swung round Bruneau's flank to continue his thrust towards the west. Having struck one first hard blow at the 1st Armoured, he left it to the approaching 5th Panzer to administer the *coup de grâce*. Bruneau, making an accurate appreciation of Rommel's intent

1. This decision exemplified the unawareness on the part of the French commanders of the speed with which the Panzers were about to move. That same morning General Sancelme of the 4th North African Division, the other component in Corap's counter-attack against Rommel, had also sent his guns to the rear.

from the consequent lull in the fighting, at 1400 ordered his division to regroup north of Florennes, facing south-east. But by the time the order reached his tanks they were inextricably engaged in heavy fighting – this time with Colonel Werner's 'Red Devils' [2] from the 5th Panzer. What that afternoon's armoured battle was like from the French point of view is well described by a subaltern fighting in a 'B' tank of the 37th Battalion:

'*En avant*!' orders the *Adour*, the Captain's tank . . . The *Gard* is on my right, the Captain is to the right of the *Gard* . . . At that moment, a shell strikes the armour on the left side! Towards the road, red lights flare up on the level of a low hedge; another shell in the armour plate! I hesitate to shoot back, because I thought it was a mistake by one of ours; then I traversed my turret towards the flames, and shoot off five high-explosive shells at the hedge, after which nothing moves any longer. I continue my advance and arrive at the woods which mark the edge of the plateau, and it is there that the battle begins. The driver shouts: 'A tank on the edge of the wood in front of us! ' It was certainly an enemy! A Mark IV on which I directed the fire of the 75 . . . Near a burning German tank, men are climbing and crawling towards the undergrowth. The whole of our left flank is crowded with big German tanks; I can make them out more or less indistinctly, because they are camouflaged, broadside on and immobile.

At this moment the co-driver of the Captain informs me that the Captain, wounded in the stomach and in the legs, is handing over the command to me. The new Mark IVs burst into flames under our fire, but my radiators are themselves smashed in; my 75 is hit on the side of the muzzle, and remains in a position of maximum recoil; I continue with the 47. Feeling myself harassed, I try to change position and to move myself in a thicket further to the south. The wood is being hammered by a 105-mm., and shell-holes open up not far from us. From a distance, I can make out the *Gard*, the door of whose turret is open . . . On my right a knocked-out tank of the 28th; the line of German tanks form a semi-circle of vehicles which I estimate in number at between fifty to sixty.

I give the order to the tanks of my company to retire . . .

---

2. So called from the insignia of the 31st Panzer Regiment.

Ourcq and *Yser* withdraw slowly, while I observe *Hérault* burning . . .

By the late afternoon the 37th Battalion was reduced to four 'B' tanks; its sister, the 28th, had only two left in fit state to comply with Bruneau's order to withdraw; while the 26th could muster less than a score of its light tanks. Only the 25th (light) Tank Battalion remained more or less intact, having lost its way the previous night and arrived too late to take part in the action. Thus was the first of General Georges's 'rooks' destroyed as an effective force. The tank crews of the French 1st Armoured had fought bravely and well, and claimed to have knocked out some hundred German tanks.[3] But they had been squandered, not in a bold armoured counter-stroke, but piecemeal in a battle of encounter. The division had been engaged, remarks Colonel Bardies, 'as in times gone past squadrons of *cuirassiers* were engaged, to cover a rout, in giving them the order to die'. Under cover of night the 1st Armoured crept back to Beamount, and then to Solre-le-Château behind the French frontier positions. When Bruneau saw it the next day, it had only seventeen tanks left, the remainder having lost their way or run out of fuel during the night's withdrawal.[4]

Rommel Breaches French Front

Meanwhile, sweeping around the 1st Armoured, Rommel's Panzers were now out in the open, inflicting fearful havoc upon the Ninth Army's 'soft' rear areas. On the way to Philippeville, Rommel himself noted passing:

numerous guns and vehicles [5] belonging to a French unit, whose men had tumbled headlong into the woods at the approach of our tanks, having probably already suffered heavily under our dive-bombers. Enormous craters compelled us to make several détours

---

3. The total may have been somewhat exaggerated.

4. But the fact that the 1st Armoured had virtually ceased to exist was not learned by Ninth Army H.Q., No. 1 Army Group, or G.Q.G. until much later.

5. Very probably the artillery and supply echelons that Bruneau had sent to the rear.

through the wood. About 3 miles north-west of Philippeville there was a brief exchange of fire with French troops occupying the hills and woods south of Philippeville. Our tanks fought the action on the move, with turrets traversed left, and the enemy was soon silenced. From time to time enemy anti-tank guns, tanks and armoured cars were shot up. Fire was also scattered into the woods on our flanks as we drove past.

Already by midday Rommel had occupied Philippeville, and was pushing on to Cerfontaine six miles beyond, thereby breaching in one swift bound Billotte's and Corap's 'intermediate line' even before it could be occupied. Men and machines were exhausted. One of his Panzer commanders records:

A number of vehicles broke down, even my command vehicle could no longer keep up and I had to have it towed by a truck . . . I'm dead tired . . . two days and three nights, not a moment of rest, food consists of two slices of bread, a hellish thirst. Next day we are to have a rest.[6] The vehicle badly needs a service, wire has wound itself around the drive wheel, and the batteries are run down . . . We look like pigs, muddy, sticky and without a shave for several days. I am tottering with fatigue, and have to help myself with Pervitin tablets. The radio operators can only be kept awake with difficulty.

But Rommel was a hard taskmaster. Furious to discover that Bismarck's weary riflemen were lagging nearly ten miles behind the tanks, creating a gap into which enemy elements were infiltrating, he turned about and headed eastward to chase them up. Along the route Rommel had covered that morning, he found two tanks which had broken down:

Their crews were in process of collecting prisoners, and a few who had already come in were standing around. Now hundreds of French motor-cyclists came out of the bushes and, together with their officers, slowly laid down their arms. Others tried to make a quick getaway down the road to the south.

I now occupied myself for a short time with the prisoners. Among them were several officers, from whom I received a number of requests, including, among other things, permission to keep their batmen and to have their kit picked up from Philippeville, where it had been left.

---

6. This was optimism!

His mission accomplished, Rommel headed westwards once again at high speed, and just short of Cerfontaine he met

a body of fully armed French motor-cyclists coming in the opposite direction, and picked them up as they passed. Most of them were so shaken at suddenly finding themselves in a German column that they drove their machines into the ditch and were in no position to put up a fight.

From his Panzer lager at Cerfontaine, 'looking back east from the summit of the hill, as night fell, endless pillars of dust could be seen rising as far as the eye could reach – comforting signs that the 7th Panzer Division's move into the conquered territory had begun'. Rommel's losses for that day had totalled just fifteen killed; he had advanced over seventeen miles, taken 450 prisoners, knocked out or captured seventy-five tanks, and struck a decisive blow against the Ninth Army, and its hopes for a counter-attack.

The Ninth Army Breaks

At 0400 on the 15th Billotte had informed Georges on the telephone that 'the Ninth Army is in a critical position'. By nightfall on the same day its condition was one of rout, all along its fifty-mile front. Describing the effect of the German bombing, a staff officer of the 18th Division recounts:

we passed through clouds of smoke from a petrol convoy which had just been bombarded by a plane and was burning along the road close to the route. Elsewhere an artillery group had been attacked while on the march. On the road and elsewhere there was a series of enormous bomb craters and very numerous corpses of horses, which indicated that the attack had been devastating . . . On the road to Fraire, there arrives upon us at full gallop a group of disbanded artillerymen. Halted, they declared that the enemy was behind them.

Hammered since the day Rommel had first set foot across the Meuse, the 18th Division now dissolved. Having lost most of his staff, its commander, General Duffet, spent the day roving the battlefield, in an attempt to regroup his scattered units. With a handful of men he ended the day trying to set up a defence at Beaumont, just inside the Belgian frontier, through which the remnants of the 1st Armoured were retreating. On his right, General Hassler's 22nd Division, which had given no particularly commendable account of itself the previous day against the German infantry forcing the Meuse at Givet, shared a similar fate. 'Aircraft do not cease to follow us, to bombard us and machine-gun us,' recorded one of its battalion commanders.

We passed through Couvin, where all kinds of columns were mixed up together . . . the disorder worsened, and our men, in whom fatigue had exceeded anything that one could imagine, mounted on any vehicles they encountered, despite their officers who attempted to stop them. But understanding that this was the only way of pulling out a force completely exhausted, I gave them the order to allow them to do this . . .

But at the exit to Couvin, we were once again attacked by enemy machine-guns. There were scenes of horror which occurred with women, children, lying alongside the road, dead or wounded, stretched out in the ditches. Grown men also fell . . . the planes came in quantity, machine-gunning and bombarding in turn, increasing the confusion.

By nightfall this division consisted of nothing but fragments, straggling back over the frontier. Thus General Martin's XI Corps had all but vanished. Nevertheless, he was ordered by Corap to 'do everything possible to halt the enemy on the frontier line'. It was an impossible demand. As General Martin notes, 'the first task was to get the engineers to open the doors of the bunkers!' But the keys to the bunkers, locked up when the Ninth Army moved forward on the 10th, had disappeared – either with units that had been dispatched elsewhere, or on the persons of local mayors who had themselves taken off among the growing stream of refugees.

To the north the 5th Motorized Division covering Yvoir, though not heavily engaged that day, was also forced to withdraw in mounting disorder after its flank had been exposed by the breaking-up of XI Corps. In Corap's northern sector there thus remained only General Sancelme's 4th North African Division, and the fate of this fine unit on the 15th was particularly poignant. After its admirable defence against Rommel at Anthée on the 14th, the division had been pulled back to hold the Hemptinne–Philippeville line. But deprived of artillery support – since Sancelme, like Bruneau, had sent his guns to the rear – it had been unable to assume a proper defensive position before being sliced up by Rommel in his drive around the flank of the 1st Armoured. The experience of Lieutenant Édouard Leng, a reservist officer of the 13th Zouaves, pushed off the roads by the retreat of General Martin's H.Q. the previous day, was perhaps typical:

From the early hours of the morning, I fought on the Vodecée crossroads and at Villers-le-Gambon, enduring fire from German tanks and Stukas, and finding myself almost without contact with the other elements of the division. Towards 1830 hours, we received the order to withdraw in the direction of Philippeville . . . Closely pursued by the enemy in the course of this movement, sustaining losses in both men and weapons (which were almost out of ammunition), with two other officers and a group of our men I ran into a score of German tanks at Vachefontaine, about one kilometre south-east of Philippeville . . . We were encircled, and any resistance became useless.

Other tanks of the 7th Panzer overran the H.Q. of the 25th Algerian *Tirailleurs* at Philippeville itself, and an hour later reached the divisional command post at Neuville, from which General Sancelme only narrowly escaped behind a barricade of anti-tank guns. Cut off from his regiments, that afternoon he dispatched three separate liaison teams to Martin's H.Q. But none returned. By the end of the 15th, the 4th North African, like the 1st Armoured, was no longer an effective fighting force.

Havoc at Monthermé

Further south on XLI Corps front, the break-up of Corap's army proceeded with even more dramatic swiftness. Here the repercussions of Corap's order to withdraw behind the line Rocroi–Signy-l'Abbaye proved particularly disastrous, for the 102nd Division, whose colonial machine-gunners from Indo-China and Madagascar had so valiantly been holding Reinhardt at bay in the Monthermé peninsula during the past two days, was a fortress unit devoid of transport, while the 61st Division to the north had insufficient vehicles, and these were not close enough at hand for a quick get-away. During the small hours of the 15th at Monthermé, German engineers equipped with flame-throwers and riflemen of the 6th Panzer crept up to within a few yards of the bunkers held by a gallant colonial rearguard. At 0330 hours they attacked under a powerful artillery barrage. While it was still dark the Germans were through the first defences, and by 0830 they had captured the French reserve positions. Immediately the hitherto stymied tanks of the 6th Panzer began to swarm across the Meuse at Monthermé. At this moment a French truck loaded with a thousand desperately needed anti-tank mines arrived at the front, tragically late. With considerable courage the driver persisted in trying to push through to his destination, but was caught by tanks 'which opened fire and the truck blew up with a formidable explosion'. Upstream from Monthermé, the German 3rd and 23rd Infantry Divisions completed their river crossings and began erecting bridges to get Reinhardt's other Panzer division, the 8th, across the Meuse.

Now Reinhardt more than made up for the time he had lost on the previous four days of crawling through the Ardennes and battling his way into the Monthermé peninsula. The transport-less 102nd Fortress Division, forced to abandon all its guns and even its machine-guns, was overtaken and rounded up with incredible speed. Rushing out from the Monthermé bridge-head, the motor-cyclists of the 6th Panzer roared past

a French munitions dump, and past numerous guns which stand abandoned on the road. The enemy has had no time in which to take them with him in his flight. Also in the wood to the right a battery all ready to fire has been abandoned. It must have been completely surprised ... Near the leading group, a few carbine shots ring out. Then the enemy soon comes out with raised hands from the bushes. Some thirty men were there, and four Negroes. They are muddy and unshaven, and their eyes are full of fear.

On reaching Arreux, some six miles from Monthermé,

Frenchmen come out from cellars and surrender of their own accord . . . In Renwez it is the same story. The French give themselves up without having fired a single shot.

On the left of the 6th Panzer, motorized infantry occupied the sprawling twin cities of Charleville–Mézières. Karl von Stackelberg, a war diarist travelling with them, noted that 'the shops were closed and barred, the houses locked up. All the inhabitants had flown, and we moved through lonely and dead quiet streets.' Later he was astonished to meet a French column marching in the opposite direction, in perfect order, headed by a captain:

They had, however, no weapons and did not keep their heads up . . . They were marching willingly without any guard into imprisonment. Behind this first company which I saw followed new groups, ever new groups . . . There were finally 20,000 men, who here in the sector of our corps, in this one sector and on this one day, were heading backwards as prisoners. Unwillingly one had to think of Poland, and the scenes there. It was inexplicable. How was it possible, that after this first major battle on French territory, after this victory on the Meuse, this gigantic consequence should follow? How was it possible, these French soldiers with their officers, so completely downcast, so completely demoralized, would allow themselves to go more or less voluntarily into imprisonment?

Everywhere on the far side of the Meuse where Reinhardt's Panzers had passed, Stackelberg encountered the same indescribable havoc:

All along the side of the road lay dead horses, abandoned baggage waggons, from which the cases had tumbled down, their contents strewn about the ground, rifles thrown away, steel helmets, saddles and all kinds of other equipment. I saw dead Frenchmen lying in the ditches. I saw abandoned guns, riderless horses roaming about, and often this scene escalated to regular barricades compounded of vehicles, guns and dead horses that had all been shot up together.

Reaching the small village of Brunehamel, close to where the command post of the French corps commander, General

Libaud, had been that morning, Stackelberg found more barricades manned by dead Frenchmen and a deathly silence broken only by the crackling of flames. In the middle of a street a horse with crazy eyes stood unmoving; as Stackelberg approached it, it suddenly collapsed and died. In another village he came upon two German soldiers playing that old hit of the Phoney War, 'We'll Hang Out Our Washing on the Siegfried Line', on a 'liberated' gramophone. As the tinny music blared out, a tearful French colonel watched the forlorn columns of prisoners file past. Interrogated by Stackelberg, they expressed hopeless amazement at the speed with which the Panzers had overrun them.

By 1100 hours, the commander of the 42nd Half-Brigade which had defended Monthermé was captured; of its right-hand neighbour, the 52nd Half-Brigade, only ten officers and 500 men remained from its established strength of seventy and 2,600 respectively. The following day, the divisional commander, General Portzer himself, was rounded up, and the total strength of the division then numbered no more than 1,200. This marked the end of the 102nd as a fighting force.

The fate of the 61st Division, which had not been subjected to any serious frontal assault, was still less distinguished. Outflanked, its 'soft' transport was overhauled by Reinhardt's racing Panzers in the kind of action tankmen dream about. On one road near Brunehamel alone, four tanks ran up and down a column of forty French vehicles, shooting them up. A hundred men surrendered. Just as the Germans were beginning to run short of ammunition, another column of seventy-five vehicles was sighted and duly destroyed. When joined by the main force the following day, the four tanks and their crews numbering thirteen had, between them, accounted for five hundred prisoners and several hundred vehicles. Under this kind of treatment, the 61st, another 'B' division, broke up like its sisters at Sedan. Its commander, General Vauthier, reported sadly to Ninth Army H.Q. the following day that there was only himself left, though in fact during the course of the 16th some seven to eight hundred men straggled back, with three light machine-guns between them, while other survivors of the 61st were picked up as far away as Compiègne over the succeeding days. By the end of the 15th, it could be said that Corap's XLI Corps had also ceased to exist.

In the heady spring sunshine, the extraordinary scenes on every side of a disintegrating enemy began to induce an entirely new mood in the German troops. Rapidly vanishing was the nervous apprehension of the legendary *furia francese*, of the insuperable victors of 1918; its place was taken by a kind of intoxication, the light-heartedness of the excursion, that swept the Panzers on at an increasingly reckless speed. 'A perfect road stretches before us,' wrote a member of the 6th Panzer, 'and no enemy fliers over us. The air is completely dominated by our own fliers. A wonderful feeling of unconditional superiority. We rush on at 50 m.p.h. to Montcornet on the Serre. In front of the town there is a short collision with a French company, who give themselves up almost without fighting.' Against somewhat stronger opposition, Montcornet itself was captured by nightfall. Since the morning, Reinhardt's Panzers had covered thirty-seven miles from the Meuse, bringing them to within a bare half-hour's drive of the H.Q. of Ninth Army itself, at Vervins to the north-west. It was by far the most outstanding advance made by the Germans so far, and even Reinhardt seems to have been taken by surprise. At midnight he ordered the 6th to halt at Liart – seventeen miles *east* of the point they had already reached that evening. Corap's 'intermediate line' had been smashed wide open, from top to bottom.

Back to Sedan: the Battle for Stonne

But Reinhardt would not have had his lucky break had it not been for the earlier successes, on either side, of Rommel and particularly Guderian. One now returns to Sedan, still the key sector. On the morning of the 15th, two separate battles confronted Guderian: an offensive, break-out battle to be fought by the 1st and 2nd Panzers westwards from Singly–Bouvellemont and a dynamic defensive battle by the Grossdeutschland Regiment (principally) facing southwards at Stonne.

All through the night of the 14th–15th, General Georges had

chafed at the way Huntziger was employing the 3rd Armoured
Division which had been rushed up to help him. At 0600 he
telephoned Second Army to confirm his order of the previous
night, calling for a vigorous counter-attack, and added: 'Its
execution is rendered even more indispensable by the situation
of the Army on your left' (i.e. Corap). Passing these instructions on to General Flavigny, Huntziger (though by now he
would have been much happier to remain on the defensive)
called for a 'tank-supported' attack on the Bulson–Sedan axis.
At 1130 hours (note the further loss of time), Flavigny ordered
the 3rd Armoured and 3rd Motorized Divisions to attack at
1500 hours. They would move in three systematic bounds: the
first taking them to the line Chémery–Maisoncelle–Raucourt,
the second to the heights south of Bulson, and the third back
on to the La Marfée–Pont Maugis position commanding the
Meuse. It was to be carried out along the methodical, classical
lines of an 'infantry backed by tanks' operation such as had
been taught at the École Militaire ever since 1918. No initiative was allowed to the executants, and typically the whole
operation was placed under the command of an infantryman
– Bertin-Boussu of the 3rd Motorized rather than Brocard of
3rd Armoured.[7] Meanwhile, the 3rd Armoured, deployed to
form 'corks' the previous evening, had become dispersed over
a wide area on both sides of the Ardennes Canal. It was additionally suffering from an unusual number of technical breakdowns, which perhaps reflected both the newness of its
equipment and the inexperience of its crews. By 1430 hours
Brocard was telling Flavigny that he could not get his 'B' tanks
into position in time. The attack was consequently postponed
until 1730 hours. It was the same old story that had bedevilled
all the French counter-strokes to date.

True to its training, the Grossdeutschland did not just sit
still and wait to be attacked by the French. Early in the morning it was pushing forward up on to the high ground on both
sides of Stonne, with orders to establish its defence line around

7. As one French military historian, Colonel le Goyet, remarks, by now
Brocard 'no longer commanded anything. He had simply become a provider
of tanks.'

this key village. This unexpected movement further helped throw Flavigny off balance, and he was forced to commit piece-meal in the defence of Stonne some of the tanks and infantry that were being husbanded for the afternoon's set-piece attack.

Stonne sits on a steep hill, surrounded by undulating country on which thick woods and scrub alternate with small patches of open moorland. Seen from a distance, in May 1940 its clustered houses gave the impression of an impregnably forti-fied hill-town from the Middle Ages. Possession of it would provide an attacker with an indispensable point of departure, while for a defender it constituted a secure position from which he would be hard to dislodge. All through the 15th the battle swayed back and forth at Stonne in some of the most violent fighting yet seen on the Sedan front, with the village itself changing hands several times in the burning May heat.

Moving up with the 10th Panzer, one company commander related to his tank crews how his grandfather had died at Sedan with Moltke in 1871, while his father had been killed fighting in the same area in the First War. He added: 'And if I die that is the end of a military clan.' Near Raucourt his tank ran into French anti-tank guns. Commanding from an open turret, he brought his gun to bear, but was evidently beaten to it by a French weapon. His tank halted, and one of his men found him being supported by his crew, his head smashed by the French shell. The tragic saga had been completed. But with the 10th Panzer's tanks still only partly deployed across the Meuse, for the Germans it was essentially an infantryman's day at Stonne, and the Grossdeutschland was by no means having an easy time of it. Towards midday, General Schaal of the 10th Panzer received from it 'alarming reports' of French tank attacks.

It was very largely thanks to the impressive celerity with which the Grossdeutschland was able to deploy its anti-tank guns (once more an attribute of the excellence of Wehrmacht training, at its best, in 1940) that the regiment was not overrun at Stonne on the 15th. Lieutenant Beck-Broichsitter, com-manding the 14th Anti-Tank Company, gives a vivid descrip-tion of the fighting that day. Moving into the village after a Stuka attack, we find abandoned houses, overgrown gardens, romantic old springs . . . a high water-tower standing apart from the rows of houses dominates every place in the village. We go along the village streets. Grenadiers of all companies are running about independently. They have no orders. A shot-up German tank lies in a ditch. An officer and a sergeant are standing with pistols nearby. One of the tank crew lies in a dusty black uniform nearby on the grass, dead. His face is yellow. From the water-tower there comes rifle fire! A cloud of dust rises from the road. A French tank comes towards us. We spring behind a house; it thunders past very close . . . The edge of the village comes under machine-gun fire from the water-tower. Hidden guns are firing often unsuspected from the wooded hill behind us – it's a completely confused situation!

After the company had brought up three of its light 37-mm. anti-tank guns, six French tanks appeared and a bitter duel ensued. Several of the tanks were knocked out, but one of their shells lodged in a wall close to where Beck-Broichsitter was standing:

the shots come gradually closer; single French tanks are bringing fresh infantry. In the gardens their strength is difficult to estimate. The situation is becoming critical, the fighting will of the soldiers is slackening in the heavy fire. All are at the end of their strength, because of the fighting since 10 May.

The German fire begins to slacken off. After a fresh French attack from the water-tower, more tanks appear from a different direction.

The situation is very serious [continues Beck-Broichsitter]. The other anti-tank section have their hands fully occupied with the enemy on their front. How are we going to stop these new attacking tanks? The fire gets even heavier, everything seems to be burning! On the street lie our dead, and more and more wounded disappear to the rear! . . .

About ten French tanks roll in on a wide front. At some 25 m.p.h., the drivers swing their vehicles about, and then fire. They are firing from the water-tower, the three guns are hit in the middle of the road; immediately there are wounded, but the section holds! The duel begins! In an hour-long running battle,

Hindelang's section stops with their fire the attacking infantry as well as the flank fire from the water-tower and also from the wooded hill. The fight for the village slackens. Against the tough French attacks some of our rifle companies gradually crumple away. Self-propelled guns help again and again . . . four heavy infantry guns are brought into open positions, and fire with 15-cm. shells on the water-tower. But it does not budge. The losses are getting greater. Some of the anti-tank guns are shot full of holes. They carry on shooting.

Beck-Broichsitter's guns now come under fire from three of the 3rd Armoured Division's 32-ton 'B' tanks:

at 100 metres, one of them shoots up the gun; then it machine-guns the wreckage. The commander is wounded – it is Sergeant Kramer, his gun layer is badly wounded, the other dead. Kramer, himself wounded, crawls under machine-gun fire to the gun layer and drags him with unspeakable difficulty into a house.

The fire of the three heavy tanks threatens to wipe out the anti-tank section. But it remains in position. One moment, one of the colossuses crosses the front. The left gun commander, Senior Corporal Giesemann, discovers in the middle of its right side a small-ribbed surface; apparently it is the radiator! It is not much bigger than an ammunition box. He aims at it. A tongue of flame shoots out from the tank . . . Both gun commanders now fire only at this small square in the side of the 32-tonners. The left gun is shortly afterwards wiped out by a direct hit. Now Hindelang retreats with the one remaining gun into the village. The three 32-tonners are knocked out!

According to the Grossdeutschland regimental history, *Ober-feldwebel* Hindelang's action saved the front at Stonne that day, for which both he and Beck-Broichsitter were later awarded the Ritterkreuz. The 14th Anti-Tank Company's losses during this ten-hour battle numbered one officer and twelve men dead and sixteen men wounded. Twelve of their vehicles and six out of twelve guns were destroyed, while they claimed to have knocked out thirty-three French tanks. From the German point of view, the situation at Stonne undoubtedly seemed critical at one time. Visiting the Grossdeutschland while a French attack was actually in progress, Guderian himself remarks that 'a certain nervous tension was noticeable'.

Shortly after 5 p.m., Graf von Schwerin, the regimental commander, was reporting to General Schaal that his men had been
forced out of Stonne again and that they were 'in a state of
complete physical exhaustion and hardly fit for combat'. All
available rifle companies from the 10th Panzer were rushed up
to support the flagging Grossdeutschland, while armour was
dispatched to meet a new French attack by an estimated fifty
tanks in the direction of Raucourt. Then, at 1800 hours, the
10th Panzer War Diary reported a fresh 'strong enemy armour
thrust on Chémery', adding the comment that this move was
'considered to be extremely dangerous, because in the event of
success it would strike the westward swing of XIX Corps in the
flank'.

Precisely what, in fact, had constituted the French effort
which caused the Germans such concern? During the morning, just one battalion (the 45th) of H-39 light tanks and a
company of 'B' tanks from the 3rd Armoured, plus one battalion of infantry, had been thrown into the reflexive counter-
attacks attempting to check the Grossdeutschland's movements
upon Stonne. Then, at 1730 hours, Flavigny's long-awaited set-
piece attack went in. But, in the words of General Ruby, it was
reduced to 'a fist blow'. Of the armour, only the 39th Battalion
of 'B' tanks and a handful of H-39s moved, and no sooner had
they entered into action than General Brocard gave the order
calling off the attack. Brocard's other two tank battalions,
deployed to the west of the Ardennes Canal, never joined in the
counter-stroke that day. As the German accounts testify, those
of the French tank crews that did see action fought well;
Captain Aulois, a First War veteran commanding one of the
'B' tank companies, having lost four of his tanks near Stonne,
was dragged badly wounded out of his wrecked machine and
'congratulated' by his captors on the admirable action he had
fought. But what Flavigny's force *might* have achieved had it
struck with all its available strength, even as late as the afternoon of the 15th, can also be deduced from the gravity with
which 10th Panzer H.Q. viewed the thrust on Chémery by this
one mere handful of tanks. Writing after the war, General
Hoth (Rommel's corps commander) reckoned that, in the

postponement of Flavigny's operation, 'the French missed a favourable occasion; this counter-attack, conducted in a resolute manner, would have transformed defeat into victory'.

It was certainly the last 'favourable occasion' to be granted on the Sedan battlefield. That evening Brocard was sent by Huntziger to swell the ranks of sacked generals. Both the French and the exhausted Grossdeutschland recoiled from Stonne. But early the next morning the Germans re-entered it against only 'slight resistance'. Later that day relief for the Grossdeutschland arrived in the form of the 29th Motorized Division,[8] the first of Wietersheim's XIV Motorized Infantry Corps that had been hastening up behind Guderian. It was, says Kielmansegg, 'a very welcome relief and certainly a necessary one for the worn-out defenders of the southern front'. The Grossdeutschland had lost nine officers and ninety-four other ranks killed; thirty officers and 429 other ranks were wounded or missing – probably the heaviest casualties of any German unit in the campaign so far.[9] But the crucial battle for Stonne had been won. Colonel von Schwerin had more than deserved the case of champagne wagered with Guderian. All that remained on the 16th was the mopping-up of the scattered tanks belonging to the 3rd Armoured, which had been so dismally cast away by the French command.

1st and 2nd Panzer: Bitter Resistance

In comparison with the flamboyant performance of Reinhardt's XLI Panzer Corps in their break-out from Monthermé, the progress achieved by the 1st and 2nd Panzers during the 15th looks almost unimpressive. Their energies were chiefly absorbed in completing the complicated change of direction imposed by Guderian and in smashing the last elements of resistance which stood between them and the soft interior of France. Of what did these elements consist?

The previous day General Georges had summoned General

8. One of the crack German divisions that was later lost at Stalingrad.

9. Though they were light compared with any equivalent action at Verdun in 1916.

Touchon – a much-wounded hero of the First War, when he had
commanded a regiment of the Chasseurs Alpins – and dispatched him to the front to take over an 'Army Detachment'.
His ambitious orders were to 're-establish liaison and weld the
flanks of the Second and Ninth Armies by co-ordinating the
activities of the units in the area'. Touchon appears to have
frittered away the 14th, calling on various subordinate commanders in his new zone of operations, and only reaching Huntziger's command post by 1600 and Rethel at 1900 hours. The
next day, having set up his own command post at Château
Porcien, at 1400 hours he promulgated his first order, which
was 'to hold at all costs the second line at Liart, Signy-l'Abbaye,
Poix–Terron and Bouvellemont'. He then set off to find General
Libaud of XLI Corps. But Libaud's headquarters camp was
deserted. Returning to Château Porcien, Touchon was shot at
by enemy armour near Rozoy-sur-Serre, and made a narrow
escape. He decided to withdraw his command post to Hermon-
ville, some ten miles north-east of Rheims.

The forces initially placed at the disposal of 'Army Detachment Touchon' (later to become the Sixth Army) were XLI
Corps (the southernmost unit of Corap's Army), General Etchberrigaray's 53rd Division, Chanoine's cavalry *groupement*, the
14th Division, and later the 2nd Armoured Division, plus the
valueless shell of Grandsard's X Corps. We have already
examined the fate of XLI Corps at the hands of Reinhardt's
Panzers during the 15th, and seen how the confusion of repeated counter-orders on the 14th had diminished the effectiveness of the 53rd Division, which, as a 'B' unit, was modest
enough even before the tide of battle caught up with it. The
tragic, futile saga of the 2nd Armoured Division, the last of
General Georges's 'rooks', will be followed later. The 14th
Division, commanded by General de Lattre de Tassigny, who
had led a company at Verdun and was to become a *Maréchal
de France* and one of the great heroes of the Liberation, was
one of the finest infantry units in the Army. But, sent from
Lorraine, it had just arrived at Château Porcien, on the Aisne
west of Rethel, with the result that only one of its regiments,
the 152nd, could reach the front in time to take part in the

day's fighting. Thus it was that the main resistance against Guderian's swinging lunge on the 15th was put up by this one regiment around the village of Bouvellemont and, just to its north, by Colonel Marc's 3rd Spahi Brigade at La Horgne.

On the other side, the hardest fighting once again fell to the redoubtable Colonel Balck and his riflemen of the 1st Panzer. All day he hammered away against a magnificent defence put up by the Spahis and de Lattre's men. At one point Balck's troops, already much fatigued by their unremitting efforts of the past days, seem to have become extremely dispirited by their losses. More than half their officers were either dead or wounded, and many companies were little above half strength. They had received hardly anything to eat or drink during a day of burning heat. Some of the officers complained at the new demands being made on the regiment; Balck alone was fully aware that what now confronted them was the very last of the French defensive lines. 'Suddenly', wrote one of his N.C.O.s, with perhaps just a touch of hero-worship, 'there appeared our regimental commander. Like a tower in the battle he stood between us, equipped with only a field cap, a walking cane, gasmask and a pistol. Quickly he put himself in the picture, and immediately produced the order expected by us all.' Visiting Balck in the burning ruins of Bouvellemont the following day, Guderian tells us:

Ammunition was running low. The men in the front line were falling asleep in their slit trenches. Balck himself, in wind-jacket and with a knotty stick in his hand, told me that the capture of the village had only succeeded because, when his officers complained against the continuation of the attack, he had replied: 'In that case I'll take the place on my own!' and had moved off. His men had thereupon followed him. His dirty face and his red-rimmed eyes showed that he had spent a hard day and a sleepless night.

By nightfall on the 15th, de Lattre's regiment, abandoning Bouvellemont, was forced to fall back towards Rethel. Though it had claimed some twenty German tanks, all its anti-tank guns and a third of its men were lost. At La Horgne, the 3rd Spahis had fought back with perhaps even grimmer determination, fully atoning for their disastrous withdrawal from the Semois three days previously. Attacked by both tanks and infantry, the brigade resisted until 1800 hours, when it had been literally wiped out. Colonel Marc had been captured at his post, while his two regimental commanders, Colonels Burnol and Geoffroy, were both killed. Out of thirty-seven officers, twelve were killed and seven wounded; casualties among the other ranks was roughly proportionate. For his leadership that day, Balck was awarded the Ritterkreuz and singled out for the rare privilege of a special mention in the Wehrmacht communiqué.

Although the resistance at La Horgne and Bouvellemont succeeded in checking the impetus of the 1st Panzer, to the north the main weight of the 2nd Panzer smashed through the disordered elements of the 53rd Division without much difficulty, and by the close of the day its reconnaissance detachments were already making contact with Reinhardt's Panzers at Montcornet. The Signy-l'Abbaye–Poix–Terron line, which Touchon had only that afternoon ordered to be held 'at all costs', was no longer anything more than an entry in a staff officer's log-book. Guderian's route westward lay open, with virtually no obstacles ahead of it. Of even more fundamental significance was the fact that, whereas twenty-four hours previously the German bridgeheads across the Meuse had consisted of three isolated bulges, they now formed one continuous pocket sixty-two miles wide – with no bottom. It is thus perhaps hardly an exaggeration to say, as has more than one French historian, that 15 May was the day France lost the war.

French 2nd Armoured Cut in Two

On paper, there remained General Bruché's 2nd Armoured Division. But of all the units sent to stem the German breakthrough, none was subjected to a sadder or more wasteful Calvary. Formed in January 1940, the 2nd Armoured had, like its sisters, been located in the Champagne area on 10 May. The next day Georges had earmarked it to reinforce the Second Army, along with the 3rd Armoured, but then appears to have forgotten about it for the next forty-eight hours. On the afternoon of the 13th, Georges finally dispatched it towards Charleroi in the tracks of the 1st Armoured and *away* from the main danger area at Sedan where Guderian had already crossed the Meuse. Because of the shortage of tank transporters, the tanks and other tracked vehicles were sent by train on flat-cars while the wheeled transport constituting the supply echelons went by road under their own steam; furthermore, as the movement of the 1st Armoured had taken up most of the available railway flat-cars, the loading of Bruché's tanks at Châlons station was protracted from the afternoon of the 14th to the morning of the 15th, and little aided by the repeated German bombing attacks. Consequently, the 2nd Armoured became thoroughly scattered over a wide area just at the worst possible moment. Reporting early on the morning of the 14th at First Army H.Q. in Valenciennes, Bruché was forced to admit to General Blanchard that he did not know where his various units were, or in what order they would arrive. The poor man was then told that his division had now been put at Corap's disposal. The next day, when Bruché's liaison officer reported to Ninth Army H.Q., pointing out that the change in plan now made it impossible to attack before midday on the 17th, he was told 'The 2nd Armoured no longer belongs to us. It has been given to the "Army Detachment Touchon", to whom we are transmitting your report.' Meanwhile, on General Georges's instructions, the road column which had just reached Guise was redirected eastwards to Signy-l'Abbaye, the southern anchor of Corap's 'stop-line', while the tanks were to be unloaded at Hirson, as soon as they reached it, and then to go under their own power to Signy.

But just at the time when this manoeuvre – so complex that it would have required all the skill of a Guderian – was being executed, Reinhardt's Panzers were already tearing through Signy on the way to Montcornet. Caught on the road at Blanchefosse (near Brunehamel) at about 1700 hours on the 15th, one artillery battery of Bruché's division had ten out of its twelve guns overrun by tanks; another tractor-drawn battery, sent by road since there were no flat-cars for its guns, simply disappeared into thin air. In effect, Reinhardt, without realizing it, had driven a wedge slap through the centre of the 2nd Armoured. The road column, having progressed farther than the armour, was forced southwards and took refuge beyond the Aisne at Rethel. Moving in a south-easterly direction from the rail terminal at Hirson, the tanks made a totally unexpected first contact with the Panzers along the Liart–Rozoy road, and had promptly headed away – towards the north. Thus by dawn on the 16th, almost all of General Bruché's armour lay scattered over a vast area between St Quentin and Hirson on one side of Reinhardt's Panzer thrust, without any means of supply and having lost half its supporting artillery. On the other side, south of the Aisne, was General Bruché himself, with all the wheeled transport of the division, one gun battery, a company of H-39 light tanks, four solitary strayed 'B' tanks, and two companies of Chasseurs. So the third and last of Georges's powerful 'rooks' had simply broken up before it could even be committed to the battle. To make matters worse, for a considerable period both General Georges and Touchon were to remain disastrously unaware of the true state of affairs with the 2nd Armoured.

Giraud Replaces Corap

At dawn on the 15th, Billotte had telephoned Georges: 'The Ninth Army is in a critical position ... It is absolutely essential to put some life into this wavering army. General Giraud, whose vigour is well known, appears to me to be best fitted to take on this difficult task.' In a telephone call with the unhappy Corap later in the morning, Georges realized that he had 'lost his sang-froid', and that evening what broken fragments there remained of his army were removed from the old colonial soldier. 'I left at 0400 hours on the 16th,' wrote Corap, 'heartbroken.' [10] Giraud, his successor, is described by Beaufre as having been 'our most ardent commander'; less flatteringly by

10. Huntziger retained his command throughout, though in retrospect it is difficult to see that he handled the battle any more brilliantly than Corap, who had faced the far greater test.

General Alan Brooke as a Don Quixote who 'would have ridden gallantly at any windmill regardless of consequences' and who 'inspired one with little confidence when operating on one's left flank'. But more than Quixotic ardour was required to restore the situation on the Ninth Army front, and would the elements of Giraud's own Seventh Army, which had survived the Breda fiasco and were now following him to the Ninth Army, prove sufficient to plug the gaping holes that had been rent there? That night Giraud sent a first disquieting message to Billotte, summing up the situation as he found it:

I have no news of XI Army Corps. Sancelme's division (the 4th North African) appears to have elements in the region to the west of Philippeville. No news of the 18th and 22nd Divisions, which seem to be disorganized. Vauthier's division (the 61st) has abandoned Rocroi and is withdrawing to the second position . . . the 1st Armoured Division has this morning struck a blow in the Mettet region. It is to strike another blow in the region of Philippeville, but I have received no information. *Mon impression est grave*, especially on my right because of the rapid advance of the Panzers.

Then, in the middle of the night, Giraud received the devastating news of the arrival of the Panzers at Montcornet, just twelve miles south of Army H.Q. at Vervins.

Meanwhile in the North . . .

In northern Belgium, the B.E.F. was again attacked by the German Sixth Army, whose orders were to 'prevent consolidation of the Allied forces' on the Dyle Line. Once again the Germans were driven off. At the close of play, Lord Gort had cause to be satisfied with the B.E.F.'s performance, and the troops – seeing only their immediate front – were confidently aware of no reason why they should not continue to sit on the Dyle indefinitely. To their right a small breach was made during the afternoon on the French First Army front, but by and large the line from Antwerp to Namur held well. It was, however, the sudden exposure of Blanchard's right wing caused by the disintegration of the Ninth Army which abruptly became the dominant factor. At 1800 hours on the evening of the 15th, General Billotte, recognizing for the first time the full gravity of the German breakthrough on the Meuse, decided to retire the whole Allied line in the north back to the Escaut, the position which the Allies were to have held originally before Gamelin imposed the more ambitious Dyle Plan. The withdrawal would take place in stages of three nights, to be completed by 19 May. Blanchard was promptly informed of Billotte's intention. Gort, on the other hand, only learned of it at 0500 the next morning when, disquieted at the news trickling in from the south, he sent a senior officer to No. 1 Army Group H.Q. who happened to see there the order before its dispatch. Gort then sent Major-General Needham, head of the British Military Mission at Belgian Army H.Q., to inform the Belgians what was afoot. But Needham was seriously injured in a car accident, so that the unfortunate Belgians did not hear of Billotte's intention until 1000 on the 16th. Gort's confidence in the French High Command was further shaken, while the Belgians were greatly embittered; their Deputy Chief of Staff, General Derousseaux, claims it was 'my worst memory of the campaign. The General Staff was stunned by it.' When the troops of the B.E.F. heard of Billotte's order to retire, after their successful holding operation of the past two days, they too were 'stunned' – and greatly disappointed. No one could possibly comprehend just what had happened in the south.

R.A.F. Bomb Ruhr: Reynaud Pleads for More Hurricanes

In the air war on 15 May, a number of extremely important events took place. At 0630, General Têtu had rung through from General Georges's H.Q. to order d'Astier to switch air priority from the Second to the Ninth Army, though it was symptomatic of the self-delusion still prevailing in the higher echelons of the French Command that he should have added: 'I am told that the situation of the Ninth Army is less serious than one might believe; its withdrawal is a controlled operation.' But what in fact the Allies were able to put into the air that day in support of this new priority now reflected all too faithfully the grim losses of the previous five days. To cover the whole of the North-East Front and Paris, General d'Astier could mount no more than 237 serviceable single-seater fighters, 38 night fighters and 38 bombers. By midday, he was forced to admit that half of his fighter capacity had been knocked out by enemy bombing. In all, his *aviation de chasse* could only send up somewhere over 200 sorties that day, compared with 340 on the 14th; they claimed twenty-one enemy planes for a loss of seven. This was hardly enough to shelter Corap's Army from the Stukas plaguing it as relentlessly as flies upon carrion.

Of France's remaining bombers, just six Léo 45s were thrown in to support Flavigny's counter-attack in the Sedan sector, while nine Bréguets from *Groupement* 18 bombed Reinhardt's armour debouching from Monthermé. With all notions of ground-level attack now abandoned, the Bréguets released their bombs from a height of over 1,500 feet; all returned safely to base, a fact which raised the morale of the *Groupement* – though apparently without its examining too closely just how effective the results had been. Typical of the feebleness of French air effort on the 15th was the nocturnal bombing of one Heinkel base by a solitary French aircraft, which dumped its missiles in woods more than a quarter of a mile from the barracks and then headed for home.

Meanwhile the relentless bombing of French reinforcements and supply columns continued. All over northern France the roads told the same story of troops caught on the move, the wounded soldiers crying for help amid piles of abandoned equipment. Day by day the sinister Arado observer planes, which seemed immune to small-arms fire and were never chased off by Allied fighters, stalked French reinforcements moving up to the line, until the Heinkels and Dorniers were ready to pounce.

The British record for the 15th was hardly more outstanding than the French. After their appalling losses of the 14th,[11] the vulnerable Battles were in the process of being withdrawn from daylight operations, so that the day's main effort consisted of

11. According to Churchill, by the night of the 14th there were only 206, out of 474, serviceable R.A.F. aircraft left in France.

some dozen Blenheims striking at Rommel's columns near Dinant, an attack reported neither by Rommel nor the divisional War Diary. But that night an operation was mounted which, although it did absolutely nothing to influence the course of the battle, was certainly to change the character of the war. Outraged by the Luftwaffe's razing of Rotterdam, the British War Cabinet banished the scruples that had hitherto restrained it from launching a strategic bombardment of the German Ruhr. It persuaded itself that such a heavy bomber attack by night would, in the first place, force the Luftwaffe to divert fighters from France to protect the Ruhr, and secondly, that the German outcry for retaliation would result in some of the bombers which were breaking up the French Army to such deadly effect being redirected against the British Isles. With somewhat less altruistic motives, the Air Staff also had at the back of its mind the hope that, daylight bombing having been proved so ruinously expensive, cheaper returns could be gained by night. Accordingly, that night ninety-six Wellington, Whitley and Hampden bombers were dispatched to north-west Germany. Of these, seventy-eight were directed against oil plants; but, in the words of the R.A.F. official history, 'Only twenty-four of the crews even claimed to have found them.' Like so much of its subsequent history, this first attempt at strategic bombing had only the most negligible results. Not one single plane or anti-aircraft gun was deflected from France. Goebbel's propaganda machine indeed howled for vengeance, but this would not be exacted until after the fall of France, until the Blitz on London.

That same day a second decision of strategic, indeed of historic, importance was taken in London. At the time of the German onslaught, ten of Britain's all too few fighter squadrons were committed in France, and on 13 May the equivalent of two more Hurricane squadrons had been dispatched. Accounts by German bomber crews testify to the impact made by the Hurricane pilots, who tended to press home their attacks with much greater energy than the French pilots in their outclassed Moranes; yet this was all a drop in the bucket. On the evening of the 14th, Reynaud telephoned Churchill with a new note of

urgency in his voice, to beg that another ten fighter squadrons
be sent to help re-establish the line at Sedan. The next day this
request became the subject of bitter controversy within the
Cabinet. Air Chief Marshal Dowding, of Fighter Command,
vigorously objected to the dispatch of any more of his squadrons to France. His face white with strain, Dowding rose from
his seat and walked round the long conference table until he
came up behind Churchill's chair. Years later Dowding remarked: 'I think some of the others thought I was going to
shoot him'; but all he did was to place in front of the Prime
Minister a single sheet of paper with a graph on it. It predicted
what would be the probable rate of loss over the next ten days
if further Hurricanes were sent to France. On the tenth day,
the graph line touched the zero point. If the current rate of
wastage were to continue over another fortnight there would
no longer be 'a single Hurricane left in France or in this
country', Dowding solemnly told Churchill. The graph, he says,
'did the trick'. In an atmosphere highly charged with emotion,
the Cabinet was reluctantly swung over to Dowding's side.

Meanwhile, in France the close of 15 May brought with it a
new threat to the A.A.S.F. A score of fighters were lost just protecting the forward bases from the incessant Luftwaffe attacks,
and now some of these airfields were seriously endangered by
the advancing Panzers. Shortly before midnight Air Marshal
Barratt decided to shift southwards a number of the menaced
combat units, an awkward move to make in mid battle with the
limited transport facilities available to him. At the same time he
closed down his own Advanced H.Q. at Chauny and retired
back to Main H.Q. at Coulommiers.

Kleist and Guderian at Odds

Behind the scenes of the German command, where one might
have presumed to find jubilation after such a promising day,
contrary to every expectation the prevailing tone was one of
uncertainty and discord. Its overt expression took the form of a
third fundamental disagreement between Kleist, the commander of the Armoured Group, and Guderian. The more

cautious Kleist wanted to confine Guderian to a small bridge-head west of Sedan and to build up forces within it before con-tinuing the next stage of the advance. That night Kleist's H.Q., says Guderian,

ordered a halt to all further advance and to any extension of the bridgehead. I neither would nor could agree to these orders, which involved the sacrifice of the element of surprise we had gained and of the whole initial success that we had achieved. I therefore got in touch, prsonally, first with the Chief of Staff of the Panzer Group, Colonel Zeitzler, and, since this was not enough, with General von Kleist himself, and requested that the order to stop be cancelled. The conversation became very heated and we re-peated our various arguments several times.

Thoroughly enraged, Guderian shouted down the telephone a pointed comparison to the Marne in 1914, when (at least ac-cording to the view widely accepted in German military circles) an untimely interference from the High Command had caused the German armies to halt and turn about on the very brink of victory. It was a reminder, notes Guderian 'that was no doubt not very well received' by his superiors. However, Kleist, with some reluctance, gave way once again, restoring to Guderian the 'freedom of movement' he demanded.

Chapter 15

'We Have Lost the Battle!'

16 May

Only he is vanquished who accepts defeat.
FOCH

The enemy has not succeeded in breaking through our battlefront and emerging from the Sedan–Mézières region. He has thrown wave upon wave, division on division, into the furnace. Our plains, our fields, our roads are filled with his corpses. . . We must say this and say it again and cry it out to the four winds of France's skies: 'He wanted to break through, as he wanted to at Verdun, and he did not get through!'
L'Époque, 16 May

South-west of Namur our divisions extended their successes on the west bank of the Meuse and once again struck at French armoured forces. South of Sedan, French counter-attacks, which included the employment of the heaviest tanks, were warded off.
Wehrmacht communiqué, 16 May

A certain number of German fighting vehicles were able to push right forward, but they were not strong enough and operated like lost children. . . The German tanks will soon have no more petrol or ammunition.
Havas, 17 May

Round Sedan the French were still holding the positions they took up yesterday after containing the enemy attack there. On the left bank of the Meuse the situation is less clear, though such progress as the Germans may have made there has been relatively slight.
The Times, 17 May

On this seventh day of the campaign, abruptly the scene of predominant interest shifts from Corap's and Huntziger's broken fronts to the higher councils of war on either side, where from now on leaders would find themselves striving desperately to keep up with the incredible tempo of events. For the Germans, the rapidity of the advance was accompanied by fresh doubts and fears of setbacks to come. For the Allied High Commands, it was the night of 15 May and the early morning of the 16th which at last brought home the extent of the disaster on the Meuse. But before coming to this tardy moment of awakening, it may be as well to retrace the activities which had ensued at Vincennes and La Ferté on the preceding days.

Was Gamelin to Blame?

Having made his plans and troop dispositions, Gamelin, as C.-in-C., had then in effect left it to General Georges, the North-East Front commander, to do the best he could with them. The relationship was not unlike that of Generals Alexander and Montgomery at Alamein (except that one must not forget the deep-seated dislike Gamelin and Georges held for each other), and doubtless if Sedan had gone as well as Alamein, historians would now regard Gamelin as a warlord of distinction. On 10 May, Gamelin revealed himself as well pleased with the apparent form the German offensive was taking, and during the first three days had busied himself with 'matters of overall organization', with a particular emphasis on Holland, to which, through his 'Breda Variant' brainchild, he felt personally committed. Although we have seen how badly informed he was kept on the course of the battle, he refrained from making more than one trip (on 11 May) to see Georges at La Ferté. Then he had learned with 'some astonishment' of Georges sub-delegation to Billotte of his 'powers to co-ordinate' the movements of the B.E.F. and the Belgian Army. Although criticizing Georges's order as an 'abdication', he went along with it on the grounds that 'it is often better to accept a *fait accompli* than to risk hampering a commander's actions'. On the 12th he deliberately kept away from La Ferté, explaining that it would have been 'improper' for him to go there while Georges was away visiting the front in Belgium. The next morning, when Guderian was about to cross the Meuse at Sedan and Rommel already had a toe-hold at Houx, Gamelin revisited Georges and claims (in his memoirs) to have been 'shaken by the realization that no major reserves appeared to have been sent to the front'. But nothing is on record to indicate that Gamelin intervened, or made any alternative suggestion at this point. On the 14th, he was at La Ferté both morning and afternoon and records that he was astonished to discover there had been no reserves immediately behind Sedan when the Germans attacked, and also that, 'for reasons that I have been unable to elucidate', Huntziger had failed to launch his counter-attack. Again, although he claims that his 'presence there was necessary from a point of view of morale', Gamelin still appears to have made no personal intervention at La Ferté that day. On returning to Vincennes, he could do nothing (according to Colonel Minart) to enlighten his own G.Q.G., beyond stating the fact that the Meuse crossings 'seemed incomprehensible, inexplicable', and that there had been 'grave errors of execution'. On the morning of the 15th, during another visit to La Ferté, Gamelin was surprised [1] to hear that Georges had given the Ninth Army the order for a general withdrawal from the Meuse.

Such were the confusion and duplication of duties existing in the French command network, that it is still not entirely clear as to who was ultimately responsible – Gamelin or Georges – for the various orders sent out during the crucial days of 10 to 15 May. If, as Generalissimo, Gamelin was not aware of the specific measures Georges was taking to counter the German threat on the Meuse, the responsibility for this rests upon him, just as, in the final analysis, he cannot escape blame for *allowing* Georges to keep him so incompletely informed as to the real state of affairs at the front. But Gamelin *must* have been aware at least of the movements of Army reserves ordered by Georges, and assuming this then either he should have intervened if he disapproved of these movements, or else one has to conclude that they had his tacit support. Gamelin never did intervene, for which, in his memoirs, he advances the rather feeble reason 'that a commander-in-chief executes badly what he does not understand'.[2] On the other hand, nothing in his

1. The words 'surprised', 'shocked', 'astonished', appear with revealing frequency in these sections of the Gamelin memoirs, *Servir*.

2. A retort originally attributed to one of Napoleon's generals upon whom he had wanted to impose his own plan of campaign.

copious apologia indicates that he would have handled his reserves other than Georges did. Thus although he may criticize (*ex post facto*) the tardiness with which Georges dispatched his reserves, it seems fair to accept that Gamelin did endorse the direction in which they were sent. Having established this, it may be useful briefly to summarize the troop movements between 10 and 15 May for which Gamelin and Georges were jointly responsible.

Altogether seventeen divisions and two brigades, representing more than 300,000 men, received orders committing them to battle. On 10 May the 1st Armoured was sent to the First Army; 11 May, two more divisions to First Army, and another two dispatched to protect the northern flank of the Maginot Line; 12 May, yet another two divisions to First Army, two (the 3rd Armoured and 3rd Motorized) to Second Army,[3] while one (the 53rd) was removed from direct control of the Ninth Army and sent to back up the front behind Mézières. On 13 May, one division (the 2nd Armoured) was sent to First Army, and one (the 36th) to Ninth Army, but only to replace the 53rd removed from it the previous day, and in fact events overtook the 36th before it could ever reach its destination, so that it remained stuck on the Aisne. On the 14th, out of nineteen different movement orders, sixteen involved a change of direction, and among these no less than seven divisions had their missions altered within twenty-four hours, the consequences of which were to prove particularly disastrous to such units as the 53rd Division and the 2nd Armoured. That same day the 14th Division (under de Lattre) was sent to bolster the Ninth Army; but, like the 36th, it too never arrived and was left holding the Aisne under Touchon's command. By the end of the 14th, orders had been issued dispatching to Huntziger's Second Army eight fresh divisions, with the object of preventing any rolling-

3. Although they were sent with the primary purpose of protecting the northern end of the Maginot Line, the dispatch of these two units to Sedan was perhaps Georges's happiest stroke; as already seen, it was the fault of the local commanders, not Georges, that they were so misused. A less happy stroke was Georges's change of mind about the 2nd Armoured, also earmarked on 11 May for Sedan, which, two days later, was ordered northwards to First Army.

up of the Maginot Line from the north; of these, half were to remain unemployed during the decisive battle. Finally, on 15 May, one division (the 1st North African) was detached from First Army and sent down to reinforce the Ninth. Thus the total reinforcements ordered up by the French High Command read as follows:

To First Army: 5 divisions, of which 3 were subsequently redirected.

To Second Army: 8 divisions, 4 of which played no part in the decisive battle.

By contrast, however, the Army most sorely in need of reinforcement – Corap's Ninth – did not receive one single division until 15 May, when it was far too late. Nothing could illustrate with greater clarity how completely Georges and Gamelin had been deceived by the 'matador's cloak', how completely they had misread German intentions. And the end of the deception was not yet in sight.

At Vincennes, 15 May had begun with renewed fears of a German left hook on the Maginot Line via Switzerland, with Intelligence from Berne reporting the situation along the German frontier now to be 'critical'. It was, says Colonel Minart, 'a gloomy day, interminable, smelling of death'. The communiqués arriving from La Ferté continued to be non-committal, but their very laconicism was becoming increasingly suspect, while liaison officers dispatched from Vincennes were treated with a marked brusqueness. On liaison duty between Vincennes, La Ferté and Doumenc's headquarters staff at Montry himself that day, Minart sensed 'that our command organization was steadily breaking down, and that a paralysis was creeping up, hour by hour'. Within the grim fortress it was more than ever like being in 'a submarine without a periscope'. Nevertheless, ugly rumours direct from the front were beginning to filter through to Vincennes in increasing quantity. Although at meals 'everything was done to avoid painful subjects', what Minart describes as 'the obsessing perspective of defeat' made its way, unspoken, through the dark corridors of

G.Q.G. The nervous tension that day was further played upon by mysterious comings and goings, private telephone conversations between Gamelin and Georges, and a call from Reynaud's office purporting to relate to an urgent intervention made to the British Government. Gamelin himself, though still externally serene, gave the appearance of a man 'stricken by a dull and pervasive fear', and increasingly sought the insulation afforded by his *chef de cabinet*, Colonel Petitbon, and his A.D.C.s. Still he declined to intervene directly in the battle.

At La Ferté, General Georges's attention during 15 May appears to have been principally concentrated on the fighting around Stonne and Flavigny's belated counter-attack. That evening, at 1700 hours, he personally telephoned the commander of XVIII Corps holding Huntziger's *right* wing, with the emphatic order: 'You must hold at all costs the anchor position Inor–Malandry. Upon this can depend the whole outcome of the war.' Inor–Malandry was the line upon which Huntziger had disastrously fallen back during the night of the 14th; its significance was that it protected the northern flank of the Maginot Line, for which purpose Georges had sent those eight divisions. Herein lay the key to Georges's thoughts that day. First it had been the threat to the Gembloux Gap; now it was the outflanking threat to the Maginot Line which stood paramount in Georges's mind. Meanwhile, as Guderian, preparatory to his swing westward, was on the defensive at Stonne, the reports reaching Georges from Huntziger sounded as if the French were more than holding their own in this sector. Gradually, towards the evening of the 15th, a new note of quite ill-founded hope seems to have begun to replace the terrible debility that Georges had displayed the previous day. On the basis of Georges's renewed optimism, Gamelin was inspired to conclude that day's signal to the C.-in-C.s of the North African and Levant theatres with the following absurdly unrealistic summary:

To sum up, the 15th seems to show a lessening in intensity of enemy action, which was particularly violent on the 14th. Our front, which was 'shaken' between Namur and the area west of Montmédy, is gradually pulling itself together.

Gamelin: 'Suddenly His Eyes Were Opened'

That evening, Gamelin delivered a similarly encouraging report to the War Cabinet. But at about 2030, shortly after Daladier, the Minister of National Defence, had returned from the meeting to his office in the Rue Saint-Dominique, Gamelin was on the telephone with an entirely different note in his voice. For the first time the Joffrian sang-froid, the sugary tone of reassurance which he customarily reserved for his political masters, had vanished. What combination of events and intelligence led to this sudden change of heart is not quite clear; in all probability it was caused by a report from a G.Q.G. staff officer, Lieutenant-Colonel Guillaut. Gamelin had dispatched Guillaut that day as his personal liaison officer to the Ninth Army, the only occasion so far when he had adopted such a measure, and reporting back Guillaut stated that

The disorder of this Army is beyond description. Its troops are falling back on all sides. The Army General Staff has lost its head. It no longer knows even where its divisions are. The situation is worse than anything we could have imagined . . . The roads are choked with routed troops.

According to Pertinax, up to this moment Gamelin 'seems to have cherished the illusion that everything could be "patched up". Suddenly his eyes were opened.' Now he knew the Germans had consummated their breakthrough, while the major part of the French reserves were irrevocably committed, or had already been partly destroyed. William Bullitt, the American Ambassador, was with Daladier when Gamelin telephoned from Vincennes. Obviously caught off balance by the change in the Generalissimo's demeanour and the tale of disaster that he had to tell, Daladier was heard by Bullitt to exclaim: 'No, what you tell me is not possible! You are mistaken; it's not possible!' When the extent of the catastrophe revealed by Gamelin had sunk in, Daladier shouted again down the telephone: 'We must attack soon!' 'Attack! With what? I have no more reserves.' The conversation ended with the following exchange:

'Then it means the destruction of the French Army?'

'Yes, it means the destruction of the French Army!'

Daladier then demanded an explanation, after which Gamelin stated: 'Between Laon and Paris I do not have a single corps of soldiers at my disposal.'

Within an hour of this dramatic conversation, General Georges at La Ferté was receiving the first 'stupefying' news that Reinhardt's Panzers had reached Montcornet. For the French High Command, the whole picture was suddenly transformed. No longer was the main threat pointing at the Maginot Line, but – of course – at Paris herself! Late that night a meeting was convened by Paul Reynaud in the Ministry of the Interior, at which Daladier, General Hering, the elderly Military Governor of Paris, and Lieutenant-Colonel Guillaut, representing Gamelin, were present. In a thoroughly panicky atmosphere the first measures for defending the capital, and for the possible evacuation of the Government, were discussed. To begin with, the decision was taken to withdraw forty squads of Gardes Mobiles from the armies and place them at the disposal of General Hering – to maintain order in Paris.[4]

Reynaud Takes a Hand

Meanwhile, the head of the civil Government, Paul Reynaud, had already arrived independently at his own sombre conclusions on the Battle of the Meuse – and much earlier than his discredited Generalissimo. At 1745 on 14 May, Reynaud had wired an urgent message to Churchill in London. The chronological context of this message needs to be noted carefully; it was sent *before* anyone in Paris could possibly have known that Rommel had smashed the counter-attack by the 1st Armoured; *before* Reinhardt had broken out from Monthermé; *before* Flavigny had launched his action towards Sedan; only a matter of hours after Guderian himself had made up his mind to swing westwards; and while General Georges was still very much preoccupied with the notional threat developing against the Maginot Line. Said Reynaud to Churchill:

4. It was revealing that the first measure taken to defend Paris should have concerned the preservation of order, presumably against a popular revolt by the Left, such as had been a perpetual bugaboo since the Commune of 1871.

Having just left the War Cabinet, I am sending you, in the name of the French Government, the following statement:

The situation is indeed very serious. Germany is trying to deal us a fatal blow *in the direction of Paris* [author's italics]. The German Army has broken through our fortified lines south of Sedan . . .

Between Sedan and Paris, there are no defences comparable with those in the line which we must restore at almost any cost . . .

The Germans could only be stopped, Reynaud concluded, by isolating the Panzers 'from their supporting Stukas'. And for this, more fighters were desperately needed. 'It is essential,' Reynaud urged Churchill, 'that you send immediately ten additional squadrons. Without such a contribution, we cannot be certain that we shall be able to stem the German advance.'

On having Reynaud's wire relayed to him, General Ironside, the British C.I.G.S., ordered that a liaison officer be sent direct to Georges's H.Q. 'to find out what the real situation is'; but later that day he noted that 'we could get nothing out of' either Gamelin's or Georges's H.Q. Reynaud, he thought, was being 'a little hysterical'. There is no doubt that the French leader was not in a good state, physically or mentally. He had not shaken off the depressing aftermath of his influenza; the strain of the previous weeks of political juggling had told on him; and his condition was not improved by Madame de Portes constantly importuning him with suggestions for running the war, and France, or with requests for advancement for friends or sons of friends. Élie Bois describes him in these days as being

worse than haggard. The nervous mannerism peculiar to him – a jerky movement of the head from right to left – was more in evidence than usual. His voice was weary and the brilliance of his glance unhealthy.

Because of the estrangement existing between Reynaud and the Generalissimo, whom he had been on the brink of sacking, his communications with Vincennes were just as unsatisfactory as Gamelin's with Georges. Paul Baudouin tells of an absurd situation when, having heard from his Military Secretary, Colonel Villelume, of Corap's collapse on the morning of the 15th, Reynaud had been unwilling to telephone direct to General Gamelin in order to avoid a breach with M. Daladier, who is hypersensitive in matters of this sort . . . He therefore rang up Daladier to ask him what were Gamelin's counter-measures, to which Daladier replied, 'He has none.'

After Colonel Villelume had in fact rung up Vincennes for information, Gamelin's *chef de cabinet*, Colonel Petitbon, snapped back: 'If this goes on, I shall not give any information at all.' [5] From the start, however, Reynaud, in his profound distrust of Gamelin, had relied upon his own 'spies'. The information they brought him, compounded with his small man's hyperdeveloped intuition, led him to conclusions closer to reality, even though they may have been tinged with 'hysteria', than either Gamelin or Georges. When he told Churchill on the 14th that the defences between Sedan and Paris had been 'broken', he also spoke with the technical knowledge of a Cassandra who had long preached, and studied, the possibilities of armoured warfare. He knew that

If our front were broken . . . *everything was lost* [Reynaud's italics]. There was no question of a repetition of the Battle of the Marne. We had cast our lot in favour of a continuous front. We had to abide by such a decision.

At 0730 on the 15th, the morning after he had received the French Prime Minister's first wire, Churchill records:

I was woken up with the news that M. Reynaud was on the telephone at my bedside. He spoke in English, and evidently under stress. 'We have been defeated.' As I did not immediately respond he said again: 'We are beaten; we have lost the battle.' I said: 'Surely it can't have happened so soon?' But he replied: 'The front is broken near Sedan; they are pouring through in great numbers with tanks and armoured cars' – or words to that effect.

Still evidently half-asleep, Churchill replied reassuringly:

5. This incredible episode appears at least to have steeled Reynaud to one resolve, though rather late in the day. 'It is time to put an end to this comedy,' he told Baudouin. 'I must be Minister of National Defence. Daladier will have to go to the Ministry of Foreign Affairs or resign.'

'All experience shows that the offensive will come to an end after a while. I remember the 21st of March, 1918. After five or six days they have to halt for supplies, and the opportunity for counter-attack is presented. I learned all this at the time from the lips of Marshal Foch himself.' Certainly this was what he had always seen in the past and what we ought to have seen now. However, the French Premier came back to the sentence with which he had begun, which proved indeed only too true: 'We are defeated; we have lost the battle.' I said I was willing to come over and have a talk.

After this more alarming communication, Churchill promptly rang up Ironside (who was then in the process of talking to Gort) to relay Reynaud's message, commenting that the French premier had seemed 'thoroughly demoralized' and that he (Churchill) had told him 'to keep calm'. Ironside informed Churchill that 'we have no extra demands from Gamelin or Georges, both of whom were calm, though they both considered the situation serious'. Churchill tells us that he now personally 'rang up General Georges, who seemed quite cool, and reported that the breach at Sedan was being plugged. A telegram from General Gamelin also stated that although the position between Namur and Sedan was serious, he viewed the situation with calm.' With a candour that would have looked well if encountered in the memoirs of General Gamelin, Churchill admits ingenuously:

Not having had access to official information for so many years, I did not comprehend the violence of the revolution effected since the last war by the incursion of a mass of fast-moving heavy armour.

Thus on 15 May the judgement of Gamelin and Georges prevailed over that of Reynaud in Churchill's appreciations. At the Cabinet meeting convened to consider the French plea for more fighters, Churchill did not overrule Dowding's arguments that the home defences should on no account be further weakened. Britain's decision to hold back her fighter squadrons will ever remain a source of extreme bitterness in France, but the influence exerted upon this decision by the misleading 'calmness' of the French C.-in-C.s in these early days cannot be overlooked.

By the morning of the 16th, however – the day of general awakening – Churchill too had begun to appreciate the full grimness of the situation in France. A new S.O.S. sent late on the 15th by Reynaud announced tersely: 'Last evening we lost the battle. The way to Paris lies open. Send all the troops and planes you can.' Churchill remarks that, although 'no clear view could be formed of what was happening, the gravity of the crisis was obvious. I felt it imperative to get to Paris that afternoon.' Accordingly, at about 1500 hours he flew off in an unarmed Flamingo at a steady 160 m.p.h., accompanied by General Ismay and the Vice-C.I.G.S., General Dill.

Vincennes, 16 May: The News is All Bad

At Vincennes, 16 May began with a seemingly endless succession of dismal tidings. 'Just as the day of the 15th had been a day of waiting on the fringe of events, so that of the 16th with one blow plunged the command post of the commander-in-chief into the atmosphere of the battle itself,' says Colonel Minart. After news had come through in the small hours that the Panzers were now nearing Laon, just eighty-two miles from Paris, 'it was as if the old fort, witness of so many historic scenes, were pounded by the first breakers heralding the tidal wave which was about to engulf France. Never had the situation seemed so grave.' At 0630 hours, Gamelin issued a desperate order instructing all troops 'to hold out even when encircled, to constitute centres of resistance'. Still the information being passed on via Georges remained at a minimum, and at 1015 Vincennes learned that telephonic communication with Blanchard's First Army had been cut off. But there now followed a series of direct communications from the front abruptly bringing Gamelin in immediate contact with the battle. First, Lieutenant-Colonel Ruby of Huntziger's staff telephoned on his own initiative to report on developments around Stonne, the failure of the 3rd Armoured counter-attack and the sacking of General Brocard. It was the first time since

10 May that any such detailed report had reached Gamelin
without being filtered through La Ferté. Almost immediately
afterwards a call came in from Amiens, from the Chief of Staff
of the Second Region, explaining that he had, 'in view of the
extreme gravity of the situation, decided to get directly in touch
with Vincennes'. Giving an itemized account of the German
forces which had passed through Montcornet, he then described
the 'withdrawal in disorder of units of all arms' from Corap's
army into the eastern areas lying under the Second Region's
jurisdiction. Already some 20,000 men, among them fugitives
from the 61st Division, had reached Compiègne; another call
from the Second Region two hours later elevated the figure to
30,000. Again, this was the first precise news about the Ninth
Army to reach Gamelin; coming from a non-combatant command such as the Second Region, it was as grotesque as if a
British C.I.G.S. had to rely upon Aldershot Command for information about an enemy invasion of Kent. Finally, towards
the end of the morning, General Touchon's Chief of Staff
telephoned to reveal the full extent of the breach the Panzers
had made.

Evacuate Paris?

Everything seemed to confirm that the Germans were now
moving on Paris at a horrifying speed. Early that morning
Reynaud was with Daladier when Gamelin telephoned to warn
him that 'the Germans may be in Paris tonight'. According to
Baudouin, Gamelin then disclaimed any responsibility for the
safety of the capital, as from midnight – 'which', Reynaud
observed to Baudouin, 'is a polite way of washing his hands!'
Gamelin telephoned the same warning to Georges Mandel, at
the Ministry for the Colonies, supposedly adding by way of
explanation that the Army, 'permeated with Communism', had
not held. At 1000 the senile Military Governor of Paris,
General Hering, evidently in a state of collapse, sent a letter to
Reynaud:

Dear Prime Minister,
    In the present circumstances, I deem it wise, for the purpose of

preventing any disorder, to suggest that you order the evacuation of the Government ... I should be obliged if you would inform me of your decision as soon as possible.[6]

Once again, it is curious to note that, by singling out the danger of civil 'disorder', the Governor of Paris obviously sensed at his back the spectre of the Popular Front and of a resurrected Commune as a threat no less great than that of the approaching enemy.

At midday, Reynaud summoned a meeting attended by General Hering, M. Langeron (the Prefect of Police), the leaders of the Senate and Chamber of Deputies – Jeanneney and Herriot respectively – and those Ministers who happened to be available, including Daladier, de Monzie (one of the most committed 'softs' in the Cabinet), Dautry, the Minister of Arms Production, and Clemenceau's old lieutenant, the cold and utterly unshakable Georges Mandel. The French leaders met amid an atmosphere of undisguised panic. Thick columns of smoke arising from Ministries that were already beginning to burn their secret files brought home all too brutally the fact that, for the third time in living memory, Paris was directly menaced by the vile Boche and his diabolical war machine. Could anything now stop it? Everyone spoke at once. Some wild suggestions were put forward, including one that shallow-draught warships should sail up the Seine to defend Paris. Governor Hering explained the measures he had taken to defend the city, but he had no explosives. There was discussion about destroying industrial plants, but this was rejected on the grounds of the working-class riots which such measures might provoke. Reynaud, showing signs of being thoroughly alarmed, had come to the meeting prepared to order that the Government leave Paris for Tours at 4 o'clock that afternoon, and was drafting a proclamation calling upon the populace also to

6. The next day, when the panic had temporarily abated, Hering wrote anew to Reynaud:

'It was my duty, yesterday, to suggest to you the departure of the Government and the Chambers from Paris. You have decided to remain. My heartiest congratulations.

Yours respectfully,
Hering.'

evacuate the city. But Daladier reckoned that the cure would
be worse than the disease, and was resolutely opposed, on
psychological grounds, to any Government departure; Dautry
declared dramatically 'we shall fight in the streets and everywhere'; Mandel, who appears throughout to have shown the
most self-control,[7] was also silently obdurate; finally, de
Monzie clinched matters by announcing that there was simply
not enough transport to carry out a large-scale evacuation.
Another call from Reynaud to Gamelin (who was meanwhile
allocating four divisions, plus another three light infantry divisions earmarked for Norway, for the defence of Paris) ascertained that the Government could still have until midnight
before deciding about its departure. Reynaud's resolve now
hardened. He declared that the Government 'ought to remain
in Paris, no matter how intense the bombing might be', though
he then added, somewhat delphically, that 'it should, however,
take care not to fall into the enemy's hands'.

The Civilian Front

Meanwhile, sparked off by the panic rife within the French
Government and the High Command, for the first time since
10 May alarm had begun to spread among the civil population.

Except for an occasional twinge of uneasy disquiet, life in
Paris – and in the provinces for that matter – had run on since
10 May with remarkable normality and calm. Going to see the
first night of Bernstein's *Elvire* on the evening of 10 May,
Vincent Sheean recalled that there had been only a score of
people in the theatre, and those few 'wept a good deal'. But
thereafter such displays of emotionalism vanished rapidly. The
theatres remained open (until 20 May) and flourished. The
restaurants were filled, often with functionaries evacuated at
the beginning of the war who, bored to death with exile in the
provinces, had drifted back to Paris. Shops in the Rue de
Rivoli kept up a busy trade in china Aberdeen terriers lifting
a leg on a copy of *Mein Kampf*. But there was nothing which

7. 'What a man!' one of Mandel's colleagues remarked to Élie Bois that
day. 'What a pity he's not Prime Minister!'

had distracted Parisian minds from the approaching peril more
than this particularly wonderful springtime itself. On returning from Brussels, Clare Boothe wrote:

Paris in the spring was still Paris in May-time. The air was sweet
and in the gardens of the Luxembourg and the Bois, the unstartled
birds sang . . . in the gilded corridors of the Ritz although now
nearly all of them had gone, one or two bosomy old women with
bleached hair and painted faces and less imagination than their
sisters still minced along cuddling their pedigreed dogs. Taxis
tooted on the boulevards, glasses clinked on the marble tops of
the bistro tables . . .

News and Censorship

As a preserver of civilian illusions, hand in hand with the
insidious beguilements of the spring of 1940 stalked the
shadowy, mute and all-powerful intermediary figure of the
French censor. The organs of censorship resided under the
Ministry of Information, in the Hôtel Continental. There one
of the most powerful figures was the 'official spokesman', a
Colonel Thomas, whose closely cropped hair, moustache and
pince-nez reminded one British war correspondent of the unhappy Dreyfus; he was supported by a number of hard-faced
ladies who had taken to sporting small imitation scissors in
their hats. Right from the opening of hostilities, Gamelin had
made it clear that he did not care to have journalists at the
front, and every effort had been made to limit their contacts
with the fighting troops to a minimum. The experiences of a
group of British war correspondents attached to the Second
Army on 10 May seem fairly representative. Because of the
bureaucracy of censorship, their 'eve of battle' stories did not
reach London until Huntziger's men were in full retreat; over
the next critical days they were permitted no nearer the front
than Vouziers, receiving their news through the medium of a
captain in charge of Huntziger's press section, who addressed
them 'as if giving a conference on military strategy', and who
seems to have been no better informed on events at the front
than they themselves. The little extra they were able to glean

of what was really happening came from the incoherent mouths
of refugees. Then, when Army H.Q. withdrew from Senuc, they
were dispatched back to Paris, a nightmarish train journey lasting eighteen hours during which they were bombed and strafed.

Thus the Allied Press was largely dependent upon the information percolating through Colonel Thomas and his minions,
and upon unilluminating official communiqués, while dispatches
based on these hand-outs had to be reprocessed, scissored and
blue-pencilled in the Hôtel Continental. Often British correspondents found that the copy ultimately reaching their papers
at home added up to little more than gibberish. One of the
journalists attached to the Second Army, Gordon Waterfield of
Reuters, claims that they were forbidden even to mention the
existence of refugees, and that when he referred to the Maginot
Line as being 'almost impregnable', the word 'almost' was
swiftly excised.

Over the long term, the severity and mendacious editing of
French censorship meant that, for historians, documentation
of those world-shaking days of May 1940 was even slimmer
than it might have been. But its immediate result was the complete deception of the French public, so that when the truth
finally seeped through, the impact was all the greater. On the
11th and 12th, there had been nothing disturbing to read in the
newspapers. On the 13th, a few fragments of bad news began
to find their way past Colonel Thomas, but not enough to cause
anxiety. On 14 May, Arthur Koestler picked up *L'Époque* in
a train to read Kerillis declare:

The spirit of the heroic days of 1916 has returned; yesterday, in
reconquering an outer fort of Sedan, our troops have shown a
bravery worthy of the glorious days of Douaumont.

Chilled by the words, he went off to tell his friend, Joliot-Curie:

'They are at Sedan.'
'Sedan? You are dreaming . . . I did not know you were such
a *paniquard*.'

But as Koestler left Joliot-Curie's laboratory, *Paris-Midi* had
just come out, with the words 'We have evacuated Sedan'

blazoned across the front page. 'That,' declares Koestler, 'was the moment when the chair under us broke down.' That same day, Alexander Werth of the *Manchester Guardian* recorded 'gloom at the office', while on the 15th he went to hear Colonel Thomas announce that the situation 'is not unlike that of March 1918. The situation is serious; but it is neither critical nor desperate.' To his diary, Werth confided: 'God, fancy saying that on the second day of the attack on France!'

In the Provinces

In fact, intellectuals like Koestler and journalists like Werth, in sensing the imminence of catastrophe, belonged to a slim minority, and it was not until the 16th that alarm began to assume any serious proportions among the public of Paris. That the picture was similar in the provincial centres of the north is testified by an excellent and detailed account of life in Amiens during these days, provided by Pierre Vasselle. According to its author, that beautiful Sunday of 12 May had passed in the utmost tranquillity. During the next day, Whit Monday, some Belgian cars began to appear in the city, but this was regarded as part of the plan for evacuating the fortified areas of Belgium and provoked no anxiety. Some people, however, thought they could hear gunfire when the wind blew from the east. On the 14th, the delay with which the official communiqués appeared to be reporting events caused some uncertainty, and there was talk about evacuating women and children. The number of itinerant Belgians increased. But life continued unchanged; the shops were full, and children made ready to return to school after the Whitsun holidays. The 15th also passed without incident. There were reports that Arras had been badly bombed during the night; some cars with AF (Aisne) and NA (Pas-de-Calais) number plates now joined in the Belgian traffic, but it still flowed smoothly through the city, and there was no move towards any organized evacuation. The sun continued to shine down, brilliant and hot as in July. The earliest moment of serious disquiet came that evening with the first official admission that the Germans had crossed the Meuse between Namur and Mézières. Then on the morning of the 16th word got around that it was no longer possible to get St Quentin on the telephone. The cars bearing AF and NA plates multiplied, and those of their occupants who paused at cafés were subjected to intense questioning. By midday, cars were beginning to pour out of Amiens towards the west, greatly favoured by the superb weather.

16 May: Panic Hits Paris

Amiens, however, remained a good deal calmer than Paris that day. From the earliest hours ugly rumours had begun to ripple through the city: 'Rethel has been overrun', 'The Boches are at Laon', 'They'll be in Paris this evening'. For confirmation of the worst, one only had to drive through the Place de la Concorde, where the Ministry of the Marine was frantically heaping its files on to Navy lorries. There was suddenly a tremendous run on walking-shoes and suitcases at the Galeries Lafayette. Senator Bardoux, on his way to the Chamber of Deputies, noted that at half past ten 'I did not have a bad impression; Paris seemed normal. But at a quarter past twelve, my impression was quite different. The requisitioning of buses, the increase in the traffic and the arrival of refugees had made Paris frantic.' From every direction the first heavily-laden motor-cars began to appear on the roads, and throughout the day the traffic built up as more and more Parisians sought to escape from the city while there was still time.

There were of course cases of calm, where it seemed that nothing, not even war, could ruffle the immortal face of Paris in springtime; Alexander Werth observed that day 'several art students on the Quai painting pictures of the Île de la Cité, one of them in uniform'.

Probably the worst centre of rumours and panic was the Assembly itself. Outside, one of Reynaud's Ministers was greeted that morning by a group of 'spivs', who 'looked towards the Madeleine, "waiting", they said, "for the arrival of the enemy"'. Inside, Senator Bardoux on his arrival found that

the corridors were invaded by a disgusting crowd, dirty and badly dressed, malodorous and enveloped in smoke. The gravest rumours were circulating – and hawked about moreover by two quaestors, Barthe and Perfetti. 'The Germans have entered Laon and Rheims. They are advancing in a motorized column, flanked to right and left by two armoured divisions. They will be in Paris this evening.'

Other prominent politicians assured him that the broken line on the Meuse had been held by two Parisian divisions which had been 'got at by the Communists'.[8] These had 'disbanded' after being attacked by tanks and flame-throwers, and the fugitives from them were now marching on Paris 'to proclaim revolution'. The Paris taxis (shades of the Marne!) were being mobilized for an unspecified purpose that night. Pierre Mendès-France, back on leave from Syria, recalls how one Minister he knew

spent literally the whole morning telephoning his friends to advise them to leave the capital immediately. He was particularly concerned about the Jews, painting a lurid picture of the risks they were likely to run,

while Bois claims that even Herriot told a friend: 'Before two o'clock I advise you to leave Paris.'

Reynaud Addresses the Assembly

At three o'clock that afternoon, Reynaud was informed by telephone that the corridors of the Chamber were seething with excited Deputies now spreading 'the wildest rumours' to the effect that the Government's departure from Paris was imminent. He decided to go and address the Chamber himself. To Bois, who saw him just before he spoke, Reynaud 'looked like a man taxed to the uttermost by fatigue, distress and responsibilities', but he managed to summon up the courage that had apparently deserted him in the morning. With some prevarication, he hotly denied that there was any truth in the rumours that the Government had been contemplating flight, declaring 'We shall fight before Paris; we shall fight in Paris, if need be!'

8. The 71st was specifically mentioned. This was the thesis to which even Reynaud, in his memoirs written after the war, continued to subscribe.

When he got up to speak, his manner struck listeners as 'very noble, very firm'. Hitler, he said,

means to win the war in two months. If he fails he is doomed, and he knows it . . . The period we are about to pass through may have nothing in common with the one through which we have just passed. We shall be called upon to take steps that only yesterday would have seemed revolutionary. Perhaps we shall have to change both methods and men. For every weakness there will be the penalty of death.

On this draconian line, the Deputies rose to their feet and applauded long and loudly. Herriot, the President of the Chamber, ended this dramatic meeting amid renewed applause with the words: 'France is alive to the grandeur and tragedy of this ordeal. She will live up to her past and her destiny!'

Churchill in Paris

Such was the atmosphere as Churchill landed in Paris. 'From the moment we got out of the Flamingo,' says Churchill, 'it was obvious that the situation was incomparably worse than we had imagined. The officers who met us told General Ismay that the Germans were expected in Paris in a few days at most.' Ismay was 'flabbergasted'. Driving through the streets of Paris, he noticed that 'the people seemed listless and resigned, and they gave no sign of the passionate defiance that had inspired the cry "*Ils ne passeront pas!*" in the previous struggle . . . There were no cheers for Churchill.' At half past five, Churchill's party arrived at the Quai d'Orsay for a meeting attended by Reynaud, Daladier, Gamelin and various others. 'Everybody was standing,' recalls Churchill.

At no time did we sit down around a table. Utter dejection was written on every face. In front of Gamelin on a student's easel was a map, about two yards square, with a black line purporting to show the Allied front. In this line there was drawn a small but sinister bulge at Sedan.

According to French accounts of the meeting, Churchill expressed surprise at the gravity of the situation, confessing that 'he did not quite understand what stage had been reached when he heard that the Government was thinking of leaving Paris'. Reynaud, says Paul Baudouin, then

> beckoned to General Gamelin, who, like a good lecturer, took his stand by the map, and gave an admirable discourse, clear and calm, on the military situation . . . His ladylike hand marked here and there on the map the positions of our broken units and of our reserves on the move. He explained, but he made no suggestions. He had no views on the future . . . While this was going on M. Daladier remained apart, red in the face, drawn. He sat in a corner like a school-boy in disgrace.

Daladier interrupted to admit in an aside to Baudouin: 'The mistake, the unpardonable mistake, was to send so many men into Belgium.'

Noting that, after Gamelin had spoken for about five minutes, 'there was a considerable silence', Churchill continues his recollection of the meeting with an immortal passage:

> I then asked: 'Where is the strategic reserve?' and, breaking into French, which I used indifferently (in every sense): *'Où est la masse de manœuvre?'*
>
> General Gamelin turned to me and, with a shake of the head and a shrug, said : *'Aucune.'*
>
> There was another long pause. Outside in the garden of the Quai d'Orsay clouds of smoke arose from large bonfires, and I saw from the window venerable officials pushing wheel-barrows of archives on to them.

> The air outside was filled with whirling scraps of charred paper – projected pacts, State secrets of the highest order, all intermingled with meaningless inter-departmental memos. Every once in a while another heavy packet of documents, thrown from the upper storeys of the Quai d'Orsay, would strike the ground with a dull thud in front of the Allied statesmen's eyes. *'No strategic reserve?'* repeated Churchill.

> *'Aucune.'* [9] I was dumbfounded. What were we to think of the

---

9. French accounts of this exchange broadly agree with Churchill's, with the exception that Gamelin claims that, when speaking of the strategic reserves, he did not say 'There are none', but 'There are no longer any'.

great French Army and its highest chiefs? It had never occurred to me that any commanders having to defend five hundred miles of engaged front would have left themselves unprovided with a mass of manoeuvre . . . What was the Maginot Line for? It should have economized troops upon a large sector of the frontier, not only offering many sally-ports for local counter-strokes, but also enabling large forces to be held in reserve; and this is the only way these things can be done. But now there was no reserve. I admit this was one of the greatest surprises I have had in my life. Why had I not known more about it. . .?

Why indeed! The question certainly pointed up an appalling gap in liaison existing between the two Allies. Several times in his bewilderment Churchill returned to the window to gaze distracted at the curling wreaths of smoke rising from the bonfires of French State documents. 'Still the old gentlemen were bringing up their wheel-barrows, and industriously casting their contents into the flames.' Then he would return to fire questions at the French leaders: why were the Allied armies retreating from northern Belgium, thereby abandoning Brussels and Louvain? Should they not, on the contrary, be counter-attacking the northern flank of the German breakthrough? Surely, 'This is the moment to advance and not retreat,' he reiterated. He hesitated to take the threat of the German tanks so seriously; as long as they were not backed up by strong infantry units they were just 'so many little flags stuck in the map', unable either to support themselves or to refuel.

According to Baudouin, Reynaud, 'seeing that the English Prime Minister did not appear wholly to grasp the seriousness of the situation', took over Gamelin's place at the easel, explaining:

'The hard point of the German lance has gone through our troops as through a sand-hill.' He pointed out the importance of the battle in progress in the bulge marked in red on the map. He twice said, 'I assure you that in this bulge there is at stake not only the fate of France but also that of the British Empire.'

Turning back to Gamelin, Churchill asked point-blank: 'When and where are you going to counter-attack the flanks of the

Bulge?[10] From the north or from the south?' Gamelin's reply was: ' "Inferiority of numbers, inferiority of equipment, inferiority of method" – and then a hopeless shrug of the shoulders.' There was no argument. Here was the admission of the bankruptcy of a whole generation of French military thought and preparations.

The French now turned the heat on Churchill to help stop the gap which the Panzers had ripped. He must send still more fighter squadrons. Churchill replied at length, pointing out how disastrously the very outcome of the war might be affected if the defences of the British Isles were denuded. He referred to the grievous losses the R.A.F. had suffered during the daylight bombing of the Sedan bridges, contrasting them with the felicitous results and small losses of the recent night raids on the Ruhr. He revealed that four more fighter squadrons were in fact already on their way to France,[11] but ended by declaring firmly (and pointedly): 'It is the business of the artillery to stop the tanks. The business of fighters to cleanse the skies (*nettoyer le ciel*) over the battle.' Having lasted two hours, the meeting ended. 'This was the last I saw of General Gamelin,' wrote Churchill, dismissing him with the withering epitaph 'no doubt he has his tale to tell'.

On repairing to the British Embassy for dinner, Churchill instructed Ismay to telephone to London that the Cabinet should assemble at once to consider an urgent telegram which he was about to dictate. With a touch of John Buchan, Ismay carried out this order in Hindustani, having previously arranged for an Indian Army officer to be standing by in London. At 2100 hours Churchill's telegram was dispatched. Stressing 'the mortal gravity of the hour', he estimated 'At least four days required to bring twenty divisions to cover Paris [12] and

10. Ismay observed that 'boolge' was the nearest Churchill could approach in French.

11. This had been sanctioned by the Cabinet just before Churchill's departure from London that day, despite the views of Dowding.

12. It should be expressly noted that, by the night of 16th, there was no considered thought by either Churchill or the French leaders that the German thrust might be aiming at the Channel and not at Paris.

strike at the flanks of the Bulge.' Describing the burning of files, which had made so strong an impression on him, Churchill went on:

I consider the next two, three, or four days decisive for Paris and probably for the French Army. Therefore the question we must face is whether we can give further aid in fighters . . . I personally feel that we should send squadrons of fighters demanded (i.e. six more) tomorrow, and, concentrating all available French and British aviation, dominate the air above the Bulge for the next two or three days, not for any local purpose, but to give the last chance to the French Army to rally its bravery and strength. It would not be good historically if their requests were denied and their ruin resulted.

Prophetic words!

At about 2330 the reply came back – in one single word of Hindustani, '*han*', or 'yes', via Ismay. The British Cabinet had agreed to the call for the six extra squadrons. Churchill immediately

took Ismay off with me in a car to M. Reynaud's flat. We found it more or less in darkness. After an interval M. Reynaud emerged from his bedroom in his dressing gown.

A scene now ensued with Churchill putting on his most powerful histrionic performance in a deliberate attempt to inspirit his French colleague. It reminded Ismay of parents watching their children open presents; Churchill 'was about to give Reynaud a pearl beyond price, and he wanted to watch his face when he received it'. He insisted on reading out with great emphasis the telegram he had sent to London. Reynaud thought it was 'admirable'. Following this, says Churchill, 'I told him the favourable news. Ten fighter squadrons! I then persuaded him to send for M. Daladier.' This proposal, Ismay observed, did not greatly please Reynaud. But Daladier arrived; Churchill read through his telegram once again, and repeated the Cabinet's response. 'Daladier,' Churchill continues, 'never spoke a word. He rose slowly from his chair and wrung my hand.' Churchill now launched into what Reynaud described as 'a forthright harangue on carrying the war to the enemy'. One of the French eye-witnesses records Daladier as being 'crushed, bowed down with grief; Reynaud silent and with his head erect, like some small broken piece of machinery', while Churchill paced back and forth, exhorting them: 'You must not lose heart! Did you ever suppose we should achieve victory except after dire set-backs?' Warming to his subject with true Churchillian vehemence, he began to exert a potent charm over his important audience. 'Crowned like a volcano by the smoke of his cigar,' wrote Baudouin in his diary, Churchill declared

that even if France was invaded and vanquished England would go on fighting . . . Until one in the morning he conjured up an apocalyptic vision of the war. He saw himself in the heart of Canada directing, over an England razed to the ground by high explosive bombs and over a France whose ruins were already cold, the air war of the New World against the Old dominated by Germany . . . Mr Churchill made a great impression on Paul Reynaud, and gave him confidence. He is the hero of the war to the end.

Meanwhile that same evening the French radio was broadcasting a confident and assertive address by Reynaud, which revealed an almost excessive swing from his mood of the early morning. 'The absurdest rumours have been put about,' he assured the French public.

It has been said that the Government intends to leave Paris: that is false. The Government is, and will remain, in Paris . . .

It has been said that the enemy was in Rheims. It has even been said that he was in Meaux, whereas he has merely managed to form a broad pocket, south of the Meuse, that our gallant troops are striving to fill in.

We filled in plenty in 1918, as those of you who fought in the last war will not have forgotten!

In this new frame of mind, before the day was over Reynaud was also warning his colleagues that the Government might have to be prepared to go, at a moment's notice, to North Africa, to continue the war from there.

The Ten R.A.F. Squadrons

Next morning Churchill flew back to England, feeling that perhaps he had managed to 'revive the spirits of our French friends, as much as our limited means allowed'. But in fact what he, Dill and Ismay had seen and heard that day in Paris gave birth to an irremediable lack of confidence in the French High Command. From now on British policy assumed an increasingly sober view of the Battle of France. 'Encouragement' towards the French would go hand in hand with retrenchment at home; operations at Narvik (which were beginning to look most hopeful) would be suspended, so as to enable a build-up of the home forces; the Local Defence Volunteers would be formed to deal with German parachutists; and a sharp line would be drawn on the dispatch of any more fighter squadrons to France. As it was, after the atmosphere of jubilation which Churchill had deliberately fostered by the manner of his announcement, the facts about the six extra squadrons promised to France were to come as a grave disappointment.

During Churchill's absence on the 16th, Air Chief Marshal Sir Hugh Dowding had followed up his stand of the previous day with an important and strongly worded official letter to the Air Ministry, reminding them 'that the last estimate which they made as to the force necessary to defend this country was 52 squadrons, and my strength has now been reduced to the equivalent of 36 squadrons'. At the emergency Cabinet meeting summoned by Churchill from Paris that night, although Ironside had 'recommended that we should send all we could – up to ten squadrons', saying that 'it was a battle that might lay France low and we must not stand out', the Chief of the Air Staff, Sir Cyril Newall, had strongly backed Dowding. He finally produced a rabbit out of the hat in the form of a conversation with Barratt's H.Q. in France, which had pointed out that their bases could, in any event, accommodate only three more squadrons. In view of the fact that the A.A.S.F. was being forced by the Panzers' advance to abandon some of its fields that day, this was an argument difficult to refute. It was thus agreed that, as a compromise, the six additional Hurricane squadrons

should be concentrated in the south of England and should fly
to France daily (three in the morning, and three relieving them
in the afternoon) for operations over the battlefield. The British
Official War History explains: 'Thus the equivalent of ten extra
squadrons for which the French had asked was operating from
French or English bases by the 17th.' But considering the short
maximum range of the fighters of 1940 (300 miles for a Hurricane), this was by no means the same as what the French
thought they had been promised on the night of 16 May; based
on England, the Hurricanes certainly could not, as Churchill
had envisaged, 'dominate the air above the Bulge for the next
two or three days'. In any case, such was the superiority now
achieved by the Luftwaffe that a hundred-odd fighters could
not possibly tip the balance. Moreover, as Churchill had
pointedly remarked to the French, it was only on the ground
that the Panzers could be stopped.

Vincennes: 'A Wind of Panic'

How, after all the comings and goings of this eventful day, did
Gamelin and Georges now propose to eliminate the 'Bulge'?

In the course of the important political happenings on the
afternoon and evening of the 16th, more fragments of bad news
had kept on arriving at Vincennes. Liaison officers brought with
them depressingly uniform accounts of the 'bad appearance' of
troops. Even in the suburbs of Paris, the bars and bistros, says
Colonel Minart, were 'filled with topers in uniform of all arms.
Disorder, indiscipine reigns everywhere.' In G.Q.G. itself,
Minart records something like a 'wind of panic' blowing by the
end of the day:

Colonel Petitbon[13] had sited in the court of the fort itself, pointed
in the direction of the great south portal, a 75-mm. gun arrived
from no one knows where, which would have been better used
elsewhere. Secretaries were rapidly initiated in the service of this
cannon.

This order Minart considered as indicative of just how com-

13. Gamelin's *chef de cabinet*.

pletely everybody had lost their heads. One staff officer had
even 'had his kit brought down to his office so that he could
carry it away with greater ease in case of flight'. Meanwhile,
Gamelin himself, 'sad and unoccupied, inspiring a profound
pity, came and went between his chief staff officers and his
A.D.C.s, endeavouring to grasp at some intangible fetish.
Nobody dares tackle him.'

Nor, for that matter, was Gamelin yet prepared to tackle
General Georges and take control of operations out of his
hands, despite his (*ex post. facto*) grumblings at Georges's
handling of operations and the fact that one army commander
(Corap), one corps commander (Martin), and three divisional
commanders had already been (or, in Martin's case, were about
to be) sacked for their responsibility in the disaster on the
Meuse. Meanwhile, by the end of the 16th, both Gamelin and
Georges continued deluded as to the Germans' strategic goal.
Paris was now their overriding fixation. Yet at the same time
fresh alarums from Switzerland combined with renewed hard
fighting at Stonne still kept alive in the backs of their minds
nagging fears for the safety of the Maginot Line, with the
result that they could not quite bring themselves to deploy elsewhere all those idle reserves and interval troops guarding the
Line. No serious thought was given to the possibility that Rundstedt might be heading for the Channel coast with the aim of
encircling and annihilating the Allied armies now in northern
Belgium.

From General Georges's North-East Command, two important orders went out during the 16th. The first, 'General
Order No. 14', specifically referring to the enemy thrust 'in the
general direction Givet–Paris', decreed that Billotte's armies
were to 'make every effort to re-establish themselves' along the
line running from Antwerp through Charleroi, Anor,[14] Liart,
Signy-l'Abbaye and Omont to the anchor position at Inor. But
this meant that the armies in northern Belgium were to continue to hold the Germans frontally, regardless of any possible
threat to flank – or rear – while the line from Liart to Omont

14. On the fortified line behind the French frontier, in Ninth Army's
sector.

had already been broken through the previous evening. The order then prescribed that, in the event of it proving impossible to re-establish the 'continuity' of this front, the French forces were to 'oppose any lateral extension of the enemy by holding all the passages over the Aisne and the Oise, as far as their confluence'. Georges's 'Special Order 93', however, called for 'a counter-attack by tanks' on the morning of the 17th aimed at 'cleaning up' the whole area between Hirson–Liart and Château Porcien on the Aisne. The attack was to be conducted by Giraud, using the 1st and 2nd Armoured Divisions with reinforcements from the 1st Light Mechanized and the 9th Motorized Divisions, which had belonged to his old Seventh Army. From the south, General Touchon was to attack with the 'de Gaulle group', about which more remains to be said later. Was this, then, to be the concentrated action against both flanks of the 'Bulge' which Churchill had urged? Alas, no. Georges was totally misinformed as to the true state of the units designated to take part. The 1st Armoured had lost most of its tanks, while the 2nd was split in two and dispersed, and de Gaulle's group was literally being assembled that very night under the fanciful title of the '4th Armoured Division'. Furthermore, as far as the 2nd Armoured was concerned, Georges's instructions were mutually contradictory in exactly the same sense as Flavigny's handling of the 3rd Armoured on its arrival south of Sedan: on one hand, it was expected to launch a counter-attack; on the other hand, its scattered tanks were being called upon to 'cork up' the various river crossings along the River Oise. Once again, as events would swiftly prove, France's waning armoured strength was about to be thrown away in penny packets.

At the Front: Stonne Again

On Guderian's front, the fighting at Stonne continued to see-saw back and forth fiercely throughout the 16th. During the night of the 15th–16th, a fresh local attack mounted by General Flavigny succeeded in pushing two companies of 'B' tanks into the village, where they destroyed some dozen German tanks. But as so often before, infantry and tanks were poorly co-ordinated, so that by midday the occupying French infantry were once again pushed out of Stonne by German counterattacks. That day the battered Grossdeutschland Regiment pulled out of the line for its well-earned rest,[15] to be replaced by the first of the infantry divisions hastening up by forced marches in Guderian's wake. On the way, they encountered scenes of destruction caused by accurate French artillery fire such as were seldom to be seen elsewhere behind the German lines during the whole campaign:

shell-hole upon shell-hole, shot-up tanks, motor-cycles; in one vehicle . . . the driver is still sitting at the wheel, half his skull torn away, a terrible sight.

Huntziger's men swiftly noticed the difference between the second-line German relief troops and the magnificent élite that had stormed Sedan. 'The prisoners,' says Ruby, 'are sorry specimens.' One letter found on a young officer revealed: 'Our losses are very heavy . . . the French artillery decimates entire companies. We are fed up with this.' But still the French could make no perceptible headway. 'The fighting,' Colonel Ruby tells us, 'took the form of a war of position.' From the French point of view, at Stonne this was quite the wrong 'form'; yet now, in what was still the most sensitive part of the German front, Huntziger no longer had the armoured striking power for a serious counter-stroke. At this point, Huntziger and his Second Army are left behind by the rapidly flowing tide of battle and assume but a minor role in this story; Huntziger, now ensconced with his H.Q. in one of the sinister forts at Verdun, reappears only to place his name on the document of capitulation which had had its beginnings at Sedan.

Guderian Breaks Through

To the north-west of the static battlefield around Stonne, the right-wheel of the 1st and 2nd Panzers moved into top gear on the 16th. Guderian, now restored his 'freedom of movement' by

15. The Grossdeutschland's next battle would be against the British at St Omer on 23 May.

Kleist, was himself riding up with the leading tank company in a signals half-track, repeatedly intervening in the conduct of the advance. Although Luftwaffe reconnaissance could provide no clear-cut picture of the situation to the west, it was rapidly becoming clear to the men with the armoured spearhead that there was no longer any defending force worthy of the name ahead of them. 'One had the impression,' wrote Captain Kielmansegg, with the staff of the 1st Panzer, 'as if he [the enemy] were staring half-paralysed, half-hypnotized at the original breakthrough area at Sedan.' Driving up from Sedan, Kielmansegg noted that, as far as Bouvellemont, where Balck had fought so hard an engagement against de Lattre's men the previous day,

there was not a place that was not either shot to pieces or burnt, in which only a few houses could offer a possibility of accommodation. The smell of burning lay everywhere in the air, and in many places the flames had still not been extinguished. Then suddenly all this ceases. There is neither any sign of the enemy nor of our own troops anywhere. A wonderful spring morning ... which is not characterized by fliers in the sky but by singing birds ... In this peaceful landscape, human beings were absent. Everything is dead and empty, not even the old people have remained ... the second thing that I remember is the bellowing cattle in the fields and in the cowsheds.

The troops were ordered to milk the swollen udders of the cows whenever possible, but 'by now the speed of the campaign seldom made this possible'.

'We were in the open now', wrote Guderian, and the realization acted like the most potent of stimulants on his jaded troops. Driving through to Montcornet that day,

I passed an advancing column of the 1st Panzer Division. The men were wide awake now and aware that we had achieved a complete victory, a break through. They cheered and shouted remarks which often could only be heard by the staff officers in the second car: 'Well done, old boy', and 'There's our old man', and 'Did you see him? That was hurrying Heinz', and so on. All this was indicative.

In the market-place of Montcornet, Guderian found General
Kempf of the 6th Panzer, which had captured it the previous
night. With three Panzer divisions now pouring through this
one centre and no boundaries laid down by Kleist, it was imperative to allot new routes to the various divisions. Guderian
and Kempf settled these between themselves and then 'ordered
the advance to go on until the last drop of petrol was used up'.
By the end of the day, the leading elements of Guderian's corps
had reached Marle and Dercy on the River Serre, over forty
miles from that morning's starting point and fifty-five miles
from Sedan. Corps H.Q. was established at Soize, just east of
Montcornet. To the north, Kempf, after capturing Vervins –
the former site of Corap's Army H.Q. – had pushed his reconnaissance units as far forward as Guise on the Oise. (Meanwhile, back on the Meuse, the 3rd Infantry Division, after a
hard fight, had just completed its bridge at Nouzonville, thereby
enabling Reinhardt's other Panzer division, the 8th, to get its
tanks across the river, which it hitherto had been unable to do.
Fresh, and having suffered negligible losses, it now sped forward
to catch up with its sister division.) Behind Guderian's and
Reinhardt's Panzer divisions there was, however, so the Official
History of the 1st Panzer tells us,

hardly a single German soldier to be found, except for a few
supply services, up to 25 to 30 miles behind the 1st and 2nd Panzer
Divisions. Munitions and petrol were brought up over a single
very thin, almost unprotected supply road. They were also, however, tanked up from petrol dumps and public petrol stations captured from the French.

By the night of the 16th, the foremost infantry divisions were
only just reaching the Sedan area. Here was a situation to alarm
sober minds back at Armoured Group H.Q. and beyond –
though not the impetuous Guderian.

During the 16th, offensive actions against Kleist's advancing
Armoured Group by French formations, disorganized as they
now were, amounted to almost nil. After several days of rest
behind the Maginot Line at Longwy, the 3rd Light Cavalry
Division had returned to the front via Rheims and was under

orders to join in de Gaulle's thrust into the southern flank of the 'Bulge' which Georges had ordered for the 17th. On the 16th the divisional commander, General Petiet, decided to send a reconnaissance in force towards Montcornet. On reaching Dizy-le-Gros, some five miles short of Montcornet, it ran into the 2nd Panzer and was badly battered late that afternoon. The cavalry force was dispersed and did not rejoin the division until two weeks later, while only two and a half platoons of motor-cyclists and armoured cars were able to disengage themselves. Guderian, in Montcornet at the time, speaks of an entire tank company taken prisoner, which he mistakenly states belonged to General de Gaulle's division'.[16] Meanwhile, a battalion of dragoons in Hotchkiss medium tanks, dispatched by Petiet to take up a defensive position near Sissonne, encountered no Panzers, but was almost overwhelmed by an unstoppable flood of fugitives from broken French units. Another battalion of dragoons was ordered to occupy the village of Liesse and make contact with de Gaulle's force, supposedly concentrating in the Forest of Samoussy, just east of Laon. It arrived in Liesse just as the curé, 'a big old man with an energetic expression and a moustache cut sharply above his upper lip, locked up his church and pulled out'. At about 1900 hours the dragoons met a solitary tank belonging to de Gaulle. Three hours later machine-gun fire was heard, indicating that the Panzers were already close.

And what of General Bruché's bisected 2nd Armoured Division, supposedly preparing for its attack against the northern flank of Kleist's 'Bulge' the next day? Because of the chaos on the railways, some of its trains were halted near Bohain *west* of the Oise, so that when the order came to disembark they found themselves on the wrong side of the river and were ordered by Giraud (in accordance with the defensive part of Georges's Order No. 14) to disperse and 'cork-up' the crossing points. (Meanwhile, the fine brigade of Somua tanks from the 1st Light Mechanized Division, which was on its way southwards through Belgium, was stuck at Soignies (north-east of

16. De Gaulle's attack was not due to begin until the following day. Guderian would err again later in attributing an action to de Gaulle.

Mons) by a breakdown in the Belgian railways.) [17] The rest of
the 2nd Armoured's tanks left on the north side of the 'Bulge'
found themselves disembarking at scattered points between
Étreux (on the Oise), Le Nouvion and Hirson, completely out
of touch with Bruché at divisional H.Q., which was now safely
south of the Aisne, and receiving conflicting instructions from
half a dozen different commands. Two companies of 'B' tanks
disembarking at Le Nouvion received orders on the 16th (before
receipt of Georges's No. 14) direct from General Giraud to
strike southwards at once towards Montcornet. There followed
a saga which revealed sadly the mechanical deficiencies of
France's best tank. At Le Nouvion, 2nd Lieutenant Perré, son
of the division's second-in-command, found that his 'B' tank,
Tempête, would not shift into fourth gear. On reaching Voul-
paix, it had only third gear left and was abandoned by the
remainder of the company. Perré spent the morning trying to
repair his tank, and towards 1500 hours, hearing that the enemy
had already captured Vervins, he decided to limp on regardless,
in third gear. But, coming to a hill, the motor rebelled. To his
agreeable surprise he then met another tank, *Martinique*,
which was having fan trouble. Like the blind leading the blind,
the two tanks took turn to tow each other. Then, just as
Martinique was giving up the ghost for good, they came upon
Aquitaine and *Toulon*, which, also broken down, were being
nursed along by *Bourrasque*.

It was now midnight. *Martinique* and *Aquitaine* were set on
fire, while *Bourrasque* managed to tow the two surviving tanks.
They advanced for three hours, passing ten German tanks
which failed to recognize them. At 0500 on the 17th, *Bourrasque*'s petrol pipe broke under the strain. Just at that moment
the tanks were attacked by lorried infantrymen. These were
driven off by the tanks' machine-guns; then a few minutes later
two men – French prisoners – came up with a white hand-
kerchief, calling up the tanks to surrender. They were sent back
with a burst of fire, and the Germans moved away. Its petrol
pipe repaired, *Bourrasque* alone remained roadworthy and

17. Caused, apparently, by posters instructing engine drivers to take off to
their homes.

moved off, destroying two German vehicles that came too close. The commanders of the two immobilized 'B' tanks, Perré and Rollier, then ordered their crews to escape and make for the French lines, taking with them the tank machine-guns. All through the 17th the two commanders stayed with their tanks, manning the 47-mm. turret. That evening Perré blew up a German ammunition truck and then knocked out a light tank with an armour-piercing shot. Meanwhile Rollier chalked up two tanks and a car. That night, running out of ammunition, they blew up *Tempête* and *Toulon* and, after watching from a ditch as a column of sixty Panzers trundled past, finally made their way back to the French lines at La Fère.

The few fighting elements of the 2nd Armoured south of the Aisne had meanwhile been absorbed by General de Lattre, and he put them to use defending Rethel. On the evening of the 15th, a Chasseur reported to de Lattre that three 'B' tanks from the 2nd Armoured were in mechanical difficulties just north of the river. During the night de Lattre had them brought in and positioned guarding bridges over the Aisne. The next day, *Téméraire* spotted an enemy staff car approaching at almost point-blank range. A well-placed round from the 47-mm. gun destroyed it, and in the wreckage was found a German colonel who had had his foot shot away. On him was a briefcase containing the whole of Guderian's order of attack for the following day, together with detailed itineraries for the Panzer columns. The documents were at once dispatched – supposedly to G.Q.G. Hearing the roar of enemy motors to the north-east of Rethel, the crew of *Villers-Brettonneux* were horrified to discover simultaneously that the 47-mm. gun was jammed, while a swollen cartridge could not be rammed home in the breech of the hull 75-mm. The co-driver finally bashed it into place with a tremendous blow from a hammer, in time to halt an enemy column with a couple of shots. Thirteen German trucks were then shot up. Without being knocked out themselves, the three 'B' tanks kept up their action for four days and nights, thereby forming the backbone of de Lattre's spirited stonewalling defence at Rethel. But this was not what these offensive weapons were there for, and de Lattre's fight, admirable as it was, in fact did no more than hold one of the gate-posts through which the stampede had already passed.

Rommel: the Avesnes Raid

On Rommel's front the 16th began modestly enough, so much so that around the middle of it the new Ninth Army Commander, Giraud, was beginning to derive utterly false hopes that the front had been 'stabilized'. But it was to end with the most spectacular German exploit of the day – possibly of the whole campaign – and one which, more than any other, was to establish Rommel's reputation. His principal task that day was to smash through what he always subsequently referred to as the 'Maginot Line'. The Line proper terminated at Longwy, but Rommel too, like the Allied Press, seems to have fallen for French propaganda of the Line having been extended to stretch from Switzerland to the sea. In fact, what faced him was a shallow belt of anti-tank obstacles and pill-boxes which had been run up behind the French frontier during the winter; they had now been manned hastily in part by remnants from Martin's broken XI Corps, who, for reasons already noted, had even encountered difficulties in occupying many of the pill-boxes. Rommel, however, seems to have regarded this line as a serious barrier and to have concentrated his forces for a heavy and deliberate blow to smash through it. By mid-morning he was still preparing his plans when, quite unexpectedly, in walked the army commander, Kluge. On his way forward, Kluge had been reassured by the scenes he had witnessed:

troop detachments are closing up, the rear services are moving forwards, prisoners marching back. Once again there is evidence of the defeat, for numerous French tanks lie shot up in the terrain on both sides of the road. One sees the effect of the German Stuka attacks along the road, with bomb craters particularly numerous at the crossroads. The hits lie mostly in the immediate neighbourhood of the road. Vehicles and horses that have been hit have been pushed to one side, and craters on the edge of the road have been rapidly filled in. The artillery fire of the early morning has meanwhile died away . . . men of the army staff . . . take prisoner two Frenchmen, who, according to their story, have been wandering around in the woods south of Anthée for three days. In their troop they have received no regular food for the last days. They seem to be strongly impressed by the effect of the German attack.

Coming across an abandoned French camp, his staff noted the horses still left tethered to trees, or else wandering about serenely grazing. Everywhere there were signs of utter panic. Arriving at Rommel's H.Q., Kluge – perhaps rather censoriously – 'was surprised that the division had not already moved off'. Rommel then elaborated on his plan for a set-piece attack on the 'Maginot Line', to which Kluge gave his complete approval.

One of the first units to encounter Rommel's advance upon the French frontier was the remains of General Duffet's hard-tried 18th Division, the same that had first felt the bite of Rommel at Houx. After a brief stand they were rounded up at noon. Duffet himself lost contact with his troops and, like a lost soul, wandered from command post to command post in search of them all through the following day. Finally, with a handful of men, he escaped through the German lines, arriving back in Paris to place himself at Gamelin's disposal again. Early on the 16th, General Sancelme of the 4th North African was also a commander without a division. While withdrawing from Neuville the previous night, deprived of any information about its formations, divisional H.Q. heard the dread cry of 'Here come the Panzers!' There was a shot from an anti-tank gun, and a tank was discovered, knocked out. It turned out to be a French Hotchkiss, the crew of which had been killed – the leading vehicle of a company (presumably belonging to the 1st Armoured) which had not been engaged in that day's battle, and was now also retreating across the frontier. Taking the tank company along with him, Sancelme arrived at General Martin's command post on the morning of the 16th, where he was greeted with some amazement, because it had already been assumed that the whole division had been taken prisoner. Still he could gain no news about it; nevertheless Martin ordered him to install what remained of his division in a defensive posture at Anor, and then (with total inaccuracy) informed Giraud [18] that 'the 4th North African has just arrived with all its infantry and a portion of its artillery'. By this time, after the appalling strain of the past week, Martin seems to have been making little sense. Having issued these and other orders to hold fast, in the afternoon he received unconfirmed (and inaccurate) reports that the Germans were already threatening the bridges behind him on the Sambre and upper Oise. Without reference to Giraud, he now ordered an unconditional withdrawal back across the Oise – the line which Georges's Order No. 14 was just decreeing should be held at all cost.

Of the 4th North African, about all that in fact reached Anor (on the 17th) was a colonel and a thousand of his *Tirailleurs* who had escaped through the German net at Philippeville, though losing the whole of the regimental H.Q. After a seventy-mile march, without rations, they were then forced to turn and face the Germans in a state of complete exhaustion. This was the tragic end of a division which had acquitted itself bravely. That same night, General Sancelme was taken prisoner with his staff at La Capelle.

Rommel was across the French frontier, travelling, as on the previous day, in Rothenburg's command tank. Moving towards the village of Clairfayts, the tank column was warned that the road through it had been mined, so

we bore off to the south and moved in open order across fields and hedges in a semi-circle round the village. There was not a sound from the enemy, although our artillery was dropping shells at intervals deep into their territory . . . Suddenly we saw the angular outlines of a French fortification about 100 yards ahead. Close beside it were a number of fully-armed French troops, who, at the first sight of the tanks, at once made as if to surrender. We were just beginning to think we would be able to take it without fighting, when one of our tanks opened fire on the enemy else-

18. Who, after Vervins had been overrun by the enemy, was in the process of moving Army H.Q. back to Wassigny behind the Sambre–Oise Canal.

where, with the result that the enemy garrison promptly vanished into their concrete pill-box. In a few moments the leading tanks came under heavy anti-tank gunfire from the left and French machine-gun fire opened over the whole area.

Taking up the story, one of Rommel's tank commanders describes coming up against one of the French bunker positions towards evening:

It spits fire. Two vehicles knocked out; and also from the right an anti-tank gun fires and hits the command tank of the heavy company. The radio operator has a leg shot off, commander unhurt. I am close by with my tank, but take cover. Enemy artillery fires heavily on us with medium-calibre guns. How are we going to get through the bunker line? Big question. In front of us is a thick wire entanglement, behind it a broad and deep Panzer ditch, and in the middle of the road anti-tank obstacles have been built. Are there still further obstacles? The only possibility; to blow up the anti-tank obstacles, and then rush through, hoping for luck. Meanwhile divisional commander [Rommel] as ever accompanies us in our attack in a tank. Explosion, silence full of apprehension, then two Very lights, the road is passable. Now with a rush shooting wildly between the bunkers. There are one or two casualties, but the mass get through.

Heavy artillery fire now plastered the French fortified zone. Under cover of smoke, engineers crept up to demolish the anti-tank 'hedgehogs'. Rommel watched as another assault troop dealt with the pill-box ahead of him:

The men crawled up to the embrasure and threw a 6-pound demolition charge in through the firing slit. When, after repeated summonses to surrender, the strong enemy garrison still did not emerge, a further charge was thrown in. One officer and 35 men were then taken prisoner, although they shortly afterwards overcame the weak assault troop and escaped, after French machine-guns had opened fire from another pill-box.

Slowly the sky darkened and it became night. Farms were burning at several points in Clairfayts and farther west. I now gave orders for an immediate penetration into the fortified zone, and a thrust as far as possible towards Avesnes.

With jubilation, Rommel wrote in his diary:

The way to the west was now open . . . We were through the
Maginot Line! It was hardly conceivable. Twenty-two years before
we had stood for four and a half long years before this self-same
enemy and had won victory after victory and yet finally lost the
war. And now we had broken through the renowned Maginot
Line and were driving deep into enemy territory. It was not just
a beautiful dream. It was reality.

Now the fighting took on an entirely different character, that
of a mad nocturnal pursuit. There was a bright moon, and
Rommel ordered his tanks to advance at top speed, firing on
the move to discourage any enemy anti-tank gunners or mine-
laying parties. 'We'll do it like the Navy,' he said. 'Fire salvoes
to port and starboard.'

In the moonlight we could see the men of the 7th Motor-cycle
Battalion moving forward on foot beside us. Occasionally an
enemy machine-gun or anti-tank gun fired, but none of their shots
came anywhere near us.

The French were clearly taken by surprise, first that Rommel
should have broken through the frontier fortifications with
such speed, and secondly that, against all the rules, he should
be continuing the advance by night:

The people in the houses were rudely awoken by the din of our
tanks, the clatter and roar of tracks and engines. Troops lay
bivouacked beside the road, military vehicles stood parked in
farmyards and in some places on the road itself. Civilians and
French troops, their faces distorted with terror, lay huddled in the
ditches, alongside hedges and in every hollow beside the road. We
passed refugee columns, the carts abandoned by their owners, who
had fled in panic into the fields. On we went, at a steady speed,
towards our objective.

As always, Rommel was leading the raiding party in much
the same way that, as a young captain, he had led his infiltrators
behind the Italian lines at Caporetto. Occasionally he transmitted a brief radio message to his divisional staff, well to the
rear. Towards Avesnes, progress became slower:

Military vehicles, tanks, artillery and refugee carts packed high with belongings blocked part of the road and had to be pushed unceremoniously to the side. All around were French troops lying flat on the ground, and farms everywhere were jammed tight with guns, tanks and other military vehicles . . . Always the same picture, troops and civilians in wild flight down both sides of the road.

On reaching Avesnes, the small town from which Ludendorff had directed the Germans' last-gasp offensive of March 1918, Rommel appreciated that it might be occupied by strong French forces. Nevertheless, he ordered the Panzer column to thrust forward at full speed. In fact, in Avesnes Rommel's advance-guard caught the remnants of Bruneau's 1st Armoured, on its way to La Capelle, completely offguard. There was a disagreeable moment for Rommel when some of the surviving 'B' tanks managed to push into a gap in the Panzer column, 'shooting wildly around them'. Several German tanks were knocked out; then, as dawn was coming up, Lieutenant Hanke – the diehard Nazi who had proved himself on the Meuse – moved in with his Mark IV and polished off the remaining 'B' tanks. Out of the whole of the French 1st Armoured Division, only three tanks crept off the battlefield. Later that day its artillery was also mopped up; with the exception of one battery, it had not fired a solitary shell. Having lost his division, General Bruneau 'gave his staff officers their freedom', and himself disappeared into the night. The following night he too was captured, east of St Quentin, by two engineers of the 6th Panzer.

After cleaning up in Avesnes, Rommel signalled corps H.Q. for further orders. There was no reply. He decided to continue the headlong rush and try to seize Landrecies and its crossing over the Sambre, eleven miles west of Avesnes. Ammunition was running out, so his column now 'drove westwards through the brightening day with guns silent'. But Rommel was convinced that the rest of his division, infantry and supplies was following up closely behind him. Once again, he passed more columns of wretched refugees mingled with utterly astonished French troops on the march:

A chaos of guns, tanks and military vehicles of all kinds, inextricably entangled with horse-drawn refugee carts, covered the road and verges. By keeping our guns silent and occasionally driving our cross-country vehicles alongside the road, we managed to get past the column without great difficulty.

One of Rommel's Panzer commanders recalled simply shouting, loudly and impudently, at the French troop columns to throw away their weapons: 'Many willingly follow this command, others are surprised, but nowhere is there any sign of resistance.' Several times his tank men were questioned, hopefully, '*Anglais*?' There was evidently one rare, recalcitrant exception, who brought out the ruthless streak in Rommel – a French lieutenant-colonel overtaken by Rommel as his staff car was trapped in the road jam. On being asked by him for his rank and appointment, 'His eyes glowed hate and impotent fury and he gave the impression of being a thoroughly fanatical type.' Rothenburg signalled to him to get in his tank. 'But he curtly refused to come with us, so, after summoning him three times to get in, there was nothing for it but to shoot him.'

Through Landrecies and across the Sambre via an undamaged bridge, the Panzer spearhead drove into a barrack full of troops. After a tank there had been swiftly destroyed, Lieutenant Hanke ordered the officers to have all their troops paraded and marched off eastwards. Almost out of ammunition and petrol, Rommel finally halted his column on a hill just east of Le Cateau, and nineteen miles on from Avesnes. It was now 0515 on the 17th. Though his tank crews were utterly exhausted, Rommel himself immediately hastened back to bring up the rest of the division.

End of the Ninth Army

Since the previous morning, Rommel had advanced nearly fifty miles. By all the existing canons of warfare, the way he had driven this thin finger, perhaps less than a mile wide, deep into the French lines by night seemed almost an act of recklessness. But its effect on an already demoralized enemy was quite devastating. Over the two days of the 16th and 17th, Rommel's own casualties amounted to one officer and less than forty men and N.C.O.s, while some 10,000 enemy prisoners were counted and a hundred tanks knocked out or captured. The wider consequences of the 'Avesnes Raid' were even more significant; by seizing their starting-off points, it shattered what little prospects there were for the counter-strokes on the northern flank of the 'Bulge' scheduled to take place on the 17th, and, by capturing the bridge at Landrecies, it breached the Sambre–Oise line which Georges in his Order No. 14 had been determined to hold come what may. Finally, it virtually administered the *coup de grâce* to the Ninth Army. The fate of II Corps and its solitary division, the 5th Motorized, was a case in point. On the left wing of the Ninth Army, this formation had played only a marginal part in the battle so far. During the afternoon of the 16th, General Bouffet (the corps commander) ordered Boucher (commanding the 5th) to withdraw on Avesnes that night. Almost immediately afterwards a violent air attack wiped out II Corps H.Q., killing Bouffet and nearly all his staff. Shaken, the 5th Motorized began to withdraw in some confusion. Then, on reaching Avesnes, it was stopped dead by Rommel. Panic sown by fear-ridden fugitives spread like fire in the dark. In the vivid words of General Doumenc, out of the ensuing chaos the division emerged 'volatilized'. Gone was the last of the divisions originally under Corap's command.

As Victor Hugo wrote of Waterloo, 'There faded away this noise which was a great army.'

Chapter 16

The Panzers Halt

17 May

We can always recover ground, but never lost time.
FIELD-MARSHAL GRAF VON GNEISENAU

. . . the spokesman of the French Ministry of Information, referring to reports of a penetration of the French lines by German
armoured columns, said that 'a marked improvement' had taken
place in the situation.

He described the penetration of the German armoured columns
as being 'in a long straight line,' and said that some short lapse
of time had been necessary before measures were taken to deal
with this armoured column, owing to the necessity of collating
reports of its progress to enable the Allies to make the counter-
blow as hard as possible.
The Times, 17 May

There is no ground for a suggestion that the French Army showed
itself 'overwhelmed' by the striking force of the German
armoured divisions and bombers [at Sedan]. It is true that they
lost ground in several places and had their line of advance ruptured; but that is only the inevitable outcome of the advantage
the attacker has in choosing his point of attack. The French
General Staff were prepared for such a temporary reverse; and
more are bound to occur before the Allies succeed in stabilising
the front.
Manchester Guardian, 17 May

All Quiet on the Kurfürstendamm

Inside Germany, the tremendous developments of the first
week of the campaign had aroused astonishingly little excitement. True, as part of the German deception campaign, the
full scope and direction of the breakthrough had been extensively played down. Not until 15 May did the Wehrmacht
communiqué even mention that the Meuse had been crossed
at Sedan, and then it was subordinated to news about the capi-

tulation of Holland. That same evening German radio commentators also dwelt at length on the glories of the Dutch surrender, adding almost *en passant* that 'the crossing of the Meuse south of Namur . . . offers the best prospects of threatening the fortress of Namur from the flank and of taking the northern sector of the Dyle Line from the rear'. Nevertheless, announcements of such triumphs as the conquest of Holland, the capture of Liège and the seizure of Fort Eben Emael were given tremendous emphasis – interpolated with loud fanfares and occasional bursts from the *Deutschlandlied*, or 'We Sail Against England' – and it was quite clear from the occasional hints dropped by Berlin officialdom that other startling successes were being scored at the front.

Yet by comparison with the electric days of August 1914, the lack of enthusiasm among the German public amounted almost to apathy. On 10 May, housewives gave the appearance of being principally concerned with laying in provisions for the Whitsun holiday. William Shirer, sensitive as always to the prevailing temper of the Berliners, noted how few even 'bothered to buy the noon papers which carried the news' that day. Two days later he recorded: 'A typical Sunday in Berlin to-day, with no evidence that the Berliners, at least, are greatly exercised at the battle for their thousand-year existence'. As a modest air-raid precaution, cafés were closed at 11 p.m. instead of 1 a.m., and dancing was *verboten* for the time being. The next day, Shirer's diary begins to reveal a sense of astonishment at the speed of events:

May 13. Astounding news . . . No wonder a German officer told me to-day that even the *Oberkommando* was a little taken aback by the pace . . .
May 14. We're all a little dazed to-night by the news. The Dutch Army has capitulated – after only five days of fighting. What happened to its great water lines . . . ?
May 15. Very long, stunned faces among the foreign correspondents and diplomats to-day. The High Command claims to have broken through the Maginot Line near Sedan . . . it seems almost incredible . . .

May 17. What a day! What news! . . . I would not have believed
it except that the German land army has seldom misled us . . .
At the *Rundfunk* to-night I noticed the military people for the
first time spoke of a 'French rout' . . .

But still the window-shoppers on the Kurfürstendamm, the
strollers peacefully enjoying spring in the Tiergarten, continued to betray no visible excitement.

Hitler Nervous: Halder Confident

It was quite otherwise within the various headquarters of the
German High Command. The hard-pressed Allied leaders
would have been amazed, and encouraged, could they but have
seen the nervousness, apprehension and confusion which by 17
May prevailed at the summit of the enemy camp – in sharp
contrast to its very tangible successes. When one recalls the
positions taken during the drafting of *Sichelschnitt*, a marked
change in attitudes now becomes apparent among the German principals. Hitler for one – the gambler whose audacity
had previously terrified his professional advisers – was showing
signs of losing his nerve, whereas the cautious, professional
Halder was now bursting with confidence.

On 10 May the Führer had taken up his battle H.Q. in an
austere nest of concrete works belonging to the Siegfried Line
amid the bleak uplands of Münstereifel. Even the mess was
located in a bunker, while the focal point was a small wooden
hut, no more than twelve feet square, serving as a map- and
briefing-room where all the most important O.K.W. conferences took place. According to Jodl's testimony at Nuremberg,
life at the *Felsennest* resembled

a cross between a cloister and a concentration camp . . . a martyrdom for us soldiers; for it was not a military headquarters at all,
it was a civilian one and we soldiers were guests there . . .

Although Brauchitsch and Halder had their O.K.H. H.Q.
close at hand, so deep-rooted had Hitler's contempt for his
Army General Staff become that contact between the two
headquarters was minimal, and strained. The Luftwaffe con-

tinued to roar overhead, and Army units heading for the front poured down the roads past the *Felsennest*, but Hitler remained curiously remote from the battle, informed largely through the eyes of the sycophantic Keitel, who tells us that he 'was on the road literally every other day, mostly in the area of Rundstedt's Army Group', of which the new Chief of Staff, General von Sodenstern,[1] was an old friend of Keitel's.

On 16 May, Hitler was already showing visible concern for the safety of the lengthening left flank of the Panzer breakthrough. The infantry divisions marching up to protect it seemed to be arriving much too slowly. Jodl noted that Hitler that day 'was pressing hard for the transfer of all armoured and motorized formations from Army Group B to Army Group A', while he was heard bellowing down a field telephone at Reichenau, commander of the Sixth Army, for procrastinating over the release of Hoeppner's XVI Panzer Corps.[2] This and other interferences in the Army's conduct of the campaign added to the tension already existing between Hitler and the O.K.H. Meanwhile Halder, its Chief of Staff, who had long since abandoned his cautious pessimism about *Sichelschnitt* (once he had been persuaded as to its intrinsic military virtues), in no way shared Hitler's alarm for the left flank. Here lay the essential difference between the rational intellect of the professional and the irrational, instinctive functioning of the unschooled genius. In his diary for 16 May, Halder wrote with manifest satisfaction that 'the breakthrough is developing along completely classical lines'. Following with scrupulous care the Intelligence reports from 'Foreign Armies West', which on the whole proved to be highly accurate, Halder noted that there was still no sign that the French were throwing their main reserves into battle, while by 1900 hours that evening incoming reports stated that all attacks [3] against the left flank had been warded off. By the next day, fresh intelligence from 'Foreign Armies West'

1. Successor to Manstein.
2. Which had been striking at Prioux's Cavalry Corps and the French First Army.
3. Referring presumably to Flavigny's action.

made it quite obvious to Halder that there was also little danger now of a serious Allied counter-attack on the northern flank of the 'Bulge'. In the opening entry for the 17th, Halder wrote in his diary that the 'picture shows clearly that the enemy has still not taken any major measures to close the breakthrough gap'. He noted that the French had brought up 'at least six divisions' along the Germans' critical southern flank, but 'here we do not intend to attack, and his forces do not suffice for an attack'.

In his new mood of complete confidence, Halder then went on to give voice to an opinion which signified a radical departure from the original *Sichelschnitt* blueprint, as well as representing a remarkable swing of the pendulum from his own earlier mood of conservative caution. So well did the overall situation seem to be developing, thought Halder, that 'one may conclude that we can now consider continuing the operation towards a *south-westerly direction*'.[4] In his view, France could at this point be smashed in one single battle, instead of the two separate operational phases called for in Manstein's thinking. To Bock's Army Group 'B' alone would fall the task of 'encircling and annihilating the enemy north of the Sambre', while Rundstedt's Army Group 'A' should now swing away eccentrically to roll up the French to the south-west, with a possible right hook enveloping Paris. He could see no conceivable threat to the southern flank, 'because for the time being the enemy is too weak'. Accordingly, at 1030 hours he telephoned Rundstedt's Chief of Staff, Sodenstern, instructing him not to halt on the Oise, and not let his forces become pinned down along the southern flank. At midday, the O.K.H. C.-in-C., Brauchitsch, was summoned to Hitler and evidently experienced another of those disagreeable sessions that so discomfited him. Says Halder laconically:

Apparently little agreement of ideas. The Führer emphasizes that he sees the main danger coming from the south. (At present I don't see any danger at all!) Therefore infantry divisions must be brought up as quickly as possible to protect the southern flank.

---

4. Author's italics.

Rundstedt Supports Hitler

Distrustful as ever of his O.K.H. advisers, Hitler then set off himself that afternoon to see Rundstedt at his H.Q. in Bastogne. Arriving in a state of extreme nervousness, Hitler found Rundstedt's views closely approximating to his own. (Indeed, in retrospect one may well wonder to what extent Rundstedt, in his recurrent anxiety, was the principal breeding ground for Hitler's loss of nerve, not only during the period of 17 to 19 May, but also later at the time of the historically far more consequential 'halt order' before Dunkirk.) The utterances of all three Army Group commanders show them to have been completely taken aback by the initial successes of *Sichelschnitt*; after the Meuse crossings, Bock exclaimed 'The French seem to have taken leave of their senses', while by 18 May, Leeb, obviously overwhelmed by the speed of the German advance, was writing in his diary 'It's fantastic!' But Rundstedt seems to have been the most surprised of the three; his loyal Chief of Operations and biographer, General von Blumentritt, refers to the Meuse crossings as a 'miracle which Rundstedt could not understand'. At various crucial moments, Rundstedt shows himself to have been almost as strongly conditioned by his personal experiences of 1914–18 as any of his French opposite numbers. His own unit having come within sight of Paris in 1914, he could not forget how Kluck's misguided change of direction had forfeited the victory apparently within Germany's grasp, and upon no other German senior officer had the French Army's capacity to recuperate from shattering reverses and fling itself into a devastating riposte left so ineradicable an impression. Any talk about a deviation to the south-west[5] immediately aroused in him the worst memories of Galliéni's lethal attack on Kluck's

5. Although events proved Halder to have judged the threat to the southern flank more accurately than either Rundstedt or Hitler, his proposed 'two in one' operation might well have dangerously dispersed the Panzers and their indispensable air support. This opportunism of Halder's was typical of what traditionally provided German staff planning with both its greatest tactical strength and its strategic weakness, and, at its worst, had led to the disaster on the Marne and Ludendorff's final catastrophe in 1918.

flank which was the prelude to the Marne. His esteem for the French General Staff remained unshakably high, and (so Blumentritt tells us) from the earliest moments of the breakthrough he and Sodenstern had lived in expectation of the wily enemy launching 'a great, surprise counter-offensive by strong French forces from the Verdun and Châlons-sur-Marne area, northwards towards Sedan and Mézières'.

Already by 15 May the Army Group 'A' War Diary is expressing Rundstedt's concern about his southern flank:

the question has arisen for the first time as to whether it may not become necessary temporarily to halt the motorized forces on the Oise . . . the enemy is in no circumstances to be allowed to achieve any kind of success, even if it be only a local one, on the Aisne or later in the Laon region. This would have a more detrimental effect on operations as a whole than would a temporary slowing-down of our motorized forces.

The War Diary continues:

The extended flank between La Fère and Rethel is too sensitive, especially in the Laon area . . . an open invitation for an enemy attack . . . If the spearheads of the attack are temporarily halted, it will be possible to effect a certain stiffening of the threatened flank within twenty-four hours.

In consequence, Rundstedt had issued orders to Kleist on 16 May instructing the Armoured Group to mark time and *not* cross the Oise before the 18th. Now Hitler in his visit to Army Group H.Q. on the following day accorded Rundstedt his complete support, declaring:

the decision at the moment depends not so much on a rapid thrust to the Channel, as on the ability to secure as quickly as possible an absolutely sound *defence* on the Aisne in the Laon area and, later, on the Somme . . . All measures taken must be based on this, even if it involves temporary delay of the advance to the west.

Fortified by his talks with Rundstedt, Hitler drove back to the *Felsennest* with renewed rage against his O.K.H. advisers. That night Halder summed up in his diary: 'A very disagreeable day. The Führer is enormously nervous. He is anxious about our own success, doesn't want to risk anything and would therefore be happiest to have us halt.' His visit to Army Group 'A', added Halder, 'has only caused unclearness and doubt'. From the O.K.W., Hitler's devotee Jodl concurred. 'A day of great tension,' he wrote. 'The C.-in-C. of the Army [Brauchitsch] has not carried out the decision of building up as quickly as possible a new flanking position to the south . . . Brauchitsch and Halder are called immediately and ordered peremptorily to adopt the necessary measures at once.' Halder was forced to abandon the 'south-west operation'; though, bravely, he still clung to his original viewpoint.

Kleist Orders Guderian to Halt

Meanwhile, what was the net effect of all this discord at the top on the actual executants and their conduct of operations? As previously noted, Kleist, the Armoured Group commander – activated by Rundstedt – had already made two unsuccessful attempts to put a brake on Guderian. There was little love lost between the two generals, with their totally different personalities and doctrines of warfare, and during the last argument (on the night of the 15th) tempers had risen. Then, very early on the morning of the 17th, Guderian received a message from Armoured Group H.Q.:

the advance was to be halted at once and I was personally to report to General von Kleist, who would come to see me at my airstrip at 0700 hours [German]. He was there punctually and, without even wishing me a good morning, began in very violent terms to berate me for having disobeyed orders.[6] He did not see fit to waste a word of praise on the performance of the troops. When the first storm was passed, and he had stopped to draw breath, I asked that I might be relieved of my command.

The angry Kleist, says Guderian, was 'momentarily taken

6. Presumably those initiated by Rundstedt on the 16th, instructing the Panzers to mark time while allowing the infantry flank protection to catch up.

aback', but then he nodded and ordered Guderian to hand over to his most senior divisional commander, General Veiel of the 2nd Panzer.

Guderian was shaken to learn that Hitler himself, the former fairy-godmother of the Panzer arm, 'who had approved the boldest aspects of the Manstein plan and had not uttered a word against my proposals concerning the exploitation of the breakthrough, would now be the one to be frightened by his own temerity'. Guderian signalled to Rundstedt, announcing his intention to fly to Army Group H.Q. that afternoon to report on what had happened. Back came the answer: Guderian was to remain at his headquarters and await the arrival of General List, commander of the Twelfth Army, 'who had been instructed to clear this matter up'. Meanwhile, until List arrived, Guderian's Panzers were also to stay put. On his arrival early that afternoon, List

asked me at once what on earth was going on here. Acting on instructions from Colonel-General von Rundstedt he informed me that I would not resign my command and explained that the order to halt the advance came from the O.K.H. and therefore must be obeyed.

Guderian's vehement exposition of the true state of the French collapse on his front (backed up by similar views expressed by the other Panzer corps commander, Reinhardt) seems to have persuaded List and, through him, to have at least partially reassured Rundstedt. But not Hitler. Finally, List, with Rundstedt's approval, produced an admirable compromise. He ordered Guderian:

Reconnaissance in force to be carried out. Corps headquarters must in all circumstances remain where it is, so that it may be easily reached.

Thus, while giving Guderian enough latitude to stifle his petulance, Rundstedt must have thought that, by immobilizing Guderian – as he would never lead his Panzers 'from the rear' – he would have effectively halted the advance. But he did not know Guderian; meanwhile, through what appears to have been connivance at junior levels between the O.K.H. staff and Rundstedt's, 'reconnaissance in force' was formally defined as being inclusive of all but the rear echelons!

Guderian's 'Blind Eye'

A delighted Guderian was now provided with exactly the blind eye he required. Obediently, his corps H.Q. remained at Soize, but

a wire was laid from there to my advanced headquarters, so that I need not communicate with my staff by wireless and my orders could not therefore be monitored by the wireless intercept units of the O.K.H. and the O.K.W.

The 'reconnaissance in force' was set in motion. After the best part of a day's inaction, by the evening of the 17th the Panzers were rolling forward again, unbeknown to Hitler and the High Command. It was a splendid piece of inspired military insubordination.

Among the Panzer troops themselves, however, there was no doubt that the halt order of the 17th was regarded as an unmitigated blessing. It was, points out Kielmansegg, 'the first real day of rest since the beginning of the campaign'. As well as enabling the outdistanced infantry and supplies to catch up, here at last was an opportunity to get some badly needed sleep, to grease up the tanks and replace their numerous worn-out parts. But if there had been no such ruthless and self-assured commander as Guderian to keep the advance rolling, if Rundstedt had had subordinates sharing his anxieties on the 15th and 16th, could events have taken a less unhappy turn for the French? Colonel Goutard, the French military historian, is one who thinks that such a two-day respite 'might perhaps have given our Command time to collect itself'.

De Gaulle: 'The Chance to Act'

17 May, the day the Panzers halted, was also the day appointed by Georges for the first co-ordinated attacks on the

'Bulge' from north and south. But in fact it was solely de Gaulle's group that made any concerted effort. Then aged forty-nine – exactly a year older than his fellow Scorpion, Rommel – and still a full colonel, this haughty, totally dedicated figure, who had chosen to return to his tanks rather than accept a political appointment as Secretary to Reynaud's War Cabinet, had only received command of the 4th Armoured Division on 11 May. As de Gaulle himself remarks, the division 'indeed did not exist', and its various elements were only gradually arriving from distant points. On the 15th, de Gaulle was summoned to Georges's H.Q. and informed that General Touchon was endeavouring to establish a defensive front barring the way to Paris; operating from the Laon area, the 4th Armoured was to 'gain time' for Touchon, and it was left to de Gaulle to decide how. General Georges, 'calm, cordial but visibly overwhelmed', sent him on his way with the words:

There, de Gaulle! For you who have so long held the ideas which the enemy is putting into practice, here is the chance to act.

De Gaulle hastened to Laon, where the next day he was joined by an embryo staff and the scattered remnants of General Petiet's 3rd Cavalry. A dismal spectacle greeted him:

Miserable processions of refugees crowded along all the roads from the north. I saw, also, a good many soldiers who had lost their weapons. They belonged to the troops routed by the Panzers during the preceding days. Caught up, as they fled, by the enemy's mechanized detachments, they had been ordered to throw away their arms and make off to the south so as not to clutter up the roads. 'We haven't time,' they had been told, 'to take you prisoner!'

At the sight of this routed rabble and 'at the tale, too, of that contemptuous piece of insolence of the enemy's', de Gaulle declares in his war memoirs,

I felt myself borne up by a limitless fury. 'Ah! It's too stupid! The war is beginning as badly as it could. Therefore it must go on. For this, the world is wide. If I live, I will fight, wherever I must, as long as I must, until the enemy is defeated and the national stain washed clean.' All I have managed to do since was resolved upon that day.

Having carried out a reconnaissance, de Gaulle decided he would try to sever Guderian's communications by striking for the important road junction at Montcornet, some twenty miles north-east of where his group was assembling. He would attack the next morning 'with whatever forces might have reached me'. By dawn on the 17th, he had received just three battalions of tanks. Two of these consisted of light Renault R-35s, mounting the obsolete short-range 37-mm. gun; only one (the 46th) was a 'B' tank battalion, and this had but recently been converted from light tanks. It had never taken part in tactical manoeuvres, and had had only one firing practice with the 75-mm. gun. There was also one company of modern D-2 light (16 ton) tanks, equipped with the powerful 47-mm. gun. In the course of the day one solitary infantry battalion, the 4th Chasseurs, would arrive, transported in buses that were highly vulnerable from the air. In sharp contrast to Guderian's lavish equipment, de Gaulle's 4th Armoured had no proper anti-aircraft weaponry, nor could it call upon any air support worth the name.

Nevertheless, at daybreak de Gaulle set forth on his mission, through the 'sad columns' of Army fugitives, clad in a leather jacket and puffing incessantly at a cigarette, an exacting leader of his improvised division. Amid the harsh setting of mechanized warfare, there is a certain note of romance as its two great French and German protagonists, de Gaulle and Guderian, confront each other on the field of battle for the first time. The day began well for de Gaulle, with his tanks sweeping all before them up the road from Laon to Montcornet. Advancing through Dizy, Captain Idée, commanding the independent company of 'D' tanks, observed with pride the professional way in which his fourteen tanks were deploying themselves, but was concerned to see only two of the battalion of 'B' tanks which should have been on his right. At Chivres, Idée's tanks overran a German reconnaissance column amid scenes of frightful carnage:

Hell breaks loose. There are their motor-cycles, their passengers inert, crumpled up in the side-cars or slumped over the handlebars; a truck in flames; an armoured car knocked out by our 47s; infantrymen mown down while they were withdrawing behind a farm; yet another armoured car, shot up on the road to Machecourt. Chivres is cleaned up, we continue towards Bucy. A feeling of success.

Another German column of soft vehicles was overtaken and left 'a long line of fire', and at 1500 hours de Gaulle's tanks fought their way into Montcornet, 'destroying everything which had had no time to flee'.

De Gaulle's Attack: the German View

Here the command post of the 1st Panzer came close to being overrun that day. General Kirchner had himself become a casualty two days earlier when a vehicle had run over his knee as he lay catching up on a few minutes of badly needed sleep. Since then, he had lain immobilized, 'cursing and with a menacing expression, on a stretcher near the situation map', but refusing to relinquish command and relying heavily on his two staff officers, Wenck and Kielmansegg. Leaving his command post at Lislet just outside Montcornet, Kielmansegg was driving alone to the division's advanced H.Q., some eight miles to the west:

As I came out of Montcornet and continued along the main road – the division's only route – I saw several German soldiers running back towards me. They were engineers, who insisted that French tanks were coming behind them. I was disinclined to believe it, because the direction in which they pointed lay towards our own front! My ordnance officer, however, who had meanwhile hastily driven up a hill, confirmed it. There was no longer any time to consider where the tanks were coming from. I ordered the engineers, who had already laid some mines, to set up a barricade at the entry to Montcornet.

The town was filled with all kinds of vehicles, including Kielmansegg's own ammunition columns, which were piling up on top of each other. Having established an *ad hoc* defence,

Kielmansegg rushed at full speed back to Lislet, which was left completely open to the French tanks. Here he found 'lying blissfully and peacefully ignorant in the warm sunshine, a field service ammunition column halted in two of the roads leading to the village, and waiting to push on ahead'. Kielmansegg shouted at them to turn about. While they were reversing, the *Feldwebel* he had posted as a look-out ran up:

'They're coming, *Herr Hauptmann*, they're coming! ' Soon I too heard shooting. At the same moment it occurred to me that among the other orders I had forgotten to inform my runner and clerk, who were in accommodations somewhere further off . . . then, the last one to leave, I pulled out of the still very quiet Lislet, as the first French tanks swung round into the village streets. Under these circumstances prudence was the better part of valour, for even with the best will in the world, one cannot hold up a dozen enemy tanks with a pistol.

Kielmansegg then hastened back to warn Guderian's H.Q. at Soize. On his way, he met a few German tanks coming out of workshops. These he immediately ordered to head for the oncoming French; meanwhile some flak guns also opened up fire from the heights behind Lislet. Several of de Gaulle's tanks were knocked out and the remainder beaten back, but Kielmansegg notes that about twenty-five had actually got in behind the 1st Panzer's fighting troops. Among the German casualties was Kielmansegg's fellow staff officer, Major Wenck, wounded on his way back from attending the sulphurous meeting that morning between Guderian and Kleist. On returning to Lislet, Kielmansegg found it 'burning from one end to another, two shot-up French tanks stood in the village itself and several others lay before Montcornet and Lislet. My H.Q. was somewhat battered.' Later in the afternoon there was a second tank attack, this time led by four heavy 'B' tanks. But

In spite of the fact that my light flak guns (which I had brought up in the interim) could not penetrate their thick armour, by firing at the tracks of the French machines they forced them to turn about. Here [claims Kielmansegg], the lack of fighting spirit of the enemy became abundantly clear to us; German tanks against so weak a defence would certainly not have turned round.

Captain Idée's account of the close of the day's operation strikes a depressingly familiar note:

1900 hours. Petrol is running low. The 'B' tanks have just turned about. They are leaving Lislet. The infantry had not been able to follow them, and what can we do without them? There must be some infiltration at our rear. The enemy platoon commanders have a terribly enterprising air about them.

His company of 'D' tanks then withdrew, though he noted proudly that he had lost only one machine in the fighting. Meanwhile, another column of de Gaulle's tanks had been stopped dead on the River Serre and forced to retreat from Montcornet by German self-propelled guns firing across the river, which de Gaulle with his lack of artillery was unable to engage. On its way back to its starting-point, the 4th Armoured, unprotected by any air cover and desperately short of anti-aircraft guns, was attacked remorselessly by waves of Stukas. Captain Idée recalls the incendiary bullets ricocheting by the thousand off his armour as he thought grimly: 'We shall not get out of this. I am blinded by sweat. I wipe myself with my sleeve – and the medallion of Ste Thérèse which I carry on my wrist smiles at me. I kiss it.' Idée survived, though he lost one more tank from the air attacks. Now the alerted German armour began skirmishing in the rear of de Gaulle's force.

We were lost children twenty miles in advance of the Aisne [says de Gaulle], we had to put an end to a situation that was, to say the least, risky.

What did de Gaulle Achieve?

Thus ended de Gaulle's first action, within the same twenty-four hours that it had begun. Two days later he would attack again, this time due northwards from Laon, and with further reinforcements, but with no greater success. In view of the

fame which his armoured operations of 1940 were later to
receive at the hands of the Gaullist *mythomanes*, thereby
creating the second of the four pillars on which his historical
reputation rests,[7] it may be useful to analyse briefly here just
what was achieved at Montcornet on 17 May. De Gaulle
himself states that his attack had left 'several hundred German dead and plenty of burned-out lorries on the field. We
had taken 130 prisoners. We had lost less than two hundred
men.'[8] But again unsupported by any infantry follow-up and
with no backing on either flank, it could hardly be described
as anything more than an armoured raid of ephemeral consequence. It is doubtful whether it gained any breathing-space
for Touchon's covering force to establish itself, and it certainly did not, as some Gaullist historians would claim, bring
Guderian's advance to a halt. (As has already been seen, an
entirely different explanation lies behind the German halt on
the 17th.) From Kielmansegg's account, it is clear that the
surprise of de Gaulle's attack did create some momentary
alarm within the 1st Panzer, but the German archives disclose
none of the note of real concern to be found in the reports on
the earlier defensive battles around Stonne, or the still greater
anxiety which was to be evoked by the British counter-attack
at Arras on 21–22 May. After the war, Kleist stated revealingly to Liddell Hart:

It did not put us in any such danger as later accounts have suggested. Guderian dealt with it himself without troubling me, and
I only heard of it the day after.

Doubtless Guderian had his own motives for not informing

7. The first pillar, roughly speaking, is constituted by de Gaulle's reputation as an *avant-garde* military thinker of the inter-war period; the second,
by his performance as an armoured commander during the Battle of France;
the third, by his career as leader of the Free French from 1940 onwards; and
the fourth, by his achievements in the post-war world as President of France.

8. It should be noted in passing that de Gaulle's account of the action has
to be drawn entirely from his own memoirs, in so far as he alone of the
French Armoured Division commanders of 1940 steadfastly refused to
testify at any of the sessions of the official Serre Commission investigating
(in 1947) the failure of French armour in 1940.

Kleist, but the fact remains that the German High Command knew nothing of de Gaulle's counter-thrust until the order to resume the advance had already been promulgated. Considering its state of extreme nervousness, if de Gaulle's blow on the southern flank *had* been forceful enough to make itself heard at Rundstedt's H.Q., the reaction of the German High Command would almost certainly have been such as to impose an extension of the 'halt order'. For the relative impact of de Gaulle's attack on the German breakthrough, one is reluctantly reminded of Johnson's dictum: 'A fly, Sir, may sting a stately horse and make him wince; but one is but an insect, and the other is a horse still.' Under the circumstances and with the force available to him, it seems unlikely that de Gaulle could have been expected to inflict *more* than an insect bite,[9] and he certainly led his division at all times with the utmost personal courage. But the facts hardly justify his own elliptic boast made in London on 1 March the following year:

I know of a certain armoured division, improvised in the midst of combat, which inflicted on the Germans exactly the same treatment that their eleven *Panzer-Divisionen* inflicted on us . . .

French Attacks from the North

On paper, the attacks on the northern flank of the 'Bulge' which Georges had decreed for the 17th, to link up with de Gaulle's action, sounded impressive enough. But in fact, for reasons already outlined, they amounted to nothing. The 1st Armoured had ceased to exist – although Georges still remained ignorant of its true state – and what forces might have been available had been deprived with one stroke of their starting-point by Rommel's night advance to Le Cateau and thrown on the defensive. Still dispersed over a wide area behind the Oise, the French tank battalions of General

9. The fact that de Gaulle's counter-attack, feeble as it was, should have gone down in the records as the one bright armoured effort by the French perhaps serves to emphasize how pathetic were those which the other three French armoured divisions had carried out previously.

Bruché's 2nd Armoured Division were given no chance to regroup themselves before Kleist's halt order came into effect, and were simply committed in packets guarding various crossing-points. Shortly after dawn they were attacked by advanced elements of the 2nd Panzer and succeeded temporarily in beating them off from the bridges in the vicinity of Moy, although the 1st Panzer managed to seize the important Oise bridge at Ribemont just as Guderian and Kleist were in the midst of their wrangle. The French 2nd Armoured remained throughout the 17th a division without a commander, with General Bruché frantically roaming around in search of his lost sheep, and himself in turn being vainly sought by General Giraud. Meanwhile Giraud's 9th Motorized Division, part of his former command, also found itself dispersed during the night of the 16th in consequence of Rommel's 'Avesnes Raid'. Arriving on the Oise, it received no order from Giraud to hold the bridges and fell back as soon as the enemy presented itself, abandoning the bridges at Hirson and Guise. With Landrecies and Ribemont already in German hands, this meant in effect that the line of the Oise–Sambre, on the retention of which Georges had placed so much store the previous day, was already compromised. General Didelet's 9th Motorized managed to regroup during the course of the 17th, and was instructed (hopefully) by Giraud to destroy 'the few squadrons of German tanks' (i.e. Rommel's) which were reaching out towards Le Cateau. Giraud then added: 'I order the bridge at Landrecies to be taken by a night attack.' The other division from the 'old' Seventh Army, the 1st D.L.M., much depleted from the fighting around Breda, was also in no position to attack that day. Thus once again what had been designated as a day of counter-attack by the French High Command ended with the forces everywhere (with the exception of de Gaulle) on the defensive.

Rommel Consolidates

One of the legion of prisoners to be taken by Rommel during his 'Avesnes Raid' was Lieutenant Georges Kosak of the 4th

Light Cavalry, who had already had one lucky escape from Rommel's advance guard east of the Meuse on the 11th. Captured at Maroilles, some six miles west of Avesnes, Kosak managed to escape a second time by wading down a stream in water up to his neck. Reaching Wassigny, he was rushed to General Giraud's H.Q. where he was cross-examined. Giraud and his staff appeared astonished to learn from him that the Panzers were already in force at Maroilles. So, for that matter, was Rommel's own corps commander, General Hoth, who that morning, to Rommel's amusement, ordered him to 'continue' his attack *towards* Avesnes. For Rommel, the 17th was spent in consolidating his gains of the previous night and early morning and rounding up prisoners, but it was not devoid of excitement. There was an anxious moment in the early morning when, after halting outside Le Cateau, Rommel discovered that in fact 'only a small part of the Panzer Regiment and part of the Motor-Cycle Battalion' had been following his lead. Displeased, he sent an officer back to the rear at once:

Then I tried myself to drive back to establish contact, but soon came under anti-tank fire from Le Cateau and had to return. Meanwhile, Rothenburg with part of Panzer Battalion Sickenius had been in action with French tanks and anti-tank guns on the hill east of Le Cateau, but had soon disposed of them. I returned to the Panzer Battalion, which had meanwhile formed a hedgehog.

After further elements of the Motor-Cycle Battalion had arrived, Rommel felt that the situation at Le Cateau was secure, and still believing that the rest of the division was somewhere close behind, he hastened off in his signals vehicle, escorted by a single Mark III tank, to bring it forward:

On the way we came across several stranded vehicles belonging to the Motor-cycle Battalion and Panzer Regiment, whose crews told us that it was wise to go carefully in Landrecies as a number of our vehicles had been fired on there by enemy tanks. I then drove on [eastwards] at high speed to Landrecies, where the Panzer III, which was in the lead, lost its way in the town. When at last we reached the road to Avesnes, we saw a German vehicle standing in the road, a hundred yards ahead, where it had been shot up by enemy guns. There must have been a French tank or anti-tank gun somewhere around, but we had no time for a long palaver and so – through! As we drove past, wounded motor-cyclists shouted frantically to us to take them along. I could not help them, unfortunately – there was too much at stake.

Then, near Maroilles where Lieutenant Kosak had fallen into German hands, the escorting Mark III broke down. It could hardly have been a more awkward moment, for

Alongside the road there were French officers and men bivouacked close beside their weapons. But they had apparently not yet recovered from the fright which the German tanks had spread and so we put them on the march so far as we could by shouts and signs from the moving vehicle. There were no German troops to be seen. On we went, at top speed, through Maroilles. East of the village we suddenly discovered a Panzer IV, which had been stranded by mechanical trouble and had its 75 mm. gun in working order. We sighed with relief. A Panzer IV was a strong protection at such a moment.

A short time later Rommel spotted a motorized rifle company on the horizon, travelling fast down the road from Marbaix, midway between Maroilles and Avesnes. Thinking that this meant further detachments would be following in its wake, Rommel pushed on further towards Avesnes, 'but found nothing'. At this moment,

a French car came out of a side-turning from the left and crossed the road close in front of my armoured car. At our shouts it halted and a French officer got out and surrendered. Behind the car there was a whole convoy of lorries approaching in a great cloud of dust. Acting quickly, I had the convoy turned off towards Avesnes. Hanke swung himself up on the first lorry, while I stayed on the crossroad for a while, shouting and signalling to the French troops that they should lay down their arms – the war was over for them. Several of the lorries had machine-guns mounted and manned against air attack. It was impossible to see through the dust how long the convoy was, and so after 10 or 15 vehicles had passed, I put myself at the head of the column and drove on to Avesnes.

Here Rommel at last encountered the lagging elements of the 7th Panzer. One can imagine that they were administered a rigorous dressing-down. It was not until approximately 1500 hours that Rommel's own H.Q. reached Avesnes and unit after unit began to occupy the territory overrun the previous night. In the course of this move, Rommel tells us that his gunners

successfully prevented 48 French tanks [10] from going into action just north of Avesnes. The tanks stood formed up alongside the road, some of them with engines running. Several drivers were taken prisoner still in their tanks. This action saved the 25th Panzer Regiment an attack in the rear by these tanks.

Having arranged the deployment of the 7th Panzer to his satisfaction, Rommel says he then 'took an hour and a half's rest'. But he was soon restored, and (according to one of his tank officers) at Le Cateau that evening, Rommel

gathered together the Panzer commanders and gave orders in his classic manner: 'Our further line of march – Le Cateau–Arras–Amiens–Rouen–Le Havre!' We were somewhat shocked by this unreasonable demand, because we were completely exhausted by the battles of the last days and lack of sleep. It was thus almost welcome to us that the execution of this order initially failed, because our tanks had almost no more petrol.

Between the long narrow tongue formed by Rommel's foray and the hernia formed by Reinhardt's and Guderian's Panzers in the Oise bend, on the 17th German infantry divisions smashed through the Anor and Trélon gaps, thereby breaking the last of the 'Maginot' extension along the Belgian frontier. Guarding the first, the remnants of General Hassler's 22nd Division were scattered into the Forêt de St Michel; at Trélon, it was the 1st North African Division, sent down as reinforcements from the First Army on 15 May, which suffered, and by the following day two of its battalions had been reduced to some 260 men each.

On Reinhardt's front, crossing tracks with the 6th Panzer,

10. Probably belonging to the 1st D.L.M.

the 8th had at last entered the battle and was pushing along the upper Oise south of La Capelle before the halt order came into effect. To the south, tanks of the 6th under Colonel von Ravenstein seized an undestroyed bridge at Origny against weak resistance. That evening its bridgeheads at Hauteville and Neuvillette were sharply attacked by 'B' tanks of the 2nd Armoured. Once again, the official German accounts relate how ineffective the German anti-tank weapons were against the thick French armour; one 'B' tank was apparently hit twenty-five times before it was immobilized by a shot in the tracks. The 6th Panzer War Diary adds scornfully that 'if German crews had been sitting in those superior French tanks', the bridgeheads would have been hard to hold. Finally, by nightfall, they were secured by bringing up those deadly 88-mm. flak guns.

Before the halt order came into effect, Guderian's 1st Panzer had taken Ribemont on the Oise and Crécy-sur-Serre.[11] By nightfall on the 17th, the Germans were in occupation of most of the promontory of land contained within the rivers Serre, Sambre and Oise. From Landrecies southwards to Moy on the Oise, some six miles north of its confluence with the Serre, the various Panzer commanders, under guise of the 'reconnaissance in force' permitted by Kleist, had established a number of important bridgeheads across Georges's river barrier. Guderian for one was poised ready to resume his march towards the Channel the moment Kleist gave the signal.

German Infantry Man the Flanks

Meanwhile the German infantry divisions, whose role in 'picketing' the walls of the 'Bulge' formed so vital a part of the German design, were at last beginning to reach their positions during the day's halt. At Stonne, far back at the root of the breakthrough where the French were still attacking, General Forster's VI Army Corps had arrived, which meant

11. Not to be confused with the Black Prince's Crécy-en-Ponthieu, near Abbeville.

that the motorized divisions of General von Wietersheim's XIV Army Corps could now move forward to hold the flank at Rethel, where de Lattre was fighting resolutely, but defensively. Also at last released from its defensive role at Stonne was Guderian's 10th Panzer, which now hastened forward to rejoin the main armoured phalanx. In the course of the 17th it was already passing Rethel to ·its south. Two days later Wietersheim would once again be 'bumped' westwards by the arrival of the Brandenburgers of III Corps, marching southwestwards from Charleville-Mézières. And so it continued, with the German flank protection divisions always coming up just before the French reinforcements, bombed and strafed on their approach routes and generally disorganized, could possibly insert themselves in the vacuum between the Panzers and the following echelons, as Hitler and Rundstedt had feared they might.

The manning of the flanks of the 'Bulge' (or the 'Panzer Corridor', as it was about to become) was undeniably an organized triumph on the part of Halder and the O.K.H., and its contribution to the overall success of *Sichelschnitt* has perhaps never received sufficient acclaim by historians. But it also reflected a notable triumph of endurance by the ordinary German foot-soldier. During those days, on every highway to the rear of the advancing Panzers the picture is the same: on one side of the road, the endless dejected columns of French captives limping eastwards; on the other, the companies and battalions of young Germans, bare-headed and with sleeves rolled up, as always singing on the march '*Sollte ich einst liegen bleiben auf blutdurchtränktem Feld*' [12] or that old favourite from by-gone times, '*Siegreich wollen wir Frankreich schlagen*' [13] – and marching, marching, marching. For them, there is little motor transport. Supplies and baggage are brought up on horse-drawn drays, but the infantry move on their feet – an illustration of how, behind the thin armoured veneer of the superb élite forces in the Wehrmacht, relatively few in number, in 1940 the great mass of its divisions were

12. 'If I should ever lie dead on a blood-soaked field'.
13. 'Victoriously we'll roll over France.'

probably less well equipped with the panoply of modern war than either the French or British. Up and down the marching columns dart the *Feldwebel,* keeping route discipline, herding on the stragglers, while at their back are the battalion commanders, Rundstedt and ultimately Hitler, all exhorting the hard-pressed infantry to greater efforts. In the heat and dust of that relentlessly sunny May, the strain of the prolonged marches day after day is immense; wrote one German footslogger, 'The first fifteen kilometres a day are a country walk, the next ten an exertion and the remainder – into the evening – sheer torture.'

Slowly the German engineers were getting the captured railway networks running again; by the 17th, there were troop trains already coming up as far as Libramont in the Ardennes; three days later, they had reached Dinant. At the same time, the Luftwaffe was leapfrogging its bases forward so that its squadrons were always there to provide the advancing Panzers the close support they needed. The organization functioned with superlative smoothness; experiences in Spain and Norway paid off. Close up behind the Panzer spearheads came special Luftwaffe task-forces, with the function of putting back into service at top speed all captured enemy airfields. They were followed by signals units that had been training all winter so that they could lay cables from vehicles and motor-cycle sidecars moving at 21 m.p.h., thus providing immediate communications with the Luftwaffe's new forward bases. But the backbone of the whole operation was the workhorse Ju-52, in which spares, fresh crews, bombs and ammunition were flown into airfields within hours of their capture from the Allies. Even fuel came up this way; by siphoning out its own tanks and carrying an additional seven big drums, each Ju-52 could fly in nearly a thousand gallons a trip (a noteworthy feat in those days), enough to keep a Messerschmitt squadron in the air for an hour.

Allied Air Forces Withdraw

On the other side of the lines, the withdrawal of the Allied air forces during the 16th and 17th proceeded with considerably less smoothness. By the 16th, Barratt had been forced to evacuate his A.A.S.F. bases astride the Aisne. Fortunately they had somewhere to go, as – with commendable foresight – some grass landing-fields had been prepared around Troyes during the months of the Phoney War. But they had virtually nothing to go in, despite Barratt's urgent representations of the past winter. As the R.A.F. official history comments:

its transport resources were still hopelessly insufficient for a simultaneous move of the kind now required. Six hundred vehicles short even of its official complement, the Force would have been crippled but for two pieces of good fortune.

The first of these was that the Germans did not try to cross the Aisne southwards, and the second the fact that the A.A.S.F. in some mysterious way managed to 'borrow' three hundred new American lorries from the French, which 'in spite of protestations' they kept until the final evacuation. Airfield accommodation was also aided by the 'rolling-up' of four of the worst hit [14] of Barratt's ten bomber squadrons. Barratt himself moved his H.Q. from its dangerous position in the path of the Panzers, at Chauny west of Laon, back to Coulommiers south of the Marne. On the 17th, the Air Component backing Gort in the north was also forced to withdraw, and Barratt, south of the enemy 'Bulge', henceforth found himself completely out of communication with it. Two days later the Air Component would be removed to England. Needless to say, in the highly charged emotions of the moment, the withdrawal of the R.A.F. bases was widely regarded by the French as a sign that it was 'running away' – a rumour that hardly improved French morale.

At the same time as Barratt, however, General d'Astier was also obliged to move his Z.O.A.N. H.Q. back from Chauny to Chantilly. On the 16th, some ten French units had to withdraw from the Rheims–Mézières–Laon triangle, and the next

14. Two Battle squadrons (Nos. 105 and 208) had only four planes left between them; the two Blenheim squadrons (Nos. 114 and 139) had nine.

day they were followed by a further four *Groupes* of fighters
and one of bombers. It was at this point that the weakness of
the French Air Force supply organization began to show up.
General d'Astier notes that, incredibly enough, it was the responsibility of each *Groupe* to send its own pilots to the rear
to ferry up replacement aircraft; meanwhile, even at the peak
of battle, the depots closed down on Sundays and after hours!
In the chaos that accompanied the withdrawals of the Allied
air forces, air activities were reduced to a minimum – at the
worst possible moment. On the 16th, 250 sorties were flown
by French fighters (compared with 340 on the 14th), of which
only 153 were over the critical fronts; [15] on the 17th, a similar
effort was made, but also dispersed across an area stretching
from Antwerp to the Maginot Line. Only twenty-two victories
were claimed. While the Luftwaffe was launching single
attacks on communications of a hundred bombers at a time,
all that could be scraped up to support de Gaulle's attack towards Montcornet was about twelve Léos escorted by about
thirty fighters. The air supremacy of the enemy was becoming more and more marked. In the French Air Force, units
such as *Groupe* I/54 had been reduced to one serviceable
aircraft. In an encounter over Gembloux in northern Belgium
on the 17th, eleven out of twelve Blenheims from No. 82
Squadron were shot down, the sole survivor being heavily
damaged. The useless, lethal Battles had now been withdrawn
from daylight operations, and used only at night; yet, in the
words of the official historians,

In fact, so many Battle crews now dropped their bombs with no
more precise identifications of their target than that provided by
their watches, that Barratt was compelled to forbid bombing 'on
estimated time of arrival'. After that the phrase ceased to appear
in the pilots' reports. The practice, however, continued.

'Why Don't Our Planes Protect Us?'

So strained had the Allied air resources become that, among

15. The British were largely absent from the battle that day.

their many tasks, they were unable either to come to the aid of the Second Army, which was still being heavily bombed by the Germans by way of breaking up any fresh threat to the flank at Stonne, or to assist the withdrawal of the armies in northern Belgium. This absence of friendly planes above them was having its cumulative effect on the morale of the French ground troops. Their progressive despair is well summed up by an account kept by a French N.C.O., René Balbaud, moving up with reinforcements towards Maubeuge. On first being machine-gunned by enemy aircraft on the 14th, he wondered 'How the devil did these planes escape being pursued by our squadrons? Probably an accident.' The next day, after his unit headquarters had been bombed, he remarked: 'But they can't really know where it is. It's just luck. We don't, in fact, see much of the French planes.' On the 16th, following more bombing, he is questioning: 'Why don't our planes protect us? No one says it aloud any more, but everyone is thinking it.' After a night spent in hastily dug trenches, and still more bombing, he admits: 'This bombing has tired even the toughest. What can one do with light machine-guns against 150 bombers?' Finally he concludes:

Not to see the enemy face to face, to have no means of defence, not to see the shadow of a French or Allied plane during hours of bombing, this was one of the prime reasons for the loss of our faith in victory.

Meanwhile, on the morning of 17 May, there had been some disagreement between Barratt and the French High Command on the employment of the additional R.A.F. fighter squadrons promised by Churchill. Should they be used to escort Allied daylight bombing missions, or to shoot down the German bombers attacking the ground troops? The two tasks were obviously irreconcilable. General Georges pleaded that the troops could not stand up to the devastating combination of tanks and aircraft. Finally it was agreed to reduce still further the modest French daylight bombing effort, so as to concentrate on providing the ground forces with more air cover.

Retreat from Belgium

In northern Belgium the methodical withdrawal of the Allied armies began on the 16th and continued through the 17th. The 3rd and 4th Panzers of General Hoeppner's XVI Corps, still hammering away at the Gembloux Gap, were now transferred from Bock to Rundstedt's Army Group 'A', swinging south-west for Charleroi and Maubeuge to assure the northern flank of the 'Bulge'. Thus all but one of the ten German Panzers were now concentrated in the encircling thrust towards the Channel. But the bulk of Bock's forces continued to push hard behind the retreating Allies, so as to grant them no possibility of disengaging. Although the Germans were nowhere able to breach the Allied positions, over the 16th and 17th the B.E.F. experienced its hardest fighting of the campaign so far. On re-reading his diary the next day, Lieutenant-General Alan Brooke found the following entry:

I was too tired to write last night, and now can barely remember what happened yesterday. The hours are so crowded and follow so fast on each other that life becomes a blur and fails to cut a groove in one's memory.

General Prioux, depressed and annoyed at seeing most of his Cavalry Corps dispersed in small packets to fill the *ad hoc* needs of the First Army, went on the 17th to Army Group H.Q. at Douai to see Billotte, who told him: 'We are on the way to a new Sedan, and more terrible still than that of 1870.' Despite the speed with which Rundstedt's drive in the south was moving, bearing with it the threat of annihilation for Billotte's armies in the north, their withdrawal was proceeding with painful slowness. Nevertheless, on the 17th Billotte proposed that the move back to the Dendre line, scheduled to take place that night, be postponed twenty-four hours. In agreement with the Belgian High Command, Gort managed to dissuade Billotte, and the original plan was adhered to, amid some confusion and costly errors. By nightfall on the 17th, German troops were marching into Louvain and Brussels for the second time in a generation. Falling back with his unit on Maubeuge that day, René Balbaud wrote, baffled:

We don't understand. A liaison officer's driver brings strange news. The Germans, he says, have entered France at Sedan. We have no radio . . . Somehow the old jokes about our coming occupation of Germany have become scarce.

French High Command: a Bogus Calm

Back at La Ferté, General Georges came to the disagreeable conclusion during the morning of the 17th that there was now no good prospect of holding the Panzers on the Oise. Accordingly, he sent out another Special Order, stipulating:

Should No. 1 Army Group be forced to abandon the Sambre–Oise line north of La Fère, it must re-establish itself on the line of the Escaut at Valenciennes, Cambrai, Le Catelet, St. Quentin, St. Simon, the Crozat Canal, and La Fère in conjunction with Touchon's Army Detachment.

To block the approaches to Paris, Georges decided to create a 'new' Seventh Army and introduce it into the hole left by Giraud's vanishing Ninth Army, to link up Touchon's forces with the rest of No. 1 Army Group, along a line south-eastwards from Péronne on the Somme. To command this army he chose General Frère, a corps commander from a quiet sector, whom he had summoned urgently to La Ferté to receive his orders. At Frère's disposal would be some ten divisions, mostly drawn (at last!) from those standing as reinforcements behind the Maginot Line or the Alps, as well as the 3rd Light Division, which had originally been dispatched to Brest for embarkation to Norway, then recalled and placed at the disposal of Governor Hering for the defence of Paris. But on the morning of the 17th, the 'new' Seventh Army comprised only General Frère and two staff officers.

After the panic of the previous day, a kind of bogus calm descended once more on Vincennes as the dawn of the 17th brought realization that the Germans were no nearer to Paris. At 0800 hours, Gamelin received a brief letter from Daladier asking him to produce a report on the conduct of operations and his personal appreciation of the situation. This was very much Gamelin's forte, and with gusto he sat down to devote his day to preparing a copious memorandum – while the battle for France raged less than a hundred miles away. Once again, there would be no intervention in Georges's handling of the battle that day from Gamelin. After completing his paperwork, he visited La Ferté, where 'they seemed to be calm'. At this time, reassuring news was reaching Georges's H.Q. that the Panzers had been halted and were possibly even turning away from Paris. Certainly the threat did not seem as acute as it had on the 16th. Meeting General Frère, Gamelin made vague reference to a major counter-offensive he was contemplating, whereupon (says Gamelin) 'I saw his face light up; he has the soul of a great leader.'

That day Gamelin received a telephone call from Reynaud, insisting that he should draft a new Order of the Day for broadcasting to the forces. 'I showed some coolness towards this,' says Gamelin, 'having addressed two already to the troops.' However, Reynaud's wish prevailed and an Order was prepared ending on a Verdun-like note that, however, somewhat lacked conviction:

. . . Every soldier who might not be able to advance must let himself be killed on the spot rather than abandon the portion of national soil which has been entrusted him.

As always, in the grave moments of our history, the order today is:

Conquer or die. One must conquer.

GAMELIN

Meanwhile, another telegram was sent off to Churchill suggesting that perhaps the German supply columns might be impeded if the R.A.F. were to drop magnetic mines in the Meuse.

In Paris Too

The false sense of relief was general in Paris on the 17th. Senator Bardoux noted that 'this morning, the Press seem to have unwound, slightly. The taxis have received a counter-order.' Later he picked up a dangerously, falsely comforting rumour to the effect that Churchill had promised to send France every single fighter based in England. Paul Baudouin also recorded:

> The military situation appears to be no worse, possibly because the German armoured divisions have had to regroup and revictual. The truth is that everybody is optimistic because Paris is not yet under fire from the German tanks.

This showed some profundity. But, in the evening,

> the news brought by Colonel Villelume was not so good. The German columns are turning away from Paris towards the Channel ports. The enemy advance has become very rapid again, and it seems as if it cannot be stopped.

Recalled to Duty: Weygand and Pétain

Reynaud had now made a firm decision to get rid of Gamelin. But when he broached the subject at a Cabinet meeting that day, Daladier once again sprang to Gamelin's defence, and, just as at the stormy session of 9 May, no conclusion was reached. Reynaud, however, had already taken other steps in utmost secrecy. The following telegram had been dispatched to seventy-three-year-old General Maxime Weygand, commanding the French forces in the Levant:

> The gravity of the military situation on the Western Front is increasing. Please come to Paris without delay. Make suitable arrangements to transfer your functions to the high authority you may choose. Secrecy of your departure is desirable.

Weygand received it in Syria on the 17th, and immediately packed his bags.

Meanwhile, Reynaud had also sent a special envoy by night train to Madrid to bring back the French Ambassador there, another old soldier of renown – Marshal Philippe Pétain.[16]

16. Note that in the Assembly that day Laval was reported as already calling for a Government led by Pétain and Weygand.

Chapter 17

The Dash to the Sea

18-20 May

They never knew. Nobody knew anything. They were evacuating.
There was no way to house them. Every road was blocked. And
still they were evacuating. Somewhere in the north of France a
boot had scattered an ant-hill, and the ants were on the march.
Laboriously. Without panic. Without hope. Without despair. On
the march as if in duty bound.
ANTOINE DE SAINT-EXUPÉRY, *Flight to Arras*

As for the German armoured column so often mentioned during
the last few days . . . this column seems to have gone astray,
inasmuch as it moved straight forward for too long and ultimately
found itself too far away from the mass of the German army.
Daily Telegraph, 18 May

It may be assumed from the reticence of the French communiqués,
and from the sibylline ring of French newspaper comment, that
General Gamelin has his counter-thrust ready.
The Times, 18 May

Every day which elapses without a catastrophe must be regarded
as a day of victory.
L'Epoque, 19 May

The high point of the crisis is over . . . our soldiers are now
accustoming themselves to the German methods of attack and
know how to counter them.
Paris-Soir, 20 May

Panzers Advance Again

As soon as day broke on the 18th, the Panzers resumed their
advance. Over the ensuing three days 'the hideous, fatal
scythes', as Churchill so aptly called them, now encountering
steadily lessening resistance in their path, moved with a new
and terrible impetus. Such was the acceleration of events that
entries in the war diaries on both sides are reduced to a mini-

mum. Bursting out from its bridgeheads on the Oise, Guderian's 2nd Panzer Division rushed forward to grab the big city of St Quentin ten miles to the west by 0800 hours. On its left, the 1st Panzer, once again in the lead, reached Péronne and the important nearby bridges over the Somme at the end of the morning, after sweeping forward some thirty miles. More columns of retreating French troops were taken by surprise and rounded up, including several staffs who, according to Guderian, 'had arrived at Péronne to find out wnat was happening'. Meanwhile the 10th Panzer was drawing level, in order to provide mobile 'blocking detachment' (*Sperrverbände*) along that sensitive, ever-lengthening southern flank. Northwards from Guderian, Reinhardt's 6th Panzer pushed out from its bridgeheads to make the welcome discovery that the 'B' tanks of Bruché's 2nd Armoured, which had given it such a hard battle the previous day, had now 'disappeared' in a west-south-westerly direction. Reinhardt reported back:

The enemy does not represent a very serious danger . . . and his local attacks are nothing more than pin-pricks, deprived of any unified command. There is only one mission for the XLI Army Corps: to push on without bothering about either the right or the left.

Towards the middle of the afternoon, however, the 6th Panzer's 'Combat Group Ravenstein' ran into heavy resistance around Le Catelet. Once more the superiority of the French 'B' tanks made itself felt. For two and a half hours the fighting raged. Finally the last coherent units of the French 2nd Armoured, under the command of Lieutenant-Colonel Golhen, were submerged by sheer weight of numbers. Ravenstein's tanks surged into Le Catelet, where they overran the headquarters of the ill-fated Ninth Army. The entire H.Q., including the Army Chief of Staff, was taken prisoner. Only the Commander himself, General Giraud, who happened to be away at his advanced command post, *behind the Panzers*, managed to escape – temporarily. By nightfall Reinhardt's corps had established itself astride the main road some six miles south of Cambrai. Summing up the day's events (after the war), the reluctant Kleist admitted that Ravenstein's engagement had been 'the only noteworthy incident' to confront the Armoured Group.

On the northern flank of the 'Panzer Corridor', the 5th Panzer (still lagging behind Rommel) captured the fortress of Maubeuge and encountered fierce resistance in the Forest of Mormal from the 1st North African Division and the 1st D.L.M., which had been sent down from Prioux's Cavalry Corps for the abortive French counter-stroke of the 17th. Confused fighting continued in the forest during the next day.

Rommel too fought one brisk engagement that day. Shortly after midnight on the 17th he had received orders to push on towards Cambrai, fifteen miles down a ruler-straight road from Le Cateau. Some six hours later, however, the adjutant of Rothenburg's 25th Panzer Regiment, still stuck out on the tip of the tongue left by Rommel's 'Avesnes Raid', arrived at H.Q. to report that 'a powerful enemy force' had established itself midway between Landrecies and Le Cateau. He had managed to get through under cover of darkness in an armoured car, but Rothenburg's line of communications was now threatened, and he was in urgent need of petrol and ammunition. Rommel promptly set his remaining Panzer battalion in motion towards Le Cateau, 'with orders to push through to the regiment and get the ammunition and petrol up to it.' Needless to say, he then followed closely in its wake. He soon caught up with it, and found its tanks in action against French armour barring their way. Says Rommel:

Violent fighting developed on the road and there was no chance of outflanking the enemy position on either side. Our guns seemed to be completely ineffective against the heavy armour of the French tanks.[1]

After watching the action at close range for some time, he disengaged the tank battalion and struck out with it southwestwards. Again they ran into French armour and slowly fought their way through. It was not until midday that

1. These were presumably Somuas from the 1st D.L.M.

Rommel finally reached Rothenburg, who reported that he had held his ground against heavy enemy tank attacks, but was 'now incapable of further movement'. For some reason, the petrol and ammunition column had not followed Rommel; thus

> I was not at that moment in a position to help him . . . Meanwhile, French heavy artillery had begun to lay down a heavy barrage on our hedgehog position. Their fire was accurate and part of the position had to be vacated.

Despite the evident precariousness of his situation, Rommel – like Reinhardt – appears to have recognized that the French attacks represented desperate 'pin-pricks' rather than any serious, co-ordinated counter-attack. Accordingly, he ordered Rothenburg's Panzer Regiment to 'form up' for the attack on Cambrai even before the arrival of the supply trains was assured. Revictualling of the main body of Rothenburg's regiment did not take place until some hours later, towards the evening. In the meantime a composite battalion of motorized infantry was already streaking out towards Cambrai, led by only a few tanks and two troops of self-propelled flak guns. It was a calculated risk,[2] typical both of Rommel and of the revolutionary dynamism of the Wehrmacht, which had already carried so much before it. According to Rommel:

> the battalion advanced over a broad front and in great depth straight across the fields to the north-west [of Cambrai], throwing

---

2. The episode later caused something of a domestic furore, in itself illustrative of the stresses which the campaign was beginning to impose upon the Germans. Rommel's extremely competent Staff Major, Heidkaemper, complained to him in a memorandum that, as divisional commander, he should have stayed farther to the rear. Furious, Rommel confided to his wife:

'I shall have to have him posted away as soon as I can. This young General Staff Major, scared that something might happen to him and the Staff, stayed some 20 miles behind the front and, of course, lost contact with the fighting troops which I was commanding up near Cambrai. Instead of rushing everything up forward, he went to Corps H.Q., upset the people there and behaved as if the command of the division were no longer secure. And he still believes to this day that he performed a heroic deed.'

A few days later, however, Heidkaemper was forgiven.

up a great cloud of dust as they went. Tanks and A.A. guns scattered fire at intervals into the northern outskirts of Cambrai. The enemy in Cambrai, unable in the dust to see that most of our vehicles were soft-skinned, apparently thought that a large-scale tank attack was approaching the north of the town and offered no resistance.

By nightfall the town was firmly in Rommel's hands. Following along his route later, a German war correspondent described a twelve-mile swathe of wreckage:

tanks, trucks, guns, command vehicles, horses and also human beings – in fact everything that found itself retreating on this road. Most numerous of all are the vehicles, which were surprised in the middle of the road by the advancing Panzers, and which drove into the ditches and were dispatched. It was a picture of horror that no one could ever forget.

Here and there were French tanks with whole slabs of their turrets ripped away, presumably the result of near-hits from Stuka bombs detonating their ammunition, while on one airfield near Cambrai some forty-two French planes were counted, shot up on the ground by the Luftwaffe. The 7th Panzer's losses for the 18th amounted to thirty-five killed, including four officers.

Hitler Comes Round

Back at the German High Command, oblivious of events at the front, the argument of the previous day had meanwhile continued on an even higher note. At 0900 hours, there was a meeting at Hitler's H.Q., attended by Brauchitsch and Halder, at which (according to Halder) there was 'an extremely unpleasant discussion.' Hitler was still displaying 'an incomprehensible anxiety' about that southern flank: 'He rages and bellows that we are on the way to wrecking the whole operation and heading for the danger of a defeat.' Then, around midday, news arrived at O.K.H. that Antwerp, Cambrai [3] and St Quentin had been captured. Apparently without further

3. This was obviously somewhat premature, as Rommel did not in fact take Cambrai till much later in the day.

reference to Hitler, Halder issued orders for the Panzers to 'win the line Cambrai–St Quentin', and push on westwards with reconnaissance forces. At a second meeting with Hitler at 1700 hours, Halder explained the new situation 'and demanded freedom of movement. This was accorded.' (By this time, however, it could do little to alter operations at the front.) Thus, says Halder acidly and with a certain smugness; 'the correct thing finally came to pass; but with ill temper all round and in a form that, seen from the outside, gave the appearance of being a measure concluded by the O.K.W.' – i.e. by Hitler.

The following day the German radio announced the capture of St Quentin and Le Cateau and claimed that since 10 May 110,000 prisoners had been taken – not including the Dutch Army.

Giraud Captured

On the French side, there was no sign of any consolidated effort on the 18th. There was in fact but little available for one. General Georges's armoured divisions had virtually ceased to exist: the 1st had been destroyed by Rommel; the 2nd, split in two, had been blotted out piecemeal; the 3rd, reduced to a fraction of its strength, was still operating feebly and fruitlessly in the Stonne area; while de Gaulle's *ad hoc* 4th Armoured Division, licking its wounds from its blooding on the 17th, was preparing for a second action on the 19th. As for the 6th Army, Touchon's 'blocking' force formed behind the Aisne, it stood guarding the unthreatened road to Paris, but as its function was purely defensive it could in no way influence the tide of the Panzers flooding to the coast. The futility of its role is depicted by Hans Habe, an Austrian refugee who had volunteered for the French Army and whose division had been pushed up into the Le Chesne sector, at the root of the 'Panzer Corridor', just twenty miles south of Sedan. 'Our officers, to be sure, spoke of a counter-offensive', he says, 'but no one believed them.' For three weeks they sat passively on their position:

They said we were going to spend some time in the Forest of Noirval . . . we seriously discussed where we should be sent on furlough after forty days in the front line.

It sounded like the Phoney War all over again.

Of the other hastily constituted 'cork', General Frère's new Seventh Army on Touchon's left, the 23rd and the 3rd Light Division arrived on the morning of the 18th, but could get only as far as the wrong side of the Crozat Canal between Ham and La Fère before having to dig in to meet the rapidly approaching enemy. North from Ham almost as far as Douai, forty miles distant, stretched a gaping hole in which lay the now worthless fragments of the French Ninth Army. Between this hole and the Channel, nothing – except for two British Territorial divisions. These, the 12th and 23rd, had been in France a month; neither fully equipped nor trained, they had been employed on line-of-communications duties between the B.E.F. and its rear bases. Their strength was equivalent to little more than half that of a normal division, and many of their field-pieces could fire only over open sights because of the lack of proper instruments. Now they too, the only units available, were flung into the hole in the dyke. The 23rd was given the task of holding sixteen miles of the Canal du Nord, from Douai and behind Cambrai where Rommel was pressing forward; the remaining fourteen miles, southwards to Péronne, was to be occupied by Frère's troops – who could never arrive in time. The British 12th Division was distributed in small packets guarding the widely separated centres of Abbeville, Amiens, Doullens and Cléry-sur-Somme. It was not much to set in the way of seven highly experienced Panzer divisions. On the evening of the 18th, a light detachment of Guderian's 1st Panzer made their first contact with British troops, the Royal West Kents, just outside Péronne. Temporarily the Germans withdrew into the town, but the British were ordered to fall back on Albert as night fell. Meanwhile, a train carrying a brigade of the 12th Division was hit that afternoon during the first Luftwaffe air raid on Amiens.

The night of 18–19 May witnessed the consummation of the tragedy of the French Ninth Army. Out of contact both with

General Frère and with most of his own troops during the 18th, General Giraud had been ordered by Billotte to pull back his H.Q. to Le Catelet, but, as 'the only way of maintaining morale', he insisted on staying put himself in his command post at Wassigny, fifteen miles to the east, with a minimum of staff. At 1600 hours he decided to withdraw to Main Army H.Q. at Le Catelet, little knowing that it was about to be overrun by the 6th Panzer. Accompanied by two of his officers, he got to within six miles of Le Catelet when he heard reports that German armour was in the neighbourhood. For the next three hours the group worked their way across country by compass. Arriving at the burning town of Le Catelet, Giraud and his group exchanged shots with a Panzer detachment. They then took refuge in a wood, and Giraud ordered his companions to separate. Slowed down by a wound acquired in the First War, Giraud was picked up by a French column, with a gun-carrier in the lead, into which he climbed. More German tanks were encountered, the first being knocked out by Giraud's gun-carrier. Later Giraud was forced to seek refuge in an isolated farmhouse. At 0600 hours on the 19th it was surrounded by German troops, and Giraud was forced to surrender: according to the French, to a group of tanks; according to the War Diary of the 6th Panzer, to the men of one of its field kitchen units. That same day the division also captured General Bruneau, the commander of the annihilated French 1st Armoured Division. Giraud's command had lasted exactly three and a half days. He had done the best he could in an already hopeless situation.

With the disappearance of Giraud, the Ninth Army, which the portly General Corap had taken into battle just nine days earlier, also disappeared. One of Gamelin's liaison officers, returning from the front, reported:

Complete disintegration. Out of 70,000 men and numerous officers, no single unit is commanded, however small . . . at most 10 per cent of the men have kept their rifles . . . Out of the thousands we sifted, it wasn't possible for me to form one company for the defence of the bridge at Compiègne. However, the losses had not seemed to be high. There were no wounded among the thousands of fugitives . . . they don't understand what has happened to them. The sight of an aeroplane induces terror in them. Service troops broke up before the infantry and it was they who spread disorder everywhere.

Covering the B.E.F. sector for the *New York Times*, Drew Middleton encountered some of the tattered remains of the Ninth Army straggling through Amiens:

They were the clerks, the cooks, the anti-aircraft, and the heavy artillery of the Army that had been decisively beaten and routed. As they sat on their horse-drawn carts in their dirty uniforms, they did not look like soldiers but like gypsies.

It was not a heroic epitaph.

Fugitives and Refugees

The spectacle of broken French soldiers who had lost touch with their units, or were simply on the run, was becoming common throughout northern France as the Panzers speeded their advance. One typical Odyssey was that of Jean Muray, a gunner on leave at Signy-le-Petit in the Ardennes when the Germans attacked. He and several hundred others were told to await transportation back to their divison, but it never arrived. On 15 May, fugitives from the battle on the Meuse began to pass through Signy, and the rumble of guns was audible in the distance. Finally a sergeant-major distributed one rifle to every five men and ordered them to try to make for safety in small groups. Still lugging their heavy leave kit with them, Muray's group headed westwards. Soon they joined up with a retreating column commanded by a lieutenant; it was all that was left of an artillery regiment mauled on the Meuse, plus a sprinkling of a few infantrymen. They had already been on the road for three days, rifling what food they could from abandoned villages. During the night of the 16th, says Muray:

We marched incessantly, with a surprising continuity for two long hours, and then the column suddenly stopped. A powerful light was fixed upon us at a turn in the road . . . profiting from

this unhoped-for halt, men sat down on the side of the road. A
quarter of an hour passed. Then an officer came to the back of
the column, to announce that we were prisoners and that we
must throw away our arms. In front of us was a machine-gun
carrier. The commander had already been taken away by the
Germans . . . I threw my rifle away in the ditch. How simple this
had all been . . .!

A short time later, Muray and his companions realized that
the Germans had all departed, taking with them only the commander of the column, so they resumed their flight. Passing
through a wood they heard a fusillade of shots, then came on
some civilian refugees whom stray soldiers were contemplating
shooting as spies. There was also a twenty-year-old infantryman who had been beaten up and was in such a state he
could not explain which unit he came from. He was taken
along with the fugitives, under escort. The next day, on
reaching Brunehamel, strewn with dead horses with horribly
distended stomachs – the remnants of a column shot-up during Reinhardt's break-out from Monthermé – Muray and his
group were surrounded by Germans. Trying to flee across
some fields, he was shot in the thigh and taken prisoner.

The luckier Army fugitives made their way not only as far
as Amiens, where Drew Middleton saw them, but to the very
gates of Georges's G.H.Q. at La Ferté. A 'centre of regroup-
ment' was set up, but there were simply not enough military
policemen to cope with the numbers. Stories circulated of
fugitives, including several officers, being shot at Mont-
Valérien – *pour encourager les autres*. Certainly the demoralization they caused as they straggled through the villages and
towns, throwing away their arms and leaping on to any available horses or cars, was extreme.

But whatever emotions the disbanded military might exact,
the condition of the civilian refugees driven from their homes
by nameless fears was incomparably more pitiful. At one
point it was estimated that as many as 2 million Dutch and
Belgians and nearly 8 million French refugees were on the
roads; some nine-tenths of the population of a city like Lille
departed. During the first five days of the battle, the French

kept the Belgian frontier closed. Then the human flood burst into northern France, resembling more one of the great migrations fleeing before the Barbarian in times of yore than any event hitherto seen in modern Europe. The number plates on the cars of the refugees, telling the truth the censors were trying to hide, in turn set more and more in motion as they realized the speed at which the Barbarian was approaching.

Pierre Mendès-France, back on leave from Syria, watched the fleeing hordes pour through his home town of Louviers (south of Rouen), of which he was mayor:

During the first few days, we had seen high-powered American cars driven by uniformed chauffeurs. Their occupants, elegant women with hands resting on their jewel-cases . . . then came the older, shabbier cars . . . a day or two later came the most extraordinary procession of veteran cars . . . then came the cyclists, mostly carefree young people . . . there were also the pedestrians, sometimes whole families . . . last of all came the heavy waggons of the peasants from Flanders; they advanced slowly, laden with the sick and the aged . . . strings of these waggons stretching for a mile or more would represent the combined evacuation of an entire village, with its mayor, its priest, the old schoolmaster, the policeman. It was a colossal uprooting.

At first there were no soldiers among the refugees; later whole detachments 'were swept into the great river of humanity which flowed towards the west and the south'. Apart from the most common sights of the countless wheezing old crocks, their roofs heaped high with mattresses, and the huge lumbering hay waggons with the family grouped under the shade of an umbrella (they reminded Simone de Beauvoir of 'a tableau staged for a ceremonial procession'), almost everything that could move took part in the exodus. There were racy Paris tourist buses, with '*Paris la Nuit*' still written up on the side, furniture vans and fire-engines, ice-cream carts and hearses, and pathetic pedestrian groups pushing battered prams laden with the precious acquisitions of a lifetime. Those without any transport besieged the railway stations. Around the station at Amiens, Maurois found

a torrent of refugees . . . seated on their bags, on sidewalks, on pavements, they made an immense human carpet worked in dull and lifeless colours. They had emptied the larders of the restaurants, the ovens of bakeries, the shelves of the groceries, as completely as necrophagous insects clean out a corpse.

There were refugees who had made a similar pilgrimage at least once before; to a French officer caught up in the retreat, one old man remarked plaintively: 'I'm eighty-two. Eighty-two, do you hear? I went out in '70. I went out again in '14. I thought all the same they'd let me die at home, in my own house.' On the road, the wretched columns of refugees were alternately bombed and machine-gunned by German planes, and pushed off the road by Allied units trying to get up to the front. As the exodus gathered momentum, the condition of the refugees deteriorated, and their plight did not always bring out the best in human nature. Lieutenant Georges Kosak of the cavalry was involved in a sadly typical scene during the retreat from Charleroi. A huge man

tries to pass four abreast with an enormous chariot which is too heavily laden, drawn by six magnificent animals. He strikes with his whip at everything which is in range. The enormous vehicle, bulging with packs, pitches and jolts, and ends by getting hooked up with and upsetting a wretched cart drawn by a little donkey; then he sends two wheelbarrows and a child's pram into the ditch amidst cries of protest and despair. People leap on to him, but the man is a real colossus, at least six feet tall, with a red face, and wide shoulders. Some women and old men try to master the brute, but he grabs his whip by the small end and strikes with the heavy end against the spines of these wretched people. Why was such a Hercules not at war?

In the end, Kosak drew his pistol on the brute. He blenched, dropped his whip, and abandoning his ponderous vehicle disappeared at top speed.

Initially, the civil population treated the refugees with kindness. In Paris, Clare Boothe noted, 'The stations were full of volunteers. Tireless, white-faced little French Boy Scouts helped them off the trains and stacked their bicycles and bundles in careful confusion.' Then, as the numbers multiplied and locust-like they denuded the countryside of foodstuffs, kindness turned to hostility. By the end of May, says Fabre-Luce, the French 'had expended their pity. They now greeted the new arrivals with closed faces.' Requests for bread, petrol, or even somewhere to sleep, were increasingly met with refusal. In their turn, the refugees often showed undisguised hatred towards the French troops they encountered on the road, which at times seemed to exceed what they felt for the enemy. A German officer overtaking the wretched refugees in their thousands during the rapid advance claimed: 'They don't hate us, and they don't love us. For them everything has come upon them as an act of God; they don't concern themselves with the causes of catastrophe.'

The 'Fifth Column': Myth or Reality?

To the Allied forces the encumberment of the refugees on the roads presented an impossible problem. Reinforcements desperately needed at the front were held up for hours at a time; wounded soldiers died in ambulances trapped in endless traffic blocks. The military police tried to force the refugees to camp in the fields during the day, but gradually they would drift back on to the roads. Short of actually gunning them down, the troops were helpless. Meanwhile the plight of their kinsmen had a markedly depressing effect on the French troops, and even on the British, fighting though they were on foreign soil. 'This continual sight of agonizing humanity drifting aimlessly like frightened cattle becomes one of the worst of daylight nightmares,' General Alan Brooke confided to his diary:

One's mind, short of sleep, is continually racked by the devastating problems of an almost hopeless situation, and on top of it one's eyes rest incessantly on terrified and miserable humanity cluttering the lines of communication on which all hope of possible security rest.

Earlier the B.E.F. had worked out an elaborate scheme for evacuating some 800,000 inhabitants from the industrial areas of northern France, but as Panzers curled around their escape routes westward, Brooke encountered these unhappy evacuees crowding back towards the east:

many women were in the last stages of exhaustion, many of them with their feet tied up with string and brown paper where their shoes had given out . . . I was informed by the Prefect that these were the 800,000 people whom we had evacuated westward. They had run into the German armoured forces, and into rumours of these forces where they did not exist. Like one big wave, the whole of this humanity, short of food and sleep and terrified to the core, was now surging back again and congesting all roads at a moment when mobility was a vital element.

The mass exodus of the refugees proved to be one of Hitler's most successful 'secret weapons' of the French campaign. To what extent was it a diabolically contrived policy of the Germans? What were the motivating causes behind this mass migration? In Allied countries during and after the campaign, it was widely believed that German radio broadcasts and 'Fifth Column' activity had been responsible for getting the refugees in motion, and that the Luftwaffe had then kept them moving by deliberately strafing them. Dr Goebbels's 'terror' propaganda was undoubtedly angled at sowing panic among the civil population, but no one in Germany calculated on the migration attaining such a scale. German troops frequently affected surprise that the neutral Belgians and Dutch whom they were coming to 'protect', as well as the French civil population, should regard them with such fear, but they forgot how deeply engrained were memories of German 'beastliness' in occupied territories during 1914–18. Superimposed on these memories was the impact made by news films of German terror-bombing during the Spanish Civil War and in Poland, not to mention the more recent example of Rotterdam. Many reliable witnesses [4] testify to the fact that refugee columns *were* machine-gunned and bombed in open country. Possibly the strafing could on occasions be attributed to inexperienced pilots genuinely mistaking the refugee columns for troops, and on others to the viciousness of individual Germans. But there is little to suggest that

4. Among those already mentioned in this story, just to name a few, are General Prioux, Drew Middleton of the *New York Times* and Gordon Waterfield of Reuters.

it was Luftwaffe policy. The refugees, however, *expected* to be attacked from the air, and this added to the uncontrollability of their panic. Maurois tells a pathetic story of a Belgian woman who, 'having noticed that our lorries and tanks were camouflaged with branches, had picked up four leaves and spread them neatly in line along the top of her baby-carriage'.

The stories, widespread at the time, of a vast malevolent network of 'Fifth Columnists' mingling with the refugees and transmitting bogus instructions to propagate terror also rarely stand up to examination. Louis de Jong, a Dutchman who made a sober and careful assessment of the whole 'Fifth Column' background, goes so far as to declare of France: 'In not a single concrete case have we any evidence that the flight of the population was furthered by false orders circulated by enemy agents.' It is impossible to avoid the conclusion that many of the allegations in this context stemmed from an instinct on the part of the authorities to explain away their own failings. Often it was the very people who should have attempted to curb the mass panic who led the exodus. Accounts of the scene behind the Ninth Army front frequently refer to gendarmes passing through the villages and telling inhabitants 'You must leave.' At the huge Pechiney works near Compiègne, the managing director (according to Senator Bardoux) took the entire factory into flight with him. In the north, Saint-Exupéry, watching the refugees teem past as if 'a boot had scattered an ant-hill', asked them:

'Who ordered you to evacuate?'
It was always the mayor, or the schoolteacher, or the mayor's clerk. One morning at three the order had run through the village: 'Everybody out!'
They had been expecting this. For two weeks they had seen the passage through their village of refugees who no longer believed in the eternity of their homes . . . The villagers were on the move. And no one so much as knew why.

And so the chain reaction passed from hamlet to village, from town to city. In view of the appalling dislocation the refugee hordes caused the Allied war effort, it was a grave failure

on the part of the French and Belgian Governments not to
have taken drastic measures. They could, for instance, have
stopped the sale of petrol, closed the Belgian frontier completely to civilian traffic, and used the radio to *order* the
population to remain at home, instead of as a means to fill the
ether with tranquillizing dance music and untruthful communiqués.

No less powerful a 'secret weapon' in Hitler's armoury was
the much-vaunted 'Fifth Column' – or the *belief* in its sinister
ubiquity. 'Spy-mania' had gripped France during the darkest
moments of defeat in both 1870 and 1914, but never more
devastatingly than in 1940. Shortly after the collapse of the
Ninth Army, a group of journalists were trying to make their
way out of Cambrai. Percy Philip of the *New York Times*
was dragged out of a train by some soldiers after it had been
bombed, his war correspondent's uniform, blue eyes and fair
hair having given rise to suspicions that he was a German
parachutist. He was about to be shot out of hand when some
gendarmes arrived and confirmed that his papers were in
order. But they would take no responsibility for his safety,
because of the 'dangerous mood' of the crowd. Philip finally
escaped with the aid of three French Army doctors. About
the same time, Maurice Noël of *Le Figaro* was seized while
bicycling through a French village. Like the *tricoteuses* of
the Revolution and the harpies thrown up by the Commune,
women seem to have led the mob, shrieking, 'The newspapers
have told us to kill all parachutists.' An Arab soldier announced to Noël: 'I can tell by your accent that you are not
a Frenchman.' Then the police intervened. On searching him
they found a box of white powder which Noël carried as a
remedy for indigestion. At once the crowd shouted: 'There it
is! There is the explosive!' To demonstrate that it was not,
Noël lit a match, but before he could put it to the bicarbonate
of soda three police officers and a dozen bystanders flung
themselves on him, 'in a desperate attempt to save the police
station from total destruction'. Noël was only saved by the
intervention of a courageous mayor.

Episodes such as these multiplied with the panic that spread before the approaching Panzers. In the early days of the fighting, a demolition squad of the Belgian Chasseurs Ardennais was arrested while retreating over the French frontier, disarmed, and placed in grave danger of being shot. In Paris, Fabre-Luce recorded:

The songstress whom one applauded under a French name is in a concentration camp at the Vel' d'Hiv; she was German. The professional anti-Nazi whose diatribes against Hitler one used to read in the newspapers has been arrested; he was a spy.

There were frequent cases of Allied flyers being manhandled, but particularly dangerous was the predicament of the rounded-up 'aliens' like Arthur Koestler. From cells bursting with 'Fifth Columnists' at Abbeville, twenty-two such prisoners were arbitrarily taken out and shot near the city bandstand. Out of a group of Belgian refugees shot without trial at Abbeville, the Fascist leader, Leon Dégrelle, was one who evidently escaped notice. 'As for the spy problem, we have solved that,' one French soldier declared to an American correspondent. 'We simply shoot all the officers we do not know!' That this was no idle boast is confirmed by Major Barlone, who wrote in his diary for 22 May: 'Our orders are to shoot all spies and strangers who are unable to justify their presence', and later:

Dispenser Charbonnier, at our hospital, had five persons shot, one a beautiful young girl; by showing lights and curtains of different colours, they had guided German aircraft, signalling to them and thereby causing fires in the neighbouring chemical factory.

To what extent *was* there an organized 'Fifth Column' working away ahead of the Panzers? Insisted Major Barlone:

The Fifth Column really does exist; every night blue, green and red lights appear everywhere. A regiment cannot remain two hours in a tiny spot without being invariably bombed with enormous bombs.

At the time, the vast majority of Frenchmen agreed with

him, and certainly the list of deeds attributed to various insidious underground agencies cover an imposing range.[5] The stories started in Poland, where it was rumoured that the *Volksdeutsch* had ambushed Polish troops and insinuated mustard gas into the water the troops washed in, and there were reports of German spy-planes dropping poisoned chocolates and cigarettes.[6] In Holland, the *fact* of the handful of 'Brandenburgers' in purloined Dutch uniforms multiplied a thousand times with incredible rapidity. On 16 May, the distraught Dutch Foreign Minister, van Kleffens, himself assured the Press in Paris that parachutists had descended on his country 'by the thousand', clad in 'French, Belgian and British uniforms, in the cassocks of priests and in the garb of nuns or nurses'. Here began the legend of the 'nuns in hobnailed boots'. In Belgium, the Security Service warned that parachutists in civilian clothes had landed in various places, and it requested that all placards advertising 'Pasha' chicory be removed from telegraph poles, etc., because on their reverse side 'drawings have been found which can give the enemy valuable information'. After the Germans had traversed the Ardennes, word went round in France that they had been able to do so at such speed only because the Fifth Column had prepared secret petrol dumps in advance of the Panzers. The débâcle at Sedan was immediately followed with rumours that the Meuse bridge had been abandoned intact to the enemy through treachery;[7] that officers detailed to blow them up

5. Some French Press reports referred categorically to 100,000 German agents as having been deployed in the Low Countries and Luxembourg alone.

6. The story of the Polish 'poisoned chocolates' is an interesting example of how, in an atmosphere of rampant terror, even the craziest allegations can gain wide credence and reappear in countless different contexts. After the invasion of Holland, orders went out for all 'unexplained' chocolates to be instantly destroyed; in France, Alexander Werth's diary for 21 May reveals this entry:

'Another woman says they dropped poisoned sweets at the Gare d'Austerlitz the other day, and that one child died after eating one.'

7. This assumption was perpetuated by no less a person than Paul Reynaud, who, in his 'the Fatherland is in danger' speech of 21 May, erroneously

had been mysteriously shot down by disguised German agents. Here, and on many subsequent occasions, local disasters were attributed to bogus orders telephoned by 'Fifth Columnists', and purporting to come from some staff officer, or from the mayor of a village ordering its evacuation. General Spears relates a typical story (told him by Saint-Exupéry, 'who said he could vouch for its truth'), of how

a group of the best heavy guns in the French Army, the 155-milli-metre Rimaillots, was halted near Laon when a pale-faced Staff Officer appeared declaring he had come post-haste from Corps H.Q. to say that a German Panzer division was converging on them and would be there in a matter of minutes, and the Corps Commander adjured them as good Frenchmen not to allow their guns to fall into enemy hands. Within a few minutes 35 of these priceless guns had been damaged beyond repair. No such order had been sent from Corps H.Q.

This dissemination of false orders was one of the commonest activities for which the Fifth Column was held responsible, and its consequence was often that orders transmitted by genuine but unidentified officers were simply disobeyed – all adding to the chaos of the French command network.

Another common allegation was that German agents sig-nalled to invisible aircraft, or to other agents. Looking out from Montmartre one night, Peter de Polnay claims 'I saw sig-nals in morse all over Paris. The Fifth Column was at work.' Hans Habe writes of a suspicious sergeant-major who used to disappear mysteriously every evening and whom he claims was later discovered

giving signals to German planes under the pretext of lighting his pipe. According to some he was shot on the spot by an artillery lieutenant . . . I never saw him again.

Only a fraction of these specific allegations of Fifth Column activities has ever been substantiated. None of the works

---

declared that 'Through unbelievable faults, which will be punished, bridges over the Meuse were not destroyed.' (According to General Doumenc, *all* the Meuse bridges were blown.)

written analytically in the aftermath of the war sustain the legend. Brigadier-General Telford Taylor, who served with the U.S. Army Intelligence in Europe during the Second World War and was later Chief Counsel at the Nuremberg Trials, states that 'careful investigations . . . have abundantly proved that in Holland, as in Norway, the reports of subversion and sabotage were uniformly exaggerated and often utterly groundless'. De Jong puts the total number active in Holland at one thousand, including about one or two hundred Dutch citizens. He adds:

it is worthy of note that in not one of the German documents bearing on the preparations for the offensive is there so much as a single passage referring to such a Fifth Column.

As in Holland, in Belgium there was a smattering of 'Rexist' traitors who may have helped the Germans, and de Jong mentions Abwehr agents who were infiltrated into Belgium as 'refugees'; these he also numbers at between one and two hundred. In Luxembourg, as has already been seen, the German 'tourists' who flowed over the frontier before the invasion did help the Panzers by preventing demolitions and disrupting communications. But apart from a few Abwehr sabotage squads attempting to infiltrate with the refugees – and about whose achievements little is known with accuracy – no serious effort seems to have been made by the Germans to operate a Fifth Column in France. De Jong categorically refutes the myth of 'bogus orders': 'Nowhere has it appeared that false instructions were circulated by the Fifth Column.'[8] At least two French generals, Menu and Ruby (who was Huntziger's Chief of Staff), also scoff at the notion of Fifth Columnists being responsible for the chaos and confusion on the Meuse. Says General Menu:

We say emphatically that we do not believe in this argument . . .

8. Walter Schellenberg, the famous S.S. Intelligence operator, boasted that he had been responsible for sending out 'false news items' in French over powerful German transmitters, but he makes no claim, however, of bogus orders having been among his repertoire.

Was he an agent of the Fifth Column, the officer of X Corps, who telephoned at the end of the afternoon of 13 May that the Panzers were at Chaumont and then at Bulson? . . . We say: No.

A Swiss historian, Eddy Bauer, goes as far as to declare: 'One thing is, however, clear: that in France there never was a Fifth Column.'

On the German side, out of the welter of personal memoirs and war narratives published since 1945, the sheer absence of allusion to organized Fifth Column work in France is in itself instructive. The Abwehr, to be sure, had its network of 'V-men', spies and informers inside France, but these seem to have been strictly limited both in numbers and quality, and for the most part established in haste at the beginning of the war. From its own accounts, the Abwehr depended for its actual intelligence more upon the less romantic forms of espionage, such as aerial reconnaissance and signals interception. The fact is that Canaris's Abwehr proved itself, throughout most of the war, to be one of the least effective organs of Hitler's war machine; added to which the German character has seldom shown a marked propensity for the subtler forms of underground warfare.

There were a number of diverse reasons why the bogy of the Fifth Column became magnified out of all proportion in France. There was the impact of Goebbels's propaganda coupled with the boasts of Hitler himself:

In the midst of peace [he had declared – or so the faithful Rauschning told the world], troops will suddenly appear, let us say, in Paris. They will wear French uniforms. They will march through the streets in broad daylight. No one will stop them. Everything has been thought out . . . We shall send them across the border in peace-time. Gradually. No one shall see in them anything but peaceful travellers.

In this form of psychological warfare, the Nazis were aided in the West by its knowledge of the precedent for subversive actions which the Sudeten Czechs created in 1938; but not least they were also succoured by the panic-inspiring utterances of Allied leaders, such as van Kleffens on the hobnailed nuns, or Reynaud declaring that the Meuse bridges had been captured undestroyed, and proclaiming (on 13 May) that all German combatants caught out of uniform would be shot on sight.[9] But, as with the refugee exodus, even the Nazis never quite expected to get such returns with the 'Fifth Column' bogy as they did.

There was also the cumulative effect of Hitler's string of lightning successes, enhanced by rumours of his armoury of 'secret weapons'. Surely, there had to be some simple answer to explain these successes? How had Norway and Denmark succumbed so easily? Had Fort Eben Emael been taken by means of some deadly nerve gas or death-ray? Had the Germans crossed the Meuse with some kind of amphibious tank kept afloat by compressed air? Were they using sixty-ton tanks with such heavy armour that nothing could penetrate? These were all stories that made the rounds. But where else could an explanation be found to all these devastating successes? Could it lie in the Fifth Column? In treason?

'Nous sommes trahis!'

Treason! Faithfully that terrible word reappears on French lips the moment there is a major disaster, revealing one of the less admirable national traits. Gallic pride can never admit that the nation has been collectively at fault; inevitably, she has been betrayed by an individual or a faction. Repeatedly during the Franco-Prussian War, and again in the most adverse moments of 1914–18, the expression 'Nous sommes trahis' – 'We are betrayed' – rings out sombrely across the ramparts. But the soil had never been more fertile for such an interpretation of France's woes than in May 1940. Clare Boothe relates a conversation with an elderly Red Cross nurse, who asked her:

'Madame . . . you are an American?' I said: 'Yes,' and she went

---

9. The Nazis retorted that for every one shot, they would execute ten French prisoners. 'Nice pleasant people the Germans,' commented Shirer. 'That takes us back a thousand or two years.'

on: 'Then you must tell me the truth: *qui nous a trahis*? Who has betrayed us?' . . . That was the first time I heard the word '*trahi*' ('betrayed') in Paris. At first it was no more than a whisper, like the little winds that come in the dim days before the hurricane.

Then, as the débâcle at the front escalated, it became 'a sullen roar'. All the suspicions and mutual mistrusts of Third Republic France bred by Stavisky, the *Croix de Feu* and the Popular Front now surged to the fore. On entering Paris with the victorious German Army at the end of June, William Shirer was assured that there had been 'treachery in the French army from top to bottom – the Fascists at the top, the Communists at the bottom'. The Left accused the *Cagoule* [10] of having conveniently established arms and fuel dumps for the Germans beyond the Meuse; the Right blamed the catastrophe there on Communist influence. The defeatists and 'softs' in the Government were men bought by German money; the right-wing generals were also bought. And so the nightmare fantasy of the pervasive Fifth Column spread, in ever-widening ripples. Even intellectuals such as Simone de Beauvoir seemed prone to believe in it ('Had there been treachery?' was her immediate reaction on hearing of Corap's defeat. 'No other explanation seemed possible.'), and from London General de Gaulle later cloaked it with historical respectability. For those in high places, treachery and the Fifth Column provided an admirably convenient explanation for otherwise inexplicable disasters. Almost on the last page of his copious memoirs, Gamelin appends, and apparently endorses, a report blaming the break-up of the 55th Division at Sedan on those bogus orders put around by 'parachutists', and at the time he made repeated allegations about the responsibility of the Communists. Whatever the Communists may have done to augment demoralization, both inside and outside the French Army, they never, however, constituted a Fifth Column in its conventional sense. It was indeed 'what is false within' that principally betrayed France.

10. The extremist organ of the right-wing 'Leagues', which, just before the war, had perpetrated one or two minor bomb outrages.

Real or imagined, however, the role played by the 'Fifth Column' in the defeat of France should never be underestimated. What it meant to the simple French fighting man was eloquently summed up by René Balbaud, a senior N.C.O.:

We felt ourselves spied on, betrayed on all sides . . . When we learned that the Germans had entered France, our first reaction was to think once more of betrayal. We talked of generals being retired, of the Commander-in-Chief being replaced. And so? But, real or imagined, these betrayals all had the same result: collapse of the Army's morale. We talked of King Leopold . . . And our aircraft? Vanished into dreamland. Betrayed. And our equipment, said to be tip-top, but which we never saw a sign of? Betrayed. Well, why fight? Everyone we trusted had betrayed us.

The French Now Know: the Germans Are Heading for the Channel

18 May was the day that the French High Command at last knew for certain that the Germans were heading for the Channel – that they were swinging away from Paris, while covering their flank defensively along the Aisne. As already noted, on the 16th orders containing the complete itineraries for the Panzers were taken off a badly wounded German colonel near Rethel. There is some mystery about their subsequent fate; the German documents were apparently handed to General Touchon's (Sixth Army) H.Q., but for some reason – perhaps simply the chaos existing in French channels of communication – they were immediately passed on to La Ferté or Vincennes. On the 17th, the *Deuxième Bureau* at Billotte's No. 1 Army Group H.Q. intercepted a German signal in clear which also disclosed that the thrust was aimed at the Channel and not Paris; again, this intelligence does not seem to have made its way promptly back to G.Q.G. That same morning another German staff officer with similarly revealing orders destined for the 1st Panzer was captured by a formation of the French 2nd Armoured Division. The divisional second-in-command, Colonel Perré, set off towards Compiègne to take them to the Ninth Army Commander.

General Giraud. But Giraud could not be traced. Colonel Perré also seems not to have thought about transmitting this valuable booty directly to G.H.Q., reasoning that it would arrive too late to be of any use. Thus it was not until well on into the 18th that the sum of all this intelligence reached Georges or Gamelin, confirming the rumours of the previous day. By this time even the Germans were no longer making great efforts to conceal the true objective of *Sichelschnitt*. Shirer spotted an item in a Berlin newspaper hinting

that the German armies now converging on Paris from the north-east may not try to take Paris immediately, as they did in 1914, but strike north-west for the Channel ports in an effort to cut off England from France.

Gamelin Still Hesitates and Pétain Arrives

The rumours that Hitler was turning away towards the Channel ports had provoked a fleeting, ill-founded elation among Parisians. Shares on the Bourse fluttered briefly upwards. 'Maybe he's going to England first' were the whispers overheard by Clare Boothe. Gamelin himself may not have subscribed to this view, but there was no doubt that on the 18th he struck his staff as being 'in better form than on the day before. Visibly the Commander-in-Chief had pulled himself together.' In the mind of the faithful staff officer of Joffre, the man who had actually prepared the orders preluding the immortal victory of the Marne in 1914, a chord was struck. By swinging away from Paris and presenting such a long, open flank, were the Germans about to commit the same error as Kluck in 1914? Thoughts parallel to those which had plagued the minds of Hitler and Rundstedt now began to preoccupy Gamelin. At Vincennes it was sensed that the Generalissimo was about to produce his master-stroke. That afternoon (the 18th) aerial reconnaissance reported a 'complete vacuum' in the Laon–Montcornet area immediately behind the cutting tip of the Panzers. But still Gamelin hesitated.

Visiting La Ferté that morning, Gamelin affects to have found none of the newly regained composure which his own staff were detecting in him. The atmosphere at Les Bondons struck his tidy mind as 'extremely detrimental to regular work'. In the office of Georges's Chief of Staff, General Roton, 'utter disorder' reigned, with staff officers continually coming and going through it. The situation was hardly better in the room where Georges himself presided, and he betrayed to Gamelin 'incontestable signs of lassitude'. The monastic Generalissimo wondered how his subordinate could possibly 'dominate events' in such an atmosphere of chaos where no reflection was possible. He voiced his misgivings privately to General Doumenc. After making conventional noises of loyalty to Georges, Doumenc expressed agreement and said he thought the time was approaching when Gamelin should take direction of the battle into his own hands. Gamelin replied, 'Of course, let me know the right moment' – as if this had not long since passed him by. After a further, inconclusive discussion with Georges about restoring the 'continuity of the front', Gamelin was warned that Reynaud and Daladier were coming to visit him at 1500 hours that afternoon, and he sped back to Vincennes.

At the appointed hour, Daladier arrived, but no Reynaud. On telephoning his office, Gamelin learned that Reynaud – accompanied by Marshal Pétain, newly returned from Madrid – had left a good hour earlier. Consternation! Had the Premier been involved in an accident? Finally, word came through ('brusquely', says Gamelin) that Reynaud and Pétain had gone to see Georges first. Gamelin and Daladier were to await their arrival. The two passed the time in 'affectionate and confident conversation', with Daladier (in the words of Gamelin) displaying 'the soul of a good Frenchman'. It was, he admitted, 'the first time for ten days that I had remained without any precise occupation' – which seems a curious admission at such a moment in Allied fortunes.

At 1820 hours, after more than three hours had passed in chat between Gamelin and Daladier, Reynaud arrived with Pétain. According to Reynaud's account, on the earlier visit to La Ferté, General Georges had explained the situation to us on a large map, which, with his hand covered by a grey glove, he pulled up and down on its roller. We saw on the map the positions of the Armies, and, prominently marked, those of the ten Panzer divisions. Two or three times he broke off his account to tell us, his brown eyes brooding sorrowfully on us: 'It is a difficult situation.'

At Vincennes, Gamelin treated Reynaud and Pétain to a similar run-down on the situation. When the eighty-four-year-old Marshal climbed back into his car, he clasped Gamelin's hand warmly and murmured, 'I pity you with all my heart.' As Reynaud had made no reference to his intentions for the Generalissimo's future, the full meaning of Pétain's expression of sympathy was not apparent until the following day. Gamelin then returned to his office to sign the wordy report which he had been preparing at Daladier's behest. He had still made no move to assume control of the battle.

For the French High Command, the 18th ended with extremely grave news reaching Georges's G.H.Q. from General Billotte. 'We had hoped to be able to contain them today, but we were twenty-four hours too late,' said Billotte. Seeing little prospect now of sealing the hole which gaped between the French First Army and General Frère's *ad hoc* Seventh Army, Billotte added ominously: 'One must reflect upon the conduct to adopt in the event that our forces should find themselves separated.' In his final order for the day, Georges spoke hopelessly of the importance of 'envisaging the prolongation of our barrage along the Somme, from Péronne to the sea' – a measure which in itself certainly 'envisaged' no means of halting the Panzers before the Channel. Finally, on the following day, de Gaulle's 4th Armoured was to make another jab into the southern flank of the Panzers along the axis Laon–Crécy-sur-Serre.

On the political scene that Saturday, Reynaud invited Pétain to join his Government as Deputy Premier. Pétain accepted. According to Reynaud, when he told the Senate that the 'Victor of Verdun' was now at his side, there were widespread shouts of 'At last!' Spears, who had not seen him since the First War, describes the eighty-four-year-old Marshal shortly after his return to France as being

> still erect but so very much older, and in plain clothes which emphasized the break with the past . . . but he seemed dead, in the sense that a figure that gives no impression of being alive can be said to be dead . . . when occasionally I looked towards him he seemed not to have heard what was being said.

From now on this venerable but pessimistic old soldier, tragically recalled from the glorious past, was to play a role of increasing weight in France's fate.

Upon Pétain's acceptance Reynaud now proceeded to the first stage of reshaping his Cabinet. Daladier at last was ousted from the Ministry of National Defence, which Reynaud took over himself, handing to Daladier the Quai d'Orsay as a sop. The tough Georges Mandel, Clemenceau's old hatchet man, was transferred from the Colonies to the Interior, a key post when civilian morale was gravely threatened. But to take the lead part in his reshuffle, Reynaud was still awaiting the arrival of General Weygand.

19 May: de Gaulle's Second Chance

In his orders for 19 May, Guderian stated: 'The Commander-in-Chief of the Army [Brauchitsch] has explicitly approved further advances by Group Kleist.' His XIX Panzer Corps was to seize bridgeheads over the Canal du Nord to the west; at the same time, looking ahead to the second phase of the Battle of France, it was to establish bridgeheads over the Somme between Ham and Péronne, in order to make ready 'to swing south-west when the time comes'. The progress registered on the 19th would, as it happened, be less spectacular than that of the previous day. The divisions' technical priorities enforced a day essentially of badly needed consolidation and regrouping in preparation for the final lunge to the coast.

Despite all the good omens, the 19th began on an anxious note for Guderian. At 0135, XIX Panzer Corps H.Q. received a radio message reporting that the fuel depot at Hirson had been 'burnt out'. This was extremely serious news, as it was from here that Guderian's tanks were to be refuelled that night. Consequently, they would have no more than *one day's ration of fuel*. Later in the morning the 10th Panzer reported that its attack against Ham had failed. Then Luftwaffe reconnaissance revealed the massing of some hundred tanks south of Crécy-sur-Serre. This was accompanied by a report that one of the 'blocking detachments' had been overwhelmed by an enemy attack on the south flank.

De Gaulle had begun to move forward at dawn. The objective of his second attack was to strike across the Serre bridges near Crécy and then cut Guderian's line of advance through La Fère. He had received further reinforcements in the form of an artillery regiment of '75s, the famous cannon of the First War, and two squadrons of Somua tanks, bringing his armour to a total of some 150 tanks. Of these, however, only thirty were 'B' tanks, forty Somuas or D.2s, the remainder obsolete R.35s. The Somua crews consisted of a commander/gunner who had never fired the gun and a driver who had done no more than four hours' driving. With only a single battalion of infantry he was once again poorly supported.

At first de Gaulle seemed to be advancing into empty space. After overwhelming or dispersing light enemy forces, he reached the Serre within four hours. Here his tanks came up against heavy opposition. Guderian had reacted with his customary speed. 'Crécy is a fortress of anti-tank guns, an enormous ambush,' declared Captain Idée. 'The R.35s came to a halt and withdrew in a shambles. Already several are burning.' His D.2s now moved up. Just before the bridge over the Serre the first tank blew up on a mine, the second had a track blown off. In third position, Idée's own tank, the *Rocroi*, came under violent fire:

A formidable shock. The turret shakes, struck at the base. The traversing gear is jammed. The turret won't move any more. I struggle furiously with it, strike the gear, and just at the moment when I am despairing, unjam it. The turret moves. I fire. Bang! A heavy shell strikes obliquely at the top of my turret, which glows red.

As on the 17th, the infantry never materialized; so – having lost two tanks – Idée decided to withdraw. In the two days' fighting, his company of fourteen tanks had lost six destroyed and two 'missing'.

De Gaulle's misfortunes on the 19th were compounded by a piece of bad liaison that was typical of the inefficient communications existing between the French ground and air forces. To ward off the shattering Stuka attacks that had disrupted de Gaulle's first attack, General d'Astier had been called upon to provide the most powerful fighter cover that his reduced circumstances would allow. But the time of the attack was changed without d'Astier being informed. The Stukas once again descended on de Gaulle's column out of an empty sky. Answering a desperate plea for help, d'Astier ordered up every fighter patrol already in the air at the time. But by the time they arrived over the Serre it was too late; de Gaulle's force had been badly knocked about. Early that afternoon he received an order from Georges, instructing him 'not to commit himself too deeply, as the division was needed on another front'. Under repeated Stuka bombing, de Gaulle once more pulled his forces back in good order, behind the Aisne. In most bitter frustration, he says:

I could not help imagining what the mechanized army of which I had so long dreamed could have done. If it had been there that day, to debouch suddenly in the direction of Guise, the advance of the Panzer divisions would have been halted instantly, serious confusion caused in their rear, and the northern group of armies enabled to join up once more with those of the centre and the east.

19 May: the Germans Consolidate

From Guderian's point of view, the various local difficulties besetting him that morning, of which de Gaulle was one, imposed three choices of action: he could halt his westerly advance and establish a defensive face towards the south; counter-attack southwards with the main weight of his forces; or change nothing in his orders and continue the advance as before. Typically he chose the third possibility, leaving it to the 10th Panzer alone to block de Gaulle's attack. Once again events proved his decision right.[11] Meanwhile, as de Gaulle's attack was in progress, a corrective radio signal resolved Guderian's major anxiety; the report about the Hirson fuel depot should have read 'ready for distribution', instead of 'burnt out'! [12] The Panzers could forge on.

During the afternoon, Guderian's 1st and 2nd Panzers crossed the Canal du Nord and reached the old Somme battle-field of the First War, an event giving rise to strong emotions among the many veterans who had sat there for months on end in 1916, under gruelling attack by the British and French. There were now warnings from both men and machines that seemed to make a brief pause imperative; when the comman-der of his prize 1st Panzer Brigade, Colonel Nedtwig, col-lapsed from sheer exhaustion,[13] even Guderian had to take note. That night the main weight of his corps halted on the line Cambrai–Péronne–Ham.

To Guderian's immediate north, Reinhardt's Panzers mopped up French resistance around Le Catelet by the middle of the day after more brisk fighting. By nightfall they too stood shoulder to shoulder with Guderian in a consolidated position west of the Canal du Nord defence line. For Rommel the fast going of the previous days came to an end with the

11. Guderian's cool-headedness is all the more remarkable in that, through an error, he seems at the time to have exaggerated de Gaulle's threat. Al-though in his memoirs (*Panzer Leader*) he describes it as 'slight', he goes on to say:

'During the next few days de Gaulle stayed with us and on the 19th a few of his tanks succeeded in penetrating to within a mile of my advanced H.Q. in Holnon wood. The headquarters had only some 20-mm. anti-aircraft guns for protection, and I passed a few uncomfortable hours until at last the threatening visitors moved off in another direction.'

The fact was that, after the 19th de Gaulle disengaged to the south and did not attack again until the 27th. Furthermore, Holnon, where Guderian came in jeopardy, lies nearly twenty-five miles north-west (beyond St Quentin) from the farthest point reached by de Gaulle on the 19th. It seems more likely that the infiltrating tanks belonged to units of the dispersed French Second Armoured.

12. *Ausgabebereit* instead of *ausgebrannt*.

13. He was replaced by the indestructible Balck.

capture of Cambrai. He too was forced on the 19th to pause in order to regroup and give his exhausted crews some sleep. By nightfall he had pushed forward a bare six miles to Marquion, where the Canal du Nord crosses the Arras road. Visited by his corps commander, General Hoth, during the afternoon, the impatient Rommel asked to be allowed to mount another night attack so as to seize the vital high ground south-east of Arras, some twenty miles on, by daybreak on the 20th. Hoth demurred, on the grounds that the men could not take it. 'The troops have been twenty hours in the same place,' countered Rommel, 'and a night attack during moonlight will result in fewer losses.' Hoth yielded, and Rommel was allowed to prepare to move towards Arras shortly after midnight. On Rommel's right flank, the 5th Panzer was again sharply engaged in the Forest of Mormal with elements of the 1st D.L.M. and the 1st North African Division. But pushing on towards Solesmes, its advanced units also began to draw level with Rommel. Meanwhile, still further north the 3rd and 4th Panzers of Hoeppner's XVI Corps, now transferred to Rundstedt, were battering back the southern anchor of Blanchard's First Army in the direction of Valenciennes. Thus by the end of the 19th, after their various itineraries, all but one of Hitler's ten Panzer divisions [14] were now lined up as a dense phalanx of armour in what has been called the 'rendezvous of 19 May'. Here, just fifty miles from the sea, they stood poised for the final act of *Sichelschnitt*.

The Maginot Line: the Forgotten Army

Down in the Maginot Line, life during the previous eight days of the battle had continued very much as in the months of the Phoney War. The desperate struggle to the north left it untouched. Inside its steel and concrete turrets, observers peered out, waiting for an enemy who never came. There was an occasional long-range artillery duel, but that was about all. Then, on the 18th, General von Witzleben's First Army suddenly attacked a small fort, curiously enough called La

14. The 9th was still deployed against Antwerp.

Ferté. It lay in an awkward defensive position, and after a savage struggle La Ferté fell on the 19th. This first capture of a Maginot Line fortress was greeted with maximum acclaim by the German radio, though its strategic significance was negligible. The action, however, was not just braggadocio. It was carefully and deliberately timed, for the French High Command had at long last given the order to withdraw the hitherto immobilized 'interval troops' as reinforcements for the battle in the north. Here, then, was a warning not to go too far in denuding the Maginot Line – one which, as the Germans expected, the French High Command would be bound to heed; by the end of May it was actually *sending back* precious tanks to help guard the forts.

The Luftwaffe Ascendant

In the air, the 18th and 19th witnessed a further marked deterioration of Allied strength.[15] By the 19th, General d'Astier's Z.O.A.N. could count no more than 170 serviceable fighters, and because of damage to the telephone lines, it was becoming increasingly difficult for his group commanders to bring their planes into action. There were still six *groupements* of bombers left, but two consisted of Amiots and Blochs, which could only be used by night; of the three equipped with Léos and Bréguets, two were on the move, while the third was caught (on the 19th) by the Luftwaffe just as it was about to take off on a mission and lost two-thirds of its machines; the sixth, consisting of newly arrived American Glenn Martins, was waiting to have the bomb-release mechanisms fixed. As far as the British were concerned, on the 18th Barratt's Advanced Air Striking Force was still virtually out of action on account of its move. The following day telephone contact between Barratt and the Air Component with the B.E.F. had been severed by the German advance, and Lord Gort agreed with the Air Ministry that it should now be withdrawn to operate from

15. Although, on the 18th, *L'Époque* felt inspired to claim: 'The German Air Force loses some of its advantage every day. Nowhere does it now have mastery of the air.'

southern England. Within two days nothing but a few Lysander liaison planes remained in France. The evacuation of the Air Component was, alas, carried out in such haste that most of its ground equipment and stores had to be abandoned to the enemy. A total of 261 Hurricanes had flown with the Component; 75 had been destroyed, but only 66 of the remainder returned to England. The balance of 120 consisted of damaged machines that also had to be abandoned in France. Thus in ten days' operations over northern France alone, Britain had lost 195 Hurricanes, roughly a quarter of her entire strength of modern fighters. Henceforth based on Kent and under control of the Air Ministry, the Component was now too far removed from the battle to provide effective collaboration with the B.E.F., and its activities were largely limited to night operations of doubtful value.

The R.A.F. continued to pound the Ruhr by night with its heavy and medium bombers, and continued to deceive both itself, the Government and the public as to the results. *L'Œuvre* spoke on 19 May of 'catastrophic effects' reported by eye-witnesses; the disorganization following the raids was claimed to have 'almost crippled the movement of reinforcements to the front over the past twenty-four hours'. In his diary General Ironside quoted a pilot who 'said that over Hamburg he could read a book at 10,000 feet. They also touched up the Ruhr again, finding very little A.A. defence guns', a statement that perhaps reveals just how lightly the Germans were taking these raids. Passing Cologne aerodrome on the 19th, William Shirer noted:

It was packed with planes, but the hangars had not been touched. Beautifully camouflaged with netting they were. Obviously these night attacks of the British have failed not only to put the Ruhr out of commission, but even to damage the German flying fields. A phony sort of war the Allies still seem to be fighting.

Meanwhile, Churchill was grumbling to his Chief of the Air Staff at the Allied impotence to strike at the Panzers which were doing all the damage: 'Is there no possibility of finding out where a column of enemy armoured vehicles harbours during the dark hours, and then bombing?' On the evening of the 19th, twenty Chance-Vought dive-bombers belonging to the French Navy and based on Boulogne and Berck were thrown in for the first time to help the forces desperately engaged in the Forest of Mormal, but ten of them were shot down, the remainder badly holed, and the effect on the Panzers apparently was minimal. With the steady extension of the 'Panzer Corridor' and the decreasing number of Allied planes available, it was becoming more and more difficult to pinpoint the spread-out enemy columns. Early on 19 May, reconnaissance spotted a large armoured force (presumably Rommel's) moving in the direction of Arras, but no bombers were on hand at the time, and the Panzers were allowed to move on unmolested. The next morning two R.A.F. bomber squadrons were dispatched from England to attack Panzer columns spotted at 0830. The first reached the target area at 1130 and bombed a column moving westwards; shortly afterwards the second could find nothing at the same point. Both had in fact arrived too late to attack the initially designated target, an advanced unit of the 6th Panzer, which was by then well dispersed.

On the German side, the Luftwaffe was now well established in Belgian airfields close behind the front, so that its Stukas were able to fly as many as six or seven missions a day, thereby multiplying its already imposing numerical superiority. Apart from this never-failing tactical close support work, the medium bombers of the Luftwaffe were concentrating effectively on smashing up the French railway system by which Georges was trying to bring up reinforcements to the Aisne and the Somme. At midday on the 19th, a powerful force of German bombers struck savagely at Amiens, 'softening up' for the next day's Panzer attack. The city appears to have been all but undefended, whether by fighters or anti-aircraft guns. Four-fifths of the population had already left the threatened city, but casualties were heavy; fortunately twenty ambulances manned by volunteers of the American Field Service happened to be passing through the city and were able to help with the wounded.

Retreat from Northern Belgium

In northern Belgium, the Allies completed their withdrawal behind the Escaut Line on the 19th, with the Belgian Army in position from Terneuzen on the coast down to Oudenaarde. Below them, the B.E.F. occupied a strong position on the Escaut as far as Maulde on the French frontier. The 5th Division had been pulled back to Seclin, just south of Lille, as Army reserve, and on the night of the 19th Gort ordered the 50th Division, minus one brigade group, to concentrate north of Arras on the Vimy Ridge of First War fame. Here it was 'to prepare for offensive action'. South of the B.E.F., Blanchard's First Army had the task of holding a 'mole' anchored on Condé-sur-l'Escaut, Valenciennes and Bouchain, around the end of which the irresistible flood of the Panzers swirled westwards. Bombed repeatedly during the last stage of its withdrawal, the B.E.F. was extremely tired. Lieutenant Miles Fitzalan-Howard, with Montgomery's 3rd Division, recorded in his diary what was a typical experience for those days: 'In five nights I have had eight hours sleep; 18th. up all night; 19th, up till 3, sleep till 7; 20th, up till 3, sleep till 7; 21st up; 22nd in bed.' Nevertheless, the B.E.F. was in much better shape than Blanchard's forces, which had consistently borne the brunt of the fighting in the north since the first encounter with the enemy, and had suffered higher casualties than either the British or the Belgians.

Retiring across the French frontier near Condé, Major Barlone was one of those who experienced a momentary sense of relief:

There at least, behind our defences, we can breathe. But refugees, fleeing towards the interior of France, tell us that our pill-boxes are unoccupied. During a long halt, giving my mare a chance to rest, I gallop forward on another horse and am astonished to find our blockhouses empty.

The staff of Barlone's divisional H.Q. (the 2nd North African) billeted itself in the town of St Amand, where fewer than fifty civilians remained. The troops, according to Barlone, were permitted to take from the houses anything they need, for we know that the Germans will be here within a few days. The officers can dip into the cellars of the Hôtel de Paris, on the Place du Beffroi, to their heart's content; a sentry stands at the door and only officers are allowed to enter.

Despite the faulty discipline implicit in this surprising admission of legalized looting by 'officers' only, Barlone states that the morale of his men was good; they were 'bewildered rather than discouraged'.

The same was also true of Prioux's Cavalry Corps, despite the repeated drubbing it had taken from the Panzers. But the troops were dead tired, and it required all the energy of the officers to prevent them from sleeping at their posts. The 1st D.L.M. was still fighting bravely far away in the Forest of Mormal, though nominally it was supposed to be under Prioux's control; many of his other tank companies had been farmed out in supporting roles to other divisional commanders who, despite Billotte's strict orders to the contrary, were now proving reluctant to return them to their rightful master. Therefore, with his Cavalry Corps thus debilitated, Prioux was surprised to receive an order from Georges at midnight on the 18th, instructing him to 'attack tomorrow, 19 May, in the direction Cambrai–St Quentin with a view to breaking up the armoured elements operating there' – i.e. the bulk of nine German Panzer divisions. It was one more revelation of just how hopelessly out of touch the French High Command was with realities at the front. Prioux at once sought out Billotte to explain precisely why he would be unable to comply.

Are the British Leaving?

Early in the afternoon of 19 May, an important telephone conversation took place between Generals Georges and Billotte, while Georges was in session with Gamelin and a British delegation headed by General Dill. In the course of it, Billotte remarked, according to General Roton, 'I learn that the British are said to have decided to fall back on Calais in three or four stages, and to evacuate.' The supposition was erroneous, based on a misunderstanding between Billotte's and Gort's staffs; nevertheless it illustrated the direction in which Gort's thoughts were beginning to run. The various factors governing the British decision to evacuate the B.E.F. concern this story only marginally. They require mention, however, so far as they touch upon the last Allied counter-stroke that had any prospect of slicing through the Panzer Corridor and releasing the armies about to be encircled in the north.

During his visit to Paris on the 16th, Churchill had miraculously managed to boost the sagging sipirits of Reynaud and Daladier. But he and his entourage had themselves returned to London profoundly alarmed by what they had seen and learned, more so than they revealed to their ally. The very next day Churchill wrote a minute to Neville Chamberlain, as Lord President of the Council, asking him to examine in general terms 'the problems which would arise if it were necessary to withdraw the B.E.F. from France'.

At this moment, Ironside was revealing in his diary that he for one no longer had much confidence in the ability of the French to halt the Germans:

We have lived in a fool's paradise. Largely depending upon the strength of the French Army. And this Army has crashed or very nearly crashed . . . At the moment it looks like the greatest military disaster in all history.

If the German advance continued, the B.E.F.'s line of communications through Amiens would be threatened, and in this eventuality Britain would be forced to try 'to evacuate the B.E.F. from Dunkirk, Calais and Boulogne'. It was, thought Ironside, 'an impossible proposition'. Nevertheless, that day he suggested to the Admiralty that they begin collecting all small vessels.

Then, on the night of the 18th–19th, there was a critical meeting betwen Lord Gort and General Billotte. At about midnight the French Army Group commander drove to Gort's command post at Wahagnies. For the past week, the B.E.F. had received no orders from Billotte; it was the first time that he had come to confer with Gort and report on the full extent of the crisis. Hitherto the French had tended to regard both Gort and Britain's small contribution to the land-war effort with a certain amount of contempt. Now suddenly, in this moment of crisis, it was apparent that France would have to rely upon the 'amateur' but relatively intact B.E.F. to play a key role in future strategy, and accordingly its commander assumed a new importance in French eyes. Gort's experiences over the past week had already greatly reduced his confidence in the judgement of the French High Command, and what Billotte now told him only confirmed his gloom. According to Gort, Billotte described:

the measures which were being taken to restore the situation on the front of the French Ninth Army, though clearly he had little hope that they would be effective. Reports from the liaison officers with French formations were likewise not encouraging: in particular I was unable to verify that the French had enough reserves at their disposal south of the gap to enable them to stage counter-attacks sufficiently strong to warrant the expectation that the gap would be closed.

What if the gap could not be closed? Then nine German Panzer divisions would be curling round the unprotected rear of Gort's nine divisions. Two alternatives presented themselves to Gort: he must withdraw either to the line of the Somme or to the Channel coast. The first had the obvious advantages that the B.E.F. would be falling back on its lines of communication, and would keep in touch with the French; on the other hand, it meant that the Belgian Army would be forced to relinquish Belgian soil or its allies – and, should evacuation of the B.E.F. finally become inevitable, it would obviously be that much more difficult if the Channel ports were abandoned. But if the B.E.F. *did* fall back on the Channel, this

would involve the departure of the B.E.F. from the theatre of war at a time when the French might need all the support which Britain could give them. It involved the virtual certainty that even if the excellent port facilities at Dunkirk continued to be available.

it would be necessary to abandon all the heavier guns and much of the vehicles and equipment.

Henceforth Gort would be torn between a desire to aid the French loyally in their attempts to counter-attack, and concern at not letting his nine divisions, the cream of the British Army, be cut off from the sea. However, what Billotte had revealed to him of his prospects for 'closing the gap' were so discouraging that, on the 19th, Gort warned the War Office that it might have to consider evacuating the B.E.F. 'I realized that this course was in theory a last alternative,' said Gort. 'Nevertheless, I felt that in the circumstances there might be no other course open to me.' That same day the War Office and the Admiralty began joint discussions, under the code name of 'Dynamo', on the 'possible but unlikely evacuation of a very large force in hazardous circumstances'.

Exit Gamelin

19 May was a Sunday. Although the French Government placed its hope for a miracle that day in two earthly champions – de Gaulle who was atacking on the Serre, and Weygand momently expected from Syria – the soul of France turned instinctively to Notre-Dame, as it had done when the Governor of Paris had invoked the aid of its patron Sainte Geneviève at the worst moment of the Siege in 1870: as it had done during countless other crises in the long course of French history. That day there was a moving service of intercession attended at Notre-Dame by the entire Government and representatives from the whole of French public life. Outside on the parvis was also gathered a large congregation 'that aroused the emotions by its piety and unanimity', said Senator Bardoux. There was 'a splendid evocation of the saints of France, while the relics of Sainte Geneviève, of St Louis were paraded . . . each of the saints was invoked and the crowd responded in chorus. Bullitt [the American Ambassador], who was in the front pew, was unable to hide his tears.'

There would be no divine intervention that day on behalf of General Gamelin. It was to be 'the last day of my military existence', although he had no inkling of this as it began with a telephone call from General Doumenc, at about 0500 hours. 'I thought it was pointless waking you earlier', said Doumenc, 'but I have the very clear impression that the time has now come for you to intervene. I can't say any more over the telephone.' Gamelin replied that he would be at Les Bondons at eight o'clock. 'Today, the hour has come,' Gamelin declared dramatically in his memoirs. 'I hope that it is not too late.' Arriving at Les Bondons, Gamelin found Georges still agitated and depressed in the extreme, amid an atmosphere of chaos similar to what he had seen the previous day. Colonel Minart, on liaison to Georges that day, describes the scene vividly:

A large number of officers of all ranks, in particular several generals, some very busy, others downcast, come and go in the different rooms of this enchanting property of Les Bondons . . . Telephones, maps (events have moved so quickly that the maps of Finland and Norway have not yet been removed from the walls) dossiers, scribbling-pads, notebooks of all sorts are spread out, as if for a jumble sale.

A grand piano was heaped high with képis, while nearby liaison officers from the various armies were ringed about by interrogators:

Some of them, having succeeded in passing through the enemy columns, have achieved remarkable deeds . . . adding to the disorder, through the thin partitions of this bungalow of *grand luxe* there filters a noise of typewriters, the ringing of telephones, the inadequately silenced noises of motor-cycles housed outside, the musty smells of the kitchen or blocked lavatories, the infantile waggeries of orderlies, secretaries or chauffeurs, witnesses that were generally unaware of – and too close to – this decomposition. One had the impression of attending a consultation without hope of a hundred done-for doctors, specialists of different kinds brought in *in extremis* to a dying man who had already been given up.

Gamelin announced to Georges diplomatically that he felt it necessary now, 'as Allied Commander-in-Chief, to formulate a general scheme of manoeuvre'. Asking for a pen, he then retired to a small room to draft his famous 'Personal and Secret Instruction No. 12', his first and last intervention in the battle. Some of his staff, says Gamelin, wanted him to take matters entirely in his own hands. 'But I did not want to inflict upon General Georges this humiliation in front of everyone. I was anxious to maintain "form", to preserve his *amour-propre* and his authority' – perhaps a curious consideration at this moment of French destiny.[16] Accordingly, Gamelin began self-effacingly:

Without wishing to interfere in the conduct of the battle now being waged, which is in the hands of the Commander-in-Chief of the North-East Front . . . I consider that, at the present time:

1. There are grounds . . . for extending the front of our Eastern Armies and those covering Paris towards the west, and for maintaining the link with No. 1 Army Group.

2. That, as regards No. 1 Army Group – rather than let it be encircled, we must act with extreme audacity;[17] first by forcing, if necessary, the road to the Somme, and secondly, by throwing in particularly mobile forces against the rear of the Panzer divisions and the motorized infantry divisions which are following them. It seems that there is, at present, a vacuum behind this first echelon.[18]

3. To prepare with all available resources an offensive against the bridges at Mézières . . .

4. The complete strength of the French and British aviation must now devote itself to joining in the battle . . .

5. Everything depends on the next few hours.

M. GAMELIN

16. Gamelin later chided Georges for the lack of gratitude he showed towards this concern for his 'susceptibilities'.

17. Gamelin originally wrote 'we must get away from classical notions', but altered it on the objection of his staff.

18. Like Gamelin (and, before him, Hitler and Rundstedt), Churchill had also arrived at the same conclusion; on the 19th he wired Gamelin in colourful terms:

'The tortoise has protruded its head very far from its shell. Some days must elapse before their main body can reach our lines of communications. It would appear that powerful blows struck from the north and south of this drawn-out pocket could yield surprising results.'

This was hardly the language of a supreme warlord, of a Joffre or a Foch, vigorously grasping the reins in his hands; it seemed almost more like a justification before the court of history. The vaguely worded concept of striking at the rear of the Panzers was obviously correct, but it had come hopelessly late in the day. A 'few hours' was more than the Allies had left at this point, and where now were the 'particularly mobile forces' called for by Gamelin's plan?

At 0945, Gamelin put his signature to what General Roton termed his 'military testament'. Having read it out in a 'calm and measured voice' to Georges's assembled staff, he then went for a stroll in the garden of Les Bondons with General Vuillemin of the Air Force, while Georges began acting upon 'Instruction No. 12'. Afterwards he stayed for a 'quick lunch' with Georges, produced by the chef who had cooked for Pétain a generation and a war earlier. 'Dispirited like all of us by the defeat, he had put all his frustrated patriotism into the confection of a true wedding banquet,' recalled one of the staff officers present; but the lunch assumed more 'the atmosphere of a funeral repast ... Then came the dessert, a huge raised pudding covered with *cheveux d'ange*. It was grotesque and pathetic.' Only Gamelin seemed to eat with a good appetite.

Returning to Vincennes, Gamelin's party (according to Colonel Minart) found that

all activity had practically halted as if on the eve of a move. Everybody, thinking about his own personal affairs, was packing in all haste. The cupboards were practically empty. The '75 cannon installed in the court had been withdrawn. At the first signal, Vincennes could be evacuated like a fireman's barracks.

In the setting, a travel-worn General Weygand arrived, at about half past three. He informed Gamelin simply that he had been summouned to Paris by Reynaud, and had been instructed to put himself in the picture. Gamelin described the situation to him. Then, he asked permission to call on Georges. As he left, he remarked to Gamelin enigmatically: 'You know Paul Reynaud doesn't like you?' Weygand was followed by a visit from a broken General Corap, to whom Gamelin expressed a few sympathetic words and an assurance that his 'honour as a soldier was beyond question'. Towards nine o'clock that evening, a car arrived bearing an emissary from Reynaud. He handed to Gamelin a letter succinctly announcing his replacement by Weygand, and thanking him for services rendered 'in the course of a long and brilliant career'.

Early next morning, 20 May, Weygand arrived at Vincennes to take over. In the C.-in-C.'s office, overlooking the moat where the Duc d'Enghien had been shot, an unusual exchange took place between the two generals – if one may accept Gamelin's version of it. Gamelin expressed his belief that 'the execution of my order is the only solution to save the situation', to which Weygand apparently replied, tapping his notebook, 'But I have the secrets of Marshal Foch!' 'I could have retorted,' says Gamelin, 'that I had those of Marshal Joffre and they had not sufficed.' With hurt feelings, Gamelin noted that during the brief final interview Weygand could not bring himself to express 'one word coming from the heart'; he did not even seem to recall that 'it was I who had obtained for him the command in the Levant in August 1939'. On this sadly petulant note Gamelin left Vincennes forever. Weygand thought he was 'manifestly relieved at being spared a heavy responsibility'. The dismissed Generalissimo said goodbye to no one. A few inquisitive secretaries watched his departure discreetly from the windows. The sentries saluted. Some of those watching felt that the gloomy courtyard at Vincennes had just witnessed yet another execution. Gamelin then returned to the ground-floor flat in the Avenue Foch which he had bought for his retirement, and began mulling over his memoirs. The war went on.

Enter Weygand

The new Commander-in-Chief who now held the waning fortunes of the Allies in his hands was seventy-three at the time of his appointment. Supposedly of Belgian parentage, he was illegitimate and to this day his parentage remains a subject of speculation. Some have it that he was the offspring of a Belgian industrialist and a Polish woman; others that Leopold II, the exploiter of the Congo, was his father; while a strong faction contend that the unhappy Emperor Maximilian and a Mexican woman were Maxime Weygand's parents.[19] Mexican blood would certainly have explained the high cheek-bones and deep-set eyes that gave him an increasingly un-French look as he grew older. A small, dapper man with a foxy face (he reminded one Englishman of an 'aged jockey') that revealed a quick intelligence, Weygand had passed into the cavalry through St Cyr. Right at the beginning of the First War he had been picked by Foch, more or less at random, as his Chief of Staff, and had remained with the Marshal, like a constant shadow, until the Armistice, and after. He had thus never commanded troops in battle, and, as Spears remarked of him, between this and being a Chief of Staff was 'as different as riding in the Grand National from taking photos of its jumps'. On leaving Foch's side he went to Poland, where his admirers consider him to have been chiefly responsible for the great Polish victory of 1920 against the Russians. In 1923 he was appointed High Commissioner in Syria, and then in 1931 became Commander-in-Chief of the French Army. Retiring in 1935, he was called back in 1939 (by Gamelin) to return to Syria as military commander.

Weygand was very much that particularly French creature, a 'political general'. He was almost as deeply committed to the Right wing as he was to the Catholic Church. Clemenceau described him as being 'up to his neck in priests', and he often seemed to harbour an inquisitional notion that sinful France would be required to suffer for her wickedness. It was also Clemenceau who had once issued the warning: 'Look out. If ever a *coup d'état* is attempted, it will be by him.' On more than one occasion Weygand had addressed meetings of de la Rocque's *Croix de Feu*, and at one time it was whispered that passionate conservatism had carried him as far as relations with

19. As a variation on this theme, the German radio promptly claimed on Weygand's appointment that he was the son of Maximilian by a Saarlander, thus claiming good German blood for the poor misguided general.

the *Cagoulard* terrorists. Certainly, during the Russo-Finnish War he had been in the van of those anxious to 'have a go' at the Bolsheviks. Spears claimed that Weygand had 'only two preoccupations: his haunting fear of revolution, and his dislike of Reynaud'. Both were to have their effect on his conduct of the war as Generalissimo.[20] Reynaud in his turn had little love for Weygand; about the best thing he could say about him in his memoirs was that he 'had the gift of explaining things clearly'. Why, then, had Reynaud called forth the elderly general at this most dire moment? He was, in de Gaulle's caustic words, 'a brilliant second' who had never commanded troops in action; he had not had the advantage of studying the German *Blitzkrieg* technique at first hand, as had, for instance, General Huntziger; and out in the Levant he had not kept himself in particularly close touch with events since 10 May.[21] The fact was that his selection was first and foremost an act of patriotism, intended by Reynaud to tap and draw strength from the 'Verdun stream' flowing through the French soul. In the popular mind, if Pétain represented honour and endurance in adversity, Weygand was still Foch's right hand – and Foch signified victory and *la gloire*. Not every French soldier, however, was thus impressed; many shared the cynicism of Lieutenant Claude Jamet who, on hearing of the new appointment, wrote in his diary:

Gagamelin. Weygand, on the contrary, he's pure blood. The spirit of Foch. 'When in danger, call for Weygand', etc. . . . what sluggishness of intellect and heart! And Weygand is summoned, regardless . . . because Foch is dead. For this 'modern war', one might just as well have called for Napoleon, the Great Condé – or Vercingetorix!

---

20. At the most critical moment in June, Weygand insisted that he be left those divisions which remained fresh 'in order to maintain order', on the assumption that, by then, the threat of revolution was more dangerous than the Germans.

21. On arriving from Syria and having first seen a map of the German advance, Weygand is reported to have exclaimed: 'If I had known the situation was so bad I would not have come' (on which Spears commented acidly, 'It meant he was thinking of his reputation.').

Certainly the emotive summoning of Pétain and Weygand to stiffen France's war effort was one measure that would back-fire badly on Paul Reynaud.

Weygand had had a gruelling flight from Syria, his aircraft constantly dogged by misfortune. On the 18th he had hoped to make Tunis in one hop, and then Paris by the evening. But there were strong headwinds, and over Benghazi (then in Italian hands, Italy being a dubious neutral) he was forced to turn back to refuel at Mersa Matruh in Egypt, thereby losing three precious hours. Finally, in landing at Étampes, the under-carriage of the plane collapsed, and Weygand had to creep out through the upper gun turret. Just at that moment there was an air-raid warning, and he did not reach Paris until 1100 hours on the 19th. Despite this harrowing journey for a man of his age, Weygand surprised those who saw him; Alexander Werth thought he 'looked good in uniform', in contrast to Pétain who was accompanying him ('Poor old boy – fancy being dragged into all this at his age.'). On arriving at La Ferté, Captain Beaufre (who admittedly became a lifelong devotee of Wey-gand) was struck by his displaying 'a swagger, a passion and a fierce will which contrasted sharply with the pale and curdled calm of his predecessor'. Almost immediately the seventy-three-year-old general astonished his new staff at Montry[22] by performing a hundred-yard sprint on the lawn.

On his first brief interview with Georges on the 19th, Wey-gand at once got an idea of just how serious the situation was. In ten days' fighting the French Army had lost fifteen divisions, and in the north another forty-five were in danger of being thrown into the sea; there were no reserves; the arsenals were almost empty. Between Valenciennes and Montmédy, the gap to be filled measured nearly one hundred miles. The proper moment for a co-ordinated counter-offensive here, assessed Weygand, should have been on the 15th or 16th; therefore it was now too late. As for the unnerved and dejected General

22. So as to be closer to the conduct of operations, but also perhaps to rid himself of the shades of Gamelin lurking in the gloom of Vincennes, Weygand decided to move his headquarters in with General Doumenc's staff at Montry.

Georges, Weygand decided that he must remain (at least nominally) at his command; it would be too complicated, as well as
too demoralizing for the Army, for him to be replaced at this
point. But in contrast to Gamelin, from the beginning the
actual conduct of the battle would be in his, Weygand's, hands.
Meanwhile Gamelin's 'Instruction No. 12', decreed only that
morning (the 19th), was cancelled. Returning from Georges's
H.Q., Weygand had gone to Reynaud's office in the evening
and, having told the Premier that he would accept the 'heavy
responsibility' cast upon him, added pessimistically: 'You will
not be surprised if I cannot answer for victory, nor even give
you the hope of victory.' As he left, Baudouin inquired about
his immediate plans, to which Weygand replied: 'I am dead
tired, for I had only three hours' sleep at Tunis. I shall begin by
getting some sleep.' All decisions would be postponed to the
morrow. Thus passed another twenty-four of the 'few hours'
remaining to France.

On to the Channel

Monday, 20 May, was the day of Guderian's triumph. The
previous evening he had once more been granted complete freedom of movement, and at midnight he ordered his corps to
strike out for Amiens and Abbeville, prefacing his orders with
the words: 'The enemy opposite the corps front has been
defeated.' The latest aerial reconnaissance reports certainly
confirmed this view; they could find virtually no Allied formations ahead of the Panzers. On the Allied side, General
d'Astier's patrols spoke of a 'whirlpool of armour' about to
burst westwards. With the Canal du Nord behind them, there
was now no natural barrier between the Panzers and the coast
– just mile upon mile of the flat, featureless Picardy plain, a
paradise for armoured commanders.

Guderian himself was on the road at 0400 hours with the 1st
Panzer, desirous of being present at the historic moment of the
capture of Amiens. The morning began with a sharp row involving Colonel Balck, now commanding the 1st Panzer Brigade,
who had moved out from the Péronne bridgehead without

waiting to be relieved by the 10th Panzer. His successor, Colonel Landgraf, was enraged by Balck's casualness, and particularly at his retort: 'If we lost it, you can always take it again.' At Albert (a familiar name from the Battle of the Somme), the riflemen formerly commanded by Balck came up against the British troops (the Royal West Kents) for the first time. The 1st Panzer official historian describes them as having 'fought toughly and bravely without, however, being able to prevent the fall of Albert'. Swinging round the hold-up at Albert, Balck's tanks were at the gates of Amiens by mid morning, having advanced nearly thirty-five miles.

Never had the armour moved faster. 'We had the feeling,' said Kielmansegg, 'such as a fine racehorse may have, of having been held back by its rider, coldly and deliberately, then getting its head free to reach out into a swinging gallop and speed to the finishing-post as winner.' William Shirer, who that day had at last been allowed to follow in the wake of the German advance, was fascinated by the spectacle of this army on wheels, which

simply went up the roads . . . with tanks, planes, artillery, anti-tank stuff, everything . . . all morning, roads massed with supplies, troops going up . . . curious, not a single Allied plane yet . . . and these endless columns of troops, guns, supplies, stretching all the way from the German border . . . what a target! . . . Refugees streaming back along the roads in the dust and heat . . . tears your heart out . . .

Notwithstanding all the years he had observed the build-up of the new Wehrmacht in Germany, the speed and efficiency with which the German columns moved made a deep impression on Shirer:

It is a gigantic, impersonal war machine, run as coolly and efficiently, say, as our automobile industry in Detroit . . . thousands of motorized vehicles thundering by on the dusty roads, officers and men alike remain cool and business-like. Absolutely no excitement, no tension. An officer directing artillery fire stops for half an hour to explain to you what he is up to.

On an airfield outside Amiens, the Panzers nearly surprised an R.A.F. unit which had lodged there for the night, and the fighters took off literally in the face of the first German tanks. The city was almost empty; the previous afternoon the last line-of-communication troops had marched out,[23] accompanied by nuns from the Community of the Holy Family; and, at about the same time, the defeated General Corap was passing through on his way to see Gamelin. Fires caused by the previous day's bombing had raged all night, and dawn brought the Luftwaffe over again, bombing relentlessly. About all that was left holding Amiens was a battalion of the Royal Sussex Regiment, belonging to the 12th (Territorial) Division, which stood and fought to a finish against Balck's tanks, and was completely destroyed. By midday the Germans had spread a large Swastika flag in front of the post office, to show the Luftwaffe that the city was in German hands. Methodically, they then pushed on southwards to seize bridgeheads over the Somme, in preparation for Phase Two of the Battle of France. Guderian was there, as intended, to inspect the great city which even Ludendorff had failed to capture in 1918, and somehow found time to visit the cathedral before rushing off to see how the 2nd Panzers were getting on.

He discovered General Veiel and the 2nd Panzer at Albert, where they had just captured a British gun battery which had exhausted its ammunition. The division was nearly out of fuel, and was proposing to halt at Albert. Guderian says that 'they were soon disillusioned' and he ordered them at once to push on to Abbeville. Having somehow mastered their fuel problem, the 2nd Panzers reached Abbeville by 1800 hours that evening, after an advance from Albert of forty-five miles, taking by surprise a French unit drilling on its parade ground. Its tanks then broke in between positions held by Territorials of the British 35th Brigade, only a few remnants of which managed to fall back across the Somme. Abbeville too had been bombed (indiscriminately, like Rotterdam, it seems) all through the 20th, and severe damage caused. But in fact the Luftwaffe prob-

23. Surprisingly, the Gare du Nord was still sending trains off from Paris to Amiens as late as the evening of the 19th.

ably granted the hard-pressed British Territorials a respite by mistakenly bombing the bridgeheads which the Germans had seized, forcing them to withdraw that night until the error was resolved.

Because of a delay in the transmission of orders, Reinhardt's troops did not move until 0800 on the 20th. At 1300 hours they ran into their first British at Mondicourt, who – in the words of the 6th Panzer War Diary – 'in contrast to the French, cause surprise by their tough way of fighting and are only overcome after a one-hour battle'. Two hours later Ravenstein's force was again fighting a hard battle against the British 36th Brigade defending Doullens, which, though hopelessly outnumbered, managed to hold out until shortly before nightfall. Nevertheless, despite this stubborn resistance, Reinhardt's armour swept around Doullens to reach its objectives at Hesdin and Le Boisle. By the end of the day the two British Territorial Divisions, the 12th and 23rd, had all but ceased to exist.[24] Widely dispersed, and inadequately prepared as they were to encounter German Panzer divisions, each had given a good account of itself against impossible odds, as the various German accounts testified.

As agreed with Hoth the previous day, Rommel launched forth on another of his famous night attacks just after midnight on the 19th. By 0500 he had reached the village of Beaurains, two and a half miles south of Arras. But, as had happened at Avesnes, his motorized rifle regiments did not follow the armour as closely as intended. Rushing back in an armoured car to find them, Rommel was nearly trapped by French cavalry tanks infiltrating across his lines of communication. These knocked out Rommel's accompanying tanks, and for several hours he and his Signal Staff were surrounded. The situation was restored only by the arrival of an infantry regiment and artillery. Once again Rommel had the narrowest of escapes. For the rest of the day the 7th Panzer hammered unsuccessfully at Arras, held by British troops under Major-General R. L. Petre. It was Rommel's first serious check since crossing the Meuse, his casualties the highest since the 13th. On the evening of the 20th, the 7th Panzer was placed on the

24. At one point, even a mobile bath unit had been thrown into the battle.

defensive around Arras – an unusual posture for Rommel.

Meanwhile, as night descended over northern France on 20 May, Guderian's men pulled off the ace achievement of the campaign so far. Pushing out down the Somme from Abbeville, Austrians from Lieutenant-Colonel Spitta's battalion from the 2nd Panzer reached Noyelles on the Atlantic coast, not far from the Hundred Years War battlefield of Crécy-en-Ponthieu. They had advanced over sixty miles since the morning. The dog-tired Panzer crews filled their lungs with sea air and wondered in amazement at how much more they had already achieved than the Kaiser's Army before them. In ten short days they had covered two hundred miles [25] and encircled the cream of the Allied armies. What could they not aspire to! In his orders that night, Guderian told his corps: 'Today's battles have brought us complete success. Along the whole front the enemy is in retreat in a manner that at times approaches rout.'

Far back at the rear, both the O.K.H. and O.K.W. were quite taken by surprise at the news. On the 19th, Jodl had been worrying that the Allies in northern Belgium might slip out to the south, and even on the morning of the 20th Halder was expressing concern lest Bock's pressure in the north might result 'in driving the game away, as it were, past Kleist'. But at the *Felsennest*, Jodl found a Hitler 'beside himself with joy. Talks in words of highest appreciation of the German Army and its leadership. Is working on the Peace Treaty ... First negotiations in the Forest of Compiègne as in 1918.'

In Paris, Alexander Werth recorded:

Cheerful news reached me from the censors' office at night that all telephone (and telegraph?) communications between Paris and London had been broken off – lines cut; Fifth Column at work, or what? . . . Colonel Thomas said there was some heavy fighting 'around' St Quentin and Péronne. He tried to suggest that the German progress was slowing down. I've noticed that when they mention places 'round' which there is fighting, it means these places are already in German hands.

25. By comparison, it is interesting to note that in mid-April 1945, when Germany was all but defeated, the American 5th Armoured – in what was held to be a record – took *eleven* days to advance the same distance.

As usual the French censor was forty-eight hours behind with the news. For the Allies this was unquestionably the darkest day of the war so far; few in the five years to come would be darker.

Chapter 18

Encirclement

21–23 May

In the West, the greatest offensive of all time has had its first strategic result, after a series of major tactical successes; our forces have reached the sea.

    Wehrmacht communiqué, 21 May

The Germans have not yet stood the final test . . . we are the old opponent of the Marne, the old opponent of Verdun. Pétain appears to us like a symbol, a promise. Weygand brings back to us the genius of Foch.

    Le Journal, 21 May

A serious technical fault in the cable, it was learned, caused the cancellation of the public telephone service between London and Paris and beyond on Monday night and yesterday . . . A Post Office official said: 'We have no idea when the service will be restored.'

    Daily Telegraph, 22 May

The recapture of Arras may prove to be a turning-point in the present battle which will have a vital effect on the whole war.

    Daily Mail, 23 May

German High Command: More Vacillations

For the jubilant Germans, the next three days would also be potentially the most dangerous of the campaign. The vulnerable 'tortoise-head' of the Panzers was now further extended than ever before,[1] the vacuum between them and the weary, forced-marching infantry divisions greater than it had been when Hitler had lost his nerve on the 17th. Would the Allies, despite their disarray, yet be able to launch a successful counter-attack to break through the 'Panzer Corridor' before this frail wedge between their armies became a thing of steel?

1. General Schaal, for example, was reporting back in alarm that his 10th Panzer, covering the western end of the flank along the Somme, was spread out over a distance of sixty miles.

At no time since 10 May had the outcome of the battle become such a race for time. On the German side, Guderian, up in the forefront with his Panzers, was supremely aware of this. After his remarkable achievements of the 20th, he fretted that night that 'we did not know in what direction our advance should continue'. Nor, he added, had Kleist himself received any further instructions on how to proceed. In his orders for the 21st, Guderian simply told his Panzers to regroup and consolidate on the positions gained the previous day.

So the 21st of May was wasted while we waited for orders. I spent the day visiting Abbeville and our crossings and bridgeheads over the Somme. On the way I asked my men how they had enjoyed the operations up to date. 'Not bad,' said an Austrian of the 2nd Panzer Division, 'but we wasted two whole days.'

'Unfortunately,' Guderian commented bitterly, 'he was right.'

The reasons for this delay in the transmission of orders lay in renewed vacillations within the German High Command, which was again partially caught off balance by its own successes. The objective of *Sichelschnitt* had been reached, the Allied armies in the north were encircled, but the master blueprint had laid down no precise directives as to what the next step should be. Halder seemed to be still toying with notions of immediately continuing the advance southwards from the bridgeheads gained across the Somme, and leaving Bock's Army Group 'B' to 'mop up' the encircled Allied forces in the north. Meanwhile, Hitler's jubilation was once again tempered with renewed misgivings about the weakness of that southern flank, and later that day he was again lecturing Brauchitsch on the slowness of the infantry in catching up with the Panzers. It was thus not until midday on the 21st that the German High Command decided to concentrate all its forces upon reducing the Allied forces trapped in the north, so that by the time Guderian received his orders to swing northwards to seize the Channel ports the campaigning day was over. In the meantime, Rommel and the forces grouped around Arras had run into serious trouble.

554 To Lose a Battle

Allied High Command: More Delays: Ironside's Plan

In the Allied camp, where time was even more vital, the change
of command, however desirable it may have been, could hardly
have come at a worse moment. Before any forces could have
been concentrated for the attack towards Mézières from the
south and the Somme from the north, as called for by Gamelin's 'Instruction No. 12' of the 19th, the order was cancelled by
Weygand. On Weygand's first visit to Georges's H.Q. that day,
Georges had offered to give him a detailed briefing on the situation. Weygand, weary after his fatiguing trip from the Levant,
had replied 'No, tomorrow.' After his briefing then by Georges,
Weygand had taken one or two important measures. He
ordered the roads to be cleared (at last); civilians were to be
allowed to move only between 6 p.m. and midnight. Struck by
the lack of anti-tank weapons, he had ordered all the famous
'75s' of the First War to be brought out of mothballs, and used
in combination with the infantry, 'like revolvers'. The most
serious problem, as he rightly saw it, now lay not south of the
Panzer Corridor but in the north. But Weygand discovered that
all communications with the forces there were cut off; he was
only in tenuous contact with Billotte through London. Therefore, he told Georges: 'I must go and see on the spot what the
situation is.' It was Foch who had taught him 'the value of personal contact maintained at frequent intervals'. Later that
afternoon he announced to Reynaud that, if the railway were
still working, 'I will go by train to Abbeville tonight; if not, I
will go by air tomorrow morning.' Pétain, who was present,
supported Weygand's decision, saying that nothing was equal
to the presence of a commander-in-chief. Reynaud, however,
managed to dissuade Weygand from entraining for Abbeville
on the grounds that 'it would be a fatal blow to France if you
were to be taken prisoner' – which, indeed, might well have
been the case, as Abbeville was at that moment about to pass
into enemy hands. Finally it was decided that Weygand would fly
north the following morning, on condition that, Cinderella-like,
he would be away no longer than twenty-four hours. But this
would still mean the loss of two more precious days to the Allies.

Meanwhile, as Weygand was being briefed at La Ferté and the Panzers were fanning out towards the coast, on the morning of the 20th the British C.I.G.S., General Ironside, had arrived in the north on an important mission from his Government. His visit followed upon Gort's call to the War Office of the previous day warning that he might be forced to consider evacuating the B.E.F. Churchill viewed Gort's fears with considerable disfavour, and stated that the C.I.G.S., Ironside, 'could not accept this proposal, as, like most of us, he favoured the southward march'. Accordingly, Ironside was dispatched to Wahagnies to tell Gort that he was to 'force his way through all opposition in order to join up with the French in the south'. The phrasing of this brief revealed just how misinformed the Churchill Government remained, even as late as 19 May, on the true situation in France.[2] Ironside arrived at Gort's H.Q. at 0800 hours on the 20th, and promptly delivered to him a written order embodying the Government's views, which said that the C.I.G.S. would inform General Billotte and the Belgians accordingly. General Dill, already in Paris, would also inform Georges of the British view; in effect, this constituted the very first intervention by Britain in the French General Staff's handling of land strategy since the war had begun.

Ironside put his case for executing the southward march towards Amiens. Gort revealed obvious consternation. Then, according to Ironside, 'after some thought, Lord Gort did not agree. I asked him to try, but the C.-in-C. said no, he could not agree.' Firmly Gort pointed out that seven of his nine divisions were in close contact with the enemy on the Escaut; even if they could be disengaged, their withdrawal would open a gap on his left between the B.E.F. and the badly shaken Belgian Army through which the enemy would be bound to penetrate. In response to Ironside's contention that the advancing German Panzers were 'tired', Gort said he was sure the French were even more tired. Everything he had seen of the French

2. However, by way of reinsurance, on the morning of the 20th Churchill did follow up with a decree that 'as a precautionary measure the Admiralty should assemble a large number of small vessels in readiness to proceed to ports and inlets on the French coast'.

forces and their leaders in recent days increasingly led him to doubt whether they could stage 'an organized counter-offensive on a large scale'; therefore he was inclining more and more to his 'last alternative'. However, he told Ironside that he 'already had plans in hand' to launch the following day a *limited* attack southwards from Arras with his two remaining 'free' divisions. In the absence of any fresh orders from the French, he would carry out this attack. Ironside then asked Gort 'under whose orders he was now acting'.

The answer was General Billotte, who had a headquarters under the Vimy Ridge near Lens. Billotte had given the B.E.F. no orders for some eight days, nor had Gort complained to the Cabinet or to me.[3]

Asking if he could take Gort's Chief of Staff, Lieutenant-General Pownall, along with him, Ironside then set off in ill humour to see Billotte.

Gort

Like actors in a play, the minor characters of history have their moments when they advance from the rear of the stage to dominate briefly the whole scene in the full glare of the foot-lights, before receding once more into the background. Now, for the next ten days, the unassuming, bulldog figure of Lord Gort emerges to the fore as the most important in the battle, perhaps in the war at large. At the time, John Standish Surtees Prendergast Vereker, 6th Viscount Gort, was fifty-four years old. After joining the Grenadier Guards in 1905, he had earned an almost legendary reputation for bravery during the First World War. Four times wounded, nine times mentioned in dispatches, he won the Military Cross, the Distinguished Service Order and two Bars, and finally the Victoria Cross, when commanding his battalion at the crossing of the Canal du Nord

3. As further instance of the poor liaison existing between the French High Command and the B.E.F., Gort only learned indirectly on the 20th that Weygand had taken over and was now directing operations; the British Government was not consulted on the change of command.

in September 1918.[4] After the war he held various staff jobs at home and in India, and was C.I.G.S. when selected to lead the B.E.F. Up to that moment he had never commanded any unit larger than a brigade.

Utterly straightforward, with a limited intellect, he had always held himself completely aloof from any kind of extra-mural intriguing, in marked antithesis to the French 'political' generals like Weygand, or the cerebral Gamelin – or, for that matter, to his own forerunner, Sir Douglas Haig. His reaction to the reforming but perhaps too adroit Hore-Belisha (appointed Secretary for War in 1937) was typical: 'We mustn't upset the people in the clubs by going too fast.' Adored among the Brigade of Guards, where he was known by the affectionate but hardly flattering nickname of 'Fat Boy', Gort was in the eyes of Brooke, his subordinate (who could be far from uncritical of his superiors)

One of those pre-eminently straight characters who inspired confidence. He could never have done anything small or mean . . . He had one of those cheerful dispositions full of vitality, energy and *joie de vivre*, and the most wonderful charm, and was gifted with great powers of leadership . . . I could not help admiring him and had feelings of real and deep affection for him.

But, added Brooke, 'I had no confidence in his leadership when it came to handling a large force. He seemed incapable of seeing the wood for trees.' During the winter of the Phoney War, when he should perhaps have been voicing to the British Cabinet his doubt on the French Army and its strategy, Gort had busied himself tirelessly with such details as the proper use of hand-grenades, the art of patrolling at night, small-arms fire, and map-reading in the snow. Visiting his H.Q., Maurois noted in evident surprise:

Never has a generalissimo had a simpler office. A scrawled card, affixed to the door by four thumb tacks, read: 'Office of the C.-in-C.' Inside the room, which contained no other furniture, two trestles of white wood supported a bare plank. This was Lord

---

4. Close to where Guderian crossed it (in the opposite direction) on 19 May.

Gort's work table . . . Extremely active by nature, he found, in time of war, his only sport and relaxation in walking. He was to be seen at dawn on the muddy roads around Arras, his elbows close to his body, his head thrust forward.

Gort's French colleagues, as Spears aptly remarks, tended to regard him 'as a sort of friendly and jovial battalion commander' – and they treated him as such. Certainly, with his hearty demeanour, the occasionally worried expression, the breeches and the Guardsman's highly polished knee-boots, Gort did seem the image of the old-style British battalion commander, and to a large extent this was the key both to his character and his actions. On being sent to lead the B.E.F. in 1939, Gort's instructions from his Government were that he was to take his orders from General Georges, as C.-in-C. North-East Front; but if any order received from the French should appear to Gort 'to imperil the British Field Force', he would be at liberty to appeal to the British Government before executing it. Gort had interpreted these instructions with the rigid, unquestioning instinct for loyalty of a Guards battalion commander. Both during the Phoney War and after the German offensive had begun, he had observed much that had disturbed him about the French conduct of affairs, and he clearly resented the offhand way in which Georges and Billotte had never bothered to offer him anything but the minimum of consultation and information – such as the commander of a very junior formation might expect. But the French leaders were his appointed superiors and, true to his instincts, Gort doggedly accepted his lot, without exercising his right to complain or express his misgivings to his own Government. At the same time, as the situation following the German breakthrough became progressively graver, so Gort's concern grew that Churchill and his Government should appear to be unaware of just how bad things were in France;[5] but again, at least until

5. For the British Government's misconceptions, Gort must himself be held partly to blame in his failure to communicate earlier his doubts about the French conduct of the battle; he seems certainly to have erred in not complaining much earlier to Ironside about his receiving no orders from Billotte.

20 May, Gort was not inclined to challenge the fallacious view of those set above him.

Yet there was much more to Gort than just the laudable virtues of a Grenadier 'battalion commander'. He was endowed to excess with the single-mindedness which so often accompanies great personal courage, and by the third week in May this single-mindedness had taken the form of a determination to save his B.E.F. from destruction, come what may. A man who had won the V.C. as Gort had would not be deterred from pursuing what he considered to be his line of duty, regardless of the opposition, even if it should include a will as formidable as that of Winston Churchill. In 1914 it was popularly said of Jellicoe that he was the only man who could have 'lost the war in an afternoon' (although, in view of the poor subsequent performance of battleships on both sides, this claim may have been somewhat exaggerated); but in 1940 Gort, by 20 May, was certainly the man who, by forfeiting Britain's only land force, could easily have lost the war at least in a week of afternoons. It was also once said of Jellicoe that he had 'all Nelson's qualities except disobedience'. Gort, the Guardsman, would never be disobedient; but in a tight corner, his single-mindedness and courage would make him defiant – which, when clear and realistic directives from above were lacking, would amount to almost the same thing. Over the next week, the responsibility resting on Gort alone would be gigantic. Fortunately, both for Britain – and ultimately for France – events would prove that Gort had the strength to bear it.

Ironside Visits Billotte

On his way to Lens to see Billotte, Ironside had an unpleasant journey. The road was

an indescribable mass of refugees, both Belgian and French, moving down in every kind of conveyance. Poor women pushing perambulators, horsed wagons with all the family and its goods in them. Belgian units all going along aimlessly. Poor devils. It was a horrible sight and it blocked the roads, which was the main difficulty.

At Lens, Ironside found Billotte with Blanchard, the commander of the French First Army. They were both, he said

in a state of complete depression. No plan, no thought of a plan. Ready to be slaughtered. Defeated at the end without casualties. *Trés fatigués* and nothing doing.

There ensued an angry scene. The British C.I.G.S. was also, to foreign eyes, something of a caricature of an Englishman; aged fifty-nine, he had been the original prototype for Buchan's Hannay and stood 6 ft. 4 in. (inevitably, this had gained him the nickname 'Tiny').[6] In Army circles he had openly referred to Secretary of State Hore-Belisha as 'that little monkey', the Cabinet as 'the old gentlemen', and had a healthy, Kiplingesque contempt for those 'lesser breeds'. In a rage he must have presented a daunting figure before the two distressed French generals of modest stature. Ironside admits he lost his temper, and 'shook Billotte by the button of his tunic. The man is completely beaten.' He added contemptuously for the benefit of his diary: 'There is absolutely nothing in front of them. They remain quivering behind the water-line north of Cambrai while the fate of France is in the balance . . .'[7]

He then bulldozed Billotte and Blanchard into accepting the British proposal to attack towards Amiens, and (according to Ironside), 'Billotte drew himself up to attention to say that he would make an immediate plan to attack and I left him to do it.' Next, Ironside telephoned Weygand and 'told him that there was no resolution here and that there was no co-ordination. I told him that Billotte should be relieved.' Finally it was agreed (with Billotte and Blanchard) that the British and the French First Army would each attack on the 21st with two divisions. That the French were acquiescing only under Ironside's formidable pressure was obvious; before the C.I.G.S. departed for London, Gort assured him 'that they would never attack'.

On his return home, the tone of his diary entries show that,

6. One of the French present at the meeting that day, Captain René de Chambrun, says that Ironside struck him as the tallest man he had ever seen.

7. The exaggeration of this remark again indicates how incompletely Ironside and the War Cabinet in England understood how disastrous the French defeat had already been.

after his experience at Lens, Ironside at any rate regarded the situation in France with more sober realism. He writes: 'I begin to despair of the French fighting at all. The great army defeated by a few tanks.' He was increasingly despondent about the prospects facing Gort's divisions. With perhaps only another four days' food left, Ironside was doubtful whether they could even fight their way back to the Channel coast:

Situation desperate . . . Personally, I think we cannot extricate the B.E.F. Only hope a march south-west. Have they the time? Have they got the food?

'God help the B.E.F.,' Ironside added bitterly. 'Brought to this state by the incompetence of the French Command.' After seeing Churchill on the 21st, he found that the Prime Minister still 'persists in thinking the position no worse'.

Gort Goes it Alone at Arras

At Wahagnies, Gort pushed ahead with his plan to attack southwards from Arras on the 21st. Co-ordinating the operation was Major-General Harold Franklyn of the 5th Division. Known as 'Frankforce', the troops at his disposal nominally consisted of two infantry divisions (the 5th and the 50th) and the 1st Army Tank Brigade; but in the event only a much smaller force could be committed. The infantry divisions had between them only four brigades, instead of the usual three apiece. One from the 5th Division had been detached, partly to relieve the French cavalry on the River Scarpe so that they could join in the attack, and General Franklyn decided to hold its other brigade (the 17th) in reserve until after the first phase had been completed; from the 50th Division, one of its brigades was sent to bolster the defences of the Arras garrison and to hold the river line immediately east of the city. Thus when the operation actually started on the 21st, instead of two British divisions only two battalions (from the 151st Brigade, 50th Division) would in fact initiate the attack. Meanwhile, instead of the one hundred tanks at its disposal, through the mechanical wear and tear of the long marches of the past days,

'Frankforce' could only mount a total of fifty-eight Mark I and sixteen Mark II infantry tanks. Both were extremely slow machines, but heavily armoured. The Mark I carried only a medium machine-gun; the Mark II, later christened the 'Matilda', was armed with a 2-pounder gun [8] and, weighing 25 tons, had the thickest armour of any tank on the battlefields of France. 'Frankforce' would be led into battle by Major-General G. le Q. Martel, the commander of the 50th Division and one of Britain's foremost experts of tank warfare of the inter-war period.

At Gort's H.Q., what had started life as a limited operation designed simply to disengage Arras had, in the meantime, as a consequence of the forceful pressure applied by Ironside during his visit, imperceptibly escalated to the point where it was now regarded as the first blow in the concerted Allied attempt to close the gap. But none of this was revealed to either Franklyn or Martel. Their orders remained unchanged: to 'support the garrison in Arras and to block the roads south of Arras, thus cutting off the German communications (via Arras) from the east'. Little thought seems to have been given as to just what enemy strength Martel's rather slender force might expect to encounter 'south of Arras' by the 21st.

After Ironside's departure, Gort, still harbouring fears that, as he had predicted to Ironside, the French 'would never attack', had instructed his liaison officers with Billotte and Blanchard to make it clear that

If our counter-attack was not successful the French and British Armies north of the gap would have their flank turned and could no longer remain in their present positions.

Nevertheless, when at 1800 hours on the 20th there was a conference at Franklyn's H.Q. to co-ordinate the next day's operation, no representative arrived from General René Altmayer's V Corps, which Billotte and Blanchard had undertaken would attack with two divisions east of Arras, in the direction of

8. The British 2-pounder had a slightly larger calibre but considerably more hitting-power than the 37-mm. then carried on the German Mark III Panzer.

Cambrai. Shaken by Ironside's rage, Blanchard had in fact sent a special liaison officer, Major Vautrin, to Altmayer to urge upon him the importance of attacking simultaneously with the British on the 21st.[9] But, Vautrin reported back, 'General Altmayer, who seemed tired out and thoroughly disheartened, wept silently on his bed.' He told Vautrin that one had to be realistic, and that

the troops had buggered off, that he was ready to accept all the consequences of his refusal and go and get himself killed at the head of a battalion, but he could no longer continue to sacrifice the army corps of which he had already lost nearly half.

Accordingly, late that night a letter from Blanchard reached Gort telling him that Altmayer would not be able to move until the 22nd or the following night – because the roads were so badly blocked. Instead, Prioux and his Cavalry Corps would lend flanking cover to the west of 'Frankforce'.

   Prioux, who seems to have retained the most fighting spirit of any French general in these days, had indeed wanted to use his armour to slice into the Panzers' tenuous communications in a cavalry-style raid. But he had his own problems at that moment. A good part of his 1st Light Mechanised Division had been destroyed in the bitter fighting in the Forest of Mormal, and on the 19th he had been unable to reassemble those others of his tank companies, farmed out to various infantry divisions, in time to combine with de Gaulle's attack from the south. The reluctant infantry generals seem to have turned a deaf ear to the injunctions of Billotte, and finally, at 1700 hours on the 20th, he sent out a draconian order:

the greater part of the fighting vehicles have not been returned to the light mechanized divisions . . . This order will be carried out immediately. I will not hesitate to bring any formation commander who disobeys this order before a court martial!

But it came too late for Prioux to offer more than a few weak

9. Although Colonel Goutard blames Blanchard for saying in his orders to Altmayer: ' "The attack will start *from 21 May onwards*." Nothing then was imperative about the order.'

detachments of his 3rd D.L.M. to help 'Frankforce' on the 21st.

At the same time, General d'Astier reveals that his Z.O.A.N. had been called upon by Georges to lend 'powerful support' on the morning of the 21st to an operation of 'first importance' being launched against Cambrai by Blanchard's First Army. But no front, no targets, no time had been given; Georges seemed completely out of the picture and d'Astier had been unable to make contact himself with either the First Army or with the British Air Component, now back in Kent. His reconnaissance planes were either shot down or turned back, and it was not until 1600 hours on the 21st that they were able to get through, by which time they reported that nothing was happening round Cambrai. From the Air Component, just completing its move back to Kent, no R.A.F. cover was forthcoming either.[10]

Despite this confirmation of his worst fears about French participation, Gort stuck doggedly to his plans for the Arras attack, his French critics suggesting that he was 'perhaps anxious to be done with the thing'. In any case, instinct and experience decided him not to wait for the French. Thus, by 1400 hours on the afternoon of the 21st, when – after various hitches in the morning – 'Frankforce' finally attacked, the massive counter-blow called for by Ironside had been whittled down from four French and British divisions to a jab by two British battalions, Territorials at that, supported by tanks of which only the sixteen Matildas were useful against German Panzers, and with flank cover from a few squadrons of light French armour. The sad story of all the previous French counter-efforts was being repeated; the only difference was that the effects would be marginally dissimilar.

Martel's Attack

Leading it as Rommel would have done, from an open car, General Martel opened his attack by striking southwards around the west of Arras with two mobile columns. Each con-

10. D'Astier, apparently, had not yet been informed of the withdrawal of Air Component.

sisted of a tank battalion and an infantry battalion (of the Durham Light Infantry), plus a battery of field artillery and one of anti-tank guns. There was no air cover. The objective was to reach the River Cojeul that night. Almost at once the right-hand column unexpectedly came up against the enemy at Duisans.[11] The village was cleared after a fight, and a number of prisoners taken, but two precious companies of infantry and some anti-tank guns had to be left behind to hold it. The remainder of the column then pushed on towards Warlus, which it had to capture against substantial opposition. Next it took Berneville and threw an advanced guard out across the Doullen–Arras road. Here the British infantry found themselves pinned down by heavy machine-gun and mortar fire, while for twenty minutes the Luftwaffe attacked the main body unopposed. Nevertheless, Martel's tanks swept around to the left and pushed on to Wailly, where they hit the newly arrived S.S. Totenkopf motorized infantry division. But the right-hand column had shot its bolt, and that evening was forced to fall back defensively on Warlus, after heavy losses. Here an unfortunate incident took place when a detachment of Prioux's tanks attacked some British anti-tank guns, taking them for Germans. A spirited engagement followed, in which one British gun was knocked out and several men killed, and more than one French tank hit, before the French commander realized the mistake and made his apologies. Six of these tanks then played a useful role in freeing rear links with Duisans, where Rommel's tanks were threatening to infiltrate. That was about the extent of French support that day.

Martel's left-hand column also had to fight all the way, but it made faster progress and (as will be seen from Rommel's own account) inflicted heavy casualties. Occupying Dainville, its tanks smashed up a motorized column, destroying its transports, while the following infantry took a considerable number of prisoners. Two miles further on, six Matildas found little difficulty in overrunning a German anti-tank battery near

11. Motorized infantry of Rommel's 7th Panzer who were just resuming their advance north-westwards. The fact that their presence was unreported reveals the incompleteness of the hasty Franco-British reconnaissance.

Achicourt. The left-hand column then pushed on to Agny and Beaurains, and a small advanced party reached Wancourt on the River Cojeul. Throughout most of the afternoon a savage battle raged in the area of Agny-Beaurains between the heavy infantry tanks of the 4th Royal Tank Regiment and Rommel's 6th Rifle Brigade, backed by a powerful line of guns. There were heavy losses on both sides; but, like Martel's right-hand column, the left also had no troops to follow up its success or even to make good the ground won. Meanwhile, east of Arras, Brigadier Haydon's 150th Brigade (50th Division) had made a harassing raid across the Scarpe towards Tilloy, and the 13th Brigade had established a bridgehead further east in preparation for the second phase of 'Frankforce's' operation. But realizing that he could not hold the ground occupied on the first day and that Rommel's Panzers would soon be threatening his rear to the west of Arras, Franklyn decided to call off the attack. The British counter-attack at Arras had come to a halt. It had advanced a maximum of ten miles, taken more than 400 German prisoners [12] and destroyed a large number of tanks and transport; but it had lost all but twenty-six of its Mark I tanks and two of its valuable Mark IIs.[13] The remainder, with their tracks breaking from the excessive wear of the past days, had to fall back to the rear, constantly harried by Stukas.

The German View

This, in brief, is the British view of what was effectively their first major armoured engagement of the war. The German accounts reveal, however, that the drive Martel instilled into the 'Frankforce' attack, combined with the almost impenetrable thickness of the armour on the British infantry tanks, made an impression out of all proportion to the numbers involved. The S.S. Totenkopf Division apparently abandoned its first line in haste when attacked at Wailly, and even Guderian states that

12. Probably the biggest bag of prisoners taken in any isolated action against the Germans since 10 May.

13. The commanders of both the British tank battalions had also been killed.

it 'showed signs of panic', a comment not to be found previously in his forthright account of the campaign. Rommel's eye-witness account of the day's events is, as so often, the most instructive. At almost exactly the moment that Martel began his attack, Rommel had ordered Rothenburg's 25th Panzer Regiment to advance again around the north-west of Arras. He intended to accompany the tanks himself, together with his faithful A.D.C., Lieutenant Most. But once again he had to retrace his footsteps to shepherd forward his lagging infantry regiments. He could not find the 7th, but just south of Wailly,

we eventually came across part of the 6th Rifle Regiment, and driving alongside their column, turned off with them towards Wailly. Half a mile east of the village we came under fire from the north. One of our howitzer batteries was already in position at the northern exit from the village, firing rapidly on enemy tanks attacking southward from Arras.[14]

Rommel continues:

As we were now coming under machine-gun fire and the infantry had already taken cover to the right, Most and I ran on in front of the armoured cars towards the battery position. It did not look as though the battery would have much difficulty in dealing with the enemy tanks, for the gunners were calmly hurling round after round into them in complete disregard of the return fire.

But on reaching Wailly itself, Rommel found that the British tank fire had created

chaos and confusion among our troops in the village and they were jamming up the roads and yards with their vehicles, instead of going into action with every available weapon to fight off the oncoming enemy. We tried to create order.

West of the village, Rommel came across a light flak troop and some anti-tank guns, 'most of them totally under cover'. Close to this position, British tanks had shot up a Mark III Panzer, and other tanks approaching from Bac-du-Nord were pressing in closely upon Wailly. 'It was,' says Rommel, 'an

14. This was in fact the right-hand column of Martel's force.

extremely tight spot.' He watched while 'the crew of a howitzer battery, some distance away, now left their guns, swept along by the retreating infantry'. The scene was almost more reminiscent of the French débâcle at Sedan than anything previously recounted by Rommel. To restore this perilous situation, Rommel continues:

With Most's help, I brought every available gun into action at top speed against the tanks. Every gun, both anti-tank and anti-aircraft, was ordered to open rapid fire immediately and I personally gave each gun its target. We ran from gun to gun . . . Soon we succeeded in putting the leading enemy tanks out of action. About 150 yards west of our small wood a British captain climbed out of a heavy tank and walked unsteadily towards us with his hands up. We had killed his driver.

Rommel then switched the fire of his guns to another group of British tanks, knocking out several and forcing the remainder to retreat:

Although we were under very heavy fire from the tanks during this action, the gun crews worked magnificently. The worst seemed to be over and the attack beaten off, when suddenly Most sank to the ground behind a 20-mm. anti-aircraft gun close beside me. He was mortally wounded.

Lieutenant Most was the second of Rommel's A.D.C.s to fall at his side already during the campaign,[15] but this episode marked the final halting of Martel's right-hand column.

Turning now to the progress of the left-hand column, Rommel speaks of 'very powerful armoured forces' which had inflicted 'heavy losses in men and material' on his 6th Rifle Regiment:

The anti-tank guns which we quickly deployed showed themselves to be far too light to be effective against the heavily armoured British tanks, and the majority of them were put out of action by gunfire, together with their crews, and then overrun by the enemy tanks. Many of our vehicles were burnt out.

The attack was finally brought to a halt after Rommel had

15. The first, Lieutenant Schraepler, recovered from his wounds and returned to Rommel a few days later.

established a strong gun-line between Beaurains and Agny, formed from his divisional artillery and 88-mm. anti-aircraft batteries. Firing over open sights, the German field-pieces proved too much even for the thick armour of the Matildas, and once again the 88s proved their deadliness, one battery alone claiming nine tanks. Later that evening Rommel was striking with his tanks north-west of Arras at the flank and rear of 'Frankforce'. There was another fierce engagement, during which seven more heavy British tanks were knocked out, but at a cost of nine of Rommel's.

The day's fighting cost Rommel considerably more tanks than any other operation so far. His casualties amounted to 89 killed (including seven officers), 116 wounded and 173 missing.[16] For one of the few times in the campaign, German eye-witnesses, as their accounts reveal, were particularly struck by the number of their own burnt-out tanks visible on the battlefield, and it is perhaps instructive that in the German propaganda film, *Sieg im West*, Martel's action at Arras is the only Allied counter-stroke to be singled out for special mention. There is no reference to de Gaulle. That Rommel for one was even more concerned than his diaries reveal is apparent from the magnification of Martel's four battalions in his own immediate appraisals; his communiqué on the 21st speaks of being attacked by 'hundreds of enemy tanks', while situation maps marked up in his own hand display arrows purporting a counter-offensive by '*five* enemy divisions'.

Rommel's anxiety echoed back all the way up the German chain of command. His Army Commander, Kluge of the 4th Army, admits in his communiqué that the 21st was 'the first day on which the enemy had met with any real success', and he was inclined to halt any further advance westward from Arras until the situation there had been resolved. In Kleist's Armoured Group, the 6th and 8th Panzers were ordered by Rundstedt to

16. Or four times the losses suffered during the breakthrough into France. One of Rommel's battalion commanders, Major von Paris, had a very lucky escape. After his unit had been overrun by Martel's tanks, he evidently took refuge in a house, under a bed. Some British officers apparently came in and rested on the bed, and Paris was only able to get out when the British withdrew the next day.

swing back from Le Boisle and Hesdin (which they had reached) respectively, to assume defensive positions along the flank of the 'five enemy divisions', while Guderian's 10th Panzer, still badly needed to guard the southern flank of the 'Panzer Corridor', was placed in reserve, to be ready in case of emergency to move up to the Arras front. In front of the Nuremberg Tribunal, Rundstedt declared:

A critical moment in the drive came just as my forces had reached the Channel. It was caused by a British counter-stroke southward from Arras on 21 May. For a short time it was feared that our armoured divisions would be cut off before the infantry divisions could come up to support them. None of the French counter-attacks carried any serious threat as this one did.

Back at O.K.H., Halder recorded in his diary early on the 21st: 'The day begins in a quite nervous atmosphere! ... a rather heavy pressure is being exerted on the north flank of the 4th Army.' As the day ended, returning to his prevailing mood of confidence, he wrote: 'The situation on the right wing of Kluge cannot be very serious. Only local affairs ...!', but by the following morning his first entry betrays a new note of concern:

Army Group 'A' has temporarily decreed a halt ... of the Panzer movement in the direction of Calais which we ordered yesterday and will only unleash it when the situation at Arras is cleared up ... everything depends on getting the infantry quickly up to Arras and westwards.

Finally, the shock received at Arras infected Hitler himself, resulting in a new nervousness which was to contribute directly to the Germans' greatest failure of the campaign. On the Allied side, the breakdown of the operation finally convinced Gort that the only hope for the B.E.F. was to fall back on Dunkirk, rather than to try to hack its way through to the south, as Ironside and Churchill had hoped.

Weygand Flies North

As Gort was about to launch his 'Frankforce' attack, the new French C.-in-C. had departed on his trip to the northern commanders. Once again the journey (in both directions) was such as might have broken the spirit of a far younger man. Arriving at Le Bourget airport with a solitary aide, Weygand found that the authorities there 'seemed to have heard nothing of this journey. We were sent from one end of the airfield to the other.' Having wasted an hour in this manner, he took off shortly after dawn with a flight of fighters as escort. The first unmistakable sign that the enemy had broken through to the coast came when, crossing the River Canche,[17] his plane was sharply greeted with anti-aircraft fire. A little further on, his escort had to drive off some attacking Messerschmitts. Arriving safely at the airfield of Norrent-Fontes, north-west of Béthune, Weygand found it abandoned as 'unserviceable' on account of enemy bombing. He continues:

After wandering past empty hangars in which everything indicated a precipitate departure, at last we met a small soldier, very dirty but with an attractive face, who told us what had happened and asked me what he was to do with 20,000 litres of petrol about which he was greatly concerned, having received no orders.

There was no sign of any transport awaiting the Generalissimo; later it transpired that cars had been sent to collect him from Abbeville, but had arrived to find the city in flames, and returned – narrowly escaping Guderian's Panzers. At last, however, Weygand and his A.D.C. discovered an ancient military truck, of which the small soldier with the grubby face appeared to be the driver. After some misdirections Weygand found his way to a village with a functioning civilian post office,

where, after long efforts, the postmaster secured communication, abominably bad though it was, with the General Staff of No. 1 Army Group. In this way I learned that General Billotte had been trying to find me, though nobody could say in what direction he had gone.

17. Running inland from Montreuil through Hesdin. See Map 6.

Weygand then decided to take off again for Calais. While waiting for the necessary order to be given, and tortured with
hunger, he went to an inn in a half-deserted village and ordered
an omelette. He was served by a woman whose husband was
away at the front, and who told him 'she did not wish to go
away, for she did not know where to go, and what was the
use?' On the wall there was a lithograph of the signing of the
Armistice in November 1918, and from it she suddenly recognized Weygand, exclaiming: 'How can I be frightened now
you are here?' With this small encouragement, Weygand flew
on to Calais, where he learned that the King of the Belgians (as
C.-in-C. of the Belgian Army) was waiting for himself and
Billotte at Ypres town hall. Through roads appallingly en-
cumbered with refugees and Army convoys, Weygand was
driven to Ypres, which he reached at 1500 hours. King Leopold
had already arrived, but not Billotte – nor Gort. The only
British representative there was Admiral Sir Roger Keyes, who
was attached to King Leopold. Such was the unpromising confusion surrounding the advent of the new Allied Generalissimo.

In the mayor's office of Ypres town hall, there ensued what
the King of the Belgians described as 'four hours of confused
talking'. Three separate meetings took place that day. The first
was between King Leopold, attended by his A.D.C., General
van Overstraeten, and General Weygand.[18] Outside were waiting three Belgian Ministers – Premier Pierlot, General Denis,
the Minister of National Defence, and the immortal Paul-
Henri Spaak, then Foreign Minister. Later they alleged that the
King had high-handedly refused to allow them to join in the
conference and that they had only 'learned by chance' that this
meeting of Allied commanders was going to take place at all;
the King in his turn accused his Ministers of adopting 'an
aggressive and disagreeable attitude'. Consequently, in this state
of strain between the Belgian King and his Ministers, accounts
of what took place in the meeting with Weygand vary radically.
According to Weygand, he told King Leopold that the Belgian
Army, now standing on the River Escaut (Scheldt), 'had remained too long in the east' and should now retreat further

18. Reckoned by some to be the King's bar-sinister uncle.

west as soon as possible – if necessary, as far as the Yser. Leopold said this was impossible; his Army 'was too tired to do this after the forced marches it had made'. Instead, he seemed to want to 'form a vast bridgehead at Ostend'. This conflicted diametrically with the project already formulating in Weygand's mind. He wanted the Belgians to fall back and hold the line of the Yser – as they had done from 1914 onwards – so that, with the left flank shortened and secured, the B.E.F. would be free to strike southwards with all its strength. But this would, of course, mean abandoning all but a few square miles of Belgian territory. General van Overstraeten claims that, on behalf of the King, he objected that it was 'absolutely necessary to suspend withdrawal because the divisions were beginning to disintegrate under a succession of night retreats – the bane of discipline'. Weygand says that the King refused then to come to any decision: 'he said he would think it over and let me know later'. Weygand thought he detected signs already of 'profound discouragement' in the Belgian King, while Premier Pierlot, who saw Leopold immediately after his tête-à-tête with Weygand, has stated that 'The King considered the position of the armies in Flanders almost, if not quite, hopeless.' Certainly, it seems true to say that in refusing to withdraw to the Yser King Leopold was, in effect, anticipating defeat.

While this discussion was going on, through the chaos of communications Billotte had at last managed to trace Weygand's whereabouts and had arrived at Ypres. But there was still no sign of Gort or any of his staff, and Blanchard, who shared an equally vital interest in the plans being discussed, had apparently not been invited. Billotte was to be granted no opportunity to set down his own recollection of what transpired at this second meeting at the Ypres town hall – so, once again, accounts of it vary. Apparently Weygand outlined his projected scheme in the broadest terms; this would be to strike simultaneously southwards from around Cambrai and northwards from the Somme, the two thrusts meeting somewhere in the neighbourhood of Bapaume. According to General van Overstraeten, Billotte then pointed out that the French First Army was in a very confused situation, tired and severely tested,

incapable of launching an attack, and barely capable of defending itself. In his opinion, only the B.E.F. still constituted a
powerful offensive force. Weygand comments: 'I had long been
aware of the intelligence, decision, and energy of General
Billotte ... The fatigues and anxieties of the past two weeks
had left a deep mark on him, but he realized the capital importance of the manoeuvre to be carried out and shared my
view of its urgency.' But it is questionable whether Billotte
gave Weygand the full facts concerning the 'Frankforce' attack
then in progress – namely, that Blanchard had declared himself
unable to launch a two-division attack until the 22nd–23rd,
and that Gort had only been able to find one brigade group,
with which he was attacking at that very moment. If Blanchard
and Gort had been at the Ypres meeting, it seems improbable
that Weygand could have returned to Paris harbouring any
serious belief that the northern armies could ever attack con-
certedly on anything like the scale that he would be promising
in front of Reynaud and Churchill twenty-four hours later.
Once again a French C.-in-C. was to deceive his Government
with false hopes.

Gort Misses Weygand: Billotte Mortally Injured

Annoyed that Gort had neither turned up nor sent any explana-
tory message, Weygand waited in Ypres for him until 1900
hours. 'I could not go back without meeting him,' thought
Weygand, and despite his undertaking to Reynaud to return to
Paris within twenty-four hours, he wondered, 'Ought I to spend
the night where I was and try to succeed better next day?' At
this moment, Admiral Abrial, the French Commander of the
Naval Forces of the North, presented himself and, warning
Weygand that enemy bombing of airfields had now made it
impossible for him to fly out, he offered to place at his disposal
a 600-ton torpedo-boat, the *Flore*. Weygand accepted and left
forthwith for Dunkirk. There he embarked in the midst of a
violent air-raid, with the *Flore* crossing the harbour at full
speed, 'amidst fountains of water thrown up by bombs falling
in the sea, and alongside the quays set alight by incendiaries'.

After a detour via Dover, the *Flore* deposited Weygand at Cherbourg shortly after dawn on the 22nd. From there he continued his journey, and, still showing no trace of fatigue, reached Paris at about 1000 hours.

Approximately an hour after Weygand left Ypres, Gort arrived. Previously, both King Leopold and General van Overstraeten had urged that efforts be made to bring Gort to the meeting, since nothing could be decided without his views being known. In vain, Overstraeten had tried to reach him on the telephone and then had driven with Admiral Keys to Hazebrouck, where Gort was thought to be. Eventually he was tracked down to his new command post, at Prémesques, between Lille and Armentières, where he had just moved from Wahagnies. According to Gort, all he knew of Weygand's visit was a signal from Churchill to Keyes, copy to Gort, received the previous night (the 20th), which stated simply 'Weygand is coming up your way tomorrow to concert action of all forces.' A message sent by the British mission at French G.Q.G., warning that Weygand would land at Norrent-Fontes at 0900 hours, apparently miscarried; there is no record of its receipt either at B.E.F.'s G.H.Q. or Gort's command post. Meanwhile, he had spent the whole day waiting for notification of Weygand's whereabouts. Until Overstraeten's intervention, no one on the French side seems to have thought of sending messengers to scour the countryside for the British commander.

Weygand was to go into German captivity still believing that Gort 'had purposely abstained from coming to the Ypres conference'. To this day, Gort's absence remains a matter of acute controversy in France. Did he stay away in a state of pique because Altmayer had not materialized at the 'Frankforce' conference the previous night, and because the French had failed to participate in the Arras attack? J. Benoist-Méchin [19] suggests that Gort deliberately absented himself, because he had already become 'a partisan of evacuation', and any involvement

19. Benoist-Méchin's *Soixante Jours qui Ébranlèrent l'Occident* (Paris, 1956), partly written while he was serving a commuted death sentence for collaboration, contains a mass of inaccuracies, although it made a considerable impact in France.

in Weygand's offensive schemes would have placed him 'in an inextricable position'. On Gort's side, there is the fact of the appalling communications and the signal which never arrived; he had just shifted his command post, on the 21st, and his preoccupation both with the Arras counter-attack and the awkward predicament of two of his corps on the Escaut front would seem to offer sufficient excuse for not attempting to track down Weygand.[20] But principally, any such complex devious thinking as Benoist-Méchin attributes to Gort is simply out of character.

The failure of Gort and Weygand to meet on the 21st was in any event disastrous. At Ypres the third meeting of the day took place between Billotte and Gort, at which Billotte relayed Weygand's intentions. Gort in turn reported on the not very encouraging progress of the Arras operation, pointing out that all his available reserves were now committed. The Belgians were finally persuaded to fall back from the Escaut to the Lys, so as to relieve British divisions for Weygand's offensive. But this was a poor compromise; as the map reveals, the Lys line hardly offered any shortening of the front, and Gort reckoned that the switch-over could not be completed in time for the relieved divisions to attack before 26 May at the earliest. As the last meeting ended, King Leopold informed his waiting Ministers that Gort had agreed to co-operate in Weygand's offensive, but

The British General considers that the chances of the manoeuvre in which he is going to take part are practically nil. The situation is desperate . .

Thus in effect nothing specific had been decided about the proposed offensive. The Belgians had not committed themselves to withdrawing to the Yser. Gort had not heard anything that might restore his faith in the capacity of the French First Army

20. On the other hand, Weygand has been equally criticized by French historians for not waiting for Gort in Ypres; and Churchill questions the wisdom of Weygand making the journey at all, thereby sacrificing another precious day.

to join effectively in an attack, and the Belgians had certainly given him no confidence in the security of his left flank. Weygand had returned to Paris thoroughly mistrustful of Gort, and imbued with notions which Gort could swiftly have persuaded him were impracticable, had the two men but met in Ypres. The meetings broke up, according to Overstraeten, in a very depressed atmosphere.

There then followed yet another of the tragic twists of fate that had seemed to dog the Allies from the very beginning of hostilities. Shortly after the Ypres conference, some young British officers were about to appease their hunger by sharing out a bottle of milk found in a nearby farmhouse. Abruptly the door opened and in came a senior French general. Spotting the milk he exclaimed '*Ah! Du lait! Excellent!*' and without any further formality grabbed the bottle, drained it, and then departed before the Britons could register their indignation. This was Billotte, and it was probably the last time he was seen alive by any member of the B.E.F. Carrying him on through the darkness to brief Blanchard about Weygand's intentions, a few hours later Billotte's car apparently skidded and ran into the back of a refugee lorry. The driver, who was wearing a steel helmet, survived; Billotte, not so protected, was gravely injured, and after lying in a coma for two days, died. His removal from the scene could hardly have been more catastrophic for the Allies. He was the only French or British commander with the northern armies who knew of Weygand's plan at first hand,[21] and he was the one person in whom both Gort and King Leopold still had some confidence. With Billotte fighting for his life, another three days were allowed to elapse before the badly shaken Blanchard was confirmed as his successor, and General Prioux was then moved up to command the First Army. Thus in these crucial days there was to be no co-ordinating hand to harness the three Allied armies in the north to the 'Weygand Plan'. Meanwhile, demoralizing rumours swiftly ran round the

21. General d'Astier rates him as having been the most outstanding of all the French commanders, and the only one who could possibly have averted the final disaster.

French camp that the unfortunate Billotte had committed suicide.[22]

Churchill's Second Meeting with Reynaud

In Paris that afternoon, Reynaud had made a courageous – indeed, a great – speech before the Senate. For the first time he revealed to France just how grave was the situation. 'The country is in danger!' he proclaimed. 'It is my first duty to tell the Senate and the nation the truth.' Murmurs swelled into a roar; there were demands for the names of the guilty. The Premier continued, enumerating some of the terrible facts. He spoke of the 'serious failures' of the Ninth Army, condemned General Corap and disclosed that 'through unbelievable faults, which will be punished, bridges over the Meuse were not destroyed'. When he revealed the news that Amiens and Arras had been lost, Alexander Werth in the gallery recorded, 'A gasp of bewilderment rises from the senators' benches ...' The air cleared only a little when Reynaud went on to offer a source of hope:

In the midst of our country's misfortunes we can take pride in the thought that two of her sons, who would have been justified in resting on their laurels, have placed themselves at the nation's service in this tragic hour: Pétain and Weygand. (*Prolonged cheers.*) Pétain, the victor of Verdun, the great soldier with the human touch, the man who knows how a French victory can come out of a cataclysm. Weygand, Foch's man, who halted the German onslaught when the front was broken in 1918 and who was afterwards able to turn the tables and lead us to victory ... France cannot die. For my part, if some day I were to be told that only a miracle could save France, that day I should say: 'I believe in the miracle,[23] because I believe in France.'

After Reynaud's speech, as Senator Bardoux recorded, the atmosphere in the corridors was 'terrifying ... Faces are dis-

---

22. About the same time, rumours were also rife in Paris that Gamelin had done the same.

23. Werth commented sceptically: 'Reynaud's belief in miracles somehow reminds me of the Russian communiqué after the Battle of Tannenberg – "God will not desert Holy Russia".'

torted. Groups form and re-form . . .' Now at last the veils were down.

That evening Reynaud suffered fresh gloomy forebodings as to what would happen if Weygand on his journey should fall into German hands, and to Baudouin he even began to speak of General Huntziger as a possible successor. The following morning (the 22nd) he anxiously waited for Weygand to report in at the Rue Dominique. Despite his arduous experiences of the past twenty-four hours, the seventy-three-year-old General-issimo arrived full of bounce and launched into his analysis of the situation on an evident note of optimism. 'So many mistakes have been made,' he began, 'that they give me confidence. I believe that in future we shall make less.' The B.E.F., he declared, apparently without mentioning its engagement at Arras, 'is in a very good state, for up to the present it has hardly been in action. Some elements in Blanchard's army have been shaken, but . . . this army still constitutes a powerful force.' He then offered to Reynaud the plan he had outlined to King Leopold and Billotte the previous day, namely, the joint thrusts from north and south meeting at Bapaume. In conception, it was roughly the same as Gamelin's short-lived plan, contained in his 'Instruction No. 12' of 19 May; the main differences were that the pincers were to close further to the west, three days later, and it would be a heavier blow. Weygand said that he had 'thoroughly explained' his plan 'to everybody I have seen,[24] I think they understood me, and that I have convinced them. I cannot waste my strength running after armour. It is better to try this manoeuvre of a junction.' He then concluded [25] with a curiously revealing remark: 'It will either give us victory or it will save our honour.' In the coming days, the expression 'save our honour' was to appear with increasing regularity on Weygand's lips, and it indicated which way his thoughts were already beginning to turn. As Colonel Goutard acidly points out: 'As soon as it became a question of "honour", we were in a bad way!'

24. But he had not seen Gort, and Billotte was dying.
25. As the scene is recorded by the Secretary of the War Cabinet, Paul Baudouin.

Reynaud declared himself entirely in agreement with Weygand's project, and informed him that Churchill was due in Paris at 1115. After collecting the British Prime Minister, Reynaud recalls: 'At midday we went together to the stronghold of Vincennes under a sky whose very beauty seemed implacable in those tragic days.' On this second visit of immense importance to Paris, Churchill was once again accompanied by the inseparable General Ismay and General Sir John Dill, who was about to succeed Ironside as C.I.G.S. Ismay noted that, despite the change in command since their last visit, 'the *Beau Geste* flavour of the old fort was just the same – spahis with white cloaks and long curved swords, on guard duty, and the floors and chairs covered with oriental rugs'. (In the light of all these disastrous revelations of the past weeks, how anachronistic the power of the French Army must suddenly have seemed!) But Ismay was at once agreeably surprised by Weygand's appearance:

He gave the appearance of being a fighter – resolute, decisive and amazingly active, in spite of his wizened face and advanced years. He might have been made of indiarubber. One dared to hope that the Allied armies would now have the leadership that had hitherto seemed lacking.

Churchill admits to having been equally taken by the Generalissimo:

In spite of his physical exertions and a night of travel, he was brisk, buoyant, incisive. He made an excellent impression upon all.

The absence of Daladier and his aroma of absinthe was also clearly an improvement.

Weygand's Plan

The meeting, says Ismay, 'was short and businesslike'. Weygand described the situation as he had found it on his trip to Ypres, and then once more gave an exposé of his plan. This met with general agreement, and accordingly Weygand retired to draft his 'General Operation No. 1',[26] which read as follows:

(I) The forces grouped with No. 1 Army Group (the Belgian Army, the B.E.F., and the First Army) will make it their principal task to block the German advance to the sea in order to maintain contact between themselves and the remainder of the French forces.

(II) The German Army will only be stopped and beaten by counter-attacks.

(III) The forces necessary for these counter-attacks already exist in the group, the linear defence of which is much too densely held, and they are:
    some infantry divisions of the First Army;
    the cavalry corps;
    the B.E.F., which must be withdrawn from the line by extending the Belgian sector, and used as a whole.

These counter-attacks will be supported by all the R.A.F. based in France.

(IV) This offensive will be covered on the east by the Belgian Army on the Yser.

The light enemy units which are trying to cause disruption and panic in our rear between the frontier and the Somme, supported by air-raids on our aerodromes and ports, are in a dangerous position and will be destoyed.

Weygand ended his order by declaring that having been 'rounded up', the Panzers 'must not escape again'. One might as well have said the same of the Soviet spy George Blake, after he had been 'sprung' from a British maximum security prison.

To write off the seven Panzer divisions which had driven through the Allied armies as 'light enemy units' might seem to bear little enough relationship to the facts of life,[27] but it was nothing as compared to the telegram Churchill now sent to Gort summarizing the talks at Vincennes:

It was agreed:
1. That the Belgian Army should withdraw to the line of the Yser and stand there, the sluices being opened.

---

26. Which was not, however, dispatched to the now headless No. 1 Army Group until 2050 hours on the 22nd.

27. Certainly as they stood by 22 May.

2. That the British Army and the French First Army should attack south-west towards Bapaume and Cambrai at the earliest moment, certainly tomorrow, with about *eight divisions*,[28] and with the Belgian Cavalry Corps on the right of the British.

3. That as this battle is vital to both armies and the British communications depend upon freeing Amiens, the British Air Force should give the utmost possible help, both by day and by night, while it is going on.

4. That the new French Army Group which is advancing upon Amiens and forming a line along the Somme should strike northwards and join hands with the British divisions who are attacking southwards in the general direction of Bapaume.

In the first place, the Belgians had *never* agreed to withdraw to the Yser. Secondly, as both Blanchard and Gort could have pointed out to the Allied leaders, how could eight divisions, or 100,000 men, turn their backs on the enemy pressing hard from the east and attack southwards, at a day's notice? One of the 'secrets of Marshal Foch', to which Weygand had archly alluded during his valedictory interview with Gamelin, was that Foch had always known exactly the value of the forces he could throw into battle at any given moment. This was something Weygand clearly did *not* know on 22 May, despite his journey of the previous day. Thirdly, it was a gross exaggeration to speak of a 'new French Army Group ... advancing upon Amiens', as Weygand must well have known. The truth was that behind the Somme, between the coast and the Crozat Canal nearly ninety air miles to the east, there were only the five divisions that General Frère had now managed to scratch together in his new Seventh Army, plus the badly mauled 2nd and 5th Light Cavalry, and the newly arrived and unblooded British 1st Armoured Division. In a separate order dispatched by General Georges on the 22nd, these units were summoned up to take their place to the left of General Frère, under command of General Robert Altmayer.[29]

28. Author's italics.

29. Not to be confused with his brother, General René Altmayer, commander of V Corps with the First Army. On 30 May, Robert Altmayer's new *groupement* was to be designated the 'Tenth' Army.

Above all, the enticing vacuum that had existed behind the German spearhead on the 20th and 21st would no longer exist by the 23rd.

Churchill's Hopes

In Reynaud's private ear, Churchill complained that four consecutive days had been allowed to pass without Gort receiving any orders whatever. 'Ever since Weygand had assumed command three days had been lost in taking decisions. The change in the Supreme Command was right. The resultant delay was evil.' Nevertheless, carried along by the vigour with which Weygand had put his case, the Vincennes meeting (so Ismay records) 'ended on a note of restrained optimism'. Before he left, Churchill remarked flatteringly to Weygand: 'There is only one fault in you; you are too young!'

Throughout his career, Churchill would always show himself susceptible to a general who gave the appearance of being a fighter, and Weygand, in sharp antithesis to the pallid intellectualism of Gamelin, clearly struck him as such. Shaken as he had been by the dreadful revelations in Paris of 16 May, as the British statesman who had once cried out 'Thank God for the French Army!' Churchill still harboured some romantic faith in that Army. Indeed, could this magnificent weapon upon which all the calculations of British European policy had been founded since 1919, could it really be proved a broken reed by the events of just twelve terrible days? As both historian and participant, Churchill retained the memory of Foch and the 'Miracle of the Marne' and July 1918 constantly before his eyes. Surely, as on both those occasions, the French Army would spring back again at the eleventh hour? Now, if a *fighting* French general, the spiritual heir to Foch, declared that such an offensive operation was possible, then it must be tried, though without being too pragmatic. And here, as far as experience with practicalities is concerned, Churchill shares some of Weygand's own limitations. Like Wavell in Greece the following year, Weygand had been plunged into the middle of battle with no previous first-hand knowledge of the speed and momentum and utter destructiveness of a modern armoured *Blitzkrieg*; similarly, Churchill – and this must always be borne in mind when considering his actions in May 1940 – after those years in the wilderness, remote from the pragmatism of public office, had had less than a fortnight of unrelenting crisis in which to acquaint himself with the practical logistics of an army at war in 1940. Now, Weygand had rekindled Churchill's faith. In the vivid words of Spears, the Weygand Plan 'hung like a limp sail from the mast', but Churchill in his turn, 'like a new Aeolus, filled it momentarily with the power of his lungs'. (But added Spears, 'the ship did not move'.)

At 1930 that same night Churchill was back in London and holding a Cabinet meeting. General Ironside noted dejectedly that 'he was almost in buoyant spirits'. The impression Weygand had made upon him remained markedly observable, and he stuck to his belief in the feasibility of his plan. Some of Churchill's military advisers, however, were much less happy. Ironside, for one (although, as he was about to be replaced as C.I.G.S., his views no longer counted greatly with Churchill), now completely disillusioned by what he had seen on his visit to Billotte two days previously, thought that 'when it all came down to things it was still all *projets*'. The B.E.F., he said gloomily, had 'lost a chance of extricating itself'. But even Churchill's faith in Weygand's 'project' would begin to wilt in the face of events before many more hours went by.

The Panzers Drive for the Channel Ports

After the well-deserved day of rest forced upon his Panzers, Guderian was on the move again early on the morning of the 22nd. His orders now were to swing northwards and seize the Channel ports. Originally he had wanted to throw the relatively fresh 10th Panzer towards Dunkirk at full speed; this was refused him, on account of 'Frankforce's' attack at Arras on the 21st which had persuaded Kleist to keep the 10th back as Armoured Group reserve, in case the situation worsened.[30]

30. Here at least was one most tangible benefit gained by Martel's effort. What the consequence might have been if Guderian had been able to break

Guderian says 'it was with a heavy heart' that he changed his plans. The 1st Panzer, bolstered by the Grossdeutschland Regiment, which was now back in the fold after recuperating from the fighting at Stonne, was to head for Calais, while the 2nd swept up the coast to Boulogne. By 0700 hours his forces had crossed the River Authie, some fifteen miles north from Abbeville; though Guderian noted, significantly, that they could not move in full strength since units of both divisions had to be left behind to secure the Somme bridgeheads until the motorized infantry of Wietersheim's XIV Corps caught up to fill its now familiar relieving role. That afternoon there was fierce fighting on the approaches to Boulogne, and for the first time Guderian recorded being vigorously attacked by Allied aircraft, 'while we saw little of our own Luftwaffe'. Owing to the speed of the advance, the German tactical air support was now operating at long range at the same time that the battlefield was coming within comfortable radius of the R.A.F. Air Component units relocated in Kent.

But on the ground, resistance was patchy and ill organized, so that by nightfall on the 22nd, Guderian was at the gates of both Boulogne and Calais, after making another staggering advance of over sixty miles (to Calais). Kleist having in the meantime decided that the crisis at Arras was past, the 10th Panzer returned to Guderian, who promptly ordered it to replace the 1st Panzer before Calais on the morning of the 23rd. The 1st was then to hasten eastwards to strike out for Gravelines and for Dunkirk, just twenty-five miles by road along the coast from Calais. During the 23rd, however, it encountered much tougher resistance and halted that night on the Aa Canal after progressing only some fifteen-odd miles. The 2nd Panzer was also involved in heavy fighting at Boulogne, which was stoutly defended by Irish and Welsh Guards of the 20th Guards Brigade (only two days previously they had been training in Surrey) and improvised French garrison defence forces. For several hours the thick medieval ramparts of the old port kept

---

through to Dunkirk on the 23rd as easily as he did to Boulogne and Calais is not pleasant to contemplate.

even the Panzers at bay; then an '88' was brought up, and it blasted a hole in the wall through which the tanks were able to make their way. But it was not until the 25th that the 2nd Panzer was able to hoist the Swastika over Boulogne, thereby providing another important setback in Guderian's timetable for grabbing the far more important booty of Dunkirk. Meanwhile, under personal orders from Churchill not to surrender, Brigadier C. N. Nicholson held out at Calais until late on the 26th in one of the finest stonewalling actions of the British Army,[31] thereby pinning down the 10th Panzer which otherwise might also have been deployed against Dunkirk.

On the 21st, elements of Reinhardt's 6th and 8th Panzers had been ordered to swing inland to meet the threat developing at Arras, and on the next day they were in turn pushing menacingly at Gort's right flank west of the Béthune–Arras line. At the same time, once Martel's attack had been brought to a halt, Reinhardt's main force (now reinforced by a motorized S.S. division moved up from Holland) thrust northwards on a course parallel to Guderian's, so that by the end of the 23rd it too was standing on the Aa Canal, in the area of St Omer.

As soon as Rommel had recovered his breath from the shock at Arras, on the 22nd he was attacking again, using his armour in his favoured technique of slipping round the enemy flank, while his riflemen kept it pinned down frontally. At Marœuil, Rothenburg's tanks overran some British gun batteries supporting Martel's rear. They then pushed up on to Mont-St-Éloi, an important height overlooking Arras from the north-west, where they were temporarily driven off in a spirited counter-attack by a regiment of Prioux's motorized Dragoons. On the 23rd, General von Hartlieb's 5th Panzer drew level with Rommel, almost for the first time since the crossing of the Meuse, and Colonel Werner's tanks (of the 31st Panzer Regiment) now joined Rothenburg's in the flanking drive to the west of Arras. By the evening of that day Werner stood on the dominating Lorette Heights, the scene of so much bitter fighting in 1915,

31. When called upon to surrender by the 10th Panzer, Nicholson replied: 'The answer is no, as it is the British Army's duty to fight as well as it is the German's.' He later died in a German prisoner-of-war camp.

where a French war memorial bears the inscription 'Who holds the Lorette Heights holds France.' [32] Rommel's advance guard was within sight of the outskirts of Béthune and threatening the Lens road, 'Frankforce's' principal line of access to Arras. Meanwhile German motorized infantry was attacking the city itself – which was being subjected to constant dive-bombing – from three sides.

All the time more and more second-line infantry divisions were pouring into the Panzer Corridor, to plug any possible breaches that the Allies might exploit. By-passing Hoth's Panzers, Hoeppner's 3rd and 4th Panzer Divisions were now moving into line to take up positions between Rommel and Reinhardt; thus all the German armour [33] would shortly be concentrated in an arc facing eastwards, opposite (principally) the B.E.F. At the same time as the German armour was thrusting into the western flank of the encircled Allied armies, Bock's infantry divisions were also stepping up their pressure against the Escaut Line, and by the 23rd the tired Belgians [34] had been forced to abandon the anchor points of Terneuzen and Ghent.

William Shirer was there to watch the German preparations for crossing the Escaut:

Heavy artillery – and this is amazing to see – six-inch guns, pulled by caterpillar trucks, and on rubber tyres, are being hauled up a hillside at forty miles an hour. (Is this one of the German military secrets, such big guns being hauled so fast?) . . . over the front all afternoon hover two or three reconnaissance planes, German, obviously, directing artillery fire. They cruise over the battlefield unmolested . . . The lack of observation planes alone puts the Allies in a hole. In fact we do not see an Allied plane all day long.

Once again Shirer was struck by the calm organization of the Wehrmacht going about its business: 'Even the wounded seem

32. In his diary for the 23rd, Halder exclaimed: 'Notre-Dame de Lorette! The fate of France is in our hands!'

33. With the exception of the 9th Panzer, arriving from Holland, which would be deployed guarding the Somme flank.

34. Who, for the four days following Billotte's accident on the 21st, received no instructions from the French.

to play their part in this gigantic businesslike machine. They do not moan . . .' But what particularly impressed him was the morale of the German troops. It was 'fantastically good':

I remember a company of engineers which was about to go down to the Scheldt River to lay a pontoon bridge under enemy fire. The men were reclining on the edge of the wood reading the day's edition of the army daily paper, the *Western Front*. I've never seen men going into a battle from which some were sure never to come out alive – well, so nonchalantly.

In contrast, Shirer sadly recalls some unaddressed letters he had found near the recent graves of two dead French soldiers: 'They must have been written before the push began. They tell of the boredom of army life and how you are waiting for your next leave in Paris, "*ma chérie*".'

In these days the smell of victory was unmistakably in German nostrils. Rommel, in one of his brief notes to his wife, wrote on the 23rd:

Dearest Lu,
    With a few hours' sleep behind me, it's time for a line to you. I'm fine in every way. My division has had a blazing success. Dinant, Philippeville, breakthrough the Maginot Line and advance in one night forty miles through France to Le Cateau, then Cambrai, Arras, always far in front of everybody else. Now the hunt is up against sixty encircled British, French and Belgian divisions. Don't worry about me. As I see it the war in France may be over in a fortnight.

Lieutenant Karl-Heinz Mende, with one of the infantry divisions pouring into the Panzer Corridor, wrote home about the same time:

don't try to form impressions of what is happening here. What is logical and what can be estimated, that is too small a yardstick for these days; out of all that is happening there is only one thing that is certain – every day something new, every hour something new.

Reflecting the admiration many young Germans felt for the astonishing successes run up by their Führer, he speaks glow-

ingly of 'an infallible victorious deed of a genius', and later
declares: 'This war is good . . .'

22 May: the French Attack

While 'Frankforce' was having a hard time holding its ground
west of Arras, at 0900 hours on the 22nd, General René
Altmayer launched the attack originally agreed between Ironside and Billotte and which had failed to materialize the previous day. But instead of the projected two-division thrust, as
had happened with 'Frankforce' the French effort was whittled
down to one infantry regiment (the 121st, belonging to General
Molinié's 25th Motorized Division), supported by two armoured
reconnaissance groups and artillery. Striking from the east of
Douai towards Cambrai, the 121st executed its orders brilliantly, administering a hard blow to the German 32nd Infantry
Division. French light tanks penetrated quickly to the outskirts
of Cambrai. Then they were heavily bombed by formations of
Henschel 123s,[35] and strafed by cannon-firing Messerschmitts;
finally, yet again, it was German 88s firing at a range of 150
yards, that halted the French armour. Twelve hours after the
beginning of the French attack, orders came through from
First Army for it to halt and withdraw behind its start-line.
That the attack took place at all when, in theory, the First
Army and the B.E.F. should have been conserving their
strength for Weygand's 'eight-division' counter-stroke projected for the 23rd, in itself reveals the disastrous breakdown in
co-ordination which followed Billotte's fatal accident; Gort,
for one, had also not been warned of Molinié's operation.

The exercising of command in the encircled armies of the
north was becoming increasingly difficult. General Blanchard's
H.Q. had been driven out of Lens after a Luftwaffe incendiary
raid had turned the town into a sea of fire. It moved to the

35. The Henschel 123 was the old biplane dive-bomber that was predecessor to the Stuka. That it had to be thrown into the battle at all at Cambrai
is further indication of the strain that the Luftwaffe, having suffered heavy
casualties among its relatively few Stukas, was temporarily feeling on 21 and
22 May.

village of Estaires until that was bombed to pieces; then on to Attiches, which was also soon blasted by the Luftwaffe. The headquarters' power plants were destroyed, so there was no electric light or radio. Around it were constantly milling large numbers of dejected soldiers who had lost their units, their equipment and their rifles and were too tired to march any further. Under the ceaseless air attacks, there were inevitably signs of still further cracks in French morale. In Paris, Weygand told Baudouin on 23 May that he had received information that forty French officers from the armies in the north had taken refuge in London; they were to be arrested and brought back to France. There had been times recently, Weygand added, when he had 'not been able to recognize the morale of the French troops; both in conduct and demeanour they were so different from those I left when I gave up my command'.

As for the relief counter-stroke coming from south of the Somme, which Weygand had depicted so favourably at Vincennes, by the end of 23 May virtually nothing had happened. Elements of General Frère's Seventh Army 'made contact' with the river, while Senegalese troops of the 7th Colonial Division, exhausted after a twenty-mile approach march, were halted on the perimeter of the German bridgehead south of Amiens, some three miles from the city. There could be no possibility of General Robert Altmayer's new *groupement* doing anything effective for several days. There was some basis for Ironside's bitter statement that the deployment of the French forces on that side of the Somme was purely defensive, and they appeared to have 'no intention of attacking but were trying to prevent the Germans from advancing on Paris'.

Gort Decides: Save the B.E.F.

Over the past three days, Gort's frustration had been steadily mounting because of his Government's apparent inability to see how grave the situation was in the north. It reached a peak, bordering on despair, when he received Churchill's directive following the Vincennes meeting of the 22nd. How on earth, in their present state, were the northern armies to mount an eight-division effort by the 23rd? As Gort well knew, the French First Army now totalled no more than eight divisions plus the much reduced elements of the Cavalry Corps, and the most they had so far been able to produce for an attack was one regiment; the B.E.F.'s two divisions formerly kept in reserve were fighting for their lives around Arras, and nothing could be expected from the Belgians. Most annoying of all, he had not even been told in advance of the French attack; with Billotte dead and still not replaced, the absence of any overall control of the three different national forces augured extremely ill for any concerted effort. By the morning of the 23rd, the day on which the Weygand Plan called for the attack to begin, Gort had still not received any specific orders; so, resorting to a rare use of his prerogative, he sent a telegram to the Secretary of State for War, Anthony Eden, pleading that 'co-ordination on this front is essential with the armies of three different nations'. He requested that the universally respected Sir John Dill fly out that day to make an on-the-spot appreciation, and warned Eden forthrightly:

My view is that any advance by us will be in the nature of a sortie and relief must come from the south as we have not, repeat not, ammunition for serious attack.[36]

Arriving at Gort's H.Q. that morning, General Blanchard expressed agreement with this view.

Churchill's response to Gort's plea was to protest to Reynaud in a new and sharper tone about the immediate execution of Weygand's plan:

I demand the issue to the French commanders in north and south and Belgian G.H.Q. of the most stringent orders to carry this out and turn defeat into victory. Time is vital as supplies are short.

This hardly helped Gort in his own difficulties, but (although Gort could not have been aware of it) Churchill was beginning to revise his opinion of Weygand's intentions. At a Cabinet

36. The B.E.F. was placed on half rations that day.

meeting held that morning, after he sent his demand to Reynaud, Churchill pointed out 'that the whole success of the Weygand plan was dependent on the French taking the initiative, which they showed no signs of doing'. That night, when still no Allied action either north or south of the Panzer Corridor had materialized and no orders had been received by either Gort or the Belgians, Churchill followed up with an even tougher signal, addressed to Weygand via Reynaud, and asking:

How does this agree with your statement that Blanchard and Gort are *main dans la main*? . . . Trust you will be able to rectify this. Gort further says that any advance by him must be in the nature of sortie, and that relief must come from the south, as he has not (*repeat* not) ammunition for serious attack. Nevertheless, we are instructing him to persevere in carrying out your plan.

But the most reassuring communication to reach Gort in these days was one from Eden on the 23rd, which read as follows:

Should, however, situation on your communications make this [Weygand Plan] at any time impossible you should inform us so that we can inform French and make naval and air arrangements to assist you should you have to withdraw on the northern coast.

At last, it seemed to show, the Government was beginning to face up to realities. As far as Gort was concerned, here now was an opening for him to act according to his own judgement.

Gort's judgement was now already formulated. It was that the Weygand Plan would never materialize, that the French would never attack, and that the only hope of preserving anything of the B.E.F. was to fall back on Dunkirk while there was still time.[37] The French Army, at any rate in the northern pocket, was finished. Meanwhile, at Arras, Gort was faced with an immediate, compelling danger. For two days, long after any

37. Many of those close to Gort felt it was already too late; Brooke confided to his diary on the evening of 23 May: 'Nothing but a miracle can save the B.E.F. now, and the end cannot be very far off,' while Ironside wrote in much the same tone 'I cannot see that we have much hope of getting any of the B.E.F. out now.'

hope of resuming its attack had vanished, 'Frankforce' had held its own against the bulk of two Panzer divisions. Now, creeping around its flank and rear, Rommel was threatening to encircle it completely. There were only two roads still left available for its extrication. At 0700 on the 23rd, Gort ordered the withdrawal of 'Frankforce' and the abandonment of Arras. During that night the British 5th and 50th Divisions pulled back some fifteen miles,[38] behind the Haute Deule Canal north-east of Arras.

In the atmosphere of mounting recrimination between the Allies, the British withdrawal from Arras provoked considerable bitterness. It was said that – despite the fact that General Franklyn had warned the French units on either side of him – Gort had not informed Blanchard of the move.[39] It was said that the speed and depth of the British withdrawal jeopardized the French forces in this part of the line. It was said (by Weygand) that it thereby abandoned the start-line for the Weygand Plan's attack from the north, and that it demoralized the French forces by conveying the impression that the B.E.F. had renounced participation in it. But even assuming that the Weygand Plan still offered any prospect of success by the 24th, if Franklyn had not abandoned the 'start-line' of Arras, Rommel would almost certainly have enveloped it that day, plus the better part of two British divisions, as well as the remnants of the French Cavalry Corps. Whatever the truth of the matter, the British withdrawal brought from Paul Reynaud a reproachful and ominous telegram, dispatched to Churchill on the 24th:

You wired me this morning that you had instructed General Gort to continue to carry out the Weygand Plan. General Weygand now informs me that, according to a telegram from General Blanchard, the British Army had carried out, on its own initiative, a

---

38. Not, as Weygand and Reynaud claimed at the time, twenty-five miles.

39. Whether this was owing to poor communications or the precipitancy with which the move had to be made, before 'Frankforce' was completely cut off by Rommel, is not quite clear, but it seems that the British Government was also taken by surprise; Ironside comments:

'Why Gort has done this I don't know. He has never told us that he was going to do it or even when he had done it.'

retreat of twenty-five miles towards the ports at a time when our troops moving up from the south are gaining ground towards the north, where they were to meet their allies.

This action of the British Army is in direct opposition to the formal orders renewed this morning by General Weygand. This retreat has naturally obliged General Weygand to change all his arrangements, and he is compelled to give up the idea of closing the gap and restoring a continuous front. I need not lay any stress upon the gravity of the possible consequences.[40]

Reynaud's claims of the southern forces 'gaining ground towards the north' was, however, a palpable exaggeration, and there is more than an element of truth in Spears's [41] counter-charge:

I feel certain that Gort's inevitable withdrawal is being seized upon as an excuse for the fact that no French forces have advanced from the south.

Although on 24 May the Weygand Plan attack was finally fixed for the 26th, Gort's decision to withdraw across the Deule in fact marked the end both of the Plan and of any sensible hope for a break-out across the Panzer Corridor. Even if there had been no prior retreat from Arras, one is forced to conclude that the 24th would have marked the end of such hopes in any event. For already by the beginning of the 23rd the steel-capped vacuum of the 21st had become what Pertinax aptly describes as a 'solid-limbed army'. The German infantry divisions had arrived and the Panzers were now deployed to meet any threat of a break-out by the encircled Allied forces, or to thrust in with the *coup de grâce* at a moment's notice. At every point of the invested perimeter the Allied forces were on the defensive, and there was no prospect of relief from the

40. Reynaud's telegram provoked an angry, baffled query from Churchill to Ironside: 'I must know at earliest why Gort gave up Arras, and what actually he is doing with the rest of his army. Is he still persevering in Weygand's plan, or has he become largely stationary? . . . Clearly, he must not allow himself to be encircled without fighting a battle.'

41. Sent by Churchill to be his personal representative to Paul Reynaud, Spears arrived in Paris on the 25th.

south. Even if the Allies could, then, have effected a temporary break-out from the northern 'pocket', the counter-attack itself would have been extremely vulnerable to attack on both its flanks by much stronger German forces. From the German point of view, the tenuous 'Panzer Corridor' was now inviolable. *Sichelschnitt* had succeeded.

Thus faded the great Allied stratagems for a concerted counter-stroke that would sever the head of the German tortoise. All they had amounted to – the Gamelin Plan, the Ironside Plan, and finally the Weygand Plan with its aim of striking with eight divisions – had been two blows, separated by twenty-four hours, by one British infantry brigade and seventy-four tanks, and one French infantry regiment plus a few light tanks. The British attack at Arras on the 21st was but a straw in the wind, far too light to do more than throw the Germans temporarily off balance; yet the shock it caused indicates what a strong, well co-ordinated and resolutely led effort on 21 May, or preferably earlier, could have achieved. One is tempted to speculate what might have happened if Martel had disposed of even fifty instead of just sixteen 'Matildas'; if his attack could have been accompanied by one of the excellent French armoured divisions squandered so uselessly early in the battle; and possibly supported by the local aerial superiority which, for the first time in the battle, the Allies were capable of attaining on the 21st. This was the day of extreme danger for the Germans. The thinly lined Panzer Corridor was only twenty-five miles wide south of Arras; the opportunities missed at this time are implicit in a report written by the commander of the French 2nd D.L.M.:

My impression is that if I had my division intact, especially my tanks, I could quite easily reach Cambrai. But all I have is the non-armoured element.

At the same time, one is forced to conclude that, although a harder Allied punch on the 21st might have inflicted heavy losses and have stopped the Germans temporarily, they would have come on again, sooner or later; for by 21 May, in terms of men, material and morale, the French Army had already lost too much of its striking-power to be able to recuperate. But without venturing on to the hazardous quicksands of speculation, there can be little doubt as to what material results the 'Frankforce' attack at Arras *did* achieve. It upset the German timetable for the seizure of the Channel ports, without which the 'Miracle of Dunkirk' would have been born dead.

This is what, at this moment of destiny, raised Lord Gort momentarily above the level of the other Allied war leaders. It was on his own responsibility that Gort decided to attack single-handed on the 21st, and on his own responsibility that he decided to disengage on the night of the 23rd and begin the withdrawal that he knew would culminate in evacuation. As far as the overall conduct of the war was concerned, the latter was the most far-reaching decision that could have been taken in May 1940 on the Allied side, and Gort was the only person who could take it. If Gort had been a romantic visionary, a kind of Lawrence, one could conceive that in his imagination he saw those British divisions which he was about to save from the cauldron of Flanders leading the liberation of Europe four summers later. But Gort was not a visionary. Nor was he communicative, and all that can be stated with some certainty is that, by 23 May, he knew that the French Army was finished and that it was his simple duty to save the B.E.F., to fight another day, on some other field. Had the B.E.F. been wiped out in northern France, it is difficult to see how Britain could have continued to fight; and with Britain out of the battle, it is even more difficult to see what combination of circumstances could have aligned America and Stalin's Russia to challenge Hitler.

Chapter 19

The End in the North

24 May – 4 June

Since the retaking of Arras, it has been reported that Amiens and
even Sedan and other important points had been retaken by
counter-attacks.
    Daily Herald, 25 May

German military circles here tonight put it flatly. They said the
fate of the great Allied Army bottled up in Flanders is sealed.
    WILLIAM SHIRER, *Berlin Diary*, 25 May

According to an estimate by the French War Ministry, at least
2,000 German aircraft and 1,400 tanks have been lost in the
operations in Holland, Belgium and France.
    National-Zeitung, Basle, 26 May

We must be careful not to assign to this deliverance the attributes
of a victory. Wars are not won by evacuations.
    WINSTON S. CHURCHILL, speaking to the House of Commons,
    4 June

The collapse of the Weygand Plan meant that the campaign was
now lost beyond recovery. The 'decisive battle' against France
of which both Hitler and Manstein had separately dreamed had
been fought and won. Henceforth minor ripostes and local
actions of extreme gallantry would impose an occasional check
upon the German progress to complete victory, but what
follows during the next month of hostilities until the inevitable
finale in the railway coach at Compiègne is little more than a
grim and protracted postscript to the story already unfolded.
Of this postscript, its most dramatic episode, the evacuation
from Dunkirk, belongs more properly to the first act of the
Battle of Britain than to the closing scenes of the Battle of
France. Yet to complete the narrative, the events of the remaining weeks before France finally laid down her arms require to
be sketched in brief. They begin with the sequel – one of

historical importance, and still a subject of active dispute – deriving from the saga of past discord within the German High Command.

Hitler Orders 'Halt'

On 24 May, after a day in which hard pressure on the encircled Allied perimeter at all points had culminated in the British withdrawal from Arras, General Ironside observed with puzzlement in his diary:

The German mobile columns have definitely been halted for some reason or other. Rather similar to the halt they made before. It is quite certain that there is very little movement about.

Ironside was correct in his supposition. Early on the 24th Guderian and Reinhardt had secured a number of bridgeheads across the Aa Canal. Guderian was limbering up for his final drive on Dunkirk. Then, like a bolt from the blue, Guderian says:

Hitler ordered the left wing [1] *to stop on the Aa.* It was forbidden to cross that stream. We were not informed of the reasons for this. The order contained the words: 'Dunkirk is to be left to the Luftwaffe' . . . We were utterly speechless.

But as it was a 'Führer Order' and no reasons had been given for it, Guderian says that this time 'it was difficult to argue against it'. His Panzers were even instructed to withdraw from the bridgeheads they had established across the Aa. Many explanations have been given for this famous 'Halt Order', which was to last for two critical days: the muddy Flanders terrain, criss-crossed with canals and drainage ditches, was unsuitable for tanks; the Germans had to husband their depleted tank force for the next phase of the battle against the French; Hitler wanted to grant the B.E.F. a 'golden bridge' back to England, so as to ease the conclusion of a peace treaty with the British; Goering, discountenanced by the Army's brilliant successes, had demanded his share of glory for the Luftwaffe;

1. Which now contained virtually all the German armour.

and finally, the vast forces now converging on the compressed Allied pocket were administratively in a tangle. At best these are half-truths. Historians will continue to argue over the motives involved, but the facts seem to be briefly as follows.

On 23 May, Goering had telephoned Hitler at the *Felsennest*, urging him that the moment had come for the Luftwaffe to administer the *coup de grâce* in the north, after which the Army would be required solely to 'occupy the territory'. He resorted to politico-philosophic arguments, declaring that the ultimate triumph should fall to the 'National Socialist' Luftwaffe, rather than to the conservative Army; it came down to a question of Hitler's own personal prestige as opposed to that of the O.K.H. generals. Goering expressed total confidence that the Luftwaffe could indeed finish the job single-handed. Doubtless the argument made its mark with Hitler, though Jodl, the O.K.W. Chief of Operations, remarked acidly of Goering: 'He's shooting his mouth off again.'

At 1030 the next morning, Hitler went to Rundstedt's Army Group 'A' H.Q. at Charleville, which was now many miles behind the battle being fought out in Flanders. Rundstedt explained the situation in detail. He told Hitler that once again the security of the southern flank was still bothering him. According to Army Group 'A' War Diaries, 'The possibility of concerted action by Allied forces in the north and French forces south of the Somme had to be reckoned with.' He stressed the extreme nervousness which had been caused to Kleist's Armoured Group by the British attack at Arras, and pointed out that Kleist had reported up to 50 per cent of his tanks *hors de combat*, although neither he nor Kleist mentioned that the larger part of these would in fact be repaired during the next few days. What if, in the marshy Flanders terrain which Hitler and Rundstedt knew so well from twenty-five years ago, the British 'Matildas'[2] should inflict even more grievous losses on the German armour? How then would they be able to muster the tanks with which to pursue 'Operation Red', the battle to crush the still considerable French forces protecting the rest of

2. They did not know that by now there was only one battleworthy 'Matilda' left in the north.

France south of the Somme? The capitulation of the encircled Allied forces in the north was but a matter of time; preparatory groundwork for 'Operation Red' must assume priority. The previous night he had sent out a preliminary order to Kleist's and Hoth's Panzers to halt where they were the next day, in order 'to allow the situation to clarify itself and to keep our forces concentrated'. This was the burden of what Rundstedt told Hitler.

For the second time in the campaign, Hitler found himself in complete accord with Rundstedt. He was delighted by the measures the Army Group commander had already taken, and agreed particularly with the necessity to husband the armour for the next phase of the battle. Orders were thereupon sent out calling for the indefinite halt of the Panzers and bearing the stamp 'By the Führer's orders' – which made total compliance mandatory.

It was, as two eminent German historians have pointed out, a situation 'probably unique in modern German military history'. What Hitler was in fact doing (not for the last time) was deliberately short-circuiting his top Army advisers, the O.K.H. As might be expected from the stands previously taken, Brauchitsch and particularly Halder strongly disagreed with Rundstedt's and Hitler's appreciation. Already by midday on the 22nd, Halder had noted down in his diary 'a decrease in tension in the overall situation: the enemy is yielding at Arras, west of Arras our Panzers have come up against only a weak enemy'. The next morning, he was showing himself principally concerned over administrative friction between the two Army Groups, Rundstedt's and Bock's, now jostling each other in increasingly confined quarters. Noting the considerable difficulty Army Group 'A' was having in controlling its huge mass of seventy-one divisions,[3] Halder added – in what was obviously a slap at Rundstedt – 'It seems to me questionable whether it is sufficiently flexible and energetic with its staff.' Later that afternoon, doubts were exchanged concerning Kleist, who feels himself not entirely up to his task, so long as the crisis at

3. Increased to this total as a result of various transfers and additions made during the course of the battle.

Arras is not resolved. Losses in Panzers up to 50 per cent. I tell
him that the crisis will be overcome within forty-eight hours. I
know the size of the task imposed. Tenacity must be demanded.

The following day (24 May) Halder's entries continue in much
the same vein:

the power of resistance of the enemy is no longer to be rated very
highly, apart from local fighting. Thus matters will take their own
course; we must only have patience, let them mature.

That night, Halder baldly records the transmission of the
'Halt Order', adding that it was 'on express wish of the Führer!
Within the area specified, the Luftwaffe is to settle the fate of
the encircled armies! !' The exclamation marks themselves contain a wealth of meaning. Ulrich Liss, the Intelligence chief of
'Foreign Armies West', noted that the usually punctual Halder
arrived nearly an hour late for the O.K.H. evening conference,
'in a clear state of rage, such as I have never before nor afterwards seen him in. "For the decision that has just been taken,
the General Staff is not to blame ..." were his approximate
words.'

The 25th, Halder records, 'began again with unpleasant disagreements between Brauchitsch and the Führer'. Hitler, with
Rundstedt ranged behind him, steadfastly held out against any
repeal of the 'Halt Order' in the face of the strongest representations from Brauchitsch and Halder. In evident despair,
Halder wrote in his diary:

A complete upset is thus occurring. I wanted to make Army Group
'A' the hammer, and Army Group 'B' the anvil; but now 'B' is to
be the hammer and 'A' the anvil. Since 'B', however, is faced with
an organized front, this must necessarily be very costly and take
a long time. Another thing, the Luftwaffe, on which so much hope
is now being placed, is completely dependent on the weather.

The whole thing was 'more wearing to the nerves than the
entire organization of the campaign itself'.

Finally, at 1230 on the 26th, Brauchitsch was called to
Felsennest. To his great satisfaction, Hitler informed him that

he had given orders, though with certain reservations, for the Panzers to advance on Dunkirk again, in order to end the evacuation of the British there. But it would take a further sixteen hours to get them moving again. By then, says Guderian, 'it was too late to achieve a great victory'. For during the three days the 'Halt Order' had been in force, much had happened. Four British divisions and a number of French had managed to escape from the cauldron forming at the bottom of the pocket, around Lille, which they certainly would not have done had Rommel been allowed to continue his encircling thrust. The construction of a tough perimeter defence line guarding a Dunkirk bridgehead was well under way. In Britain, the 'Dynamo' evacuation fleet was assembled and, as Hitler informed Brauchitsch, the first embarkations were already being made from Dunkirk. Finally, there were the first signs of a possible break in 'Goering's weather', so crucial to the Luftwaffe if it were to 'finish the job from the air'.

Before leaving this episode, which (as Guderian rightly remarks) was 'to have a most disastrous influence on the whole future course of the war', three myths can be usefully dispatched. In the first place, the excuse that the Flanders mud was responsible for the 'Halt Order' is supported by none of the German tank experts who fought over the area; Guderian, who should have been able to judge better than anybody else, simply dismisses it as 'a poor one'. Secondly, the notion of the 'golden bridge' offered by Hitler to the B.E.F. now finds few supporters, and certainly stands directly at odds with the very definite orders given to the Luftwaffe, which were the 'destruction' of all the encircled enemy forces. The myth in fact appears to have been propagated by Rundstedt's ex-Chief-of-Staff during his interrogation by Liddell Hart immediately after the end of the war. Thirdly, the fault for the 'Halt Order' cannot be placed solely at Hitler's door. Since the war, German generaldom has been committed for various reasons, which include both self-preservation and professional pride, to blaming every war-time error and crime upon Hitler, and in this instance even Guderian is to be found disputing the view that Rundstedt was responsible for holding up the Panzers. But if anyone was primarily to blame, both on the evidence of the episode itself and of his past performance during the campaign, it was Rundstedt. In his exchange with Hitler he was a completely free agent, not a Party hack just playing back Hitler's own wishes. Rundstedt's integrity as a soldier was too great for this. He was an outstanding battle commander, but as a strategist he showed himself throughout to be almost as preconditioned by the experiences of the First World War as his French counterparts. On 24 May, it was the shock of what the British *had done*, coupled with his ineradicable fears of what the French still *could do*, which principally decided Rundstedt, and, through him, persuaded Hitler, to halt the Panzers.

Here, in this disarray within the German High Command, of which the 'Halt Order' of 24 May was the culminating episode, lay the Achilles' heel in Hitler's superlative machine and its superlative plan. Through it the B.E.F. was to be saved; if the Allies could have taken advantage of this Achilles' heel by more resolute action earlier in the battle, could still more have been saved?

The Panzers Move Again

During the Panzer halt, the German infantry formations were still keeping up an unremitting pressure on all sectors of the encircled area. For the Allies, the principal danger points were in the east along the line held by the rapidly flagging Belgian Army, and at the bottom of the pocket where the French First Army, now commanded by General Prioux, was situated. As King Leopold had finally agreed, following the Ypres conference, the Belgians had withdrawn from the Escaut to the Lys on the 25th, but almost immediately Reichenau's infantry had broken through the new line on either side of Courtrai. The next day the Belgians were trying to anchor their right wing between Ypres and Roulers. Blanchard, having succeeded Billotte, was urging them to fall back on the Yser – as Weygand had wanted originally. But the Belgian Chief of the General Staff, Michiels, declared that a further retreat was out of the question, and would only result in the disintegration of his units.

On the afternoon of the 26th, the Belgian High Command warned Blanchard: 'The limits of Belgian resistance are very close to being reached.'

On the rescinding of the 'Halt Order', Rommel's first task was to break across the La Bassée Canal east of Béthune, which was held by the B.E.F. Once again, Rommel had the armour of the 5th Panzer placed under his control. After some hard and costly fighting, by the end of the 27th [4] he had broken through the British line. The 5th Panzer surged forward to capture Armentières, while Rommel swung eastwards to meet German infantry advancing from the opposite direction. Nearly half the French First Army was now cut off in a smaller pocket around Lille. For four more days General Molinié fought an immensely courageous but hopeless action (largely with North African troops), which in fact enabled the B.E.F. and the remainder of the First Army to fall back safely into the Dunkirk bridgehead.[5] But when the jaws of the trap closed, one of those to be taken (along with some 35,000 French troops) was the valiant General Prioux, captured at his command post in Steenwerck by men of the 4th Panzer. During the fighting, Rommel once again came close to losing another of his nine lives when German heavy shells landed by mistake a few yards from his signals vehicle, killing one of his battalion commanders. On 29 May, the 7th Panzer was pulled out of the line for six days' rest and reorganization before taking part in

4. The previous day Rommel was awarded the Ritterkreuz by Hitler, principally in recognition of his exploits at Avesnes. He noted that the 7th Panzer's total losses in the campaign to date amounted to 27 officers killed and 33 wounded, and 1,500 men dead and wounded. 'That's about 12 per cent casualties. Very little compared with what's been achieved,' commented Rommel. By the end of the month, the division had only 86 tanks fit for operations, of which no more than five were Mark IVs; on the other hand, many of the tanks on the unfit list would be ready for action again in a few days.

5. In recognition of its heroic defence, the Germans allowed the Lille garrison to march out with full battle-honours on 1 June. But this tragic episode provided one more source of mounting French bitterness towards the British. Blanchard complained to Weygand that, despite his protests, Gort had taken the B.E.F. withdrawal to Dunkirk entirely into his own hands; thus, it was said, the British had left the French First Army in the lurch at Lille.

·

'Operation Red'. The encirclement of Lille marked the end of Rommel's role in the first phase of *Sichelschnitt*.

Guderian, after the lifting of the 'Halt Order', pushed across the Aa Canal to capture Wormhoudt and Bourbourgville on 28 May and Gravelines, midway between Calais and Dunkirk, on the 29th. (Meanwhile Boulogne had been captured on the 25th; Calais on the 26th, after a last-ditch resistance by the Rifle Brigade under Brigadier Nicholson.) Then, like Rommel and the 7th Panzer, Guderian's XIX Corps was withdrawn to prepare for 'Operation Red'. Bitterly he remarks of the brakes applied to his Panzers in these critical days:

What the future course of the war would have been if we had succeeded at the time in taking the British Expeditionary Force prisoner at Dunkirk, it is now impossible to guess.

French Despair

Behind the lines in France, the appointment of Weygand and his flight to Flanders had been accompanied by another brief flicker of optimism. It was to be the last. On 23 May, Alexander Werth in Paris observed that the bookstalls along the *quais* had reopened and that workmen were busy completing the pedestal of one of the statues on the Pont-du-Louvre – which struck him, under the circumstances, as being rather 'queer'. At a cocktail party two days later he found people expressing confidence that things were 'going far better'; there was talk that 'Weygand has organized his Somme front; that the Flanders and Somme armies will, within the next twenty-four or forty-eight hours, join and cut the German pincer, and that Hitler made a mistake in not attacking Paris on 16 May.' On the 26th, French Army spokesmen were still deriding the 'armchair strategists' who concluded that the Flanders armies had been encircled. The following day, Werth recorded a further sign of continuing normalcy in the shape of Picasso – 'dark jealous mistress and all' – holding forth at the Café Flore, but now even Colonel Thomas in the Hôtel Continental was half-admitting the loss of Calais, while 'the juncture of the Somme and Flanders armies is no longer even mentioned'.

In this last week of May, defeatism began to spread unchecked in France. The signs of despair assumed varied shapes; Vincent Sheean first sensed it on visiting the Quai d'Orsay, when he spotted that one of the grand old *huissiers*, the guardian dragons defending the portals of French diplomacy, had allowed his heavy silver chain, the badge of service, to fall askew so that it was almost dropping off one shoulder. 'It was an arrow pointing toward disaster; anybody who ever knew those stiff, proud lackeys of the Third Republic would have known by this that the Republic was dying.' Arthur Koestler, in between arrests as a suspicious 'alien', discerned the advent of despair in

The onslaught on the railway stations. The disappearance of the buses and taxis from the streets. The melting away of the town, as if infected with consumption. The tommy-guns of the 'flics' at the street corners. The peculiar glance of the people in the Underground, with the dim candles of fear lit behind their eyeballs. The parachutist scare. The Fifth Column psychosis.

Then he was rearrested, along with the leading German anti-Nazis who had sought refuge in France, some of whom now began to take cyanide.

General Spears phrased his first reports to Churchill on much the same lines. Churchill, he said,

had been misinformed when told Paris was getting angry. The city was fast emptying of the well-to-do ... the populace was merely bewildered and apathetic. There was absolutely no sign of the effervescence and excitement that had vibrated through the city in the early days of 1914.

At the same time, from deep within the Maginot Line, Lieutenant Claude Jamet was sadly reflecting:

In whom – officer or soldier – have I discovered a true sacred fire, a sincere ardour, the dedication of one's whole being towards one solitary goal? The sole and complete will to 'make war' – and to win it? Oh yes, we should be vexed to be beaten . . . But how can one get worked up about something that one simply cannot imagine?

On Sunday 26 May, there had been a repetition in Paris of the solemn religious invocations of the previous week. The relics of Ste Geneviève had been displayed in front of the Panthéon, the resting place of the great men of France's past; but for Senator Bardoux, who was again present, the spectacle there of the 'stricken and silent crowd, which has lost its voice so that it can longer even sing the *Marseillaise* and recites the litanies mechanically, is incapable of comforting me. The shadow of 1870 is spreading over the country.'

Belgium Capitulates

As the news got around that the B.E.F. was beginning to embark from Dunkirk, French despair was accompanied by an emotional rift, now rapidly widening, between the Allies. Spears, ever sensitive to the prevailing atmosphere after a lifetime of experience in French affairs, says that on his arrival

for the first time I sensed a break in the relationships between the two nations, no more perceptible than a crack in crystal, but going right through, irreparably. We were no longer one.

The implications of the widening breach were equally horrifying to neutral observers. 'I watched with fear the hatred of the French for the English growing by giant leaps and bounds,' wrote Clare Boothe. 'Many people now quite openly blamed the whole horrible fiasco on the British High Command.'

On 28 May, France learned of another cause of rancour. In the small hours of that morning, Belgium had surrendered. The surrender of the Belgian Army on its left indeed provided the final blow to Prioux's First Army in the Lille pocket (it also left a gaping hole between the B.E.F. and the sea); but from the hints dropped by King Leopold and General Michiels for the past several days, it should have been abundantly clear to the French High Command that it was only a matter of hours before Belgium succumbed. Nevertheless, in the despair of the moment, Reynaud reacted with ferocity. Broadcasting to the nation that night, he declared that Leopold had laid down his arms 'without warning General Blanchard, without a thought or a word for the French or British troops who went to the aid of his country in response to his agonized appeal'. He rated it 'a deed without precedent in history'.[6] Anger towards the defaulting ally swept through France. Listening to Reynaud's broadcast in a bistro, Gordon Waterfield observed two women burst into tears, crying *Les salauds, les salauds!* Parisians threw Belgian refugees out of their houses, countrymen set fire to their wretched carts, French refugees heckled and buffeted them in stations and on the roads.

Weygand and the 'Separate Peace' Lobby

Within Paul Reynaud's Government, the twin viruses of defeatism and anti-British sentiment had established themselves even before they had begun to cast their malaise in wider circles. 24 and 25 May were critical days, and they marked a kind of watershed. Henceforth, Weygand, the 'political general', is to be found exerting an influence over French councils far transcending his military functions as Generalissimo; it was he, not Pétain, who first assumed lead of the 'separate peace' lobby. At 1030 on the 24th, Weygand arrived for a meeting in the Prime Minister's office at which Baudouin and Pétain were also present. According to Baudouin, who reveals himself increasingly in support of Weygand, the new C.-in-C. whispered to him on entering: 'The situation is very serious, for the English are falling back on the ports instead of attacking to the south.' Weygand claimed that he was not surprised by the British manoeuvre, for on the previous evening General Ironside's tone over the telephone had made an unfavourable impression upon him. 'I would willingly have boxed his ears,' he exclaimed to Baudouin. In the course of his conference with Reynaud, Weygand still appeared to be adhering to his original plan, despite

6. At first, Churchill's reaction was far more restrained. He told the House of Commons that he had no intention of passing judgement on the King; and Duff Cooper, the British Minister of Information, declared on the B.B.C. that the Belgians had 'fought bravely ... suffered heavily', and that it was no time for recriminations. Later, however, under strong French pressure, Churchill swung round to condemning King Leopold in much the same terms as Reynaud.

the British withdrawal from Arras. Then, at 1800 hours that evening, Weygand telephoned Baudouin from Vincennes, where he was with General Georges, and asked him to come and see him.

On Baudouin's arrival, Weygand confided that the situation caused by the British withdrawal now seemed much graver than it had in the morning, and as a result he saw himself forced to abandon his plan of two days previously. Weygand, says Baudouin, 'seemed to me overcome by the defection of the English'. He had summoned Baudouin because he wanted him to explain this to Reynaud and also to point out to him the condition in which the French Army would find itself if the forces in the north capitulated. It would then consist of only some fifty divisions, of which eighteen were immobile fortress units, and it would have to hold a front from the Somme to the Maginot Line nearly 350 miles long. Weygand described this remaining force as a 'wall of sand' which would soon be pierced by the enemy. He then outlined to Baudouin his plans for the future:

the French Army ought to resist desperately on the Somme and Aisne positions. Then, when the enemy has broken this resistance, what is left of the French Army should continue to fight where it stands until it is annihilated, *to save the honour of the French flag.*[7]

Weygand repeated to Baudouin what he had told Reynaud that morning, namely, that it had been 'criminal' for France, the previous September, to have declared war without any of the means for carrying it on. Baudouin then expressed his doubts as to whether the Army's morale was up to waging any new desperate struggle on the Somme and the Aisne:

Would it be possible to apply the measures envisaged by the General to save the national honour?

I said to him, 'We have only one object – to get France out of the ordeal which she is undergoing so as to allow her, even if defeated in the field, to rise again' ... With tears in his eyes, the General told me that he shared my fears.

7. Author's italics.

After this meaningful exchange, the two men parted in wide agreement with each other. The fateful word 'armistice' had never once been mentioned, but, as Reynaud points out, this was clearly what was in both their minds, behind the talk about 'saving national honour'.[8] Weygand had now been in command for just four days.

At noon on the following day, 25 May, discussions were held in Reynaud's office lasting two and a half hours. Before they began, Churchill's emissary, General Spears, had arrived to present his credentials to Reynaud, whom he had known well in the past. Reynaud says Spears, launched in with some acid comments on 'how British generals always made for harbours'. Spears begged him 'to set his face against recriminations', saying that the only hope for France and Britain now was to 'act together as brothers':

Reynaud nodded his head in approval. He got up once or twice, his small figure very erect, the shoulders of his black jacket thrown back, and walked up and down, his hands behind his back. Several times he stretched his neck and turned his head to one side as if putting on too high and too tight a collar. His Chinese eyes, always ready to emphasize his wit with a twinkle, did not smile ... He looked not in the least rattled. I said to myself as I had often done before: 'This is a likeable, gallant little man.'

To Spears and to members of the French Government with whom he spoke that day, Reynaud declared – as he was to declare repeatedly in the ensuing weeks – that he would fight, tooth and nail, to the end. Reynaud then invited Spears to attend the session of the War Cabinet which was about to take place.

Inside Reynaud's office, Spears found Marshal Pétain, General Weygand, Admiral Darlan and Paul Baudouin waiting. Weygand had with him a liaison officer from Blanchard's H.Q., a Major Fauvelle, whom he requested should be heard. Says Spears:

8. At the Commission of Inquiry in 1949, Baudouin admitted that he 'was certain ... on 24 May that the struggle was lost', and that he considered Weygand was of the same opinion.

The idea of defeat, or even the shadow of such an idea, never crossed my mind, but, as Commandant Fauvelle told his story in fragments, revealing an appalling state of affairs, and as I realized that his catastrophic defeatism seemed to some extent at least to be accepted as the reflection of the real position, I felt cold fingers turning my heart to stone … In my view nothing short of throwing Fauvelle out of the window would have been adequate.

Fauvelle ended his pessimistic report on Blanchard's situation by declaring 'I believe in a very early capitulation', which provoked a censure for exceeding his brief simultaneously from both Reynaud and Weygand. The discussions continued with Weygand expressing utmost gloom over the prospects of the French Army 'retreating in good order and defending successive positions' in the face of a new German attack. According to Spears, Weygand then turned on Reynaud, and 'with a voice like a saw' said: 'This war is sheer madness, we have gone to war with a 1918 army against a German Army of 1939. It is sheer madness.'

During this and other conferences of such extreme gravity, Spears was shocked to note the number of interruptions on the French Prime Minister's 'harmonium-like telephone'. If it was not his mistress, Hélène de Portes, the caller appeared to be some Parliamentarian requesting 'that his son-in-law serving in the north should be transferred to a part of the front where there were fewer Germans'. Spears found this revelation that the 'Republic of Pals' still prevailed in France horrifying:

The Chairman of a reputable board in the City of London would never allow himself to be interrupted at a meeting where he was discussing the retail price of soap with his colleagues, to deal with a personal question. But here we were, when the fate of France was in the balance, interfered with in this way.

At the same time, Spears admits that his admiration for Reynaud's courage grew, when, following this first meeting, 'I gradually came to appreciate what he was up against, the defeatism in high places and the trance into which France had fallen.'

After Spears departed, a second, still more important meeting [9] of the French War Cabinet was held at the Élysée that
evening, at which President Lebrun was also present. Weygand
opened with a brief and gloomy résumé of the disastrous course
of military operations since 10 May. He claimed still to be
adhering to his 'plan' for the north–south operation towards
Bapaume (despite what he had confided to Baudouin the previous day), now due to begin on the night of the 26th–27th, but
he was hardly optimistic any longer and he regarded it as 'my
duty to prepare for the worst'. At this point, Reynaud interrupted to announce receipt of a telegram from Churchill that
afternoon, which now confirmed the retreat of the British from
Arras, and recognized that the northern forces were to all
intents and purposes surrounded and their communications
cut – save for Ostend and Dunkirk. Weygand continued with
his report, forecasting the course of events that would follow
the loss of the northern armies. France would find herself
'called upon to fight against odds of three to one'. She must
fight a last-ditch stand on the Somme–Aisne position; here
'each section of the Army must fight to the last to save the
honour of the country'. Weygand concluded by repeating yet
again his reproaches about France's unpreparedness to declare
war.[10] 'It is probable,' he prophesied (according to Reynaud),
'that she will pay dearly for this imprudence.' It was time to
think of the resurrection of the country.

President Lebrun [11] now intervened to voice for the first time
the unspoken thought in the mind of Weygand and his supporters. What if the French armies were scattered and destroyed as Weygand envisaged? 'Of course,' he said,

9. The principal source here is Baudouin, who in his role as Secretary was
the only one to take notes; caution must therefore be exercised in accepting
exactly what transpired.

10. Referring to Weygand's own stewardship during the 1930s as French
C.-in-C., Reynaud remarks that he 'took great care not to recognize the
responsibility he bore for the "great mistake" which he denounced'.

11. Of the President of the Republic's role in these days, Mandel made
this caustic comment to Spears: 'He raises his hands to heaven and weeps.
Il pleure.'

we have signed engagements [12] which prevent us from concluding a separate peace, but if Germany makes any relatively advantageous offer we ought nevertheless to examine it closely and objectively.

Weygand expressed sympathy with the President's point of view, and thought that the Government ought to take up this issue with the British right away. Pétain questioned whether there was in fact complete reciprocity of obligations between the two countries; after all, had not Britain put only ten divisions into the field while eighty French divisions were fighting? On the same theme, General Vuillemin of the Air Force [13] stated that while the French were losing some thirty machines a day, R.A.F. fighters had hardly been engaged at all. Although at times B.E.F. troops on the ground might have shared the same view, it was hardly a true picture. Nevertheless, Vuillemin continued that there were only sixty-five British fighters on the Continent while six hundred were kept in England for the defence of the island. 'It is said,' he claimed, 'that during the last three days the English have sent a hundred fighters a day over the Continent, but I have not been able to verify the statement. I do not know in any detail what has been done by the English fighters in France.' [14] M. Campinchi, the Minister of

12. Referring to the Franco-British Declaration signed by Reynaud in London on 28 March (see above p. 215).

13. Vuillemin, who seems never to have recovered from the shock the Luftwaffe prepared for him on his visit to Germany in 1938, seldom contributed at War Cabinet sessions; instead, says Spears pungently, he 'just looked on with the bewildered washed-out eyes of an ancient celluloid doll floating on the opaque waters of the bath it seemed bewildered to find itself in'. '*Vuillemin, nul comme d'habitude*', was Baudouin's verdict.

14. On 21 May it had in fact been agreed that the R.A.F. should henceforth support the armies in the north, with d'Astier's Z.O.A.N. backing the Somme and Aisne fronts. During the last week of May virtually the whole of the R.A.F. Bomber Command's strength of some 500 bombers was continuously employed. The official R.A.F. history states that, from 22 May onwards, 'something like two hundred fighter sorties a day were flown from England over northern France'. Some of Dowding's most treasured possessions, the Spitfire squadrons earmarked for the defence of Britain, were even drawn into the battle by the end of May. In the course of the whole campaign, only ten out of Britain's total of fifty-three fighter squadrons were not engaged in France; of these ten, two were committed in Norway, three

the Marine, injected the ingenious suggestion that, if France wanted to conclude a separate peace without British consent, she might be freed of her obligations if the present French Government, which had signed the joint declaration, were simply to resign. The session ended with Reynaud announcing that he would fly at once to London and that he would explain France's military plight clearly to Churchill. Weygand and his supporters urged that Reynaud should specifically raise the question of the Franco-British Declaration. There was no discussion of whether, in the event of defeat in France, the French Government might follow the example of the other invaded nations and go into exile in London, or elsewhere.

As a result of these meetings of the 25th, Reynaud says, 'if I did not know all, at least I knew ... that Pétain and Weygand were in favour of asking for an armistice on the day the battle of France was lost, and of allowing the Government to be captured in Paris'. In London the next day, he relayed to Churchill the full gravity of France's dilemma and the problem now confronting him from the 'softs' within his own Government. He also expressed concern that Mussolini was about to bring Italy into the war against France. What could Britain do to help here? Reynaud declared his own determination to fight on to the end, but he declined to raise the deli-

---

were night-fighters and two were non-operational. Though General Vuillemin may not have been aware of it, the Germans certainly noticed R.A.F. intervention in the battle in the north from 22 May onwards. Jacobsen and Rohwer write:

'... for the first time VIII Air Corps was compelled to admit that its Stukas had suffered heavy losses from the unexpected appearance of numerous British fighter planes. Many R.A.F. planes until now held back for the defence of the United Kingdom had obviously been flown from their bases in south-east England, and taken part in the air war on the Continent. With this, the situation in the air suddenly grew critical.'

Meanwhile, as far as the French air effort was concerned, as late as 30 May the Minister of Air, M. Laurent-Eynac, revealed that, in all but fighters, the French Air Force was actually *stronger* in numbers than on 10 May; 660 aircraft had been lost, but 571 new machines had been delivered. According to French sources, by the Armistice of 22 June the French Air Force was *still* stronger and better equipped than it had been on 10 May.

cate issue demanded by Weygand. At 1930 that evening he was
met at Le Bourget by Baudouin, who at once asked him:

'What did you say of the necessity in which we may shortly find
ourselves of breaking off the fight? In what conditions will the
English free us from our promise?' 'I was not able to put the
question,' he replied. I told him that he had done wrong; that he
had not fulfilled the mission with which the War Committee had
entrusted him.

If so junior a Minister [15] expressed himself in these terms to
the Prime Minister of France, it is in itself indicative of the
growing ascendancy of Paul Baudouin. Behind Baudouin one
may descry the shadowy agency of the Comtesse de Portes, his
political patroness, indefatigable, inflamedly anti-British and
already dedicated to a separate peace, but (for once) apparently
unable to use the weapons of the boudoir to influence her
lover, Reynaud, determined as he now was on fighting to the
end.

   During Reynaud's absence in London, Pétain had called
upon Baudouin. He revealed to Baudouin that he too did not
believe in a fight to the finish. The old Marshal who had gained
his reputation for husbanding the lives of his men at Verdun
thought that it was 'easy and stupid to talk of fighting to the
last man; it is also criminal in view of our losses in the last war
and of our low birthrate'. He felt that a part of the Army must
be saved; for without it 'to maintain order a true peace is impossible'. In the days to come, these last words were to corres-
pond faithfully with Weygand's own views.

From the South: the Last Allied Attack

Thus in Paris the days of 24–26 May saw the crystallization of a
'separate peace' lobby, of which its hard core was formed by
the Weygand–Pétain–Baudouin axis. It was a turning-point in
the affairs of France. From now on the lobby would be increasingly conscious of its combined strength against Reynaud.

   15. As Secretary to the War Cabinet, Baudouin's official status was that
of Under-Secretary.

It was also the time when the fire which Churchill had thought he detected in Weygand on the 22nd finally flickered out. On the 27th, the long-awaited effort from the south began. Under the reinstated General Grandsard (formerly of X Corps), the 7th and 4th Colonial Infantry divisions, backed by a scattering of Somuas, attacked towards Amiens. They got to within sight of the city, apparently causing the German defenders some passing anxiety; then, after suffering heavy losses, the French colonial troops (many of them Senegalese with no battle-training) were thrown back to their start-line by an enemy counter-attack. On the 28th, de Gaulle executed his third offensive action with customary courage and dash, supported by the British 51st (Highland) Division, this time against the German bridgehead around Abbeville. De Gaulle claims:

there was an air of victory on the battlefield. Everyone held his head high. The wounded smiled. The guns barked joyously. The Germans before us had fallen back after a pitched battle.

Five hundred German prisoners were claimed, but once again the attack petered out on the second day, without the German bridgehead having been erased, and certainly without any incursion having been made into the Panzer Corridor. The French forces along the Somme now resumed their defensive posture.

Herewith faded the last Franco-British offensive effort, and the final flicker of the 'Weygand Plan'. Its author had lost hope well before it began. On the 29th, while de Gaulle was still attacking towards Abbeville, Weygand presented a memorandum to the War Cabinet in which he made an unfavourable comparison with the lost war of 1870. At that time, when the regular armies had been crushed, France had been able to raise *ad hoc* forces which had 'prolonged the resistance for five months and saved the honour of France'. Now, even if the equipment were available for fresh armies, 'the enemy would not allow us the time to organize them'. Pétain congratulated Weygand on his memorandum, and approved its contents. Weygand then said to Reynaud: 'I hope to stand on the Somme–Aisne line, but it is my duty to tell you that I am not sure of being able to do so.' His meaning was now abundantly clear; he would fight one more battle, 'to save the honour of France', and then that would be the end. Reynaud replied to Weygand's memorandum with a resolute written rejoinder in which, for the first time, he declared his intention of continuing the war, if necessary, from North Africa.

Dunkirk

During these days, Gort, with dogged determination and deflected neither by Blanchard's pleas nor Churchillian growls, was beginning the evacuation from Dunkirk of the force upon which would depend the immediate safety of Britain, and the ultimate salvation of France. Although Gort had been acting (at any rate until 26 May) in direct opposition to his will, Churchill wrote of him later in *The Second World War* in magnanimous terms:

Confident in his military virtue, and convinced of the complete breakdown of all control, either by the British and French Governments or by the French Supreme Command . . . In all this Lord Gort had acted upon his own responsibility. But by now we at home, with a somewhat different angle of information, had already reached the same conclusions.

Accordingly, on the 26th Gort received official notice from the War Office 'to operate towards the coast forthwith'. Few then held hopes of saving more than a fraction of the B.E.F.; Ironside was reckoning in private that the British would be lucky to get out 30,000 men,[16] and Gort himself signalled back in reply to the War Office's instruction of the 26th: 'I must not conceal from you that a great part of the B.E.F. and its equipment will inevitably be lost even in best circumstances.' On 28 May Churchill warned the House of Commons to 'prepare itself for hard and heavy tidings'. Certainly, without Gort's decision to disengage from Arras and without Hitler's 'Halt Order' to the Panzers, the probability is that few in excess of

16. The German High Command itself erroneously estimated that the encircled Allied forces in the north totalled no more than 100,000 all told.

Ironside's pessimistic calculation would have been rescued.

The story of the 'miracle of Dunkirk' has been told and re-told. Little needs to be added here. During the three-day respite afforded by the halting of the Panzers, Gort had managed to throw up a strong protective shell around the Dunkirk bridgehead. But it was in the air that the holding of the bridgehead was predominantly decided. The R.A.F. now threw in every single plane available. Day and night its bombers blasted the attacking Germans, while fighter pilots flew sometimes as many as four sorties a day. Altogether the British fighter cover totalled 2,739 sorties while the evacuations lasted. For the first time since the campaign began, the cruelly beautiful 'Goering's weather' that had so aided the Luftwaffe now deserted it; during at least half of the nine-day epic of Dunkirk, fog and bad visibility limited flying. On the good days the Luftwaffe, considerably weakened by the losses and strain of three weeks constantly on the offensive,[17] found itself sorely pressed by the furious concentrations of aircraft that the R.A.F., flying from bases just across the Straits of Dover, was able to put in the air over Dunkirk. Only two days, 27 May and 1 June, did the Luftwaffe enjoy outstanding success. Each day that went by proved Goering's boast that he could 'finish the job' to be a little further from realization.

By the evening of 27 May, the disappointing total of only 7,669 men had been embarked from Dunkirk. But·the next day the Royal Navy began to be reinforced by the vast armada of small boats collected from all over the South Coast of England, and that day's figure reached 17,804. On the 29th, the arrival of French warships helped hoist the day's results to 47,310; and so on, until a peak of 68,014 was reached on 31 May. That day Gort himself sailed for England, having been issued strictest orders by Churchill to hand over to one of his corps commanders as soon as the B.E.F. left in France was down to the equivalent of three divisions.[18] That same day, Churchill was in Paris again attending a meeting of the Supreme War

17. Some bomber *Gruppen* could now only put fourteen to sixteen aircraft in the air, instead of thirty.
18. General Blanchard followed on 1 June.

Council and was able to tell it that the astonishing figure of 165,000 men had already been evacuated. Weygand promptly questioned, in what Spears describes as a 'high, querulous and aggressive' voice, 'But how many French? The French are being left behind?' When Churchill revealed that only 15,000 of these had been French, not unnaturally there were resentful comments. (In fact, it transpired that Blanchard – to Gort's amazement – had received *no orders* from Weygand to begin evacuating French troops until 29 May.) At the meeting of the 31st, Churchill promptly decreed that henceforth the evacuations should proceed on equal terms between the British and the French – '*bras dessus bras dessous*' as he put it in his robust French.[19]

By the morning of 3 June, the last British troops were embarked. The Germans were within a mile and a quarter of the sea, but still held back by a courageous French rearguard. At dawn the next day, the last ship left Dunkirk, taking with it a final contingent of French soldiers. The remarkable total of 337,000 men, of whom 110,000 were French, had been got out of the *Sichelschnitt* trap, at a cost of six British and two French destroyers, as well as many lesser craft. But the knowledge that 30,000 French troops, the last of the rearguard, had to be abandoned to the Germans, in addition to the many thousands forced to surrender in the Lille pocket, was to provide another lasting source of anti-British bitterness in French hearts.

Although, as Churchill warned the House of Commons on 4 June, 'Wars are not won by evacuations', Dunkirk will always be regarded by the British as one of the great triumphs of the

19. It was also at that meeting that Churchill delivered one of his greatest orations, with the intent of boosting the morale of the French Government. 'The peoples of France and Britain,' he declaimed, 'were not born to slavery, nor can they endure it. It is impossible that a temporary Nazi victory should bring to a final conclusion the glorious histories of France and Britain.' Britain, he insisted, would 'carry on with the war if every building in France and Great Britain is destroyed. The British Government is prepared to wage war from the New World if through some disaster England herself is laid waste. The British people will fight on until the New World re-conquers the Old. Better far that the last of the English should fall fighting and *finis* be written to our history than to linger on as vassals and slaves.'

island race. But to the French, for whom, in any case, water was a hostile rather than a friendly element, Dunkirk could only represent defeat, and desertion by an ally. But it was Hitler who, in terms of overall war strategy, suffered the most injurious defeat at Dunkirk.

Chapter 20

One Last Battle

5–22 June

. . . defeat is a thing of weariness, of incoherence, of boredom. And above all of futility.
ANTOINE DE SAINT-EXUPERY, *Flight to Arras*

One can only think with a shudder of our unawareness during the past eight months, in which our noblest duty seemed to consist of making the leisure hours of the soldiers at the front pleasant.
L'Œuvre, 30 May

Soldiers of the West Front!
Dunkirk has fallen . . . with it has ended the greatest battle of world history.
Soldiers! My confidence in you knew no bounds.
You have not disappointed me.
ADOLF HITLER, Order of the Day, 5 June

While the German Army suffers unheard-of losses, the French Army remains intact.
Radio Strasbourg, 12 June

'Operation Red': the Opposing Forces

At midnight on the day Dunkirk fell, Hitler decreed that bells throughout the Reich should be tolled for three days in celebration of the end of this 'greatest battle in world history'. An hour later, on 5 June, the O.K.W. communiqué announced: 'The second great offensive is being launched today.' To be in at the kill, Hitler had moved westwards from his headquarters at the *Felsennest*. Before doing so, he ordered that the entire area in the Eifel should be preserved as a 'national monument'; every room was to be kept unchanged, every name-plate to remain upon its door. On a rare note of concord and satisfaction, Halder wrote in his diary for the 4th: 'In the evening a

glass of wine with the C.-in-C. at his country residence.[1]
Wonderful eventide peace, harmonious atmosphere!'

In the six days of rest since they had been withdrawn from
the northern battle, the German Panzers had been completely
reorganized and redeployed with superb flexibility. For the
final battle, they were now divided into five armoured corps,
each consisting of two Panzer divisions and one of motorized
infantry. Three of these corps were given to Bock, still standing on the right of the German line, and two to Rundstedt, who
was now facing the French from east of Laon to the northern
anchor of the Maginot Line at Montmédy. On the far right of
the German line, along the lower Somme, were Rommel's 7th
Panzer and the 5th, once again with Hoth as the corps commander. Then, facing Amiens and Péronne, came Kleist's
Armoured Group, now comprising two armoured corps;[2]
further east, facing the Rethel area along the Aisne, came
Guderian, now promoted to command his own Armoured
Group of two corps.[3] Altogether, from the sea to the Meuse,
the Germans mustered some 104 fully-manned divisions.

Against this, along a front 225 miles long, Weygand could
dispose of only forty-three infantry divisions,[4] plus three much
reduced and only partially reconstituted armoured divisions,
and three similarly weakened D.L.C.s. Twenty-five of Weygand's available infantry divisions had been pulled out
(belatedly) from the Maginot Line area, but another seventeen
still remained there. In addition, there were the British 51st
(Highland) and 1st Armoured Divisions; the latter was now
down to about a third of its strength, and its armour consisted

1. Together with Hitler, Brauchitsch and the O.K.H. had also moved
westwards on to Belgian territory, west of Givet on the Meuse.

2. Containing the 9th, 10th, 3rd and 4th Panzers.

3. The XXXIX and XLI Panzer Corps, containing Guderian's old 1st and
2nd Panzers and Reinhardt's 6th and 8th.

4. According to Weygand's figures, French losses up to the fall of Dunkirk
amounted to the equivalent of

24 infantry divisions (including 6 out of 7 motorized);

3 out of 3 D.L.M.s;

2 out of 5 Light Cavalry Divisions (D.L.C.s);

1 armoured division.

chiefly of lightly-clad cruiser tanks. On their way were two more divisions (one of them Canadian), the only two equipped formations now left in the British Isles. In the air, French production and American consignments had helped replace a good part of the losses suffered; Glen-Martin bombers and new Dewoitine 520 fighters, mounting a cannon and four machine-guns, were seen in the air for the first time. General d'Astier's Z.O.A.N. could now mount 125 bombers, of which 93 were modern and suitable for daylight operations, and about 225 fighters. To General Vuillemin's pleas for another twenty R.A.F. squadrons, the British had continued to present a firm front. But by 5 June Barratt's A.A.S.F., after falling to a total of thirty aircraft by 20 May, had once more risen to a total of a hundred (thirty fighters and seventy bombers), a fact not generally appreciated in France at the time. Some 250 bombers from Bomber Command in England were also used in support of operations in France. In all, d'Astier says that 980 aircraft were engaged in the second phase of the battle, but the pilots and the organization needed to keep them in the air were desperately thin on the ground.

Thus Weygand assessed his total strength at a maximum of sixty divisions, while, against what the Luftwaffe could throw in, he regarded his air forces as 'ridiculously weak'. For the main strength of the 'Weygand Line' behind the Somme and the Aisne, Weygand – at last abandoning the ruined 'continuous front' philosophy – relied principally on a 'chequer-board' system of 'hedgehogs'. Each 'hedgehog' consisted of troops well dug-in around a natural obstacle (a village or wood) and armed with 75s which were to be used in an anti-tank role. Many of them First War weapons brought out of retirement, the 75s were to be pointed 'like revolvers' at the enemy armour. The 'hedgehogs' were designed to hold out even when surrounded or by-passed by the enemy. Behind them were *groupements de manœuvre* constituted from the few remaining units of Allied armour. It was at last an attempt at a defence in depth, but unfortunately the 'Weygand Line' lacked the forces with which to provide anything like the depth needed to halt Panzers. True to his belief that he should fight one last battle, 'for the sake of honour', and then persuade the Government to sue for peace, Weygand had prepared no succeeding positions on which to fall back once the 'Weygand Line' was broken.

The French Fight Back

The German plan called for Bock to open the attack on 5 June and Rundstedt to follow four days later. At once Bock's forces ran into unexpectedly tough resistance. Desperate as their situation was, the French defenders fought back with a determination and a spirit of sacrifice that had not been seen on the Meuse. No longer did the screaming Stukas bring panic in their wake. The French gunners stayed and died with their 75s, knocking out considerable numbers of German tanks. Karl von Stackelberg, the military diarist who had followed the German advance all the way from Nouzonville on the Meuse, wrote: 'In these ruined villages the French resisted to the last man. Some hedgehogs carried on when our infantry was twenty miles behind them.' Both at Amiens and Péronne, Kleist's two Panzer corps were prevented from breaking out of their bridge-heads, after managing to advance only a few miles; and even Rommel had been halted most of the day at Hangest and Le Quesnoy in the marshes of the Lower Somme. By the end of the day, Weygand was impressed by the fact that his troops had held their own better than expected. There were grounds for hope. But the cost had been high, and the material odds were enormous. A sequence in the German film, *Sieg im West*, taken at this time shows a monster German self-propelled gun (probably 150 mm.) reducing a solitary French sniper in a house, with shot after shot at point-blank range. Nothing could demonstrate more clearly the disparity of might between the two sides in these desperate days.

Rommel Again

On the 6th, the French once again stopped Kleist south of Amiens and Péronne. In these two days of battle, one of his Panzer corps had some 65 per cent of its tanks disabled. But disaster overtook the French on the flank. It was precipitated by

Rommel, who broke through west of Amiens after some fierce fighting and advanced twenty miles southwards from the Somme. The next day (his wife's birthday), Rommel swept forward another thirty miles to Forges-les-Eaux on the Beauvais–Dieppe road and only twenty-five miles from Rouen. With his customary swiftness to adapt himself to new situations, Rommel had mastered Weygand's 'chequer-board' system by taking his division cross-country so as to avoid the French 'hedgehogs', leaving them to be dealt with by the following infantry. His advance that day split in two General Robert Altmayer's Tenth Army, of which one of the units left on the coastal flank was the British 51st (Highland) Division. Next, on the 8th, Rommel pushed on to take Elbeuf on the Seine, thereby sealing off the great city of Rouen. He wrote to his wife on the 9th in high spirits: 'Two glorious days in pursuit, first south, then south-west. A roaring success. 45 miles yesterday,' and on the 10th:

Our successes are tremendous and it looks to me inevitable that the other side will soon collapse.

We never imagined war in the west would be like this.

The 5th Panzer had meanwhile captured Rouen, and on Rommel's left the Lower Seine had been reached by the XXXVIII Infantry Corps, commanded by General Erich von Manstein – allowed at this late date to participate in the triumph which owed so much to his genius. Rommel was now ordered to countermarch to the north-west, swing around Rouen, and head for the sea near Fécamp in order to cut off the retreat of Altmayer's isolated left wing. After another sixty-mile advance, Rommel reached the coast in a day, and began to push back up it towards Dieppe. At the small port of St Valéry-en-Caux he fell upon the cut-off part of Altmayer's army, then attempting to form a bridgehead prior to evacuation. But no ships arrived, and on 12 June the Allied garrison surrendered. That day Rommel took 40,000 prisoners, including twelve generals. They included the whole of the 51st Highland Division, with its commander, Major-General Fortune – one of Britain's finest fighting units.

On the 14th, Rommel occupied Le Havre. Then, after two days' rest, he was ordered to advance on Cherbourg, passing through terrain which, as a Field-Marshal and almost exactly four years later, he would be called upon to defend against American tanks enjoying almost the same numerical superiority that the Germans had had in 1940. On 17 June he established an alleged all-time record, by advancing 150 miles in a single day. Two days later he accepted the capitulation of Cherbourg. This was the end of the campaign for Rommel and the 7th Panzer, nicknamed by the French the 'Phantom Division'. In six remarkable weeks, it had captured 97,648 prisoners, together with 277 guns, 458 armoured vehicles, and over 4,000 trucks. Its own casualties had totalled 682 killed (including the relatively large number of 52 officers), 1,646 wounded and 296 missing, while its loss in tanks was only 42 complete write-offs.[5]

Guderian Again

On 9 June, Rundstedt's attack had duly gone in. In an Order of the Day to the French armies that morning, Weygand declared: 'We have come to the last quarter of an hour. Stand firm.' The German assault was led by Guderian's Armoured Group, which, after a 150-mile march largely retracing the route of his victorious advance, was concentrated on either side of Rethel. Meanwhile, the main weight of the Armoured Group belonging to his former chief and antagonist, Kleist, was also being switched eastwards to the Aisne, after being checked south of Amiens and Péronne on the direct route to Paris. In contrast to the Meuse crossings, this time the infantry were to attack first and seize bridgeheads across the Aisne before Guderian committed his Panzer divisions. But, says Guderian,

At 1200 hours [German] I received messages from the front on either side of Rethel that the Rethel attacks had failed. My ob-

---

5. By the end of May, Rommel in fact had only 86 tanks (of which just 5 were Mark IVs) fit for operations, out of his complement of 218. But many of the remainder were back on the road within the next few days.

servers from the other fronts reported that the infantry had only succeeded in establishing a single bridgehead, a small one a mile to a mile and a half deep, in the neighbourhood of Château-Porcien.

Once again, the French defenders were fighting back heroically; de Lattre de Tassigny's tough 14th Division alone claimed some 800 German prisoners. If only Grandsard's men could have put up the same kind of resistance at Sedan, when the odds had been so much less in favour of the Germans! Guderian now decided to move tanks of the 1st Panzer into the solitary bridgehead under cover of darkness. The next day the armour pushed out of the bridgehead, but made only slow progress; in the afternoon a hard tank-versus-tank battle was fought around Juniville against the remnants of Guderian's old adversary, the French 3rd Armoured Division. Colonel Balck personally captured the colours of a French regiment, but Guderian admitted to having suffered heavy casualties. On the 11th, Guderian records that the 1st Panzer progressed 'as though this were a manoeuvre'. French resistance on the Aisne sector of the 'Weygand Line' was clearly coming to an end. Soon Reinhardt's two Panzer divisions, then Kleist's four, were across the Aisne, thrusting southward in an irresistible mass of armour. By nightfall, Rheims was reached; the following morning (12 June) Guderian captured Châlons-sur-Marne.

Paris Abandoned

The capture of Rouen in the west and the crossing of the Marne in the east now meant that Paris, the sacred capital, was irretrievably compromised. On 3 June, Paris was bombed for the first time and over 250 people were reported killed. By the 8th, the sound of distant cannon had become almost continuous. For the third time in seventy years, Paris began to resemble a city under siege. 'The restaurants emptied,' said Fabre-Luce. 'The Ritz, abandoned by its last clients, looked like a palace in a spa on the day the baths closed down.' The following day, G.Q.G. North-East packed up at Les Bondons and departed for less commodious lodgings at Briare, on the upper reaches of the Loire. The next night (10 June), the French radio announced: 'The Government is compelled to leave the capital for imperative military reasons. The Prime Minister is on his way to the armies.' At midnight, the car containing Reynaud and his new Under-Secretary of State for National Defence, General Charles de Gaulle, left for the future seat of Government at Tours. Behind them an endless stream of refugees poured out along the Boulevard Raspail. Ilya Ehrenburg, who, as a correspondent representing Hitler's Russian ally, remained, was moved to compassion while, as he watched, 'An old man laboriously pushed a handcart loaded with pillows on which huddled a small girl and a little dog that howled piteously.' In contrast, de Gaulle relates how in the course of his arduous journey through the night, past a long stationary line of refugees,

suddenly a convoy of luxurious, white-tyred American cars came sweeping along the road, with militiamen on the running-boards and motor-cyclists surrounding the procession; it was the Corps Diplomatique on its way to the châteaux of Touraine.

It was dawn by the time Reynaud and de Gaulle reached Orléans.

Until this moment, the French Government had kept on repeating in Gambettaesque terms that it would fight in front of Paris and behind Paris, and only that weekend it had announced that the city had been placed 'in a state of defence'. Every fifty yards or so down the Champs-Elysées buses had been placed diagonally, with the object of preventing German airborne troops from landing. Then, on the night of the 11th, Weygand decided to declare Paris an 'open city'. That Paris should have capitulated without a struggle while Warsaw, London, Leningrad and Stalingrad opted to accept battle and be devastated has ever since remained a source of contention; at the time there were many loyal Frenchmen who, like André Pertinax, considered its capitulation 'quite unprecedented' and pointed out that 'in 1870–1 the war had continued in the provinces only as a result of the capital's heroic resistance'. By 11 June, the situation was such that there would, however, have been little military advantage gained in fighting for Paris, stone by beautiful stone. But psychologically, its abandonment struck a grievous blow to what remained of French morale. André Maurois recalls being warned, on 10 June, that Paris would not be defended: 'At that moment I knew everything was over. France deprived of Paris, would become a body without a head. The war had been lost.'

As the Germans approached Paris, a drizzle of rain fell on the capital, after the long weeks of peerless weather. Early on the morning of 14 June an officer on the staff of Küchler's Eighteenth Army, Lieutenant-Colonel Dr Hans Speidel,[6] received two French officers who came under flag of truce with instructions to deliver up the capital. Later that morning troops of the German 87th Infantry Division, led by an anti-tank gun detachment which occupied the Hôtel de Ville and the Invalides, made a bloodless and orderly entry into Paris. Following in its wake just three days later, William Shirer felt an ache in the pit of his stomach at the sight of the familiar but lonely streets: 'I wished I had not come. My German companions were in high spirits.' Going round the Place de l'Opéra, he noted

for the first time in my life, no traffic tie-up here, no French cops shouting meaninglessly at cars hopelessly blocked. The façade of the Opera House was hidden behind stacked sandbags. The Café de la Paix seemed to be just reopening. A lone *garçon* was bringing out some tables and chairs. German soldiers stood on the terrace grabbing them.

The following day, he observed that there was already 'open fraternizing' between German troops and Parisians:

It seems funny, but every German soldier carries a camera. I saw them by the thousands to-day, photographing Notre-Dame, the

---

6. Four years and a few weeks later, Speidel, now a Lieutenant-General, was defending Paris against the Americans and Free French as Chief of Staff, Army Group 'B'. After ending the war in a Gestapo prison camp, he returned to Paris in 1951 to negotiate the rearmament of Federal Germany. In 1957 he was in Paris again, as the first German Commander of Allied Land Forces in Europe.

Arc de Triomphe, the Invalides . . . Two newspapers appeared yesterday in Paris, *La Victoire* (as life's irony would have it) and *Le Matin* . . . It [*Le Matin*] has already begun to attack England, to blame England for France's predicament!

The day after Paris fell, Halder entered in his diary: 'Another important day in military history!' Verdun, the mighty fortress and spiritual symbol for which hundreds of thousands of German lives had been spent in vain in 1916, had fallen after twenty-four hours' fighting and at a cost of less than 200 dead. For the Germans the campaign was rapidly becoming a pursuit down the highways of France. Rommel was rushing from Le Havre to Cherbourg. On the 14th Guderian entered St Dizier, to find Colonel Balck relaxing peacefully on a chair in the market-place; by the 15th the 1st Panzer had captured the old fortified town of Langres and pushed on to Gray-sur-Saône in the foothills of the Jura. The next day Guderian's columns took Besançon, and on the 17th (his birthday) Guderian learned that his 29th Motorized Division had reached the Swiss frontier at Pontarlier. At the same time Kleist's armour, pushing along the upper Seine, had taken Dijon. The Maginot Line – that exorbitant Great Wall – and the powerful forces [7] guarding it were now turned and completely isolated from the rest of France which the Line had been built to protect. Like the triangle-player in a school orchestra waiting for his solitary bar of music, the moment had at last arrived for the Maginot Line. Attacked on all sides, little aware in their deep, sunless caverns of what was happening in the rest of France, the defenders of this white elephant of French interwar policy fought on until the very end. Not one of the major fortresses of the Line actually succumbed.

Mussolini Declares War

As if France's cup were not full enough, the scavengers, scenting that her wounds were mortal, had moved in. Mussolini had long been champing at the bit to grab a piece of French territory, as well as a crumb of the glory. He told Marshal Badoglio:

7. Four armies totalling 400,000 men.

'I need only a few thousand dead to ensure that I have the right
to sit at the peace table in the capacity of a belligerent.'
Several times President Roosevelt had interceded with the
Duce, sending firmly worded pleas for Italy to remain neutral.
But Hitler's reluctance to have Mussolini as a co-belligerent
(with good reason, as it later turned out) carried more weight.
Finally, Mussolini could bear the postponements no longer. 'I
can't just sit back and watch the fight,' he exploded at the
beginning of June. 'When the war is over and victory comes I
shall be left empty-handed!' On 10 June, the day the French
Government left Paris, Italy declared war on France, bringing
forth from Roosevelt the angry condemnation that 'the hand
that held the dagger has stuck it in the back of his neighbour'.
Italy's act had little military consequence. After five days of
fighting before the Armistice was signed, an Italian army of
thirty-two divisions had barely dented France's Alpine Front,
held by General Olry and three divisions; on the Côte d'Azur
the Italian invasion was held up by a French N.C.O. and seven
men.[8]

The Soldiers: Last Resistance

For the French soldiers, the retreat seemed to go on without end:

You could catch the smell of the earth, the smell of a good June
rain [wrote Hans Habe], the smell of sweating horses, the smell
of the starched white blouses of the peasant girls. And then your
eyes turned back to the flood of limping soldiers, trying in vain to
look like men in the presence of the fleeing women. You saw
children screaming desperately or still as death; officers' cars
blowing their strident horns and trying to open a path; bright
cavalry uniforms on nervous, weary horses; wagons with their
sleeping drivers; cannon without ammunition; the whole disordered
funeral procession of a disintegrated army.

In these last terrible days, the quality of resistance was mixed.

8. A squadron of R.A.F. Wellingtons, sent to Marseilles to bomb northern Italy, found, however, that it also had to contend with the French;
lorries were driven on to the airfield to prevent the bombers taking off, in
anxiety at possible Italian reprisals against French targets.

But perhaps it was almost miraculous that, under the circumstances, soldiers could be persuaded to fight at all. At Vierzon, it is said, a tank officer wanting to defend the city was lynched by angry burghers. There were signs of mutiny in some units, while disbanded soldiers were reported to be robbing passers-by in the forests near Paris. There were also revelations that, whether through incompetence or lack of will, France had never reached right down into the depths of her military potential. As the Germans advanced, they came upon huge depots of weapons, ammunition, clothing, fuel and even new tanks which appear, inexplicably, never to have reached the armies. At the same time Spears, on his way to the Government's final resting place at Bordeaux, wondered angrily at the fact that 'nearly all the towns and villages I passed through were full of gaping, idle soldiers . . . How came it then that we were constantly told that all resources and man-power had been exhausted?' The validity of such reproaches may never be determined. Yet amid all the adverse accounts from these days of France's expiring agony, one episode at least will always leap forth from French history books in a blaze of glory, the kind of glory belonging almost to a past age. On 19 June, the day Pétain was asking for an armistice, Bock's Panzers had reached Saumur on the Loire, the site of the famous cavalry school. Though still under instruction, the young cadets decided that they would not allow the school to fall without a fight. Armed only with training weapons, they held the Saumur bridges for two whole days against Panzers, until at last their ammunition ran out.

Doubtless there were other such epics of hopeless heroism, which will never now be recognized.

The Politicians: Last Resistance

While the German mobile columns were thrusting and tearing into the entrails of France, branching and re-branching like the tendrils of some rampant fungus or a nightmare man-eating plant, a bitter political struggle was being waged within Allied councils. Though forced to be more or less an impotent spectator at this stage of France's agony, Britain's position was a relatively simple one. Every hour that France remained in the fight delayed the German invasion of Britain by an hour – an hour in which Britain would be rearming herself to meet the attack. Should not the undefeated French armies withdraw into a Breton redoubt, where, supplied by the Royal Navy, they could hold out until, in due course, new armies from Britain, the Empire and possibly America came to their aid? Or if all hope failed in metropolitan France, would not the French Government and what remained of the army transfer itself to North Africa, there to recuperate behind the joint shield of the French and British Navies? These were the anxious hopes of Britain. But above all, Churchill and his Government were concerned at the fate of the French fleet. If this were to fall into enemy hands, it would mean the end for Britain, the end for everybody.

On 11 June, Churchill made his fourth visit to France, in response to an urgent summons from Reynaud, who had just established himself at Tours. The meeting itself was at Briare; among those present were, as usual, Pétain and Weygand, and – for the first time – General de Gaulle, whom Reynaud had brought into his Cabinet from the front line in an attempt to strengthen his position against the 'softs'. With the exception of the calmly phlegmatic de Gaulle, Spears recalls that

The Frenchmen sat with set white faces, their eyes on the table. They looked for all the world like prisoners hauled up from some deep dungeon to hear an inevitable verdict.

Churchill at once urged that Paris be defended: 'I emphasized the enormous absorbing power of the house-to-house defence of a great city upon an invading army.' Weygand countered by demanding that every available British fighter squadron be thrown into the battle. 'Here,' he said (according to Churchill), 'is the decisive point. Now is the decisive moment.' No, replied Churchill, adamantly; the decisive moment would come when the Luftwaffe hurled itself against the British Isles. This can hardly have been encouraging to French ears, nor any more so Churchill's promise that, if France could hold on until the spring of 1941, Britain would send her twenty to twenty-five fresh divisions. Spears says, mildly, that he was aware of Reynaud's 'suppressed irritation' at the inadequacy of this offer. Reynaud remarked pointedly: 'No doubt history will say the Battle of France was lost through lack of aircraft.' 'And through lack of tanks,' retorted Churchill.

Weygand, having made it clear all along that he would fight his one last battle, was all defeatism: 'I am helpless, I cannot intervene for I have no reserves ... *C'est la dislocation.*' He repeated what he had told the Army in his proclamation of 9 June: 'We have come to the last quarter of an hour.' [9] Weygand concluded by giving his opinion that France might soon have to ask for an armistice. According to Churchill, Reynaud snapped back: 'That is a political question.' Then Churchill, deeply moved by the agony of the French, erupted into a new explosion of inspired, visionary oratory, once more declaring Britain's determination to fight to the end. Prophetically, he added:

It is possible that the Nazis may dominate Europe, but it will be a Europe in revolt, and in the end it is certain that a regime whose victories are in the main due to its machines will collapse. Machines will one day beat machines.

Then, without waiting for an answer to it, he threw in the question that was obviously uppermost in his mind: if France's armies were to succumb, what would the French Navy do?

After the meeting ended, Churchill took aside General Georges, the French general on whom, from pre-war days, he placed the greatest reliance. He was shattered to discover that Georges was now largely in agreement with Weygand. At dinner that night, Churchill, turning in a friendly manner to Pétain, said: 'Think back! We went through difficult times in 1918 but we got over them. We shall get over these in the same way!' Pétain replied coldly:

9. Spears records that, in this moment of extreme gravity, 'fancy came to my rescue ... I saw Big Ben with a French General's cap on, marking time at the double, chiming the last quarter of an hour incessantly, at ever accelerating speed, while the dial of the clock became Weygand's face.'

In 1918, I gave you forty divisions to save the British Army. Where are the forty British divisions that we would need to save ourselves today?

The question was unanswerable. Churchill and his advisers returned to London, anticipating the worst.

The 'Softs' versus the 'Hards'

Behind the scenes of the French Government, the struggle between the 'softs' and the 'hards' raged on. On one side was Reynaud, backed principally by the cold, unconquerable will of Georges Mandel, by Campinchi (Navy) and Marin (Minister of State), and now by de Gaulle, all determined to be loyal to the Anglo-French Declaration to fight to the end in France and to continue from North Africa.[10] Against them were arrayed Weygand, Pétain, Baudouin, Chautemps and Ybarnegaray (the latter two Ministers of State without Portfolio) – and Hélène de Portes – all the time bringing over new recruits to their side. The case of the 'softs' was that it was imperative to negotiate a separate peace at once; the validity of the Anglo-French Declaration was questionable, because although (in the views of some) she had pushed France into the war, the British had not upheld their part of the bargain, by keeping back the R.A.F. in Britain and by evacuating the B.E.F.

To his song about fighting one last battle to 'save honour', Weygand had added a new refrain. Haunted by the precedent of the Commune (which he was almost old enough to remember), he now began expressing fears that in the wake of defeat would follow revolution. This prospect clearly seemed to afflict him more than surrender to the Germans.[11] On the 12th he

10. Whether or not a French continuation of the war in North Africa would have been swiftly followed up by a German invasion, and therefore disastrous to the Allies in the long run, lies beyond the scope of the present book.

11. This repetition of history is interesting. One of the considerations urging General Trochu and the French leaders to hasten capitulation to the Prussians in January 1871 had been the threat of left-wing revolt in Paris – which, indeed, came to pass.

warned the Cabinet to remember 1917 in Russia, when 'soldiers formed *soviets* in the regiments and in the armies'. He urged that Army divisions be kept intact, so as to 'maintain order'. The following day, Weygand announced that he had received a telegram via the Ministry of the Marine, stating that 'serious disturbances have broken out in Paris, and that Thorez has installed himself in the Élysée'. President Lebrun jumped, and the rest of the Cabinet were aghast, except for Mandel, who, as Minister of the Interior, declared with crushing certainty: 'There are no riots in Paris and M. Thorez, M. le Président, will not sleep in your bed this evening.' But the era of the Popular Front had planted one last paving-stone on the way to France's downfall.

For all their disagreements during the inter-war years, Pétain was now completely at one with Weygand, both in his fears about 'internal order' and in the need to stop the fighting. Ever since Verdun, horror of the losses suffered by 'his' French soldiers had left an ineradicable mark upon the eighty-four-year-old marshal. There is something infinitely pathetic about Pétain in these days. Except for when any mention of the troops and their suffering would snap him to life, there were long periods when he seemed not to be aware of what was going on. Reynaud notes in his memoirs that after Weygand had delivered his account of the fighting at the Cabinet meeting of 9 June,

Marshal Pétain said nothing. He seemed to be asleep, prostrated. I questioned him. 'Don't you want to express an opinion, Marshal? These gentlemen are anxious to hear you.' 'I've nothing to say,' he replied.

Listening to 'that thin voice and cough' on the radio, Arthur Koestler was reminded of 'a skeleton with a chill', and somehow it was such images of the grave and the snows of yesteryear that most struck people on encountering Pétain in these days. Making his first call on the Marshal at his office near the Invalides, Spears was struck by the complete 'sense of unreality' there: 'it was as dead, as somnolent, as the chambers of a provincial lawyer on a Sunday afternoon'. On a later visit in

June, the impending fall of Rouen made Spears remark to Pétain that what France needed was another Joan of Arc. The name promptly roused Pétain, who asked Spears whether he had ever read his speech about Joan of Arc ('When was it, in 1937, '38?'). Bringing down a bound volume of typescript from a bookshelf, he proceeded to read out the complete speech in a dull monotone. Spears was unable to recall a single sentence; but what he did remember

was the terrible sadness I felt as I watched him, a sadness now based on pity for a very old man for whom I had, till so recently, felt the deepest affection and regard. He was infinitely pathetic in his childish satisfaction as he read.

Even more saddening, Spears reflected, was the enormous influence Pétain wielded in France; what French man or woman in these days, he wondered, was not saying, 'He will save us as he did at Verdun.' The next day Spears warned Churchill that he was certain the Marshal would never leave France; there would be no question of his following any French Government into exile.

General Spears, in his illuminating, vivid account of this page of history, speaks of Reynaud staggering not only under the burden of his own responsibilities, but 'the additional cross of the entourage with which he had handicapped himself. He was like those savage warriors who, not contented with the wounds inflicted by the enemy, gash themselves with knives.' The source of perhaps the most crippling wounds Reynaud received from his entourage was the one which in these terrible days should have lent him the most comfort – his mistress, Hélène de Portes. The same ruthless, relentless energy she had once applied to pushing her chevalier to the top rung of the political ladder was now devoted to the cause of obtaining an early separate peace. Following the Government to Tours, then to Bordeaux, the Comtesse de Portes was everywhere, plaguing the Prime Minister incessantly, without mercy, in a manner that astounded the British officials who came in contact with her. Paul Baudouin, who was completely her man and came to represent her will within the Cabinet, wrote with the utmost restrained chivalry: 'if she acted as the controller of the Cabinet, her one desire was to save the country by defending and fortifying the man she admired.' Certainly the impression one gets from those others who were present is that Reynaud was never for a moment left alone, never allowed to make a decision or an appointment without Hélène de Portes being party to it. In the middle of deliberations of the War Cabinet she would ring him on his private telephone; if, in despair, he should disconnect it, she would summon ushers to take in written messages to him, and finally she would often burst into the council chamber herself. On one occasion at Tours, Spears (who admittedly was no devotee of the Countess) was astonished to see her in the courtyard of Reynaud's residence, clad 'in a dressing gown over her red pyjamas, directing the traffic from the steps of the main entrance'. This was relatively harmless; but on another occasion Spears also found her intercepting one of Reynaud's stenographers and reading over his shoulder a most important and top-secret communication from Churchill.[12] Again, when a secret telegram from the French Embassy in London had been missing for some hours, Reynaud's *chef de cabinet* from the Quai d'Orsay, Roland de Margerie, eventually produced it with the hushed whisper 'It was in Madame de Portes's bed.'[13] In Spears's opinion, as he left France, it was Reynaud's mistress who did him the greatest harm, because she 'had imposed on him as collaborators the men who were now his bitterest opponents'.

The Breaking of Reynaud

Certainly, she must have greatly added to the physical and nervous strain imposed on Reynaud in these last days. By 12 June, Reynaud was beginning to break. That night he was per-

12. This was, in fact, his eleventh-hour proposal for an indissoluble Franco-British Union.

13. It was hardly surprising that de Margerie was in the habit of characterizing her, uncharitably, as 'ugly, *mal soignée*, dirty, nasty and half-demented, and a sore trial to me'.

suaded by the 'softs' to telephone Churchill and ask him to fly to Tours, once again, to discuss the prospects that France would conclude a separate peace with Germany. The following afternoon Churchill arrived, accompanied by Halifax and Beaverbrook. According to Churchill, over lunch Baudouin 'began at once in his soft, silky manner about the hopelessness of the French resistance'. Only if the United States declared war on Germany might it now be possible for France to continue. After lunch, Churchill was received at the Prefecture by Mandel, who in marked contrast to Baudouin was

energy and defiance personified . . . He was a ray of sunshine. He had a telephone in each hand through which he was constantly giving orders and decisions. His ideas were simple: fight on to the end in France, in order to cover the largest possible movement into Africa.

Then Reynaud arrived. The meeting began with the French declaring that the position of the Army was desperate. Now Reynaud put the fateful question to the British Prime Minister; would Britain agree that France, having nothing further to contribute to the common cause, should be released from the Joint Declaration and be permitted to negotiate a separate peace? Spears, watching him closely, noted that Reynaud no longer mentioned the possibility of fighting on in Africa:

he was a very different man from the cheerful, determined little chap of a few hours ago. For a moment I saw him as a ventriloquist's dummy voicing the views – of whom? Pétain? Weygand? Could it be Madame de Portes?

Meanwhile, according to Élie Bois, the Countess was trying to get into the conference room. Prevented from doing so, she grew impatient and sent for Baudouin:

'Tell Paul that we must give up – give up. We must make an end of it. There must be an armistice! Tell Paul so, won't you? – from me. I insist on it.'

In response to Reynaud's agonizing question, Churchill expressed his understanding of France's predicament. In no case would Britain waste time in reproaches and recriminations. But that was a different matter from consenting to release France from her pledge. He added, however, a solemn promise that was to be fulfilled five hard years later: 'If England won the war France would be restored in her dignity and her great-ness.' As a final suggestion, Churchill urged that Reynaud send one last new appeal to the President of the United States, with which Britain would identify herself. Reynaud agreed, but made it clear how grave matters would be in the event of an un-favourable reply. With that, Churchill returned to London; it was the last time that he would set foot on French soil for four years. After the meeting, Reynaud was violently reproached, for raising the separate peace issue, by Mandel and the Presi-dents of the Senate and Chamber of Deputies, Jeanneney and Herriot; the latter was in tears. In the meantime Baudouin was insidiously putting it about that Churchill had released France from her engagement. Later that evening when Spears saw Reynaud, he was struck by how 'ghastly' he looked, 'with a completely unnatural expression, still and white'. By the end of that day, he was convinced that 'the possibility of France remaining in the war had almost disappeared'.

The Plea to America

During the small hours of 14 June, Reynaud dispatched his appeal to President Roosevelt, making it dramatically clear that 'unless you can give France firmly to understand, in the hours ahead, that the United States will enter the war in the very near future, the destiny of the world will change'. In other words, France would capitulate. It was the last of a series of communications, ranging from the beseeching to the admonish-ing, addressed to the President by the British and French Premiers. At the beginning of June, Roosevelt and General Marshall had rushed through a deal whereby Britain purchased some six hundred freight-cars of First War arms and ammuni-tion; this was virtually everything the U.S. Army could spare at the time, but none of it was to reach Europe before France fell.

In harbouring any anticipation whatever that the United States could instantaneously send him 'clouds of planes', or ever declare war on Hitler, Reynaud was under a hopeless delusion.[14] The fact was that America, no more prepared to play a role in Europe than she had been during the past twenty years, had no planes to send; and with the Presidential election coming up in November, no politician alive could have brought America into the war that June. Roosevelt's response to Reynaud's appeal was bound to be negative.

The Last Quarter of an Hour

On 14 June, the day the Germans entered Paris, the Government of the Third Republic departed for its final seat at Bordeaux. Reynaud was clearly reaching the end of his tether, and seemed to have lost all his old vigour in dealing with the 'softs'. He kept on repeating that everything depended on Roosevelt's answer to his telegram. He would try one last ploy, however, within the confines of his Cabinet. That afternoon he proposed to Weygand that, like the Dutch, France should seek a military capitulation, 'binding only the army but leaving the Government freedom of action'. Weygand was outraged. 'I refuse,' he declared indignantly, 'to bespatter our colours with this shame!' But this was a political decision, beyond the prerogative of a Commander-in-Chief, and, as Churchill points out, Reynaud would have been within his rights to have dismissed Weygand. It was a decision, however, that he no longer had the strength or the will to take. Next, Camille Chautemps suggested a compromise solution: why not ask the Germans what their conditions of armistice would be, remaining free to reject them? The proposition had a dangerously Faustian smell about it; said

14. For this, the American Ambassador in Paris, William Bullitt, must be held greatly to blame. In an age when Ambassadors carried weight and were more than merely the post-office clerks they tend to be today, Bullitt appears to have sinned by misleading both his own country and France as to the true situation in the other. Washington was persuaded by Bullitt that France's fighting capacity was much greater than it was, while through him the French Government was led to expect far greater aid than could possibly have been forthcoming from the United States at that time.

Churchill, 'It was not of course possible to embark on this slippery slope and stop.'

When the Chautemps proposal was relayed to London, Churchill's reply was that Britain would give her consent for France to ascertain the terms of an armistice, *'provided, but only provided, that the French Fleet is sailed forthwith for British harbours pending negotiations'*.[15] Britain, in her resolve to continue the war, would in no way associate herself with such an inquiry.

That evening Reynaud received Roosevelt's answer. Spears was with him when it arrived:

As he read it he grew still paler, his face contracted . . . 'Our appeal has failed,' he said in a small toneless voice, 'the Americans will not declare war.'

Meanwhile in England, de Gaulle, who had flown there on the 14th to ask for shipping to transport troops to Africa to continue the fight there, had impressed upon Churchill the need for some 'dramatic move' to keep his Government in the war. In the words of Churchill, de Gaulle 'suggested that a proclamation of the indissoluble union of the French and British peoples would serve the purpose'. So, on the afternoon of Sunday 16 June, such a 'Declaration of Union', of staggering historical implications, was duly drafted and approved by the Cabinet. De Gaulle then dictated it over the telephone in person to Reynaud.

With him in Bordeaux, Spears records that as Reynaud put down the telephone 'he was transfigured with joy, and my old friendship for him surged out in a wave of appreciation at his response, for he was happy with a great happiness in the belief that France would now remain in the war'. A Cabinet meeting was immediately called. But Reynaud's colleagues did not share his elation. From the front, reports had arrived that the Germans were at the gates of Besançon and Dijon. Baudouin claims that the French Ministers were 'stunned' by the British offer: 'It in no way satisfied our expectations. It did not loosen

15. Churchill's italics.

the stranglehold on the country.' Chautemps declared that he 'did not want France to become a Dominion'. In the middle of the discussion, an usher entered with a cryptic note ('I hope that you are not going to play at being Isabella of Bavaria!') [16] hastily scribbled by Hélène de Portes, giving Reynaud the last orders he would receive from her as Prime Minister of France. Suddenly the tough little Frenchman with the mandarin face collapsed. Physically and mentally exhausted, he could no longer stand up to the 'softs'. No vote was taken on the British 'Declaration of Union' proposal; Churchill's telegrams concerning the safety of the French fleet were not even presented to the Cabinet. Reynaud announced his intention to tender his resignation to the President. He would propose that Marshal Pétain be sent for.

At about eleven o'clock that night, President Lebrun relates that he told the eighty-four-year-old Marshal:

'Well, there it is. Form a Government.' Without hesitation the Marshal opened his briefcase with a characteristic gesture, showed me a list and said to me: 'Here is my Government.' I must say that, despite the deep sadness of the moment, all the same I felt a small ray of comfort. I recalled those difficult negotations about forming administrations . . . and here I had one given me ready made . . . I thought that this was excellent.

Two hours later Pétain called for the Spanish Ambassador, Señor de Lequerica, and requested him to approach the Germans about an armistice. Later on that morning of 17 June, Spears – his mission ended – prepared to fly back to England. By a prearranged plan, de Gaulle (only just returned from his own journey to England) came to the airstrip, affecting to see Spears off. After the engines had started up, Spears reached out a hand as if to say goodbye and yanked de Gaulle into the

16. Isabella was Queen of France from 1389 to 1435; she gave her daughter, Catherine, in marriage to King Henry V of England, whom she recognized as heir to the King of France, and is generally held responsible for the surrender of France to the English. Isabella was buried, without honours, at St Denis.

plane. Georges Mandel was less fortunate; attempting to get
to North Africa and set up a 'Government in exile' there with
other leading politicians among the remaining 'hards', he was
arrested and returned to France. Four years later he was
murdered by Vichy Milices. De Gaulle alone 'carried with
him', said Churchill, 'in this small aeroplane, the honour of
France'.

In France, the news that Pétain had requested an armistice
was greeted by emotions of widespread relief. 'At last, the
nightmare is about to end' was the common reaction. Crowds
of refugees gathered around the Government buildings in
Bordeaux to cheer the old Marshal. People wept publicly in
grief, and in gratitude.

In Germany, the immense events of the past weeks seem to
have provoked, at least on the surface, astonishingly little excitement. At the end of May, Shirer recalled three Germans
betting him that the Wehrmacht would be in London within
three weeks, but a week later, as the battle round Dunkirk was
about to end, he admitted that the scene in Berlin 'confounds
me'. Strolling down the Kurfürstendamm in the evening, Shirer
found it

jammed with people meandering along pleasantly. The great side-
walk cafés on this broad, tree-lined avenue were filled with thousands, chatting quietly over their *ersatz* coffee or their ice-cream.
I even noticed several smartly dressed women. To-day, being the
Sabbath and a warm and sunny June day, tens of thousands of
people, mostly in family groups, betook themselves to the woods
or the lakes on the outskirts of the city. The Tiergarten, I noticed,
also was thronged. Everyone had that lazy, idle, happy-go-lucky
Sunday holiday air.

Shirer was equally taken aback at the lack of elation the nor-
mally excitable Berliners displayed on hearing the unbelievable
news that Paris had fallen. The city took it

as phlegmatically as it has taken everything else in this war. Later
I went to Halensee for a swim, it being warm and I feeling the
need of a little relaxation. It was crowded, but I overheard no

one discussing the news. Out of five hundred people, three bought extras when the newsboys rushed in, shouting the news.

He added: 'It would be very wrong, though, to conclude that the taking of Paris has not stirred something very deep in the hearts of most Germans. It was always a wish-dream of millions here.'

Chapter 21

Aftermath

Can it be that France has had her day like Athens, Rome, Spain or Portugal in the past? Is it Germany's turn now? No. Our virtues and our culture, which only twenty years ago proved so strong and full of life, have not been killed by a mere handful of politicians.

MAJOR D. BARLONE, *A French Officer's Diary*

There are no Allies any more. There remains only one enemy: England!

Final Wehrmacht communiqué, 25 June 1940

FRENCH SIGN PEACE TREATY: WE'RE IN THE FINALS.
Newspaper vendor's sign in London, 1940

The Clearing at Réthondes: Hitler's Revenge

Shortly before noon on 20 June, Pétain received radio instructions from the Germans for the dispatch of the French armistice delegation. They were to present themselves 'at the Loire bridge near Tours' early that evening. There would be a temporary cease-fire in the area. After some argument, the unfortunate General Huntziger, erstwhile commander of the Second Army, had been selected to lead the delegation. Reluctantly he accepted. His orders were to break off talks instantly if the Germans called for the surrender of the French fleet or the occupation of any colonial territory.

So great was the cluster of refugees and military traffic on the roads that Huntziger and his convoy did not reach the appointed rendezvous until late that night. A German escort then whisked them, with no time for sleep or any proper meal, to Paris, where they arrived at 7.30 a.m. They still had no clue as to the site chosen by the Germans for the cease-fire negotiations. Then, after only a few hours' pause, they were driven on to Compiègne, some fifty miles north-east of Paris. Finally, just after three o'clock that afternoon, the cavalcade halted at the clearing in the forest at Réthondes. There stood the historic *wagon-lit* where, in November 1918, Marshal Foch and Weygand himself had received the defeated German emissaries. With characteristic efficiency, German Army engineers had hacked down the wall of the museum housing the railway coach and brought it out to where it had stood twenty-two years earlier. A large Swastika was draped over the monument to the 1918 Armistice. The cycle of revenge could not be more complete. France had chosen as the setting for the final humbling of Germany in 1919 the Versailles Hall of Mirrors where, in the arrogant exaltation of 1871, King Wilhelm of Prussia had proclaimed himself Kaiser; so now Hitler's choice for the scene of his moment of supreme triumph was to be that of France's in 1918.

When Huntziger and his co-delegates, dazed and weary from the journey, realized they were being led to Foch's *wagon-lit*, they were deeply shocked. Together with his Service chiefs, plus Ribbentrop and Hess, Hitler had already arrived at the clearing. In warm sunshine he strode up to the great granite block and meticulously read the inscription on it:

'HERE ON THE ELEVENTH OF NOVEMBER 1918 SUCCUMBED THE CRIMINAL PRIDE OF THE GERMAN PEOPLE ...'

Fifty yards away, Shirer was intently studying Hitler's expression through binoculars:

It is afire with scorn, anger, hate, revenge, triumph. He steps off the monument and contrives to make even this gesture a masterpiece of contempt ... Suddenly ... he throws his whole body into harmony with his mood. He swiftly snaps his hands on his hips, arches his shoulders, plants his feet wide apart. It is a magnificent gesture of defiance, of burning contempt for this place now and all that it has stood for in the twenty-two years since it witnessed the humbling of the German Empire.

Then Hitler led the way into the railway coach.

After the French delegation had seated itself, Keitel began proceedings by reading out a brief preamble, explaining that the site had been chosen as 'an act of reparatory justice'. France was now defeated; in her armistice terms, Germany's chief aims were to prevent any resumption of hostilities and to provide herself with the requisite conditions for pursuing the war against Britain. When Keitel had finished, at 3.30 p.m., Hitler got up, gave a Nazi salute and marched out to the strains of *Deutschland über Alles*. Keitel now handed the French delegates copies of the German terms. No discussion was to be allowed. Huntziger and his team returned to Paris late that night, and over an infuriatingly bad telephone line relayed the armistice terms to Weygand in Bordeaux. To Pétain, Weygand described the terms as 'harsh but not dishonouring'. All through the night and most of the next day Pétain's Cabinet debated the terms. An extension of the deadline was granted, ill-humouredly, by Keitel. Finally, at 8.50 p.m. on Saturday 22 June, the armistice was signed at Réthondes. The shooting would officially end at 35 minutes past midnight on the 25th. In a voice seized with emotion, Huntziger, addressing Keitel, said he hoped that, 'as a soldier', the German leader would understand how onerous this moment was for him. Keitel then declared: 'It is honourable for the victor to do honour to the vanquished.' He asked those present to stand in silence for a minute, in honour of the fallen on both sides. 'Military honour,' commented Weygand, 'was safe.'

As the delegates emerged from the *wagon-lit*, the observers outside in the clearing felt a drop of rain fall. The skies had become heavily overcast. Soon the drops grew to a violent storm. The few black flags hung out by French householders drooped limp and sodden. The wonderful days of sunshine, 'Goering's weather', that extraordinary run of good fortune which had so assisted the Germans in their conquest, had at last broken with a vengeance. In the darkening sky lay auguries for the future: Britain was not yet suing for peace, and in exactly one year to the day Hitler would be sending his victorious legions to their doom in Russia.

Immediately the armistice had been signed, German engineers prepared to move Foch's *wagon-lit* in triumph to Berlin.[1] With a barbarity worthy of Genghis Khan, Hitler decreed that, except for Foch's statue, the site should be totally razed. He

1. Where it was later destroyed in an R.A.F. air-raid.

then set off on a tour of First World War battlefields, together with two old comrades from the company in which he had served as a corporal, taking in some of the Maginot Line forts – like any German tourist – before returning to Berlin to organize the celebrations that would suitably commemorate this astonishing victory. For Hitler, as for many of his soldiers, the war was over. France, the arch-enemy, was prostrate at last; Britain no longer counted, she would fall like a plum from a tree in due course. Russia did not exist; America did not exist. Ever since that day of humiliation at Versailles, it was France alone that had obsessed German thoughts. Karl-Heinz Mende summed them up well when, writing home about the Armistice, he said: 'The great battle in France is now ended. It lasted twenty-six years.'

The Price

What had been the cost of this earth-shaking last round of the 'great battle'? When the figures were added up, during the six weeks' fighting German casualties amounted to

killed	27,074
wounded	111,034
missing	18,384

Thus despite repeated Allied and neutral reports of hecatombs of German casualties, the overall total of just over 150,000 was equivalent to not much more than a third of the number of men Germany lost at Verdun in 1916, in one single battle of the First World War. During the three decisive weeks up to Dunkirk, German casualties (as claimed by the Wehrmacht) were reported to have totalled approximately what Britain suffered during the first day of the Somme alone. Even the losses of its élite formations, which had been in the forefront of the battle, were comparatively light (at least by First War standards): Rommel's 7th Panzer, for example, lost a total of 2,273 in killed and wounded; the Grossdeutschland Regiment, 1,108 (including 221 killed) out of its complement of 3,900 men; and the losses of one of the most constantly engaged infantry divisions, the 3rd, had totalled no more than 1,649. On the other hand, as the cost of the Wehrmacht's enormously successful doctrine of 'leading from the front', a relatively high proportion of the German dead – 5 per cent – were officers. The strain imposed by the tempo of the campaign also extended its casualties; one was Colonel Werner, commander of the 31st Panzer Regiment (5th Panzer Division), who died of a heart attack shortly after the armistice.

On the Allied side, French losses during the six-week campaign are estimated [2] at somewhere in the region of 90,000 dead, 200,000 wounded and 1,900,000 in prisoners and missing. British total casualties came to 68,111, Belgian 23,350, and Dutch 9,779. While the Luftwaffe lost 1,284 planes, R.A.F. losses amounted to 931, of which 477 were priceless fighters. French losses in the air are difficult to assess. One reasonable French figure puts the number of planes lost in combat at 560, of which 235 were destroyed on the ground. It was months before the victorious Germans could even count up the vast piles of captured war booty of all descriptions. Among the guns taken were some 7,000 French '75s' of First War vintage, many of them only brought out of retirement in the last desperate hours of the battle; nevertheless, slightly modified by the Wehrmacht, four summers later they would be used with deadly effect to halt British and American tanks landing on the Normandy beaches.

Tears and Celebrations

At thirty-five minutes past midnight on the 25th, the cannon ceased firing and something like the silence of the grave descended on France. Already the endless lines of weary, footsore, broken-spirited refugees had begun to retrace their footsteps, to find out what had happened to their homes. Foodstuffs were in seriously short supply, transportation and other public services had broken down, but in some respects French life reverted – at least temporarily – to normality with surprising speed, just as it had done after the defeat of 1870. On the day after the armistice was concluded, a German war correspon-

2. Because of the confusion of the collapse, there are discrepancies here.

dent (Stackelberg), lunching in a restaurant in Lyon, was astonished to observe a bourgeois French family at the next table going through the important ritual of their Sunday lunch as if nothing in the world had happened. They spent approximately half an hour

bent over the menu, discussing the food, and then at length and with great seriousness discussed city gossip. It struck me as remarkable that their thoughts on this day should not assume other lines, but the meal was something very important for them.

Returning to Paris from Compiègne, William Shirer was intrigued to find that along the Seine 'The fishermen were dangling their lines from the bank, as always. I thought: "Surely this will go on to the end of Paris, to the end of time." ' Ilya Ehrenburg also watched Paris coming back to life, in an implausible kind of way:

The Germans bought souvenirs, smutty postcards, pocket dictionaries in the little shops. Notices appeared in restaurants: *'Ici on parle allemand.'* Prostitutes lisped *'Mein Süsser'*.

In the countryside Simone de Beauvoir registered surprise at the conqueror's good behaviour; they

did not cut off children's hands; they paid for their drinks and the eggs they bought on the farms, and spoke politely . . . As I was reading in a field two soldiers approached me. They spoke a little clumsy French, and assured me of their friendly feelings towards the French people; it was the English and the Jews who had brought us to this sorry pass.

By and large, the German troops appeared to be kind and helpful. The Gestapo, the Sicherheitsdienst, and all the apparatus of Nazi terror had yet to arrive.

Meanwhile, in England, once it was apparent that Hitler was not going to follow up Dunkirk with an immediate invasion, the shock of defeat turned into a kind of relief that, somehow, strangely enough, life had at least become simpler. King George VI spoke for many when he wrote to his mother: 'Personally, I feel happier now that we have no allies to be polite to and to

pamper.' There was, after all, something to be said for being 'in
the finals' – to quote the headline which one Cockney news-
vendor chalked up on his stand.

For the victorious German troops in France, the first summer
days after the armistice indeed seemed like a halcyon time of
insouciant rapture. They clambered up the Eiffel Tower, gazed
down at Napoleon's tomb, clicking cameras everywhere, like
tourists of any country at any time. On the wreckage-strewn
Channel beaches, they kicked off their jackboots to paddle in
the warm water, gazing across at a defiant but impotent enemy.
As the cease-fire came into force, the ascetic Halder noted from
his desk: 'Now begins the administrative work.' War production was cut back, and there was talk of massive demobilization
of the Army. It was also a time of mutual congratulation, and
of thanksgiving and celebration, rather than of preparation for
any further fighting. Even the icy Molotov (while reaching out
with one hand for the Baltic States and the Roumanian prov-
ince of Bessarabia, as Russia's self-awarded 'tip' for her benev-
olent neutrality) had sent Hitler 'the warmest congratulations
of the Soviet Government on the splendid success of the German Wehrmacht'. On 17 July, the Grossdeutschland paraded
in triumph through Paris, to hold a thanksgiving service in
Notre-Dame.[3] The next day in Berlin, a victory parade marched
through the Brandenburger Tor, for the first time since 1871.
Then, on the 19th, Hitler in a solemn ceremony at the Kroll
Opera House promoted twelve of his triumphant generals to
the rank of Field-Marshal.[4] Such an inflation of military pomp
had never been seen during the time of the Kaiser; but nor had
such victories.

3. It subsequently received orders from Keitel banning all such religious
services.

4. These were; Keitel (the O.K.W. Chief of Staff); Brauchitsch (Army C.-
in-C.); Rundstedt, Bock and Leeb (the three Army Group commanders);
Reichenau, List, Kluge, and Witzleben (Army commanders); and Milch,
Kesselring and Sperrle from the Luftwaffe. Conspicuously absent from these
so honoured was Halder; Shirer, watching the scene, thought him the
'saddest figure' there.

Shadows: the Flaws of Victory

Yet already there were shadows. As young Lieutenant Mende wrote home: 'I feel full of peace within this enemy country, and yet also I feel a certain anxiety about this not entirely finished war.' When in the course of the Berlin victory celebrations Hitler remarked to his sober-faced financial wizard: 'Well, Herr Schacht, what do you say now?', Schacht, sibyl-like, had simply replied: 'May God protect you!' Meanwhile, thousands of miles away in Chicago, Roosevelt was being nominated by the Democratic Party to run for a third term. For 28 June, the twenty-first anniversary of the signature of the Versailles Treaty, Hitler had planned a further act of humiliation for prostrated France by holding a massive parade in front of the palace, followed by an oration delivered inside the Hall of Mirrors. But it was cancelled; there were fears (which even Goering could not allay) that the R.A.F. might also attend. Meanwhile, it was not until 17 June, the day of the Grossdeutschland's thanksgiving ceremony in Notre-Dame, that the O.K.H. issued its first orders for 'Operation Sea-Lion' – the invasion of England. Then, on 29 July, Jodl gathered together some of the senior O.K.W. staff officers in a railway restaurant car, ensured that all windows and doors were closed, and informed them that Hitler had it in mind to attack Russia the following spring.

Soon Hitler's astounding achievements in France would turn to dust as the diamond brilliance of *Sichelschnitt* was shattered by the fatal flaw latent within it. In his appreciation drawn up for the Kaiser, which prepared the ground for the German attack on Verdun in 1916, Falkenhayn, the German Chief of Staff, had recognized Britain to be Germany's principal enemy. By 'bleeding white' the French Army at Verdun, he had argued, Britain's 'best sword would be knocked out of her hand'. The U-boat blockade would do the rest, in due course. Now Hitler had succeeded where Falkenhayn and all the Kaiser's generals had failed. Britain's 'best sword' lay shattered on the ground. But Hitler and the planners of genius who had created *Sichel-schnitt* had in reality thought no further ahead than Falkenhayn; no contingency plan had been prepared whereby a tottering Britain might be invaded immediately after success had been achieved in France. By mid July, when the first O.K.H. plan was drafted, it was already too late. The Germans had missed the bus, as Chamberlain would have said. The two great errors of the otherwise perfect *Sichelschnitt* – this original fault of high strategy, and the tactical fault of the 24 May 'Halt Order' which allowed the B.E.F. to escape from Dunkirk – in conjunction added up to one thing. Britain would remain at war, inviolate. And as long as Britain was there, it was inevitable that sooner or later the immense power of the United States would be brought in too. But like so many of his generation of Germans, their vision blinkered by the memories of 1914–18 and of the shame of Versailles, Hitler could see only France and 'the last decisive battle' which would have to be fought there.

In fact, as one now sees it in the perspective of time, Hitler's astonishing triumph over France was to be the direct source of his greatest disaster. After France, the mighty warrior nation which had defeated Germany in 1918, had been overthrown with such ease, what nation on earth could stand up to the Wehrmacht? So Hitler in 1941 was convinced that, while reducing his war production and demobilizing part of his forces, and without furnishing his cohorts with any winter equipment, he could knock out Russia in one lightning campaign. But although in many ways their doctrine of war may initially have been as faulty as that of the French, the Russians would be able to make a retreat equivalent to a French withdrawal from Sedan across the Pyrenees and down to Saragossa, before launching any major counter-offensive. What might even Gamelin and Weygand have achieved, had they but disposed of such space over which to manoeuvre and behind which to form fresh armies? Even more lethal to the Germans than their self-assuredness derived from the easy success in France was the supreme reliance Hitler now placed in his own infallibility. He saw himself as having been proved right in his audacity over the cautiousness of his professional advisers during the planning of *Sichelschnitt*; and, in retrospect, he saw how wrong had been the strategic assessment in battle of even those like Rundstedt whose judgement he trusted most. In his unquenchable animosity towards the O.K.H., he could not admit that it was in fact not he but Halder who during the campaign had been right. So Hitler became less and less inclined to accept the advice of his military experts, and more and more to rely on his own intuition, until finally it led him to the point of no return at Stalingrad.

French Post-mortems

For four grim years, France disappears from the forefront of the battle. 'The choice is always between Verdun and Dachau,' wrote a severe French critic of 1940, Jean Dutourd. Unable to face the prospects of another Verdun in 1940, it was indeed Dachau that became France's fate. In their hundreds of thousands, Frenchmen were shipped off to the concentration camps or to slave labour inside the Reich. With superb psychological cunning, the Nazis divided the conquered country geographically in two, thereby imposing yet another enduring source of division upon those that already plagued France. In the act of liberation, her old and new Allies would inflict at least as much damage upon France's cities and countryside as had the Luftwaffe, and the prostrate nation could hardly be subjected to greater humiliation. But there were many Frenchmen who did not agree that the final battle to save national 'honour', which so obsessed General Weygand, had yet been fought. Using every device and subterfuge they slipped off to join de Gaulle's Free French in England, or the 'Normandie-Niemen Squadron' in Russia; later, with Anglo-American support, the Resistance would rekindle the flame of 'honour' inside France itself.

Who, and what, were responsible for France's catastrophe in 1940? Could the game have been played differently? At what point did disaster become irremediable? The questions are still asked and re-asked, and the answers become no simpler with time. But post-mortems are irresistible. The Riom Trials, held under the auspices of the Vichy Government in 1942, attempted to saddle the blame for the lost war upon earlier French

Governments. The questions asked were loaded; no official
record was made of the proceedings; the 'trials' were finally
adjourned and then dropped. Equally inconclusive and incomplete were the 2,500 pages of the 'Serre Report', based on the
findings of the French official Commission of Inquiry which sat
from 1947 to 1951. It did its best to exculpate the politicians of
the period, but it could not even agree as to whether it was the
breakthrough on Corap's or Huntziger's front which precipitated the military catastrophe on the Meuse. However, as this
present book has tried to show, more than any individual or set
of individuals was to blame. Two doctrines and two philosophies
and the past events of a generation were involved. Since the 'day
of glory' of 14 July 1919, almost every throw of the dice had
resulted in advantage to Germany and loss to France. Upon
Hitler's reoccupation of the Rhineland, unchallenged, in 1936,
the road to disaster was clearly signposted. Three years later
France went reluctantly to war, while she was herself still close
to a state of civil war, with morale (as Mandel admitted to
Spears during the last days of defeat) 'sapped by the feeling of
the last twenty years that there would be no war because France
could not stand another bleeding like that of 1914', and (in the
words of Weygand) with a French Army of 1918 facing a
Wehrmacht of 1939.

Before the decisive battle itself opened, there were two other
chronological milestones on France's road to disaster. In
August 1939, the signature of the Ribbentrop–Molotov Non-
Aggression Pact effectively removed any prospect of Germany's
military potential being split by a war on two fronts; a month
later, this was compounded by France's unwillingness to come
to the aid of her solitary Polish ally, by launching an offensive
in the west. Thus, from October 1939 onwards, France had no
option but to remain on the defensive and wait to be attacked.
When the attack came the following May, the preponderance
of strength – with all factors taken into account – was immeasurably greater on the German side than at any time during
the First World War. Therefore, there is a fatalistic view which
regards the Battle of France as having been lost even before it
was begun. Might France still have been defeated even if the

Germans had not marched to the masterly blueprint of *Sichelschnitt*, if they had simply utilized a crude replay of the Schlieffen Plan of 1914? Possibly.

On the other hand, in war Fate contains many surprises. For all its impressiveness, the Wehrmacht of 1940 was a more fragile instrument, less consistently solid throughout, than the Kaiser's Army of 1914; nor did it have the same weight of resources behind it. On almost every occasion when Allied troops in 1940 came up against the ordinary infantry divisions which comprised the great mass of the Wehrmacht, they held their own. Acutely limited in their fuel supplies, the Panzers could not have fought a protracted campaign without a major reorganization. Then there is the prime consideration of the steadfastness of the German High Command, about which much has already been said. It is always held that the Younger Moltke lost the First War on the Marne because his nerve failed. Yet there were times during both the Norwegian and the French campaigns when the German High Command of 1940 revealed itself to be potentially little less impressionable than Moltke. What, then, if the steel tip provided by the few Panzer and motorized divisions could have been blunted, the nerves of the German High Command shaken by one sharp reverse? Might the German onslaught have been brought to a temporary halt, perhaps long enough for the Allies to reorganize their forces into a more coherent defence? The impact Rundstedt's Ardennes Offensive of 1944 made upon the Allies indeed suggests how even such a last-gasp effort (and against a far greater relative superiority than the Germans possessed in May 1940) can at least win time.

It was *time* that was the vital element which – more than weapons, even perhaps more than morale – France most lacked in 1940. After the battle had been engaged, the afternoon of 15 May, the sixth day of fighting, marks the moment of almost certain military defeat. This was the decisive day that saw the failure of the first French counter-attacks, to which had been dedicated the main weight of her armoured reserves, and the day on which it was clear that the Germans could not be prevented from breaking out of their Meuse bridgeheads. For the

French armour to have concentrated for a blow effective
enough to have halted the Panzers on the 15th, the necessary
dispositions would have had to be decreed by the 12th. But with
the essential French reserves dispersed as they were in the line-
up for the Dyle–Breda Plan's advance into Belgium, this would
have proved virtually impossible. The French ripostes were
almost bound to be too late. The speed with which Panzer warfare developed in 1940 certainly proved the validity of the
dictum of Moltke the Elder: 'One fault only in the initial deployment of an Army cannot be made good during the whole
course of the campaign.' On top of this must be added the
tremendous significance of the Luftwaffe's supremacy in the
air, which (although later in the war the Germans were able to
conduct an imposing defence in the teeth of far greater Allied
tactical air superiority) constituted a decisive factor at this stage
of the Second World War. Apart from the lethal effect of the
close-support Stukas, the Luftwaffe's far-ranging medium bombers were what finally denied the French High Command the
time it needed to commit its reserves to battle, at the right
moment and the right place.

The odds against France opposing *Sichelschnitt* in 1940, with
any successful defence and even allowing for the element of
the unexpected, remain enormously high. When all is said and
done, the strategic brilliance of the German plan and tactical
skill with which it was executed will always make it one of the
classic campaigns of history.

What Happened to Them? The Victors

So immense were the universal consequences of the Fall of
France that one tends to lose sight of the leading actors in the
tragedy. On the German side, there were countless thousands
of all ranks who, like Rommel's two ace commanders, Rothenburg [5] and Bismarck,[6] either fell later in the war or else ended
in disgrace with the Nazi hierarchy. Rommel's own subsequent
career is well known; the legendary hero of the desert war

5. Killed in Russia.
6. Killed in the Western Desert, once again fighting under Rommel.

yields to the disillusioned Field-Marshal conducting a hopeless defence of northern France against the Allied invasion of 1944, and finally to the critic of the régime forced to take poison or be shot by the Gestapo. Curiously enough, of all the commanders of the ten Panzer divisions which proved so decisive in France, Rommel alone later rose to great prominence; Kirchner, for instance, who had led the enormously successful 1st Panzer, ended the war as a corps commander. On the other hand, his junior, the tough and ruthless Lieutenant-Colonel Hermann Balck, was to become a full general commanding an Army Group in France (in 1944–5), and one of a handful of Germans to be awarded the highest grade of the Ritterkreuz decoration.[7]

Guderian, promoted Colonel-General in September 1940, was given command of the Second Panzer Army, which he led in the battle for Moscow during the autumn of 1941. After the failure of the campaign, he fell under a shadow and was transferred to the reserve. The strain of the past years had left its mark and in 1942 he began to suffer from heart trouble. Following the bomb attempt of 20 July 1944, Guderian – always politically acceptable to Hitler – was given the job once held by Halder as Chief of the O.K.H. General Staff, until in March 1945 he too was finally dismissed. In poor health in his last years, he died in 1954, aged sixty-six. His portrait still hangs in a place of honour in the barracks of Panzer units of the present-day Bundeswehr. Kleist led the First Panzer Army into the Ukraine in 1941, and became another of Hitler's Field-Marshals. Manstein was also promoted Field-Marshal and justly came to be rated as Germany's ablest field commander; he fell into disgrace with the Führer on the same day as Kleist – 30 March 1944.[8] Rundstedt led Army Group South at the start of the Russian campaign in 1941, and it was he who (reluctantly) commanded the last German offensive of the

7. 'Knight's Cross with Oak Leaves, Swords and Diamonds'.

8. After the war, Manstein, sentenced to a lengthy imprisonment for war crimes, was at first reluctant to speak to any Allied interviewers. When he did, in old age, he would often express surprise that anything particularly brilliant should be seen in his plan, *Sichelschnitt*: 'After all,' he remarked once, 'We just did the obvious thing; we attacked the enemy's weakest point. The hopeless French reconnaissance won us the Battle of France; just that.'

winter of 1944–5 – over terrain which he knew so well from 1940. After the war he was imprisoned in England, but released in 1949. He died, aged seventy-eight, in 1953. Hitler's *bête noire*, Brauchitsch, was sacked after the failure to take Moscow, when Hitler himself took over command of the O.K.H., thereby ending, once and for all, the independence of the German General Staff. After the war, Brauchitsch was to have been arraigned on war crimes charges, but died (in 1948) before a trial could be held. Franz Halder lost his job in 1942, after yet another disagreement with Hitler; implicated with the 'resistance' in the 1944 bomb plot, he was found inside Dachau by the Americans in 1945.

The Vanquished

For the French leaders, defeat was followed by long years of frustration or imprisonment, of recrimination by their compatriots and of attempts to justify their own roles in the battle. Many lived to considerable ages. On his replacement by Weygand, Gamelin had rejoined his wife in their 'comfortable, modest ground-floor flat in the Avenue Foch which we had bought in 1937, in anticipation of the moment of my retirement'. As the Germans approached Paris, Gamelin wrote to Weygand informing him that he was leaving for his sister's house in the country; but he would naturally be available to return at any instant. He was hurt to receive no acknowledgement from Weygand. After confinement in various châteaux, from 1943 onwards Gamelin found himself in Buchenwald, together with Daladier, Blum and President Lebrun. All survived, and in 1945 Gamelin threw himself tirelessly into the publication of three hefty volumes of memoirs and apologiae, entitled *Servir*. He died in 1958, aged eighty-six. General Maxime Weygand, after a brief interlude as Minister of National Defence in Pétain's Government, was sent to Algeria as Delegate-General. Here he acquitted himself with distinction, maintaining the spirit of the Army there while keeping the Germans at bay. Later he too was imprisoned by the Germans, and later still by his own countrymen, for a short period.

He died in 1965, at the venerable age of ninety-eight, mistrustful of the British, and shrewdly alert (though rather deaf) to the very end.

Unlike Gamelin and Weygand, General Georges left no memoirs. Before vanishing finally into oblivion, he reappeared briefly and contentiously in the intrigue-ridden world of Algiers in 1943; the Allies, having imported him from France, soon came to regard him (in the words of Anthony Eden) as 'a reactionary old defeatist' and pensioned him off. The unhappy General Corap also made no attempt to justify himself against the charges made publicly by Reynaud, which led him to a nervous breakdown. He was later cleared at the Riom Trials, and died, in silence, at his home in Fontainbleau in 1953. Huntziger, commander on the fatal field of Sedan and leader of the armistice delegation, also had no opportunity to write his side of the battle; he was killed in a plane crash in 1941. Among the French generals taken prisoners-of-war, General Giraud managed to escape [9] from Königstein Castle, where he was interned with General Prioux. He too made his way to Algiers and, with American backing, established himself briefly as a rival claimant to de Gaulle for the leadership of the Free French. General Frère died of maltreatment in a German concentration camp.

Of the British participants, Lord Gort, although he had succeeded in saving so many of his men, was shattered by what had happened to the B.E.F. Not favoured by Churchill, he received no further fighting command, whereas his juniors in the B.E.F. – Brooke, Alexander and Montgomery – rose to the highest summits of fame. Probably Churchill was right; Gort was not the man to lead or organize a modern, mechanized Army. But no one deserved greater recognition for the incalculable services he had rendered Great Britain, and the Allied cause. Wars, however, 'are not won by evacuations'. Later, Gort was made Governor-General of Malta at a time when the island's position seemed hopeless; here, once again, was a challenge for which his tenacious courage was supremely adapted. His career ended as High Commissioner in Palestine at the end of the war;

9. He had also escaped from a German P.O.W. camp in the previous war.

but soon after his appointment his health broke down and he died in 1946, aged sixty.

Reynaud and Pétain

Of all the major figures of this epoch, none seem so closely shrouded in tragedy as the two French Premiers, Reynaud and his successor Pétain. A few days after the armistice, there had been a scandal when two emissaries were caught trying to smuggle out to America gold and jewellery belonging to the Comtesse de Portes – apparently unbeknown to Reynaud. On 28 June, Reynaud was driving in the south of France with the woman for whom he had worked so hard, and whose love was now about all that was left to him. To distract him from his misery, she persuaded him to take the wheel. Almost immediately the car swung off the road, into one of the plane trees lining it. A heavy suitcase hurtled forward from the back of the car to strike Hélène de Portes in the neck. She was killed instantly. Reynaud suffered only minor injuries. When he regained consciousness in hospital and was told of her death, he is said to have remarked simply: *'Elle était la France.'* The remaining war years Reynaud spent in German prisons, narrowly escaping the fate of his fellow inmate, Georges Mandel. After the war he re-entered politics, devoting himself to the cause of European unity, and once more became a Minister. His first wife having died, he remarried in 1949 (aged seventy-one) and begot three children, the youngest born when he was approaching eighty. Still exercising regularly in the private gymnasium he had constructed in his Paris apartment, Reynaud lived to be eighty-seven. He died in 1966.

Alas for him, Pétain lived to be even older, the receptacle of France's dishonour, abandoned by his colleagues of the generation which should have been in control of the destiny of France, and later condemned by them for allowing members of the defeated nation to be marched to the Nazi slave-labour camps. As Paul Baudouin deserted him, the old Marshal said with tears in his eyes: 'Pity me. You are going, but I, at eighty-four, must stay and lead this sort of life.' Finally, aged ninety-

five, he too died in an austere French prison in 1951. By one of
the strange quirks of fortune, seven years later at the age of
sixty-eight, Pétain's erstwhile protégé and the man who had
gone to continue the fight from England while Pétain capitulated, General de Gaulle, would be summoned back from old
age, just like Pétain, to take over the reins of France after
younger men had abdicated.

Scars of Battle

In a way, the physical scars left by these cataclysmic six weeks
of 1940 seem not to have lingered on as did those of Verdun.
The court at Vincennes which housed Gamelin's *Thébaïde*,
though destroyed by the Germans, has now been rebuilt at last;
the villages and towns of France seared by the Luftwaffe (and
again by the liberating British and Americans) have long since
been rebuilt. At Dinant on the Meuse and Bouillon on the
Semois, German and French tourists come by the bus-load each
summer to visit the pseudo-medieval Citadel and crusader
Godefroy de Bouillon's Keep, perhaps pausing midway to
admire the fantastic panorama from Monthermé's Roche-à-
Sept-Heures. But there is little enough to suggest the events of
thirty summers ago. Noirefontaine, whence Guderian planned
his crossing of the Meuse, is now a resting-place recommended
by the idyllic *Route de Bonheur*. At Sedan itself, the battlefield
where France's Third Republic was first engendered and subsequently killed, it is easier to find reminders of the battle of
1870 than of 1940. There are calvaries celebrating the gallant
charge of General Margueritte's *cuirassiers* and the Maison des
Dernières Cartouches at Bazeilles, and there are war memorials
and cemeteries dating from 1914–18. But 1940 has left none of
the pock-marked, lunar shell-fields and the ghost-ridden atmosphere that one feels will characterize Verdun for all time.
Down on the Meuse at Sedan, where the heaviest fighting took
place, a few concrete bunkers (now used as cow-stalls by local
farmers) still bear the marks of blows delivered by the German
flak and tank guns seeking out their embrasures. But all too
many of them reveal little sign of damage – a mute testimony

to the fact that Grandsard's 'B' reservists did not stand fast like the men of Verdun. In any case the battle did not rest here long enough for the scars to be lasting. At Houx, the weir over which Rommel's motor-cyclists crept is still there; the island is itself a camping ground, frequented by young Germans not born in 1940. It is not easy to discover locals who can recount precisely what happened on the Meuse during those glorious May days.

As the revolutionary nightmare of Paris in May 1968 subsequently revealed, the wounds of political self-division – the heritage of the Commune and the Popular Front, with the schisms of Pétainist–versus–Gaullist now superimposed – linger unhealed in France. But where perhaps the invisible scars lie deepest are in the relations between the former allies, Britain and France. After 1945, disillusion and mistrust at the French performance in 1940 played their part in Britain's determination never again to rely upon other peoples' forces for her own security. She would loyally contribute to the collective security of NATO, but at the same time she would build her own costly Maginot Line of atomic weaponry and call it the 'independent deterrent'. (Fortunately, unlike France's, Britain's 'Maginot Line' has been allowed to lapse into graceful obsolescence without ever being put to the test.) Meanwhile, in the irony of history, it was the Germans who pushed Britain out of the continent of Europe in June 1940; but, within the Common Market framework of the 1960s, it was France who prevailed upon the Germans not to let Britain back in again.[10] Yet this was no accident of fate, nor just the resentment of the once humiliated towards the superciliousness of the unvanquished. In France, the consequences of Dunkirk do not cease to engender suspicions that, if the going ever gets too tough in Europe, whether in military or economic terms, Britain will always be tempted to pull out, as she did in 1940. Will it ever be said that, in saving the B.E.F. and thus winning the war, Britain perhaps lost the peace for herself?

10. As a further piece of irony, it was the statesman – Charles de Gaulle – who had sold to the French Government the amazing notion of an 'indissoluble union' between Britain and France in the darkest hour of June 1940 who kept the door to Europe barred to Britain while he lived.

Though it remains vivid and fresh in the memories of many men now barely middle-aged, historically that May of 1940 now seems to have belonged so much more closely to 1918, to the world of Foch and the Kaiser than the one we live in today. In some respects the figures involved in the great drama of *Sichelschnitt* are seen to march back and forth across a screen almost as dimly distant as that of the Crimea. The weapons they used have become as outdated as the national causes they represented. How many centuries ago can it have been that Vietnamese fought and died for France at Monthermé, Algerian *Tirailleurs* at Philippeville, Senegalese at Amiens? How much has changed within these three decades! The French and British Empires have ceased to exist. The German Reich is split into a Soviet satellite and a secondary power. Both emerging from the Second World War as defeated nations, France and Germany have at last discovered a common denominator; in consequence, relations between them have become more harmonious over a longer period than at any time since Louis XIV came to the throne. The Army of a reconditioned but truncated Germany now provides France (and Britain) with her 'best sword' in Europe. In face of a docile Germany, France herself is – in appearance, and temporarily – the continent's most powerful political force west of the Elbe. But all this is irrelevant. In the modern world, the combined influence of the three chief belligerents of 1940 adds up to little when weighed against the might of the two new super-powers which maintained their neutrality, through military impotence, during the Battle of France.

Back and forth through Dinant and Sedan the prosperous, well-fed burghers of the Common Market flock in their Citroëns and their Mercedes, apparently oblivious to all the misery perpetrated in this tiny blood-sodden corner of France during the past hundred years. Watching them it is sometimes hard not to wonder: did the First Sedan, the Battle of Verdun, the Second Battle of Sedan *have* to be fought before Germany and France would lower the frontier barriers between their two countries? Perhaps Hitler's blood-curdling prediction in *Mein Kampf* that Germany would have to fight 'one last decisive battle' against France has come true in a sense that he indeed could never have foreseen. Certainly this Franco-German battle *must* have been the 'last'; the facts of life today are such that one cannot possibly conceive of there being any repeat. At last *finis* seems to have been written to the saga wherein the ancient rivalry between France and Germany set the tempo of world affairs. But at what a cost!

London, Ashington, Château de Rougemont

Bibliography

Part One: Books

Abetz, Otto, *Das Offene Problem* (Cologne, 1951).

Abshagen, Karl Heinz, *Canaris* (London, 1956).

Accart, J. M., *Chasseurs du Ciel* (Paris, 1945).

Allard, Paul, *L'Énigme de la Meuse: La Vérité sur l'Affaire Corap* (Paris, 1941).

Armengaud, A., *Batailles Politiques et Militaires sur l'Europe* (Paris, 1948).

Astier de la Vigerie, Francois d', *Le Ciel n'était pas Vide* (Paris, 1952).

Balbaud, René, *Cette Drôle de Guerre* (Oxford, 1941).

Bardies, R. M., *La Campagne de 1939–1940* (Paris, 1947).

Bardoux, Jacques, *Journal* (1 Sept. 1939–15 July 1940) (Paris, 1957).

Barlone, D., *A French Officer's Diary: Aug. 1939–Oct. 1940* (Cambridge, 1943).

Baudouin, Paul, *Private Diaries: March 1940–Jan. 1941* (London, 1948).

Bauer, E., *Der Panzerkrieg* (Bonn, 1965).

Baumbach, Werner, *Zu Spät* (Munich, 1949).

Bayet, A., *Pétain et la Cinquième Colonne* (Paris, 1944).

Beaufre, Gen. André, *Le Drame de 1940* (Paris, 1965).

Beauvoir, Simone de, *The Prime of Life* (London, 1963).

Bekker, Cajus, *Angriffshöhe 4,000* (Oldenburg, 1964).

Benoist-Méchin, J., *60 Days that Shook the West* (London, 1956).

Bernard, H., *La Guerre et son Évolution à Travers les Siècles* (Brussels, 1957).

Bloch, Marc, *Strange Defeat* (Oxford, 1949).

Blum, Léon (1), *De Munich à la Guerre: 1937–1940* (Paris, 1965).

—— (2), *Mémoires* (Paris, 1955).

Blumentritt, G. von, *Von Rundstedt: The Soldier and the Man* (London, 1952).

Bois, Élie J., *Truth on the Tragedy of France* (London, 1940).

Bongartz, Heinz, *Luftmacht Deutschland* (Essen, 1939).

Boothe, Clare, *European Spring* (London, 1941).

Borchert, Hubert, W., *Panzerkampf im Westen* (Berlin, 1940).

Bräck, Hermann, *Als Kampfflieger über Frankreich* (Berlin, 1942).

Brogan, D. W., *The Development of Modern France* (London, 1940).

Bryant, Arthur, *The Turn of the Tide* (London, 1957).

Bucheit, Gert, *Der Deutsche Geheimdienst* (Munich, 1966).

Carron, Lucien, *Fantassins sur l'Aisne* (Paris, 1943).

Chambrun, René Aldebart, Comte de, *I Saw France Fall* (New York, 1940).

Charles-Roux, F., *Cinq Mois Tragiques aux Affaires Étrangères* (Paris, 1949).

Chastenet, Jacques (1), *Les Années d'Illusions: 1918–31* (Paris, 1960).

—— (2), *Déclin de la Troisième: 1931–38* (Paris, 1962).

—— (3), *Le Drame Final de la 3e République: 1938–40* (Paris, 1963).

Chautemps, C., *Cahiers Secrets de l'Armistice: 1939–1940* (Paris, 1963).

Christophe, E. C., *Wir Stossen mit Panzern zum Meer* (Berlin, 1940).

Churchill, W. S., *The Second World War*, vols. i and ii (London, 1948–9).

Clark, Douglas, *Three Days to Catastrophe* (London, 1966).

Conquet, Gen. Alfred, *L'Énigme des Blindés* (Paris, 1956).

Conrad, Florence, *Camarades de Combat* (New York, 1942).

Dolléans, E., *Histoire du Mouvement Ouvrier* (Paris, 1939).

Douglas, Sholto, *Years of Command* (London, 1966).

Doumenc, Gen. Aimé, *Histoire de la 9e Armée* (Grenoble, 1945).

Draper, Theodore, *The Six Weeks War: 10th May–25th June* (Methuen, 1946).

Ehrenburg, I., *Eve of War: 1933–41* (London, 1963).

Ellis, Major L. F., *The War in France and Flanders* (London, 1953).

Fabre-Luce, A., *Journal de la France*, vol. i: *Mars '39–Juilliet '40* (Trévoux, 1940).

Fauvet, Jacques, *Histoire du Parti Communiste français de la Guerre à la Guerre: 1917–1939* (Paris, 1964).

Fechner, Fritz, *Panzer am Feind* (Gütersloh, 1942).

François-Poncet, André, *The Fateful Years* (London, 1949).

Fuller, Major-Gen. J. F. C., *Decisive Battles of the Western World*, vol. iii (London, 1956).

Galland, Adolf, *Die Ersten und die Letzten* (Schneekluth, 1953).

Gamelin, Gen. Maurice, *Servir: Les Armées Françaises de 1940*, 3 vols. (Paris, 1946).

Gauché, Maurice Henri, *Le Deuxième Bureau au Travail* (Paris, 1953).

de Gaulle, Gen. Charles (1), *Vers l'Armée de Métier* (Paris, 1935: London, 1946).

—— (2) *War Memoirs*, vol. i: *The Call to Honour, 1940–42* (London, 1955).

Gontaut-Biron, Ch. A. de, *Les Dragons au Combat* (Paris, 1954).

Gorce, P.-M. de la, *The French Army* (London, 1963).

Görlitz, Walter (1) *Der Zweite Weltkrieg, 1939–1945*, 2 vols. (Stuttgart, 1951).

—— (2), *The Memoirs of Field-Marshal Keitel* (London, 1965).

Goutard, Col. A. (1), *The Battle of France, 1940* (London, 1958).

—— (2), *La Guerre des Occasions Perdues* (Paris, 1956).

Grandmougin, Jean, *Histoire Vivante du Front Populaire, 1934–39* (Paris, 1966).

Grandsard, C., *Le 10e Corps d'Armée dans la Bataille 1939–40* (Paris, 1949).

Greenwall, H. J., *When France Fell* (London, 1958).

Guderian, Heinz (1), *Achtung – Panzer!* (Stuttgart, 1937).

—— (2), *Panzer Leader* (London, 1952).

—— (3), *Mit den Panzern in Ost und West* (Stuttgart, 1942).

Guérin, Daniel, *Front Populaire: Révolution Manquée* (Paris, 1963).

Habe, Hans, *A Thousand Shall Fall: May–Dec. 1940* (London, 1942).

Halder, Franz, *Kreigstagebuch*, 3 vols. (Stuttgart, 1962–4).

Harsch, Joseph C., *Pattern of Conquest* (London, 1942).

Hartog, L. J., *Und Morgen die Ganze Welt* (Gütersloh, 1961).

Hassell, C. A. U. von, *The Von Hassell Diaries: 1938–44* (London, 1948).

Haupt, Werner, *Sieg ohne Lorbeer* (Holstein, 1965).

Hautecler, G., *Le Combat de Chabrehez, 10 mai 1940* (Brussels, 1955).

Hébrard, J., *25 Années d'Aviation Militaire* (Paris, 1947).

Heinkel, Ernst, *Stürmisches Leben* (Stuttgart, 1953).

Herriot, Édouard, *Épisodes, 1940–44* (Paris, 1950).

Heusinger, Gen. A., *Befehl im Widerstreit: Schickalstunden der Deutschen Armee, 1923–45* (Tübingen, 1950).

Ironside, General Sir E., *The Ironside Diaries* (London, 1962).

Jacobsen, H. A. (1), *Decisive Battles of World War II: The German View* (London, 1965).

—— (2), *Fall Gelb* (Wiesbaden, 1957).

Jamet, Claude, *Carnets de Déroute* (Paris, 1962).

Jong, Louis de, *The German Fifth Column in the Second World War* (London, 1956).

Kammerer, A., *La Vérité sur l'Armistice* (Paris, 1944).

Klein, Burton H., *Germany's Economic Preparation for War* (Cambridge, Mass, 1959).

Kielmansegg, J. A., Graf. von, *Panzer zwischen Warschau und Atlantik* (Berlin, 1941).

Koeltz, Louis, *Comment s'est joué notre Destin* (Paris, 1957).

Koestler, A., *Scum of the Earth* (London, 1941).

Kosak, Georges, *Belgique et France, 1940* (Paris, 1946).

Laure, Gen. Émile, *Pétain* (Paris, 1947).

Lebrun, Albert, *Témoignage* (Paris, 1945).

Lee, Asher, *The German Air Force* (London, 1946).

Lerecouvreux, M., *Huit Mois d'Attente, Un Mois de Guerre* (Paris, 1946).

Leverkuehn, Paul, *German Military Intelligence* (London, 1954).

Lévy, L., *Truth about France* (London, 1941).

Liddell Hart, B. H. (1), *Memoirs*, vols. i and ii (London, 1965).

—— (2), *The Other Side of the Hill* (London, 1948).

—— (3), *The Tanks*, vol. ii : *1939–45* (London, 1959).

Liss, U., *Westfront, 1939–40* (Neckargemund, 1959).

Lossberg, Gen. B. von, *Im Wehrmachtführungsstab* (Hamburg, 1950).

Lyet, Pierre, *La Bataille de France* (Paris, 1947).

Maassen, Heinz, *Über die Maas* (Düsseldorf, 1942).
Maine-Lombard, Pierre, *Ceux du Béton* (Paris, 1957).
Manstein, Field-Marshal F. E. von, *Lost Victories* (London, 1958).
Manteuffel, Gen. Hasso E. von, *Die 7 Panzerdivision im Zweiten Weltkrieg* (Cologne, 1965).
Maurois, André, *Tragedy in France* (New York, 1940).
Mellenthin, Major-Gen. F. W. von, *Panzer Battles, 1939–45* (London, 1955).
Mende, Karl-Heinz, *Briefe aus dem Westen* (Berlin, 1940).
Mendès-France, Pierre, *The Pursuit of Freedom* (London, 1956).
Mengin, Robert, *No Laurels for de Gaulle* (London, 1967).
Menu, Charles Léon, *Lumière sur les Ruines* (Paris, 1953).
Middleton, Drew, *Our Share of Night* (New York, 1946).
Minart, Col. Jacques, *P.C. Vincennes: G.Q.G. Sector I* (Paris, 1945).
Montreuil, J., *Histoire du Mouvement Ouvrier en France* (Paris, 1947).
Monzie, A. de, *Ci-devant* (Paris, 1942).
Moulton, J. L., *The Norwegian Campaign of 1940* (London, 1966).
Mueller-Hillebrand, Gen. B., *Das Heer, 1933–45* (Darmstadt, n.d.).
Müller, K. J., *Das Ende der Entente Cordiale* (Frankfurt-am-Main, 1956).
Murawski, Erich, *Der Durchbruch im Westen* (Oldenburg, 1940).
Muray, Jean, *La Ballade des Tordus* (Paris, 1943).

Narracott, Arthur Henson, *War News Had Wings* (London, 1941).
Namier, L. B., *Europe in Decay* (London, 1950).

O'Neill, Robert J., *The German Army and the Nazi Party* (London, 1966).
Osterkamp, Theo, *Durch Höhen und Tiefen Jagt ein Herz* (Stuttgart, 1952).

Paquier, Pierre (1), *L'Aviation de Bombardment Française en 1939–40* (Paris, 1948).
—— (2), *Combats de Chasse* (Paris, 1946).
Pertinax, A., *The Gravediggers of France* (New York, 1944).
Picht, Werner, *Das Ende der Illusionen* (Berlin, 1941).
Prételat, Gen. G., *Le Destin Tragique de la Ligne Maginot* (Paris, 1950).

Prioux, R., *Souvenirs de Guerre* (Paris, 1947).

Prittie, Terence, *Germans against Hitler* (London, 1964).

Rauschning, H., *Hitler Speaks* (London, 1939).

Reile, Oskar, *Geheime Westfront: Die Abwehr, 1935–45* (Munich, 1962).

Reynaud, Paul (1), *Au Coeur de la Mêlée* (Paris, 1951); translated as *In the Thick of the Fight, 1939–45* (London, 1955).

—— (2), *La France a sauvé l'Europe* (Paris, 1947).

—— (3), *Mémoires: Venue de ma Montagne* (Paris, 1960).

Richards, D. J. and Saunders, H. St G., *The Royal Air Force, 1939–45*, vol. i : *The Fight at Odds* (London, 1953).

Ritter, G., *Carl Goerdeler und die Deutsche Widerstandsbewegung* (Stuttgart, 1956).

Rocolle, Lt.-Col. P. P. F., *Le Béton a-t-il trahi?* (Paris, 1950).

Romains, Jules, *Seven Mysteries of Europe* (New York, 1940).

Rommel, Field-Marshal E., *The Rommel Papers*, ed. B. H. Liddell Hart (London, 1951).

Rossi, A., *Une Page d'Histoire: Les Communistes Français pendant la Drôle de Guerre* (Paris, 1951).

Roton, G., *Années Cruciales* (Paris, 1947).

Rowe, Vivian, *The Great Wall of France* (New York, 1959).

Ruby, Gen. Édouard, *Sedan, Terre d'Epreuve* (Paris, 1948).

Saint-Exupéry, Antoine de, *Pilote de Guerre* (Paris, 1942).

Salesse, Lt. Col., *L'Aviation de Chasse Française en 1939–40* (Paris, 1955).

Sarraz-Bournet, Col. Jacques, *Témoignage d'un Silencieux: G.Q.G., 2e Bureau* (Paris, 1948).

Schlabrendorff, Fabian von, *The Secret War Against Hitler* (London, 1966).

Seive, Fleury, *L'Aviation d'Assaut dans la Bataille de 1940* (Paris, 1948).

Sendtner, K., *Die Vollmacht des Gewissens: Die Deutsche Militäropposition im Ersten Kriegsjahr* (Munich, 1956).

Serre, C. (*rapporteur*), *Les Évenements survenus en France de 1933–45*, 5 vols. (Paris, 1947).

Serrigny, Gen. Bernard, *30 Ans avec Pétain* (Paris, 1959).

Seydewitz, Max, *Civil Life in War-Time Germany* (New York, 1945).

Sheean, James Vincent, *Between the Thunder and the Sun* (New York, 1943).

Shirer, William L. (1), *Berlin Diary, 1934–1941* (London, 1941).
—— (2), *The Rise and Fall of the Third Reich* (London, 1962).
Spaeter, Helmuth, *Die Geschichte des Panzerkorps Gross-deutschland*, vol. i (Duisburg-Ruhrort, 1958).
Spears, E. L., *Assignment to Catastrophe*, 2 vols. (London, 1954).
Sponeck, Thedor Graf von, *Mit Schnellen Truppen an 6 Fronten* (Leipzig, 1943).
Stackelberg, K. von, *Ich War Dabei, Ich Sah, Ich Schrieb* (Berlin, 1940).
Starcke, Gerhard, *Die Roten Teufel sind die Hölle!* (Berlin, 1941).
Stoves, Rolf, *1 Panzer division, 1935–1945* (Bad Nauheim, 1962).
Strohmeyer, Kurt, *Stukas* (Berlin, n.d.).
Supf, Peter, *Das Buch der Deutschen Fluggeschichte* (Berlin, n.d.).

Taylor, A. J. P. (1), *English History, 1914–1945* (Oxford, 1965).
—— (2), *Origins of the Second World War* (London, 1961).
Taylor, Telford, *The March of Conquest* (New York, 1959).
Teissier du Cros, Janet, *Divided Loyalties* (London, 1962).
Thompson, Laurence, *1940* (London, 1966).
Tippelskirch, Admiral Kurt von, *Geschichte des Zweiten Welt-kriegs* (Bonn, 1951).
Tissier, P., *The Riom Trial* (London, 1942).
Tournoux, J. R., *Pétain and de Gaulle* (London, 1966).
Tschimpke, Alfred, *Die Gespenster-Division* (Munich, 1940).

U.S.A.F., *German Air Force Operations in Support of the Army* (U.S.A.F., 1962).

Vasselle, Pierre (1), *La Tragédie d'Amiens: mai-juin 1940* (Amiens, 1952).
—— (2), *La Bataille au Sud d'Amiens, 20 mai–8 juin* (Paris, 1948).
Voisin, Pierre, *Ceux des Chars* (Lyons, 1941).

Walter, G., *Histoire du Parti Communiste Français* (Paris, 1948).
Warlimont, Gen. W., *Inside Hitler's Headquarters, 1939–1945* (London, 1964).
Waterfield, Gordon, *What Happened to France* (London, 1940).
Webster, Sir Charles and Frankland, Noble, *The Strategic Air Offensive against Germany, 1939–45* (London, 1961).

Weiss, Wilhelm (ed.), *Der Krieg im Westen* (Munich, 1941).

Werth, Alexander, *The Last Days of Paris* (London, 1940).

Westphal, Gen. S., *The German Army in the West* (London, 1951).

Weygand, Gen. M. (1), *Recalled to Service* (London, 1952).

Weygand, J. (2), *The Role of General Weygand* (London, 1948).

Wheeler-Bennett, John W., *The Nemesis of Power* (London, 1953).

Wittek, E. (ed.), *Die Soldatische Tat: Berichte von Mitkampfern des Heeres in Westfeldzug, 1940*, hrsg. vom Generalstab des Heeres (Berlin, 1941).

Young, Desmond, *Rommel* (London, 1950).

Part Two: Periodicals and Miscellaneous Sources

L'Armee: La Nation
Lt.-Gen. Nyssens, 'Lord Gort avait raison', May 1953.
Major Jean Godet, 'Rommel en Belgique', July–Aug. 1958.

Revue Défense Nationale
Gen. Ély, 'La leçon qu'il faut tirer des opérations de 1940', Dec. 1953.

Revue d'Histoire de la Deuxième Guerre Mondiale
R. Villate, 'Le changement de commandement de mai 1940', Jan. 1952.

Louis Marin, 'Gouvernment et commandement, mai–juin 1940', Oct. 1952.

Lt.-Col. le Goaster, 'L'action des forces aériennes', June 1953.

P. Dhers, notes on the Comité de Guerre du 25 mai 1940, June 1953.

Jean Vanwelkenhuyzen, 'L'alerte du 10 janvier 1940', Oct. 1953.

J. M. d'Hoop, 'La politique française du réarmement', April 1954.

J. Willequet, 'La politique belge d'indépendance, 1936–40', July 1958.

Gen. Rollot, 'La bataille de Sedan', Oct. 1958.

Gen. Rollot, 'L'offensive de Sedan: les rapports franco-belges', April 1960.

Gen. Tournoux, 'Les origines de la ligne Maginot', Jan. 1959.

E. Wanty, 'La défense des Ardennes en 1940', April 1961.

Gen. de Cosse-Brissac, 'L'armée allemande dans la campagne de 1940', Jan. 1964.

Lt.-Col. le Goyet, 'La percée de Sedan, 10–15 mai 1940', July 1965.

Revue Historique de l'Armée

Gen. Guderian, 'La campagne de France', vol. 1, 1947.

Lt.-Col. d'Ornane, 'Le XIX Corps blindé allemand dans les Ardennes en 1940', vol. 3, 1955.

Col. P. Lyet, 'Témoignages et documents, 1939–40', vol. 1, 1960.

Lt.-Col. le Goyet, 'Le XIe Corps Armée dans la bataille de la Meuse, 10–15 mai, 1940', vol. 1, 1962.

Col. P. Lyet, 'A propos de Sedan, 1940', vol. 4, 1962.

Lt.-Col. le Goyet, 'Contre-attaques manquées, Sedan, 13–15 mai 1940', vol. 4, 1962.

Col. P. Lyet; 'Les Tirailleurs malgaches à Monthermé, mai 1940', vol. 4, 1963.

Lt.-Col. le Goyet, 'L'engagement de la 2e Division Cuirassée Française', vol. 1, 1964.

Lt.-Col. le Goyet, 'Rethel 1940', vol. 4, 1964.

Col. Cailloux, 'Campagne de France 1940: la contre-attaque qui n'eut jamais lieu, 19–25 mai', vol. 3, 1966.

Alte Kamaraden

'Über die Maas am 15 Mai 1940', no. 9, 1959.

Deutsche Soldaten-Zeitung

A. Rothe, 'So war die erste grosse Panzer schlacht . . .', May 1952.

Militär-Wochenblatt

Sergeant-Major Schulze, 'Erste Einfass vor Sedan', April 1941.

Maj.-Gen. Aschenbrandt, 'Der Einsatz der französischen 4 Panzer-Division', July 1942.

First Lt. Grubnau, 'Brückenschlag über die Maas westlich Sedan für den Übergang einer Panzer-Division', Jan. 1941.

Militärwissenschaftliche Rundschau

Lt.-Col. Soldan, 'Der Durchbruch über die Maas am 13 Mai 1940', Nov. 1940.

Individual account from the war on the West Front, 1940.

More individual accounts, 1940.

Schweizerische Militär-Zeitschrift

Ulrich Liss, 'Der französische Gegenangriff gegen den deutschen Maas-Durchbruch im Mai 1940', 1958.

Contemporary newspapers and magazines.

Federal German Archives, Koblenz; War Diaries of German units.

Supplement to the *London Gazette*, 10 October 1941 (Lord Gort's dispatches).

Reference Notes

The foregoing Bibliography contains the principal published works, books, periodicals and unpublished official sources, used either to a greater or lesser extent by the author. But it represents only the small visible tip of the iceberg of an immense volume of words which have been written about the Fall of France, in all its aspects. Works relating to the 'Fifth Column' alone would easily fill the preceding pages several times over.

As far as source material is concerned, the book falls into two fairly independent sections: 1919–40 (Part One), and the battle itself (Part Two). Of the great mass of histories and memoirs covering the inter-war period from which I have directly or indirectly benefited, I have not attempted to list the more obvious; the titles appended below refer chiefly to works quoted or specifically alluded to, and which I feel may be of use to a reader desirous of reading further.

In Part Two, there are certain works which I have kept by my side throughout, and can recommend for their particular value. One of the best military sources on the campaign from the French side remains Colonel Goutard (the English edition, however, is a heavily abridged version of the French); he is fair, generally accurate and critical enough not to have endeared the author to the French military establishment. Less accurate and more biased, but of considerable interest in the chronological relation of political events, is Benoist-Méchin (also reduced in translation, from three volumes to one). On the German side, Werner Haupt's *Sieg ohne Lorbeer* is one of the best general accounts of the campaign. Another source used extensively throughout is General Roton, who is particularly useful on French High Command decisions; meanwhile, for details of the actions in which they themselves were involved, Rommel and Guderian (2) are indispensable and generally trustworthy. Considering the little time that Rommel had to bother with keeping up a diary, as an eye-witness account he remains quite outstanding.

I have also made constant and extensive use of the War Diaries of various German units, now located in the Bundesarchiv in Koblenz. Among the most interesting of these is a bound copy of Rommel's own orders and reports, together with situation maps kept up in his own hand,[1] which was presented to Frau Rommel by the 7th Panzer and subsequently handed by her to the Bundesarchiv. For a pictorial memory of the campaign, I used the numerous illustrated volumes produced on either side, and derived particular value from the official German film, *Sieg im West*, the first of the major wartime documentaries, which – despite its propaganda content – contains excellent material.

Much of the mass of battle accounts requires to be treated with suspicion. Many are based, second-hand, on other (second-hand) narrations, and have not necessarily gained accuracy in the retelling. Some written very close to events have the invaluable stamp of the unprocessed, fresh memory – such as Clare Boothe's impressions and William Shirer's *Berlin Diary*. Others inevitably suffer from the distortion of the passions of the moment – such as the bitter post-defeat reminiscences of French writers who tend to see a Fifth Columnist and a traitor in every command post, or the boastful, superman accounts emanating from Nazi Germany and often published for propaganda purposes when the war was going against Hitler. Nevertheless, neither of these categories is without value. For the reasons outlined in the Preface, I have been wary about using unpublished 'I was there' material; on the other hand, my researches were helpfully supplemented by the responses to various correspondence and interviews on specific points. I have referred to these below under the general title of 'personal correspondence'.

On specific and recurrent war topics, there were also certain standard books used consistently. *For fighting on the French Ninth Army front (up to May 16th)*: Doumenc and Menu. *The Second Army Front*: Ruby, Grandsard and Menu. *The war in Northern Belgium and Holland*: Prioux, Ellis, Fechner, Christophe. *The war in the air*: d'Astier, Paquier (1), Bekker, Richards (for R.A.F. especially), Seive, Salesse, Tissier, Accart. In the source notes below, therefore, I have not necessarily made repeated allusion to these works each time the relevant topic comes up; and similarly with the general references (e.g. Goutard) mentioned earlier. The following notes list solely the principal source material utilized in each chapter. Works to be found in the Bibliography bear the

1. *Geschichte der 7 Panzer-Division im Westfeldzug.*

author's name only; where there are more than one by the same
author, the appropriate number is given; where a work is not listed
in the Bibliography, the title is given in full.

Part One

Chapter 1
The 1919 Victory Parade: *Illustrated London News, The Times,
Le Matin, Le Figaro*. French post-war illusions and stresses:
Chastenet (1) & (2), Brogan, Taylor (2), Churchill i.

Chapter 2
The French Army, Verdun and the Maginot Line: Rocolle, de
Gaulle (1), Beaufre, Prételat, Horne (*The Price of Glory*), Rowe,
Rodolphe. State of Army in 1935: Chastenet (1) & (2), Brogan,
Ruby, Beaufre. Armoured doctrine and foreign policy: Conquet,
Guderian (1), Taylor (2), Reynaud (1), Liddell Hart (1), Namier.
Hitler reoccupies Rhineland: Shirer (1) & (2), Churchill i, Armen-
gaud, Taylor (2), Reynaud (1), Grandmougin, Beaufre, Osterkamp,
Rocolle.

Chapter 3
Hitler rearms: Shirer (1) & (3), Wheeler-Bennett, O'Neill, Klein,
Gauché, Demeter (*The German Officer Corps*). Guderian and the
Panzerkorps: Guderian (1) & (2), Michael Howard (ed.) (*The
Theory and Practice of War*), Rauschning. The revolutionary
Wehrmacht: Shirer (1) & (2), Wheeler-Bennett, Taylor (2),
O'Neill, Churchill i, Prittie, Guderian (1). Anti-militarism in
France: Chastenet (1) & (2), Fauvet, Beauvoir. French political
scandals: Chastenet (1) & (2), Grandmougin, Pertinax, Bois. Be-
ginnings of 'civil war': Horne (*The Price of Glory* and *The Fall
of Paris*), Pertinax, Taylor (1), Chastenet (1) & (2), Brogan, Lévy,
Fauvet, Montreuil, Grandmougin, Walter, Ehrenburg.

Chapter 4
French industrial unrest and the Popular Front: Montreuil,
Walter, Lévy, Chastenet (1) & (2), Grandmougin, Fauvet, Beau-
voir (*The Blood of Others*), Pertinax. France rearms: Roton, Con-
quet, Rowe, Serre, Goutard (1), Pertinax, Reynaud (1), Tissier,
Namier, Conquet, Tournoux, de Gaulle (1), Mengin, Gamelin i &
ii, Beaufre, Grandmougin, Chastenet (2), Gauché. The Luftwaffe:
Lee, Galland, Heinkel, Osterkamp, Bongartz, Bekker, Seive,

Taylor (1), Douglas, d'Astier, François-Poncet. The French Air
Force: d'Astier, Maurois, Brogan, Seive, Churchill i, Tissier,
Gamelin i, Armengaud, Paquier, Salesse. Widening political rifts
in France, the 'Fifth Column': Brogan, Namier, Chastenet (2),
Spears i, Pertinax, Lévy, Bloch, Rauschning, Menu, Bayet, Abetz,
Bois. Fall of Popuar Front and rise of Communists; Chastenet (2),
Grandmougin, Lévy, Walter, Fauvet, Rossi, Beauvoir, Pertinax.
The rush towards war: Taylor (2), Chastenet (2) & (3), Pertinax,
Churchill i, Klein, Reynaud (1), Fabre-Luce, Shirer (1).

Chapter 5
War begins: Chastenet (3), Fabre-Luce, Shirer (1), Seydewitz,
Klein, Harsch, Barlone, Maurois, Pertinax. The 'Saar Offensive'
and Poland: Allied periodicals, Gamelin iii, Goutard, Rowe,
Lerecouvreux, Prételat, Rodolphe, Minart, Spears i, Chastenet (3),
Guderian (2), Balbaud, Liss, Lossberg, Blumentritt. The Phoney
War: Fabre-Luce, Waterfield, Pertinax, Boothe, Sumner Welles
(*Time for Decision*), Beauvoir, Koestler. Life at the front, French
Army morale: French periodicals (see Bibliography, Part II),
Fabre-Luce, Pertinax, Barlone, Spears i, Jamet, Sarraz-Bournet,
Koestler, Barlone, Lerecouvreux. Impact of Nazi and Communist
propaganda: Chastenet (3), Fabre-Luce, Conrad, Greenwall,
Spears i, Rossi, Bois, Koestler, Ehrenburg, Pertinax, Bardies,
Walter.

Chapter 6
Gamelin: Menu, Spears i, Romains, Maurois, Bardies, Bardoux,
Gamelin i & ii, Pertinax, de Gaulle (2), Minart, Baudouin. French
command and Georges: Goutard, Minart, Roton, Beaufre, Spears
i, Sarraz-Bournet, Gauché, Weygand (1), Pertinax, Bardies. Gamelin's strategy: Doumenc, Gamelin i & iii, Roton, French periodicals, Jacobsen (1), Ellis, Goutard, Lyet, Reynaud (1), Minart,
Draper, Prioux. The 'Mechelen Incident': Jacobsen (2), Koeltz.
French neglect of Polish lessons: Armengaud, Gauché. Finland
and other distractions: Taylor (1), Koestler, Bois, Clark, Gamelin
iii, Bardoux, Bois, Ironside, Weygand (1), Pertinax, Beaufre,
Fabre-Luce.

Chapter 7
Fall Gelb: Jacobsen (1) & (2), Koeltz, Warlimont, Ellis, Westphal,
Manstein, Goerlitz (1), Liss, Telford Taylor, Haupt, Blumentritt,
Heusinger, Guderian (2). Halder and the 'Resistance': Krausnick

'(*Schicksalfragen der Gegenwart*), O'Neill, Prittie, Görlitz (1), Sendtner (*Vollmacht des Gewissens*), *Von Hassell Diaries*, Namier. Manstein and his plan: Blumentritt, Westphal, Manstein, O'Neill, Liddell Hart (2), Koeltz, Jacobsen (2). Finalizing *Sichelschnitt* plan: Jacobsen (2), Koeltz, Liss, Warlimont, Telford Taylor, Guderian (2), Lossberg, Abshagen.

Chapter 8

Norway: Moulton, Reynaud (1), Churchill i, Koeltz, Telford Taylor, Taylor (1), Lossberg. Allied Government crises: Gamelin iii, Boothe, Bois, Fabre-Luce, Baudouin, Chastenet (3), Pertinax, Churchill i. Daladier, Reynaud and Hélène de Portes: Bois, Pertinax, Fabre-Luce, Maurois, Spears i & ii, Harold Nicolson (*Diaries* ii), Baudouin, Chastenet (3), Sheean, Boothe. Strength of opposing forces by May 1940: Goutard, Jacobsen (2), Menu, Conquet, Lyet, Tissier, Bauer, Guderian (2), Roton, Bardies, d'Astier, Gamelin i, Lee. French line-up on the Meuse: Ruby, Menu, Goutard, Allard, Prételat, Gamelin i. French military unpreparedness: Lerecouvreux, Goutard, Maurois, Menu, Grandsard, Ruby, Conquet, French periodicals, Doumenc, Draper, Bauer, Allard, Gauché, Bernard, Beaufre, Prételat. Allied reconnaissance and German deception: Accart, Salesse, Bauer, Liss, Gauché, Lossberg, Jacobsen (2), Abshagen, Bartz (*Die Tragödie der Deutschen Abwehr*), Leverkuehn. Last days in France and Germany: Boothe, Fabre-Luce, Bardoux, Gontaut-Biron, de Beauvoir, *Von Hassell Diaries*, Seydewitz, Shirer (1), Warlimont, Halder, German periodicals, Sendtner.

Part Two

Chapter 9

Beginning of German offensive 10 May: Stackelberg, Kielmansegg, Flack, Reile, Sponeck, Spaeter, Osterkamp, Bekker, Draper, Liddell Hart (2). German advance into Ardennes: Stoves, Spaeter, Starcke, Halder, Manteuffel, Lerecouvreux. German 'special operations', 'Brandenburgers', and Eben Emael: Leverkuehn, Abshagen, Bucheit, Jong, Haupt, Strohmeyer, Hartog, Lossberg, Bekker, Telford Taylor, Purnell's *History of the Second World War*. Allies move into Belgium: Ironside, Minart, Reynaud (1), Boothe, Baudouin, Chastenet (3), Prioux, Bryant, Menu, Kosak, Gontaut-Biron, Ruby, Lerecouvreux.

Chapter 10

Fighting in Ardennes, 11 May: Manteuffel, Kosak, French periodicals, Stoves, Halder, Goutaut-Biron, Guderian (3), Mende. Allied progress in northern Belgium: Lyet, Bardies, Middleton, Roton. French High Command reactions: Draper, Roton, Minart, Goutard, Gamelin i, Weygand (1).

Chapter 11

War in Holland and northern Belgium, 12 May: Picht, Ironside, Draper, Benoist-Méchin. Guderian crosses Semois: Weiss, Stoves, Christophe, Lerecouvreux, Conrad. Corap withdrawn from Ardennes: Kosak, Manteuffel, French periodicals. Rommel crosses at Houx: French periodicals, Manteuffel, Tschimpke, Lyet. Huntziger prepares for Guderian's attack at Sedan: Conrad, Lyet, Minart, d'Astier, Gamelin i.

Chapter 12

Rommel, background: Young, Rommel, Lossberg, Mellenthin. Corap: Chastenet (3), Allard, Draper, Maurois. Rommel's bridgehead at Dinant: in addition to Rommel himself, Manteuffel, Draper, Borchert, Young, Tschimpke, Minart. Guderian's preparations at Sedan: Spaeter, Stoves, Christophe, Liddell Hart (2), and here as well as later Grandsard, Ruby, Menu, Goutard. Luftwaffe bombing at Sedan: Lee, Telford Taylor, Bekker, Richards & Saunders, Goutard, Salesse, d'Astier, Stoves, Guderian (2), German periodicals. The crossings at Sedan: *Sieg im West* (film), Draper, German periodicals, Guderian (2) & (3), Wittek, Haupt, Spaeter, Mellenthin, Stoves, Weiss, Christophe. The French view: in addition to Roton, Goutard, Menu, Ruby, Grandsard, also Lerecouvreux, Gamelin i & iii, Conrad, French periodicals, Bardies, Draper, Doumenc. French High Command reactions: Minart, Baudouin, Gamelin i & iii, Beaufre, Ironside.

Chapter 13

Rommel consolidates his bridgehead: Manteuffel, Tschimpke, Young, Bardies, Allard, Draper, Minart, German periodicals, Wittek. First French counter-attacks at Sedan: Spaeter, Mellenthin, Stoves, Guderian (3), German and French periodicals. Guderian decides to swing westwards: Guderian (2), Halder, Stoves. Allied air attack on Sedan bridges: Richards & Saunders, Haupt, d'Astier, Paquier (1) Kielmansegg, Bekker, Ellis, Tessier, Guderian (3). French 3rd Armoured Division at Stonne: Spaeter, Serre, Lerecouvreux, Roton, French periodicals, Waterfield.

Guderian and Kleist at odds: Guderian (2), Halder, German War Diaries. Holland capitulates: Draper, Bekker, Telford Taylor, Sponeck. French High Command reactions: Bardies, Minart, Menu, Spears i, Gamelin i, Reynaud (1), Ironside, Werth.

Chapter 14
The French 1st Armoured Division and Rommel's break-out: Serre, d'Astier, Starcke, French periodicals, Bardies, Tschimpke, Borchert, German periodicals, Manteuffel, personal correspondence. Reinhardt breaks out at Monthermé: German periodicals, Guderian (3), Stackelberg. Fighting at Stonne: Spaeter, Wittek, Lemelsen (*Die 29 Infanterie-Division*), French periodicals, Serre. 1st Panzer breaks out at Sedan: Guderian (3), Kielmansegg, Stoves, Lemelsen (op. cit.), Draper, French periodicals, Doumenc, Bardies. R.A.F. begin bombing Ruhr, Reynaud asks for more fighters: Paquier (1), Richards & Saunders, Ellis, d'Astier, Müller, Webster, Narracott, Bräck, Churchill ii, Douglas. Kleist's 'Halt Order' of 15 May to Guderian: Guderian, Goerlitz (1), Goutard (1), personal correspondence, French periodicals, Halder.

Chapter 15
French High Command actions, 10–15 May: Gamelin i & iii, Bois, Baudouin, Beaufre, Minart, Menu, Bardies, French periodicals, Goutard, Bardoux, Ironside, Churchill ii, Reynaud (1), Lyet, Draper, Hartog, Pertinax. Reynaud and Churchill, 15–16 May: Bois, Baudouin, Benoist-Méchin, Reynaud (1), Ironside, Churchill ii, Gamelin iii. French Government actions of 16 May: Baudouin, Herriot, Reynaud (1), Draper, Bois, Monzie, Gamelin iii. French censorship: Sheean, Boothe, Chastenet (3), Vasselle (1), Koestler, Waterfield, Bois, Werth. First panic in Paris: Sheean, Mendès-France, Bardoux, Hartog, Werth, Bois, Herriot, Benoist-Méchin. Churchill in Paris, 16 May: Benoist-Méchin, Churchill ii, Spears i, Chautemps, Baudouin, Reynaud (1), Ironside, General Ismay (*Memoirs*), Ellis, Douglas, Müller, Taylor (1), Richards. French High Command decisions, 16 May: Mellenthin, Minart, Roton, Doumenc, Lyet, French periodicals, Bardies. Guderian's breakthrough, 16 May: Gontaut-Biron, Lerecouvreux, Ruby, Kielmansegg, Stoves, Spaeter. French 2nd Armoured Division's operations: Serre, Voisin, French periodicals, personal correspondence, Bardies, Roton, Doumenc. Rommel's 'Avesnes Raid': principally Rommel, and Doumenc, Rocolle, Menu, Roton, Borchert, Goutard, German periodicals, Manteuffel.

Chapter 16
The German High Command, 10–17 May: Murawski, Wehrmacht communiqués, Shirer (1), P. C. Ettighoffer (*44 Tage und Nächte*), Halder, Warlimont, Goutard, Heusinger, Jacobsen (1), German periodicals, Ellis, Guderian (2), Haupt, Telford Taylor, personal correspondence, Blumentritt, Mellenthin, Manteuffel, Kielmansegg. De Gaulle's first counter-attack: Serre, de Gaulle (2) Tournoux, d'Astier, Gontaut-Biron, Voisin, Stoves, Kielmansegg, French and German periodicals, Mengin, Bardies, Roton, Bauer. Panzers consolidate: Doumenc, Manteuffel, Kosak, Prioux, Stackelberg, Guderian (2), Haupt, Lemelsen (*Die 29 Infanterie-Division*). Waning Allied air effort, effect on land forces: Webster & Frankland, d'Astier, Richards & Saunders, Narracott, Balbaud, Paquier (1). Retreat from northern Belgium: Prioux, Ellis, Balbaud, Bryant, Jacobsen (1). French High Command and Government actions: French periodicals, Weygand (1) & (2), Gamelin iii, Minart, Doumenc, Baudouin, Bardoux, Roton.

Chapter 17
Panzers advance again: Stoves, Churchill ii, Draper, Jacobsen (1), Christophe, Manteuffel, Starcke, Haupt, Halder, Murawski, Wehrmacht communiqués. End of Ninth Army and capture of Giraud: Vasselle (1), Habe, Draper, Doumenc, Guderian (2), Ellis, Minart, Middleton, Roton. Fugitives and refugees: Accart, Sarraz-Bournet, Muray, Mendès-France, Bardoux, Jong, Kosak, Koestler, Waterfield, Maurois, Carron, Beauvoir, Chambrun, Bryant, Kielmansegg, Boothe, Chastenet (3), Bardies, Chautemps, St.-Exupéry. The 'Fifth Column': Barlone, Jong, Waterfield, Habe, Vilfroy (*The War in the West*), Werth, German archives, Tissier, Spears ii, Conrad, Pertinax, Reile, Telford Taylor, Menu, Ruby, Lerecouvreux, Reynaud (1), Rauschning, Shirer (1), Beaufre, personal correspondence, Bayet, Koestler, Gamelin iii, French periodicals. French High Command recognizes German objective: Minart, Roton, French periodicals, Baudouin, Weygand (1), Voisin, personal correspondence, Baudouin, Gamelin iii, Reynaud (1), Bardoux, Spears i, Ironside, Benoist-Méchin. Operations on 19 May: French and German periodicals, Kielmansegg, d'Astier, de Gaulle (2), Salesse, Voisin, Halder, Gontaut-Biron, Vasselle (1), Wittek, Ellis, Stoves. Fighting on Maginot Line: Prételat, Rowe, Picht, Benoist-Méchin. Withdrawal from northern Belgium and rumours of British evacuation intent: Ellis, Roton, Prioux, Reynaud (1), French periodicals, Barlone, Draper, Lyet, Richards & Saunders,

Ironside, Detrez & Chatelle (*Tragédies en Flandres*), Churchill ii, Benoist-Méchin. 'Instruction No. 12' and end of Gamelin: Minart, French and German periodicals, Roton, Reynaud (1), Gamelin i & iii, Beaufre. Weygand takes over: Lévy, Reynaud (1), Spears i & ii, Greenwall, Werth, Beaufre, Jamet, Bois, Waterfield, Weygand (1) & (2), Baudouin, Minart. Germans reach Channel: Manteuffel, d'Astier, Kielmansegg, Stoves, Draper, Bryant, Shirer (1), Telford Taylor, Guderian (3), Lyet.

Chapter 18
German 'pause' of 21 May: Halder, Goutard (1), Telford Taylor, Guderian (2). Allied High Command, Ironside's plan: Reynaud (1), Lyet, Baudouin, Detrez & Chatelle (*Tragédies en Flandres*), Benoist-Méchin, Chambrun, Ellis, Ironside, Weygand (1), French periodicals, Müller, Churchill ii, Gort's dispatches. Gort, background: Draper, Thompson, Spears i, Ellis, Maurois, Bryant. The Arras attack: Detrez & Chatelle (op. cit.), d'Astier, Bardies, Bryant, Chambrun, Draper, Ellis, Prioux, Roton, Weygand (2), Telford Taylor, Goutard, Guderian (2), Churchill ii, Gort dispatches, Reynaud (1), Jacobsen (1), Flack, Halder, Mellenthin, Haupt, Manteuffel, Rommel, Starcke, *Sieg im West*, German archives, personal correspondence. Weygand's visit to Ypres: Baudouin, Churchill ii, Weygand (1) & (2), Reynaud (1), French periodicals, Bardies, Ellis, Lyet, Benoist-Méchin, Beaufre, Goutard (1), Bauer, Hartog. Reynaud and Churchill in Paris, 22 May: Bois, Bardoux, Werth, Goutard, Baudouin, Draper, Roton, Weygand (1), Reynaud (1), Churchill ii, Ellis, General Ismay (*Memoirs*), Ironside. German operations, 22 May: Christophe, Shirer (1), Mende, Stoves, Manteuffel, Ellis. French counter-strokes, 22 May: Detrez & Chatelle (op. cit.), d'Astier, Bekker, Prioux, Ellis, Lyet, Roton, Weygand (2), Goutard (1), Gort dispatches, Bardies, Vasselle (2). Gort withdraws: Ellis, Churchill ii, Gort dispatches, Weygand (1), French periodicals, Draper, Richards, Detrez & Chatelle (op. cit.), Bryant, Prioux, Weygand (2), Telford Taylor, Bardies, Reynaud (1), Ironside.

Chapter 19
The German 'Halt Order' of 24 May: Taylor (1), Ellis, Halder, Rommel, Telford Taylor, German periodicals, Guderian (2), Fechner, Haupt, Goutard (1), Bekker, Blumentritt, Warlimont, Heusinger, Benoist-Méchin, Churchill ii. Growing French despair, rancour among Allies: Werth, Jamet, Bardoux, Spears i, Koestler,

686 Reference Notes

Picht, Sheean, Waterfield, Telford Taylor, Prioux, Draper, Boothe, Baudouin, Benoist-Méchin. Weygand, beginnings of 'separate peace' lobby: Waterfield, Telford Taylor, Draper, Baudouin, Benoist-Méchin, Müller, Chautemps, Spears i, Reynaud (1). French Cabinet session of 25 May: Müller, Baudouin, Spears i, Reynaud (1), Benoist-Méchin. Footnote on air strengths: Bauer, Baudouin, Jacobsen (1), Ellis, Paquier (1), Richards & Saunders. French attacks from south, fading of Weygand plan: Goutard, Vasselle (1) & (2), Benoist-Méchin, Weygand (2), Reynaud (1), Baudouin, Draper, Churchill ii. Dunkirk: Jacobsen (1) & (2), Bekker, Spears i, Draper, Lyet, Ellis, Weygand (1), Ironside, Richards & Saunders, Gort dispatches, d'Astier, Goutard, Benoist-Méchin, Churchill ii.

Chapter 20
'Operation Red' begins: Draper, d'Astier, Weygand (1), Warlimont, Spears ii, Goutard, Richards, Churchill ii, Halder, Reynaud (1), Telford Taylor, *Sieg im West*, Manteuffel, Rommel, Guderian (2), Benoist-Méchin. Paris falls: Draper, Shirer (1), Werth, Telford Taylor, Ehrenburg, Waterfield, Maurois, Fabre-Luce, Benoist-Méchin, Halder. Italy attacks: Reynaud (1), Benoist-Méchin, Goutard, Richards & Saunders. Last resistances: Draper, Spears i & ii, Chastenet (3), Benoist-Méchin, Beaufre. Political struggle between 'softs' and 'hards': Spears i & ii, Churchill ii, Benoist-Méchin, Bois, Koestler, Lévy, Weygand (1), Reynaud (1), Baudouin, Benoist-Méchin, Maurois. Reynaud at breaking-point, his plea to America: Spears ii, Bois, Benoist-Méchin, Baudouin, Boothe, personal correspondence, Reynaud (1), Churchill ii. Reynaud resigns: Reynaud (1), Spears ii, Benoist-Méchin, Churchill ii, Baudouin, Shirer (1), Chastenet (3).

Chapter 21
The armistice: Shirer (1) & (2), Halder, Mende, Warlimont, *Sieg im West*, Weygand (1), Benoist-Méchin. Casualties: Haupt, Manteuffel, Chastenet (3), Werth, Picht, Ellis, Webster & Frankland, Richards & Saunders, Tissier, Starcke, Spaeter, personal correspondence. First days after cease-fire: Stackelberg, Halder, Beauvoir, Ehrenburg, Shirer (1), Middleton, Thompson, Spaeter, Mende. Shadows of defeat for Hitler: Mende, Warlimont, Shirer (1) & (2), Telford Taylor, Blumentritt, Jacobsen (1), Klein, Murawski, *Sieg im West*, Bauer, Ellis. Post-mortems: French & German periodicals, Spears i, Jong, Habe, Doumenc, Ellis, Goutard (1), Telford Taylor,

Koestler, personal correspondence. Subsequent careers of principals: Reynaud (1), Gamelin ii, Prioux, Telford Taylor, Baudouin, d'Astier, Benoist-Méchin, Greenwell, Harold Nicolson (*Diaries* ii), personal correspondence, *The Times, Chambers Encyclopaedia, Encyclopaedia Britannica.*

Index

698 Index

Index of Military Units